A SHORT HISTORY OF THE
RENAISSANCE IN EUROPE

A SHORT HISTORY OF THE RENAISSANCE IN EUROPE

MARGARET L. KING

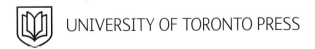 UNIVERSITY OF TORONTO PRESS

Library and Archives Canada Cataloguing in Publication

King, Margaret L., 1947–
        A short history of the Renaissance in Europe/Margaret L. King.—Third edition.
Revision of: King, Margaret L., 1947–. Renaissance in Europe.

Includes bibliographical references and index.
Issued in print and electronic formats.
ISBN 978-1-4875-9309-4 (hardback).—ISBN 978-1-4875-9308-7 (paperback).—
ISBN 978-1-4875-9310-0 (html).—ISBN 978-1-4875-9311-7 (pdf).

        1. Renaissance. 2. Humanism. 3. Civilization, Western—Classical influences. 4. Europe—History—1492–1648. 5. Europe—Civilization. 6. Europe—Intellectual life. I. Title. II. Title: Renaissance in Europe.

CB361.K56 2016   940.2'1   C2016-901854-7
                                         C2016-901855-5

We welcome comments and suggestions regarding any aspect of our publications—please feel free to contact us at news@utphighereducation.com or visit our Internet site at www.utppublishing.com.

North America
5201 Dufferin Street
North York, Ontario, Canada, M3H 5T8

2250 Military Road
Tonawanda, New York, USA, 14150
ORDERS PHONE: 1–800–565–9523
ORDERS FAX: 1–800–221–9985
ORDERS E-MAIL: utpbooks@utpress.utoronto.ca

UK, Ireland, and continental Europe
NBN International
Estover Road, Plymouth, PL6 7PY, UK
ORDERS PHONE: 44 (0) 1752 202301
ORDERS FAX: 44 (0) 1752 202333
ORDERS E-MAIL: enquiries@nbninternational.com

Every effort has been made to contact copyright holders; in the event of an error or omission, please notify the publisher.

The University of Toronto Press acknowledges the financial support for its publishing activities of the Government of Canada through the Canada Book Fund.

Printed in Canada.

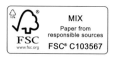

CONTENTS

MAPS

ILLUSTRATIONS

FIGURES, GRAPHS, AND TABLES

Figures

Graphs

Tables

ACKNOWLEDGMENTS

I have been living with the idea of the Renaissance for more than 50 years: longer than the 34 years I have been a mother, or the 40 I have been married, or the 40 I was employed by the City University of New York. In that long career, I have been informed and inspired by many scholars and students—far more than it is possible to name here, but I will name three who have been an unfailing source of inspiration and guidance: Paul F. Grendler, Paul Oskar Kristeller (1905–1999), and Albert Rabil, Jr. To them I am forever grateful. I am grateful as well to my new collaborators at the University of Toronto Press, whose idea it was to give this book on the Renaissance a renaissance of its own in a new and revised edition.

My father, deceased in 2012, always encouraged me in these scholarly labors he did not quite understand—he had been a builder of power plants—but accepted nonetheless and lined the products up on his bookshelf. Here's another one, Dad. To my husband and sons and all my family, all my love forever. To my granddaughter Madeleine, I hope you will like the pictures in this book, which is for you.

Margaret L. King
Douglaston, New York

INTRODUCTION
THE IDEA OF THE RENAISSANCE

Writing the history of the complex and protean idea of the Renaissance is a project as daunting as it is essential. It is not like writing the history of the Soviet Union, baseball, or the Platonic tradition, since there is scarcely anyone who doubts that these things existed or that they belong to a certain time and place. No such certainty prevails when it comes to the Renaissance. Not only do scholars not agree what the Renaissance is, they are not sure when or where or even *if* it took place.

CONTEMPORARY VIEWS

The people who lived during the era we call the Renaissance—extending from approximately 1300 to 1700—knew they were living in an extraordinary age. The fourteenth-century poet and scholar Francesco Petrarca (Petrarch; 1304–1374; see Chapter 2) looked back to the great achievements of the ancients, after which he saw only bleak decline until his own day in which, he believed, the world was becoming "modern" to the extent that it revived and relived antiquity. The sixteenth-century painter and historian of art Giorgio Vasari (1511–1574; see Chapter 4) detected the beginnings of a new vitality, an ability to understand and imitate nature itself, beginning in the last years of the thirteenth century and the early years of the fourteenth. The humanist scholars who "recovered" or "discovered" those ancient works that had been "lost" (rather, neglected) over the intervening years since the collapse of the Roman Empire often spoke of *renovatio* (renewal) and *rinascita* (rebirth).

THE MODERN UNDERSTANDING OF THE RENAISSANCE

Contemporaries did not, however, use the term "Renaissance," a French word meaning "rebirth" and applied from the eighteenth century by art critics to the classicizing style of the fifteenth and sixteenth centuries. For the French historian Jules Michelet (1798–1874), who entitled the seventh volume of his 17-volume work on the history of France *Le Renaissance* (1855), "Renaissance" took on a larger meaning as a turning point in Western history—although Italy and the earlier stages of the Renaissance interested him little, and his Renaissance began instead with explorer Christopher Columbus (1451–1506) and reformer Martin Luther (1483–1546). The concept of the Renaissance won its modern currency in the work of the Swiss historian Jacob Burckhardt (1818–1897; see discussion under "The 'Medium' Renaissance" below), whose *Die Kultur der Renaissance in Italien* (1860) circulated widely across the Atlantic in the English translation of S.G.C. Middlemore as *The Civilization of the Renaissance in Italy*.

Since Burckhardt defined the Renaissance as a key era in European history originating in Italy, many scholars have examined his arguments and agreed with, opposed, or reframed them in diverse ways. Their views of the Renaissance fall generally into three categories: small, medium, and large. The small-sized Renaissance constitutes a revival of classical forms and ideas. The medium-sized Renaissance involves a broader cultural resurgence. The large-sized Renaissance constitutes a historical era in itself, a period of two or three centuries that stands between the Middle Ages and the modern world.

THE "SMALL" RENAISSANCE

Adherents of the most restricted notion of the Renaissance focus on the revival of classical antiquity, especially in the arts and in thought and especially in Italy. They point to the artists who began to formulate new ideas about the relics of the ancient past littered about in the city of Rome, that had, for centuries, been understood primarily as the home of the papacy. Those artists sketched and imitated the arches, sarcophagi, and statues that had survived from a pre-Christian era and incorporated those forms into the Christianized culture of their own age. Scholars also note how Italian authors from the late thirteenth century followed classical models, as did the poet Dante, whose journey through the afterworld recorded in *The Divine Comedy* was guided by the Roman poet Virgil. They see humanism, an intellectual movement that was grounded in the serious reading of classical texts, as the chief characteristic of Renaissance thought.

Proponents of this view of the Renaissance extend from the nineteenth-century German scholar Georg Voigt (1827–1891), whose *Die Wiederbelebung des classischen Alterthums, oder das erste Jahrhundert des Humanismus* (1859; *The Rebirth of Classical Antiquity, or the First Century of Humanism*) established this interpretive pattern, to the contemporary, prize-winning author Ronald G. Witt, whose *In the Footsteps of the Ancients: The Origins of Humanism from Lovato to Bruni* (2000) systematically uncovers the early appropriation of the classical tradition by Italian thinkers of the thirteenth and fourteenth centuries. The many works of the great historian of Renaissance philosophy Paul Oskar Kristeller (1905–1999) fall in this category as well, among them the essays collected in the volume *Renaissance Thought and Its Sources* (1979). Kristeller stresses continuities with traditions of medieval thought while noting the changes in emphasis that accompanied the close study of classical texts in the fifteenth and sixteenth centuries and constituted the humanist movement. Anthony Grafton's many explorations of Renaissance thought probe how Europeans of the Renaissance era read and understood the classical texts which transformed their outlook; his *Joseph Scaliger: A Study in the History of Classical Scholarship* (1983) is classic.

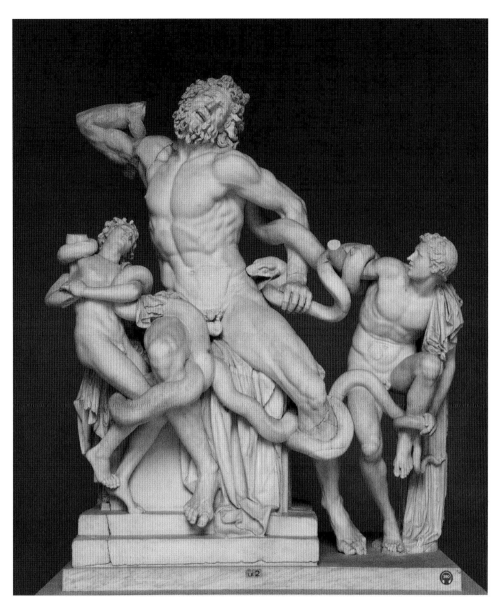

Laöcoon and His Sons, c. 50 CE. **Marble, height 6 ft (1.84 m). Vatican Museums, Rome.**

Found in 1506 in the ruins of the palace of the Roman Emperor Titus (r. 79–81 CE), this emotionally charged representation of the death of the Trojan priest and his sons is a product of the Hellenistic era. It was one of the most significant Renaissance discoveries of ancient sculpture.

    Critics of this view of the Renaissance are those medievalists who see earlier revivals of classical antiquity in the arts and thought—as in the creation of Romanesque style in architecture and sculpture in the eleventh and twelfth centuries, and in the enthusiastic study of recovered classical texts in the twelfth and thirteenth centuries. The keynote work of this "revolt of the medievalists" is *The Renaissance of the Twelfth Century* (1927) by Charles Homer Haskins (1870–1937). Many medievalists (especially those whose specializations are non-Italian) emphasize the great creativity of late-medieval civilization, whose innovations they view as continuous with the early stages of modernity. They continue to be deeply skeptical that there was such a thing as a great, preeminent Renaissance.

THE "MEDIUM" RENAISSANCE

Adherents of a middling notion of the Renaissance are aware of the revival of classical models but see a broader cultural movement in process as well, an exuberant unleashing of energies that encompassed a sharpened sense of individual dignity and a conscious reinvention of society and the state. Burckhardt's *The Civilization of the Renaissance in Italy*, as has been noted, first presented these claims for the Renaissance. Burckhardt saw the Renaissance as a moment of awakening—"the discovery of the world and of man" (a phrase borrowed from Michelet)—expressed in the bold and inventive development of personality in key cultural actors. Such extraordinary individuals were creators for whom even the state was a work of art, a product that bore the particular imprint of its founder.

For Burckhardt and other nineteenth- and early-twentieth-century scholars, these exuberant individuals were essentially indifferent to or hostile to Christianity; their Renaissance, these experts concluded, was "pagan." More recently, scholars in the Burckhardtian tradition have countered this judgment, pointing to the continued force of Christian thought and attitudes in the Renaissance. *In Our Image and Likeness* (1970) by Charles Trinkaus (1911–1999), while Burckhardtian in its stress on the notion of a dynamic self seen as a central and defining theme of humanist thought, also credits the humanist outlook as genuinely Christian.

Adopting Burckhardt's hypothesis of the Renaissance as a moment of civilizational change, some early twentieth-century scholars, shaped by Marxist theory, identified a different cause for the cultural shift. Foremost among these was the German sociologist Alfred von Martin (1882–1979), whose *Soziologie der Renaissance* (1932; *Sociology of the Renaissance*, 1944, 2015) identified the Renaissance as the "first modern bourgeois epoch." Like Burckhardt, he recognized the dynamism and spirit of innovation that characterized the merchant patrons and amateurs of the early Renaissance but attributed that surge of creative energy to a rapidly developing capitalism and not to some form of spiritual rebirth. Von Martin's thesis was writ large, and applied to the development of artistic style, by Hungarian art historian Arnold Hauser (1892–1978). Hauser's multi-volume *Sozialgeschichte der Kunst und Literatur* (1953; *Social History of Art*, 1951, 1999) includes an interpretation of the evolution of Renaissance art keyed to the consciousness of the Italian merchant elite.

Among the Renaissance figures Burckhardt admired were the audacious builders of despotic states, which he likened to works of art. Some twentieth-century scholars agreed. Eugenio Garin (1909–1999), in his *Der italienische Humanismus* (1947; *Italian Humanism: Philosophy and Civic Life in the Renaissance*, 1965), and Hans Baron (1900–1988), in his *The Crisis of the Early Italian Renaissance: Civic Humanism and Republican Liberty in an Age of Classicism and Tyranny* (1955, 1966), viewed Renaissance humanists (many from republican Florence) as contributors to a new, secular politics centered on the free individual and an ideal of liberty. These "civic humanists" might, in fact, be seen as the originators of modern political thought, a possibility explored by J.G.A. Pocock (*The Machiavellian Moment: Florentine Political Thought and the Atlantic Republican Tradition*, 1975) and Quentin Skinner (*The Foundations of Modern Political Thought*, 1978). All of these authors conceived of political ideals and models as outgrowths of the dynamic cultural changes brought on by the Renaissance.

THE "LARGE" RENAISSANCE

Adherents of the broadest notion of the Renaissance see it as an age defined by certain artistic and cultural tendencies but an era, nevertheless, that was much more than the product of its creative elites. These scholars speak of the economy or society of Renaissance Italy or Renaissance Europe, although neither society nor economy could be said to have experienced a "Renaissance." Thus we have such important works as Samuel K. Cohn, Jr.'s *Women in the Streets: Essays on Sex and Power in Renaissance Italy* (1996), Thomas Kuehn's *Law, Family, and Women: Toward a Legal Anthropology of Renaissance Italy* (1991), and Sharon Strocchia's *Death and Ritual in Renaissance Florence* (1992).

In works such as these, the art and thought of the Renaissance are not a primary focus. Yet its cultural determinants characterized the era as a whole, so that authors considering gender, ritual, and society, nevertheless, accept the frameworks of "Renaissance Italy" or "Renaissance Florence." The same is true of the even larger notion of "Renaissance Europe," as seen in such works as the enormous *The Civilization of Europe in the Renaissance* by John R. Hale (1994) that impressionistically surveys the politics, economy, society, religious movements, philosophy, and art of two centuries of European history.

"EARLY MODERN" VERSUS "RENAISSANCE"

Whereas the authors just named are comfortable in accepting the concept of the "Renaissance" to define the era whose social and cultural processes concern them, other historians resist the term "Renaissance" altogether. For them, to accept the concept of "Renaissance" is to accept the primacy of the artistic and intellectual activities that characterized it, while they see those activities as irrelevant or as subordinate to the mass movements, political structures, and ideological currents that principally concern them. These scholars have adopted the term "early modern" to indicate the centuries between the Middle Ages and the modern world—primarily the sixteenth and seventeenth centuries. We have, for instance, from Eugene F. Rice, Jr. (although Rice was also an author of important works on the Renaissance), in collaboration with Anthony Grafton, the second edition of the overview *Foundations of Early Modern Europe, 1460–1559* (1994). Many recent works of French, German, or English history in this period, especially of histories of gender or class, likewise prefer the term "early modern" rather than "Renaissance." Even for works about Italy, the home of the Renaissance, this is the case, such as Deanna Shemek's *Ladies Errant: Wayward Women and Social Order in Early Modern Italy* (1998).

Avoiding the term "Renaissance" in favor of "early modern" is understandable in view of the many developments in the era from 1300 to 1700 that are independent of the Renaissance if conceived primarily as an episode of artistic and intellectual innovation. The story of schools and universities, the book trade that serviced those institutions, and the print technology developed from the fifteenth century are a case in point. The Renaissance is not responsible for any of these phenomena. Similarly, developments in popular culture, shifts in the role of women, changes in ritual behavior, all of which are important subjects of study for scholars of the period, have little to do with the Renaissance.

The Protestant and Catholic Reformations, likewise, are movements distinct from the Renaissance, as are the development of the modern nation state, absolute monarchy, and the scientific revolution of the sixteenth and seventeenth centuries. So, too, the exploration and conquest of the New World, the European penetration of Asian and African markets, the development of protoindustrialization, and the great shift in European urbanization from the Mediterranean region to northwestern Europe are all autonomous from the Renaissance, although contemporary with it. The Renaissance should not loom so large, it seems, in our journey through past time if all of these other changes constituting the early modern experience were also underway.

THE RENAISSANCE PRESENCE IN "EARLY MODERN" HISTORY

And yet, even if autonomous in origin, none of these phenomena are wholly separable from the Renaissance. Printing developed in the German lands within an artisan tradition but quickly was put to use in Renaissance Italy to publish Latin and Greek and contemporary humanist and literary works. The Renaissance did not cause women's roles to change, but women's place and capacity became a major theme of Renaissance literature. Popular culture became distinct from elite culture in this era largely because elite society embraced the new pedagogy of the Renaissance and its new standards for proper behavior. Although the Renaissance did not trigger the religious revolutions and counterrevolutions, the major Protestant and Catholic apologists—including the key figures Martin Luther (1483–1546) and John Calvin (1509–1564)—were trained humanists, and the school and university curricula devised by reformers followed humanist principles. In the end, the central Renaissance intellectual phenomenon of humanism both powered the Reformations and assisted in their diffusion.

The Renaissance did not in itself encourage the development of absolutism, but advocates of absolutist rule read the classical and contemporary works the Renaissance made available and employed humanist rhetoric in its defense. Renaissance thinkers were not themselves, for the most part, scientists, but the founders of Europe's scientific revolution had been trained in classical thought and garnered new concepts from ancient Greek books. Although the Renaissance did not trigger the drive to open up the Atlantic and the Pacific to European trade, the authors of travel literature, tracts on economics and cartography, critiques of the enslavement of Indigenous peoples, and all the other literary manifestations of European expansion had read the texts that humanist scholarship made current and employed the rhetoric imparted by humanist teachers to speak about those events. Meanwhile, the experiences of Europeans were reflected in artistic and dramatic productions that belong to the story of the unfolding Renaissance.

The historical events and processes of the "early modern" age cannot be, as some scholars might wish, surgically detached from the elite civilization of the Renaissance. The Renaissance, in fact, extended from Scandinavia to the Balkans, Bordeaux to Buda and Pest, and even to the distant European settlements in the New World, lending its distinct shading to regional cultures.

THE RENAISSANCE AND THIS BOOK

The argument returns to the Renaissance as a valid construct, spurred by innovations in the realms of art and thought but embracing many and touching on very nearly all the events and developments of the period from 1300 to 1700. The author of this book, clearly, does not share the doubts some scholars have expressed about the existence or the importance of the Renaissance. She believes that the Renaissance was a phase of Western history of such tremendous importance that students living far from its epicenter and several centuries afterward should devote an entire semester to its study. In so doing, they will learn not only about the Renaissance that unfolded in Europe between 1300 and 1700 but about the problem of cultural renewal: why it happens; why the energy it unlooses is momentous; how it changes everything about it.

The Renaissance, it is assumed in this volume, emerged because of the very special circumstances present in Italy from the twelfth century. Those circumstances encouraged a large number of artists and thinkers to integrate the values of classical antiquity into medieval culture, grounded in the Christian values (themselves rooted in ancient Judaism) they inherited. This was the second and final moment in the history of the West when the Judeo-Christian and classical traditions would coalesce. The first was in late antiquity as Christianity spread and became integrated with classical civilization before the collapse of the western zone of the Roman Empire.

This second and definitive reintegration of two ancient cultural traditions permitted European civilization to develop into its modern form. That civilization remained dominant until, in the twentieth century, it was challenged by modernism and then post-modernism, movements that called for the repudiation of both its classical and Christian pasts. Before that denouement, it was the civilization of the Renaissance, extending and evolving through the Enlightenment and into the nineteenth century, with its ancient past unforgotten, that characterized Western civilization at its height—the civilization that yielded the liberal ideals of the democratic West.

The preceding outlines the assumptions that underlie the meaning of the term "Renaissance" in the present volume. Why, then, the present title *A Short History of the Renaissance in Europe*? It has been chosen because the other likely titles have been rejected with cause. "The Renaissance," it could be argued, claims too much. The Renaissance is not a disembodied entity that floats free of time and space: it first occurred in a specific place Italy for identifiable reasons. Yet "The Italian Renaissance" has also been

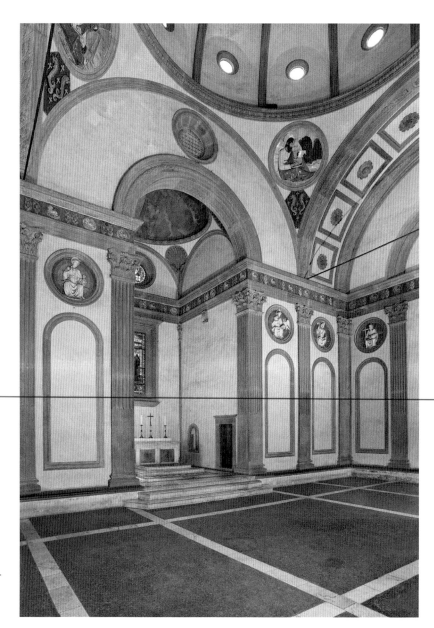

Brunelleschi, Pazzi Chapel interior, 1429–61. Santa Croce, Florence.

This freestanding chapel built adjacent to the Gothic-style Franciscan Basilica of Santa Croce for the patrician Pazzi family epitomizes the Renaissance adoption and interpretation of classical forms.

rejected. The first two centuries of the Renaissance unfolded almost exclusively in Italy. Nevertheless, its Italian roots are only part of the story, which must also trace the diffusion of Italian Renaissance thought to other settings, which were already undergoing renewal of their own native cultures. "The European Renaissance" suggests a monolith, when, in fact, the Renaissance unfolded differently in different settings: here combined with religious reformation, there primarily musical and dramatic, elsewhere a matter of philosophy and texts, and elsewhere again involved wholly with the rituals and pretenses of the monarchical court.

THE STRUCTURE OF THIS BOOK

And so, this volume is entitled *A Short History of the Renaissance in Europe*. It traces how a civilization was born in Italy through the work of artists and thinkers, was transformed by the political and social changes experienced by the peoples of that peninsula, and then was transformed again in each region, city, and court of Europe beyond the Alps to which it was carried by willing emissaries and involuntary exiles. Chapters 1 and 2 describe the evolution of Italian society from late Roman days through the mid-fourteenth century, delineating the conditions that would give rise to a burst of cultural energy. Chapters 3 and 4 introduce the intellectual and artistic dimensions of the Italian Renaissance. Chapters 5 and 6 explore the social and cultural world within which the Renaissance unfolded: the neighborhoods and associations, gender roles and the interplay of genders, the structure and hierarchy of the official church, and the great dynamism of popular religious belief.

Chapters 7 and 8 describe the political evolution of the Italian states and the dislocations that occurred with the French, Spanish, and imperial invasions of the late fifteenth and early sixteenth centuries. The political defeat of Italy did not put an end to the artistic and intellectual expression of the Italian Renaissance, but it was transformative. The works of Niccolò Machiavelli (1469–1527) and Baldassare Castiglione (1478–1529) testify to the political diminution of the region, which then is seen to continue as a leader in the arts and of ideas into the early seventeenth century.

Chapters 9 through 11 see the Renaissance travel beyond the Alps and beyond the context of the Italian city-state. In Chapter 9, the Christian humanism represented especially by Desiderius Erasmus (c. 1466–1536) is seen to temper Italian classicism with the values of the *Devotio Moderna* (New Devotion), a product of the Low Countries that stressed genuine and personal piety. That Christian humanism, in turn, both promoted and stood apart from the message of the first of the reformers, Martin Luther, whose repudiation of the Roman Church was uncompromising and definitive.

Chapter 10 reviews the different social contexts of the Renaissance beyond the Alps—the kingdom, the court, the city—and, region by region, describes the transformation of Renaissance civilization in new settings conditioned by diverse native cultures. Chapter 11 considers three of the great cultural shifts of the sixteenth and seventeenth centuries: exploration and encounter, the development of science, and the broadening of the horizons of the learned, which now included even women, who, in turn, claimed their own place in Western civilization. All of these even if not of the Renaissance were preconditioned by the Renaissance, which had integrated the sum total of the intellectual traditions of the West into a pluralistic, dynamic, and flexible whole.

FEATURES

Accompanying this 11-chapter narrative is a series of features that are meant sometimes to deepen the reader's understanding of the account and sometimes to explore related issues that provide insight into the era but do not form part of the primary exposition. There are three kinds of these features: Focus and Voice boxes, and mini-boxes.

Twenty-five Focus boxes explore collateral issues using both words and images. A Focus box on "Personal Space," for example, describes the appearance of the scholar's study as an aspect of the development of humanism, the principal intellectual movement of the Renaissance. Similarly, a Focus box on "Warriors for Hire" looks closely at the phenomenon of the *condottiere*, the paid commander of a mercenary force who was often the very effective instrument of military power for the Renaissance city-state.

Twenty-two "Voice" boxes present excerpts from contemporary texts that add depth to the reader's understanding of the people and issues named in the chapter. Voice boxes provide a closer look at such matters as the thought of Petrarch; the patronage activity of Isabella d'Este (1474–1539), the marchioness of Mantua; and the threats of riot, crime, and plague to the Renaissance city-state. As the Renaissance moves over the Alps, Voice boxes explore aspects of French and Spanish literature, the Protestant and Catholic reform movements, and the development of scientific thought.

Eighteen mini-boxes, many containing statistical data, provide an at-a-glance summary of particular aspects of Renaissance culture and society. Among other things, they display the patterns of wall-building in Renaissance cities during a period of economic expansion; provide comparative data about the sizes of libraries from the fourteenth to sixteenth centuries; track the prosecution of homosexuals over two peak decades in Renaissance Florence; show patterns in the persecution of Protestants in Antwerp; and document the expansion of the numbers of the literate as the Renaissance yields to modern times.

Each chapter, finally, provides timelines, maps (except Chapter 5), and suggestions for further reading (both primary and secondary), which further assist the reader to place the information delivered by the narrative in a framework of time and space.

YOU, THE AUDIENCE

This book—narrative and features—is designed for you, the audience, whether you are a secondary-school or college student, an advanced student or casual reader who wishes a brief and coherent introduction to the origins, course, and significance of the Renaissance in Europe. It introduces many major figures and events since the complexity of the era cannot be understood if only generalizations are provided. At the same time, it tries to avoid dense discussions of ideas or events that can be explored later, if the reader wishes, in the boundless, rich literature on specific aspects of Renaissance politics, society, and culture.

Twenty-first-century readers, especially students, have many claims on their attention. Even within the field of history, they might want to explore first their own national past, or gain an acquaintance with other civilizations around the globe. The author of the present volume does not suggest that the Renaissance is more important than these. But she would argue that a clear understanding of the Renaissance will help any reader understand how the Western world, its civilization built on the twin foundations of Judeo-Christian and classical cultures, came to expand from 1500 to 1900 and attain world dominance and why even today, in an era of globalization, the Renaissance very much matters.

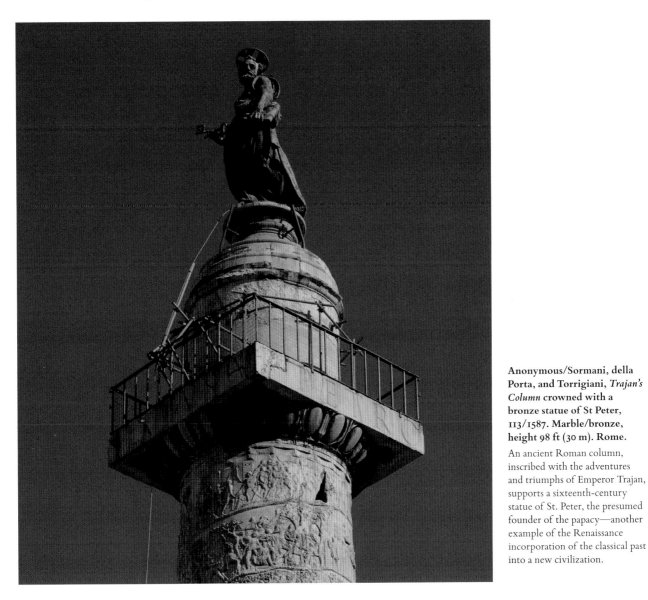

Anonymous/Sormani, della Porta, and Torrigiani, *Trajan's Column* crowned with a bronze statue of St Peter, 113/1587. Marble/bronze, height 98 ft (30 m). Rome.

An ancient Roman column, inscribed with the adventures and triumphs of Emperor Trajan, supports a sixteenth-century statue of St. Peter, the presumed founder of the papacy—another example of the Renaissance incorporation of the classical past into a new civilization.

ONE

ITALY AND ROME: FROM ROMAN REPUBLIC TO *SECONDO POPOLO* (c. 500 BCE–c. 1300 CE)

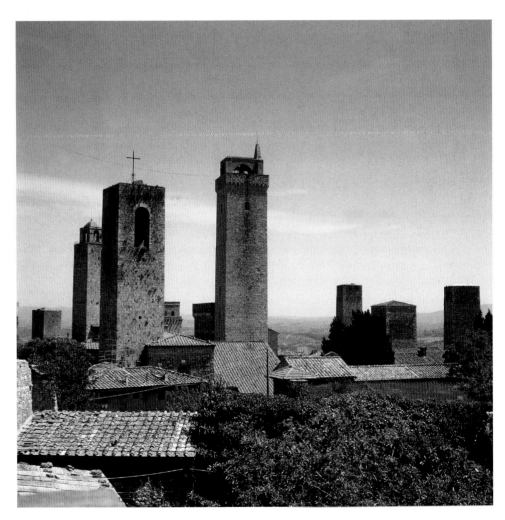

San Gimignano, Tuscany

As was common in northern Italy, towers belonging to *consorterie* (clans) of urbanized nobles bristled against the skylines, signifying the military power, prestige, and intentions of their owners.

On February 15, 1944, when World War II was still 18 months away from its awful close, an Allied army faced a German force encamped at Monte Cassino (see pp. 6–7), a **monastery** founded in 529 by St. Benedict of Nursia (c. 480–547). The Allied bombardment destroyed the monastery—its fourth destruction. Previously, in 577, it had been sacked, gutted, and burned by the German tribal people called **Lombards**, and then again in 883 by Arabic **Muslims** called **Saracens**. In 1349 it was flattened by an earthquake, an act of hostile nature contemporaneous with the even more devastating **Black Death** then stalking Europe.

Each time it was destroyed, the abbey was rebuilt. It can be visited today in its fifth incarnation, 80 miles south of Rome. Monte Cassino links the ancient world with the medieval civilization that ensued. It also links the ancient world with the Renaissance of classical forms and ideas, which occurred after 1300, and with our own world, modern and postmodern, negligent of what was once so carefully preserved.

Monte Cassino is not unique. Sites spread throughout Europe, and particularly in Italy, contain the memory of past civilizations and especially of that span of time between the Roman Empire at its height and the resurgence of classical learning and sensibility more than 1,000 years later. This chapter will provide an overview of the transitions that occurred from ancient times to about 1300 CE, as Roman civilization yielded to the civilization of the Middle Ages and medieval civilization grew and changed, making way for the transformation of the Renaissance yet to come.

The chapter will explain, first, how the Italian peninsula became romanized over the 500 years before the advent of the Common Era (CE) under the leadership of a people with a special talent for military and political organization. It will turn next to the cultural and economic upheavals of the third and fourth centuries CE and the disintegration of Roman political institutions under the pressures of invasion in the fifth and sixth centuries. The chapter then describes the reorganization of the peninsula during the medieval era under the authority of bishops, popes, and emperors, and the concurrent processes of commercial revival and urbanization. Finally, it considers the communal revolution that began in the eleventh century, powered by economic revival, which created the vigorous urban institutions of northern Italy that were the framework for the Renaissance.

THE ROMANIZATION OF ITALY

In 510 BCE, as one of the peninsula's Latin-speaking tribes, which inhabited a village on the Tiber River, prepared to depose its foreign ruler, the Etruscan King Tarquin the Proud (r. 534–510 BCE), there was no nation called Italy. (Indeed, there was no such nation until 1871.) The slender boot-shaped peninsula that dips into the Mediterranean Sea about midway from west to east was peopled by many different inhabitants at different stages of cultural development.

In the south, around the toe and heel of the peninsula, the many flourishing cities were peopled principally by Greeks. They were the descendants of Greek colonists who had come two and three centuries earlier. The large mountainous island of Sicily, poised off the toe of the peninsula, whose one large fertile plain fed its people, was home to Greeks, Carthaginians, and indigenous people. The center of the peninsula was occupied by tribal peoples often in competition with each other: Oscans, Volsci, Samnites, and Latins. Settled north of the Arno River were the Etruscans, who spoke a non-Indo-European language and who may have descended from Near Eastern peoples. Still further north, in the fertile valley of the Po, groups of migrant Celts had settled.

The peoples of Italy were diverse in language, occupation, and culture. The citified Greeks of the south consumed luxury goods from the Near East and performed tragedies and comedies in their theaters. The warrior tribes of central Italy plundered their rivals or grazed herds of cattle and sheep. The Etruscans were producers of iron ore and implements, imaginative architects, and hearty banqueteers—to which events they brought their wives, which shocked the Greeks, who generally separated the sexes at mealtime.

These peoples of Italy competed among themselves for land and for dominion. Oriented toward commerce and the sea, the Greek city-dwellers sought mainly to defend themselves, often hiring mercenary armies to do so. The contending peoples of Sicily called on the assistance of Italian or Carthaginian allies. The Etruscans, who, like the Greeks lived in **city–states**, with their more advanced culture and iron technology, extended their control of neighbors to the south. In 510 BCE, when the united villagers of Rome expelled their Etruscan overlord, it seemed very likely that they would soon be recaptured. Instead, the Romans consolidated their position in central Italy. As Rome expanded, the northern boundary of dense habitation was pushed further north, bringing under the Roman umbrella the whole of the region that today is identified as the nation of Italy.

They did this, in part, by force, and in part, by political skill. They defeated the Latins (their former allies), the Oscans, and the Samnites. Departing from the norm of ancient conflict, they did not enslave those they defeated. Though they demanded tribute, they did so in the context of a mutual relationship that was as bold as it was novel. They arranged contracts with the peoples they conquered, extending to them different privileges of association with Rome: full citizenship, partial citizenship, commercial rights. As a result, the conquered tribes of central Italy became the friends and allies of the Romans. Although their status was subordinate, they had not been crushed and did not hate their conquerors. More, they enjoyed the protection that Rome was able to confer. By about 200 BCE, the Italian peoples that Rome had conquered had become culturally Roman, and they had begun to think of becoming formally Roman as well.

Rome was less gentle toward the Etruscans to the north and Greeks to the south. Nevertheless, once the Punic Wars against Rome's arch-rival Carthage had been won (in 146 BCE), and the empire was expanding toward Greece and the Near East, Italy had become Roman. The tiny village built on seven hills overlooking the Tiber River had tamed the other regions of Italy. They, in turn, could make their claims on Rome. By 89 BCE, 40 years before Julius Caesar (102/100 44 BCE) crossed the Rubicon to precipitate

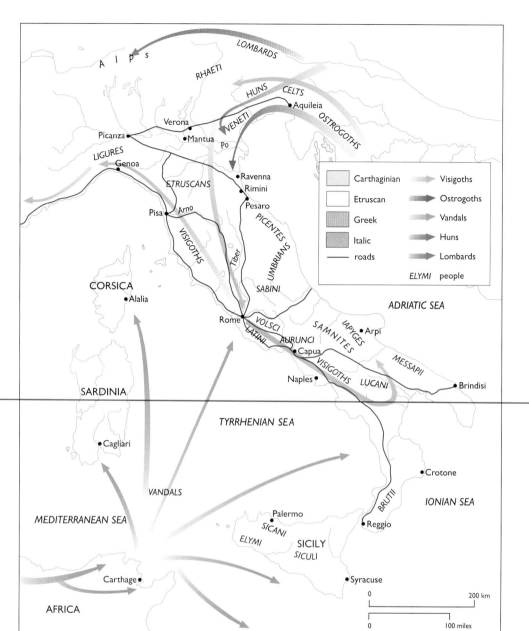

The Peoples of Roman Italy

This map tells the story of Italian peoples at the beginning (c. 500 BCE) and end (5th to 6th centuries CE) of the Roman era. Around 500 BCE, Etruscan, Greek, and Italic peoples inhabited the peninsula, but they became romanized by the beginning of the empire (c. 27 BCE). Roman unity was by then expressed in its extensive road network (shown here). During Rome's last centuries, new and hostile peoples arrived from Asia, northern Europe, and North Africa: the Ostrogoths and Visigoths, Vandals, Huns, and Lombards.

both a civil war and the great transformation of Rome from republic to empire, the Italians south of the Po River had rebelled against their masters, asking for the privilege of citizenship, and that privilege had been granted. Northern Italians received the same privilege in 49 BCE, the same year as Caesar's decisive crossing.

Over the next centuries, during which the Roman Empire reached its furthest boundaries and Roman civilization reaped its greatest achievements, Italians, like Romans, were involved in the creation of literature, history, and law and enjoyed and used the roads, aqueducts, bridges, sewers, and colosseums that were the hallmarks of the Roman presence. The orator M. Tullius Cicero (106–43 BCE) came from Arpinum, some 70 miles from Rome; the historian Livy (Titus Livius, 59/64 BCE–17 CE) came from Padua, in the northeast corner of the peninsula; the poet G. Valerius Catullus (84–54 BCE) from nearby Verona. Two hundred years later even immigrants from Spain or Africa might be "Roman" as the city on the Tiber became a world metropolis and extended the privilege of citizenship far beyond its borders.

It was a thoroughly romanized Italy, then, that began to suffer a progressive decline in economy and culture from the third century CE and the invasions and destruction of the fifth and sixth centuries.

INVASION AND DESTRUCTION

From the third through the sixth century CE, the cosmopolitan, urban, expansive, and tolerant civilization of the Mediterranean world changed utterly and with it, Italy, the heartland of the Roman Empire. Initially, the imperial borders were hard to manage. In time, they broke and fell. Emperors found it difficult to rule; they were raised to power by a political faction or an army and often were born far from Rome or even Italy. A low point was reached when Emperor Aurelian (who, characteristically for this era, reigned a mere five years from 270 to 275 CE, but for his achievements was accorded the title *restitutor orbis*, "restorer of the world") built a new ring of defensive walls for the city of Rome, signaling the vulnerability of the capital itself. The walls stood for centuries, but did not, in the end, protect the city: they were breached by **Goths** in 410 and Vandals in 455, two of the Germanic peoples whose armed migrations contributed to the weakening of the empire.

In these years, although bureaucrats, generals, and merchants carried on much as they always had, the bonds of imperial rule were loosening. By 476, a German Gothic king ruled Italy and the Western Empire; by 540, the attempts of Justinian (r. 527–565), emperor in the East, to reclaim Italy from the Goths resulted in the devastation of Italy; by 568, German Lombard dukes and kings dominated the peninsula. Roman Italy was no more.

Early Migrations

The story of the movements of peoples who came to settle in Italy as Rome fragmented is important. The history of the Old World, the most densely inhabited parts of Afro-Eurasia, is to a great extent a history of migrations. These regions were inhabited because creatures of the new genus *homo* pushed out of Africa tens of thousands of years ago to settle in West, South, and East Asia, Anatolia, the Balkans, and western Europe. The Stone Age settlements of hunters and gatherers gave way to villages of pastoralists and agriculturalists, and then, by 3500 BCE in the Mediterranean zone (and somewhat later in India and China), to cities of artisans, merchants, aristocrats, priests, and kings.

MONTE CASSINO: MOUNTAINTOP REFUGE IN AN AGE OF TURMOIL

In 529 the Roman nobleman Benedict of Nursia, who had become a monk during the last years of Rome's imperial sway in western Europe, took refuge in a mountaintop tower near the city of Cassinum (destroyed 35 years earlier by the Goths), halfway between Rome and Naples. There, in the tower, he composed his *Rule* for monks, which became the basis of Western monasticism. There too, on the site of the dismantled temple of the god Apollo, he established the monastic community of Monte Cassino. As elsewhere, the Christian institution of the monastery became the repository of both Christian and Roman traditions amid the ruins of ancient cities and the wreckage of ancient systems of value.

Benedict never again left Monte Cassino, where he received as a visitor the Ostrogothic king Totila and where he was buried next to his sister, St. Scholastica, the abbess of a nearby nunnery. The autograph copy of Benedict's *Rule* remained within the community for about 300 years as the monks fled into exile and then returned home until, at

last, around 900 it was destroyed. For Monte Cassino had a long and tumultuous history, emblematic of the fortunes of human institutions in Italy—and Europe—during the period between the disintegration of the Roman Empire and the reestablishment of order during the Renaissance.

Monte Cassino flourished after Benedict's death until 577, when it was pillaged by Lombards. The ravaged community reunited in Rome under papal protection. It was still residing there during the **papacy** of Gregory the Great (r. 590–604), who organized the spread of Benedictine monasticism, the creation of Monte Cassino, to northern Europe. Only in 718 did the monks return to Monte Cassino to regroup and rebuild, erecting a new church over the tombs of Benedict and Scholastica. In 786 Monte Cassino welcomed to its community the Lombard scholar and poet Paul the Deacon (720–799), who wrote a history of the Lombard kingdom to 744, an indispensable source for modern historians of the early Middle Ages, and a commentary on Benedict's *Rule*.

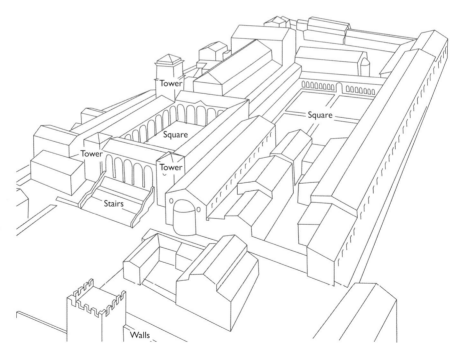

Plan of Monte Cassino

A new invasion in 884, this time by Saracens, caused the monks to seek exile once again. Again they returned, in 949, to their mountaintop refuge, where they now resided in safety for nearly 400 years. The zenith of Monte Cassino's history was reached under Abbot Desiderius (r. 1058–1087), who later reigned as Pope Victor III (r. 1086–1087). At that time, more than 200 monks resided at the monastery, which supported schools of manuscript copyists and illuminators—for Monte Cassino was one of the most important sites for the preservation and reproduction of the books rescued from the fall of the ancient world. Desiderius had the abbey and church reconstructed with great magnificence, bringing in artists from many parts of Italy and using new mosaic techniques imported from Byzantium. More reconstruction followed the devastations caused by an earthquake in 1349, just one year after the Black Death had ravaged the region. In the sixteenth and seventeenth centuries, Renaissance and **Baroque** artists added their contributions to the architectural and painting programs. The complex became a splendid monument, a worthy home for the invaluable library the monks had accumulated, and a tribute to its founder Benedict.

In 1799, Monte Cassino was again pillaged, this time by Napoleon's soldiers, and then suppressed in 1866 by the new, secularizing Italian government of the Risorgimento (Resurgence), the movement of national unification. Still a national treasure, it preserved its irreplaceable library under the protection of the Italian government until 1944, when, having been occupied by the Nazis, it was wholly destroyed by the US army of liberation.

Monte Cassino was the most important, but not the sole, monastic refuge from the tumult that prevailed from late antiquity through the late Middle Ages. The Roman statesman and scholar Cassiodorus founded the monastery of Vivarium around 540, where he retired until his death, accumulating a library and himself writing works that preserved the memory of the Roman past. In the northern part of the peninsula, near Piacenza, the Irish monk and refugee Columban (543–615; later canonized) founded a monastery at Bobbio around 612. It, too, became a center of learning and the home of an important library that possessed about 700 tenth-century manuscripts, subsequently dispersed mostly to other Italian libraries. In retreats such as these, the legacy of antiquity was preserved until it could be digested anew by the humanists of the Renaissance.

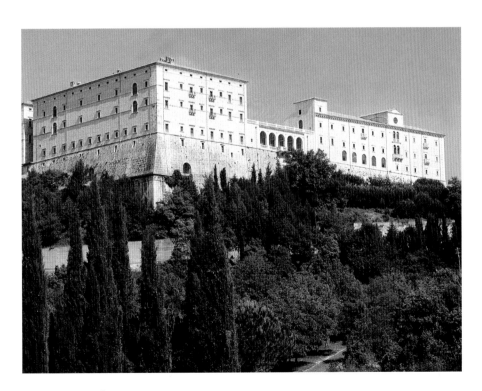

Monte Cassino, Italy

From Africa, again, in the fourth and third millennia BCE, speakers of Semitic languages swept into Mesopotamia in the Near East, the Fertile Crescent bounded by the Tigris and Euphrates Rivers. Perhaps from Anatolia, in the third and second millennia BCE, speakers of an Indo-European language spread west and north into Europe and east and south into India and Iran. Among them were a people called "Italic," who lent their name and their language to the inhabitants of that peninsula. In the last millennium BCE, the Celtic peoples pushed into western Europe, the Balkans, and Italy. All this time, across the southern steppes of Asia, nomadic tribes swept east on the horses they had domesticated to harry the borders of China and west to survey the tempting prospects of the wealthy urban centers of the Mediterranean lands. Soon they, too, would come in search of pasture, plunder, and the lure of civilization.

In the fourth century, one of these Asian steppe peoples, the Huns, erupted into Europe. Under King Attila (c. 406–453 CE), they caused havoc in central Europe, Gaul (modern France), and Italy before abandoning a push into Italy in 451. But the Huns had a terrible impact long before Attila's strike. They terrified the eastern Germans (and incidentally the Slavs, inhabitants of northeastern Europe) who had recently migrated to the Balkans. As the Huns drove westward, a mixed force of German Goths prodded and then entered the Roman Empire in the Balkans and inflicted a terrible defeat on an imperial army at Adrianople in 378. German horsemen routed imperial infantry and raised the specter of what lay ahead: a showdown between the less advanced but militarily superior peoples from beyond the zone of civilization and the practiced Roman war machine.

Germanic Incursions

In the fifth century, Germanic tribal armies and steppe raiders poured into the Western Empire. Vandals and Sueves swept past the Alpine border of Italy to settle in Iberia and in the case of the Vandals, crossing at Gibraltar into North Africa. Ostrogoths and Visigoths (eastern and western Goths, respectively) appeared in Italy, and Visigothic leaders created kingdoms in southern Gaul and Iberia. Burgundians, Allemanni, and Franks moved south and west into west Germany and modern France; Angles, Saxons, and Jutes crossed the English Channel to destroy the remnants of Roman rule in Britain. Rome itself, as noted above, was sacked in 410 by the Goths and in 455 by the Vandals. Italy became the plaything of German warlords who proclaimed obedience to the Eastern emperor at Constantinople.

In 476, with the expulsion of the last nominal Western emperor, the Germanic king Odoacer (r. 476–493) took charge. Ruling with the support of the Roman senate, he attempted to regain Roman supremacy in Dalmatia and Sicily. When the Ostrogoth Theodoric (r. 493–526), encouraged by the Eastern emperor Zeno (r. 474–491), invaded in 489, however, Odoacer was doomed. He took refuge in Ravenna, then the Italian imperial capital, as Rome had become too vulnerable. Theodoric, having conquered nearly all of the peninsula, amiably invited his rival to dinner—and there he killed him.

The reign of the Ostrogoth Theodoric as king of Italy still did not destroy Roman culture in Italy. Although an Arian, and thus considered a **heretic**, Theodoric was Christian, and Christianity won converts under his rule. The Roman senate continued to meet, and Theodoric patronized two of the senators, both learned men, who would be pivotal figures in the transmission of Roman civilization to medieval Europe. One was Boethius (Anicius Manlius Severius Boethius, c. 475–525), an interpreter and translator (into Latin) of the logical works of Aristotle (384–322 BCE) and author of *The Consolation of Philosophy*. This work, read constantly over the next thousand years, was written in prison where Boethius, who had been consigned there by Theodoric on a false charge of treason, was later executed. The other learned senator was Cassiodorus (490–583). After an adult career spent as senator, landowner, and political advisor, he retired to a monastery of his founding to record in writing his memories of Roman antiquity.

On Theodoric's death, the kingdom of Italy was left to his successors. This gave Justinian, emperor in the East (later the **Byzantine** Empire), an opportunity to snatch Italy from German rule as he was also hoping to rescue North Africa. His general Belisarius (c. 505–565) led a large army to North Africa in 533 and swiftly reconquered the region from the Vandals. In 535 he crossed to Italy. Justinian's so-called reconquest of Italy, however, was bloody and destructive.

By 540 Belisarius had won—or so it seemed. But then a resurgence of Gothic strength, especially under the last Ostrogothic king Totila (r. 541–552), resulted in further mayhem. Whereas the Ostrogothic regime had been fairly mild during the reign of Theodoric, vengeance now drove the German leaders to merciless and unrelenting violence. By 550 only Ravenna and a few other outposts remained in Byzantine hands. Justinian sent a new general, Narses (c. 478–c. 573), to reclaim Italy and destroy Totila, both tasks accomplished by 552. He became imperial prefect of a ruined Italy and served until he was recalled for his cruelties by Justinian's successor. At Justinian's death in 565, much of Roman Italy had been reconquered, but it would soon be lost again. The story of the Gothic Wars, which destroyed the lands they were meant to preserve, are well-known through the narratives of two contemporary historians: the Roman aristocrat Cassiodorus and the Byzantine scholar Procopius (c. 499–565), advisor to Justinian.

Italy was still vital in the fourth and fifth centuries, but the years of devastation left it impoverished by the middle of the sixth century. As the hostilities ceased, a new horror came in the form of the bubonic plague that would strike Europe again in 1347. The epidemic resulted in further depopulation and demoralization and recurred several times in the century. It was a gravely weakened Italy that was invaded again in 568, this time by the Germanic Lombards. Lombard chieftains seized the northern zone, creating a kingdom of Italy, its king crowned by an iron crown. They pressed on toward the south, where lesser leaders called "dukes" set up autonomous principalities. The Byzantine Empire retained a mid-section of the peninsula, reaching as far as Venice on the Adriatic coast. Meanwhile, the pope, as the bishop of Rome was now called, was building a new power base around Rome.

500 BCE–1 BCE

510 BCE Romans depose their Etruscan ruler, King Tarquin.

340 BCE Romans defeat the Italian states of the Latin League then make lenient peace terms.

146 BCE Carthage's defeat leaves Rome the dominant power in the Mediterranean.

44 BCE Julius Caesar is assassinated.

27 BCE Octavian (as Augustus) becomes the first Roman emperor.

1 CE–499 CE

c. 110 The Roman Empire reaches its greatest extent under Emperor Trajan.

270 Emperor Aurelian builds city walls to defend Rome from attack.

284–305 Emperor Diocletian's measures fail to halt the Roman Empire's decline.

313 By the Edict of Milan, Emperor Constantine grants tolerance to Christians in the Roman Empire.

330 Constantine makes Constantinople his new capital.

374 Ambrose becomes Bishop of Milan, exercising authority over religious and secular matters.

391 Emperor Theodosius I privileges Christianity in the Empire, banning cults considered pagan.

410 Goths led by Alaric enter Rome, sack the city.

455 The Vandals attack and loot Rome.

476 The last Roman emperor in the west, Romulus Augustus, is deposed. The Germanic leader Odoacer takes power in Rome.

493 The Ostrogoth King Theodoric kills Odoacer and holds sway.

500–999

523 Boethius writes *The Consolation of Philosophy*.

529 St. Benedict founds the Monte Cassino Monastery, the first house of what would later be known as the Benedictine Order.

535–552 Emperor Justinian reconquers Italy.

c. 540 Roman historian Cassiodorus promotes a mix of classical and sacred learning.

568 Lombards overrun much of Italy; Venice is founded by refugees fleeing from them.

590–604 Pope Gregory I the Great systematizes church ritual, expands the papal role.

756 Frankish King Pippin defeats the Lombards, gives Ravenna to the pope, creating the first papal state.

768 Charlemagne becomes King of the Franks.

800 Pope Leo III crowns Charlemagne as Emperor of the Romans.

962 Frankish King Otto I becomes emperor.

1000–1350

1075 Pope Gregory VII in *Dictatus papae* asserts the pope's power, including the right to invest bishops.

c. 1080 The "commune" movement begins, bringing Italian cities under local magnates' rule.

1095 Pope Urban II proclaims the First Crusade to free Jerusalem from Seljuk Turks.

1122 Concordat of Worms ends the Investiture Controversy with a compromise between pope and emperor.

1138 Florence becomes a commune.

1176 Lombard League, formed by Italian communes, defeats Emperor Frederick Barbarossa at Legnano.

1204 Venetians plunder Constantinople in the Fourth Crusade.

1215 Under Pope Innocent III, the Fourth Lateran Council reforms monastic orders.

1226 A Second Lombard League is organized against Frederick II.

1266 Charles d'Anjou kills Manfred, ending Hohenstaufen rulers' attempts to dominate Italy.

1309 Pope Clement moves from Rome to Avignon, France, where successive popes stay until 1376.

CATHEDRAL AND MONASTERY

Even before the Germanic and Lombard invasions, Italy had begun to acquire a new infra-structure that would remain in place even as the official institutions of Roman governance and security failed. That infrastructure belonged to the new Christian church, whose fragmented and vulnerable communities of the first century grew progressively stronger despite episodes of vicious persecution until, in the fourth century, it received official protection under Emperor Constantine (r. 306–337) and privileged status under Emperor Theodosius I (r. 379–395). Over the centuries, capable and powerful leaders emerged to guide the new church. Most of them held the title of bishop, and they presided over large churches called cathedrals.

Bishops were authoritative figures, in part, because they were understood to be the successors of the apostles (a Greek word meaning "those sent out") of Jesus of Nazareth, surnamed the "Christ," or "the Anointed One." According to Christian scripture, Jesus, after his crucifixion and his resurrection, commissioned the original apostles: "And Jesus came and said to them, 'All authority in heaven and on earth has been given to me. Go therefore and make disciples of all nations, baptizing them in the name of the Father and of the Son and of the Holy Spirit, and teaching them to obey everything that I have

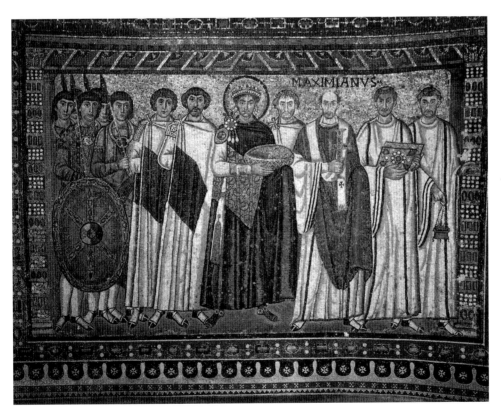

Justinian and His Retinue, c. 547, **mosaic. San Vitale, Ravenna.**

This image speaks of the Roman world changed after Justinian's reconquest. The Emperor is a remote, disembodied figure—quite unlike heroic characterizations of earlier emperors. He is flanked by ministers, soldiers, and a representative of the church. The medium is mosaic, dazzling in its brilliance but suggestive of a reality distanced, like the Emperor himself, from the things of this life.

commanded you. And remember, I am with you always, to the end of the age'" (Matthew 28:18–20). Paul (d. c. 64), the first missionary of the church, numbered among the first apostles. He planted Christian communities throughout the Near East and Greece and died, it is thought, in Rome.

The Authority of the Bishops

As the first generation of apostles met their deaths, a far more numerous generation of leaders emerged, known as bishops. These were the authoritative leaders of new Christian communities, empowered to set standards for membership in their community, overseeing the training and confirmation of new converts, and expelling those who failed in their Christian duties. They also managed church finances; organized the extensive machinery of benevolence that provided for the poor, the sick, the orphaned and the widowed; and appointed deacons, the subordinate officials who administered these projects. They were responsible for the installation of other bishops and the training and ordination of priests, who performed the **sacraments** of baptism and the mass (the liturgy of the Eucharist, the central rite of **Catholic** Christian worship) for all Christian congregants. They promoted the cults of local martyrs (those who died during the Christian persecutions of the first three centuries CE) and saints (holy persons of exceptional virtue and miraculous accomplishment), arranged for processions of the citizenry on festal days or, in times of crisis, for the feeding and housing of pilgrims en route to holy places in Rome or Jerusalem.

A bishop's authority extended over a territory comprising several congregations, called a **diocese**, the term used in the Roman Empire for a subdivision of a province. Within that territory, he had juridical rights over church personnel according to a body of specialized church or "canon" law, which rapidly developed. He also had the right to discipline ordinary church members through the practices of penance and absolution, which also became sacraments. Under the bishop's authority, separate parishes, administered by priests, tended locally to the needs of the faithful. Above him, holding authority over any number of subordinates, was the archbishop, whose jurisdiction might extend to very large areas (defined as, and sometimes identical to, the preexisting Roman province). The clergy of the whole of Britain, for instance, reported to only two archbishops.

In the early centuries of the church, the archbishops and bishops of the Eastern Empire, especially those at Antioch, Jerusalem, and Alexandria, were immensely important figures. Bishop Athanasius of Alexandria (293–373), for instance, persecuted heretics and was the primary architect of the important concept of the Trinity. Those in the west were at first less imposing, although in time, the bishop of Rome and the archbishop of Milan became more and more powerful. How the bishops related to the secular state differed in the Eastern and Western Empires. In the East, from Constantine onwards, the emperor was not only powerful but intimately involved with ecclesiastical policy. Ecclesiastical and lay (non-church) figures were closely related: the emperor boosted his clergy, and the clergy supported the emperor. In the West, Roman state power was increasingly in disarray, and the Germanic kings who asserted their authority by force were often not only short-lived but also heretical—most adhered to the anti-Trinitarian "Arian" heresy. Here, therefore, the bishops often exercised power despite, and in place of, any established government. The roots of a powerful and independent clergy in the West are deep.

They are especially deep in Italy. Here, in a populous region that had a long and intense experience of Roman rule, there were many bishops, approximately as many as there were major cities. In addition, Milan, Aquileia, and Ravenna, all metropolitan centers of Roman provincial administration, were archbishoprics. The term "metropolitan" came to designate not only the urban center but also the archbishop's office—a significant identification of the two realms. The Italian bishops became the effective rulers of Italy's cities as political authority dissolved. Not only did they administer the churches and clergy, but they managed urban grain stores, policed local markets, and raised and funded armies. Under their rule, the cities recovered from the gross depopulation of the sixth and seventh centuries and entered a new phase of growth.

The career of St. Ambrose (339–397) tells much about a bishop's role in the century before the fatal invasions of the West began, when Roman rule was already weakening. Born to a family of the Roman senatorial elite, he occupied a government position in Milan, northern Italy. In 374, over a period of just eight days, he was promoted from his secular office to bishop of the city. In that role, he wielded far more power over the citizens and exercised a far greater influence on the future of Europe than he would have done as an agent of the fading Roman state. Ruthlessly promoting Catholic Christianity in his territory, he restricted opportunities for Arian worship and pagan participation in civic life. Asserting the supremacy of clerical over political authority, a case he eloquently argued in his funeral orations for two emperors, he rebuked Theodosius I for his brutality against the citizens of Thessalonica. In his literary works and musical compositions, he published an ideal for the Christian clergy and enriched the early liturgy of the church. In his service to the Milanese, he mapped out the course by which, when Rome crumbled, a well-ordered, inspired, and confident church would pick up the reins of governance.

The Origins of Monastic Life

In these centuries that saw at once the enervation of Rome and the progress of Christianity, bishops were not, however, the only source of new energy; there were also the monasteries. These were, like the Western church itself, latecomers to Italy. The first monasteries grew out of the eremitic movement, in which Christians, inspired by the example of the martyrs who gave their lives for the faith and by the evidence of a crumbling world order, went out into the deserts of Egypt or Syria to live as hermits—a word derived from the Greek term for "desert-dweller." While the hermits sought by ascetic discipline to transcend earthly concerns and begin to live with God apart from the world, other Christians began to live apart from the world in the first monasteries, or communities, of solitary monks.

In these communities, whose occupants denied themselves many earthly comforts and subjected themselves to stern disciplines, the ascetic expectations were not as harsh as for the hermits. The monasteries took on other tasks. As self-sufficient enclaves set apart from urban life (especially as urban centers shrank in size and function), they had to cultivate their own food. They cleared land, managed drainage and irrigation projects, introduced new agricultural technology, and improved grain yields. They took on the functions of hospitals, schools, and inns; and they became the principal storehouses in Europe of the literary legacy of antiquity, copying and recopying ancient scrolls on parchment pages that were bound in books and placed on the shelves of the first libraries of the Western world.

Although there were separate impulses onditioning the development of monasticism in Gaul and Celtic Ireland, European monasteries came to develop this cultural role primarily in Italy due to the organizational work of St. Benedict of Nursia. His *Rule* for monks and the monastic organization would become nearly universally observed over the next three centuries. He followed the monastic models of Egypt and Gaul but adapted them for the Italian milieu, emphasizing not so much heroic asceticism as sound governance and community life in isolation from the world. While worship of God remained the monk's primary task, Benedict's *Rule* permitted ample food, moderate drink, and sufficient (if interrupted) sleep. Yet it insisted that the monk on entrance commit to residence in a single monastery, secluded from those outside, as well as to vows of poverty, chastity, and obedience; and it subjected all the monks, as "brothers," to the primacy of an abbot, or "father," whose rule was absolute.

Benedict's *Rule* was first used at the monastery he himself founded at Monte Cassino (see pp. 6–7). In time, it became the model for most of the monasteries of Italy, including, in a kind of hybrid format, the great monastery at Bobbio, originally founded by the Irish missionary Columban about 612. From Italy, the Benedictine rule spread to central and western Europe and for several centuries became the standard form of monastic organization. Benedictine monasticism was successful because of its clear system of governance, its austere but reasonable standards, and its great wealth. This wealth was the net product of the many endowments made to the monasteries by wealthy families that died out without children, or that believed, as many then did, that as the Roman state—the "City of Man" in the words of St. Augustine (354–430)—failed, the "City of God," of which the monastery was the perfect emblem, was bound to win.

From the sixth through tenth centuries, as Roman institutions fragmented, it was the monasteries and

Lombard and Byzantine Italy, c. 700

By the end of the sixth century, the Rome of Caesar and Augustus was no more. Germanic Lombards dominated the Italian peninsula, north and south, and the island of Corsica, while the Byzantine Empire retained fragile control over central Italy and the Veneto, the Dalmatian coast, parts of the south, and the islands of Sicily and Sardinia.

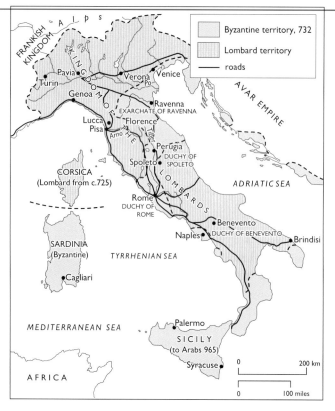

cathedrals that governed Italy, sustained the reduced remnants of civic life in depopulated urban centers, and nurtured the intellectual and literary legacy of the ancient world in their conversations, their new productions, and above all, in their preservation and reproduction of ancient books. These institutions, so unlike the original Roman institutions of family council and senate, became the vehicles by which Rome survived until the city was "reborn" centuries later.

EMPEROR AND POPE

During the period of Roman disintegration, as petty warlords struggled among themselves and ordinary folk sought refuge, two visions survived that would have tremendous importance for the development of western Europe and especially for Italy. The first was the idea of "empire": a political entity of transnational scope that would continue in the West the legacy of ancient Rome, set apart from the Byzantine Empire, which was increasingly seen as remote and unhelpful. The second was the idea of the papacy as a spiritual kingdom, the realm of God on earth, equipped with titles and territories to rule. Papacy and empire grew slowly, at times in cooperation, but ultimately in conflict, as each laid claim to be the greatest political force on the continent. By 1250 the empire's claim to rule Italy or to manage the pope had failed. Though it seemed as though the pope emerged victorious, the papacy was also to suffer a catastrophic loss of authority. Wedged between the zones of emperor and pope, the Italian city-states made their own claims for autonomy and freedom.

The Development of the Holy Roman Empire

With the Western Roman Empire in disarray, the Eastern Empire remained strong, centered in its bastion at Constantinople, and in time called Byzantine (after Byzantium, the original city that preceded the rebuilt capital of Constantine). The German chieftains who seized power in Italy in the late fifth and sixth centuries did not dare to call themselves "emperor." They acknowledged the overlordship of the Eastern emperors in Byzantium, who were occupied with the defense of their own realm and were glad to dispatch such titles as "patrician" or "protector"—a cheap currency of honor. The new Lombard kings who established themselves in the north of Italy received no such honor. They were the enemies of the Byzantine realm in Italy, centered at the exarchate of Ravenna, which still held the south and central territories of the peninsula as well as most of the Adriatic coast. The popes were confirmed in their office by the Byzantine emperors and remained loyal to the Eastern Empire—until that empire could no longer protect them.

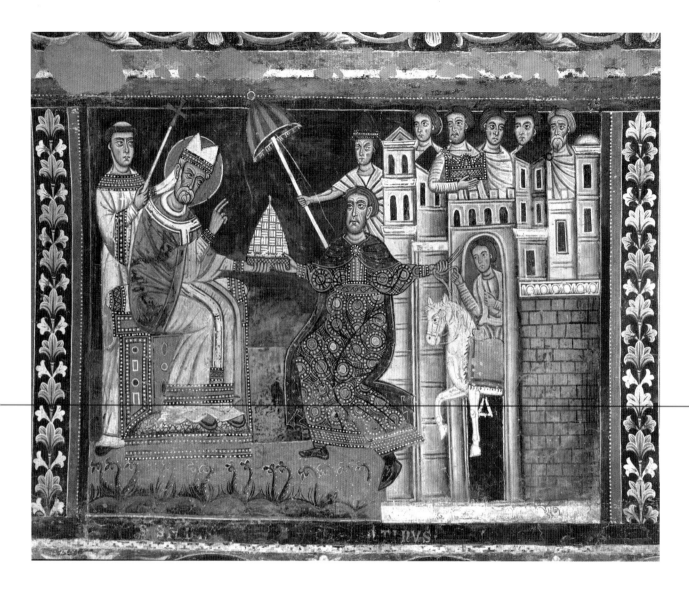

Donation of Constantine, **12th century, fresco. Santi Quattro Coronati, Rome.**

Painted during the medieval contest between pope and emperor, this fresco asserts the superiority of church over state. Emperor Constantine, kneeling unstably at the center, has yielded his throne, and here his crown, to Pope Sylvester.

Under Byzantine rule in a German-dominated Italy, the early popes enlarged the conception of the papacy. The Roman bishopric was already viewed as special in the first and second centuries because of the presence (and it was thought martyrdom) there of the apostles Paul and Peter. In the post-Constantinian period, when the church was first tolerated and then established, the popes began to argue for the unique authority of the Roman bishop. Pope Leo I (r. 440–461), surnamed "the Great" and later canonized, was the foremost architect of the papacy in late antiquity, attaching its claims for supremacy to its identification with Peter. After the Lombard invasion, Pope Gregory I, also a saint and also surnamed "the Great," laid the groundwork for a medieval papacy that would have considerable independence from secular authority. In addition to his many theoretical and pastoral works, Gregory labored to stem the Lombard advance, convert the German invaders and settlers, and reorganize the papal lands.

His successors adopted his understanding of the papacy's political and military role. In 739 and 751, when Byzantine authority on the peninsula was in full retreat and the Lombard threat loomed, Roman popes invited the Frankish rulers Charles Martel (c. 688–741) and Pippin III (d. 768) to halt their advance and protect the church. In 756 Pippin granted the pope territorial possession of lands in central Italy formerly belonging to the Byzantine exarchate. In the meantime, a papal forger had created a document—the so-called Donation of Constantine—which recorded the fictional donation of the Italian lands to the pope (then Sylvester III) by the newly converted (and miraculously healed) Emperor Constantine. The popes would frequently wield that document in their struggles with secular rulers to back up their claims to authority to rule in Italy and elsewhere.

Yet the pope remained unequipped with an army. The papacy's need to find a kingly protector in Italy was the springboard for the creation of what would become the **Holy Roman Empire**, conceived as a western European successor to ancient Rome. The phenomenon evolved slowly, however. When Pippin III's son Charlemagne (r. 768–814), like his father and grandfather, descended to Italy in the pope's service, the pope placed a crown on his head (on Christmas Day, 800) and called him "emperor." Though Charlemagne took the title of emperor, there was, as yet, no empire. More than a century later, in 962, following his triumph over a great Magyar invasion, the Eastern Frankish King Otto I (r. 936–973) was crowned emperor—yet at this point the concept of the empire, which was vague at best, included only the German lands and northern Italy. The emperor enjoyed preeminence among European kings but did not pretend to rule western Francia or other parts of Europe nor to be of equal status with the Byzantine ruler. (Charlemagne's successors had divided the Frankish kingdom into a western zone, later to become modern France, and a large eastern German zone.) By the next century, the Western Empire began to call itself the "Roman Empire." Under the audacious Emperor Frederick Barbarossa (r. 1152–1190) in the twelfth century, it was deemed the Holy Roman Empire.

During the tenth and eleventh centuries when the conception of empire was expanding, the emperors were more powerful than the popes. Although many of them journeyed to Rome to receive their crown from the popes, it was the emperors who were the de facto representatives of God's power on earth and to whom the popes were subordinate. These early emperors deposed and installed popes as they saw fit. At the same time, they had the support of the abbots of the great monasteries of Europe, for whom the empire was central to a Christian universe. Bishops were particularly important to them. Emperors installed bishops who could serve as effective agents of the state in part because they were

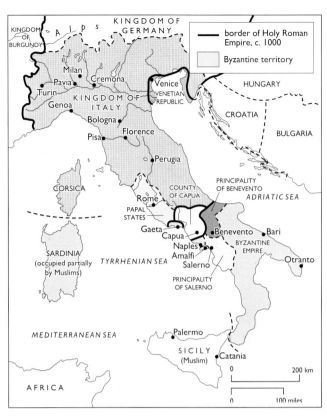

Decentralized Power in Italy, c. 1000

A fading Byzantine presence and a weakening Lombard kingdom permitted the Papal States and revived urban centers to stake their claims to power in Italy around the turn of the millennium.

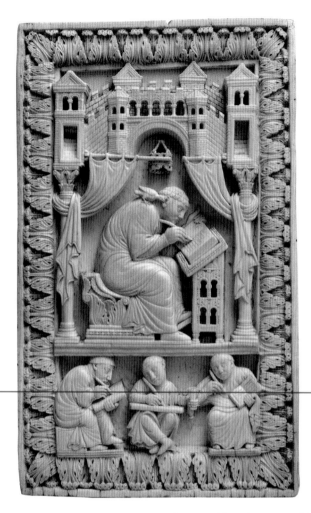

Gregory the Great, 10th century, ivory panel. Kunsthistorisches Museum, Vienna.

Amid great disruption, the Roman aristocrat and author who became Pope Gregory I the Great, stemmed the Lombard advance, converted the German invaders, and reorganized the papal lands. This ivory carving shows the pope, later canonized, energetically applying himself to his writing.

literate. They also conferred upon them the *spiritualia* (spiritual things): ritual items that were the symbols of their authority.

Gregory VII and the Drive for Papal Supremacy

In 1073 a new pope came to power who had a higher vision of the papal office and a plan for the reform and professionalization of the church. Gregory VII (r. 1073–1085) was determined that the emperors should not interfere with the realization of the church's objectives. With the support of the recently arrived Norman (French) rulers of Sicily and southern Italy, who had expelled the Saracens and Byzantines from these regions in 1071 and 1072, and in the absence of powerful intervention from the north, Gregory and his successors asserted their own claims to preside in Europe.

The papal drive for supremacy was linked with and powered by a drive for reform. Christian monks had long since been assigned (although they certainly did not always observe) certain standards of behavior because an ascetic mission was central to monasticism. The same was not true of the priests and prelates—"secular" clergy—who lived in a worldly setting among ordinary people. The eleventh-century program of papal reform targeted those vices to which the secular clergy were particularly prone: selling church offices, or **simony**; procuring church positions for relatives, or **nepotism**; and keeping concubines (often disguised as housekeepers and referred to as "priests' wives"). The wholesale pursuit and punishment of clergy who fell short of these newer, more exacting standards amounted, arguably, to a second conversion of Europe. The aim was to equip a purified clergy to lead the consciences of ordinary Christians who, just at this juncture, were becoming more numerous and mobile.

The aim was also to make the clergy wholly obedient to the pope and not the emperor, even though it was the emperor who chose and installed most of his bishops. This imperial practice of lay investiture became a particular target of the reform papacy. Gregory VII fired off a condemnation of the practice in 1075 in his succinct, but daring, manifesto of papal authority, the *Dictatus papae*. That manifesto triggered the Investiture Controversy, which lasted from 1076 to 1122, a showdown between pope and emperor, especially Gregory VII and Henry IV (r. 1054–1105/1106) of the Hohenstaufen dynasty. The conflict was eventually resolved, in part by the Concordat of Worms in 1122 by which time both Gregory and Henry were dead. It was decided that only a papal representative could invest a bishop, but the emperor could have episcopal elections conducted in his presence—and thus presumably control the selection of those bishops who would be invested by another hand.

Pope Gregory's *Dictatus papae* touched on issues broader than that of the lay investiture of bishops. It was a statement about the papacy as an institution and of papal supremacy over emperors and kings. Among its 27 numbered principles were the following:

> 2. That the Roman pontiff alone can with right be called universal.
> 8. That he alone may use the imperial insignia.
> 9. That of the pope alone all princes shall kiss the feet.
> 10. That his name alone shall be spoken in the churches.
> 11. That this is the only name in the world.
> 12. That it may be permitted to him to depose emperors.
> 19. That he himself may be judged by no one.

(E.F. Henderson, trans., *Select Historical Documents of the Middle Ages*. London: George Bell and Sons, 1910, pp. 36–37)

Gregory's vision of the supreme right of the pope and of the grand claims of the papal monarchy was given life by his later successor, Pope Innocent III (r. 1198–1216). Under Innocent III, the medieval papacy reached its height and the Papal State was reorganized. At the Lateran Council of 1215, Innocent asserted the pope's power to clarify doctrine for the entire church.

It was this energetic and ambitious papacy that held sway in Italy from the late eleventh to the early thirteenth century—precisely when northern Italian cities grew strong and wealthy and eager for their own autonomy. The German emperors had other ambitions, however. Having weathered the Investiture Controversy, which greatly weakened their prestige, they sought to revive their power by rebuilding their territorial empire, especially in the Italian lands from which they had retreated during the years of conflict. They wanted not only to reassert their prerogatives as lords but also to collect dues and fees from the now-affluent citizens and artisans of the Italian north. During the twelfth and thirteenth centuries, the emperors—notably Frederick Barbarossa and Frederick II (r. 1220–1250)—pursued this aggressive Italian strategy. In the end, and in part because of papal support for the northern cities, they failed to regain that foothold in Italy. By 1250 the Holy Roman Empire had weakened, becoming a loose federation of German states. At that moment, in contrast, the papacy was at the peak of its power. As new urban and national states emerged in Europe, however, its ascendancy would endure not much longer.

The Communes Emerge in Italy, c. 1100

By 1100, although the Holy Roman Empire had titular authority over much of Italy (while the south had been conquered by Normans), northern Italy was becoming transformed by the communal revolution. Later in the century, 16 communes would unite in the Lombard League and defy the emperor. The largest of approximately 40 communes are shown here.

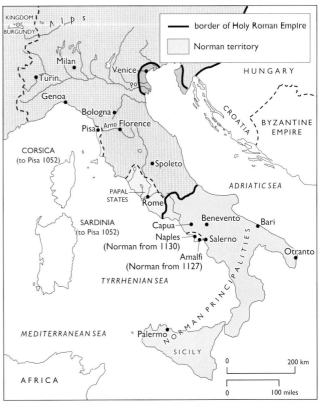

COMMERCE AND REURBANIZATION

As successor to the empires of the ancient Mediterranean world, Rome was the hub of a great commercial network, even though the Romans themselves were not innovative either in production or trade. Grains, oil, and wine were the most basic Mediterranean commodities, and these, together with the ceramic pots, bowls, and cups that held them, passed through all the ancient centers. Rome herself, an immense city of between one to two million inhabitants at its peak around 200 CE, was fed by the peasant farmers of Sicily, Egypt, and the Black Sea region. From the edges of the empire came slaves (Africa, Europe) and metals (Britain, Spain); from further east, exotic goods—gems, perfumes, spices, and especially silks—which were by the imperial era carried by land from China along central Asia's well-marked and maintained Silk Road. From the ports to the inland towns and cities, goods and money circulated, spreading and creating wealth.

Decline of the Roman Economy

This lively commercial system began to suffer disruption in the third century as migrating peoples and political failure pressured the Roman world. It suffered even more from the reforms that Emperor Diocletian (r. 284–305) instituted during his critically important reign. His restructuring of imperial and military organization brought order to a shattered empire. His economic policies, however, had deleterious effects. Diocletian raised taxes, attempting to derive the maximum possible profit from the agricultural sector, but the result was the resentment of a peasant population already pressed to the limit. He levied price controls on many products and commodities, which tended to slow down the pace of exchange and encouraged smuggling and evasion. He tried to maintain the supply of urban officials and artisans, many of whom were tempted to flee the towns and cities, ordering that none could leave their trade. Worse, he compelled them to raise their sons to follow them in the same roles and trades even if those activities had become unrewarding or useless. Thus, Diocletian's heavy taxation and iron regulation probably contributed to the weakening of the Roman economy.

The Roman economy in the Western Empire descended into chaos during the next two centuries as the empire languished and failed. Invasion and war exacerbated already serious difficulties. Commerce stagnated and withered, and the standard of living plummeted with it. The material conditions of life sank to those of a much earlier, pre-imperial era. Many people fled the cities—including the officials and artisans who had been declared bound to their occupations—to new settlements in remote or fortified settings. Coins, especially the valuable gold coins that were necessary in high-volume exchanges of goods, drained from the West to the East. In the Western region, small denominations of silver coins sufficed for the exchange of basic goods, or else, the barter transactions of a "natural economy" took the place of monetary exchange altogether. Slaves who escaped or who could no longer be maintained negotiated new labor contracts with landowners, becoming

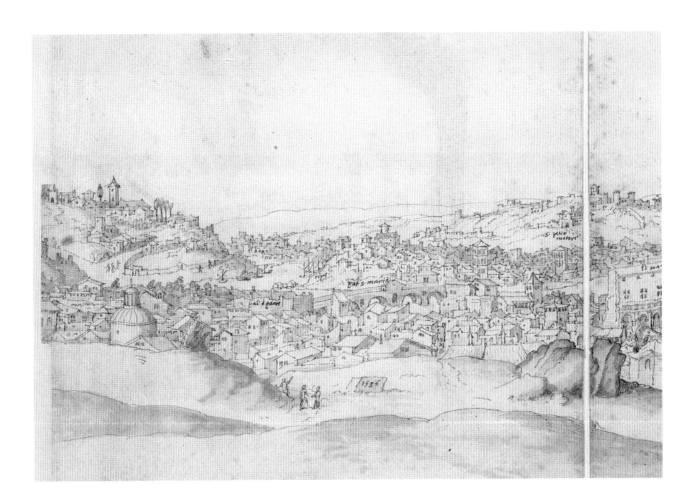

coloni (colonizers), forerunners of medieval serfs. The great landowners and barbarian chiefs fused together into a new social elite, the armed and horsed European nobility. Housed in their fortified country stations, they maintained order and became, in effect, the new rulers of a post-Roman age. Thus authority became fragmented and the land feudalized.

Italy, which had known a flourishing city life during the empire, deurbanized. Under the empire, there had been about a hundred places officially designated towns, or *municipia*, in northern Italy. Three-quarters of these survived into modern times. Yet during the bleakest medieval centuries, they lost so many people and functions that they nearly ceased, in effect, to be urban. Within their circuits of walls, populations shrank, leaving zones of waste land and ruined buildings around a smaller core of inhabitants who tended to cluster around the cathedral or the port, vacating the peripheral neighborhoods. Rome itself shrank from between one and two million occupants at its height to about 800,000 at the time of Constantine, 90,000 at the time of Gregory the Great (c. 600), and a mere 35,000 at the time of the Investiture Controversy (c. 1100). A vast sector of the ancient Roman city was dubbed the *disabitato* (disinhabition); its inhabitants having been sucked away to live near the banks of the Tiber and in the Vatican complex, it remained as empty as the surrounding countryside.

Panorama of Rome from the Capitol, 1534–1536. Staatliche Museum, Berlin.

This illustration reveals the most striking characteristic of the city of Rome in the Middle Ages—the *disabitato*. Large swathes of land within the walls of the former world capital were wholly uninhabited and allowed to revert to pasture or agriculture.

HOW TO SUCCEED IN BUSINESS: THE *COMMENDA* CONTRACT AND METHODICAL BOOKKEEPING

As the Italian cities sprang into activity at about 1000, their merchants devised techniques to facilitate the conduct of business. Borrowing at first from the Byzantine and **Islamic** models, they developed distinctively Italian commercial instruments and practices.

In between a loan and partnership contract, the Italian *commenda* was a written agreement between a cash-rich sedentary, or passive, partner and a cash-poor merchant venturer. In the example that follows, the "passive" or sedentary partner contributes two-thirds and the merchant one-third of the capital toward the voyage. On the merchant's return, both parties share the profits equally. In the event of loss, both parties lose their investment, in capital and labor.

Venice, August, 1073

I, Giovanni Lissado of Luprio, together with my heirs, have received in collegantia [the Venetian commenda] from you, Sevasto Orefice, son of Ser Trudimondo, and from your heirs, this amount: £200 Venetian. And I myself have invested £100 in it. And with this capital we have acquired two shares in the ship of which Gosmiro da Molino sails as captain. And I am under obligation ... by this agreement and understanding of ours ... to put to work this entire capital and to strive the best way I can. Then, if the capital is saved, we are to divide whatever profit the Lord may grant us from it by exact halves, without fraud and evil device.... And if all these goods are lost because of the sea or of hostile people ... may this be averted—neither party ought to ask any of them from the other; if, however, some of them remain, in proportion as we invested so shall we share.

(R.S. Lopez and I.W. Raymond, Medieval Trade in the Mediterranean World. *New York: Columbia University Press, 1955, pp. 176–177*)

Written nearly four centuries later, Benedetto Cotrugli's *On Commerce and the Perfect Merchant* (1458) provides tips for success based on the accumulated experience of Italian business practice. Here he describes the need to keep careful accounts.

Mercantile records are the means to remember all that a man does, and from whom he must have, and to whom he must give, and the costs of wares, and the profits, and the losses, and every other transaction on which the merchant is at all dependent....

Therefore the merchant ought to keep three books, that is, the ledger ... the journal ... and the memorandum.... And the ledger ought to have its alphabetical [index] through which one may quickly find any account written in the said ledger....

In the journal you shall reconstruct methodically all [your] capital, item by item, and you shall carry it forward in the ledger.... And when you have finished writing the said ledger, you shall settle all accounts opened in it, extract from them all balances ... to the debit or likewise to the credit....

In the memorandum you ought to note every evening or morning before you leave your home everything you have traded and transacted on that day because of your commerce.... And you should further note that you ought to keep always with you a small notebook ... in which you shall note day by day and hour by hour even the minute [detail] of your transactions....

And therefore I warn and encourage any merchant to take pleasure in knowing how to keep his books well and methodically.... Otherwise your commerce will be chaos, a confusion of Babel—of which you must beware if you cherish your honor and your substance.

(Lopez and Raymond, Medieval Trade, *pp. 375–378*)

The Flourishing of Maritime Trade

With Rome's decline, as commerce stalled and cities shrank in Italy, the Mediterranean Sea still served its ancient function as a highway of goods and services, the nerve center of the Old World. It did so, however, without the participation of the people of the Western Empire. Byzantine merchants were busily trading and voyaging in the seventh, eighth, and ninth centuries; the West, in contrast, was almost entirely detached from the system of world commerce. Byzantine gold coins, replacing those of the old empire, became the standard currency in the Mediterranean, and Byzantine warehouses stored the luxurious goods brought in largely from the east. In addition, the Byzantines learned from the Chinese how to nurture silkworms and produce silk cloth so that Constantinople itself became a new center for textile manufacture. They also opened up new trade routes to the north. Goods from the Russian forests found their way to Constantinople down the Volga and Don river systems and were exchanged for valuable products in that capital, whose population reached about 500,000 by the time of Emperor Justinian.

A century later, newcomers challenged Constantinople's dominance of Mediterranean trade. Armies of Arab followers of the Prophet Mohammad (c. 570–632) swiftly conquered the southern tier of the lands of the old Roman Empire. From 632 through 750, Arabic Muslims (called Saracens by the Europeans) burst forth from the Sinai Peninsula to seize neighboring Mesopotamia and the **Levant**; swept westward to claim the northern rim of North Africa, the entire Iberian Peninsula, and patches of territory north of the Pyrenees; and eastward to occupy Asia as far as the Indus River. The Byzantine Empire was reduced to its core: Greece and the Balkans south of the Danube, Anatolia, and the southern tip of Italy. It had lost the former Roman provinces of the Middle East and Africa to the new Muslim conquerors and would soon lose all the major Mediterranean islands, while in a further humiliation, the central Italian exarchate of Ravenna, another Byzantine foothold in the West, was lost to Germanic Lombard invaders of that peninsula.

Under Umayyad caliphs ruling from Damascus until 750, and then Abbasid caliphs from Baghdad, Islamic civilization flourished and trade revived. Constantinople, its population reduced to one-tenth its size before the Arab invasion, was no longer the sole destination for merchant voyagers. Now they sought as readily the ports of Alexandria (Egypt) and Valencia (Spain) on the Mediterranean, Córdoba (Spain) on the Guadalquivir River, Baghdad on the Tigris, and Damascus, the endpoint of the caravan routes from the east. Meanwhile, Saracen pirates harassed Byzantine and other European ports, attacking but not conquering the coastal cities of Italy and Greece and twice besieging Constantinople itself, in 674–678 and 717–718. Byzantine fleets responded as best they could, policing the Mediterranean and offering some protection to the new territorial lords of the remnants of the Roman Empire.

Yet in time, recovery came. Beginning in the ninth century, resourceful adventurers from the European west took their ships out onto the Mediterranean, first as pirates and then as merchants. They emerged from four coastal cities of Italy—Amalfi, Pisa, and Genoa on the west, and Venice on the east—with access to basic commodities that could be traded abroad and whose political and social circumstances permitted them to nurture diminutive merchant ventures. (Around this time, as well, in the small stretch of Christian Iberia that had been reconquered from Islamic rule, the merchants of Barcelona ventured into the ring of Mediterranean trade.)

Amalfi, southeast of Naples, which had begun to flourish under Byzantine rule during the Lombard period, was the first of the Italian port cities to develop. Its merchants carried grain, timber, and slaves to Arabian ports, taking their profits in gold coins used to buy expensive silks in Constantinople for resale in the west. Soon they grew rich. Amalfi was soon eclipsed, however, by Pisa and Genoa, whose merchant ships muscled aside their competitors on the Mediterranean. Pisan and Genoese sailors cleared the Tyrrhenian and Ligurian Seas west of the Italian peninsula of Saracen pirates, recovered the islands of Corsica and Sardinia, and settled merchant colonies on the shores of Africa, the Levant, the Black Sea, and in Constantinople itself. Pisa's fortunes climaxed early, in the eleventh and twelfth centuries, when, in one grand space, the celebrated monuments that bespoke the city's primacy were erected: its cathedral (begun 1064), **baptistry** (1152), and famously leaning tower (1173). Genoa eventually rivaled and outstripped Pisa, by 1150 becoming the leading naval power on the Italian west coast. On the east coast, meanwhile, around 1000, Venice threw off nominal Byzantine overlordship, purged the Adriatic Sea of pirates, and opened a clear naval highway to Constantinople and the Levant. Soon Venice rivaled Genoa in all its targeted areas of commercial advance, surpassing it by 1400 to emerge as the last and greatest of the Italian maritime republics.

The Expansion of Trading Networks

Exchanging at first cheap, bulky goods—salt, metals, fish—for the refined products of eastern ports, at great risk and marginal profit, Italian merchants gradually extracted enough capital to develop and expand their enterprises. Not only did they extract commodities from the interior of the peninsula for sale abroad, they also stimulated in those regions the manufacture of goods, including textiles, iron tools, and weapons, which would in time generate higher profits. These, in turn, permitted the importation of more valuable merchandise—silks, spices, gems, gold, furs—to be sold locally in the Italian interior and transshipped across the Alps. Italian merchants profited, too, from their role in the crusades (principally in the period from 1095 to 1291) as transporters of supplies and carriers of knightly armies from northern Europe to the Levant. From their modest beginnings in the late 900s, by the end of the crusading era, the Italian mercantile states had challenged, and even displaced, both Arabs and Greeks on the main routes of Mediterranean trade.

The bold and dangerous merchant ventures sent out from these coastal cities had dramatic consequences. Not only did those cities themselves revive, but so did the entire hinterland of northern Italy. Beneficial climatic conditions, and after 1000 the absence of foreign invasions, assisted the economic revival. It was commerce above all, however, that triggered growth, both in the agricultural sector (where surplus could now be sold, permitting the development of some crops specifically for export) and in the urban sector (where artisans could multiply and manufacture goods beyond the immediate needs of local residents). The population of the countryside exploded, and excess laborers and excess nobles alike moved into the prosperous cities, which began to expand into the waste and ruins of their disinhabited zones and fill up to the limits of their walls.

The Italian urban revival in the eleventh through thirteenth centuries, the consequence of commercial and maritime projects that began in the ninth and tenth, was the achievement of anonymous adventurers whose efforts can be hailed as heroic. They ventured into an unknown and often hostile sea, with the most wretched ships and unpromising merchandise, simply because the risk involved was less burdensome than the stagnation of not doing so. Had they not ventured forth, Italy, and perhaps Europe, would have remained a backwater, as it was in the centuries after the dissolution of the Western Empire. Instead, they began the commercial expansion and urban revival that would produce Italian cultural preeminence in the Renaissance and the explosive creativity of European civilization thereafter.

THE COMMUNAL REVOLUTION

The economic awakening of northern Italy in the eleventh and twelfth centuries resulted in the creation of a new social stratum: a citizen elite, composed of wealthy merchants and urbanized nobles, bound together by ties of mutual self-interest and marriage alliances. This new social group launched a "communal" revolution that transformed the political map of Italy and that had important implications for the later development of Europe.

Nowhere else in Europe did this hybrid phenomenon emerge. It was much more common that the warrior nobility and burghers pursued their different paths, each giving the other only a wary glance. In Italy, things were different. The nobles were not great landowners but **vavassors** (vassals of vassals). Their profession was violence and their aspirations were as great as their status was low. Finding that their lands by themselves, although a mark of status, did not provide sufficient wealth, these noblemen moved into the cities, attracted by the success of merchants (some of whom were also of noble status), the *cives* (citizens), who were actively engaged in the new commercial system and rapidly acquiring great wealth. Within a generation or two, the noble immigrants had built fortified urban palaces for themselves, featuring tall spare towers, which, clustered together, were a hint of the violence that was the nobleman's hallmark. They congregated as clans, or *consorterie*, forged alliances with

THE BIRTH OF THE COMMUNE: DATES OF FORMATION OF 14 COMMUNES	
Pisa	1080s
Lucca	1080s
Milan	1081
Parma	1081
Rome	1083
Pavia	1084
Piacenza	1090
Arezzo	1098
Genoa	1099
Pistoia	1105
Verona	1107
Bologna	1123
Siena	1125
Florence	1138

(Based on L. Martines, *Power and Imagination: City-States in Renaissance Italy*. New York. Alfred A. Knopf. 1979, p.18)

other nobles, and intermarried with the wealthy cives. They came to be described as the *grandi* or **magnates**—the "great men" of the city.

Alliance of the Magnates

The magnates quickly realized that in order to benefit most fruitfully from the possibilities of commerce they would have to seize power and rule the city themselves. But seize power from whom? Most northern Italian cities were ruled by bishops, who had provided security and guidance to communities that were abandoned and isolated when Rome dissolved and Italy was overcome by invasions from the north. Now, the bishops' rule seemed burdensome to men who wanted urban policies to support the commercial activities of its citizens. Many of the bishops, moreover, were agents of the remote emperors (some of whom were even German-speaking).

In a combined drive against the authority of both bishops and emperor, from the late eleventh into the early twelfth century, the magnates of the budding cities of northern Italy joined together as a sworn brotherhood to seize power and jointly rule what they now called their *communis* (**commune**), the term itself communicating the collective action that these leaders undertook. In the decade of the 1080s, communes formed rapidly in five major inland cities: Lucca, Milan, Parma, Rome, and Pavia; Pistoia and Verona followed in 1105 and 1107; and the three Tuscan cities of Bologna, Siena, and Florence in 1123, 1125, and 1138 respectively. By 1100, the great port cities of Pisa and Genoa were communes, too, and Venice soon afterwards. Their political leaders saw as among their chief objectives the security of their citizens and the development of commerce.

Communal government followed the pattern of what we would today call republicanism. There was an elected consul, or consuls, a term borrowed from the constitution of republican Rome. There was an assembly of all the people—for this purpose defined as all adult male citizens—that would occasionally be summoned to approve the decisions of a council made up of elected magnates. (The elections generally took place by a process of drawing names from a bag that had been previously scrutinized by a special committee.) Hundreds of standing and ad hoc councils and committees were created, such as the Forty of Justice, the Eight of War, the Twelve Good Men, the Commissioners of the Salt Tax, and the Gentlemen of the Night (in charge of policing the streets after dark). Secretaries recorded the deliberations of the councils and committees and drew up treaties or official letters to rival cities. And then there was a host of minor bureaucrats, notaries, and servants.

Behind all of this machinery of government was the power of the magnates, whose interests the government was created to serve. These interests were sometimes beneficial for all the inhabitants of the city when, for instance, grain was procured and stored in advance of a famine or when new commercial ventures were launched—and sometimes not. Although this communal system of government was republican, in the sense that no single king or lord or tyrant could rule unchecked, and all decisions were made by a duly elected or appointed council or committee, it was not democratic. The city's

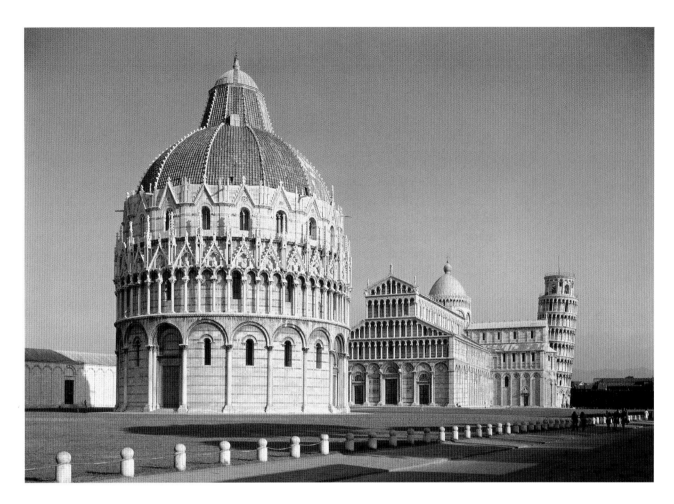

inhabitants—merchants below the level of the great magnate entrepreneurs, artisans, and laborers, not to mention foreigners, prostitutes, beggars, and the desperately poor—had no role whatsoever in the political process.

Pisa Baptistry, 1153–1265; Cathedral, begun 1063; Campanile, 1174–1271.

Built at the height of the communal era, Pisa's major monumental buildings—the related ecclesiastical structures of baptistry, cathedral, and bell tower—express in their sheer mass and material expense the power and wealth that the city commanded in the early phases of Italian mercantile expansion.

Triumph of the Lombard League

Communes were formed to replace the arbitrary rule of unelected and often foreign ecclesiastical or imperial officials and to resist the taxation of cities by a German monarch. The communal revolution must therefore be viewed as forming part of the history of the liberation of human societies from tyranny. Certainly this is how communal leaders viewed their role. They had the opportunity to put words to action when Emperor Frederick Barbarossa decided to force the communes of Italy to submit to his power. He instructed his agents in Italy to reverse the tide of communal revolution and restore his regalian rights, certain taxes and gestures of obedience that marked the political subordination of the Italian cities to imperial rule. In 1154, he came in person to see that the deed was done, with a knightly army behind him; there were four subsequent expeditions.

In 1167, to defend themselves against Frederick's incursions, the northern Italian communes joined together in the *Lega Lombarda* (Lombard League) armed and equipped by the magnates who were both trained warriors and city magistrates. They had the full support of Pope Alexander III (r. 1159–1181), who was at this point eager to protect papal rights against an encroaching empire. Initially, the Lombard League consisted of 16 cities, later 20, including the major centers of Milan, Venice, Mantua, Padua, Brescia, and Lodi.

The imperial and communal forces met on the battlefield of Legnano in 1176. Astonishingly, the League forces won—a triumphal landmark in the history of autonomous republics, albeit limited republics, over monarchy. By the Treaty of Constance of 1183, Frederick agreed to grant the Italian cities substantial communal autonomy and freedom from fees in exchange for the acknowledgment of imperial overlordship—an overlordship the cities proceeded to ignore.

The triumph of the Lombard League did not end the conflict between urban (and papal) and imperial interests. Over the next generations, factions within cities would war with each other. The **Ghibelline** party, named after a German imperial fortress, claimed allegiance to the emperor, and the **Guelf** party, named after a German family opposed to the imperial Hohenstaufen dynasty, claimed allegiance to the pope who had supported communal resistance to the emperor. Cities, too, would declare themselves Guelf or Ghibelline, depending on whether they were more or less dominated by a warrior nobility or in rivalry with a pro-papal or a pro-imperial enemy. Italy remained in turmoil as the economy soared, cities competed for political might, and a new stratum of aspiring merchants developed an appetite for power.

THE COMING OF THE *POPOLO*

The communal revolution attempted to replace the rule of bishops and their imperial overlord by self-rule by self-appointed leading citizens, whose regimes stood in opposition simultaneously to monarchy, theocracy, and feudalism. It was an impressive achievement. Within a century of the first stirrings of the dissident communes, however, there emerged another social group that launched a second even more radical revolution.

As the thirteenth century dawned, the merchants and artisans who had been busy developing new enterprises and enriching themselves in the economic boom inherited from the eleventh and twelfth centuries, wanted a share of the political system that was exclusively commanded by the sworn members of the commune, who considered themselves both rulers of the city and "the city" itself. The new men who knocked on the doors of the communal councils and committees called themselves the ***popolo***—a term with resonant meanings. While popolo means "the people," it also means a city's population, that is, the people of Florence, Milan, or Lucca. It can also mean "the people" in the sense that Abraham Lincoln employed the word in the Gettysburg Address more than 600 years later: "government of the people, by the people, for the people." It further suggests a humbler social group, the *ordinary* people, as opposed to the magnates, the rich and powerful. All of these meanings came into play when the newly wealthy merchant and artisan strata of the northern Italian cities clamored to participate in the governance of their cities. As one modern historian has termed the popolo, it was the first truly revolutionary class in modern history.

Merchant Guilds

Just as the noblemen and wealthy citizens who had joined together to form and rule the commune found strength in solidarity, so too did the hosts of the popolo who began to form merchant **guilds** soon after 1200. Set up for practitioners of certain trades or crafts, these guilds were among the first to form in modern Europe. They included associations of very wealthy men who engaged in long-distance commerce, such as bankers and spice merchants whose merchandise was necessarily shipped to Italy from Asia. Other high-status merchants were those who imported and then refinished, to a luxury grade, the wool cloth produced by the artisans of northern Europe; those who coordinated the production and sale of home-produced wool textiles; and goldsmiths and spice dealers. Judges and notaries, who were professionals rather than merchants, had equivalent status. Somewhat lower on the social scale were the practitioners of ordinary crafts, producers of items of lesser value or less well-esteemed professionals: butchers and bakers, barrel-makers and masons, physicians and grammar school teachers.

The guilds formed in order to protect and advance the interests of their members. They were institutions of professional certification, setting standards for the craft and assuring the competence of new members, or "masters." They had judiciary functions, settling disputes among members and disciplining members for shoddy work or unfair competition. They had charitable functions, gathering and disbursing funds to pay for the funerals of members and to support their widows and children. They had ritual functions, taking part as an organization in civic performances (which they sometimes funded) and religious processions. In performing these functions, they developed a complex bureaucracy, an interlocking system of committees and councils. The mechanisms of guild self-government were similar in form and function to the mechanisms of communal government. The guilds of the Italian popolo accentuated this similarity, electing officials to offices much as did the commune and creating councils of their own that operated much as a shadow, or alternate, government, theoretically subordinate to the external government of the commune.

Just as the guilds formed a shadow government within the larger framework of communal government, they also created a shadow military. They did so, from the perspective of the guildsmen, in self-defense. Whereas the merchants and artisans of the popolo on the whole were not naturally a militant group, the members of the communal elite were. That magnate class, it will be remembered, was initially an amalgam of an urbanized warrior nobility with a narrow circle of privileged cives. When those two

THE BATTLE OF LEGNANO, 1176: THE TRIUMPH OF THE LOMBARD LEAGUE

In 1158 Frederick I, called Barbarossa ("red beard"), having resolved matters at home, launched a series of expeditions to Italy. His aim was to recover his regalian rights, the rights due him as overlord of northern Italy—a legacy of the medieval conquest of the Lombard kings by Charlemagne and the subsequent crowning of the Holy Roman Emperor with the Iron Crown of the Lombard Kingdom.

Frederick razed Milan, the greatest of the inland communes (cities), which succumbed after a nine-month siege in 1162, and announced his demands at the Diet of Roncaglia: taxes and tariffs, the take from judicial confiscations, and fees accruing from official appointments; the profits from mines, fisheries, and salt-works; a half share of all found treasure. The restoration of these privileges would have brought Barbarossa much-needed income. But his goals were even larger: to systematize the financial and military organization of northern Italy so as to exploit fully the region's wealth and compel its obedience. These demands outraged the other communes of northern Italy—as did the sight of Milan in ruins.

In 1167, 16 cities of northern Italy formed the *Lega Lombarda* (Lombard League) to resist the emperor's attempts to reclaim his titular rights in the region. Four more joined the League subsequently. The League, including the principal cities of Milan, Venice, Padua, Brescia, and Mantua, enjoyed the important backing of Pope Alexander III (r. 1159–1181), an advocate of papal authority against imperial ambitions in the aftermath of the Investiture Controversy of the previous century. Frederick's 1167 descent into Italy was jinxed by plague. His 1174 expedition brought the temporary submission of the Lombards. His 1176 expedition, however, resulted in a monumental setback.

On May 29, 1176, the forces of the League met those of Barbarossa at the Battle of Legnano, not far from Milan. It was one of those great historic occasions where the newly constituted militia of a dynamic upstart historical actor confronted a long-established and official power. The battle began when several hundred Lombard knights faced a group of imperial soldiers while the rest of the Lombard forces, an assemblage of mounted knights and peasant infantry, rallied around their *carroccio* (a multi-purpose cart that served as presidium, supply train, portable altar, and honor guard). They were joined by extra forces from Milan. This larger group threw itself at the imperial flank, which was overcome. Barbarossa himself was unhorsed and put to flight.

Barbarossa's loss at Legnano compelled him to settle with Pope Alexander III. In 1177, Alexander and the emperor met in Venice, where the latter, in front of a large multitude of witnesses before the great **basilica** of San Marco, recognized the pope's authority and received the papal kiss of peace. A truce between Barbarossa and the League lasted until 1183, when all participants agreed to the Peace of Constance. At Constance, although Barbarossa gave up many of the regalian rights he had craved at Roncaglia, he was able to maintain the principle of imperial overlordship and the payment of some kind of tax or tribute. The League cities, however, won a substantial victory. Barbarossa granted to "the cities, territories, and persons of the League, the regalia and other rights within and without the cities, as you have been accustomed to hold them." In addition, Frederick granted a general amnesty, recognized the right of the Italian cities to organize as a league, and permitted the cities to build walls and fortifications within and outside their boundaries.

The League was renewed in 1198 and 1208. It only became active again, however, in 1226 when faced with another aggressive imperial opponent, the formidable Frederick II (r. 1220–1250). Securely based in southern Italy and Sicily, Frederick aimed to restore imperial authority in northern Italy—much as had his grandfather and namesake Barbarossa. Frederick defeated the League forces at Cortenuovo in 1237. The struggle continued until Frederick's death in 1250, at which point the League dissolved.

But it revived in other forms. During the nineteenth century, the theme of the Lombard League resonated as a reminder to the contentious leaders of different Italian regions to put aside local ambitions for the sake of the nation. In this climate, Giuseppe Verdi (1803–1901) created his opera *La battaglia di Legnano* ("The Battle of Legnano"), still performed today. In recent politics, an insurgent northern Italian political party called the Lombard League—with its origins in the very same region of Italy from which the twelfth-century alliance sprang—has made its power felt. The endurance and recurrence of the Lombard League and the memory of its great triumph at Legnano confirm the statement of American author William Faulkner: "The past isn't dead. It's not even past."

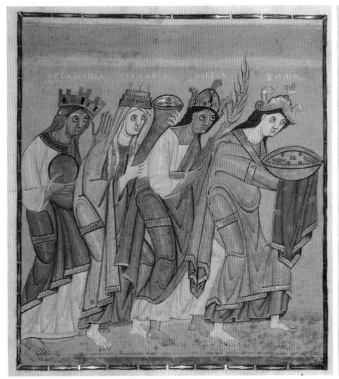 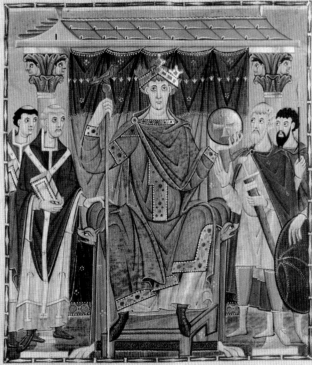

Otto III receiving tribute from four regions of the empire, led by Italia, c. 1000, manuscript illumination. Bayerische Staatsbibliothek, Munich, Germany.

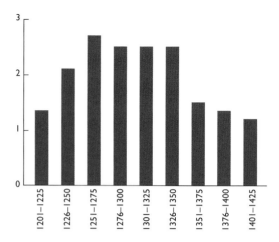

Cost of Land Rental, Pistoia, 1201–1425

Land costs rose steadily during the thirteenth century, a period of continued economic expansion, and remained high, though below their peak, in the early fourteenth. The Black Death caused a collapse of land values, which sagged persistently. It took centuries before they regained their thirteenth-century highs.

(David Herlihy, *Medieval and Renaissance Pistoia: The Social History of an Italian Town, 1200–1430*. New Haven, CT: Yale University Press, 1967, p. 135)

elite urban strata fused—a fusion achieved primarily through marriage alliances—the ruling cadres retained their capacity for violence and its symbols: horses, weapons, and above all the towers and tower societies that clustered related and allied families together.

Against the looming wall of magnate strength, the popolo felt the need to arm itself. It formed militias, organized by guild membership and neighborhood residence, each section led by a *gonfaloniere* (standard bearer). In Florence, in which these institutions of the popolo reached their most elaborate form, the four neighborhood gonfalonieri followed a superior commander, the *gonfaloniere della giustizia* (standard bearer of justice). When violence threatened from the magnate rulers of the commune, the church bells of the neighborhood districts rang out, and the guildsmen militias would assemble in their ranks behind their gonfalonieri and their chief.

The potential violence of the guildsmen threatened communal elites. The magnates fought back by terrorizing the guildsmen by random acts of violence—kidnap, rape, murder—while they continued to maintain exclusive control of governmental councils and committees. The popolo had two goals that were interrelated: the stemming of the tide of magnate violence and the opening up of government councils to participation by the guild members. In achieving the latter goal, the guilds often had the support of the pope, and thus the guild movement became closely associated with the Guelf party, opposed to the imperial Ghibelline party.

Conflict between Pope and Emperor

The battle between pope and emperor, which resumed in 1226, assisted the cause of the popolo. The emperor in question was the brilliant and powerful Frederick II (grandson of Barbarossa), called the Great and *stupor mundi* (the wonder of the world), descended on his mother's side from the Byzantine emperor. This cosmopolitan ruler held the south of Italy, assuming kingship in 1197 of the Two Sicilies—the kingdoms of Sicily and Naples–Apulia—inherited from the Normans who, a little more than a century earlier, had taken the region from Arab and Byzantine overlords. He acquired the imperial title in 1220 and soon began to announce his claim to Lombardy and to menace the rest of the peninsula. Guelf and Ghibelline factions were roused into action and the Lombard League, which had triumphed over Frederick's grandfather, was reconstituted with papal backing.

Allied with the northern cities and employing foreign armies, the pope waged war on Frederick, **excommunicating** him in 1239 and deposing him in 1245—ineffective weapons against this imperturbable aggressor. When Frederick died in 1250, the war continued against Frederick's son and successor as king of Sicily, Conrad IV (r. 1250–1254), Conrad's son Conradin (r. 1254–1258), and then against Frederick's illegitimate son Manfred (r. 1258–1266), who seized the Sicilian kingdom and was excommunicated by the pope. The pope invited the French nobleman Charles d'Anjou to assume the crown of Sicily and be the loyal servant of the papacy. Charles defeated and killed Manfred at Benevento in 1266, ending the imperial pretense to lordship in Italy.

The Rebellion of the Popolo

What followed, for a brief century, was the triumph of the popolo and its chief defender, the pope. The pope replaced the imperial Hohenstaufens in the south with a cooperative French dynasty linked to the crown, and the cities of northern Italy retained their autonomy. In many of them, the popolo rose up in rebellion against the communal magnates and established city governments that can best be called republican. Like the communal governments that preceded them, they were powered by councils and committees, to which members were elected by scrutiny and lot. Like their predecessors, they were exclusive; only guild members could participate in government. Yet the system of governance they created was more progressive than that of the communes. Although it was far from democratic, it involved a significant portion of the population—perhaps one-third—compared to the one, two, or ten per cent of the more narrowly hierarchical communal regimes. Nor did it enforce its decrees with the threat of violence as had the warrior nobility.

The classic case of the revolt and triumph of the popolo is found in Florence—the city that would become, a little more than a century later, the home of the cultural movement of the Renaissance. The Florentine guildsmen seized power in 1250 and declared their new regime to be that of *Il popolo*, one might say the "People's Republic." As the sign of their political success, in 1252 this commercial elite minted the **florin**, the first gold coin to be produced in Europe (outside of Byzantium) since the time of the Roman Empire.

Betrayed by exiled Florentine magnates to the rival Ghibelline rulers of Siena, the government of the people in Florence fell in 1260. It returned from exile in 1268, triumphed yet again, and installed the regime of the *Secondo popolo* (the Second People's Republic), which continued in place until 1494, although the realities of power shifted over time. In 1293 the leaders of the *Secondo popolo* passed the Ordinances of Justice, which allowed for the exile of unruly magnates, denied noblemen access to government councils, and ordered the destruction of the private towers of the noble clans, the emblems of their warrior status. Besides the ***campanili*** (bell towers) of the churches and cathedral, only one tower stood, that of the Palazzo Pubblico (public palace), a monument to the republican principle where the elected guildsmen called "priors" lived during their terms in office.

The guild republicanism of the popular governments of the thirteenth and fourteenth centuries, surpassing the magnate republicanism of the eleventh and twelfth centuries, ultimately derived from the Italian context in which it grew: the Roman past, still living in the ruins of walls, roads, and aqueducts, and in the fabric of the churches; Roman law, still living in law books preserved, recopied and newly interpreted by an energetic generation of scholars; and the stimulus of money that dissolved old hierarchies of power because republicanism could not claim prestige by birth, office, or spiritual privilege, but only by the work of hands and brain and the willingness to venture afar and take exceptional risk.

CONCLUSION

The Renaissance—a "rebirth" or "renewal" of antiquity—would occur in Italy because ancient Rome had in some ways never died. Although the political authority of Rome collapsed and its economy crumbled, its physical and institutional structures remained. Rome lived on, much as did the Roman legacy contained in the books that were housed, read, and recopied in Monte Cassino, potent links between the past and the future.

By 1300, 800 years after the collapse of the Roman Empire in the West, the cities of northern Italy had experienced a surge of economic and political development that prepared them for an era of rapid and brilliant cultural innovation. The next chapter explores the vital world of the popolo in the century between its emergence as a dominant social and political force and the arrival of a natural enemy that could not be withstood—the Black Death.

SUGGESTED READINGS

Primary Sources

Benedict, St. *The Rule of St. Benedict: Insights for the Ages.* Edited by Joan D. Chittister. New York: Crossroad, 1992. The rules for living in a monastic community set forth in the sixth century and still used as a guide for the spiritual life.

Boethius, Ancius Manlius Severinus. *The Consolation of Philosophy.* Translated by P.G. Walsh. Oxford: Oxford University Press, 1999. Written in captivity by a former Roman senator, it encapsulates ancient values of transcendent reason and anticipates the medieval embrace of the inner life.

Lopez, Roberto S., and Irving W. Raymond, trans. and ed. *Medieval Trade in the Mediterranean World: Illustrative Documents Translated with Introduction and Notes.* 3rd ed. New York: Columbia University Press, 2001. A treasure house of contracts, bills of sale, laws, and chronicles testifying to economics of life from 1000 to 1300.

Michael of Rhodes. *The Book of Michael of Rhodes: A Fifteenth-Century Maritime Manuscript.* Vol. 2, Transcription and Translation. Edited by Pamela O. Long, David McGee, and Alan M. Stahl. Cambridge, MA: MIT Press, 2009. A Venetian mariner reports on his experience in both merchant and military fleets, discussing shipbuilding practices, naval technology, and portolan charts.

Secondary Sources

Abulafia, David, ed. *Italy in the Central Middle Ages: 1000–1300*. Oxford: Oxford University Press, 2004. A collection of essays exploring the development of the city-states of northern Italy, the kingdoms of the south, and developments in the economy, the family, literature, religion, and more.

Duggan, Christopher. *A Concise History of Italy*. 2nd ed. Cambridge: Cambridge University Press, 2014. The best recent survey, with chapters on the late Roman through medieval periods.

Herlihy, David. *Medieval and Renaissance Pistoia: The Social History of an Italian Town, 1200–1430*. New Haven, CT: Yale University Press, 1967. Herlihy masterfully describes a late-medieval society by using the number of sheep, land prices, and movements of people.

Holmes, George, ed. *The Oxford History of Italy*. Oxford: Oxford University Press, 1997. A collection of essays synthesizing recent work.

Hyde, J.K. *Society and Politics in Medieval Italy: The Evolution of the Civil Life, 1000–1350*. New York: St. Martin's Press, 1973. The developing cultural life of late-medieval urban centers.

Jones, Philip J. *The Italian City-State: From Commune to Signoria*. Oxford: Clarendon Press, 1997. A recent, exhaustive, and authoritative study.

Krautheimer, Richard. *Rome: Profile of a City, 312–1308*. Princeton, NJ: Princeton University Press, 1980. Based on architecture, mosaics, and urban structures, this book reconstructs Constantine's and the papacy's transformations of Rome.

Kreutz, Barbara M. *Before the Normans: Southern Italy in the Ninth and Tenth Centuries*. Philadelphia: University of Pennsylvania Press, 1991. Investigates the early development of southern Italy, soon to be outpaced by dynamic northern communes.

La Rocca, Cristina, ed. *Italy in the Early Middle Ages, 476–1000*. Oxford: Oxford University Press, 2002. Collection of essays illuminating the complex and not always negative changes effected especially in northern Italy during an era of foreign infiltration and conquest.

Mazzaoui, Maureen Fennell. *The Italian Cotton Industry in the Late Middle Ages, 1100–1600*. Cambridge: Cambridge University Press, 1981. Studies the manufacture and commerce of a key textile, linking the Latin West with Byzantine and Islamic trade.

Metcalfe, Alex. *The Muslims of Medieval Italy*. Edinburgh: Edinburgh University Press, 2009. Focusing on Sicily from the Arabic conquest until the dissolution of the Muslim community in the thirteenth century, considers the interactions between Latin Christians and Arab Muslims during an era when the latter indelibly marked the culture of southern Italy.

Tabacco, Giovanni. *The Struggle for Power in Medieval Italy: Structures of Political Rule, 400–1400*. Translated by Rosalind Brown Jensen. Cambridge: Cambridge University Press, 1989. A study of power relations on the Italian peninsula.

Waley, Donald. *The Italian City Republics*. 4th ed. London: Routledge, 2009. Basic account of the evolution from commune to republic.

Ward-Perkins, Bryan. *From Classical Antiquity to the Middle Ages: Public Building in Northern and Central Italy, 300–850*. Oxford: Oxford University Press, 1985. Studies the continuities in public life from imperial collapse through early medieval reconfiguration.

Wickham, Chris. *Early Medieval Italy: Central Power and Local Society, 400–1000.* Ann Arbor: University of Michigan Press, 1989. Studies the tension between larger and local political formations.

Wickham, Chris. *Framing the Early Middle Ages: Europe and the Mediterranean, 400–800.* Oxford: Oxford University Press, 2006. At just under 1,000 pages, a comprehensive and probing account of the unraveling of Roman antiquity in multiple regions of Europe and its periphery, with particular attention to the evolution of states, aristocracies, and peasantries.

TWO

AN AGE OF REPUBLICS (c. 1250–c. 1350)

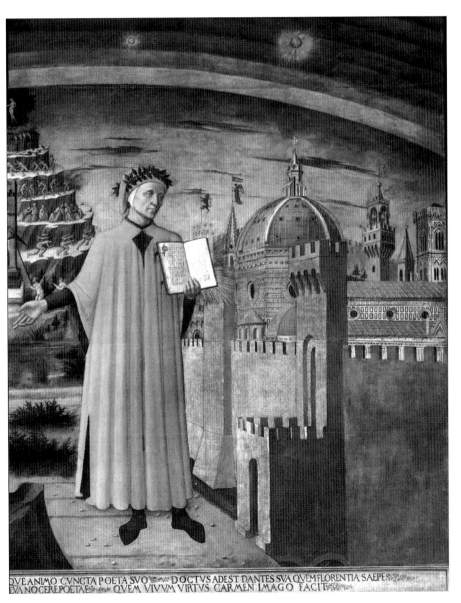

Domenico di Michelino, *Portrait of Dante Alighieri, The City of Florence, and the Divine Comedy's Allegorical Representation* (detail), 1465, oil on canvas, 7 ft 7 in × 9 ft 6 in (2.3 × 2.9 m). Santa Maria del Fiore (Duomo), Florence.

On the left is purgatory where souls seeking salvation toil upward to the Garden of Eden. On the right is the Cathedral of Florence (built a century after Dante's death). Dante is linked through his book with the Christian vision of the Middle Ages and the robust innovations of the dawning Renaissance.

Things were going well for ordinary people in northern Italy in the years after 1250—especially for the artisans and merchants, the people in the middle between the warlords whose towers pierced the skyline in both country and city and the transient or desperately poor. Things were going so well that work could be neglected for a while. The Florentine banker Giovanni Villani (c. 1276–1348), accordingly, went on a pilgrimage to Rome to celebrate the jubilee year of 1300. What he saw of the ruins of the greatness of Rome spurred him to reflect upon his own city, where energy and industry and the swift pursuit of opportunities had resulted in growth and abundance:

> But in view of the fact that our city of Florence, daughter and offspring of Rome, was mounting and pursuing great purposes, while Rome was in its decline, I thought it proper to trace in this chronicle the origins of the city of Florence ... and to relate the city's further development.... And thus in the year 1300, on my return from Rome, I began to compile this book.
>
> (G. Villani, *Chronicle*, in F. Schevill, trans. *Medieval and Renaissance Florence*, Vol. 1. New York: Harper Collins, 1963, p. 36)

And so he did, composing his *Chronicle*, a flowing narrative of the history of the city, with colloquial asides on any matter that occurred to the author. Among these were the comments he famously made about the Florentine economy, providing us with the most complete account we have of an Italian city on the eve of the Renaissance. He spoke first of the population:

> From the amount of bread constantly needed for the city, it was estimated that in Florence there were some 90,000 mouths ... [and in addition] some 80,000 men in the territory and district of Florence. From the rector who baptized the infants ... we find that at this period there were from 5,500 to 6,000 baptisms every year.... We find that the boys and girls learning to read [numbered] from 8,000 to 10,000, the children learning the abacus and algorithm [subjects necessary for commercial careers] from 1,000 to 1,200, and those learning grammar and logic [equivalent to advanced secondary studies] ... from 550 to 600.
>
> (Villani, *Chronicle*, p. 41)

And then of economics:

> The workshops of the *Arte della Lana* [the wool-makers' guild] were 200 or more.... The [warehouses] of the *Arte di Calimala* [the wool-importers and refinishers' guild] ... were some twenty.... The association of judges was composed of some eighty members; the notaries were some six hundred; physicians and surgical doctors, some sixty, shops of dealers in spices some hundred.... There were then in Florence 146 bakeries.... Every year the city consumed about 4,000 oxen and calves, 60,000 mutton and sheep, 20,000 she-goats and he-goats, 30,000 pigs.
>
> (Villani, *Chronicle*, pp. 41–42)

Not long after recording these data, in one of the most extensive and precise among all premodern documents of urban life, Villani noted in 1348 that a new epidemic had broken out in Italy: "a great pestilence, from which, if one fell ill, he but rarely escaped." With this event, his *Chronicle* ends, although it was continued by his brother and nephew through 1364. Villani himself perished in the Black Death.

The flourishing urban civilization that Villani observed is the subject of this chapter. The Renaissance that was yet to emerge would do so within urban centers constructed by the merchant leaders of the Italian republics. Their international ventures and local production created the wealth that was necessary for the Renaissance innovations. They oversaw a wave of new buildings, which gave expression to advancing merchant interests and ambitions. In this charged environment, a young generation of thinkers, artists, and writers created new ideas and forms of expression that were both original and daring—a prefiguration of the great cultural innovations soon to come. Yet the tremendous dynamism of the century after 1250, the culmination of the merchant advance, would soon be halted by the capitulation of all but a few of the northern Italian cities to despotism and by the implacable epidemic of bubonic plague which struck defenseless Italy in 1348.

This chapter begins with a closer look at the economic and social conditions of two of those republics which would, in the next century, emerge as Renaissance centers: Florence and Venice. It will then consider the cultural changes accompanying this outburst of commercial energies: the vigorous construction of walls, buildings, and urban spaces and the creation of a vital urban consciousness and culture. The chapter ends with the two processes—the turn toward despotism and the advent of the plague—that brought this proto-Renaissance era to a close.

FLORENCE: BANKING AND WOOL

As the Florentine popolo advanced in the thirteenth century, it specialized in two enterprises that generated enough wealth to transform Florence from a minor center to one of the leading cities of Italy and of Europe. These enterprises were banking and wool.

Banking

Like many merchant groups, the leaders of the Florentine popolo enjoyed the support of the pope and proudly proclaimed themselves to belong to the Guelf party. A close relationship with the papacy meant, however, more than political and military support. It also brought the opportunity to act as the pope's fiscal (tax) agent. The activity of Florentine merchants as the collectors of church tithes, or taxes, throughout Christendom propelled some merchant companies into the profession of banking. Profiting on each exchange of currency, they became the most important bankers in Europe, sustaining whole states.

FLORENCE: CITY OF WOOL AND REFINEMENT

The Venetian merchant who set out in 1073 (see p. 22) with 300 Venetian lire to trade in perilous waters abroad had produced nothing of his own to offer eastern distributors of luxury goods. Venetian merchants bought and sold for maximum profit; they were not manufacturers of things.

Florentine merchants, too, bought and sold goods, snaring a profit where they could. By 1300, however, some Florentine merchants had become manufacturers of woolen cloth. They were not the only wool manufacturers; they had rivals in the Low Countries and in many other Italian centers. Yet Florentines were the leading manufacturers of wool, the most important European product and the engine of its economic growth from the Middle Ages into the Industrial Revolution—which began as a revolution in textile manufacture.

It was the complexity of wool manufacture—the many and different steps between shearing the sheep and selling the cloth, including washing, combing, carding, spinning, fulling and dyeing, weaving—that opened a pathway to immense profits for entrepreneurs who could manage the buying and selling of raw material and the finished product as well as coordinate the great number of subordinate workers (about one-third of the whole labor force) that the process required. Not only did they need to know how to manage money and organize workers, they needed to know their product. A desire to have the highest-quality material is revealed in this letter by a Florentine merchant describing with what extraordinary care he and an associate selected the "twelve yards of good blue cloth" his friend had requested:

> First we looked around in the cloth factories, where occasionally one may find some nice remnants at a discount, but we didn't see anything we liked. Then we visited all of the retail shops which sell for cash … [where we found] a way to examine the finest and most beautiful cloth in each shop, and we also seized the opportunity to compare these pieces side by side. From them all, we chose a cloth from the shop of Zanobi di Ser Gino. There were none that were better woven or more beautifully dyed.

> (G. Brucker, *Renaissance Florence*. Berkeley: University of California Press, 1983, p. 220)

That demand for quality, that sense of refinement, is also evidenced in another arena of Florentine life: city planning.

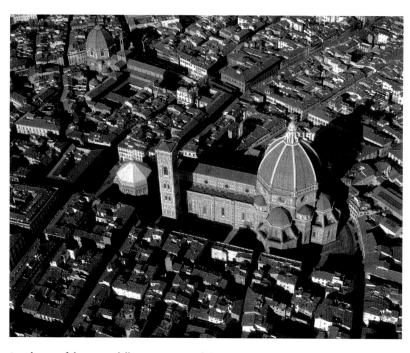

Aerial view of the Piazza della Signoria toward the Duomo, Florence.

This chapter has told the story of the city's expanding walls, and the building of the Cathedral and Palazzo Pubblico. Those two projects were part of a much larger building campaign launched by the victorious popolo of the thirteenth-century revolutions.

The wall project testifies to the magnitude of their vision. The last circle of walls, whose construction extended over a 50-year period from 1284 to 1333, enclosed an area six times as great as the previous ring and was far larger than the population, then near its premodern peak, required. With its 73 towers and 15 fortified gates, it was a statement of civic monumentality, the outcome of a choice both political and aesthetic.

Meanwhile, the city-planning commission of 1282 to 1283 launched a project that resulted in the building of the new cathedral (begun in 1296), the Palazzo Vecchio (1298), the Church of Santa Croce (1295), the **Campanile** (1334), the Orsanmichele (1340), and the Loggia dei Lanzi (1378, Lancers' Arcade). This was a banquet of architecture, a reworking of the configuration of the city at its center, a manifesto by the ruling popolo. Private building followed the public model, adding splendid residences for the leading citizens to the civic panorama that they had collectively planned and constructed.

In 1403 and 1404 the humanist Leonardo Bruni (1370–1444; see Chapter 3) wrote a *Panegyric to the City of Florence* which praised Florence for its government, citizenry, location, laws, cleanliness, and so on. Among the most interesting passages are those describing the beauty of the city—a beauty stemming from the consciousness of quality, the sense of refinement, of all those who participated in its building:

> What in the whole world is so splendid and magnificent as the architecture of Florence? … Almighty God, what wealth of buildings, what distinguished architecture there is in Florence! Indeed, how the great genius of the builders is reflected in these buildings, and what a pleasure there is for those who live in them.
>
> (B.G. Kohl and R.G. Witt, *The Earthly Republic*. Philadelphia: University of Pennsylvania Press, 1978, p. 139)

The homes of the citizens were magnificent in their architecture and decoration:

> Indeed, what could be more pleasant and more beautiful to the sight than the entrance courts, halls, pavements, banquet halls, and other interior rooms of these homes? … In these living quarters you find beautiful chambers decorated with fine furniture, gold, silver, and brocaded hangings and precious carpets.
>
> (Kohl and Witt, *The Earthly Republic*, p. 140)

Bruni invites the visitor to come and look, and to look carefully. Visitors to other cities view just a few public buildings, which are like an "outward bark." If they stray from the busy center, or try to look at the interiors and not just the exteriors of the city's buildings, "instead of houses they will find only small huts, and behind the exterior decorations only filth." But in Florence beauty is diffused everywhere:

> Therefore, the sort of careful scrutiny that brings shame to other cities only serves to raise the esteem held for Florence, for behind the walls of the buildings of Florence there are no fewer ornaments and no less magnificence than there is outside; nor is any one street better decorated or more handsome than another, but every quarter shares in the beauty of the city. Hence, just as blood is spread throughout the entire body, so fine architecture and decoration are diffused throughout the whole city.
>
> (Kohl and Witt, *The Earthly Republic*, p. 141)

The revolutionaries and wool producers who led the city of Florence knew quality in cloth and in art. The energy that drove them to create a new kind of civic life also drove them to define a new aesthetic vision.

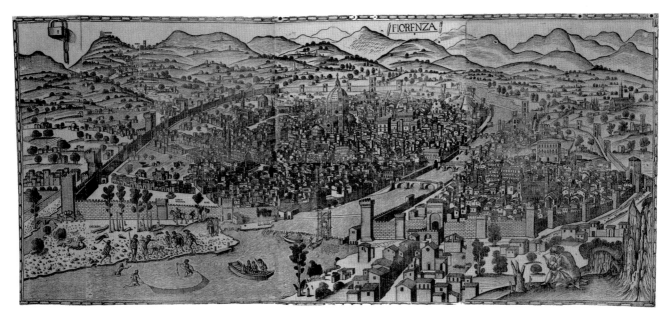

Francesco di Lorenzo Rosselli, Chain Map of Florence, 1471–1482, woodcut, 11 × 17 in (29 × 44 cm). Galleria degli Uffizi, Florence.

The Bardi and Peruzzi banks, for example, lent the great fortunes to King Edward III of England (r. 1327–1377) that funded the opening phases of the Hundred Years' War. Although both companies failed after 1342, when Edward refused to pay the debt, and further disasters put a momentary halt to Florentine endeavor in this area, it resumed again some years later. From the late 1300s, the Medici family accumulated as bankers the fortune that in 1433 permitted their descendant Cosimo de' Medici (1389–1464) to seize control over the merchant oligarchy then ruling the city.

Wool and the Wool Guilds

Relations with the papacy also gave Florentine entrepreneurs the opportunity to expand their role in textile manufacture. Florentine merchants were already importing woven wool textiles from Flanders, which they refinished as luxury cloth and sold to eastern markets. In 1268, the year in which papal forces decisively defeated imperial ambitions in Italy, the Angevin rulers, whose armies had achieved that victory and who replaced the Hohenstaufen dynasty in the Two Sicilies, made the raw wool yielded by the extensive sheep-herding enterprises of that region readily available to Florentine merchants. Florentine merchants now organized an enormous and complex wool-manufacturing industry in Florence. That industry pioneered the manufacture of textiles on a large scale, and wool became one of the two most important manufactured products (the other being metal, especially weapons) that Europe could sell profitably in foreign markets.

Because of the importance to the Florentine economy of wool manufacture, which at its peak in the early fourteenth century involved as many as one-half of the city's population, the wool merchants were significant figures. They organized themselves into two guilds considered among the *arti maggiori* (major guilds): the Calimala guild of wool-cloth refinishers and international exporters, and the Lana guild of wool producers. These merchants acted as purchasers, organizers, and sellers of the finished textile. For its actual manufacture, which required as many as 15 processes from the cleaning of the raw wool to the final fulling and dyeing, they hired a complex array of *sottoposti* (subordinates).

Some of the sottoposti, such as the fullers, dyers, and weavers, were artisans themselves, housed in their own shops and sometimes employing their own assistants and apprentices. Others were manual laborers, including women principally employed as spinners, who worked in their own city houses or country cottages. These people washed, combed, carded, spun, and transported the wool at different stages of the manufacturing process. The labor of many *sottoposti* contributed to the manufacture of the eventual textile, whose sale required the further labor of many agents engaged in shipping and selling the finished product. The wool merchant stood at the center of this hive of productive and commercial activity. He was an entrepreneur of the first order, deserving that designation perhaps more than any other of the bold and venturesome merchants of the age.

The Guilds and Civic Life

Sharing the same niche in the social order as the wool merchants were the other guildsmen of the *arti maggiori*: the bankers, judges and notaries, physicians and apothecaries, silk merchants, and furriers. Below the seven *arti maggiori* were 14 lesser guilds: those of the butchers, bakers, wine sellers, blacksmiths, and the like. In practice, the boundaries of these guilds were fluid. A merchant might be enrolled in only one or several guilds if his enterprises caused him to engage in the buying or selling of commodities proper to different crafts. In addition, merchants and artisans alike might own commercial and residential space, which paid rents, and shares in the city's *monte*, or publicly funded debt, which paid regular interest.

Once the Florentine system of governance reached its full development, the lesser guildsmen too were able to participate in civic life. The main executive body in Florence was the group of nine priors, each elected for a two-month term (lest any become too powerful and take over the state) and housed together in the Palazzo Pubblico. Of this group, six were elected from the major guilds and three from the minor. In the same way, guildsmen of both categories were eligible to serve on the many councils and committees that made the major domestic and foreign policy decisions. Although all guildsmen did not have equal access to government positions, about one third of these artisans and merchants held public office at one or several points in their careers. In that role they acquired an experience of public affairs that was extraordinary for this era and inconceivable outside of the kind of urban society that flourished in northern Italy.

Yet Florentine government was by no means democratic. An inner circle of oligarchs controlled elections and channeled policy discussions. Although several thousand adult male citizens of guild status formed the politically active class, the mechanism of "scrutiny," which decided which of those citizens should actually be considered for office, and selection by lot (presumably random and thus fair, but often in reality manipulated) meant that the real rulers of the city were a circle of a few hundred oligarchs. A further limitation on free political participation was the activity of the Guelf party, which intervened in government to ensure a continuing fidelity to the principles of the Guelf triumph in the thirteenth century, when papal and urban forces vanquished those of the Holy Roman Emperor (see Chapter 1).

Revolt of the Ciompi

If all guildsmen were eligible for public office, but not all actually served, it remains true that only those enrolled in a guild had access to public life. So critical was the matter of guild membership to political representation that it triggered one of the most important rebellions in premodern European history, the revolt of the **ciompi**. The ciompi were the (unguilded) wool workers from the unskilled to highly skilled, who worked as *sottoposti* to the wool merchants of the Lana guild. In 1378 the ciompi rose up in armed rebellion,

VENICE: CITY OF ST. MARK AND OF SHIPS

The islands of Venice were home to a scattered community of fishermen when, driven in great numbers by the Lombard invasions that began in 568, refugees started arriving from northern Italy. Suddenly populous centers, these lagoon settlements fell under the authority of the Byzantine Empire, which, in the eighth century, approved the first dukes or **doges** of Venice. In the ninth century, after the Byzantine exarchate at Ravenna disintegrated and Byzantine power waned, the doges transferred their capital from the island of Malamocco to a more protected position on the island of Rialto. Soon these lagoon dwellers constituted themselves as the city of Venice, and the doges ruled with effective independence of Byzantine authority.

From the tenth through thirteenth centuries, Venice built up a commercial empire that extended to the Near East and North Africa. From humble fishermen, many citizens became wealthy merchants, and during these centuries of expansion, the city was built—hard to do on marshes and sand bars always threatened by the sea. The guidebook author Francesco Sansovino, writing in the sixteenth century, explained how:

> Now, the foundations of all the buildings are made of the strongest oak piles, which last for ever under the water because of the slimy bed and even bottom of the marsh. These are driven into the earth and then made firm with thick cross-planks. The space in between the piles is filled in with various cements and rubble, which sets and makes the foundations so stable that they support any bulky or tall building without moving a hair's breadth.
>
> (D.S. Chambers and B. Pullan, eds., *Venice: A Documentary History, 1450–1630*. Toronto: University of Toronto Press, 2001, p.24. © RSA)

On such foundations, the merchants of Venice built their palaces, which doubled as warehouses. The first level opened onto the water so that boats could be brought in for loading and unloading.

The great project of public building began in the ninth century. At the point where the Grand Canal that snakes through the center of Venice opened into the harbor, a resplendent complex took form. In 829, the remains of the body of the evangelist San Marco (St. Mark) were brought back from the East, and a new church—San Marco—was built adjacent to the doge's residence to house the precious relics of the city's new patron saint. The original church was destroyed by fire and replaced in 978. This second structure was replaced in the eleventh century by the magnificent building that still stands today, notable for its grand spaces, its extraordinary mosaics, its bronze doors, and, atop the facade, the four bronze horses brought from Constantinople to adorn San Marco, the great basilica of once-subject Venice.

The doge's palace, not only a residence but the seat of government and justice, went through many more transformations. The ninth-century castle, destroyed by fire, was replaced and achieved noteworthy form by 1177 when the Venetian doge hosted the peace-making meeting of Emperor Frederick Barbarossa and Pope Alexander III (see Chapter 1). This structure, however, was rebuilt, restored, and extended over the next four centuries to create the building which visitors now see. Faced in a pattern of rose and white marble, sporting **Gothic** ogival (peaked) arches and classical staircases, it is a fabulous blend of Romano-Venetian, Byzantine, Renaissance, and Islamic elements.

The San Marco complex stands at the mouth of the Grand Canal. At its midpoint, the Canal is arched by the Rialto Bridge, the central hub of Venetian enterprise, though the bridge itself remained wooden and unremarkable until the sixteenth century. Around it swirled the commercial life of Venice: the exchange of iron and salt, gold and treasure, timber and wine, meat and fish, brought in by fishermen from the neighboring islands, as Marino Sanudo wrote in the late fifteenth century:

> They bring as much fish here as can be sold in a day and in the evening none is left, the cause of it being that everyone spends, and everyone lives like lords. And in this city nothing grows, yet whatever you want can be found in abundance. And this is because of the great turnover in merchandise; everything comes here, especially things to eat, from every city and every part of the world.
>
> (Chambers and Pullan, *Venice*, p. 13)

Near the tip of Rialto Island, in the other direction from San Marco, lies the Arsenal, the state-run shipbuilding enterprise that powered Venice's commercial success. The word "arsenal" was derived from the Arabic *darsina'a*, meaning a "house of manufacture," a witness to Venice's extensive relations with the Islamic world. Begun in the twelfth century to supplement the many private boatyards and to organize the government's own fleets, it was in full operation in the fourteenth century, when the poet Dante (1265–1321) was among its visitors (see his *Inferno*, Canto 21). It was continually extended and revamped through the sixteenth century, so that it came to occupy a sizable part of the whole city fabric. Sanudo informs us:

> The Arsenal … covers a great area … surrounded by very handsome walls, and here great galleys for the war fleet are continually being built…. Almost a thousand workmen labour here every day…. There are covered building-yards for galleys with water surrounding them, so that they can be launched and floated.
> They can then leave the Arsenal and join the Grand Canal…. Here there are a great number of carpenters or shipwrights for the galleys; smiths also work here, making all the iron fittings; in conclusion, whatever is required of every skill is here.
>
> (Chambers and Pullan, *Venice*, p. 19)

From its sparkling center at San Marco, to the commercial bustle at the Rialto Bridge, to the vast shipbuilding factory that was the Arsenal, Venice was proud and independent—at the time that Sanudo wrote, and for almost 1,000 years in all, "a free city, a common home to all men … never subjugated by anyone, as have been all other cities."

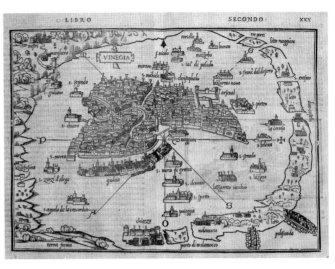

Perspective plan of Venice and the Lagoon, 1528.

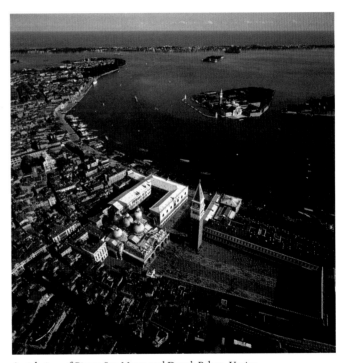

Aerial view of Piazza San Marco and Doge's Palace, Venice.

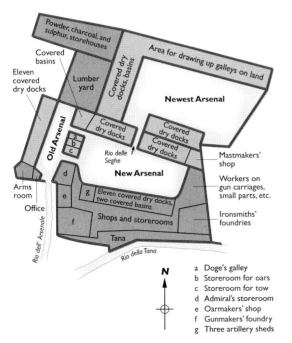

Plan of Arsenal, Venice, c. 1560.

seizing the government palaces. They compelled the oligarchy to permit the upper strata of these workers to form three guilds, in addition to the 21 major and minor guilds, and thus gain access to political office. About 13,000 new citizens of Florence were created from the previously disenfranchised ciompi.

As guild members, the ciompi were able to compete for seats in the councils where, once represented, they pressed for their particular political demands. These included especially the right of the three ciompi guilds to elect three of the nine priors, the executive officers of the Florentine state; the limitation of punishment by mutilation and imprisonment for debt; and the reform of taxation, involving the replacement of the interest-paying forced loan with a direct tax on property. These demands together aimed to empower ordinary workers and to correct the economic and social disabilities suffered by the workers. It would be at least four centuries before a European worker population again gained the rights demanded by the Florentine ciompi at the end of the fourteenth century.

The rights they did win they held only for a moment. A few months after the initial ciompi revolt, members of the traditional guilds led by the butchers (often a factor in urban violence because of their deadly skill with sharp-edged weapons) waged battle against the ciompi guildsmen. The three extraordinary guilds were dissolved, and the oligarchy once again took charge. By 1382 all relics of ciompi participation in public life had been eliminated.

From the original victory of the popolo through the political crises of the fourteenth century and on to the covert despotism of the fifteenth century, when members of the Medici family manipulated the machinery of government, the oligarchy that controlled Florence's affairs of state became increasingly narrow. Yet the city remained a republic and one in which ordinary men had experience of public affairs to a remarkable extent.

VENICE: SHIPBUILDING AND TRADE

In Venice, too, although power was restricted to certain groups, the politically privileged group was of merchant origin. Like Florence, Venice was an autonomous republic during the period 1250 to 1350. As one of the coastal cities that had begun, even before the age of communal revolutions, to penetrate the trade networks of the eastern Mediterranean, it had developed a set of economic priorities and a system of governance that differed from those of Florence and of many other inland popular republics. Where Florence's wealth derived from its banking and wool-manufacturing activities, Venice's derived from trade, which required a giant commitment to the construction of ships and the management of fleets. Venice was, above all, as the eminent historian Frederic Lane has described her, a "maritime republic."

1250–1275

1250 Guilds control Florence, establish a "popular" Guelf government.

1252 Florence introduces the florin.

1260 The popular government in Florence falls to pro-imperial Ghibellines.

1260 The Scaligeri (della Scala) family takes control of Verona.

1262 Ottone Visconti becomes archbishop of Milan, beginning his family's dominance of the city.

1264 Obizzo d'Este becomes ruler of Ferrara, to be controlled by his family for 300 years.

1265 Dante Alighieri is born in Florence.

1266 Florentine author Brunetto Latini writes *Les livres du trésor* in exile in France.

1268 Popular rule is restored in Florence with the *Secondo popolo*.

1276–1300

1277 Archbishop Ottone, of the Visconti family, becomes ruler of Milan.

1277 Mastino della Scala becomes governor of Verona, starting the Scaligeri family's rule in the city.

1284 Gold ducats are first minted in Venice.

1285 Pisa declines after its fleet is defeated by the Genoese.

1293 Florentine Ordinances of Justice bring magnates under strict control.

1289 Florence defeats Arezzo at the Battle of Campaldino to become the main Tuscan power.

1296 Work begins on the building of the Cathedral of Florence.

1297 Membership of Venice's Grand Council is declared hereditary.

1300 Dante completes *Vita nuova*, the story of his love for Beatrice.

1301–1325

1301 Dante leaves Florence, spends the rest of his life in exile.

1304 Birth of Petrarch.

1306 Giotto begins work on Arena Chapel frescoes, Padua.

1306 The independent city of Pistoia is taken over by Florence.

1307 Dante begins work on *The Divine Comedy*.

1309 Reconstruction of the Doge's Palace in Venice begins.

1310 Venice's Council of Ten is formed to defend the state against conspiracy.

1313 Birth of Boccaccio.

1318 Jacopo da Carrara becomes Padua's "perpetual captain."

1321 Death of Dante.

1324 Marsilius of Padua's treatise on government *Defensor pacis* states the church should be subordinate to princes.

1326–1355

1328 Ludovico Gonzaga becomes ruler of Mantua; his family will control the city for 300 years.

1329 Albertino Mussato writes the tragedy of *Eccerinis*.

1334 Giotto is appointed master of works for the city of Florence.

1341 Petrarch produces love poems, *Le rime*, and is crowned poet laureate in Rome.

1342 Repudiation of debts by King Edward III ruins the Florentine Bardi and Peruzzi banks.

1342 French nobleman Walter of Brienne seizes Florence, to be driven out in 1343.

1345 Work begins on Florence's Ponte Vecchio.

1348 Bubonic plague, the Black Death, sweeps through Italy.

c. 1350 Boccaccio works on *The Decameron*.

1355 Doge Marino Falier is executed by the Council of Ten for seeking to establish personal rule over Venice.

The Growth of Venice

In the quiet of the lagoons off the Adriatic shore during the centuries of invasion and disruption, Venetian boatmen began to venture down the coast and up the rivers, offering the basic commodities that they had for sale: fish and salt. In exchange for salt, they acquired timber and some metal goods from inland sites; and in exchange for these, at ports of call south and east, they acquired small quantities of the high-cost goods from the east that could fetch high prices at home: spices, dyestuffs, silks, gems. By about 1000, Venice officially achieved independence from the Byzantine Empire to which it had been nominally subject, gaining the freedom it needed to expand further. Venetian merchants built larger ships that carried more varied merchandise longer distances and experimented with new kinds of commercial contracts that aided the extension of credit to fund merchant ventures while evading church restrictions on moneylending (usury).

A wealthy merchant elite took command of the instruments of government, which it guided, so as to support mercantile interests. The harmony between the Venetian state and Venetian commerce was complete. Venice became a commune in the eleventh century when its *dux* (leader) or, in the local dialect, *doge*, ceased to be a monarch and became a figure increasingly controlled by the broader oligarchy, from which he himself emerged. It did not, however, undergo a revolution by the popolo. Although there were guilds in Venice, the guildsmen never approached in wealth or status the great merchants, who engaged in international commerce but who were not themselves manufacturers or specialists in any commodity.

The main manufacturing activity in Venice in this era was shipbuilding. The product was not a commodity that could be offered for sale but the great cogs and galleys that carried whatever merchandise one might wish. The cogs were large, round ships that though slow could efficiently and comfortably carry the bulky, cheap goods, such as timber, from the Italian interior. The galleys were long and sleek, rowed by three oarsmen to a bench, so that they did not need to depend on sails to enter a harbor or to advance in calm seas. Since their speed was an advantage in a battle, the galleys were generally armed and were sent on the most dangerous missions.

Shipbuilding and the State

Shipbuilding became an especially vital enterprise in Venice when, from the 1290s, the state itself began to fund and organize fleets of merchant galleys that traveled in convoy escorted by warships. In spring and late summer each year, fleets left Venice to go to Romania (the formerly Roman parts of the Mediterranean, now the Balkans, Greece, and islands), the Levant, and Alexandria in Egypt. Soon after 1300, in the trail of Genoese galleys that had pioneered the route in the 1270s, Venice sent out convoys of state galleys bound for English and Flemish ports, connecting with the other great late medieval trading network, the **Hanseatic League**. Venetian merchants leased fractions of the space on these state galleys, while Venetian sailors, free laborers who manned the oars, doubled as soldiers ready to defend the fleet. Young Venetian noblemen might serve their first public function as "gentlemen of the quarterdeck," minor officers on board, while experienced noblemen served as captains and admirals. The convoy system greatly increased the security, and thus the profitability, of international trade for the merchant elite.

The state that had so great an interest in trade that it organized armed merchant convoys at public expense needed also to take an interest in the mass construction of ships. Venice, accordingly, built a unique complex called the *arsenale* (Arsenal), the word taken from the Arabic term for "place of manufacture." In artificially made pools connected by canals that led out to open water, special government workers—carpenters, sail-makers, caulkers, and designers—constructed sturdy, efficient galleys with assembly-line efficiency. In the complexity of worker organization, in the analysis and management of subtasks, in the provision of materials and scheduling and management of outcomes, the shipbuilding operation of the Arsenal matched or exceeded the system of wool manufacture in Florence. Certainly they both looked ahead to the large-scale enterprises of the industrial era. Not all ships produced in Venice, of course, came from the Arsenal shipyards. Individual entrepreneurs, in private shipyards, saw to the construction of cogs, which generally carried less valuable merchandise and did not travel in convoy; individual merchants commissioned space on these as well, for different types of voyages.

The Venetian Nobility

The greatest merchants, however, were those most intimately involved in the mechanisms of the state, and the state oversaw the production of ships and the organization of the galley convoys that were essential to Venetian commerce. In 1297 this interdependence of merchant elite and government apparatus expressed itself in a remarkable act. The representatives present in the Grand Council—the largest council of the state—voted that the membership of that body would henceforth be "closed." Only descendants of the families present at the time of the closing would be eligible for membership on the council. The *serrata* (closing) of the Grand Council took a generation or more to be fully accepted and established as law. But established it was, and thus Venice, which had begun as a village of fishermen and refugees without social distinction and had grown to become a merchant republic, now turned its merchant class into an official, hereditary nobility.

The Venetian nobility created by the serrata was not and would never become an elite equivalent to the warrior nobility of the feudal societies of Europe. Its origins in commerce, in the dynamic of the quest for profit, would never disappear, even though as commercial opportunities dwindled centuries later, many Venetian nobles retired to leisurely lives as country gentlemen. But this artificial nobility continued to function as a closed elite. In 1381, some 80 families who had contributed notably to the war chest supporting Venice's desperate struggle with rival Genoa were enrolled in the official nobility. With this one exception, the Venetian nobility was a closed caste from the early 1300s until the 1640s, when wealthy individuals were able to purchase entrance to the patriciate to bolster state revenues. Although persons of all social backgrounds might prosper in Venice, they could not aspire to participate in the government at the decision-making level. Some educated members of the highest stratum of the non-noble citizenry were, however, permitted to hold the positions of secretary and chancellor to the various councils and considered it a great honor to approach close to power, while never wielding it, in those roles.

Since 1000 Italian urban life had been moving in the direction of openness, toward an expanding and active citizenry. Venice took a different course; was there no protest? Virtually none. In 1310 angry at the exclusions instituted by the serrata, the nobles Biamonte Tiepolo and Mario Quirini joined in a conspiracy. It was quelled, and the incident led to the formation of the Council of Ten, a standing government committee whose main function was to oversee state security. In 1354 a second conspiracy formed around the figure of the doge himself, Marino Falier (1274–1355), who hoped to restore a ducal monarchy. The Council of Ten discovered this rebellion as well, and Falier was executed in 1355. In the sequence of the portraits of all the doges which were painted on the walls of the government council halls, his portrait was blackened over. Otherwise, Venice was uncannily and conspicuously tranquil—*la Serenissima* (the most serene republic) as it called itself. It discovered the secret of preventing rebellion by providing adequately for the needs of the citizens and not imposing on them judicial malpractice, the miseries of war, and the deprivations caused by over-taxation—hardships that elsewhere provoked the disenfranchised to revolt.

Consequently, Venice endured until 1797, one of the few city-states to survive into modern times. Like Florence, it was no democracy but a well-functioning oligarchy. In a remarkably balanced republican system of councils and committees, a noble caste governed itself and everyone else, its eye fixed on the bottom line.

URBAN RENEWAL: WALLS, BUILDINGS, AND SPACES

Along with other urban republics in the century after 1250, Florence and Venice saw a surge of building that seemed to accelerate in tempo with the fortunes of the merchant oligarchy. New churches, guildhalls, government buildings, palaces, hospitals, bridges, roads, and above all, walls sprouted up. Each new structure redefined the spaces within which the citizens pursued an existence different in kind from anywhere else in Europe.

Walls

Today a visitor to the city of Florence will very likely travel by car for some distance on a broad boulevard that rings the older part of the city. That boulevard traces the line of the outermost city walls, torn down to accommodate the industrial expansion of the nineteenth century—the first century in which the number of inhabitants exceeded the

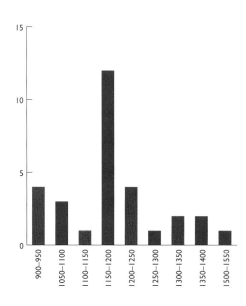

population achieved by about 1340, on the eve of the Black Death. Enormous for that era, the population then lived densely packed within the circuit of walls that had only been completed in 1333.

This last ring of walls was the third set (excluding minor alterations) built to protect the inhabitants of Florence. The first ring dated from the era of the Roman Republic. They were the walls of the original Roman *castrum* (camp) established in 59 BCE. Those ancient walls served their purpose for more than 1,000 years: throughout the career of the Roman Empire and the Gothic, Lombard, and Carolingian phases of the Italian Middle Ages. In the tenth century an extension of the Roman walls reached toward the bank of the Arno River. It was only after the population advance of the eleventh century and the establishment of the Florentine commune, that a significant enlargement of the walls was needed. That larger circuit of walls, constructed on the right or main bank of the Arno in 1172 to 1175 and extended to the left bank by 1250, enclosed an area twice as large as the expanded tenth-century walls. No sooner had it been completed than the building of a third, much larger ring began, in 1284, during the lifetime of Dante Alighieri. It was completed only a few years after his death and enclosed an area more than six times as large as the previous circle.

Rings of Walls: New Walls in 13 Italian Towns, 900–1550
(H.A. Miskimin, *The Economy of Early Renaissance Europe, 1300– 1640*. Upper Saddle River, NJ: Prentice Hall, 1975, p. 22)

To put this in perspective: the tiny Roman city was sufficient to house the people of Florence from its founding until the tenth century; but over the next 350 years, the city expanded so remarkably and rapidly that, beyond minor alterations, two major enlargements of the walls were required. The final circuit of walls would remain sufficient for a further five hundred years. The walls, by themselves, are a chronicle in stone, telling the story of stagnation, growth, catastrophe, and continuity.

Other cities expanded less dramatically than Florence, but still in rhythms that trace the patterns of its prosperity. Pisa, which reached its apex in the 1100s and 1200s and suffered a grievous defeat in 1285, lived within its Roman walls until the twelfth century, when it received a new and final belt. Pistoia's Roman walls were extended a little in the eleventh century. A much larger ring began in 1305—12 times as large as the original Roman circuit and too large for the population at that time. Unlike Pisa and Pistoia, which fell subject to Florence, independent Lucca expanded its Roman wall system in the twelfth century, completing it in 1265 and further extending it about 1400. In 1504, it began its third and final circuit, constructed in the modern style to withstand artillery attack. In all three cases, as in Florence, the widest circuit of walls was constructed at the point, or a little after it, when the city was still independent and powerful.

Buildings

Whereas city walls tell the story of urban growth and contraction, the monumental buildings within those walls tell another story: who were the city's rulers and what was its mission? The "stones of Florence," to borrow the phrase made popular as the title of a book by Mary McCarthy (1912–1989) alluding to *The Stones of Venice* an older work of English author John Ruskin (1819–1900), tell us that the city's rulers were its wealthy merchants and that their mission was to promote the pursuit of wealth and piety and to resist the claims of the warrior nobility, whom they had disgraced and expelled.

The two most important Florentine structures, both built during the century 1250–1350, marked either end of the street that was the axis of the old Roman city—today's Via dei Calzaiuoli, the street of the stocking-makers. At one end stood the Cathedral, or Duomo (dome), of Santa Maria del Fiore, with its additional buildings: the much older baptistry, which would be greatly adorned by Renaissance additions, and a free-standing bell-tower, designed by the artist Giotto di Bondone (c. 1267–1337), who will figure prominently later in this chapter. At the other end, in front of the **Piazza** della Signoria (government square), stood the Palazzo Pubblico, later called the Palazzo Vecchio (old palace), in the style of a nobleman's fortified townhouse. Much of the city's traffic passed between the massive cathedral, representing the citizens' devotion to God, and the massive Palazzo Vecchio, representing their guild-based government. Midway between the two structures was the main market place; a little nearer to the Signoria and to the Arno River was the unusual Orsanmichele, originally a granary and later a complex for the management of the major guilds. In addition to these central structures, splendid bridges and the houses of prominent citizens adorned the city.

Elsewhere, too, where merchant elites led their communities to successive heights of commercial and productive achievement, splendid and distinctive monumental buildings sprang up within the swelling belt of walls—as at Milan, Genoa, and Siena—or on its islands, as at Venice. The opposite was also true: where cities lost their freedom, the phase of exuberant monumental building stopped. Pisa's great cathedral complex, with the famous leaning tower, dates from the eleventh and twelfth centuries, but after its decisive defeat by Genoa in 1285, followed by the Florentine conquest of 1405, no memorable structures were built during the Renaissance era. Pistoia, too, was built up during the twelfth and thirteenth centuries, before it lost its independence in 1254. Lucca retained its independence in the Renaissance, except during the period 1314 to 1369 when it was ruled by despots, and from this period when Italy's fortunate cities were building public buildings, there was no great monumental architecture.

The late medieval building boom in the most dynamic republics of urban Italy sets the stage for the civilization of the Renaissance that was soon to develop.

VITA CIVILE: URBAN CULTURE IN A REPUBLICAN AGE

The explosion of economic and political energies that culminated in the twelfth and thirteenth centuries resulted not only in new forms of urban life but also in a reorientation of culture. In earlier centuries, intellectual culture, like the arts, revolved almost entirely around the communication of Christian ideas and the affirmation of the church. While religious commitments were not forgotten, ideas and the arts now came to serve the interest of the cities and their rulers as well.

The Jurists

As early as the eleventh and twelfth centuries, one group of intellectuals played a prominent role in Italian cities: the **jurists**. These were men trained in Roman law, which was fundamental to the law codes that governed the different regions of Italy as well as the law of the church, or canon law. Jurists were prominent among the citizen leaders who took part in the formation of the communes and continued to hold high status in Italian society into modern times. Jurists might or might not be churchmen. Either way, they provided valuable services to growing city-states that needed experts to compile urban law codes, to document contracts and exchanges of property, and to negotiate alliances and treaties of peace with other states. From the twelfth century, the schools of law became organized within the developing Italian universities, where law and medicine—not theology and the arts, as in France or England—were the dominant faculties. Legal professionals thus enjoyed prestige within both urban and scholarly settings, and the universities trained and certified a stream of jurists who staffed or advised the new urban bureaucracies.

In their role as advisors to urban states, some jurists entered upon the new terrain of political theory. What, exactly, was a state? From where was the right to rule such a state derived? Was rulership necessarily personal, or could it be exercised by a council or community? Were states subject to ecclesiastical power, or were they separate, secular organisms? If the latter, did they in any way owe obedience to the empire, the largest nonecclesiastical political entity of the time? Who was empowered to make law? Were new laws to be added to the Roman corpus of civil law? These were some of the issues that occupied the medieval jurists in Italy's urban setting, who quickly opened a path to modern political thought in their consideration of these matters. Two in particular made contributions to this discussion that are still profitably studied today: Marsilius of Padua and Bartolus of Sassoferrato.

Marsilius of Padua (c. 1280–c. 1343), who studied and taught at the University of Paris, returned to his native Italy to become advisor to Ghibelline interests in the 1320s—the pro-imperial, anti-papal party in an era after the ascent and victory of the popolo. Convinced of the dangers to a state of interference by ecclesiastical power, Marsilius wrote his *Defensor pacis* ("Defender of the Peace") between 1320 and 1324. A highly original work of political theory, *Defensor pacis* sketched out the contours of the modern state as an entity that was both autonomous and secular and that provided security and order to its citizens, who were the source of its power and legitimacy. Marsilius was declared a heretic and spent his later years at the imperial court, which greatly approved the anti-papal thrust of his theories. There he died, an exile from the region where such autonomous states as he described were laboratories of his political principles.

Based mainly at the University of Perugia, Bartolus of Sassoferrato (c. 1313–1357) was a commentator on the Roman civil law books contained in the *Corpus iuris civilis* (*The Body of Civil Law*). He developed a political theory appropriate for the governance of the Italian city-state, where individuals and groups who were neither monarchs nor clerics might hold power. Although very large states might be well ruled by a single king, he argued, wealthy cities (he specifically named Venice and Florence) were best ruled by combinations of prominent men, rather than by a king or even the populace at large. Drawing on the political thinking of Aristotle, Cicero, Augustine, and other church fathers, Bartolus gave theoretical justification to self-sufficient, self-governing states, although he expected these to have oligarchical rather than democratic governments.

The secular politics outlined by Marsilius and Bartolus, among other medieval authors of political works, emerge more from the urban environment of northern Italy than from the imperial ideology of the German emperors. They set the stage for modern theories of the state developed by Niccolò Machiavelli (1469–1527), Thomas Hobbes (1588–1679), John Locke (1632–1704), and their successors.

The Secretaries

Although the contribution of these jurists to Western political thought was momentous, other educated men were engaged in the service of the urban republics and made other notable cultural innovations. One of the most important tasks entrusted to the secretaries of these states was the composition of official letters. Those entrusted with these duties could write elegant Latin prose, adorned with rhetorical flourishes learned from the close study of ancient Roman literary models.

In acquiring this verbal expertise, these secretaries needed to master many ancient texts. Those who did so, and who had the education necessary to do so, formed a committed literary network within the urban community and between cities. Some of them began to compose works grounded in their familiarity with classical texts that were not specifically required by their employment. These works—poems, letters, treatises—mark the beginnings of **humanism**, the intellectual movement that would come to characterize the whole of the Renaissance. Humanism was marked by the absorption and imitation of classical texts at the highest level of quality and the creation of new works, bearing original ideas but grounded in ancient traditions that were, ironically, in tune with the needs of an advanced urban society.

The circle of Paduan secretaries that clustered around Lovato Lovati (1241–1309) and Albertino Mussato (1261–1329) is representative of the group of early humanists who were active in some northern Italian cities prior to 1350. In the shadow of the great university at Padua, a training ground for professional jurists and physicians, the city's secretaries embarked on a different kind of intellectual experience, both less technical and more literary. Lovati studied the Roman poets Lucretius (c. 99–55 BCE) and Catullus and the works of the philosopher, essayist, and tragedian Seneca (c. 55 BCE–c. 40 CE). Like the later humanists (discussed in Chapter 3) whose early mission included the recovery of the manuscripts of ancient works, he read Seneca and Livy in books that he found in neglected monastery libraries. Mussato actually composed a tragedy in the Senecan style, the first written since antiquity, based on the life of Ezzelino III da Romano (1194–1259),

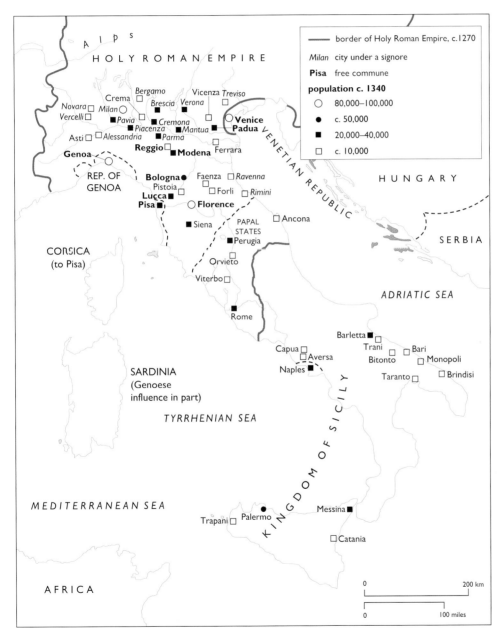

Political Diversity in Italy, c. 1250–1340

This map shows the diverse Italian political scene in the century before the Black Death. The Holy Roman Empire still made occasional claims to authority in northern Italy. Descendants of the Angevin rulers, once invited to displace the pope's Hohenstaufen opponents, ruled in the south and Sicily (see Chapter 1). The pope ruled Rome and most of central Italy. Northern Italy was fully urbanized. Some cities were ruled by a *signore* or prince; others were free communes.

YEARNING TO BE FREE: GIANO DELLA BELLA AND BOCCACCIO'S PAMPINEA

Amid turmoil and crisis, some people find new opportunities for freedom. According to the humanist and historian Leonardo Bruni, that was the response of Giano della Bella, a leader of the Florentines in the revolutionary moment of 1292 to 1293.

Here Giano arouses the assembled popolo to defy the magnates—the powerful nobles whose arrogance and crimes went unpunished—and thus ensure their liberty.

The more I think about the Republic, the more I am convinced that we must either check the pride of the powerful families or lose our liberty altogether.... It seems to me that the liberty of the people consists in two things: the laws and the judges. When the power of these two things prevails in the city over the power of any individual citizen, then liberty is preserved. But when some people scorn the laws and the judges with impunity, then it is fair to say that liberty is gone....

Therefore ... consider the crimes of the nobility: tell me, any one of you, whether you think the city is free or whether it has been for some time in subjection.... For what do we possess, that they don't want to take? ... Our very bodies, if we will only admit it, are no longer free: remember the citizens who have been beaten, chased out of their homes, the numerous examples of arson, rape, wounding, and killing in these last years. The doers of these evil deeds are so well-known and publicly recognized that obviously they ... don't care to conceal their crime.... We see men who deserve prison and torture strutting around the city with a crowd of armed retainers, terrifying us and the officials. Would anyone tell me that this is liberty?

(R.N. Watkins, trans. and ed., Humanism and Liberty: Writings on Freedom from Fifteenth-Century Florence. Columbia: University of South Carolina Press, 1978, pp. 69–73)

It is personal, not political freedom—the freedom to act to preserve life—that is envisioned by the speaker of the words that follow. They are delivered by Pampinea, a fictional character in Giovanni Boccaccio's *Decameron* ("Ten Days"), a collection of 100 stories. Here she persuades her companions to consult the dictates of reason and, rather than remain in Florence and die of the plague, act to save themselves.

Dear girls ... you must have heard often enough ... that a person who uses his just rights legitimately injures nobody. It is the natural right of everyone born to help preserve and defend his life as best he can.... Now if this is conceded by laws ... how much more justified we ought to be ... in taking every possible means to preserve our lives.... I am convinced that each one of us is in mortal terror for herself.... And it's no great wonder! But I certainly do wonder that, clever though we are, we take no measures to prevent what we have so much reason to dread. We all look ... as though we were waiting to see just how many bodies are brought in for burial....

Now, if things are as they are ... what are we doing here? What are we waiting for? ... Do we hold ourselves more cheap than everybody else? Or do we imagine our lives are linked to our bodies by a stronger chain, so that we don't have to worry that anything will hurt them? We are mistaken.... I think it would be a mighty good thing if we all left this town ... [and] go quietly to our own country places ... and there, without in the least overstepping reasonable restraint, we would take what innocent pleasure and enjoyment we could find.

(Giovanni Boccaccio, The Decameron, trans. F. Winwar. New York: Modern Library, 1955, pp. xxxi–xxxiii) a tyrant who had controlled the city of Padua as an agent of Emperor Frederick II during the latter's struggle with the papacy.

Some distance away from Padua, the home of the earliest humanists, lived the Florentine politician, poet, and master of **rhetoric** Brunetto Latini (c. 1220–1294). He had been extensively exposed to the cultural life of northern France and was well trained in the classical tradition, from which, along with his own contemporary experiences, he derived his ideas on politics, moral philosophy, and proper behavior. Brunetto Latini wrote his *Les livres du trésor* ("Book of Treasures") a general-purpose encyclopedia and guide to all things, in French. France was where Latini, a Guelf, had been exiled during the Ghibelline ascendancy in Florence in 1260 to 1267, and by this time medieval French had developed into a flexible and expressive literary language. Full of nuggets of ancient thought lifted from Aristotle, Cicero, and Seneca, Latini's *Trésor* was a primer of ancient thought and a guide to behavior in the fast-paced urban society of late-thirteenth-century Florence.

These early humanist efforts came about in the particular setting of Italy's urban society at a time of highly conscious state formation. The same matrix would also nourish the talents of some of the greatest creative geniuses Italy or Europe would ever call its own.

DANTE AND GIOTTO: INNOVATORS BEFORE THE DAWN OF THE RENAISSANCE

Their lives and work straddling the year 1300, two natives of Florence contributed remarkably to the development of the civilization of republican Italy. The literary and artistic work of Dante and Giotto in turn reflected the urban environment in which they lived.

Dante Alighieri

Born to a wealthy and substantial family and educated according to the principles laid out by Brunetto Latini, Dante Alighieri began his career as a poet. As a young man, he experimented with the *dolce stil nuovo* (sweet new style) that had recently come to northern Italy, via the Two Sicilies, from the courts of medieval France where the emotions aroused by love were the favored theme of poetic composition. In his autobiographical verse-and-prose work *Vita nuova* ("The New Life," 1295), which speaks of his inspiration by his beloved Beatrice, Dante is both a lively, engaged poet, and a full participant in civic life. The same is true of his verse discussion of philosophical notions and literary trends in *Il convivio* ("The Banquet"), which also contains a heartfelt celebration of Italian as a literary language—one which Dante's writing in large part created. In his prose work *De monarchia* ("On Monarchy"), anticipating the works of Marsilius and Bartolus discussed above, Dante argued for a secular, autonomous state.

In the meantime, Dante had become an active participant in the Florentine government and had been exiled for his association with the wrong political party, the White faction within the larger Guelf movement. In his immense *Divina commedia* ("The Divine Comedy"), written after his exile, Dante traced his own journey through the three realms of the afterworld—Hell, Purgatory, and Paradise, as they were in his day conceived— while commenting on his friends and enemies, the great shapers of history and the great

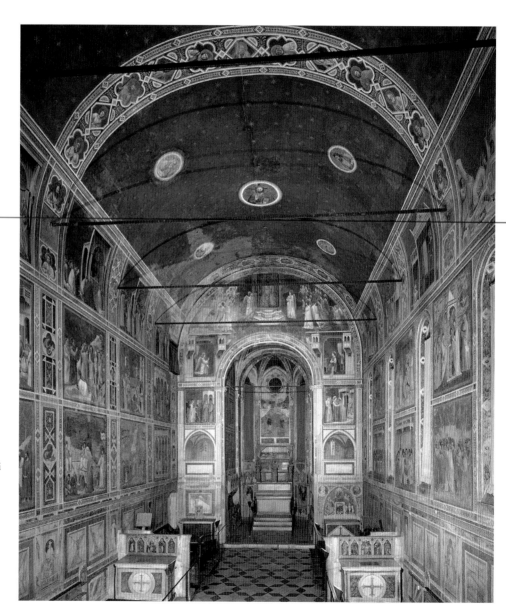

Giotto di Bondone, Scrovegni (or Arena) Chapel, c. 1305, fresco. Padua.

To the left unfolds the story of the life of Mary, mother of Christ; straight ahead, on the chancel wall, pierced by the great arch, are scenes of the Annunciation; to the right are depictions of Christ's birth, death, and resurrection.

traitors to humanity. In all of these works, Dante is the immensely gifted Florentine, aware of his city, of history, of the legacy of ideas and literature, and a figure who encompasses in his grand achievement both the whole of late medieval thought and the first fruits of the coming Renaissance.

Giotto di Bondone

Much the same can be said of Giotto di Bondone (1266/1267–1337). At first glance, the pair seem ill-suited: Dante was from an aristocratic family, Giotto was born a peasant; Dante received the broad education of the privileged, Giotto learned his art in the fields; Dante

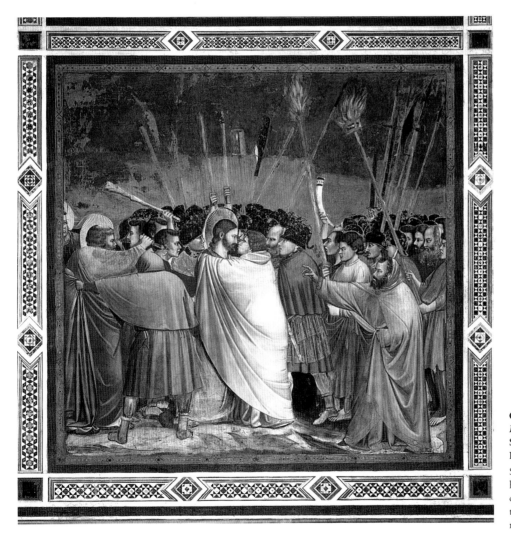

Giotto di Bondone, *The Kiss of Judas*, c. 1305, fresco. Scrovegni (or Arena) Chapel, Padua.

Showing Judas engulfing Jesus in his embrace, Giotto comments on the ironic identity of love and treachery central to the Gospel message.

was a master of words, Giotto of forms. But Giotto, like Dante, launched a new way of seeing and feeling that would have its culmination in the Renaissance; and like Dante, he projected his own experience as a citizen of a dynamic, innovative, urban society into his art.

The masters from whom Giotto learned his craft were already bringing new life to the standard patterns of the visual arts of the Italian late Middle Ages. Yet the standard patterns still prevailed: depictions of Jesus on the cross, saints and martyrs, the Virgin Mary and infant Christ, all in the poses in which they had always appeared, flat, static, and staring, as though suspended in space. These were devotional images whose purpose was to assert the authority of the figure portrayed and thus to inspire and comfort the worshiper. With Giotto, all that changed. The figures gained bulk, revolved in space, and moved across prop-like buildings or landscape whose lines and volumes added to the meaning of the scene. Above all, the figures had expression. They showed love, fear, rage, and anguish, both in the arrangement of their features and in the inclinations and tensions of the stocky, mobile bodies.

With such figures and such settings, Giotto was prepared to bring the stories of the great religious figures to life in a way they had never before been portrayed. A particularly fine sample of his work is preserved in the Scrovegni (or Arena) Chapel in Padua. This is a compact ecclesiastical building, midway in scale between the family chapel it was built to be and the vast cathedral that might have accommodated such rich embellishment. The entire interior is covered in Giotto's frescoes: the lateral, entrance, and chancel walls, from floor to lofty ceiling. The lateral walls each feature three rows of frescoes, meant to be read continuously. The sequence is read from left to right across one side, continued on the other, returning to the first for the second row, across the way once more, returning a third time to the lowest order on the first wall, and around to the opposite surface. The images on the chancel and entrance walls complete the sequence.

In all, the frescoes relate the story of the birth and life of the Virgin through the **Annunciation**, when the angel Gabriel informs the young girl that she will conceive by the Holy Spirit and give birth to a son, followed by the story of the birth, life, crucifixion, resurrection, and judgment of Jesus. Such an enormous narrative program, although unusual, is not in itself a tremendous innovation, since the surfaces of medieval churches, in sculpture and glass if not in paint, had always been used for narrative sequences. The originality lies in Giotto's conception of each individual scene, focusing on the emotional moment each evokes, and rendering that emotion in the human, architectural, and natural forms represented. When Joachim, father of the Virgin, is exiled from the temple, he is in despair. When Jesus is betrayed, he coolly stares into the face of Judas, halting the momentum of the false embrace that sweeps powerfully across the surface. When Jesus' dead body is brought down from the cross, his mother and the Magdalene softly grieve, but the angels in heaven are tormented by grief. Human experience is lifted to new heights in images of figures once seen as remote and awesome.

If the circle of Paduan secretaries were humanist innovators in their use of classical form to express new ideas in language, Giotto was a proto-humanist for whom the point of artistic representation was to gain some enlarged notion of the human spirit.

PETRARCH'S LETTER "TO POSTERITY"

Equipped with the largest personal library in Europe (see p. 75), Petrarch (Francesco Petrarca, 1304–1374) developed a unique sense of the sweep of Western civilization and his own role in it. He composed biographies of the heroic figures of the ancients—philosophers, orators, rulers, and generals—in his *De viris illustribus* ("On Famous Men"), to whom he also composed respectful, wistful, and intimate letters (see Chapter 3, which describes a letter to Cicero). He considered the issues that were pressing in his own age: the nature of the religious life, the striving for fame, the passion of love, the value of different forms of knowledge.

He also looked to the future. He thought that people of a later age might look back at the age he lived in and wonder who Petrarch was. So in 1351 he wrote a letter "To Posterity," for all those who would come after him. To conceive such a project shows the extraordinary sense that Petrarch had of himself. Running to nearly 4,000 words, it is one of the few autobiographies written prior to the modern age—preceded notably by St. Augustine's monumental *Confessions*, a late product of Christian antiquity, and by the twelfth-century philosopher Abelard's *Story of My Adversities*. Reproduced here are excerpts from the opening sections of "To Posterity."

You may perhaps have heard something about me—although it is doubtful that my poor little name may travel far in space and time. Still, you may by chance want to know what sort of man I was or what was the fate of my works, especially of those whose reputation may have persisted, or whose name you may have vaguely heard.

There will be various opinions on this score, for most people's words are prompted not by truth but by whim.... But I was one of your own lot, a little mortal man.... Youth led me astray, young manhood corrupted me, but maturer age corrected me and taught me by experience the truth of what I had read long before: that youth and pleasure are vain....

In my youth I was blessed with an active, agile body.... I can't boast of being handsome, but in my greener years I made a good impression. I had a fine complexion ... ardent eyes, and a vision that was for many years very sharp (But it failed me unexpectedly when I was over sixty, so that I was forced reluctantly to use spectacles. Old age suddenly took possession of my body ... and assailed me with its usual train of illnesses.) ...

My mind was rather well balanced than keen ... especially inclined to moral philosophy and poetry.... I devoted myself, though not exclusively, to the study of ancient times, since I always disliked our own period; so that, if it hadn't been for the love of those dear to me, I should have preferred being born in any other age, forgetting this one; and I always tried to transport myself mentally to other times....

People have said that my utterance is clear and compelling, but it seems to me weak and obscure. In fact, in my ordinary speech with friends and familiars, I have never worried about fine language.... If only I have lived well, I make small account of how I have spoken. To seek reputation by mere elegance of language is only vainglory.

(Petrarch, *Letters*, trans. and ed. M. Bishop. Bloomington: Indiana University Press, 1966, pp. 5–7)

BOCCACCIO AND PETRARCH: INAUGURATORS OF RENAISSANCE THOUGHT

A generation younger than Dante and Giotto, Boccaccio and Petrarch were two authors whose work truly inaugurated the Renaissance. Yet they achieved their intellectual formation in the earlier era of the urban republics before the great cataclysm of the Black Death. Their achievement, although bold and new, had its roots in the age of the popolo.

Boccaccio

Giovanni Boccaccio (1313–1375), son of a prominent merchant of Florence for whom a law career was planned, disappointed his father and turned instead to imaginative literature and classical scholarship. His prose and verse romances written from the 1340s delighted a large readership. Even more successful, his *Decameron*, a collection of 100 stories told over ten days by ten narrators, is both enormously amusing and highly instructive. The tales of misguided adventures, love affairs fulfilled and discovered, lecherous monks, and ignorant clerics mock corrupt practices and celebrate human courage and ingenuity. The work was an important source for Boccaccio's younger contemporary Geoffrey Chaucer (c. 1345–1400) and later authors, and it celebrates the creation of literature as an autonomous activity (breaking with the medieval pattern of literature being didactic). Boccaccio was also a literary critic: he was the first commentator on Dante's *Divine Comedy*, and his 1364 *Life of Dante*, composed barely a generation after the subject's death, remains an important source.

It is Boccaccio's scholarly endeavor, however, that marks him as a pioneer of the Renaissance. His learned work *De genealogiis deorum gentilium* ("On the Genealogies of the Pagan Gods") is not merely an encyclopedia of the figures of ancient myth. It is also an extended defense of the study of ancient literature and thought. Boccaccio argued that much can be learned from antiquity, despite the pagan concepts at its heart. He thereby undermined the arguments of clerical intellectuals who wished to limit access to classical sources for Christian readers because of the moral danger that they presented. In that the revival of classical antiquity was essential to the achievement of the Renaissance (see the Introduction), Boccaccio's defense of the value of ancient literature was an essential prerequisite for its development. After completing *De genealogiis*, Boccaccio proceeded to prove his point about the utility of classical studies by writing two collective biographies that drew heavily on ancient sources—*De casibus virorum illustrium* ("On the Fortunes of Famous Men") and *De mulieribus claris* ("On Famous Women").

Petrarch

Boccaccio and Dante composed in both Italian and Latin and in both literary and scholarly genres. So too did Francis Petrarch, whose works are unique in their exploration of the human personality and mind. Even more than those of his predecessors, therefore, they point to the mature achievement of Renaissance civilization. Petrarch was born in Arezzo where his father, a Florentine notary, had been exiled. He spent his childhood in and near Avignon, in France, where the papal court (during the **Babylonian Captivity**, 1309–1378) was located. There he received his early education and his first training in law at the university at nearby Montpellier. Later, he returned often to Italy, where he was supported by a variety of patrons, clerical, princely, and republican.

Petrarch produced an enormous number of works of immense importance for later European thought and literature. In his "Ascent of Mont Ventoux," a brief and charming account of a mountain-climbing excursion composed as a personal letter, but evidently to some degree allegorical, Petrarch broke new ground in the exploration of the self. Self-examination with the aim of moral judgment was a familiar exercise to medieval intellectuals, and Petrarch engages in this exercise, questioning whether in his life to date he had chosen the easier rather than the more virtuous path. But Petrarch's exploration goes further. Having chosen to climb to the top of a mountain in search of experience, to see the sight, to attain a goal, at the summit he reaches for the little book he carried with him always, a copy of Augustine's *Confessions*, that late classical masterpiece of the inner life. Opening Augustine at random, he happens on a passage that condemns those who look elsewhere for enlightenment and neglect the depths of their own souls. In a mere dozen pages, Petrarch strikes out on a modern path to adventure and simultaneously on the modern quest for the self.

Petrarch's letter "To Posterity," which he included among his collection of *Familiar Letters*, also displays a wholly original self-consciousness. In this chatty and reflective autobiography, written as though to friends but in fact to unknown readers long in the future who "may perhaps have heard" of him, Petrarch is confident of the work he has done, yet uncertain whether it will endure. He knows that he stands at the center of time, and just as he looks backward to the great minds who came before him, he looks forward to the future, conscious that it is through him that the legacy of the human spirit will be transmitted to his intellectual descendants.

In his several volumes of letters and many other prose works—leaving aside the immensely important body of verse that he left, including a collection of **sonnets** that are the originals of the form that would have so important a role in the development of modern European literature—Petrarch emerges as a thoughtful explorer of human subjectivity, as well as a zealous student and imitator of antiquity. Of these, perhaps none is more important than his unique work *De sui ipsius et multorum aliorum ignorantia* ("On His Own Ignorance and That of Many Others"). As the title suggests, here Petrarch admits to being ignorant—as his critics had charged—of Aristotle (so important to contemporary **scholastic** philosophers) whose value he suggests is overestimated. At the same time, he denounces the far more serious ignorance of his opponents who, blinded by the authority of Aristotle, fail to consider the state of the human spirit and its longing for the good, a worthier passion than the zeal to know. Pointing to Plato (c. 428–c. 348 BCE) as a philosopher more alert to the complexity of the human condition (whose works he knew only in part through Latin versions and synopses), Petrarch brilliantly trumps his enemies by conceding ignorance but gratefully accepting the compliment of goodness: for it is more important "to will the good than to know the truth."

Building on the work of earlier authors at this moment of cultural explosion, Boccaccio and Petrarch continued the tradition of the study of classical antiquity, linking it to the exploration of the human self and the social world the self inhabits. In the same way, the later creators of the Renaissance were to study the past and use what they found to understand the nature and potential of the human condition within the framework of their own contemporary world.

REPUBLICS AND PRINCIPALITIES

Although the first impulses of Renaissance civilization announced themselves in the unique context of the republican states of urbanized northern Italy, the Renaissance would continue to unfold in a world where republics were few and fragile. Ironically, the very social and political conditions that provided an ideal framework for the explosion of new cultural energies would soon fail. By 1300 most of the urban republics that had emerged from the struggles of the Middle Ages had succumbed to tyranny. By 1500, only four independent republics remained: Venice, Florence, Siena, and tiny Lucca. Genoa alternated between periods of despotism and independence. Of the major Renaissance republics, only Venice would survive the wars of the sixteenth century (see Chapter 8) and remain fully autonomous. It endured until 1797, when Napoleon Bonaparte (1769–1821) fulfilled his promise to be an "Attila to the Venetians" and dismantled the last of the Italian republics.

Why did so many of the Italian republics become **signorie** (states ruled by a signore, or prince), also termed principalities, despotisms, or tyrannies? The same social conflicts that permitted the commune to throw off the rule of bishop and emperor and enabled the popolo to break up the monopoly of the magnate rulers of the commune, also led to autocracy, the rule of an individual. Where civic strife continued to destabilize a city, the citizens submitted either freely or forcibly to the rule of a lord. Financial crises and wars also paved the way to a takeover by a despot. So too did the presence of a powerful nobility.

Where the nobility were an important force, cities tended to lose their republican liberties and become subject to a nobleman and his supporters. Although an urban nobility in Italy had developed as early as the eleventh century, even these urbanized families retained the tendencies to violence and exclusivity that were characteristic of this warrior class. They were able to regain power where merchant oligarchy was weak and unable to restrain them. Generally, one figure claimed the state by violence and was supported

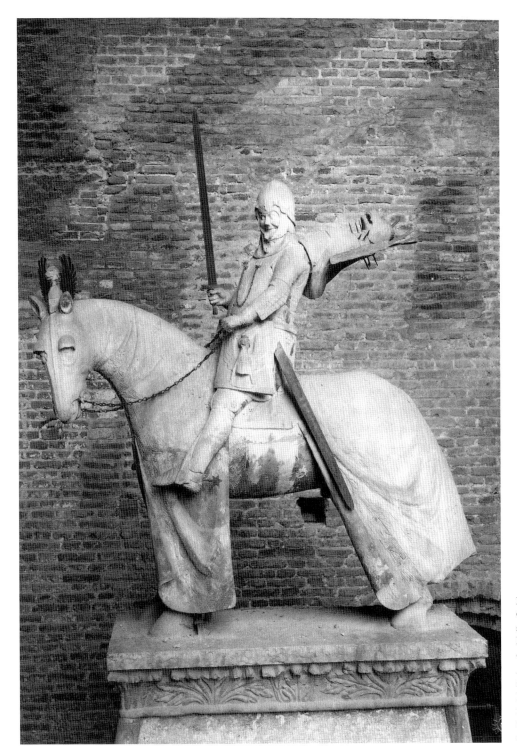

Equestrian Statue of Can Grande della Scala, 1330, sandstone with marble base, height 6 ft 7 in (2 m). Museo del Castelvecchio, Verona.

Alert, sword erect, tense body inclined backward so as to launch forward, one of the first great signori proudly rides a brilliant Renaissance representation of the horse.

by other noble followers. At Milan in 1278, for example, the archbishop Ottone Visconti (1208–1295) seized control and left the state to his nephew and descendants. The Scala in Verona, the Este in Ferrara, and the Carrara in Padua all came to power from the late thirteenth through early fourteenth centuries in the same way; Bologna and Perugia were latecomers, falling to despotic rule early in the fifteenth century (see Chapter 7).

Some despots stand out, not so much as strongman representatives of the nobility, but as unique individuals who dominated by force of personality and extraordinary intelligence or craft. Notorious was the case of Ezzelino da Romano, an agent of Frederick II in Padua, whose ruthless but clever rule inspired the Swiss historian Jacob Burckhardt (1818–1897), in his characterization of Italian politics, to speak of "the state as a work of art." Of the same cloth was Francesco Sforza (1401–1466), who by sheer force of will, it seemed, rose from nowhere to become the duke of Milan, then the largest of the Italian states. Born the illegitimate son of a minor noble, Sforza followed his father into the career of mercenary soldier. In 1446, he became *condottiere* (mercenary general) for Filippo Maria Visconti (1391–1447), ruler of Milan, in its war with Venice, and in 1448 condottiere for Venice in the same struggle. Clever, tireless, responding to every opportunity with maximum and ruthless force, he claimed his prize in 1450, riding into vanquished Milan to be greeted by the hollow cheers of its starved and disheartened populace. Once in power, Sforza used the talents of his stable of humanists, diplomats, and artists to affirm publicly what was certainly not the case: the legitimacy of his rule.

In other cities, even where noble strongmen did not seize control of the state, factional struggles were so bitter that the citizens called upon an arbiter to take control and establish peace—at which point, the arbiter himself would make his authority permanent and become a despot. This nearly occurred in Florence, that most republican of republics. In 1342 the French nobleman Walter of Brienne, "Duke of Athens" (d. 1356), was called in by the wealthier merchants and bankers who feared a popular uprising in the prevailing conditions of fiscal emergency. He seized power, declared himself signore, and so ruled—until a faction of horrified merchants banded together the following year and drove him from the city. In Venice, as we have seen (see p. 50), there were two conspiracies in the decades immediately following the momentous serrata of the Grand Council and the effective establishment of a patriciate. All the conspirators were captured and executed, including a doge, a remarkably early case of the exercise of the rule of law over a legitimate ruler.

Some republics, then, became despotic signorie, while a few managed to retain their autonomy. Meanwhile, republics and principalities alike conquered or subordinated others, as the many flourishing cities of the Middle Ages gave way to the great territorial states of the full Renaissance (see also Chapter 7). By 1450 five states would emerge as dominant: Venice, Florence, Milan, Rome, and Naples. Each gained that prepotency by a process of imperial expansion: they subordinated not only the villages and countryside that surrounded their walls, but also cities further afield. The city of Pistoia, for instance, previously a free republican oligarchy, succumbed to Florence in 1306, becoming the colonial subject of an imperialist free republic. Pisa fell to Florence a century later. In 1404 and 1405, likewise, the autonomous cities of Verona and Padua, under their Scaliger and Carrara rulers, were incorporated into the Venetian empire.

By all these processes—noble aggression, urban factionalism, and territorial expansion—many of the free cities whose history laid the foundations of Renaissance civilization lost their autonomy. Italy became a country of principalities and oligarchic republics, but it was in these states and courts that the Renaissance would flourish.

THE BLACK DEATH

Republics and principalities alike suffered a ferocious and unbearable blow when, late in 1347, the Black Death arrived. It changed the course of history in Italy and in all of Europe. It interrupted, but did not choke off, the movement in ideas and the arts that would soon blossom as the Renaissance.

The plague bacillus, *yersinia pestis*, probably assumed all three of its known forms in the European episode of the fourteenth to eighteenth centuries. Its most common form was bubonic, so called after its characteristic buboes (swellings), which led to death in most cases. The bubonic infection was carried by a particular flea (*xenopsylla cheopis*) that was carried by a particular species of rat (*rattus rattus*). The flea transmitted the disease from rats to humans. In the plague's septicemic form, the bacillus enters the bloodstream, causing death within only a few hours. In the pneumonic form, the bacillus inhabits the lungs, and the infection is spread by droplets—requiring neither flea nor rat to transmit a deadly infection that kills within a few days.

Although some recent studies have suggested that the plague was not bubonic but rather viral hemorrhagic in origin, the consensus among scholars about its origin and course is as follows. The epidemic of bubonic plague, called in Europe the Black Death, had its origin in Asia, where it caused awful slaughter. In 1347, borne by merchant galleys that had traded with Byzantium and in the Crimea, it arrived at Messina, Sicily, where rats carrying plague-infected fleas scurried from the rigging of infected ships onto Italian soil. The disease traveled throughout the winter of 1347–1348 and flared up again the following summer, when tens of thousands of lives were lost. Populations declined by rates of one-third to two-thirds. Although the plague hit the cities worse than the countryside, it hit the countryside as well, whose rural population was already weakened by waves of famine in 1339–1340 and 1346–1347.

After 1348, the plague returned to strike each new generation, though with less force. It carried off the fragile elderly and, even more tragically, the young, who had not yet been exposed to it and bore no immunity to the onslaught. Epidemics recurred in 1361–1363, 1371, 1373–1374, 1382–1373, 1390, 1400, and with declining frequency thereafter. The accumulated effects of plague left their mark in population figures: Florence shrank from between 90,000 to 100,000 before the plague to a post-plague low of approximately 30,000; Venice from 120,000 to 84,000; Bologna from 54,000 to 35,000; Padua from

Populations expressed as a percentage of peak figures before the Black Death

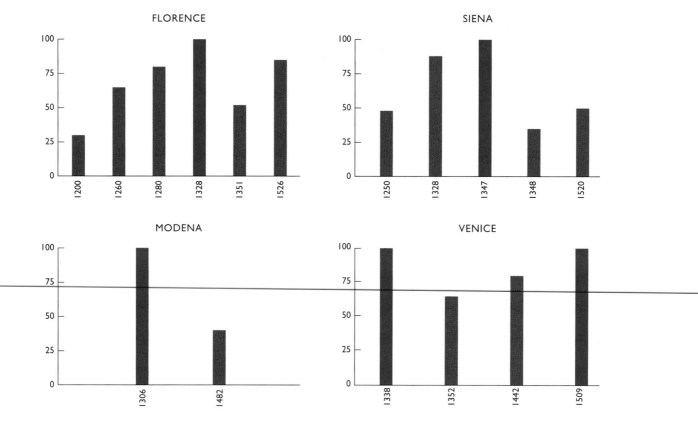

Based on H.A. Miskimim, The Economy of Early Renaissance Europe, 1300–1460. Upper Saddle River, NJ: Prentice Hall, 1975, p.75.

38,000 to 18,000; Pisa from 50,000 to 10,000. The plague remained endemic in Europe, exploding periodically even as late as 1720 when the plague hit Marseille in southern France. Thereafter, perhaps because *rattus rattus*, the species that served as the preferred host of the carrier flea, was edged out by a rival species or perhaps because improved public health strategies were able to prevent contagion, the plague died out.

When the plague first struck in 1348, the Italian population was helpless to resist it. The physicians of the day, well trained by university courses in the Greek physician Galen (c. 130–c. 201 CE) and Aristotelian theory, knew nothing of infection, contagion, or quarantine. The medicine of the day treated illness mainly through the examination of urine and the letting of blood. For the plague, there were no antidotes. Often doctors refused even to treat patients. Some, lured by high salaries, labored on, but could cure nobody. Thinking the disease was carried by miasma, or poisonous air, they recommended moderate

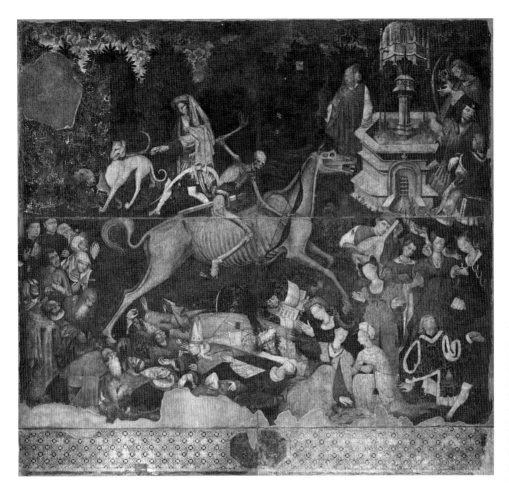

Traini (?), *Triumph of Death,* c. 1350, fresco, 19 ft 8 in × 21 ft 1 in (6 × 6 m 42 cm). **Galleria Regionale della Sicilia di Palazzo Abatellis, Palermo.**

The Black Death transformed Europe in many ways. Among them was the heightened awareness of life's fragility, as seen in this image of a skeletal death rampaging at will.

habits, filtered air, and closed windows. City governments tried somewhat more effectively to deal with plague, although they too had no theoretical understanding of the disease or its course. In different cities, officials devised methods of identifying plague-stricken households, declared quarantine, and arranged for the evacuation and burying of corpses, sometimes in mass graves. The church responded sporadically. In places, priests were available to assist the ill, to hear confessions, or to perform funeral masses. In other places, the clergy, like the citizenry, took refuge or fled. Survivors were left to bury their dead, as one Sienese householder reported:

> Members of a family brought their dead to the ditch as best they would without priest or divine office, and the bell did not sound for them. And in many places in Siena huge pits were dug and the multitude of the dead were piled within them. And I, Agnolo di Tura, called "the fat," buried my five children with my own hands. And there were those so poorly covered with earth that the dogs dug them up and gnawed their bodies throughout the city. And there were none who wept for any death, for everyone expected to die. And so many died, that everyone thought it to

be the end of the world ... and there was so much horror, that I, the writer, cannot think of it, and therefore will tell no more.

(From *Cronica senese* in A. Lisini and F. Iacometti, eds., *Rerum italicarum scriptores*, vol. xv; quoted by J. Larner, *Italy in the Age of Dante and Petrarch, 1216–1380*, p. 265)

The author Giovanni Boccaccio left a more famous description of the plague—which he observed first hand in the summer of 1348—in the introduction to the first book of his *Decameron*. This grim prelude frames the whole work of ebullient storytelling, as though the writer means to say that art must supersede experience. He describes the disease itself and its virulence, and the scenes of death and burial. Most striking, perhaps, is his description of the corrupting effect of the plague on the human spirit:

The fact was that one citizen avoided another, that almost no-one cared for his neighbor.... This disaster had struck such fear into the hearts of men and women that brother abandoned brother, uncle abandoned nephew, sister left brother, and very often wife abandoned husband, and—even worse, almost unbelievable—fathers and mothers neglected to tend and care for their children, as if they were not their own. Thus, for the countless multitudes of men and women who fell sick, there remained no support except the charity of their friends (and these were few) or the avarice of servants, who worked for inflated salaries and indecent periods of time and who, in spite of this, were very few and far between.... Between the lack of competent attendants, which the sick were unable to obtain, and the violence of the pestilence, there were so many, many people who died in the city both day and night that it was incredible just to hear this described, not to mention seeing it!

(Giovanni Boccaccio, *The Decameron: A New Translation*, trans. and ed. M. Musa and P.E. Bondanella. New York: W.W. Norton, 1977, pp. 6–7)

Critics disagree in their assessment of Boccaccio's stylish account. This introduction to his masterpiece serves as its frame, where Boccaccio links the horror of the plague to the free creation of literature—art for art's sake—that will occur when his ten fictional characters flee the dying city for the pleasant gardens of an idyllic country retreat. Clearly the plague affected the production of art and literature, just as it affected many other spheres of life. In art, the modernist historian Millard Meiss proposed, controversially, that the creative surge of the era of Giotto gave way, after the plague, to a more conservative and ordered style, which returned to the hierarchical compositions of an earlier era. Certainly, there were no significant innovations in the visual arts until about 1400.

In literature, there seems also to have been a disruption. Petrarch and Boccaccio both survived the plague onslaught and continued writing until their respective deaths in 1374 and 1375. But a new generation of literary figures did not emerge until after a pause— and then slowly, from the 1390s. From that point we can trace the renewed development of the intellectual movement that best characterizes the Renaissance: humanism. It is the subject of the following chapter.

CONCLUSION

The republican era, the century from 1250 to 1350 that began, in many Italian cities, with the triumph of the popolo and ended with the twin victories of the despot and the Black Death, was the culmination of the region's dynamic development that began about the year 1000. Population reached a peak not surpassed for centuries. Commerce and industry were both expansive and innovative. An age brimming with confidence spoke out: in French, Latin, but especially Italian, authors wrote about the household and the state; they composed poetry; they opened new paths of expression pointing to modern vernacular (mass) literature and to the intellectual movement known as humanism. After the hiatus of the plague and restructuring after the plague, it was humanism, paralleled by new ventures in the visual arts, that came to the fore.

SUGGESTED READINGS

Primary Sources

Boccaccio, Giovanni. *The Decameron*. Translated by M. Musa and P. Bondanella. New York: W.W. Norton, 1983. These stories launched a Renaissance literary tradition while commenting critically on contemporary Italian society.

Branca, Vittore, ed. *Merchant Writers: Florentine Memoirs from the Middle Ages and Renaissance*. Translated and edited by Murtha Baca and Cesare De Michelis. Toronto, ON: University of Toronto Press, 2015. Originally published in Italian by Branca and now translated into English, this collection of nine merchant memoirs and diaries illuminates the psychological and emotional world of the entrepreneurs who generated the wealth that was the precondition of Renaissance civilization.

Brucker, Gene, ed. *The Society of Renaissance Florence*. New York: Harper and Row, 1971. Documents all aspects of Florentine life, especially in the fourteenth and fifteenth centuries.

Chambers, David, and Brian Pullan, trans. and eds. *Venice: A Documentary History, 1450–1630*. Oxford: Blackwell, 1992. A compilation of documents drawn from official records, chronicles, and informal literary works.

Petrarch, Francesco. *Letters*. Translated and edited by M. Bishop. Bloomington, IN: Indiana University Press, 1966. A selection of Petrarch's letters profiling the poet-scholar in his fourteenth-century context.

Secondary Sources

Brucker, Gene. *Renaissance Florence*, rev. ed. Berkeley: University of California Press, 1983. A coherent presentation of the social and cultural foundations of Florence.

Cohn, Samuel K., Jr. *The Cult of Remembrance and the Black Death: Six Renaissance Cities in Central Italy.* Baltimore, MD: Johns Hopkins University Press, 1992. Explores how citizens of six cities responded to the trauma of the Black Death, by tracking their pious bequests.

Cohn, Samuel K., Jr. *Cultures of Plague: Medical Thought at the End of the Renaissance.* Oxford: Oxford University Press, 2009. Considering thousands of plague cases described by physicians at Milan from 1452 to 1523, argues against the identification of the Black Death as due to an outbreak of bubonic plague (*yersinia pestis*). A summation of Cohn's researches on this problem, begun in partnership with David S. Herlihy.

Green, Louis. *Castruccio Castracani: A Study on the Origins and Character of a Fourteenth-Century Italian Despotism.* Oxford: Clarendon Press, 1987. Studies the career of the ruler of Lucca whose rise and fall interested Machiavelli.

Herlihy, David. *The Black Death and the Transformation of the West.* Edited by Samuel Cohn. Cambridge, MA: Harvard University Press, 1997. Examines the plague as a medical event and as a force influencing the economic, social, and cultural transformations of Europe.

Kohl, Benjamin G. *Padua under the Carrara, 1318–1405.* Baltimore, MD: Johns Hopkins University Press, 1998. Examines one apparently beneficent signorial regime that shared power with communal leaders.

Lane, Frederic C. *Venice: A Maritime Republic.* Baltimore, MD: Johns Hopkins University Press, 1973. A comprehensive history of this important city, emphasizing shipping and commerce.

Lansing, Carol. *The Florentine Magnates: Lineage and Faction in a Medieval Commune.* Princeton, NJ: Princeton University Press, 1992. Profiles the Florentine nobles whose arrogance and violence were the targets of the new republican state.

Larner, John. *Italy in the Age of Dante and Petrarch, 1216–1380.* London: Longman, 1980. Surveys the republican period with special emphasis on cultural effects.

Marina, Areli. *The Italian Piazza Transformed: Parma in the Communal Age.* University Park, PA: Penn State University Press, 2012. Focusing on the building of communal and cathedral centers in the city of Parma during the thirteenth century, shows how elites designed the stage for a coherent urban culture in harmony with their ideals.

Martines, Lauro. *Power and Imagination: City-States in Renaissance Italy.* Baltimore, MD: Johns Hopkins University Press, 1988. Shows how the explosive energies of the republican era culminated in oligarchy, despotism, and the culture of humanism.

McLean, Alick M. *Prato: Architecture, Piety, and Political Identity in a Tuscan City-State.* New Haven, CT: Yale University Press, 2008. Studies one Tuscan city from the eleventh to the fourteenth century, considering interrelations of political formation, architectural development, public life, and popular piety.

Pullan, Brian S. *A History of Early Renaissance Italy, from the Mid-Thirteenth to the Mid-Fifteenth Century.* New York: St. Martin's Press, 1972. A master historian surveys the transition from popular takeover to the early Renaissance.

Trachtenberg, Marvin. *The Dominion of the Eye: Urbanism, Art, and Power in Early Modern Florence.* Cambridge: Cambridge University Press, 1997. Argues that the Florentine sense of urban planning begins in the republican period.

THREE

HUMAN DIGNITY AND HUMANIST STUDIES: THE CAREER OF HUMANISM (c. 1350–c. 1530)

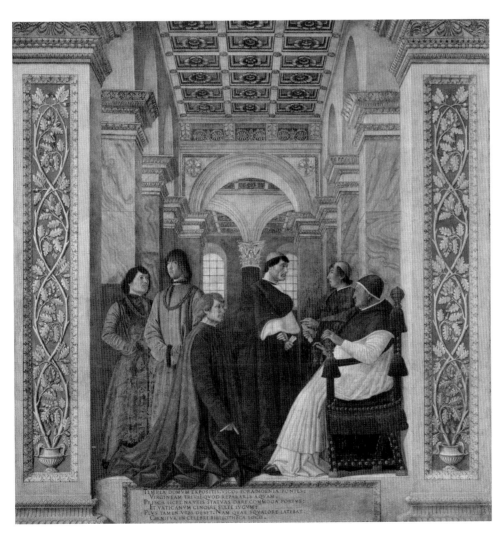

Melozzo da Forlì,
Sixtus IV Appointing
Platina, 1474–1477,
fresco, now transferred
to canvas, 12 ft 1 in ×
10 ft 4 in (3.7 × 3.15 m).
Pinacoteca, Vatican,
Rome.

In an architectural setting
governed by classical
themes, the pope appoints
his humanist secretary
Bartolomeo Sacchi, known
as Platina (1421–1481) to the
post of Vatican librarian.
This image shows the
confluence of the classical
and Christian and the
learned and powerful,
so characteristic of the
Renaissance.

Just three years before the Black Death struck, Petrarch wrote a letter to a man long dead, the Roman philosopher and statesman Marcus Tullius Cicero. Petrarch had sought out manuscripts of Cicero's letters and read them closely—so closely that he seemed to hear their author's still-living voice: "Your letters I sought for long and diligently; and finally, where I least expected it, I found them. At once I read them, over and over, with the utmost eagerness. And as I read I seemed to hear your bodily voice."

After this greeting, Petrarch rebukes Cicero: why had he meddled in politics in his final years when he might have continued safely in his country retreat, dedicated to the study and translation of Greek philosophy? For Cicero had stood up to the brutal regime that took over in Rome after the assassination of Julius Caesar in 44 BCE and was himself murdered by its agents the following year. "What will-o'-the-wisp tempted you away, with a delusive hope of glory; involved you, in your declining years, in the wars of younger men; and, after exposing you to every form of misfortune, hurled you down to a death that it was unseemly for a philosopher to die?" His rebuke delivered, Petrarch wishes Cicero "farewell forever," and closes: "Written in the land of the living; on the right bank of the Adige, in Verona, a city of … Italy; on the 16th of June, and in the year of that God whom you never knew the 1345th."

This extraordinary document, one of several that Petrarch wrote to ancient figures, reveals the attitude of the Renaissance intellectuals to the Greek and Roman past. They knew it intimately. Petrarch knew not only who Cicero was, but what Cicero thought. On the other hand, for Renaissance thinkers the past was distant—almost unreachable. One barrier was the advent of Christianity, to which Petrarch alluded in the letter above— the God whom Europeans worshiped in the age of the Renaissance most of the ancients "never knew." Other changes included the loss of Roman political institutions, the arrival of half-civilized Germanic peoples, and the emergence of commerce as the source of wealth and power. Renaissance thinkers were so close to the past they wished to relive it; so distant, that they believed that their own age was entirely new. They revered the ancients, but they were modern: the civilization they created was a wholly new creation.

Just as the Italian cities emerged from the ruins of Roman cities and were both like and unlike their ancient predecessors, so also Renaissance thinkers were grounded in ancient civilization yet built a novel and unprecedented civilization. It was their encounter with that ancient tradition and their reformulation of it that constitutes what historians call the Renaissance, or "rebirth" of the classical spirit. Much of what these thinkers created falls under the heading of humanism, the most dynamic intellectual movement of the age.

Renaissance humanists recovered the words and thoughts of the classical world. Armed with this new store of knowledge and with a masterful command of language, they reformulated the insights of Christian scholars to give a new account of the nature of the human being, human society, and the arts and sciences of civilization. The humanists were the sons of wealthy and powerful men and of middle-level merchants and notaries. Some of them were women. They wrote letters, speeches, treatises, dialogues, plays, poems, and histories. They were philosophers, theologians, bureaucrats, and mathematicians. In a later era, humanism as an intellectual movement would lose its energy and give way to a broader array of intellectual leaders—religious reformers, scientists, and litterateurs of various types. Yet between 1350 and 1530, the Italian humanists put into circulation a wealth of ideas that linked their present with the classical past and opened up the main lines of intellectual inquiry for centuries to come.

This chapter describes the humanist endeavor to revive the work of classical antiquity and the development of the curricular program of "studies of humanity" to train future generations. It considers central themes behind the humanist project, including the "dignity of man" and the introduction of the values of "civic humanism." The chapter presents the special case of female humanism and explores the relationship of humanism to philosophical studies and philological scholarship. It ends with an analysis of the "sociology of humanism," placing the humanists in their social contexts.

THE RECOVERY OF CLASSICAL ANTIQUITY

From 1414 to 1418, church leaders meeting at Constance (Konstanz, modern Germany) declared that the authority of a council was superior to that of the pope. Among those

LIBRARIES: A GROWTH INDUSTRY	
Petrarch (1340–1374)	A few hundred volumes (then the largest in Europe)
Library of Cardinal Bessarion (c. 1395–1472; donated to Venice in 1468)	800–900 volumes, of which more than 600 were in Greek
Library of Matthias Corvinus, King of Hungary (r. 1458–1490)	More than 500 volumes
Library of humanist Giovanni Pico della Mirandola (1463–1514), at his death	1,100 volumes
Library of German humanist Hartmann Schedel (1440–1514)	370 mss. and 600 printed books
Vatican Library 1443, at death of Pope Eugene IV	340 mss., of which 2 were in Greek
1455, at death of Pope Nicholas V	1,160 mss., of which 353 were in Greek
1484, at death of Pope Sixtus IV	3,600 mss.

PERSONAL SPACE: THE COMPANY OF BOOKS

Among the things to which the Renaissance gave birth was a new kind of room: a small personal space where the well educated gentleman or gentlewoman might seek quiet and the company of his or her books.

The appearance of the study or personal library in social life was documented by Renaissance artists, who delighted in depicting these unusual spaces (see p.xxx) equipped with books and the other paraphernalia of the intellectual life, with the scholar often shown gazing out the window or caught in a moment of thought, while an attentive pet stands guard. Or the images depict interesting wooden contrivances, a little like a student's carrel in today's university libraries, where the scholar sits in cocoon-like isolation, content among his learned volumes. In later centuries, the scholar's study also became the geographer's workstation, astronomer's observatory, or scientist's laboratory.

The arrival of the study is part of the story of the evolution of personalized living space. Most of humanity has lived its existence within a one-roomed residence—a hut, a cottage, a shanty, perhaps in a cave, or partially below ground. This space, sometimes shared with domesticated beasts, served the needs of peasant families: here they ate, slept, drank, kept warm, told stories, gave birth, and died. In medieval Europe, even lords and kings in their castles lived largely in one great hall where they, their retinue, their guests, and their families carried on much of the business of life.

The first specialized room was the master's bedchamber, which appeared in the castle and the burgher's townhouse from the twelfth century. Among the very wealthy, other rooms would be designated for sleeping, dining, or for private meditation and study.

Another antecedent of the study, of course, was the monk's cell. The word *cella* initially meant only a small room. In the monastery, it acquired the sense of great isolation and of intensified spiritual experience. The study of the Renaissance gentleman, however, unlike the barren purity of the monk's cell, was softened and enlivened by the presence of his books.

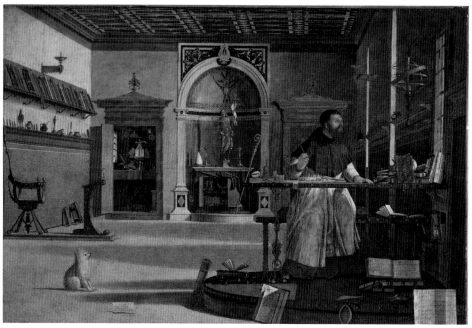

Carpaccio, *St. Augustine in His Study*, c. 1502, tempera on panel, 56 × 83 in (141 × 210 cm). San Giorgio degli Schiavoni, Venice.

A splendid example of the private study is the exquisite *studiolo* of Federico da Montefeltro, Duke of Urbino (r. 1444–1482), shown below. It is a beautifully proportioned room, modest in size (given the giant expanse of the ducal palace at Urbino), wholly lined with wood and with wood-mosaics designed to simulate shelves, open cabinet doors, musical instruments, and books. A second studiolo much like the first, from Montefeltro's residence in Gubbio, has been reconstructed within the Metropolitan Museum of Art in New York City.

It was to such a room that the patriarchal hero of the dialogue *On the Family* by humanist and artist Leon Battista Alberti (1404–1472) retreated when his day's work was done. He kept his jewels and treasures in his bedchamber but his really precious possessions in his study: "Only my books and records and those of my ancestors did I determine to keep well sealed … not in the sleeves of my dress, but locked up and arranged in order in my study, almost like sacred and religious objects. I never gave my wife permission to enter that place, with me or alone."

Not so very different, perhaps, was the little "book-lined cell" (*libraria cellula*) in her brother's palace to which the woman humanist Isotta Nogarola (c. 1418–1466) retreated when, having decided not to marry, she determined to commit herself to lifelong study. Her friend, the Venetian nobleman and statesman Ludovico Foscarini, described seeing her there amid her cherished possessions—the religious objects we might expect to find in a devout woman's private room but also her beloved books. So, too, did the cleric Matteo Bosso, who as a child used to visit her in her studiolo: "I used to come to you after school and my lessons, and … would sit in your book-lined cell, and happily hear you gently singing sweet hymns and the rhythms of the psalms."

It is to such a room, too, that the fictional character Bianca proposed to retreat in *The Taming of the Shrew* by William Shakespeare (1564–1616), a compiler of so many Renaissance themes. She promised her father: "My books and instruments shall be my company/On them to look and practice by myself."

In the same vein, the humanist Pier Paolo Vergerio (1370–1444/1445), advising the young heir to the dynasty of the Carrara lords of Padua, recommended the quiet and responsive company of books: "How bright a household is the family of books!… In their company there is no noise, no greed, no self will; at a word they speak to you, at a word they are still; to all our requests their response is ever ready and to the point."

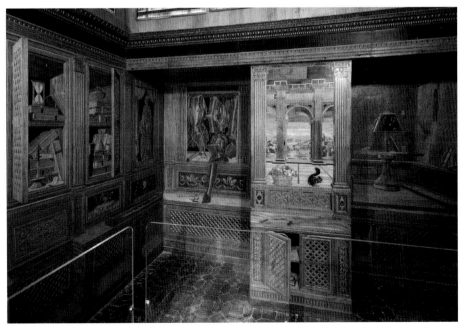

Studiolo of Federico da Montefeltro, 1476. Palazzo Ducale, Urbino.

participating was the papal secretary Poggio Bracciolini (1381–1459). In their leisure hours, Poggio and his friends scoured the monastic libraries in the area. They were on the hunt for ancient texts, works of ancient authors already well studied by educated men but also ancient works not yet known to have survived the fall of Rome. Joyfully, they found two of Cicero's speeches previously not known to them and the complete text, previously available only in fragmentary form, of the *Institutio oratoria* ("Rudiments of Oratory") by the Roman scholar Quintilian (c. 35–c. 100 CE). Scornfully, they noted the condition in which these manuscripts were found—damp, dirty, riddled by wormholes, held "like captives" or abandoned in a heap in a closet or at the foot of a flight of stairs.

Just as Petrarch felt he heard the voice of Cicero through his letters, Poggio encountered an ancient Roman when he read, or even handled, Quintilian's rhetorical handbook. The Roman past was revived as generations of humanists located, studied, and commented upon—in all, "discovered"—these ancient works.

Roman Works

Most of the Roman works known to the modern world were already in circulation during the Middle Ages. Their survival was due to the labor of trained monks who transcribed texts from the ancient papyrus scrolls to the parchment or paper leaves of leather-covered books. Most of the works of Seneca, Cicero, and Virgil, among others, were known to authors and philosophers of the twelfth and thirteenth centuries and served as the texts by which new generations acquired Latin. The "discovery" of "new" texts, therefore, important as such episodes were, was not so important as the "discovery" of familiar texts. The humanists of the early Italian Renaissance discovered new texts and old ones as well, therefore, by reading and commenting upon them with a new understanding and critical spirit.

Of the ancient Latin authors, the philosopher Seneca was the first to influence the early humanists. It was Cicero, however, who had the most powerful impact on humanism—perhaps because he was a humanist himself, the author of speeches, an interpreter of Greek philosophy, a guide to rhetorical style, and a moral philosopher who wrote on friendship, on public and private responsibilities, and on old age. The historian Livy (later, also Tacitus, c. 55–120 CE) and the poet Virgil were read and reread, and Quintilian, "recovered" by Poggio, was a guide to rhetorical style. The Latin church fathers also heavily influenced the humanists, especially Augustine, author of the deeply personal *Confessions*, and Jerome (c. 342–420 CE), translator of the Bible and master of the letter form.

From the concentrated reading of this literature, Renaissance humanists established the standard for prose style that prevailed for several centuries. The works of Cicero, above all, were a benchmark for proper style until, by the end of the fifteenth century, a highly imitative and prissy Ciceronianism aroused a wave of resisters, including the pivotal northern humanist, Desiderius Erasmus (c. 1466–1536; see Chapter 9). In the early years of the humanist movement, however, Ciceronian standards served a creative function, encouraging authors to break from the workaday vocabulary and sentence forms that had characterized late medieval Latin composition. In brief, the corpus of Latin literature served as a model of literary form, an office it would continue to perform well into the eighteenth century.

Those same works, of course, were also a trove of information about antiquity. Initially, it was a somewhat indigestible trove, since knowledge of the classical world was scanty and many works were read without context and without the assistance of those handbooks and encyclopedias with which a modern reader attempts to understand an ancient text. But the early humanists read thoroughly and often, recording words, places, sayings, and names in their notebooks, thus building up a familiarity with the world of Rome. Just as early Christian thinkers transformed the legacy of the ancient world to suit a new belief system, now Renaissance thinkers revised perceptions of Roman buildings, objects, and ideas to suit a different worldview. The medieval gloss which things Roman had acquired was stripped away, and the humanists came to see Rome whole.

Greek Works

More difficult was the recovery of the Greek tradition. In antiquity, most educated Romans knew Greek, and so the knowledge of Greek life and values traveled with Greek literature and its translations into the Roman world, including all parts of the Western Empire. At the end of the Roman era, however, knowledge of Greek virtually disappeared in Latin Christendom. It continued only at the peripheries where medieval Christians conversed with the Jewish and Muslim scholars of non-Christian Spain or with Greek scholars in Byzantium or the south of Italy. In these other two medieval civilizations, those of Islam and Byzantium, Greek studies proceeded briskly throughout the medieval era. The first translations into Latin of ancient Greek works, sometimes by way of Arabic or Hebrew, reached the European heartland in the twelfth century. Aristotle's works, nearly entire, arrived by the thirteenth. The humanists, with their superior command of both Greek and Latin, would later retranslate these.

Latin was familiar, both because it was the language of church liturgy and learned conversation, and because many of the European languages had descended from Latin and preserved much of its vocabulary. In contrast, Greek was unfamiliar as well as inherently difficult. Petrarch and Boccaccio, although aware of the importance of Greek works, never themselves learned how to read the language. They found a southern Italian who could translate Homer (c. 8th century BCE) for them, but his *Iliad* and *Odyssey* were too literal and inadequate. In the very next generation, however, the serious study of Greek in the Latin West took off. The Byzantine statesman and scholar Manuel Chrysoloras (c. 1353–1415) came to Italy, seeking support for that embattled empire as the Turks steadily advanced. While resident in Florence between 1397 and 1400, Chrysoloras began to teach the early humanists Greek. In 1415 he prepared a Greek grammar for the teaching of ancient Greek to Latin speakers, though it was not printed until 1480.

1350–1399

1358   Boccaccio completes *The Decameron*.

1374   Death of Petrarch.

1375   Death of Boccaccio.

1391   University of Ferrara founded under patronage of the Este rulers.

1397   Byzantine scholar Manuel Chrysoloras teaches Greek to humanist scholars in Florence.

1400–1449

1401   Leonardo Bruni (Aretino) writes a eulogy to Florence, *Laudatio florentinae urbis* ("In Praise of the City of Florence").

1403   Guarino Veronese studies Greek language, culture in Constantinople.

1404   Pier Paolo Vergerio writes *De ingenuis moribus et liberalibus studiis* ("On Liberal Studies and the Moral Education of the Free-Born Youth"), the first major treatise on humanist education.

1405   Christine de Pizan completes her two major prose works, *The Book of the City of Ladies*, a defense of women's character and intelligence, and *The Treasure of the City of Ladies* (or *Book of the Three Virtues*), on women's social roles.

1415   Bruni begins writing *History of the Florentine Republic*.

1420   Humanist Francesco Filelfo visits Constantinople.

1423   Vittorino da Feltre establishes a humanist school in Mantua, where children of the ruling Gonzagas are educated.

1424   Bruni gives guidelines for the humanist education of women in *De studiis et litteris*.

1427   Bruni becomes chancellor of the Republic of Florence.

1429   Guarino Veronese establishes a humanist school in Ferrara.

1431   Lorenzo Valla writes *De voluptate* ("On Pleasure"), praising pleasure as part of a Christian life.

1440   Valla writes his *Treatise on the Donation of Constantine*.

1447–1455   Pope Nicholas V encourages humanist scholars, founds the Vatican Library.

1450–1499

1451   Isotta Nogarola's *Dialogue* denies the guilt of Eve, and thus all women, for the Fall of Man.

1453   Poggio Bracciolini becomes chancellor of Florence.

1453   Constantinople falls to the Ottoman Turks; Byzantine scholars flee to Italy.

1453   Giannozzo Manetti writes humanist treatise, *De dignitate et excellentia hominis* ("On the Dignity and Excellence of Man").

1458   Humanist scholar Enea Silvio Piccolomini becomes Pope Pius II.

1462   Marsilio Ficino begins translating into Latin.

1469   Livy's *Decades* is printed, dedicated to Pius II.

1471   Ficino translates occult writings attributed to Hermes Trismegistus into Latin.

1471   Valla advocates a purer form of Latin based on classical models.

1472   Cardinal John Bessarion bequeaths his learned books to Venice.

1474   Ficino's *Platonic Theology* tries to reconcile Plato's philosophy with Christian beliefs.

1486   Pico della Mirandola flees Italy after Pope Innocent VIII declares his ideas heretical.

1493   Aldo Manuzio, founder of Aldine Press, starts printing books in Venice.

1494   Pico della Mirandola dies.

1494   French King Charles VIII seizes Florence.

1496   Pico della Mirandola's *Oratio de hominis dignitate* ("Oration on the Dignity of Man") is published.

1498   Aldine Press publishes portable versions of Greek and Latin texts.

Greek literacy gave humanism an intellectual range far beyond what the recovery of the Latin tradition had provided, if for no other reason than that the Greek written tradition was much vaster. Many more works by Greek than by Latin authors have survived, as can be easily checked in any university library by examining the shelves carrying the Loeb Classical Library: the Greek titles in their green binding dominate the shelves, dwarfing the Latin titles in red. Beyond mere expanse, the Greek tradition is rich in subjects in which the Latin tradition is weak: philosophy, mathematics, and science. In addition, the *Parallel Lives* of Greek and Roman figures by the second-century author, historian, and biographer Plutarch (c. 46–c. 120 CE) greatly supplemented Livy as a guide to the history of Rome. It would inspire many literary works for centuries to come, including some of the major plays of William Shakespeare (see Chapter 10).

Although this first generation had to master Greek from native speakers such as the Byzantine scholar Chrysoloras, by the early 1400s, a later generation of Italian-born **Hellenists** were able to teach Greek to their compatriots. Notable among these early Hellenists were two men of modest background who were able to journey to Constantinople to study Greek language and literature at its source. Guarino Guarini of Verona (Guarino Veronese, 1374–1460) followed Chrysoloras back to Constantinople in 1403 and remained there for five years, his education paid for by a Venetian nobleman. He then returned to northern Italy, eventually establishing a famous school at Ferrara in 1429 where he trained a generation of students in Latin and Greek studies before his death. Francesco Filelfo (1398–1481) also journeyed to Constantinople in 1420. He stayed there for seven years, studying with the son of Chrysoloras, whose daughter he married. Returning to Italy, where he was recognized as the peninsula's leading Hellenist, he established himself as a humanist author and critic especially at Milan, whose cultural scene he dominated for more than 40 years. After the generation of Chrysoloras, several other Greek men of letters lived and worked in Italy and produced scholarly translations, especially of scientific and philosophical texts. Italian Hellenists received a new trove of texts on the death of the Byzantine-born cardinal of the Roman Church John Bessarion (1403–1472), who left his library of more than 800 books to Venice where they became the core of the collection now in the Biblioteca Marciana (the Library of St. Mark, patron saint of that city).

THE "STUDIES OF HUMANITY"

Although there would always be fewer scholars of the Greek than of the Latin tradition, instruction in Greek became part of a new humanist curriculum that began to crystallize in the early 1400s.

The first generations of humanists nurtured the first generations of teachers of the *studia humanitatis* (studies of humanity). According to Paul Oskar Kristeller, the twentieth-century's foremost scholar of the movement, the intellectual pursuits the humanists most valued consisted of these five: grammar (the Latin language learned through Latin literature), rhetoric (the art of speechmaking but also, more broadly, of prose composition), poetry, history, and moral philosophy. These became the subjects of humanist education: roughly the equivalent of our modern humanities.

The Idea of Humanist Education

Although humanist educators referred to these *studia humanitatis* as the "liberal arts," in fact, they contrast notably with the curriculum of the liberal arts inherited from late antiquity and taught throughout the Middle Ages. In the ancient formulation, the liberal arts consisted of the *trivium* (a group of three word-focused subjects: grammar, rhetoric, and **dialectic**, or logic) and the *quadrivium* (a group of four number-focused subjects: arithmetic, geometry, astronomy, and music, or musical theory, which was based on mathematical concepts). In departing from the medieval curriculum, the humanists consigned the teaching of basic arithmetic to the schools of *abaco* (abacus), middle-level schools where boys learned the skills needed to carry on business and trade. They abandoned the teaching of more advanced mathematics and science to the universities, where those subjects were taught as part of the natural philosophy curriculum. Philosophy was one of the four curricula normally taught in the university, an invention of the Middle Ages which had developed about the year 1200; the other three disciplines taught were theology, law, and medicine.

Over the last 200 years, the subjects taught by the humanists—the "humanities"—have been reintegrated with the sciences, the social sciences (developed in the nineteenth century), and fine and performing arts. These together make up the liberal arts offerings generally encountered on the campuses of modern Western universities—although new information technologies may be demanding a redefinition of the liberal arts. From the sixteenth century, when the humanist curriculum became institutionalized, to the nineteenth century, the humanities curriculum was the standard of secondary education. The political, social, and intellectual elites of Europe began their careers with a humanist preparation.

The eventual triumph of the humanities curriculum was the work of early humanist educators. They argued that the word-based *studia humanitatis* were most apt to equip a young person with broad intellectual and sound moral qualities. They would provide models of excellent behavior, they would lay down ideals and values (those of antiquity, revived for a later age), they would instill standards of taste, and they would guide the formation of literary style. And so they did—although many an accomplished student of the humanities would prove to be personally corrupt or shallow. Whereas medieval education had prepared students for certain tasks such as monk, jurist, prelate, physician, teacher, or professor, the student trained in the humanist curriculum was a generalist.

The *studia humanitatis* was an intellectual program centered on the mastery of verbal skills and materials. A person competent in these subjects could think broadly about a range of issues and write fluently and knowledgeably about any issue that did not require a specific professional training. Precisely these abilities were valued in those who managed states or other large enterprises. Humanist teachers, therefore, were in demand to train the promising sons of merchants and professionals so that they could win good positions in the bureaucracies of city-states or the church. They were also sought after by despots and princes who wished their sons, destined to succeed them, to possess the advantages that a humanist education provided.

Humanist Educational Treatises

It is not surprising, therefore, to find that in 1404, Pier Paolo Vergerio dedicated his *De ingenuis moribus et liberalibus studiis* ("On Liberal Studies and the Moral Education of the Free-Born Youth"), the first major treatise of humanist education, to Ubertino, son of Francesco Carrara (d. 1406), the despot of Padua. In this pioneering work, Vergerio defines the subjects of instruction—especially history, moral philosophy, and poetry—and argues their benefit for the student. He identifies these humanities subjects with the liberal arts, recovering the ancient Roman meaning of the term: "We call those studies *liberal* which are worthy of a free man." The liberal arts were suited to *liberi*, free men, who were capable of ruling the state. They were understood to be more valued than the mechanical arts— the skills possessed by artisans and producers of things—which, for the Romans, were associated with slavery.

In summoning up the Roman understanding of liberal arts, Vergerio appears to be shaping a curriculum exclusively for elite students. Yet, he is apparently motivated by a deep love of learning, and he seems to be addressing all potential students, not merely future rulers. He sees classical studies as the best preparation for citizenship, recommends periods for relaxation and physical activity during the school day, and cautions against corporal punishment. Movingly, Vergerio describes the importance for the young person of developing a lifelong love of learning. We have no finer companions, he remarks, echoing Cicero, than the family of books: "In their company is no noise, no greed, no self-will; at a word they speak to you, at a word they are still: to all our requests their response is ever ready and to the point."

Following Vergerio's lead, humanist teachers were soon implementing his vision of the studia humanitatis in schools of a new kind. Vittorino da Feltre (Vittorino Rambaldoni, 1378–1446) was a pioneer in Mantua, where he was summoned by the ruler Gianfrancesco Gonzaga (r. 1407–1444) to create a school for the children of the despot's family (including his daughter) and talented boys from both noble and modest backgrounds. In 1423 he established a school named the Casa Giocosa (House of Joy). Notable at Vittorino's school, besides the rigor of both academic and athletic programs, was the assumption that valuable learning took place when master and students worked together in an intimate, personal setting.

Summoned to Ferrara by Marquis Niccolò III d'Este in 1429, Guarino established a school like that of Vittorino's in Mantua, where he developed his own educational methods. Guarino's school also trained not only the sons of the ruling family but also future leaders from many cities and foreign lands, including some scholarship students. The method of instruction was somewhat dry and tedious, at least as it is described in the

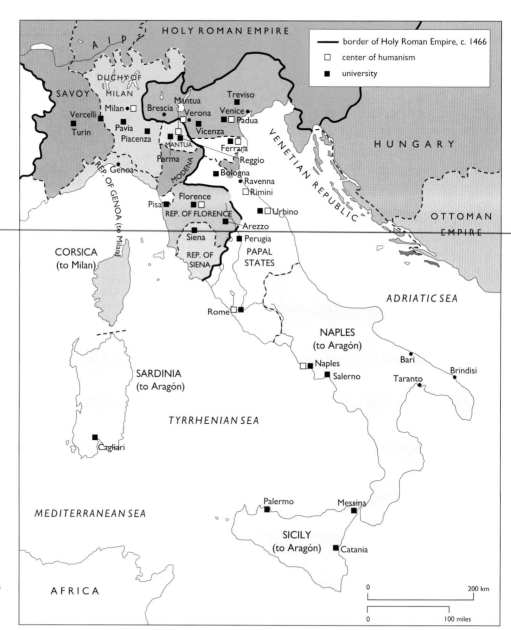

Italian Humanism

Renaissance Italy is here seen divided into a few major states that have absorbed all but a handful of the smaller cities. The geography of humanism is clear: it is concentrated in the cities of northern Italy, especially in Florence. Birthplaces of humanist figures are listed in the table of Key Figures on the facing page.

work *De ordine docendi et discendi* ("On the Method of Teaching and Learning") of Guarino's son, Battista Guarino de' Guarini (1434–1513), who succeeded his father as headmaster of the school in Ferrara.

Other advocates of a humanist education followed Vergerio's path as authors of practical treatises. In 1450 Enea Silvio Piccolomini (1405–1464), who later served as Pope Pius II (r. 1458–1464), addressed his *De liberorum educatione* ("On the Education of Boys") to Ladislas, King of Bohemia, when the latter was about 10 years old. Like Vergerio, he recommended a thorough grounding in the liberal arts and warned against models of bad style—especially the chroniclers of the history of Bohemia! Better known throughout Europe as a poet, the humanist priest Maffeo Vegio (1406–1458) also composed *De educatione liberorum et eorum claris moribus* ("On the Education of Boys and Their Moral Character").

KEY FIGURES

Verona
- Guarino Guarini (1374–1460)
- Isotta Nogarola (1418–1466)

Milan
- Francesco Filelfo (1398–1481)
- Leonardo da Vinci (1452–1519)

Padua
- Francis Petrarch (1304–1374)
- Pier Paolo Vergerio (1370–1444)

Mantua
- Vittorino da Feltre (1378–1446)

Florence
- Dante Alighieri (1265–1321)
- Giotto di Bondone (1267–1337)
- Giovanni Boccaccio (1313–1375)
- Leonardo Bruni (c. 1370–1444)
- Filippo Brunelleschi (1377–1446)
- Lorenzo Ghiberti (1378–1455)
- Poggio Bracciolini (1381–1459)
- Donatello (1386–1466)
- Cosimo de' Medici (1389–1464)
- Giannozzo Manetti (1396–1459)
- Paolo Uccello (1397–1475)

- Masaccio (1401–1428)
- Leon Battista Alberti (1404–1472)
- Marsilio Ficino (1433–1499)
- Sandro Botticelli (1445–1510)
- Lorenzo de' Medici (1449–1492)
- Pico della Mirandola (1463–1494)
- Niccolò Machiavelli (1469–1527)
- Michelangelo Buonarroti (1475–1564)

Venice
- Ludovico Foscarini (1409–1480)
- Lauro Quirini (c. 1420–1475/1479)
- Giovanni Bellini (c. 1430–1516)
- Ermolao Barbaro the Younger (1453/1454–1492)
- Cassandra Fedele (1465–1558)

Brescia
- Laura Cereta (1469–1499)

Ferrara
- Olimpia Morata (1526/1527–1555)

Rome
- Lorenzo Valla (1407–1457)
- Raphael (1483–1520)

Arezzo
- Piero della Francesca (c. 1420–1492)

For Vegio, the aim of humanistic training was above all the development of moral excellence, conceived of as a more specifically Christian enterprise than that of his predecessors. Vegio also stands out as an early opponent of corporal punishment (then a schoolroom norm) and as an advocate of education for girls.

By 1500, according to historian Paul Grendler, nearly all the Latin schools in Italy, court-based and town-based, were humanist. After 1500 the Italian model of humanist education traveled to France, the German lands, the Low Countries, and England (see Chapter 10).

THE DIGNITY OF MAN

Humanist educators proposed a new curriculum—the mastery of the *studia humanitatis*—as a preparation for life, not as a set of technical skills to prepare for a particular career. An attentive and committed reading of ancient texts would awaken resources of spirit, they believed, and cultivate more conscious as well as more informed human beings, who would, in turn, regenerate the present age. In particular, ancient texts sparked a new evaluation of the human being and an appreciation of the *dignitas hominis* (dignity of man).

The "dignity of man" theme that threads its way through humanist thought must be distinguished from the individualism that Jacob Burckhardt, the inventor of the modern conception of the Renaissance, saw as essential to the era, which he described as achieving "the discovery of the world and of man." Individualism, a modern construct, assumes that the individual is paramount and is the source of all values. Many historical figures have acted as though holding such views, including most of the heroic figures celebrated by later generations. Among these are some figures from the Middle Ages, which is often dismissed as hostile to individual thought and action. Among them, too, are renowned figures of the Renaissance, including the Florentine ruler Lorenzo de' Medici (1449–1492), surnamed *il Magnifico* (the Magnificent), the artists Leonardo da Vinci (1452–1519) and Michelangelo Buonarroti (1475–1564), and the political theorist Niccolò Machiavelli. The abundance of such dynamic individuals is the phenomenon that so impressed Burckhardt and urged him to highlight this trait as central to the Renaissance era.

Renaissance humanists, however, in their discussions of the nature and condition of the human being did not advocate this kind of modern individualism, which denies a cosmic framework and implies moral relativism. Human beings, in their conception, existed within a providential universe—one guided by God—and achieved their full perfection in affirming its moral and intellectual order. In this, their vision was essentially Christian. It was also classical. The humanists, like the ancients, viewed the human being as possessing powerful capacities of body and spirit, as capable of great and decisive action, as seeking such worthy goals as knowledge, goodness, justice, and even pleasure. (The phrase "dignity of man" is used deliberately; for the Renaissance view of women, see Chapter 5.)

Giannozzo Manetti

In 1453 the Florentine statesman and humanist Giannozzo Manetti (1396–1459) composed the work *De dignitate et excellentia hominis* ("On the Dignity and Excellence of Man") in response to contemporary debates on the issue. Using arguments from classical authors, especially Cicero; the fathers of the church, especially Augustine and Lactantius (fourth century CE); and philosophers, theologians, and physicians, including Aristotle, Peter Lombard (c. 1100–1160), and Galen, Manetti argued for the excellence of the human body, the human soul, and the whole existence of the human being. In the final section, he responded to critics of the human condition. Foremost among these was the great medieval Pope Innocent III (r. 1198–1216), whose *De contemptu mundi* ("On Contempt for the World") was a meditation on the frailties of human existence appropriate to the vision of medieval Christianity which aimed to turn people to the contemplation of the afterlife, away from the things of the world.

Innocent vividly characterized the weakness of the human body, the insecurities of human existence, and the vices of the human spirit. Manetti, in answer, laid down evidence of human capacity and common sense. The human body is born in filth and prone to illness, he argued, but is nonetheless a magnificent creation and a source of pride. It is equipped with five senses, which permit the human being to perceive the world and to know pleasure: the pleasure derived from "the untrammeled vision of beautiful bodies … from listening to sounds and symphonies and even more delightful things … from smelling the odors of flowers … from tasting various sweet and succulent viands, and … from the touch of the softest substances." It possesses, moreover, a sixth or "common sense" (a generally acknowledged concept at the time), with which it receives and evaluates the evidence of the senses and makes prudential judgments. It almost seems as if this sixth sense was the seat of human wisdom for Manetti. "What great pleasures," he wrote, derive from that sense; "words cannot express the pleasure we experience when we imagine, compare, make value judgments, remember and understand."

To Innocent's complaints about the human soul, Manetti responded with an argument Innocent himself could not have rejected. The soul is immortal, divine in origin, destined for eternity. When Manetti wrote, the concept of the immortality of the soul was not yet church teaching. It only became an official doctrine of the Roman Church in 1513—and then as a result of arguments propounded by Christian humanist philosophers. Yet the notion was certainly current in Christian thought from the late Middle Ages and in the writings of St. Paul and the church fathers as well. There is little distance, for instance, between the understanding of spirit (as opposed to the flesh) or of the victory over death posed by the Apostle Paul in his Epistle to the Romans and the later formulation of the doctrine of immortality. St. Augustine, similarly, speaks of the human mind as a template of the mind of God and of the infinite, eternal capacity of human memory.

Manetti drew from this pool of understandings and cleverly used a thinker who was not Christian at all but who spoke explicitly about the immortal nature of the human mind: the Roman author Cicero. Manetti thereby implied that both Christian and non-Christian

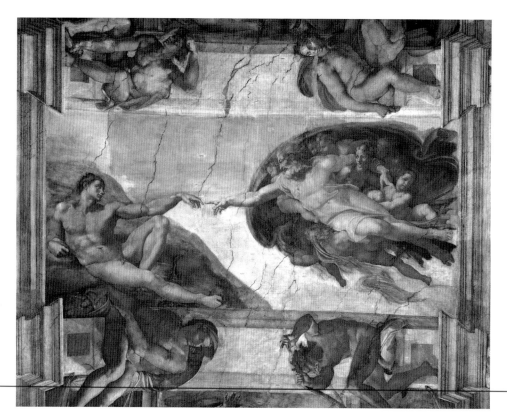

Michelangelo, *Creation of Adam*, 1510, fresco, 9 ft 2 in × 18 ft 8 in (280 × 570 cm). Sistine Chapel, Vatican, Rome.

The humanist understanding of the dignity of the human condition is eloquently conveyed in this image. God, the benign creator, extends his all-powerful hand. The languid Adam attentively awaits the divine touch that will stir his innate strength

authors foresaw the eternal destiny of the human spirit. On the basis of reason alone, Cicero came to recognize that the human spirit belongs to a changeless and undying realm beyond the natural world.

Where Innocent compared the lovely fruits of a blossoming tree to the foul, defiling "fruits" of the human body, Manetti pointed to the true "fruits" of human endeavor. These he defined as the products of human hands and minds, creations that directly imitated the actions of God, the Creator; in human creation, the combined effort of the body and the spirit, the human being experienced the fullness of God's nature.

So Manetti concluded, addressing his audience directly: "O fellow humans … you have been given a nature and a destiny of immeasurable dignity and excellence, to your rule and command have been made subject all things on earth, in the waters, of the sea, in the heavens … let our chief aim be virtue." If humans practice virtue, they will be like God "occupied in knowing, loving, contemplating," and with Him they will know "the joy of endless blessedness, of happiness unalloyed."

Pico della Mirandola

Manetti's arguments for the dignity of the human condition constitute a brilliant moment in Renaissance humanism. In it a medieval worldview is directly countered by the good sense, the homely observations, the scholarly reading, and the clever theological reasoning of this extraordinarily gifted humanist. This gemlike work was succeeded by an even more concise and breathtaking consideration of the nature of the human condition, written by the humanist and philosopher Giovanni Pico della Mirandola (1463–1494). His *De hominis dignitate oratio* ("Oration on the Dignity of Man") celebrates the various world philosophies, all of which tend toward a single truth about the universe. Pico recreates Renaissance notions of the human being in a way far more threatening to conventional assumptions than Manetti's.

Where Manetti grappled with negative views of the human being used as rhetorical devices to spur conversion to God, Pico began on the plane of ideas. He was a young genius fresh from his studies of Christian and Arabic philosophy, the Jewish mystical tradition of the **kabbalah**, and the ancient tradition of the occult. To Pico, therefore, the human being was essentially that creature uniquely able to understand and to know and through that knowledge has the capacity to approach the infinity of God. The whole species was dignified by the limitless possibilities of the philosopher's mind, which stood in for the ordinary human being in Pico's thought.

Pico's work opens with a philosophical question that is answered by a fable, a myth pieced together from Scripture and fantasy. Where is the human being's place in the universe? Is it, as Psalm 8:5 holds, at a point "a little lower than the angels"? No, replies Pico. He then explains where that place is by returning to the story in Genesis of the creation of Adam, the first man, modifying it so as to make his case for the infinite mental capacity of the human being.

In Genesis, God created human beings after five days in which he created the other living and inanimate creatures of the world. According to Pico, however, the world that God created was generated from "seeds" in his mind. This idea was derived from Greek philosophy, especially Greek atomic theory. For each creation, God, in effect, used up one of those mental seeds. By the end of the fifth day, he had exhausted them all in the task of creation, but now there was no creature created merely to contemplate and admire his wondrous creation. So God would create a special creature, unlike all the others, for that purpose. This creature, man, would not be generated from any single seed, and thus have his nature and destiny established for him even before his own birth. Instead, this creature would receive the ability to imitate any one of the seeds that had served as the resource for the divine creation. In effect, the human being from his origins was just like God—equipped with the same storehouse of possibilities that had once inhabited the mind of the Creator. God then speaks to Adam:

> Adam, you have been given no fixed place, no form of your own, and no particular function, so that you may have and possess, according to your will and your inclination, whatever place, whatever form, and whatever functions you choose. Divine law assigns to all other creatures a fixed nature. But you, constrained by no laws, by your own free will, in whose hands I have placed you, will determine your own nature.
>
> (M.L. King, trans. and ed., *Renaissance Humanism: An Anthology of Sources*.
> Cambridge, MA: Hackett, 2014, p. 57)

The moral of Pico's fable is clear. The *capacity* of the human being is infinite, since humans can ascend through the power of mind to become one with God, the Creator, and can imitate God to the extent that they choose to do so. The *nature* of the human being is a somewhat different matter: it is freedom. For human beings are the only creatures in the universe who can determine their own nature; this freedom has been granted by God in the act of creation. Pico's human being is one whose ultimate good—union with God—is achieved through a deliberate mental act. That action, however, is a free choice: the human creature is equally free to choose to descend the ladder of creation and become one with the fallen angel, the devil. Pico's optimism does not explore that possibility, which is nevertheless implied in his vision.

Pico's "Oration" was never delivered. It was composed as an introduction to the 900 philosophical theses (arguments) that he had compiled, drawn from ancient and modern, Christian, Jewish, and Muslim philosophies. He had proposed them to the intellectuals of Europe, whom he invited to Rome (offering to pay their expenses) to participate in an enormous debate, to be held in 1487. Before that event could occur, a papal commission examined the theses and found 13 of them heretical. Pico fled, to be arrested in France. In 1488, he was handed over to the custody of Lorenzo the Magnificent in Florence. There he continued to write treatises blending kabbalistic, Platonic, and other philosophical strands of thought, while divesting himself of worldly goods and drawing closer to the Dominican prophet Girolamo Savonarola (1452–1498; see Chapter 6). He died a few years later, on November 17, 1494, the same day the city of Florence fell to the French King Charles VIII (r. 1483–1498; see Chapter 7).

Pico's and Manetti's apologies for the dignity of the human condition offer different explanations for a renewed conception of humans as gifted creators, endowed with enormous gifts of body and spirit, with a magnificent destiny, should they choose it. It is an uplifting vision grounded in Christian and biblical thought, enriched by philosophical and literary traditions of the ancient world which the humanists had, in a certain sense, "discovered" anew.

CIVIC HUMANISM

In much the same way, humanists discovered anew the importance of the city for human existence and redefined the intellectual life as a civic endeavor. Humanism had its roots in city life; and humanists thought about and wrote about the lives of people in cities. Humanism had its origin, as we have seen (see Chapter 2), not in the age of the Renaissance in which it reached its peak but in the age of the popolo, of the emergent republics. The earliest humanists were laymen employed by city-states to record important decisions, write official letters, negotiate with neighbors, and design the proclamations of war or peace. It was the literary adventures of these early humanists, nurtured in a vibrant new urban context, that paved the way for Petrarch and Boccaccio, and the full-blown

BARBARO AND PICO: THE DEBATE BETWEEN PHILOSOPHY AND ELOQUENCE

Humanists represented a new type of intellectual. They were mostly laymen, and they were fascinated with the literature of Greek and Roman antiquity. They imitated those models in their own work, striving for the greatest possible eloquence.

Most of the intellectuals of medieval Europe, in contrast, were clerics; most were also university professors. They thought about God and his universe. They were not concerned with eloquence but with the precise demonstration of what was true. The intellectual activity of medieval thinkers as a whole is called Scholasticism, because it was a product of the schools and their offspring, the universities.

Scholasticism and humanism coexisted, competed, and came into conflict. An early battle took place in 1366 when Petrarch (1304–1374) was labeled a "good" but "ignorant" man by his university-trained friends. He defended himself, deploring his opponents' mindless investigations of the physical universe rather than the inner world of the human being. "It is better to will the good than to know the truth," he exclaimed triumphantly.

A second famous debate took place in 1485. The two contenders were both young aristocrats and brilliant humanists: the Venetian Ermolao Barbaro the Younger (1453/1454–1492) and Giovanni Pico (1463–1494), count of the tiny principality of Mirandola. Barbaro wrote Pico on April 5, commending him for his Latin eloquence and his Greek studies, since "there has not stood out a memorable work in good Latin done by anyone who lacked Greek letters." He then mocked the Scholastic philosophers who thought they could attain to truth without regard to the standards of Latin eloquence:

…who were not really alive in their life-time, much less will they live now they are dead … or if they live, they live in torture and reproach…. Who would not rather be non-existent than have such a reputation? One must admit of course that they said something of use; they were strong in natural endowment, in learning, in a lot of good things…. However, that which procures for an author immortal reputation is a shining and elegant style.
(Q. Breen, "Giovanni Pico della Mirandola on the Conflict of Philosophy and Rhetoric," *in* Christianity and Humanism: Studies in the History of Ideas, *2nd ed., ed. N.P. Ross. Grand Rapids, MI: Eerdmans, 1968, p. 393)*

Pico responded on June 3, defending the pursuit of truth, even if articulated only in plain language for a limited audience of experts. Pico had those uncultivated philosophers respond directly to Barbaro:

Well-spokenness is an elegant thing; we admit it … but in philosophers it is neither an ornament or a grace…. We search after the what of writing, we do not search after the how…. We do not want our style … adorned and graceful; we want it useful, grave, something to be respected…. We do not expect the applause of the theater … but we expect the silence which comes rather from astonishment on the part of the few who are looking very deeply into something … so thoroughly defended that there [is] no room for refutation.
(Breen, "Giovanni Pico della Mirandola," pp. 396–397)*

The polite duel of words between Pico and Barbaro is interesting even today. Should intellectuals seek a remote truth that no one can understand and that may not be a guide to people in their daily lives? Should they devote themselves to the mastery of rhetoric, the art of speaking and writing powerfully, which can be used indiscriminately both to teach human beings what is good and to deceive and lead them to what is evil?

Renaissance humanism of their successors. Renaissance humanists, in turn, celebrated the *vita civile* (civil life) and its values. They were in fact "civic humanists," as historian Hans Baron has named the phenomenon. Humanism reached its fruition, he argued, when the early humanist movement became integrated with the republican spirit of the Italian city-states.

Proposing New Values: Poggio and Valla

Humanism, then, was both *lay* and *urban*, even though some humanists were actually clerics and some preferred the countryside (for example, Petrarch). Given this context, it is not surprising that many humanists challenged the notion dominant throughout the Middle Ages that the "contemplative" life—the life of religious seclusion, perhaps in a monastery—was superior to the active life of merchants, artisans, and statesmen. Although Petrarch, in the fourteenth century, still praised the religious life in his *De vita solitaria* ("On the Solitary Life"), he himself was an engaged observer of both city-state and imperial politics, and he wrote a book on governance for the despot of Padua. In the next generation, the chancellor of Florence, Coluccio Salutati (1331–1406), also favored the religious, or contemplative, life in his *De religione et fuga saeculi* ("On Religion and the Flight from the World"). In 1398, however, 17 years later, he offered the contrary argument in a long letter to his friend and counterpart, the chancellor of Bologna, Peregrino Zambeccari. Zambeccari was thinking of becoming a monk to escape the memory of an unfortunate love affair. Salutati discouraged him: "Do not believe, my Peregrino, that to flee the crowd, to avoid the sight of attractive objects, to shut oneself in a cloister or to go off to a hermitage is the way of perfection." Instead, he should pursue worthy tasks in the world: "If you provide for and serve and strive for your family and your sons, your relatives and your friends, and your state you cannot fail to raise your heart to heavenly things and please God."

As the value of civic life and the possibility of leading a virtuous life while in the world became widely accepted in humanist culture, some humanists turned still more boldly against the religious values of an earlier era. Poggio Bracciolini's carefully crafted dialogue *De avaritia* ("On Avarice") presents two speakers condemning greed and in between them, one who defends it. Far from being the soul-destroying root of evil that clerics had imagined it to be, argues this speaker, greed is the dynamic force that urges people to produce, to build, and to overcome the narrow circumstances of their lives. In fact, the avaricious are essential to society. Without them, "every splendor, every refinement, every ornament would be lacking. No one would build churches or colonnades; all artistic activity would cease, and confusion would result in our lives and in public affairs if everyone were satisfied with only enough for himself." What are cities or states "if not the workshops of avarice?" This advocate of avarice is not the victor in this dialogue, but neither is he the loser. In presenting vividly the case for capitalist acquisition and competition,

Poggio (another chancellor of Florence) displayed an outlook that, centuries later, would come into its own.

In his dialogue *De voluptate* ("On Pleasure"), the humanist Lorenzo Valla (1407–1457) similarly proposed values that significantly challenged those accepted by the medieval church. Here the speakers belong to two ancient philosophical schools: Stoicism, which, like Christianity, required of its adherents self-discipline and self-denial, and Epicureanism, a byword in premodern times for scandalous self-indulgence, which encouraged its followers to enjoy the moderate pleasures of life without fear of death or retribution. In this dialogue, a Christianized Epicureanism clearly prevails: Valla appears to be informing the followers of a church whose key theme was the rejection of pleasure, that pleasure was in fact the true good.

Only the boldest humanists confronted Christian assumptions as squarely as did Poggio and Valla. Like them, however, most Renaissance humanists preferred rhetoric, the art of persuasive prose and speech-making, as being more useful for the civic life than its rival discipline, dialectic. Dialectic, or the method of logical argumentation, was the intellectual discipline essential to Scholastic philosophers, whose creative contributions peaked in the thirteenth and fourteenth centuries. The great medieval *summae*—the compendiums of theology and philosophy in which the Christian view of the cosmos was expounded—were grounded in the dialectical method. The technical and theoretical genre of the *summa* was rejected by the humanists in favor of brief works—letters, dialogues, treatises, orations—in which they could present their ideas in a challenging and engaging way. If dialectic was the necessary skill for philosophers in a university setting, rhetoric was the necessary skill for bureaucrats and amateurs in an urban setting where ideas circulated not merely among trained intellectuals but between them and the active, important men who led the city.

Praising the City: Bruni

Civic humanism, therefore, was characterized by a lay outlook, a preference for the active over the contemplative life and for secular over Christian values, as well as by a preference for the accessible, persuasive prose learned from the rhetorician over the technical, systematic prose of the philosopher in an ivory tower. Civic humanists also wrote explicitly about cities: they described them, and they wrote their histories. One such was Leonardo Bruni (c. 1370–1444), another chancellor of Florence, who occupied that position from 1427, after Salutati but before Poggio. Bruni's *Laudatio Florentinae urbis* ("Panegyric to the City of Florence") is a rhetorical oration that epitomizes the civic humanist project. It celebrates the city of Florence for its productive and creative achievements—its architecture, its setting, its people, and its governance. It is a city bursting with beautiful buildings, beautiful even in the side streets and courtyards: "just as blood is spread throughout the entire body, so fine architecture and decoration are diffused throughout the whole city."

Amid these exquisite buildings lived the free and productive citizens of Florence. They derived their excellence, Bruni continued, from their heritage: they were descended

VALLA'S LOGIC: DESTROYER OF WORLDS

The humanist Lorenzo Valla, a master of words and a committed Christian, was also a destroyer of worlds. He used his precise command of the ancient languages—Latin, Greek, and Hebrew—to question enduring assumptions that he ruthlessly proved wrong. He questioned papal claims to dominion in Italy, critiqued the standard Latin (Vulgate) translation of Scripture, and challenged prevailing moral assumptions. Two instances of Valla's destructive logic are given here.

Valla's *Discourse on the Forgery of the Alleged Donation of Constantine* exposed as fraudulent the papal claim to vast territorial possessions in Italy. Papal apologists had long pointed to a document issued to Pope Sylvester I (r. 314–336) by the Roman Emperor Constantine. On the basis of this grant, the popes held the Papal States until 1870; still today, they govern a remnant of those possessions, The Vatican City, restored to the papacy in 1929. Valla employed many tools to show that the document was an eighth-century fabrication. Here Valla argues that Sylvester was never given possession of the Roman lands:

> Or is it not certain that possession was never given?… Did Constantine ever lead Sylvester in state to the Capitol?… Did he place him on a golden throne in the presence of the whole Senate? Did he command the magistrates, each in the order of his rank, to salute their king and prostrate themselves before him? This … is customary in the creation of new rulers. Did he afterwards escort him through all Italy?… Did he go to the Germans, and the rest of the West?… I do not remember to have seen any other procedure when any one was made lord of a city, a country, or a province; for we do not count possession as given until the old magistrates are removed and the new ones substituted.
>
> (C.B. Coleman, trans. and ed., The Treatise of Lorenzo Valla on the Donation of Constantine. *Toronto: University of Toronto Press, 1993, pp. 63, 65*)

Valla's exposure of the "Donation of Constantine" had immense political repercussions. Equally important was his challenge to the moral universe of medieval and Renaissance Europe. In his dialogue *De voluptate* ("On Pleasure"), he investigates Christian, Stoic, and Epicurean concepts of the true good, thus putting Christian assumptions to the test of arguments based on pre-Christian moral philosophy. Of these, the Epicurean school was especially despised at that time. In contradiction of Christian belief, it held that human beings died irreparably and that in the absence of the hope of an afterlife they should direct their lives to the healthful pleasures of philosophy and friends. Valla's serious exploration of the Epicurean perspective challenged many Christian presuppositions. Here, the Epicurean interlocutor of Valla's dialogue questions the Christian prohibition on adultery:

> "What if you commit adultery?" What a hateful word! Why should we assail adulterers, if it pleases us to look at Nature? There is absolutely no difference between a woman's going to bed with her husband or with her lover. Exclude the difference created by that perverse word "wedlock," and you have made adultery and marriage one and the same thing…. A woman is either united with a man or by her marital partner is made a mother…. Both of these things can be effected for women by another man who is not her husband.
>
> (Lorenzo Valla, On Pleasure, trans. A. Kent Hieatt and M. Lorch. New York: Abaris Books, 1979, p. xxxviii)

Just as Valla's arguments about papal claims to sovereignty have had repercussions down to the present, so too have his moral philosophical arguments, which point to the skepticism of the **Enlightenment** and the relativism of modern times.

from ancient Romans, and specifically from the ancient Romans of the free republican, not imperial era, whose qualities as free men transferred to their descendants. Bruni took up the theme of Florence's Roman past again in his *Historiarum florentini populi* ("History of the Florentine Republic"), a full-scale work on this subject on which the author labored for nearly 30 years.

The Florentine state was the most splendid and just of all cities. It was generous to strangers and refugees, and generously assisted other cities threatened by oppression. Its own citizens fought bravely for the city's freedom. At home, its public institutions and laws were dedicated to justice and freedom. Under its admirable and coordinated system of councils and magistrates, the city had been "governed with such diligence and competence that one could not find better discipline even in a household ruled by a solicitous father." In Florence, justice was available to all and not just to the wealthy: "There is no place on earth where there is greater justice open equally to everyone," Bruni asserted. "Nowhere else does freedom grow so vigorously, and nowhere else are rich and poor alike treated with such equality."

The historian Hans Baron identified this work as a defense of the republican liberty of Florence, written in response to the imperialist aggression of the duke of Milan, Giangaleazzo Visconti (1351–1402). Bruni's stylized and stylish oration, however, cannot be taken at face value. But neither is it to be discarded as a merely rhetorical work. Certainly he exaggerated the perfections of the city and overstated the extent to which Florence provided its citizens with unstinting care and balanced justice. The city's archive holds many documents, written at about the same time as Bruni's *Laudatio*, which reveal the anguish of the poor or the oppressed as they petition for a hearing, for tax relief, or for assistance.

Nevertheless, Bruni's inflated vision of Florence is not all wrong. Florentine urbanism was perhaps the most developed in Europe, a flawless matching of public design, private architecture, and the city's mission. Among the citizens of Florence, although they included both the dizzyingly rich and the desperately poor, were a large fraction who were prosperously engaged in commerce and manufacture, providing for their families and sustaining

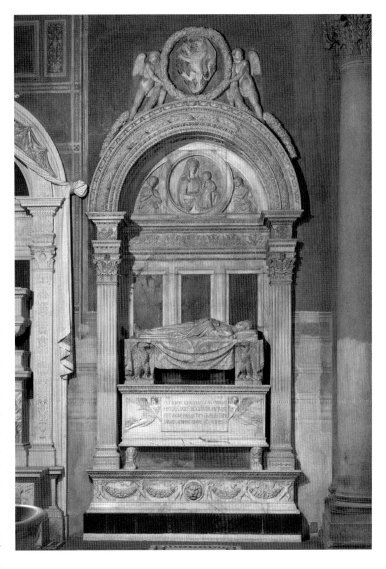

Bernardo Rossellino, *Tomb of Leonardo Bruni,* **1444–1447, marble, height 20 ft (610 cm). Santa Croce, Florence.**

Although he had requested a simple stone slab for his burial, in this sculpture the great humanist and chancellor of the Florentine republic lies in state as he did at his funeral in 1444. He holds his book, *The History of the Florentine People,* wears a laurel crown, and lies on a bier set in an elaborate architectural frame recalling a Roman triumphal arch.

the costs of an autonomous republic. The political and judicial machinery of fifteenth-century Florence would appear flawed to an American of the twenty-first century. But in the context of the fifteenth century, where arbitrary power was the norm on feudal estates and in royal and despotic courts, it was admirably fair and open.

Outside of Florence, too, humanists employed their pens to celebrate their cities and their cities' rulers. In Venice, where both humanist expression and political life were carefully controlled, patrician humanists (men born to the ruling noble class) celebrated the city's harmony—or, to use their term, its "unanimity." All social classes worked together selflessly, each serving in its way the greater goal of maintaining a city seen as flawless and ideal—*la Serenissima*, as Venice was called. Venice promoted the writing of its own history, too, and by the end of the fifteenth century had instituted the position of public historiographer as a permanent post. Each state historian, predictably, wrote about Venice's seamless history, its enduringly peaceful dedication to justice.

From the Venetian case, it is clear that the civic humanist project can descend to propaganda. When Antonio Beccadelli (called Panormita, 1394–1471) wrote in praise of King Alfonso the Magnificent of Naples (r. 1442–1458) or when Giovanni Simonetta celebrated the deeds of Francesco Sforza, we see not so much a humanist inspired by the genuine dynamism of his city as a hireling celebrating his master—in very nearly the same language. We have passed from humanism to the culture of the court (see Chapter 7).

WOMEN AND HUMANISM

The humanists were mostly male; for them ideas were a part of civic life, and civic life was imbued with thought. For those few women, however, who acquired the training to engage in humanist studies, the situation was different. They were not free to engage in public life. Not only could they not serve in any public offices or official positions in commercial organizations, they could not even freely walk about their neighborhood. Women of the middle and upper classes were understood to be under men's care—that of their father or his male kin or of their husband and his. Their place was at home. (Women of the lower social strata, in contrast, did venture abroad in the course of their work, but they, like their male counterparts, did not acquire humanist educations.)

Early Female Humanists

The first women known to be involved in humanist pursuits belonged to the minor nobility associated with the courts and cities of northern Italy. These were women who had the leisure and the wealth to study and who were protected by their status from the criticism that an ordinary woman might have encountered. Even before the turn of the fifteenth century, the Paduan noblewoman Maddalena degli Scrovegni (1356–1429) was known to be learned in Latin literature and to engage in highbrow conversation with the literati who frequented her father's house. The male humanist Antonio Loschi, later an apologist for the Visconti rulers of Milan, knew the family and celebrated her learning and her chastity. In the 1430s the noblewoman Costanza Varano (1428–1447) was sufficiently gifted in Latin that she could deliver orations. She would die before she reached 20, a wife of three years.

Costanza Varano was perhaps encouraged in her intellectual pursuits by her grandmother Battista Montefeltro Malatesta (1383–1450), the daughter of a lord of Urbino, who married into the Malatesta family that commanded Rimini, although this branch of the family ruled the small city of Pesaro. Battista was known as a composer of verses—an activity typical for the noblewomen of this milieu— and even vied in composing them with her father-in-law at court. She apparently became aware of humanism as a literary movement and hoped to become part of it. She learned Latin sufficient to deliver an oration in 1433 when Holy Roman Emperor Sigismund passed through Urbino (to which she had retired after her husband was expelled from Pesaro). She is best known, however, as the recipient of a letter from Leonardo Bruni, the male humanist chancellor of Florence, who wrote in response to her letter of inquiry to advise Battista on the progress of her studies.

Bruni's letter *De studiis et litteris* ("On Literary Study"), written in 1424, is the first major statement we have in modern times on the issue of women and education. In a misogynist age that greatly limited women's opportunities, it is remarkable for the assumption that a woman's natural ability was sufficient for advanced humanist studies. It is also remarkable for the assumption that a woman would not wish to pursue humanist studies as merely an occupation for idle hours. He advised Battista on the various fields of study. By all means, she should study the best ancient authors, both secular and sacred, and the disciplines of grammar, moral philosophy, poetry, and history (and not bother with arithmetic, geometry, and astrology, disciplines the humanists did not value). The one humanist discipline that it would be futile for her to pursue, according to Bruni, was rhetoric: it would be a waste of time for her to study its intricacies, since she was a woman "who never sees the forum" (that is, the open area in ancient Rome where orators delivered their speeches). Bruni's advice was ironic, since one of the first activities of the early humanists was to compose speeches in classical style. The role of orator was not—except in a few cases, some noted here—open to women.

Later Female Humanists: Nogarola, Cereta, Fedele

Forty years later, the humanistically trained scholar Lauro Quirini of Venice (c. 1420–c. 1475/1479), then studying philosophy at the University of Padua, addressed a letter to Isotta Nogarola reminiscent of Bruni's to Battista Montefeltro. A noblewoman from Verona, Nogarola had already won a considerable reputation for her classical learning and her Latin letters and orations. Now, having decided to remain unmarried (she lived with her mother in her brother's household), she was eager to pursue an advanced curriculum: a university-level program in philosophy. Quirini unhesitatingly plunged in, advising her

WOMEN AND HUMANISM IN RENAISSANCE ITALY

In fifteenth-century Italy, women entered the mainstream of culture. They did so by learning Latin and participating in the program of humanist studies. Humanism, in effect, was the gateway to women's full participation in intellectual life. In the sixteenth century, with the availability of print technology and the increasing use of the vernacular, many more Italian women engaged in cultural discourse, their way having been prepared by a few predecessors in the humanist era. Represented here are the three foremost women humanists of the fifteenth century: Isotta Nogarola of Verona, Laura Cereta of Brescia (1469–1499), and Cassandra Fedele of Venice (1465–1558).

Nogarola engaged a prominent Venetian nobleman, Ludovico Foscarini (1409–1480), in a debate on the relative sinfulness of Adam and Eve in the Garden of Eden (Genesis 3) when, bidden by the serpent, Eve ate the forbidden fruit of the Tree of Knowledge of Good and Evil, and when afterward, bidden by Eve, Adam, too, ate of its fruit. Nogarola argued that Adam was more guilty than Eve because Eve, a woman, was inferior to Adam in strength of character. Foscarini responded that Eve was more guilty than Adam because she lured him into sin and thus brought sin— in Christian theology, Original Sin—on the whole human race. Here Nogarola pursues the defense of Eve—and thus of womankind:

> Moreover, the woman did not eat from the forbidden tree because she believed she would become like God, but rather because she was weak and inclined to pleasure.... Thus the woman, but only because she had been first deceived by the serpent's evil persuasion, did indulge in the delights of paradise; but she would have harmed only herself and in no way endangered human posterity if the consent of the first-born man had not been offered. Therefore Eve was no danger to posterity but only to herself; but the man Adam spread the infection of sin to himself and to all future generations.
>
> (M.L. King and D. Robin, trans. and ed., Isotta Nogarola: Letters, Dialogues, and Orations. *Chicago: University of Chicago Press, 2003, pp. 146–147)*

In this letter, Laura Cereta lambasted women who wasted themselves in amusements and did not engage in the studies that would permit them to develop an autonomous self. Here she urges women to seek an education:

> For an education is neither bequeathed to us as a legacy, nor does some fate or other give it to us as a gift. Virtue is something that we ourselves acquire; nor can those women who become dull-witted through laziness and the sludge of low pleasures ascend to the understanding of difficult things. But for those women who believe that study, hard work, and vigilance will bring them sure praise, the road to attaining knowledge is broad.
>
> (D. Robin, trans. and ed., Laura Cereta: Collected Letters. *Chicago: University of Chicago Press, 1997, p. 82)*

In her path-breaking speech before the doge and senate of Venice, Cassandra Fedele defended the liberal arts and concluded by urging women to pursue knowledge even if they had no access to public careers.

> But enough on the utility of literature since it produces not only an outcome that is rich, precious, and sublime but also provides one with advantages that are extremely pleasurable, fruitful, and lasting—benefits that I myself have enjoyed. And when I meditate on the idea of marching forth in life with the lowly and execrable weapons of the little woman—the needle and the distaff—even if the study of literature offers women no rewards or honors, I believe women must nonetheless pursue and embrace such studies alone for the pleasure and enjoyment they contain.
>
> (D. Robin, trans. and ed., Cassandra Fedele: Letters and Orations. *Chicago: University of Chicago Press, 2000, p. 162)*

to read deeply in the most rigorous authors in both Latin and Greek. He had no concern about her overstepping her limits. Quirini's only caution was that Nogarola should avoid the narrower Scholastic philosophers. He encouraged her, however, to read the ancient philosophers, in Latin translation if not in the original Greek. The curriculum that Quirini urged upon Nogarola was a difficult one for even the most advanced students, and he did not doubt that she could pursue it: "Give your whole heart, then to philosophy alone, for I want you to be not semi-learned, but to have knowledge of all the good arts [i.e., humanistic studies] … as well as the science of human and divine things [i.e., philosophy and theology]." Implicit in his letter was the assumption that women, as much as men, could read and understand the most complex ideas.

Despite Quirini's open-mindedness, the issue of the different natures of male and female had not yet vanished. A few years after he wrote her, Nogarola engaged the Venetian humanist and statesman Ludovico Foscarini in a discussion of the relative guilt of Adam and Eve for their expulsion from the Garden of Eden and subsequent punishment. In the biblical account in Genesis, Eve, prompted by the evil serpent (the devil), persuades Adam to eat the fruit of the Tree of Knowledge of Good and Evil, which God had specifically forbidden. Both had eaten; but Eve was seen as especially guilty because she succumbed to the demon's persuasion and then persuaded Adam to break God's law. As a punishment, both were expelled from paradise. In addition, Adam, or "man," was condemned to work for his survival; and Eve, or "woman," was condemned to bear children in pain and to be subject to men's will.

In the dialogue Nogarola wrote recording Foscarini's arguments and her own, Foscarini used biblical, legal, and theological texts to defend the traditional view of Eve's guilt. Nogarola, however, used the same kinds of sources to prove that Eve, although guilty of tempting Adam, was by nature weaker than he; she could not, therefore, be considered responsible for her actions. In attempting to lift from Eve's shoulders the great burden of condemnation for the Fall of Man from grace, Nogarola conceded the weakness of female nature. Still, her *Dialogue* of 1451 is one of the early defenses of women by a woman, and thus a landmark in the history of feminist thought.

Far bolder in her defense of women, and especially of women who wrote, was Laura Cereta. She came from a prominent, but not noble, Brescian family. Widowed young, Cereta could devote her full attention to humanist studies, which she found as ennobling and freeing for women as for men. She demonstrated her abilities by giving orations and writing letters; the latter were widely circulated and, thus, really a public genre rather than personal correspondence. These activities aroused active criticism from men and even more from women. In response, Cereta defended women's ability to acquire learning and celebrated the benefit of education to women. She also encouraged other women to follow the hard and long road to knowledge: "For an education is neither bequeathed to us as a legacy, nor does some fate or other give it to us as a gift. Virtue is something that we ourselves acquire…. But for those women who believe that study, hard work, and vigilance will bring them sure praise, the road to attaining knowledge is broad."

The figures of Isotta Nogarola and Laura Cereta helped to break the monopoly that high noblewomen had held over female humanism. Nogarola was both wealthy and noble, but not from a bourgeois family active in urban affairs. Cereta's family was more modest still. A third great woman humanist of the Italian fifteenth century, Cassandra Fedele, came from a middle-class intellectual Venetian family with a history of service in the state bureaucracy.

Like her predecessors, before her marriage and during her widowhood, Fedele wrote in the familiar humanist genres of letters and orations. Although much of her work is conventional, her oration in praise of the liberal arts, delivered before the doge and the Venetian senate, is astonishing—a woman speaking out in support of the full humanist program. How extraordinary it must have been to the audience of that day, where a woman virtually never appeared, to observe a woman speak on these matters, when so few women learned Latin and acquired the advanced knowledge of the classics necessary to give a humanist oration. Only at the end does Fedele cease to be the neutral and genderless celebrant of the liberal arts, commenting on why a woman might devote herself to study: "And when I meditate on the idea of marching forth in life with the lowly and execrable weapons of the little woman—the needle and the distaff—even if the study of literature offers women no rewards or honors, I believe women must nonetheless pursue and embrace such studies alone for the pleasure and enjoyment they contain."

Fedele lived to the extraordinary old age of 93. During that span of years, Olimpia Morata (1526/1527–1555), the daughter of a humanist advisor to the Duke of Ferrara, lived and died. Thoroughly trained by her father at a very early age, Morata had already published works in Latin and Greek when, in 1549 or 1550, she married a German student, a Lutheran convert, for whom Italy was no longer safe (see Chapters 8 and 9). She returned with him to the German lands and died as a result of an illness, perhaps tuberculosis, that she acquired during the siege of Schweinfurt, a minor incident in the religious wars that now engulfed Europe. Her works, including a vast number of thoughtful letters, were published posthumously (it was by this time the age of print) by a learned man and family friend. With Morata, the linked chain of Italian women humanists ends.

The phenomenon of female humanism in the Italian Renaissance is limited—barely a dozen women could properly be identified as humanists, and some of these have left scant written record or none at all. Yet it is exceedingly important. With the exception of Christine de Pizan (1364–1430), a Frenchwoman of Italian origin who wrote in the first decades of the fifteenth century, the Italian women humanists were among the first authors of any age or gender to make explicit and public the issues of female capacity for education and women's full participation in the human condition. Their ideas spread during the sixteenth and seventeenth centuries, translated and transformed in the works of both male authorities and female poets, then much in fashion. Through these vehicles, they would reach the modern age, and their words continue to flow in the mainstream of feminist thought.

Nevertheless, the unavoidable focus of the women humanists upon the issue of being women detached them from the mainstream of humanist thought in the Italian

Renaissance, which would have its next important development in conjunction with new developments in philosophy and scholarly method.

HUMANISM, PHILOSOPHY, AND SCHOLARSHIP

Renaissance humanism was not a philosophy. It rejected order and consistency, qualities central to most philosophical systems and certainly to the ancient and medieval philosophies of which humanism had knowledge. Its written products tended to be occasional works, written at the behest of a patron, in response to the stimulus of an interesting event or encounter, or in the whim of a moment. Nevertheless, the humanist program had philosophical implications, which are worthy of review. Moreover, humanists opened up new approaches, especially in their confrontation with Greek texts, that had profound consequences both for the pursuit of philosophical understanding and for the development of scholarly procedures in the analysis and publication of texts.

Philosophy: Aristotle and Plato

Some central humanist concepts had philosophical implications. Most important, the humanist interest in the nature of humans and in their social and historical setting, pointed philosophical discussion in a new direction. In the medieval university, in contrast, philosophers had been almost entirely concerned with God and the cosmos. Related to the refocused concern upon the individual was a shift in the preference for pure thought, the *vita contemplativa* (contemplative life) of the monk or mystic, to a preference for useful action, the *vita activa* (active, or civil life) of the citizen. The medieval ideal was of a hermit or sage whose contact with the divine realm brought salvation to others. The humanist ideal was of a man of affairs who combined intellectual with practical insights and could, therefore, bring his knowledge of deep matters to bear upon the life of the community. If action was more important than thought, then will was more important than knowledge—an idea that conflicted with basic philosophical assumptions. The emphasis on will was also reflected in language as the humanists valued persuasion over logical demonstration, the incitement to action over mere knowledge.

Although these preferences did not amount to a philosophy, the humanist attention to texts had monumental consequences for philosophy. Critical was the recovery of Greek, which the first major humanists—Boccaccio, Petrarch—knew was essential and which the generation immediately following accomplished. Some attempted the translation of individual lives of Plutarch or other brief, narrative works. The Florentine chancellor Leonardo Bruni took on a more serious task: he retranslated works of Aristotle (then available in thirteenth-century translations used by the schools of theology run by **mendicants**) directly from the Greek. The Aristotelian works he chose to study were those of moral and political philosophy: the *Nicomachean Ethics* and *Politics* and the pseudo-Aristotelian *Economics*. He left aside Aristotle's works on physics, metaphysics, and logic, which speculated about the nature of the cosmos and provided the tools for Scholastic disputation.

The next generation, in the mid-fifteenth century, saw the more momentous translation of Plato. Except for a few isolated works, Plato had not previously been translated into Latin, with the consequence that Platonic concepts were not well-known in the West. The injection of Platonic ideas into a philosophical consensus that was essentially Aristotelian was pivotal—stimulating as well as threatening. The incorporation of Aristotelian thought with Christian assumptions was the great achievement of the medieval Scholastic philosophers. (The major Scholastic figures labored, it should be remembered, from the twelfth to the fourteenth centuries and thus did not wholly precede but rather overlapped with early humanist endeavors.) Now Platonic thought would be integrated with Christianity but in a less stable framework where Platonic concepts might also challenge Christian as well as Aristotelian assumptions.

Marsilio Ficino (1433–1499), the son of the physician to Cosimo de' Medici of Florence, was the key figure in the inauguration of Platonic studies. He was groomed from childhood to understand the philosophical texts related to the study of medicine, but in 1462 Cosimo provided the scholar with a house and a source of income to support him in the epochal task of preparing a full and definitive translation of Plato's works. This he completed within a few years. The second edition, published in Venice in 1491, became the standard Latin version for many years.

The translation of the Platonic corpus might have been achievement enough. But Ficino was heart and soul, day and night, a Platonist. He hosted gatherings of learned men of the age (all of whom were hailed as philosophers in Ficino's circle), who discussed the Platonic issues of love, rhetoric, and republicanism. In 1474 he published his *Platonic Theology*, which proved to the world at large the harmony of Platonic and Christian understandings. He extended his speculations to include magic (not yet distinguished from science) and astrology (not yet distinguished from astronomy) and the late antique Neoplatonic theorists, who blended Plato in turn with Aristotle and various later philosophical schools.

Other Schools

The rapid absorption of Plato, therefore, involved an openness to and interest in other greater or lesser, more or less exotic schools of thought. Giovanni Pico della Mirandola's interests and influences extended even further than Ficino's. Pico studied medieval Arabic and Jewish, including kabbalistic, thought, as well as "Chaldean" (Zoroastrian and Babylonian) and hermetic (mystical late antique Neoplatonist) traditions, which he blended with the Christian, Aristotelian, and Platonic traditions. Pico was an extreme eclectic for whom all philosophical and religious traditions were true, and all reflected "One Truth."

Pico was unique. Among his contemporaries and successors, though, were many more scholars whose knowledge of Greek permitted them to explore a broad array of ideas not previously accessible. They studied Plato and the Neoplatonists, both pagan and Christian, including the works of the mythical Hermes Trismegistus (the "thrice-great Hermes," a combination of the Egyptian Thoth, the god of wisdom, and the Greek Hermes) which contained many occult elements and probably derived from late Neoplatonic writings. Beyond these, they studied ancient and medieval Arabic works of astronomy and astrology, and magic. At a time when certain forms of magic were associated with witchcraft and considered demonic (see Chapter 11), other forms called "white" or "high magic" were considered benign. Alchemy, the ancestor of the scientific discipline of chemistry, was one aspect of late Renaissance magic.

While some thinkers were attracted to the occult and magical dimensions of the ancient tradition, others pursued its more strictly scientific, logical, and mathematical elements. The renewed Renaissance reading of Aristotle could lead to conclusions dramatically different from those of the thirteenth-century Scholastics. At Padua, university professor Pietro Pomponazzi (1462–1525), for instance, employed Aristotle to inquire into the principle of the immortality of the soul (promoted by Ficinian Platonism, only recently declared Christian dogma). Pomponazzi argued that since the mind (or soul) required the senses, and thus the body, to formulate its ideas, it could not be shown to outlive the body. Immortality could not, therefore, be demonstrated in philosophy—although it must, he conceded, be embraced by faith. On the basis of their close study of Greek texts, other philosophers began to lay the foundations of the scientific investigations that came to fruition from the 1540s in the movement called the Scientific Revolution (see Chapter 11). From later ancient Greek references to the works of Aristarchus of Samos (c. 310–230 BCE), for instance, the Polish priest Nicholas Copernicus (1473–1543) encountered the notion of a universe centered about the sun.

Printing

Expert Hellenists also devoted themselves to the critical study of ancient texts as part of the process of publishing them via the new technology of print, which had reached Italy in the 1470s. Although the Greek texts offered the greater challenge, Latin texts, too, received critical study in preparation for print. In addition to native Italian humanists engaged in this task were many emigré scholars from the Byzantine Empire who had escaped when the Turks conquered Constantinople in 1453. These scholars prepared the texts for print by supplying emendations of words that had been mistakenly altered in the inexact process of copying the manuscript by hand or by suggesting how fragmentary statements could have been completed. After the type was set, they proofed the printed text and constructed the book. Over the two generations before and after 1500, Renaissance editors developed the main features of published books today, including pagination and indices (though these appeared in some cases in manuscripts before the arrival of print), footnotes, and cross-references (see Chapter 9).

Among the great print shops of this transitional age was that of Aldo Manuzio (Aldus Manutius, 1449–1515). Born in Rome, Aldo received a basic humanist education and then moved to Venice, where he established his printing shop in 1493. By 1500 it was the most important press in Europe. It was Aldo's ambition to print all of the Latin and Greek texts in clean, accurate, and portable versions, smaller than the standard full-sheet folio editions. By 1515 he had published 130 editions, of which the most important were Greek texts, including a complete edition in five volumes of the works of Aristotle. There were Latin classics, too, and a few contemporary religious and literary works, including the life of the fourteenth-century saint Catherine of Siena (1347–1380; see Chapter 6) and the *Adagia* ("Proverbs") of Desiderius Erasmus (see Chapter 9). Aldo was a major employer of Greek emigré scholars, for whom Venice was a favored refuge, as well as traveling humanists. His household, where many of his assistants boarded with him, was a vital intellectual community whose importance reached far beyond Venice itself.

Textual Scholarship

The close examination of texts had purposes larger than their preparation for print. It raised significant intellectual issues. When, for instance, the Venetian humanist Ermolao Barbaro the Younger addressed the Roman encyclopedist Pliny's works in his *Castigationes plinianae* ("Castigations" or editorial questioning and correction of Pliny), his concerns rose well above the proper spelling of words or naming of flora and fauna. He was in fact on a quest for the author's meaning or intention, something that is very difficult to obtain in literary works, but nonetheless of supreme importance especially in works that convey information and not just authorial opinions.

Humanist historians, too, interrogated a larger body of source materials than had medieval chroniclers. They energetically pursued historical issues such as explanations of city origins and party identifications. The foremost example of this kind of scholar was Lorenzo Valla, whose *De falso credita et ementita Constantini donatione declamatio* ("The Treatise on the Donation of Constantine"), one of the most important literary works of the Italian Renaissance, was a model of historical criticism. In it Valla exposed as a forgery a document that purported to record the gift by the Emperor Constantine to Pope Sylvester I of the central Italian lands, which came to be known as the Papal States, territories under the secular control of the pope. The document was incorporated into the corpus of canon, or church, law in the Middle Ages. It had actually originated centuries later, as Valla showed, pointing to linguistic errors, anachronisms, misreadings of the historical record, and the improbable behavior of key figures. At that time, it was useful to the papacy, isolated and vulnerable, to secure its status by inventing an explanation for the foundation of the church's territorial dominion. Valla's exposure of this forgery embodied the critical spirit of Renaissance thought.

Valla brought the same critical spirit that he brought to the so-called Donation of Constantine to his other scholarly and philosophical works. Valla's use of Epicureanism in his *De voluptate* ("On Pleasure") as a contrast to Stoic concepts of virtue has already been noted. It was inspired by a critical spirit that aimed to probe and question the comfortable assumptions of the age. The same spirit animated his *Adnotationes novi testamenti* ("Notes on the New Testament"), which is a study of the Latin Vulgate, a fourth-century translation of the Bible from the Greek by the saint and scholar Jerome. Using the methods of textual criticism, supported by a thorough knowledge of both Greek and Hebrew, Valla demonstrated that many of Jerome's translations, which had been used and extended by the church over a thousand years to support certain kinds of practice and doctrine, had no basis in the original text. Valla's arguments were later of great interest to the reformers Erasmus and Luther (see Chapter 9).

For some historians, it is the critical spirit that humanist scholars brought to historical, literary, religious, and scientific texts that is the movement's most enduring contribution. Whereas many humanist works are now read only by specialists, their ideas have entered into the mainstream of Western thought, though in a form altered and extended by later thinkers. The critical outlook and scholarly method in which humanist scholars were innovators remains valid and alive to this day.

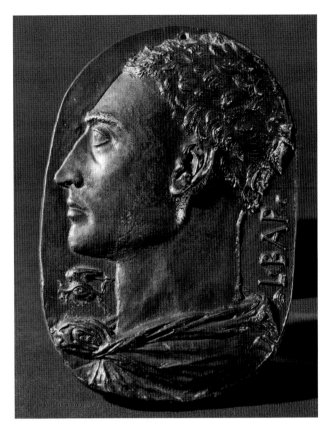

Alberti, *Self-Portrait*, c. 1435, bronze plaque, 7 × 5⅜ in (2.01 × 13.6 cm). National Gallery of Art, Washington, DC.

Alberti modeled himself in profile, an act at once of self-assertion and self-reflection befitting a humanist and leading participant in the exploration of the human condition (see also Chapter 4).

THE SOCIOLOGY OF HUMANISM

The preceding pages have sketched a profile of humanism as the defining intellectual movement of the Renaissance, showing that humanists addressed many social, political, and even economic issues that concerned their contemporaries. The question remains just how humanism related to the society of the Renaissance. This final section considers the occupations filled by humanists, the social backgrounds from which they came, and the social settings in which they gathered to exchange ideas.

Humanists most often held one of three positions: they were secretaries, teachers, or amateurs. The medieval or Renaissance secretary was not a mere clerk or receptionist, but someone who had the special confidence of a superior (a prince, a prelate, or a magistrate) and was responsible for records and correspondence and thus, often, for the rhetorical definition of policy. The origins of humanism, as has been seen, lie in the activity of the secretaries of northern Italian city–states in the age of the commune and popular republic.

In the Renaissance proper, humanists were often employed as the secretaries of city-states and principalities and in the many offices under the papal curia, or court. It has already been noted that among the major humanists were the sequence of the chancellors, or first secretaries, of Florence: Coluccio Salutati, Leonardo Bruni, and Poggio Bracciolini. The Hellenist Francesco Filelfo served as secretary to Visconti and Sforza rulers of Milan, while Lorenzo Valla and Giovanni Pontano (1422–1503) served King Alfonso I the Magnificent of Naples. The need for humanistically trained, trustworthy secretaries was so great that Venice created a special social category for the families who regularly performed this function and a publicly funded school for training their offspring.

The Venetians understood well the relation between education and occupational skills. Once the skills of the humanist came to be prized, it was necessary to train experts who could reproduce those skills by educating each new generation. Pier Paolo Vergerio, Vittorino da Feltre, and Guarino Veronese all performed this task for princely employers. Many more served in public and private schools and as personal tutors in the houses of the wealthy. The associations that young men made at humanist schools often led to lifelong friendships. They reached across the social spectrum, from burgher to prince, and invigorated the society of humanists.

Humanist amateurs include all those for whom humanist studies were a joy and commitment but whose primary occupation was not as a secretary or teacher of humanist skills. There were two main categories of amateurs: clerics, whose primary occupation was as a priest or monk, or, more commonly, bishop of the church and wealthy men, whose primary occupation was to engage in commerce or in public service as a magistrate, ambassador, general, or prince.

That some humanists received wages for their intellectual work whereas others were amateurs already points to the complex sociology of the humanist cohort. Some humanists were the sons of notaries or physicians. Solidly of the middle class, they could hope to find employment as secretaries or teachers. Others were the sons of wealthy merchants, Venetian nobility, or princes. They were more likely to pursue their humanist studies— and many did—as amateurs, while playing a prominent social role.

Clerical humanists in the lower ranks were more likely to be sons of the middle classes. Those holding the titles of bishop or archbishop, abbot or head of a religious order or patriarch, or even cardinal or pope, were likely to come from the higher social strata. There are exceptions even within the papacy. Pope Nicholas V (Tommaso Parentucelli, 1397–1455), humanist scholar and founder of the Vatican Library, was the son of a struggling physician, but his predecessor, Pope Eugene IV (Gabriele Condulmier, 1388–1447), also a humanist and patron of humanists, came from a noble Venetian clan.

The women humanists, like the clerics, might be daughters of humbler men, as were Fedele, a secretary's daughter; Cereta, a merchant's daughter; and Morata, a teacher's daughter. Or they might be daughters of noblemen, as was Nogarola.

Humanists might come from some lower burgher status than those mentioned here, but not one appears to have come from the peasantry. Humanism was a phenomenon of Italy's urban civilization.

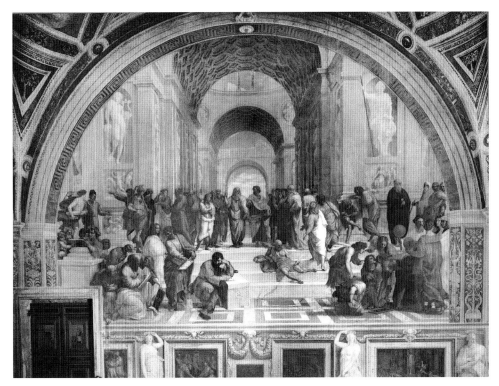

Raphael, *The School of Athens*, 1509–1511 (after restoration), fresco, 16 ft 6 in × 25 ft 3 in (500 cm × 770 cm), Vatican, Rome.

Raphael celebrates the philosophers of all eras and regions in this depiction of a gathering of the wise. Among them are the Athenian philosophers Socrates, Plato, and Aristotle; the ancient sages Pythagoras and Zoroaster; Diogenes the Cynic; and the mathematicians Euclid and Ptolemy. Plato stands at the center, his hand pointing to the heavens as the source of truth; his pupil Aristotle is next to him, reaching out his hand as he considers the moral truths of humankind.

Where did these humanists exchange their ideas? Not, for the most part, in the ivory tower of the universities, which housed the Scholastic philosophers. Nor did they very often do so in the monasteries, although in Italy, both university and monastery were often part of the urban fabric. There were, however, important circles of humanist intellectuals employed by the pope and, to a lesser extent, by cardinals and bishops. These were often visited by a humanist diplomat or emissary who stayed for dinner or for a few days. Humanists also gathered in the courts of the condottiere princes of northern Italy—Urbino, Ferrara, Mantua—and of the grand figures of the Duke of Milan and King of Naples.

In Florence the chancery was the center of humanist exchange, as were also, in the days of Ficino and the Medici, villa retreats outside the walls or urban palaces. In Venice a large number of humanist amateurs among the nobility held humanist gatherings, which the humbler secretaries and physician or clerical amateurs might attend. These, like the Florentine palace and villa retreats, were the model for the academies and **salons** that would form in the sixteenth century. They brought not only humanists together, but with them artists and musicians, poets and playwrights. The humanist movement, however important it was as a source of ideas, was just as important as a spur to other forms of literary and artistic creation.

ALDINE EDITIONS: MEETING PLACE OF MIND, MACHINERY, AND ART

Aldo Manuzio (Aldus Manutius) came to Venice around 1490 with a mission: to use the new technology of the printing press to reproduce in elegant, portable, and inexpensive volumes the classic works of Greek and Roman antiquity. In doing so, he broke new ground in a number of ways.

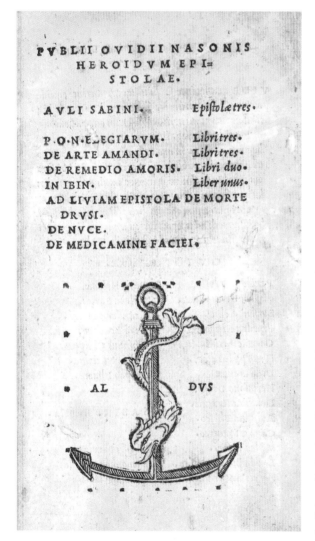

Table of Contents of 1502 edition of Ovid, in original Latin, with Aldine Editions imprint. Harold B. Lee Library, Brigham Young University, Provo, Utah.

First, Aldo's focus on the classics was itself pioneering. He had received a humanist education and was well-known in Italian humanist circles before he migrated from Rome to Venice. Most early printers, in contrast, were craftsmen who did not bring, as Aldo did, an intellectual vision to their work, which consisted largely of reproducing as many copies of the Bible and standard devotional works as possible for the maximum profit. Aldo revolutionized the printing project by grafting onto it the intellectual aims of humanism.

Second, Aldo set a standard of textual editing and production that the best publishers have honored ever since. It had only been recently that the humanists had begun to collate (systematically compare) the medieval manuscripts of ancient texts—these were the only ones that survived—purging the errors that had accumulated through the process of manuscript transmission, when the slip of a pen by a sleepy scribe might be replicated in all later copies born of that original. Now Aldo put these corrected texts into print and hired professionals to prepare others for the press—including Greek scholars who had taken refuge in Italy following the takeover of Constantinople by the Ottoman Turks in 1453.

Third, Aldo developed new, clearer typefaces for his books. The typeface used by the first German printers was the "Gothic" of medieval calligraphers. In Italy, printers sought to establish a typeface that imitated the clearer humanistic hand. Still, in early books, called *incunabula* (cradle-books) because they belonged to the infancy of print, the type was often irregular, and the text itself displayed typographical errors (errors specific to the activity of setting type), such as the transposition of letters. Aldo commissioned a transparently clear roman face as well as an italic that resembled the cursive writing of the best contemporary scribes. Both of these, and their many later variations, are still in use today. In addition, he developed a Greek font for the production of the Greek texts that he made his special goal.

Fourth, Aldo created a new type of book. Most early printed books were large, like the medieval manuscript books that were meant to rest in a single place where the few literate readers might come to consult them. In this new age, however, in addition to monks in their remote libraries and a few university professors, a large audience of middle- and upper-class male and female readers now hungered for books, especially ones that they could carry with them from room to room or while out strolling. So Aldo devised the **octavo** volume, a new format in which the large sheets of paper that were imprinted by the press were folded not just once or twice but three times, to make eight two-sided pages. These smaller, lighter books, with their clear, unburdened type, were ideal for Renaissance readers who consumed many books in rapid succession.

Over the course of his more than 20-year career in Venice, Aldo introduced these innovations as he produced an entire library of ancient and vernacular classics. Of the Roman authors, he published the Epicurean Lucretius, the orator and philosopher Cicero, the poets Ovid and Horace, the general Caesar, and many others. Of the Greeks, he published the entire extant texts of Aristotle (in 1497) and Plato (in 1513). In addition, he made available the epics of Homer and the plays of Sophocles and Euripides. In the Italian vernacular, he published the dream-epic of Francesco Colonna, the *Hypnerotomachia Poliphili* (1499), and the letters of Catherine of Siena, Italy's most important female saint (1500). Of modern works that he published, the most famous was *Adagia* ("Proverbs"), a Latin, edited collection of proverbs with commentary by the learned Netherlander Desiderius Erasmus (see Chapter 9).

Each of Aldo's books after 1502 carried his special colophon (a mark identifying the publisher, placed on the title pages and final pages of printed books). This colophon (seen opposite, which shows the title page of his 1502 edition of Ovid's works) was an arresting image of a dolphin entwined around an anchor. The emblem signified the complementary qualities of tenacity and thoroughness (the anchor) that the printer must employ in constructing a correct and lasting book and the speed and intelligence (the dolphin) that the publisher must possess to understand and evaluate the texts that will be communicated to the public. It also gave graphic expression to Aldo's favorite Roman proverb, *festina lente* (hasten slowly), imitating at once the speedy dolphin and the unmoving anchor.

During the infancy of printing, manuscript books still circulated, and some readers preferred them. They were exquisite handmade products, written specifically for one reader, and decorated with wonderful abstract designs and realistic images, or illuminations. When manuscript readers purchased printed volumes, they often hired professional artists to paint, or illuminate, them. Below is the first page of Aldo's edition of Dante's *Inferno* of 1502, richly illuminated with the famous scene of Dante's encounter with Virgil and three mythological beasts "in the middle of the journey of [his] life."

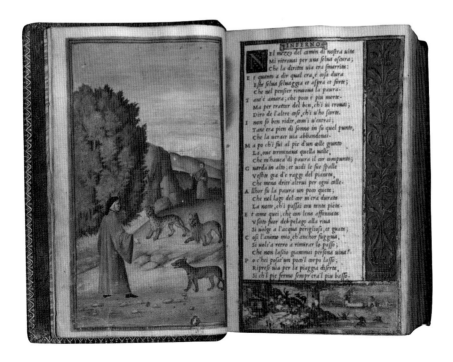

Opening page of Dante's *Inferno*, with illumination, 1502. Newberry Library, Chicago.

CONCLUSION

Humanism was the preeminent intellectual movement of the era. It informed and enlivened all other areas of culture, including the arts and sciences, and even such diverse phenomena as theater and civic processions and the design of weapons and fortifications. It also transformed the way ideas were communicated, introduced principles of scholarly method, and created the school curriculum that would prevail in the West into the nineteenth century.

Like the cities in which it flourished, humanism was ancient in origin. It derived from and was constantly sustained by the legacy of classical literature, primarily Latin, but also Greek. Classical thought lay behind its commitment to the human realm (without discarding the divine), to the active life of the citizen (while still revering the secluded life of the sage or contemplative), and to the force of the will (while still valuing the fruits of the intellect).

Yet Renaissance humanism, while it was part of the "rebirth" that was the Renaissance, was not just about the recovery of the past. It was about innovation that was grounded in the past. Perhaps no illustration of this complex relationship is more powerful than the image of Niccolò Machiavelli (1469–1527; see Chapter 8), politician, statesman, and boundlessly original author, a child of humanism though not himself a humanist, who each evening engaged with the ancients—much as Petrarch corresponded with Cicero. Exchanging his sordid country clothes for the robes of the **courtier**, he retired to his study:

> And in this graver dress I enter the antique courts of the ancients where ... I taste the food that alone is mine, for which I was born. And there I make bold and speak to them and ask the motives of their actions. And they, in their humanity, reply to me. And for the space of four hours I forget the world, remember no vexation, fear poverty no more, tremble no more at death: I am wholly absorbed in them.

> (J.R. Hale, *Machiavelli and Renaissance Italy.* London: English University Presses, 1961, p. 112)

Machiavelli lived in the past, one might say. But that past was not dead, rather, it bounded into the present to live and bear fruit once again in the hands of this man of the Renaissance.

SUGGESTED READINGS

Primary Sources

Cassirer, Ernst, P.O. Kristeller, and J.H. Randall, eds. *The Renaissance Philosophy of Man.* Chicago: University of Chicago Press, 1948. Presents texts by major thinkers on the nature and condition of the human being.

Gordan, Phyllis W., trans. and ed. *Two Renaissance Book Hunters: The Letters of Poggius Bracciolini to Nicolaus de Niccolis*. New York: Columbia University Press, 1974. An exchange of letters between two humanists who recovered and circulated classical texts.

Kallendorf, Craig, trans. and ed. *Humanist Educational Treatises*. Cambridge, MA: Harvard University Press, 2002. A new translation of the treatises originally published by W.H. Woodward in 1897, now definitively superseded. Contains Vergerio's pedagogical treatise *De ingenuis moribus*.

King, Margaret L., trans. and ed. *Renaissance Humanism: An Anthology of Sources*. Cambridge, MA: Hackett, 2014. Traces the humanist recovery of the classical tradition, visions of the self, relations to civic life, the arts, women, science, and global expansion.

King, Margaret L., and Albert Rabil Jr., trans. and ed. *Her Immaculate Hand: Selected Works by and about the Women Humanists of Quattrocento Italy*, 2nd ed. Binghamton, NY: Center for Medieval and Early Renaissance Studies, 1991. A selection of texts giving voice to women's experience.

Kohl, Benjamin, and Ronald Witt, trans. and eds. *The Earthly Republic: Italian Humanists on Government and Society*. Philadelphia: University of Pennsylvania Press, 1978. Selections by major humanists on social and political topics.

Pico della Mirandola, Giovanni. *Oration on the Dignity of Man: A New Translation and Commentary*. Translated with commentary by Francesco Borghesi, Michael Papio, and Massimo Riva. New York: Cambridge University Press, 2012. A new translation and examination of Pico's philosophical ideas.

Valla, Lorenzo. *The Treatise of Lorenzo Valla on the Donation of Constantine*. Translated by C.B. Coleman. New Haven, CT: Yale University Press, 1922. Reprint, Toronto: University of Toronto Press, 1993. A famous debunking of the documentary basis for claims to papal supremacy.

Secondary Sources

Baron, Hans. *The Crisis of the Early Italian Renaissance: Civic Humanism and Republican Liberty in an Age of Classicism and Tyranny*. 2nd ed., 2 vols. Princeton, NJ: Princeton University Press, 1966. Presents the revolutionary theory of "civic humanism."

Celenza, Christopher S. *The Lost Italian Renaissance: Humanists, Historians, and Latin's Legacy*. Baltimore, MD: Johns Hopkins University Press, 2004. Argues that Italian humanism vanishes from memory as modern students, intellectuals, and institutions become unable to understand the Latin-based civilization that was its foundation.

Hankins, James. *Plato in the Italian Renaissance*. 2 vols. Leiden: E.J. Brill, 1990. Discusses the impact of Plato on the Renaissance and subsequent European culture.

Hankins, James, ed. *Renaissance Civic Humanism: Reappraisals and Reflections*. Cambridge: Cambridge University Press, 2000. Important collection of 10 essays updating the discussion of civic humanism since Hans Baron by scholars including Mikael Hörnqvist, Allison Brown, and John Najemy, with an expert overview by Hankins.

Kristeller, Paul Oskar. *Renaissance Thought and Its Sources*. Edited by M. Mooney. New York: Columbia University Press, 1979. One of several essay collections by the most important modern scholar of humanism.

Lowry, M.J.C. *The World of Aldus Manutius: Business and Scholarship in Renaissance Venice*. Ithaca, NY: Cornell University Press, 1979. Studies Aldo's dual commitment to scholarship and the printing enterprise.

Martines, Lauro. *Power and Imagination: City-States in Renaissance Italy*. New York: Alfred A. Knopf, 1979. Reprint, Baltimore, MD: Johns Hopkins University Press, 1988. Links the Renaissance cultural project to the self-interest of Renaissance despots.

Nauert, Charles G. *Humanism and the Culture of Renaissance Europe*. Cambridge: Cambridge University Press, 1995. A thorough synthesis, extending from Italy to northern Europe.

Parker, Holt N. "Women and Humanism: Nine Factors for the Woman Learning." *Viator* 35 (2004): 581–616. Concise and insightful analysis of the preconditions for women's entry into the mainstream of Renaissance humanism.

Thornton, Dora. *The Scholar in His Study: Ownership and Experience in Renaissance Italy*. New Haven, CT: Yale University Press, 1998. Explores the meaning and construction of the private space of the study.

Trinkaus, Charles. *In Our Image and Likeness: Humanity and Divinity in Italian Humanist Thought*. 2 vols. Chicago: University of Chicago Press, 1970. Discusses the humanist concept of the individual in relation to God, exploding the notion of a "pagan" Renaissance.

Witt, Ronald G. *In the Footsteps of the Ancients: The Origins of Humanism from Lovato to Bruni*. Leiden and Boston: E.J. Brill, 2000. A reconceptualization of the early origins of humanism in the study of classical philology.

FOUR

NEW VISIONS (c. 1350–c. 1530)

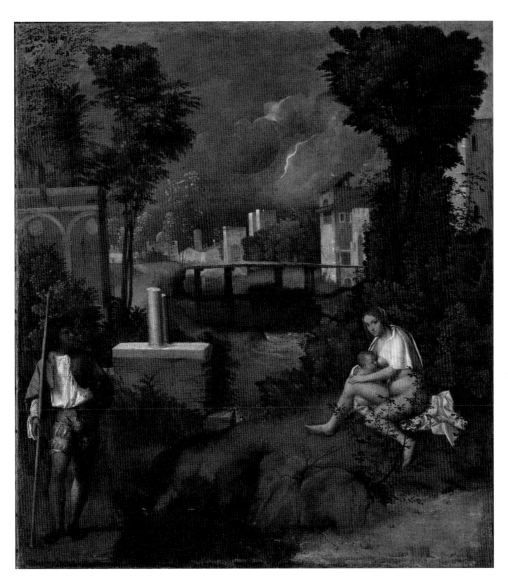

Giorgione, *La Tempesta* (detail), c. 1505–1510, oil on canvas, 32½ × 28¼ in (82 × 73 cm). Galleria dell'Accademia, Venice.

By the High Renaissance, the lessons of perspective and drawing have been fully absorbed, and in the case of this Venetian masterpiece, the standard themes of Renaissance painting have been discarded. Here subjects are not a crucified Christ or devoted Madonna but human relationships and the powerful moods of nature.

In 1401 Filippo Brunelleschi (1377–1446) lost a contest to his chief rival Lorenzo Ghiberti (1378–1455). Both artists had created a bronze plaque to be judged in a competition, depicting in relief that moment when Abraham's hand was held from sacrificing his own son in a test of his obedience to God. Both plaques, in different ways, were brilliant interpretations of great emotional depth that announced the coming of a new age in art. The winner, Ghiberti, stayed in Florence to design the north and east doors of the baptistry, the commission that was the reward for his victory. Brunelleschi, disgruntled, set out with his friend Donatello (1386–1466) for Rome. The sixteenth-century painter and biographer of the great artists of the Renaissance, Giorgio Vasari (1511–1574), reports what happened there.

> And when [Filippo] came to Rome, and saw the grandeur of the buildings and the perfection of the form of the temples, he remained lost in thought and like one out of his mind; and he and Donatello set themselves to measure them and to draw out the plan of them, sparing neither time nor expense. And Filippo gave himself up to the study of them, so that he cared neither to eat or to sleep … [and] gave himself no rest until he had considered all the difficulties of the Pantheon … and if by chance they found any pieces of capitals or columns they set to work and had them dug out. And the story ran through Rome that they were "treasure seekers," the people thinking that they studied divination [fortune-telling] to find treasures, it having befallen them once to find an ancient pitcher filled with medals.
>
> (Giorgio Vasari, *Lives of the Artists*, trans. and ed. E.L. Seeley. New York: Farrar, Strauss and Cudahy, 1957, pp. 58–59)

They were treasure seekers indeed. For with the new eyes of the artist of fifteenth-century Italy, they encountered the ruins of Rome that had stood for more than 1,000 years without imitators. By identifying, measuring, and sketching them, they sought to bring them to life again—much as the humanists had sought to restore to life, by new, insightful reading, the classics of Greece and Rome. Like the humanists, the artists of the Renaissance brought about a revolution, creating new visions of form and space unprecedented in any human civilization. Their innovations would establish the pattern of Western art into the last years of the nineteenth century.

This revolution in art unfolded over 200 years, if the early contributions of Giotto are included (see Chapter 2). Beginning about 1400, a new generation resumed his interrupted legacy of innovation. Thenceforth, in little more than a century, Italian artists crafted a distinctively Renaissance style centered on the human form displayed in three-dimensional space. They developed the technique of **perspective** that permits the representation of three-dimensional objects on two-dimensional planes and creates an ideal and abstract universe for the depiction of form. They rediscovered the portrait as an artistic form, exploring the psychology of human individuals as they served the powerful whose palaces they built, whose walls they adorned, and whose rooms they filled with beautiful things.

Meanwhile, artists themselves won status and prestige as mind and talent were recognized as key elements in the construction of culture. Artists vied, too, with and for the patrons, whose personal ambitions and wealth determined what was painted, sculpted, or built almost as much as did the creators of those products: for Renaissance art was a social product. It emerged from the inspired minds and hands of great artists; from the urban context of central and northern Italy; from the wealth generated by merchants and bankers; and from the religious and intellectual aspirations of the people.

This chapter begins by describing the breakthroughs of the fifteenth century that created a distinctly new Renaissance style. It considers the art and science of perspective, which permitted Renaissance artists to represent three-dimensional space. Turning to the social world, the text considers the forms and effects of patronage and the architectural and urban designs that were influenced by the new Renaissance style. The chapter examines how art intersected with the conceptualization of the human condition, as seen in portraiture, and with daily life, and how the role of the artist evolved. It concludes with a consideration of High Renaissance style, the culmination of the Renaissance artistic achievement.

BREAKTHROUGHS IN STYLE

In the early 1400s in Florence, startling new developments in sculpture, architecture, and painting marked the emergence of Renaissance style. The classical approach introduced by innovators like Brunelleschi and Donatello, contemporaneous with the reinvigorated classicism of **quattrocento** humanism (see Chapter 3), merged with the contemporaneous trend toward spatial and psychological realism introduced during Italy's republican age.

One of the first expressions of the new Renaissance style was the pair of bronze plaques submitted for a competition in 1401. The contest was run by the Calimala, or wool cloth refinishing guild. The guild had been given special responsibility for the embellishment of the city baptistry adjoining the cathedral. The Baptistry, a major public shrine built in honor of the city's patron saint John the Baptist, was a magnificent **Romanesque** structure of the eleventh century. It was so classical in its elements that the Florentines themselves believed it was ancient. Its domed ceiling had been decorated by Byzantine mosaicists when that art form was at its peak in Italy. The interior space was sumptuous and solemn, glittering figures lifted above by supports of massive piers, columns, and arches.

The 1401 contest was held to select the artist to be charged with the casting of two bronze doors for this gemlike building. Each competitor was to submit a sample bronze relief plaque depicting Abraham's sacrifice of Isaac, to be judged by a jury of experts. Those submitted by Brunelleschi and Ghiberti were both gloriously original, breathing a fresh inspiration not known since the days of Giotto.

What is this scene that is presented in so new and gripping a way? The plaques depict the moment when the patriarch Abraham, poised to slay his young and long-awaited

1400–1449

1401	Lorenzo Ghiberti wins contest to design bronze doors for Florence's Baptistry.
1416	Vitruvius's *De architectura* ("On Architecture"), first-century architectural treatise, is rediscovered.
1416	Donatello completes a statue of St. George for Orsanmichele, Florence.
1421	Brunelleschi begins work on San Lorenzo Basilica, Florence.
1427	Masaccio completes frescoes of the Brancacci Chapel, Florence.
1429	Brunelleschi begins work on the Pazzi Chapel, Florence.
c. 1430	Donatello creates *David*, the first nude statue in Christian Europe.
c. 1430	Birth of the Venetian Giovanni Bellini.
1432	Paolo Uccello explores striking perspective effects in the *Battle of San Romano*.
1434–1464	Cosimo de' Medici rules Florence, which becomes the leading Italian center for art.
1435	Leon Battista Alberti publishes *Della pittura* ("On Painting"), giving the first theoretical explanation of linear perspective.
1444–1482	Federico da Montefeltro is Duke of Urbino, a major art patron.
1445	Donatello begins his equestrian statue of Venetian condottiere Gattamelata.

1450–1499

1450	Alberti's treatise *De re aedificatoria* ("On Architecture") appears.
1452	Ghiberti completes the East Door of the Florence Baptistry.
c. 1455	Piero della Francesca paints *The Flagellation of Christ*.
1464	Antonio Filarete's *Treatise on Architecture* includes a plan for an ideal symmetrically designed city.
c. 1465	Piero della Francesca paints twin portraits of Federico da Montefeltro and his wife Battista Sforza.

1467	The dome of the Cathedral of Florence, designed by Brunelleschi, is completed.
1471–1484	Pope Sixtus IV spends lavishly to beautify Rome; the Sistine Chapel is built.
1474	Birth of Isabella d'Este, one of the great art patrons and collectors.
1482	Leonardo da Vinci joins the court of Ludovico Sforza, Milan.
c. 1485	Sandro Botticelli paints his allegorical work *The Birth of Venus*.
1486	The first printed edition of Vitruvius's *De architectura* ("On Architecture") appears.
1498	Leonardo da Vinci completes *The Last Supper*.

1500–1530

1501	Michelangelo creates his monumental nude sculpture of *David*.
1503	Leonardo da Vinci paints *Mona Lisa*.
1503–1513	Julius II is pope, commissions Raphael, Michelangelo, and others.
1505	Michelangelo moves to Rome to create a tomb for Julius II.
1506	Donato Bramante is commissioned to design and build the new St. Peter's Basilica, Rome.
1508	Birth of architect Andrea Palladio, future creator of the Palladian style.
c. 1508	Leonardo da Vinci paints *Virgin on the Rocks*.
1508–1512	Michelangelo paints the Sistine Chapel ceiling, Rome.
1509	Raphael is engaged to decorate Vatican rooms with frescoes.
c. 1505–1510	Venetian painter Giorgione completes *The Tempest*.
1516	Leonardo da Vinci moves to France, invited by King Francis I.
1518	Titian completes *Assumption of the Virgin* in the Basilica of the Frari, Venice.
1519	Death of Leonardo da Vinci.
1520	Death of Raphael.
1521	Michelangelo begins work on the Medici tombs, Florence.

son, is told by an angel that having proved his faith in God, he may desist, and instead, slay a ram who at that moment stirs in the bushes. Brunelleschi's Isaac expresses both horror and pain in the sharp angles of his body as he kneels to receive his father's fearsome blow. Ghiberti's Isaac, his chest swelling with pride and determination, sways slightly toward Abraham, defying him to strike. These are intense, probing examinations of a human confrontation on a matter of central importance to humankind. Both panels coax their representations of flesh, muscle, and bone to display the psychological condition of the figure portrayed.

The judges chose Ghiberti, who was then commissioned to design the north doors of the Baptistry. Completed in 1424, the north doors narrated in a fresh and vivid style stories from the New Testament, each embedded in quatrefoil frames (square with rounded corners). The following year, Ghiberti was commissioned to do a second set of doors—the east doors, later dubbed the Gates of Paradise, which tourists today crowd to see. The Gates of Paradise, with their freely conceived scenes of biblical stories and released from the quatrefoil frames of the earlier doors, announced to all that the Renaissance of the arts had arrived in Florence.

Enraged by his defeat, Brunelleschi turned his attention to architecture, employing classical forms and proportions in the renovation of old buildings and the construction of new ones. His design of a dome for the Cathedral of Florence, left unfinished in 1418 after more than a century of construction, was his most daring venture and shows how he profited from his study of ancient monuments. However, he incorporated more obvious classicizing elements in his designs for other buildings such as the Churches of San Spirito and San Lorenzo and the Pazzi Chapel (see p. 128).

While Brunelleschi revised quattrocento structures in a classical language, his friend Donatello brought his experience of Roman forms to a variety of sculptural projects. His life-sized marble statue of St. George on the facade of Orsanmichele (in Donatello's time the common hall of several guilds) is a boldly original figure. Not a knightly dragon-slayer, Donatello's George is classical in form and profoundly thoughtful—whatever he will do, he will have understood fully the meaning and consequences of his action. Here the new Renaissance classicism is married again to humanistic psychology.

The representation of the human figure and personality was significantly advanced in the medium of painting, the medium in which Giotto had first represented conscious, feeling, human forms set in a space defined by architectural structures. In the early quattrocento, the Florentine painter known as Masaccio (Tommaso di Giovanni di Simone

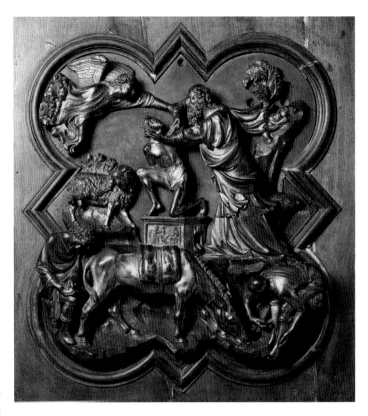

Brunelleschi, *Sacrifice of Isaac,* **1401–1403, competition panel, gilded bronze, 18 × 15 in (45 × 38 cm). Florence Baptistry doors, Museo Nazionale del Bargello, Florence.**

The anguish that Brunelleschi's Isaac experiences as his father's knife surges forward is expressed in the sharp angles of his limbs and the twisting of neck and body. Brunelleschi highlights the violence and fear inherent in this momentous drama.

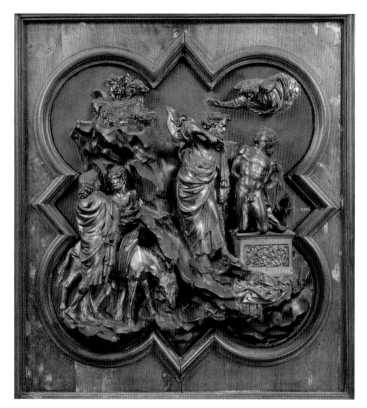

Ghiberti, *Sacrifice of Isaac*, 1401–1403, competition panel, gilded bronze, 18 × 15 in (45 × 38 cm). Florence Baptistry doors, Museo Nazionale del Bargello, Florence.

Ghiberti's Isaac is lyrically graceful, withdrawing from the knife in his father's hand even as his chest swells defiantly. The effect is profound harmony, because God will intervene in the end.

Guidi, 1401–1428) developed Giotto's legacies. His human figures in representations of biblical scenes or theological concepts were full-scale adults, in the most striking cases rendered nude, conveying power in form and meaning. Masaccio's rendition of Adam and Eve as they are expelled from Paradise (one of a series of frescoes in the Brancacci Chapel, Church of Santa Maria del Carmine, Florence) is a compelling and unusual depiction of despair— Eve looks up to God as though to ask guidance, while Adam covers his eyes and bends his head as though in painful meditation on the meaning of his disobedience. Masaccio's representation of the three persons of the Holy Trinity is awesome even as it is intensely human. A burly, nude Christ, flanked by saints and donors (one of whom points significantly to the trio), with the hovering dove of the Holy Spirit above his head is presented to view by the majestic, omnipotent Father.

By the 1420s Renaissance style had made its appearance and had established a new standard for European art. Artists would bring the new vision primarily developed in Florence to other Italian cities and ultimately to courts and cities throughout Europe. Henceforth, and until Romanticism and impressionism in later centuries introduced a new artistic language, the norms of Renaissance style would be authoritative in the Western world. In painting and sculpture, human figures would inhabit three-dimensional space and would be expressive both in their posture and in their facial expression. These art forms, and architecture as well, would draw their formal vocabulary from Roman prototypes and would achieve the kind of harmony in composition and structure that the ancients also modeled. Like the humanists, the artists of the early Renaissance were engaged in the recovery or rediscovery of antiquity, but even more, in the creation of a new vision beyond the horizon of the ancient models they pursued.

PERSPECTIVE: THE ARTFUL CONSTRUCTION OF REALITY

The visually powerful human forms that Renaissance artists created inhabited space—or so it seemed. That observed space was deeper than the boxlike cavities that Giotto had created by propping up a mountain here, a wall there, to give the illusion of recession into a distance behind the pictorial frame. How did artists of the Renaissance utilize perspective to create the illusion of lifelike space, as large as the space in an assembly room or a town square? Why did they want to do so? Were they eager to depict reality as they actually saw it? Or perhaps they wished to control the world or define a new one by mapping and enclosing space?

Whatever their motivations, Renaissance artists learned to break through the two-dimensional plane of the painted or sculpted surface, and imaginatively penetrated the third dimension extended behind it. Their three-dimensional representations of reality, so much closer to reality than the abstractions of medieval art, would be the norm until modern artists rediscovered the possibilities of the plane at the turn of the twentieth century.

Brunelleschi was the first artist known to systematically study the way a three-dimensional object appeared to the eye so that it could be reduced on a two-dimensional surface. Obtaining a reflection of the Florentine Baptistry on a flat mirror, from which he could paint the three-dimensional object, he was able to analyze the forms mathematically. He identified the **vanishing point**, the furthest point of convergence of the main lines of the image and through this point constructed the horizontal line that would be the horizon of the painting. All other lines formed rational relationships to the horizon. Brunelleschi had replicated not only how the building looked to him but the actual lines possessed both by the structure, as viewed by the human eye, and the image based upon it, in their necessary and logical relation to each other.

Brunelleschi used this new understanding in his own designs for architectural projects. His contemporary Masaccio also used it in painting. He did so, for instance, in his famous *Trinità* (see p. 123), where the lines of the barrel vault (arched ceiling forms bridging wall or column supports) depicted over the heads of Jesus and the Father converge toward a vanishing point and lend the illusion of deep space to what might otherwise be a flat representation.

The humanist and artist Leon Battista Alberti (1404–1472) systematized Brunelleschi's insights by constructing a rational, mathematically defined spatial grid that could be used for any image. Alberti's treatise *Della pittura* ("On Painting") of 1435 is in fact a treatise on perspective, designed to give basic instruction in the skill to semi-learned artists. Alberti wrote in humanist Latin style, but he also simultaneously published the work in the far more accessible Italian. He instructs his readers to imagine lines, representing optical information, extending from their eyes to all the objects in their field of vision, which he defined as pyramidal in shape. He encourages the artist to grasp this abstract and difficult concept as the necessary preparation for representing three-dimensional objects on a plane:

> Here I have related only the basic instructions of the art … which will give the untrained painter the first fundamentals of how to paint well. These instructions are of such a nature that [any painter] who really understands them well both by his intellect and by his comprehension of the definition of painting will realize how useful they are. Never let it be supposed that anyone can be a good painter if he does not clearly understand what he is attempting to do…. I hope the reader will agree that the best artist can only be one who has learned to understand the outline of

the plane and all its qualities…. There remains to teach the painter how to follow with his hand what he has learned with his mind.

(L.B. Alberti, On Painting, trans. and ed. J.R. Spencer. New Haven, CT: Yale University Press, 1956, p. 59)

With Brunelleschi, Masaccio, and Alberti having shown the way, Italian artists now regularly incorporated the principles of perspective into their compositions. Two quattrocento artists continued to experiment with optical phenomena, testing the principles of perspective in actual works of art. Paolo Uccello (1397–1475), in a bravado sequence of three canvases depicting different phases of the Battle of San Romano of 1432, took advantage of his subject matter to explore perspective effects. The bodies of the horses, the riders' lances and helmets, the corpses of the fallen, and the orange-studded trees in the background are all scattered about along the lines of the perspectival grid. The chaos of battle became a playground for receding diagonals en route to their vanishing point.

More soberly, Piero della Francesca (c. 1420–1492) explored the expressive possibilities of perspective in his rendition of the *Flagellation of Christ* (c. 1455; see p. 125). The painting is divided into two spatial zones, each defined by architectural and decorative elements. At left to the rear, in a space partly enclosed by classical architectural forms, Christ is mocked and beaten by the soldiers. To the foreground on the right, in the open and standing on a tiled pavement whose joint lines recede toward the vanishing point, are three mysterious gentlemen—aloof, perhaps unknowing, perhaps unconcerned. The spatial arrangement is not just a decorative flourish in a serious religious scene. It adds to the painting's meaning: Jesus' humiliation occurred within the framework of civic life as human bystanders pursued their business while the supreme drama unfolded.

Like the humanists, Renaissance artists looked back to antiquity for models of form. Like them, too, artists were entirely modern creators of a new reality, a reality that dwelled so clearly in the mind that it became possible to depict it on an abstract and pristine surface.

PATRONAGE AND PATRONS

During the Middle Ages, most artists were anonymous, and they were paid mostly by some agency of the church. That pattern changed in Italy during the republican age. Giotto, of course, was highly acclaimed during his lifetime; the names of his predecessors, competitors, and students were also known to the public. Nor did Giotto work only for the church. He spent four years at the court of Naples in the employment of King Robert d'Anjou (r. 1309–1313). He painted the Scrovegni Chapel frescoes for a private citizen and designed the Campanile adjoining the Cathedral for the city of Florence. Just as Giotto was a forerunner of Renaissance artistic style, his career illustrated a new pattern in the social organization of art that crystallized during the Renaissance.

The proliferation of institutions in republican Italy and the opportunities for personal endeavor and advancement were the setting for a different kind of art market. In this market, artists competed to interest the most wealthy purchasers of art. At the same time, buyers of artistic works, whether corporate or individual, ecclesiastical or lay, competed for the best, the cheapest, the most efficient, or the most cooperative artists. Art, like fine wool cloth or well-tempered steel, was bought and sold. Here we discuss the buyers, or patrons, of art.

Types of Patronage

From the earliest stages of the Italian Renaissance until modern times, patronage would be the crucial engine of artistic production and innovation. The term "patronage" comprehended a range of relationships between the art provider and the art buyer. The artist might produce works in his shop with no particular buyer in mind. He would then sell to whichever customer, or patron, admired and desired the work. Alternatively, the buyer would commission a particular work. In that case, a contract might specify materials, dimensions, details of the theme or composition, and date of delivery. In the case of very wealthy consumers of art, the artist might live in the patron's household, executing for a fee any and all projects as required. Most of the great works of Renaissance art were occasioned by the second or third of these forms of patronage.

Corporations, either secular or ecclesiastical, commissioned and paid for many of the early works of Renaissance art. Florentine public commissions oversaw the construction of the building project that sliced through the center of the city along the Via dei Calzaiuoli: the Cathedral complex, the Loggia dei Lanzi, and the Palazzo della Signoria. Similarly, commissions enabled the completion of Siena's coordinated cathedral and *campo* (main square) complexes. In Rome a series of popes supervised the reconstruction of the city that culminated in a reinvigorated Vatican complex. Guilds, too, were active commissioners of art. The bronze doors of the Florence Baptistry, as has been seen, were the special project of the Calimala guild. The wholly voluntary organizations called confraternities commissioned artwork as well, such as the *Virgin of the Rocks* that Leonardo da Vinci painted for the **confraternity** of the Conception of the Virgin in Milan. In Venice, where the state and state-linked churches were the main purchasers of art, the charitable organizations called *scuole* were also major patrons.

Increasingly, however, wealthy individuals became major patrons of art. Enrico Scrovegni enlisted Giotto to **fresco** the walls of his chapel in Padua, while Felice Brancacci of Florence commissioned Masaccio's workshop to paint his private chapel in the Church of the Carmini. In Venice, private individuals hired architects to build their splendid palaces—40 along the Grand Canal in the fifteenth century alone. Venetian individuals commissioned tombs and chapels to line the walls of the nave (long central portion) of churches, although the most elaborate tombs were those of the city's doges. In Rome, likewise, the cardinals of the church hired painters and sculptors to adorn their residences.

NEW VISIONS: SEEING IN PERSPECTIVE

The charming figures who inhabit the landscape of Giotto's magic world (see Chapter 2, pp. 59–60) seem to stand, bend, and rotate in space. The stubby rocks and mountains of rural scenes and the stage-set huts and palaces of urban ones, insisted on and delineated space. That appearance of space was new.

What Giotto achieved by suggestion, the artists of the full Renaissance learned to depict accurately and systematically through the method of linear perspective. Why and how did they do so?

Why? They wanted to depict on flat wall, panel, or canvas a world that looked as much as possible like the world that they encountered when they walked through their cities or the neighboring countryside, in much the same way that they wanted the human figures they portrayed to appear to have real faces and bodies. They craved realism: psychological realism in the representation of human subjects, spatial realism in the representation of their world. They produced this illusion of the real by investigating how the eye saw and then devised a regular, replicable system for duplicating its action on a plane surface.

Following up on early experimentation by Brunelleschi (see pp. 119–120), Leon Battista Alberti constructed a practical guide for the painter that explained how this could be done. In his *Della pittura* ("On Painting") of 1435–1436, circulated in Italian, as well as in Latin (*De pictura*), for an audience of practitioners, he describes how what the eye sees is a succession of points and lines constituting a plane—and is thus similar to the surface that the artist must paint:

> I say, first of all, we ought to know that a point is a figure which cannot be divided into parts. I call a figure here anything located on a plane so the eye can see it. No one would deny that the painter has nothing to do with things that are not visible. The painter is concerned solely with representing what can be seen. These points, if they are joined one to the other in a row, will form a line…. More lines, like threads woven together in a cloth, make a plane.
>
> (*Alberti*, On Painting, *pp. 43–44*)

From the eye, visual rays extend to the outer limits of the plane and to all the points within that outline.

> We can imagine those rays to be like the finest hairs of the head, or like a bundle, tightly bound within the eye where the sense of sight has its seat. The rays, gathered together within the eye, are like a stalk; the eye is like a bud which extends its shoots rapidly and in a straight line on the plane opposite.
>
> (*Alberti*, On Painting, *p. 46*)

The figure formed by the eye, the plane, and the rays connecting them create a "visual pyramid."

> The extrinsic rays, thus encircling the plane—one touching the other—enclose all the plane like the willow wands of a basket-cage, and make, as is said, this visual pyramid. It is time for me to describe what this pyramid is and how it is constructed by these rays…. The pyramid is a figure of a body from whose base straight lines are drawn upward, terminating in a single point. The base of this pyramid is a plane which is seen. The sides of the pyramid are those rays which I have called extrinsic. The cuspid, that is the point of the pyramid, is located within the eye.
>
> (*Alberti*, On Painting, *pp. 47–48*)

The artist-observer, looking out at the world of forms, will see many different planes at once (at the base of many different visual pyramids), each shaded distinctively by color and light. In representing objects, they must in his mind focus on the plane—the cross-section of the visual pyramid—in which they sit. They will appear smaller if they are farther away, larger if near. How large and how small depends on the grid the artist draws based on lines radiating from the "centric," or vanishing, point (where all the lines of vision will converge) to points on the base line of the surface to be painted.

> First of all about where I draw. I inscribe a quadrangle of right angles, as large as I wish, which is considered to be an open window through which I see what I want to paint. Here I determine as it pleases me the size of the men in my picture. I divide the length of this man in three parts. These parts to me are proportional to that measurement called a *braccio*, for, in measuring the average man it is seen that he is about three *braccia*. With these *braccia* I divide the base line of the rectangle into as many parts as it will receive…. Then, within this quadrangle, where it seems best to me, I make a

point which occupies that place where the central ray [from the eye to the plane] strikes. For this it is called the centric point…. The centric point being located … I draw straight lines from it to each division placed on the base line of the quadrangle. These drawn lines, [extended] as if to infinity, demonstrate to me how each transverse quantity is altered visually.

(*Alberti*, On Painting, *p. 56*)

The grid of lines that Alberti has the artist construct on the paintable surface mimics the patterns of rays that reach from the eye to the perceived plane. It is an artificial device, but it is grounded in nature. It creates a controlled and artificial world in which spatial relations and drawn forms appear as much as possible to resemble those observed in the real universe perceived by the eye.

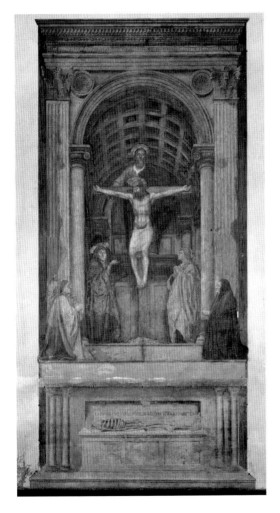 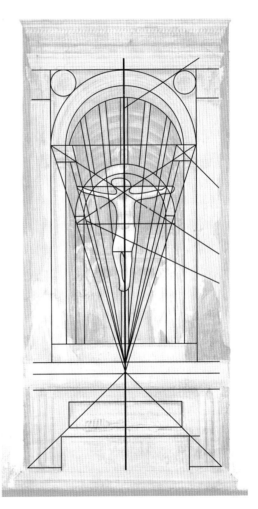

(left) Masaccio, *Trinità*, 1425, fresco detached from wall, 21 ft 10⅝ in × 10 ft 4¾ in (6.6 × 3.1 m). Santa Maria Novella, Florence.
(right) Perspective lines of Masaccio's *Trinità*.

Masaccio's *Trinità* (Trinity)—God the Father behind the crucified Jesus with the white dove of the Holy Spirit between their heads—derives much of its power from the use of perspective. The lines on the barrel vault of the architectural space that the figures inhabit recede toward a vanishing point behind Christ's head, the composition's central point. Christ's body functions as a geometrical figure inscribed in a triangle formed by extending lines from below the vertical of the cross to the two anterior column capitals of the architectural frame.

Florence and Milan

The patriarchs of the Medici family, effectively the rulers of Florence from 1433 to 1494, were the most important patrons of art in the Italian Renaissance, together accounting for nearly half of all art commissioned in that era. They required artists to paint the walls and ceilings of their palaces and villas as well as free-standing canvases for display in those buildings and to design the church they attended and their private family chapel. Whereas the Medici formed an unofficial principate, the Sforza dukes of Milan were true despots. The self-made prince Francesco Sforza, who seized the city in 1450, fostered the short-lived dynasty that ruled until 1499. The Sforza were lavish in their spending on artists as well as humanist apologists, managers of their stables and kennels, jewelers, and engineers. It was Ludovico Sforza (r. 1494–1499) who hired Leonardo da Vinci to profit from that genius's multiple talents in the visual arts, set design, and military engineering (see p. 125).

Sforza munificence had one driving motivation: the quest for status. It was this same force that drove private patrons in Florence and Venice. But for the dukes of Milan, it rose to a hectic pitch. This dynasty had seized the throne, and in the political context of Europe, where sovereignty derived from dynastic right, their right to rule was precarious. Cadres of humanists and artists labored to establish the legitimacy of their regime. The same need for legitimacy inspired the lavish spending of Alfonso I, King of Naples (who had seized his throne from the heir named by the previous ruler). His richly furnished, newly built castle became the scene for lavish musical performances and the home of a team of humanist propagandists.

Ferrara, Mantua, and Urbino

The same need to establish their legitimacy inspired the efforts of the condottieri princes of the tiny cities of Ferrara, Mantua, and Urbino. Simultaneously, they performed the roles of mercenary captains and noble patrons, creating courts that were centers of Renaissance culture and a magnet for artistic and literary talent. The Este dukes of Ferrara, who established a humanist school and supported a university, renovated their villas and built a new palace whose Sala dei Mesi (Hall of the Months) reflected like a mirror the ideal world of the court and its ruler. The rulers of Mantua (who had also launched a humanist school) had their palace walls adorned by Antonio Pisanello (1395–1455) with frescoes asserting their claim to descent from King Arthur of the Round Table. Isabella d'Este (1474–1539), the consort of ruler Francesco Gonzaga (r. 1484–1519), became one of Italy's most important patrons—the only one, equipped with a literary advisor, who minutely prescribed the content of her artistic projects.

Celebrated in the portrait he commissioned from Piero della Francesca, Federico da Montefeltro (r. 1444–1482) reconstructed his little state of Urbino as a center of arts and learning. Trained in the humanist school of Vittorino da Feltre in Mantua, this burly soldier was a lover of books. By 1482 he had amassed a library of 1,100 books, many bound

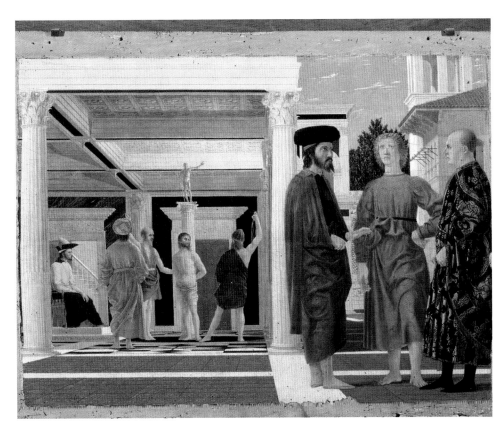

Piero della Francesca, *The Flagellation of Christ*, c. 1455, oil and tempera on panel, 23⅛ × 32¼ in (58.4 × 81.5 cm). Galleria Nazionale delle Marche, Urbino.

A study in perspective, a study in contrasts, a spiritual statement—*The Flagellation of Christ* is a complex and elusive image. While three gentlemen, dressed in Turkish, Greek, and contemporary Italian styles, converse in the foreground, Christ suffers in the background. Yet his ultimate victory is signaled by his association with the perfect mass of a column and the triumphant figure atop it.

in gold or silver. He retired to read them in his personal study or *studiolo*, one of those intimate spaces that marked the first steps toward a modern consciousness of privacy (see Chapter 3, Focus: Personal Space). When not in retirement, he roamed a palace constructed at his direction under architect Francesco Laurana (c. 1430–c. 1502), which was stuffed with art objects, musical instruments, tapestries, and fine furniture.

Music

The princely courts were also the main promoters in Italy of new developments in music. Burgundy and Flanders, not Italy, were the regions which saw the birth of Renaissance musical forms—vocal and instrumental **polyphony**, based originally on church plain-song or popular melodic themes—in the first half of the fifteenth century. But by the last decades of the fifteenth century, the Italian courts supported a staff of musicians. Both vocalists and instrumentalists, they entertained the prince's followers, provided music for dancing, or performed the solemn masses of church festivals or special occasions, such as the entry of an important personage, a wedding, or a victory. The princes of the church—the pope and the cardinals—also supported a musical staff as the music performed in the great churches gradually became transformed by the innovations that derived from experiments in secular genres. This music was accompanied by the organ, which became established in most large European churches from the fifteenth century. Meanwhile, music performance also became part of family life. The ability to sing and to play an instrument, especially the lute, was widespread among the educated, who often spent their evenings in group music-making.

ARCHITECTURE AND URBANISM

The greatest patrons of Renaissance art were arguably as much the creators of its splendid products as were the artists themselves. They were also the motivating force behind the great architectural projects of the age. Buildings define a civilization. The castles of the medieval countryside and cathedrals of medieval cities were the characteristic monuments of the age. In the Italian Renaissance, fortified towers (both of the nobility and the state) clustered around cathedral bell-towers while amid them were the urban buildings that testified to the achievements of their citizens: arcaded market places, hospitals, guildhalls. Those built during the full flowering of the Renaissance, beginning soon after 1400, displayed classical features as part of a larger project of the emulation of ancient civilization.

The Rediscovery of Classical Architecture

Italian architecture was unique in Europe in that its forms continued the traditions of antiquity without a break. Roman structures—some intact, some in ruins—remained in evidence everywhere. Large sections of Italy, moreover, had for centuries been under Byzantine overlordship, especially on the Adriatic coast and in the south. Byzantine style, which had developed from the ancient Roman style, retained the round arches and domes and other key features of classical architecture. Even before the Renaissance, therefore, Italian buildings were markedly different in form from those of the French, English, and German lands. That difference was further accentuated because the Italians built in brick, with touches of stone, marble, or mosaic for contrast, while the northerners built in stone. Even when Italy belatedly picked up the keynotes of Gothic style in the thirteenth century—ogival or peaked arches and vaults—they interpreted these in the framework of the classical patterns they never abandoned. In Italy the solid wall and the horizontal line never gave way to the pierced and windowed walls and heady verticals of northern Gothic style. An example of Italy's stubborn adherence to Roman patterns is seen in the Loggia dei Lanzi in Florence. It is a graceful Gothic structure, built in 1376–1382, but its arches are rounded. The advent of Gothic style enlivened but did not disturb the Italian classical tradition in architecture.

Nevertheless, although the classical style was well-established in Italy before the Renaissance, Renaissance theorists and working architects intensified this classicism in

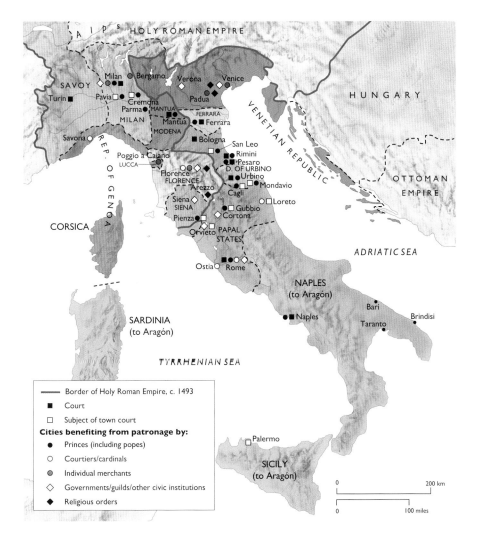

many new buildings that enriched the age. The theoretical exploration of architecture began with the rediscovery and careful study of the most important Roman treatise on the subject Vitruvius' *De architectura* ("On Architecture"), written about 27 CE and recovered in 1416. Vitruvius, in turn, influenced Italian theorists over the next 150 years. That sequence began with Leon Battista Alberti, whose theoretical work on painting and perspective has already been noted. Alberti's *De re aedificatoria* ("On Architecture"), written about 1450, was based solidly on Vitruvius. So was the *Trattato d'architettura* ("Treatise on Architecture"), composed about ten years later by Filarete (Antonio Alverlino, c. 1400–1469), as well as Sebastiano Serlio's (1475–1554) immense multi-volumed treatise *Tutte l'opere d'architettura, et prospetiva* ("Complete Works on Architecture and Perspective"), published between 1537 and 1575. In addition to these contemporary works, Vitruvius was printed in 1486

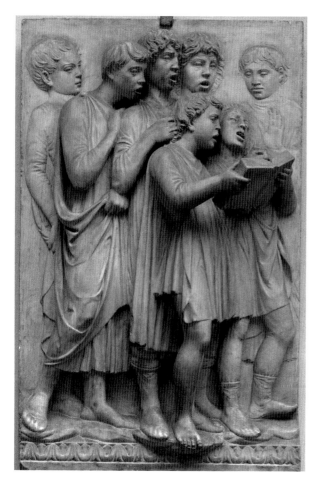

Luca della Robbia, *Cantoria* (detail), 1434, marble. Museo dell'Opera del Duomo, Florence.

A detail from one of the reliefs on the Cantoria (singing gallery), sculpted for the Cathedral of Florence, shows children and adolescents gathered around a single copy of music and singing lustily—one of the few representations of musical participation from this period.

in the original Latin and thereafter in translation in several modern languages.

This theoretical literature has in common a commitment to the Roman model in architecture. It accepts the models of classical form defined by the style of decoration of column capitals and by such structures as Roman triumphal arches, basilicas, and domes. It assumes that the harmony of the building is of crucial importance and that elements in simple geometrical proportions to each other will create this harmony. It anchors that idea of proportionality in the original relationship between the human body and the simplest hypothetical human dwelling. These principles of classical architecture remained dominant until the middle of the sixteenth century and governed the design of new Renaissance structures.

Churches

As in earlier eras, churches were a prominent type of building during the Renaissance. Since church architecture had been the type most affected by the Gothic, the introduction of classical form was particularly striking. Brunelleschi's churches boldly announced the advent of the new classicism already in the first half of the quattrocento. His Church of San Lorenzo (c. 1421–c. 1460) in Florence was a wholly classical creation strongly reminiscent of the most beautiful late antique Roman basilicas. San Lorenzo observes strict classical principles of proportion (the height of the nave is equal to twice its width), while its classical ornamentation accentuates horizontals and verticals in a sober, striking contrasting gray stone (*pietra serena*) native to Tuscany. Brunelleschi's Pazzi Chapel (1429–1460), a miniature ecclesiastical monument designed for private worship and burial in the precincts of the vast Gothic Basilica of San Croce, epitomizes early Renaissance classicism in its perfect symmetry and harmony, enlivened again by contrasts of serene Tuscan stonework.

Brunelleschi's most notable accomplishment, however, in the area of church architecture, was the design and building of the dome of the Cathedral of Florence. Begun about 1420, but finished only after his death in 1467, the dome was the final element in the construction of the Cathedral, which had been begun in Gothic style more than a century before. Brunelleschi needed to design a dome—a highly classical form—that harmonized with its medieval base. Even more daunting was the task of engineering: not since antiquity had anyone attempted to enclose so large a space under a dome. Brunelleschi's solution, which may have been based upon his observation of the Roman model of the Pantheon, involved bridging between stone beams with an interlaced brickwork pattern and required both audacity and engineering skill. His solution for this project has won the admiration of engineers, architects, and visitors to Florence, for whom the dome is the single most distinctive feature of the cityscape.

Later architects also brought classicizing elements to ecclesiastical projects. Leon Battista Alberti's Basilica of Sant'Andrea in Mantua (begun in 1472 but only finished in the eighteenth century) was striking in two regards. First, true to Roman ideals, it was based on a central plan: it was cross-shaped, like the traditional basilican church, but without the elongation of one arm. Second, its facade was modeled on the forms of the Roman triumphal arch, which were reflected in the design of the interior. In Venice Pietro Lombardo (1435–1515) and Mauro Coducci (1440–1504) designed the splendid Santa Maria dei Miracoli (1481–1489) and sober San Zaccaria (begun 1458), respectively, both characterized by their classical features. Most famously, Donato Bramante (c. 1444–1514) designed the new St. Peter's Basilica in Rome, first on the central plan, then modified with a more extensive nave. Building had begun on the revised plan by his death, although it was not finished until the next century.

Secular Buildings

Renaissance architects also introduced classical principles into their designs for secular buildings, which multiplied in type during this era. A notable newcomer was the hospital. Although there were certainly hospitals in the Middle Ages—multipurpose refuges for the sick, the poor, and the elderly—they were generally sited in nondescript outbuildings in ecclesiastical complexes. Now a surge of charitable giving for benevolent purposes called for the design of elegant quarters for much larger hospital projects. Brunelleschi, again, was a trendsetter in his design of Florence's Ospedale degli Innocenti (Foundling Hospital, 1419–1451). The first foundling hospital in Europe and the first secular building constructed in full Renaissance style, it featured a light, graceful classical arcade (a series of arches) along its facade, with an upper order punctuated by roundels (round windows or niches). The Ospedale displayed Brunelleschi's intent to use a classicizing vocabulary in an institutional setting. Still classical, and even grander in scale, was Filarete's Ospedale Maggiore (General Hospital) in Milan, begun in 1457.

The urban civilization of the Renaissance called for other types of secular buildings as well. In Venice, Jacopo Sansovino (1486–1570) created in the Piazzetta, the open space before the Gothic Doge's Palace, both the Loggetta, a small arcade at the foot of the bell-tower (1537–1540), and the Zecca (1536–1588), the city mint, subsequently converted to house the Marciana Library. Renaissance architects also built theaters, aqueducts and other water-management structures, and fortifications, which underwent radical changes during the Renaissance.

Most grandiose among the projects of secular architecture, however, were the palaces and villas designed as the residences of princes, patricians, and prelates. From the late fifteenth century, these became less like fortresses and more like luxury hotels. Equipped

BRUNELLESCHI'S DOME

The most distinctive feature of the skyline of Florence, the capital of the Renaissance, is the dome atop its cathedral. It presents a mass of spiraling curves and vertical arcs against a skyscape otherwise pierced only by verticals—the tower of the Palazzo Vecchio and the Campanile. It is a Renaissance monument atop a Gothic building (begun in 1296), a form distinctive in shape, soaring, thrusting, and elegant: "a large structure, rising above the skies, ample to cover with its shadow all the Tuscan people," wrote contemporary admirer Leon Battista Alberti. Not only was the dome beautiful, but its construction (especially difficult because of an octagonal base) constituted a triumph of engineering. It capped an expanse of space larger than had any dome since antiquity and was erected by unprecedented methods.

In 1418 a competition was held to choose the future architect of a dome for the Cathedral of Florence, and Filippo Brunelleschi (1377–1446) entered the fray. So, too, did his old rival Lorenzo Ghiberti (1378–1455), to whom Brunelleschi had lost the 1401 competition for the Baptistry's bronze doors. This time, in 1420, Brunelleschi won. He had proposed to build the dome without an interior wooden scaffold (a huge expense the cathedral supervisors hoped to avoid). No one knew how it would be done.

Brunelleschi did it by creating a herringbone plan for the courses of bricks of which the dome, above a base of native stone, was constructed. Horizontal rings of bricks (hoisted up from ground level by special machines of Brunelleschi's construction) were interrupted periodically by a vertical sequence, which bonded each row to the next. The verticals of successive courses formed an interlacing pattern as the dome arched inward and upward, supporting and reinforcing itself as it grew taller. The outer shell of the dome visible to the spectator, moreover, was supported by an inner shell, the two connected by sixteen vertical arching ribs and both anchored to the eight vertical ribs seen on the surface, which lended so much elegance to the whole structure. This invisible system of buttressing gave tremendous strength to the dome's graceful and soaring red-brick form.

A miracle of construction, the dome project was also a manifesto of classicism. Defying the Gothic forms in the supporting church below, there is nothing Gothic in the dome—except, perhaps, a whisper of elongation in its graceful, vertical thrust. The *oculi* (eyes), openings around the drum of the dome to let in light, are pure circles flanked by rectangular forms. The lantern atop the dome, which seems to pull the eight ribs together and upward, is also a showpiece of classical components: pilasters, arches, and volutes, culminating in the linear clarity of cone and ball at the zenith.

The dome was largely constructed in 1436, when its completion was celebrated in a great public ceremony that featured a choral performance directed by the famous Burgundian composer Guillaume Dufay (c. 1400–1474). The lantern was completed in 1461; the bronze ball at the summit was added in 1464.

FILIPPO BRUNELLESCHI, CATHEDRAL DOME, FLORENCE, 1420–1436

Brunelleschi's Dome (approximate dimensions)

Distance from ground to drum base	177 feet
Distance from drum base to zenith	108 feet
Distance from opposite sides of exterior octagonal base	176 feet
Height of lantern	72 feet
Weight of dome	40,800 tons
Number of bricks	4 million

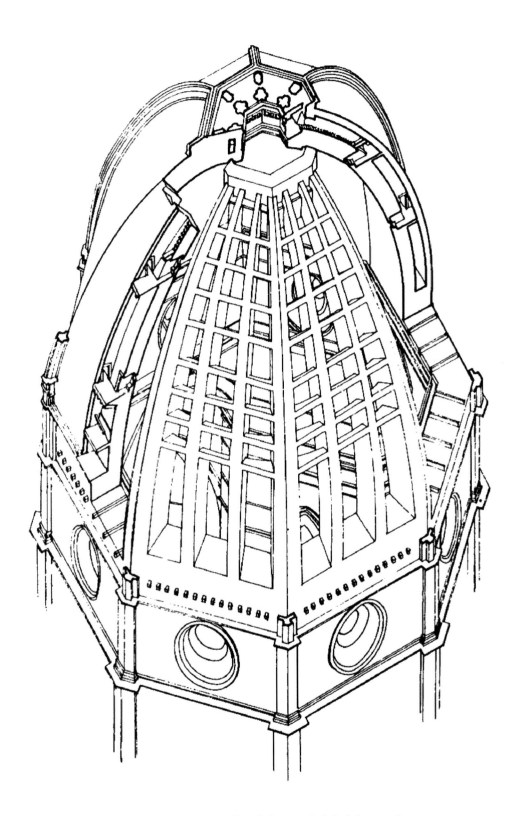

Axonometric section through dome, Cathedral of Florence, Florence.

ARTISTS AND PATRONS IN URBINO AND VENICE

Artists today may paint or sculpt whatever they like and then attempt to sell it. In the Renaissance, an artist was commissioned to create a specific product. In the first example, an artist is being commissioned by a patron, and in the second, an artist is seeking patronage.

Here the Duke of Urbino Federico da Montefeltro appoints the Dalmatian artist Luciano Laurana to direct the building of his palace at Urbino.

We judge worthy of honour and praise those men who are … versed in certain skills, and particularly in those which have always been prized by both Ancients and Moderns. One such skill is architecture, founded upon the arts of arithmetic and geometry, which are the foremost of the seven liberal arts because they depend upon exact certainty. Architecture furthermore requires great knowledge and intellect and we appreciate and esteem it most highly. And we have searched everywhere, but principally in Tuscany, the font of architects, without finding anyone with real understanding and experience of this art. Recently, having first heard by report and then by personal experience seen and known, how much Master Luciano, the subject of this letter, is gifted and learned in this art, and having decided to make in our city of Urbino a beautiful residence worthy of the rank and fame of our ancestors and our own stature, we have chosen and deputed the said Master Laurana to be engineer and overseer of all the master workmen employed on the said work…. And we thus order the said masters and workmen and each of our officials and subjects who have anything to do with the project, to obey the said Master Luciano in all things and perform whatever they are ordered to do by him, as though by our own person…. Pavia, 10 June 1468.

(P. Elmer, N. Webb, and R. Wood, eds., The Renaissance in Europe: An Anthology. *New Haven, CT, London: Yale University Press, 2000, pp. 205–206)*

Venice, unlike Urbino, was a republic, albeit a republic ruled by a restricted political class. In this environment, artistic patronage involved the complex structures of the Venetian state. Here a striving artist, hoping for a lucrative contract, petitions the doge and his councillors to permit him to paint a test piece at no charge:

I, Alvise Vivarini of Murano, being a most faithful servant of Your Serenity and of this most illustrious state, have long been desirous of showing an example of my work in painting, so that your Sublimity may see … that the continuous study and diligence to which I have applied myself has not been vain in success, but in honour and praise of this famous city. As a devoted son, I offer myself without any reward or payment for my personal labour in making a picture to surpass myself; that is, to paint in the Hall of the Greater Council in the manner in which the two Bellini brothers [Giovanni and Gentile] are working at present. Nor do I at present demand for the painting of the said work anything more than the canvas and the expenses of colours and the expenses of assistants to help me…. When I have truly perfected the work, I will then remit it freely to the judgement and pleasure of your Serenity, that from your benignity you may design to provide me with some just, honest, and suitable reward which … you decide the work to merit…. 28 July 1488.

(D.S. Chambers, Patrons and Artists in the Italian Renaissance. *Columbia: University of South Carolina Press, 1971, pp. 80–81)*

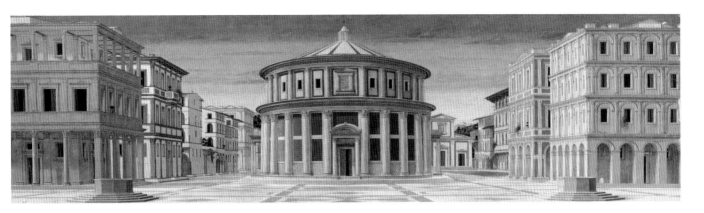

with grand rooms, staircases, arcades, and courtyards, their function was less to provide security, as in the past, or even sleeping quarters, so much as an elegant space for the display of elegant people. In Florence Michelozzo di Bartolommeo (1396–1472), a follower of Brunelleschi, designed the Medici Palace (1444–1459) while Alberti designed the Palazzo Rucellai (1452?–1470?). The Roman features and classical proportions of these buildings softened and civilized the rugged, faceless urban houses of earlier generations of the elite.

In Venice, whose Grand Canal was already lined with palaces of the nobility in Gothic style, Mauro Coducci introduced classical design in his Palazzo Corner-Spinelli (late fifteenth century) and Vendramin-Calergi (c. 1500–1509). In Rome a follower of Alberti designed the Palazzo Venezia (1455–1503), whose elegant interior courtyard was modeled on the forms of the Colosseum. Leading churchmen required many other Roman palaces and some required suburban villas, such as the Villa Farnesina (1509–1511) designed by the Sienese Baldassare Peruzzi (1481–1536) for the pope's banker Agostino Chigi (c. 1465–1520).

The villa form added broad arcades reaching out to the surrounding gardens to the luxurious palace. Villas reached a new peak in the Palazzo del Te (1525–1534), built for the dukes of Mantua by Giulio Romano (c. 1492–1546). The Venetian *terraferma* (the mainland in the vicinity of Venice and under its control) acquired a belt of villas to which the city's nobles, retired from the risks of maritime trade, withdrew for elegant conversations and serious farming enterprises. Many of these villas, famous for their exquisite classical restraint, were designed by architect and theorist Andrea Palladio (1508–1580).

City Planning

As public buildings multiplied, cityscapes were transformed. To some extent this effect was accidental. But there were also deliberate efforts to shape the appearance of cities, just as in Florence during the republican age (see Chapter 2). Some architects even conceived of ideal cities, cities that might be built in their entirety or serve as a conceptual ideal for future building. Filarete envisioned the ideal city of Sforzinda (named after the ruling Sforza dynasty of Milan), which would have cathedral, public buildings, and fortress arranged in a perfect harmonious whole.

Piero della Francesca, *Ideal City*, late 15th century, oil on panel, 79 × 23½ in (200.7 × 59.7 cm). Galleria Nazionale delle Marche, Urbino.

Piero's perspective painting of a freely imagined city square incorporates many elements from classical architecture. A fantasy city, its architectural forms resemble those that were being constructed in Italy during the same era.

In Rome, the series of popes who followed the triumphant return to the city of Martin V (r. 1417–1431) in 1420 threw their efforts into developing the city around the figure of St. Peter as founder of the Vatican. By 1590 Rome had been transformed into a city of boulevards and open spaces, rationalized and centralized, punctuated by fountains, porticoes, and statues. In that form, it became a model for the great capitals of northern Europe; the grand squares and avenues of Paris and London owe much to its inspiration.

One pope ventured beyond Rome to reinvent his native town near Siena as a new model city, replacing an ordinary village with a monument to himself and his family. Pope Pius II, originally the humanist Enea Silvio Piccolomini, called the new city Pienza after himself (Pio, the Italian form of his papal name Pius). The condottiere general Federico da Montefeltro, Duke of Urbino, commissioned the Dalmatian architect Francesco Laurana to design a palace complex that was, in effect, a complete model city. Its quality of planned perfection was captured in the fresco *Ideal City* (see above) in the Palazzo Ducale (Ducal Palace), possibly by Piero della Francesca. It is a coldly abstract imagined utopian city, foreshadowing the visionary cities of Thomas More (1478–1535) and Tommaso Campanella (1568–1639; see Chapters 8 and 9). These ventures in urbanism all opened the pathway to dramatic new thinking about urban design and management in an age when princes ruled from their bastioned capital cities or found it useful to plant new port cities or garrisoned towns as means of their control.

PORTRAITS AND PERSONALITY

In the great architectural and urbanistic projects of the Renaissance, the leaders of that civilization declared who they were and what was their domain. Painted or sculpted portraits performed a similar function for important and wealthy individuals.

The idealizing art of the Greeks did not produce realistic portraits of known historical individuals. The Hellenistic and Roman ages, however, were great ages of portraiture, especially in sculpture. The late antique fascination with human individuality waned again during the Middle Ages and only returned, along with much else that was ancient, in the quattrocento. It appears to be influenced by humanism, with its emphasis on human worth and its celebration of the great figures of ancient history. A new feature, however, was the technical advances of Renaissance artists.

Portraits and Self-Portraits

Among the first notable Renaissance portraits are two self-portraits. The first is a miniature bust of the artist Lorenzo Ghiberti, set in a medallion forming part of the ornamental border of the Florence Baptistry's east doors, the Gates of Paradise (to the right of his Jacob and Esau). But it is unmistakably a portrait, whose subject is drawn without idealization.

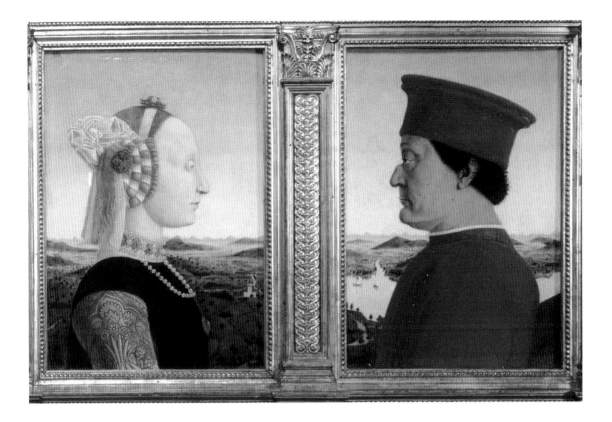

The second is a miniature on a bronze plaquette of the artist Leon Battista Alberti from 1435 (see p. 105).

The most famous early Renaissance portraits, however, are the matched, facing panels of Federico da Montefeltro, Duke of Urbino, and his wife, Battista Sforza, painted by Piero della Francesca about 1465. Both figures are portrayed in strict profile and with great attention to detail. Federico's face features his warts and a broken nose, suffered in tournament combat; Battista's pale face is highlighted by an elaborate headdress and gorgeous jewelry. Both are shown high above and at a remote distance from the misty, undulating lands over which they ruled. These are simultaneously portraits of individuals and of power.

In contrast to the strict profile view of Piero's subjects, the unnamed *Man*, who is the subject of a portrait by Antonello da Messina (c. 1430–c. 1479), is seen in quarter-profile (see p. 138), and is far more lifelike and human. The portrait was done in oil about 1475, using techniques the artist had perhaps learned from Flemish-trained masters in his native Sicily. It may be the oil medium that permits the deep expression of the eyes that makes this portrait not just an expression of selfhood but a study in the self. The portrait *Old Man with a Young Boy* by Domenico Ghirlandaio (1449–1494) from about 1480 is also lifelike and personal (see p. 180). Shown in all his comfortable ugliness, the grandfatherly man gazes tenderly at the young boy. This is a portrait of love, the depiction of which requires a mature art.

Piero della Francesca, *Battista Sforza and Federico da Montefeltro*, c. 1472, oil and tempera on panel, each 18½ × 13 in (47 × 33 cm). Galleria degli Uffizi, Florence.

The stark profiles of the rulers of Urbino are shown elevated above the landscapes they dominate, in art as in life. The realistic detail—the Duke's broken nose, the Duchess's necklace—is matched by the balanced abstract forms constituted by his hat and her headdress.

ISABELLA D'ESTE, MARCHIONESS OF MANTUA AND ART PATRON

Daughter of the ruler of Ferrara, wife of the ruler of Mantua, Isabella d'Este was a major patron of art. Her correspondence with Lorenzo da Pavia, a builder of fine musical instruments, extended from 1496 to 1515 and consists of 182 letters. It documents Isabella's efforts to acquire not only great works of art but also harpsichords, porcelains, and exotic civet cats (whose glandular secretions were used as a perfume fixative) for her rooms at Mantua. These excerpts concern two important artists and illumine the dealings behind the scenes of the production of great Renaissance art.

On Andrea Mantegna

Isabella d'Este to Lorenzo da Pavia, June 6, 1497.
I remind you to send me some varnish to varnish the painting by messer *Andrea Mantegna, as you promised to him and to me you would do, using diligence to assure that it is of good quality and let me know the cost so that I can reimburse you.*

Isabella d'Este to Lorenzo da Pavia, June 14, 1497.
Master Lorenzo, messer Andrea Mantegna received the varnish that you sent him, which pleases him greatly except that it is not sufficient, so please send two times as much as that and the faster the better, because he has already begun to varnish the painting.

Isabella d'Este to Lorenzo da Pavia, June 13, 1502.
Lorenzo, send me enough varnish to varnish Mantegna's painting, as much as the other you sent for the other painting, and let it be of as good quality as the other.

Lorenzo da Pavia to Isabella d'Este, October 12, 1506. *I was very saddened by the death of our messer Andrea Mantegna, in whom truly was lost a most excellent man and another Apelles [legendary artist of ancient Greece]; I believe the Lord God will use him to make some other wondrous work. For my part, I do not hope ever again to see a better designer and inventor.*

(C.M. Brown, Isabella d'Este and Lorenzo da Pavia, trans. M.L. King, nos. 11, 12, 60, 116. Geneva: Librairie Droz, 1982, pp. 44, 66, 99)

On Giovanni Bellini

Isabella d'Este to Lorenzo da Pavia, April 10, 1504.
Lorenzo, since I can't tolerate any longer the great villainy that Giovanni Bellini has shown me concerning the painting … that he has not completed, I have decided to ask to have my money back from him until the work is completed, which I don't believe will happen.

Lorenzo da Pavia to Isabella d'Este, April 21, 1504.
Most illustrious and excellent lady, I received your letter and on that account saw what needed to be done concerning the painting of Giovanni Bellini…. God knows how many times I asked him, not asked really but importuned, and always he responded with a "it will be done," which he delivered with a torrent of words. Finally he told me that it was nearly done.

Lorenzo da Pavia to Isabella d'Este, July 6, 1504.
This morning I spoke with Giovanni Bellini at great length, and it seems that the painting is just about finished, so that it lacks nothing; and truly it is a beautiful thing, really better than I would have believed. I know that it will please your excellency.

Isabella d'Este to Lorenzo da Pavia, July 9, 1504.
*Lorenzo, after Giovanni Bellini has finished the painting and it is as beautiful as you say, I am content to receive it and so I send … the 25 **ducats** that constitute the entire payment.*

(Brown, Isabella d'Este, nos. 87, 88, 90, 91, pp. 81–84)

Portraits of women in this period are generally less engaging as the personality of the subject tends to be overshadowed by the splendor of her ornament or the loveliness of her face. Piero della Francesca's representation of Battista Sforza is a case in point. The lovely woman represented by Antonio del Pollaiuolo (1433–1498) in his *Portrait of a Young Woman* of about 1475 is also more decorative than compelling (see p. 138). The famous *Mona Lisa* (1503) of Leonardo da Vinci says precisely little about the subject. The many women painted by the Venetian artist Titian (Tiziano Vecellio, c. 1480/1485–1567) are gorgeous, but without identity. Quite different is the 1554 self-portrait by the woman painter Sofonisba Anguissola (c. 1535–1625): she is all eyes, intelligence, and excitement (see p. 274).

Equestrian Portraits and Tombs

A particular genre of portraiture is the representation of heroic figures on horseback. This "equestrian" genre, like the portrait itself, looks back to ancient depictions of mounted generals and emperors. The theme first revived even before the full Renaissance was underway in the awkward yet expressive statue of Veronese despot Can Grande (Big Dog) della Scala (1291–1329) of about 1330 (see p. 65). In the period 1415–1420, the Venetians followed with an equestrian monument in the Basilica of the Frari (the Franciscan friars) to Paolo Savelli, the Roman condottiere who had led their armies to victory against Verona, Padua, and Vicenza in 1405. In 1436 and 1456 Paulo Uccello and Andrea del Castagno (c. 1421–1457) painted, respectively, sculptural images of the Florentine condottieri John Hawkwood (1320–1394) and Niccolò da Tolentino, each on his mount. But it was Donatello who in 1445–1450 created the first Renaissance sculpture of horse and rider, that of the Venetian condottiere Erasmo da Narni, known as Gattamelata (1370–1443), for the *piazza* in front of the church dedicated to Padua's patron saint Antonio. Modeling his horse on the bronze horses on Venice's San Marco, Donatello's Gattamelata is a man in charge of himself and his mission, as much intellect as strength (see p. 224). In contrast, the equestrian monument to another Venetian condottiere, Bartolommeo Colleoni (1400–1476), erected in 1496 by Andrea del Verrocchio (1435–1488) is all muscle and breathes violence (see p. 225). The much-admired 24-foot-tall clay model of an equestrian portrait of the Milanese Duke Francesco Sforza by Leonardo da Vinci was destroyed by French invaders in 1499. The original was never cast in bronze.

Both Gattamelata and Colleoni were memorialized after their deaths by elaborate tombs—Gattamelata's in Paduan Cathedral, and Colleoni in his own chapel at Bergamo. Tombs erected to private individuals were another kind of portraiture—an exaltation of an individual whose memory was important to family or to state. Medieval tombs, in contrast, were generally limited to saints (as shrines) and royalty. In the Renaissance, petty despots, generals, merchants, and scholars were all memorialized in the public view in the holiest places. The two Rossellino brothers, Bernardo (1409–1464) and Antonio (1427–1479), thus crafted tombs, respectively, for the humanist chancellor Leonardo Bruni in Santa Croce in Florence, completed in 1447 (see p. 95), and the cardinal of Portugal

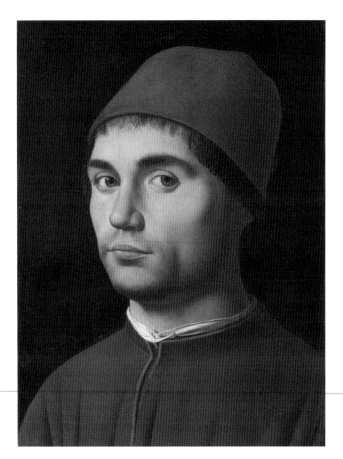

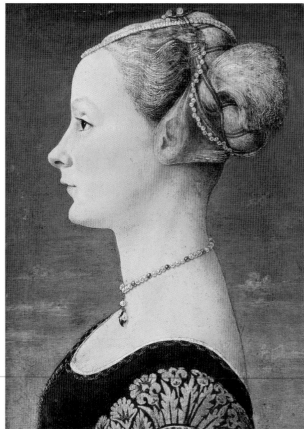

(left) **Antonello da Messina,** *Portrait of a Man,* **c. 1475, oil on wood, 14 × 10 in (35.6 × 25.4 cm). National Gallery, London.**

The rich shadings made possible by oil paints allowed the artist to explore the soul of this young man, seen in the expression of his eyes.

(right) **Pollaiuolo,** *Portrait of a Young Woman,* **c. 1465, oil on wood, 19 × 14 in (48 × 35 cm). Museo Poldi Pezzoli, Milan.**

This young woman—the details of whose coiffure, jewelry, and costume are rendered in exquisite detail—reveals little about herself.

at San Miniato al Monte in Florence, completed in 1460–1466. The Venetian Church of Santi Giovanni e Paolo, second in size in the city only to the enormous San Marco, contains sculpted tombs of 25 doges; the Basilica of the Frari contains exquisite tombs for the doges Francesco Foscari (r. 1423–1457) and Niccolò Tron (r. 1471–1473). In St. Peter's in Rome, the popes Sixtus IV (r. 1471–1484) and Innocent VIII (r. 1484–1492) had tombs sculpted by Pollaiuolo; the tomb of the warrior Pope Julius II (r. 1503–1513) was sculpted by Michelangelo (1475–1564).

ART AND THE EVERYDAY

Props from ordinary life—streets and buildings alluding to the framework of urban life, trees and mountains alluding to rural existence—were as important an element in some Renaissance paintings as the main figures themselves. Already in the paintings of Giotto, stubby, stony hills and stage-set houses framed the action of his solid, expressive characters. In the Scrovegni Chapel frescoes in Padua, for instance, a fragile one-room house is the setting for the birth of the Virgin Mary. We see both the bedroom scene within and a secondary narrative on the front porch, where a neighbor woman is greeted at the door and welcomed, like a spectator, to enter within. The lamentation for the death of Jesus by Mary and other followers, accompanied by angelic mourners aloft, is set against a downward sloping hill, its incline tracing the descent from the cross and the depressive emotions of the figures.

City and Country Settings

Urban and landscape settings became more sophisticated and plausible in the paintings of the High Renaissance. Masaccio's fresco *The Tribute Money* in the Carmine in Florence shows Jesus and his disciples inhabiting real space defined by rolling hills and a Renaissance building. Later in the century, *The Annunciation* by Carlo Crivelli (c. 1430/1435–1490/1495) virtually buries the key figures of the Angel Gabriel and the Virgin in a dense urban setting of doors, windows, arches, terraces, and street arrayed in perfect perspective. Meanwhile, the paintings of Perugino and his more famous disciple Raphael (Raffaello Santi, 1483–1520) explore the deep, dreamy landscapes of north-central Italy. Further north, Giorgione (1477–1510), in *The Tempest*, created a painting that had as its twin purposes an exploration of human relationships and a depiction of the evocative atmosphere of a storm-lit Veneto landscape (see p. 113).

Other paintings depicted cityscape or landscape in order to convey a political, historical, or mythological message. The *Effects of Good Government in the City and in the Country* (see p. 140), a fresco by Ambrogio Lorenzetti (c. 1290–1348) in the Palazzo Pubblico in Siena, shows both a prosperous city scene, with young girls dancing in the streets, and an equally prosperous countryside, with nobles on horseback and farmers bringing goods to market, the two divided by a zigzagging city wall. In the quattrocento, Paolo Uccello's three panels depicting separate scenes in the *Battle of San Romano* manipulate landscape elements to highlight the scenes of the conflict. These scenes are also exercises in the painting of figures and landscape, foreground and background, in proper perspective. The allegorical paintings of *Primavera* (Springtime) and the *Birth of Venus* by Sandro Botticelli (1445–1510) set figures of pagan goddesses, gods, and nymphs in a refined forest scene and seascape respectively. The frescoes of Vittore Carpaccio (c. 1460–1526), such as the *Healing of the Possessed Man* painted for the **Scuola** di San Giovanni Evangelista in Venice, often feature realistic cityscapes of Venice, including crowds, bridges, gondolas with gondoliers, and characteristic chimneys. Gentile Bellini (c. 1429–1507) painted a Venetian procession in the city's grand piazza in celebration of the Feast of Corpus Christi that displayed the entire hierarchy of the Venetian state in a moment equally of civic and religious ritual.

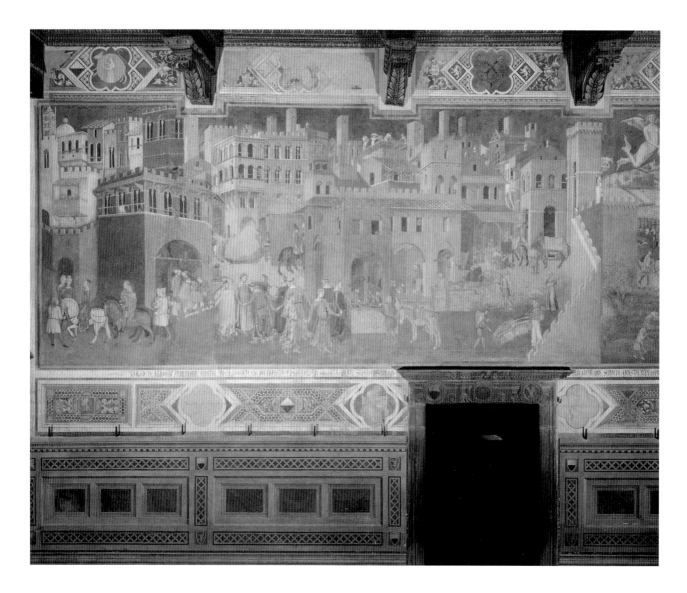

Ambrogio Lorenzetti,
Effects of Good Government
in the City and in the Country
(detail), 1339, fresco. Palazzo
Pubblico, Siena.

According to Lorenzetti, the
effects of good government are
that the men and women of
Siena may go about their daily
business—shopping, dancing,
embarking on a journey—in
security and contentment.

Interiors

With the incorporation of country and city settings, spectators could recognize their
own world in the worlds depicted by Renaissance artists. They also brought the world of
the Renaissance artist into their own homes and palaces. Even humble citizens purchased
small items of religious art for display on their walls and possessed implements or items of
furniture that were stamped, engraved, or carved with motifs characteristic of the era. In
addition to the large canvases, frescoes, or sculptures which the wealthy might commission to adorn their villas, palaces, and gardens, they also filled their residences with carved
and decorated objects. Costly tapestries woven of wool and silk and gold and silver thread
also added color and texture to large bare rooms.

This too was the era of increasingly elaborate domestic furniture and furnishings—chairs and tables but also chests and cabinets. Noteworthy, for instance, are the *cassoni di nozze* (marriage chests) in which brides carried their linens and adornments with them to the households of their new husbands. The *cassoni* were typically decorated with classically inspired scenes of marriage and fertility. As the cuisine became more delicate and artful, so too did tableware. Plates adorned with mythological or historical scenes, heraldic devices, or portraits were on hand for use and display. These were mostly of the native Italian ceramic process called majolica, but they were also imported from Islamic Spain or Asia. Cups, knives, and saltcellars were all opportunities for casting and engraving; forks were rarities at first but were used increasingly, and these, too, were preciously decorated. With the advent of such implements, the art of the Renaissance had completely penetrated the world of everyday.

FROM ARTISAN TO GENIUS: THE EVOLUTION OF THE ARTIST

The medieval artist was generally anonymous, even if that artist had designed a cathedral or a wall of stained glass. The Renaissance artist had a name, even if all that had been designed was a saltcellar or a candlestick. During the Renaissance era, the artist evolved socially from the artisan, a nameless but skilled worker, to a genius, a creator of superhuman insight and energy.

The production of works of art in Italy during this period was organized like the production of other items that, in a workshop system, was overseen by guilds. A young boy who had shown talent was apprenticed to a painter or sculptor, a builder or goldsmith. His master would train him in the same way that the candle-maker or butcher trained his apprentices. In the case of a painter, the apprentice would be introduced to the different types of product (fresco, panel) or paint (tempera, oil), the tools used to apply them, and the relative values of the ordinary hues and the precious blues and golds. As the apprentice gained skill, he might be given the task of filling in background figures in a fresco. He might also be given access to the master's personal sketchbook or other "secrets" of the trade—as the famous sketchbook of Jacopo Bellini (c. 1400–c. 1470) was used by his two sons, Giovanni (c. 1430–1516) and Gentile, and his son-in-law Andrea Mantegna (c. 1431–1506) in their own compositions. In time, an apprentice became independent and won commissions of his own.

Vasari

As works of art came to be more highly valued in the course of the fifteenth century, the name and personality of the artist gathered new importance. Giorgio Vasari's *Le vite*

In 1968, historian Peter Burke assembled, for the purpose of statistical analysis, a 600-member "creative elite" for the Italian Renaissance. The 600, born between 1340 and 1519 (plus a few of unknown birthdate), were clearly dominated by practitioners of the arts.

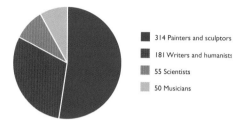

■ 314 Painters and sculptors
■ 181 Writers and humanists
■ 55 Scientists
■ 50 Musicians

Among the distinctive characteristics of this elite is the pattern of their geographical origin. They were heavily from Tuscany and the Veneto (the regions around Florence and Venice respectively); very few came from the southern part of the Italian peninsula. specifically:

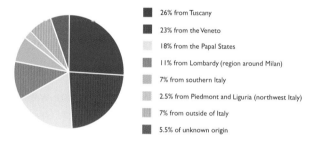

■ 26% from Tuscany
■ 23% from the Veneto
■ 18% from the Papal States
■ 11% from Lombardy (region around Milan)
■ 7% from southern Italy
■ 2.5% from Piedmont and Liguria (northwest Italy)
■ 7% from outside of Italy
■ 5.5% of unknown origin

Burke considered paternal occupations in order to judge social origins. Although these could be known for only 43 per cent of the 600-member elite, still the range of occupations is instructive.

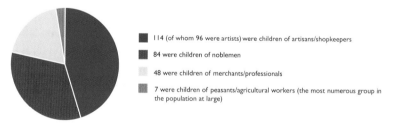

■ 114 (of whom 96 were artists) were children of artisans/shopkeepers
■ 84 were children of noblemen
■ 48 were children of merchants/professionals
■ 7 were children of peasants/agricultural workers (the most numerous group in the population at large)

(*Peter Burke,* The Italian Renaissance: Culture and Society in Italy, *rev. ed. London: Batsford, 1972; Princeton, NJ: Princeton University Press, 1987, pp. 44, 46–47, 251–252*) *de' più eccellenti pittori, scultori, e architettori* ("The Lives of the Most Excellent Painters, Sculptors, and Architects"), first published in 1550, records the looming stature of the artist. It provides lively profiles full of anecdotal incidents from which the passions, aspirations, and eccentricities of the creators of Renaissance style emerge vividly and poignantly. These are not anonymous craftsmen, but driven geniuses, torn by jealousies and longings, sometimes verging on the madness that comes with extraordinary talent.

One example, perhaps apocryphal, must serve for many: Andrea del Castagno, Vasari wrote, "great as he was in painting and design, was greater still in the hatred and envy that he bore to other painters." Having overheard praise of the work of his collaborator, Domenico Veneziano (d. 1461), in the adornment of the Chapel of Santa Maria Nuova, Andrea determined to rid himself of his rival. As Vasari tells the tale:

> One evening in summer, Domenico as usual took his lute and departed from S. Maria Nuova, leaving Andrea in his chamber drawing…. So Domenico being gone out to his pleasure, Andrea disguised himself and went to wait for him at the corner, and when Domenico came up, returning home, he struck at him with a leaden instrument, and breaking his lute, pierced him in the stomach at the same moment. But thinking he had not done his work as he wished, he struck him on the head heavily, and leaving him on the ground, returned to his room in S. Maria Nuova, and sat down to his drawing as Domenico had left him. In the meantime the servants, having heard a noise, ran out and heard what had happened, and came running to bring the evil tidings to Andrea, the traitor and murderer, whereupon he ran to the place where lay Domenico…. At last Domenico died in his arms, and it could not be found out who it was that had slain him. Nor would it ever have been known, if Andrea on his deathbed had not made confession of the deed.
>
> (Giorgio Vasari, *Lives of the Artists*, trans. and ed. E.L. Seeley. New
> York: Farrar, Strauss, and Cudahy, 1957, p. 94)

Renaissance artists not only stepped out from the pages of Vasari's books as complex and passionate individuals, but they often interacted with scholars, although they themselves were not educated as humanists. Humanists might advise on the subject and substance of commissioned works of art, suggesting attributes for the key figures, dramatic relationships, or philosophical concepts that were to be expressed in the composition. Patrons, humanists, and artists often worked in tandem in the creation of a work of art. These concerns and contacts further raised the status of the artist from the level of mere artisan to that of collaborator in a unique act of creation.

Alberti

Two artists call for special mention here: Leon Battista Alberti and Leonardo da Vinci. Both were powerful personalities of the type that crowd Vasari's pages, and both involved themselves in the world of knowledge at a level well beyond that of the older type of artisan. The illegitimate son of a prominent Florentine family in exile, Alberti was splendidly educated and gifted in many ways. For Jacob Burckhardt, creator of the modern notion of the Renaissance era, he was the prime example of the "Renaissance man." "In all by which praise is won, Leon Battista was from his childhood the first," Burckhardt wrote. He was a master gymnast, who in the cathedral once "threw a coin in the air till it was heard to ring against the distant roof"; he composed music and studied law; he was an artist and an author.

> At the sight of noble trees and waving cornfields he shed tears; handsome and dignified old men he honored as "a delight of nature," and could never look at them enough. Perfectly formed animals won his goodwill as being specially favored by nature; and more than once, when he was ill, the sight of a beautiful landscape cured him.
>
> (Jacob Burckhardt, *The Civilization of the Renaissance in Italy*, trans. S.G.C. Middlemore. New York: Modern Library, 1954. Originally published in 1878, p. 107)

Among his several other works, Alberti was the author of two important treatises on the arts, "On Painting" and "On Architecture" (see pp. 122–123), as well as the key formulator of the theory of perspective and the creator of major and pioneering architectural monuments. It is notable that Alberti tried to bridge the gap between the world of the learned, the world of those who know geometry and think abstractly, and that of the artisan, the world of those who take a tool in hand and depict what they see.

Leonardo

The illegitimate son of a country notary and a peasant woman from a small town outside Florence, Leonardo did not receive the expensive education of a humanist or university student. His training in the workshop of Andrea del Verrocchio was practical. Living in Florence during its creative peak in the late fifteenth century, however, he became aware of the currents of thought and inquiry which circulated among the learned and powerful. He, too, became an explorer, mingling in the thousands of pages of his notebooks both his observations as an artist, rendered in sketches, and the ideas of a genius who could transcend the limits of his early training. His sketches were important contributions to anatomy and botany. His theoretical insights extended to the role of the artist and the relative merits of painting and sculpture. His tireless mind produced important innovations in theatrical set design, engineering and hydraulics, and weaponry and fortifications.

In painting, Leonardo developed the technique of *chiaroscuro* (literally, "light-dark") to represent the minutely graded shadings from light to dark that appear in natural objects illuminated by an artificial or natural source. He also explored the possibilities of landscape crowded with meandering rivers, rocky mountains, misty voids, and dreamy lakes. He extended the possibilities of perspective by adding atmospheric effects to the diagrammatic precision. He painted works of monumental importance for their expressive force: *Mona Lisa*, painted in Florence (1503); *The Last Supper* (1495–1497/1498), painted during his first lengthy stay in Milan; *St. Anne with the Virgin* (1508–1513?), painted during a second, briefer visit.

Leonardo was unsettled, however, forging no real connections with any place, shifting between cities and ambitions, leaving behind him a trail of unfinished works as he accumulated his notebooks and explored new flora and fauna. After careers in Florence and Milan, he moved back to Florence and on to Rome, and back to Milan, and ended his life in France, restless to the last.

Women Artists

Among the other artists who emerged as full-blown personalities and achieved high status during the Renaissance were a few women artists, mostly from the later years of the era. Already in the fifteenth century, the nun Caterina Vegri (1413–1463) was admired for her devotional paintings as well as her mystical books and saintly life. In the sixteenth, Marietta (1560?–1590), daughter and apprentice of Venetian painter Jacopo Tintoretto (Jacopo Robusti, c. 1518–1594), gained notice. Late in the sixteenth century, Sofonisba Anguissola (1532–1625), daughter of a noble family that supported her artistic inclinations, became the first woman artist of the modern era, providing paintings (mostly portraits) on commission. In the next century, the Roman-born painter Artemisia Gentileschi (1593–1652), daughter and student of Orazio Gentileschi, a disciple of Caravaggio (Michelangelo Merisi, c. 1571–1610), brought a feminist vision to Renaissance art (see Chapter 8, especially pp. 274–275.)

THE HIGH RENAISSANCE (c. 1500–1530)

Renaissance style entered a new phase about 1500—the so-called High Renaissance. The first breakthroughs in the new style had been made by artists working in Florence. Indeed, throughout the fifteenth century, the preponderance of artistic talent concentrated in Florence, in part because of the patronage of the Medici family. Although the covert Medicean regime subsumed and largely subverted the republican machinery of government, republicanism was central to Florentine civic identity. It reared up again in the 1490s (see Chapters 6 and 7).

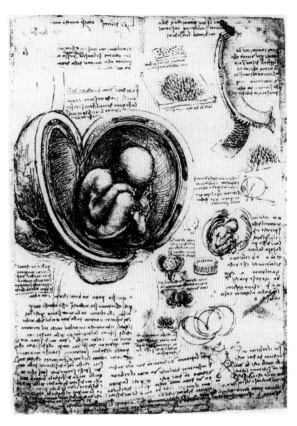

Leonardo da Vinci, *Embryo in the Womb*, c. 1510, pen and brown ink, 11¾ × 8½ in (29.8 × 21.6 cm). **Royal Collection, Windsor Castle, England.**

Leonardo's drawings are as fascinating as his paintings, stage designs, or military inventions, especially because they often straddle art and natural science. He sketched this image of a fetus in the uterus more than a century before physicians unraveled the mysteries of the human reproductive system.

By the end of the century, however, the main centers of art had shifted from Florence to Rome and Venice. In Rome, overshadowed by the papacy and the wealthy and princely cardinals, the arts celebrated the wealth and majesty of those prelates, conceived as the heirs in majesty and power of the ancient emperors. In Venice, a republic with a nominal monarch and a legally defined aristocracy, art celebrated the wealth and power of a spectrum of patrons, from the state itself to private citizens, from grand nobles to the charitable associations that served the poor. In both cities, the canvases grew larger and the ideal space represented on flat planes grew grander and more unified; figures gained bulk and force and massed together in great pyramids of form; colors were lusher, ornamentation richer. These are the signs of the High Renaissance.

Rome

The Renaissance in Rome began with the reestablishment in that city of the papacy after two consecutive traumatic experiences: the Babylonian Captivity, when the papal court removed to Avignon (1305–1378), and the **Great Schism**, when first two, then three figures were recognized as pope (1378–1415; see Chapter 6). These disturbances were settled by the Council of Constance (1414–1418), which elevated Martin V to the papacy. For the remainder of the century and until the emergence of the new challenge of the Protestant **Reformation**, the popes dedicated themselves to affirming papal supremacy by enhancing the city of Rome (see Chapter 9).

Along with their cardinals, the popes straightened and broadened streets, fixed bridges and aqueducts, built and repaired palaces and churches; they unearthed, collected, and displayed ancient sculptures and fragments; and they commissioned artists to decorate their palaces, gardens, and chapels. Eugene IV, in particular, was a collector of gems and medals, a taste shared by his fellow Venetian, later Pope Paul II (r. 1464–1471). Nicholas V preferred to collect manuscript books, which he had gathered into a new Vatican Library, now one of the foremost libraries in the world. Sixtus IV spent lavishly to restore churches, commission paintings, and enhance the Vatican center, including the construction of the Sistine Chapel, a monument to papal primacy, where Michelangelo would later labor (see p. 88).

By 1500 Rome had become the principal center of Western artistic innovation. A key figure was Pope Julius II. Julius notoriously wore a beard and armor as he prosecuted a war to restore papal dominion in central Italy, but he was as extravagant in his patronage as he was in his career. During his brief tenure, he inaugurated a series of architectural and artistic projects unprecedented in scope and expense. The architect Donato Bramante had already in 1502 created the gemlike Tempietto, a perfectly classical round temple on the presumed site of the crucifixion of St. Peter, founder of the papacy. Thus, in 1506, he was commissioned to design and build the great St. Peter's Basilica, the principal church of Latin Christendom, which was completed only in the seventeenth century. His architectural work was complemented in paintings by two major artists of the era who established the style of the High Renaissance: Michelangelo and Raphael.

Michelangelo Michelangelo's reputation as painter and sculptor was already well-established in his native Florence when he came to Rome in 1505 to design and build a tomb for Pope Julius II. It was to be a gigantic free-standing mausoleum, a work of architecture adorned by an allegory of Victory, figures of Captives, and statues of Moses and St. Paul. The project was suspended in 1506, and Michelangelo angrily returned to Florence. He returned to Rome, however, at Julius's direction in 1508, commissioned to design and paint the ceiling of the Sistine Chapel (so named after its creator, Pope Sixtus IV). Also a vast project, it featured painted figures of prophets, sibyls (ancient female visionaries), and nudes, framing nine scenes from the biblical book of Genesis, and bounded by painted elements simulating marble architecture and bronze and marble sculpture. In its sum one of the greatest achievements of all of Western art, the paintings have recently been restored and now in their brighter hues continue to attract steady throngs of visitors to Rome.

Julius's tomb, finally, remained an issue. On the pontiff's death in 1513, Michelangelo developed a revised plan for a more modest structure to be affixed to the wall of San Pietro in Vincoli. The much reduced tomb was not completed until 1545. Two of the six statues of bound captives struggling for release, never finished and never used, are in the Louvre in Paris (above). They are in their own right objects of admiration, expressions of the human struggle for survival and transcendence.

Raphael Raphael was born in Urbino and trained in Perugia. Like Michelangelo, he had established his reputation in Florence before coming to the Rome of Julius II. There he worked on the Vatican *stanze*, the papal apartments. Known as the painter of wonderfully harmonious madonnas set against luminous landscapes, Raphael now designed fresco projects on the massive scale that Vatican architecture required. *School of Athens*, for instance, in the Stanza della Segnatura, displays arrayed within a deep, vaulted, architectural setting several groups of monumental figures of the great thinkers of antiquity, including Plato and Aristotle, Socrates and Diogenes, Pythagoras and Ptolemy (see p. 113).

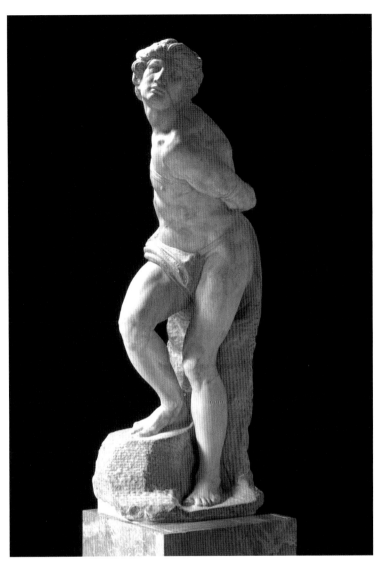

Michelangelo, *Rebellious Slave*, 1513–1515, marble, height 7 ft 1 in (2.15 m). Musée du Louvre, Paris.

Planned as one of six sculpted slaves in different postures to adorn the tomb of Pope Julius II, this heroic figure is struggling to release himself from his bonds—perhaps the bondage to the body from which the enslaved soul is released only in death.

A visual encyclopedia of the ancient tradition in thought, the painting is the fitting counterpart to *Disputation over the Sacrament* on the opposite wall, which commemorates the great theologians of the church.

Venice

The Venetian republic developed artistically according to its own distinctive rhythms. While in Florence artists were boldly pioneering a new style in the early quattrocento, Venetian palaces and churches were still being built in a Gothic style that unabashedly incorporated some novel classical elements. Panel painting, too, remained conservative and unremarkable until later in the century. At that point, as Rome flowered in the High Renaissance, Venice, too, was home to artists who had learned the classical vocabulary of central Italy. In Venice, however, High Renaissance style was less a matter of pyramidal compositions of spiraling, monumental figures, and more a matter of color, atmosphere, and mood. The contrast is seen clearly when the eye turns from Michelangelo and even the sentimental Raphael to the soft mysteries of Giorgione.

Giorgione (Big George) of Castelfranco, a village on the Venetian mainland, came to Venice as a young man and worked there until his early death. Creator of only a few works, he already showed the mark of Venetian style: the gentle beauty of human subjects, the mysterious depths of nature. His *Tempest* (see p. 113) is a landmark in painting: without a biblical or classical text, adorned at the margins by the figures of a nude woman nursing and an armed soldier, its main subject is nature itself. His *Sleeping Venus*, which he began but Titian finished, is another landmark: a female subject nude, prone, and alluring.

By contrast, Titian left many paintings and lived nearly 90 years, dominating Venetian art during that city's climactic century. Ceaselessly original, he treated every subject he undertook in a new way, introducing off-center and diagonal orientations to his compositions, mixing special hues and blending them subtly through the medium of oil glazes. In religious masterpieces, such as the gigantic *Assumption of the Virgin* in the Basilica of the Frari (see p. 187), in secular compositions, such as the compelling *Sacred and Profane Love*, and in realistic portraits, like that of Pietro Aretino (see p. 281), he created a new framework in representation that would have followers into the next centuries.

Titian lived long enough to see the destructive wars of the first part of the century and witness foreigners assume the domination of much of the peninsula thereafter—a fate Venice itself escaped. The High Renaissance yielded to new forms elsewhere in Italy during his lifetime under the compulsion of political stress. Whereas the brief and intense High Renaissance saw the wedding of art and power, later Renaissance styles evidenced the failure of that marriage (see Chapter 8).

CONCLUSION

Roughly two centuries separate the time when Giotto painted the walls of the Arena Chapel in Padua at the behest of the usurer Enrico Scrovegni and when the warrior Pope Julius II commanded Michelangelo to paint the ceiling of the Sistine Chapel. During those centuries, an artistic revolution unfolded in Italy that touched upon every aspect of its society and culture and had enormous consequences for the subsequent development of European civilization. Italy's great wealth permitted the building of churches, palaces, city centers, and whole cities. Her rulers commissioned painters to decorate walls, ceilings, studies, and churches in a new style infused with classical memories and set in a new and wholly abstract spatial frame. Her artists emerged into history from the anonymity of the craft traditions. Works of art produced in staggering abundance celebrated wealth and power, the uniqueness of the human spirit, the wonders of the human form, and the mysteries of divine love. Whereas the works of the humanists could be known only to those trained as humanists, the creations of the artists were visible to many. They had the power to transform all who gazed upon them.

SUGGESTED READINGS

Primary Sources

Alberti, Leon Battista. *On Painting: A New Translation and Critical Edition.* Translated and edited by Rocco Sinisgalli. Cambridge: Cambridge University Press, 2011. This guide to the craft includes Alberti's explanation of linear perspective.
Vasari, Giorgio. *The Lives of the Artists.* Translated by Julia Conway Bondanella and Peter Bondanella. Oxford: Oxford University Press, 2008. An invaluable biographical collection by a practicing sixteenth-century painter.

Secondary Sources

Baxandall, Michael. *Painting and Experience in Fifteenth-Century Italy: A Primer in the Social History of a Pictorial Style*, 2nd ed. Oxford: Clarendon Press, 1988. Explores how the context of daily life shaped the development of pictorial style.
Brown, Howard M., and Louise K. Stein. *Music in the Renaissance*, 2nd ed. Upper Saddle River, NJ: Prentice Hall, 1999. An updated overview of the development of musical style.
Brown, Patricia Fortini. *Venice and Antiquity: The Venetian Sense of the Past.* New Haven, CT: Yale University Press, 1996. A medieval city creates for itself a Roman past through the work of its artists and classical scholars.

Burke, Peter. *The Italian Renaissance: Culture and Society in Italy*, rev. ed. Princeton, NJ: Princeton University Press, 1999. Identifies a cultural elite of some 600 figures to assess their origins and relations and their impact on style and thought.

Campbell, Lorne. *Renaissance Portraits: European Portrait-Painting in the 14th, 15th and 16th Centuries*. New Haven, CT: Yale University Press, 1990. Traces the rebirth of portraiture in an age of assertive individualism.

Campbell, Stephen J. *The Cabinet of Eros: Renaissance Mythological Painting and the Studiolo of Isabella d'Este*. New Haven, CT: Yale University Press, 2004. Explores the paintings adorning the *studiolo*, or private space, of the leading female patron of the Renaissance.

Cole, Bruce. *The Renaissance Artist at Work: From Pisano to Titian*. New York: Harper and Row, 1983. Explains how artists learned their craft and made their paints, paintings, and sculptures.

Edgerton, Samuel Y., Jr. *Pictures and Punishment: Art and Criminal Prosecution during the Florentine Renaissance*. Ithaca, NY: Cornell University Press, 1985. Art had practical uses in the Renaissance, among them the judicial use to arouse horror in observers, deter crime, and encourage repentance.

Garrard, Mary D. *Brunelleschi's Egg: Nature, Art, and Gender in Renaissance Italy*. Berkeley: University of California Press, 2010. Shows how Renaissance artists led the way in revising the gender identities of art and nature on the threshold of the creation of modern science.

Goldthwaite, Richard. *Wealth and the Demand for Art in Italy, 1300–1600*. Baltimore, MD: Johns Hopkins University Press, 1993. Examines art as an economic commodity during the Renaissance that became a prized object by wealthy buyers.

Hollingsworth, Mary. *Patronage in Renaissance Italy: From 1400 to the Early Sixteenth Century*. Baltimore, MD: Johns Hopkins University Press, 1994. An overview of patronage in Florence, Venice, the princely courts, and papal Rome.

Kent, F. W. *Lorenzo de' Medici and the Art of Magnificence*. Baltimore, MD: Johns Hopkins University Press, 2004. A new look at Lorenzo de' Medici's role as patron and consumer of the arts, showing the vast extent of his activity.

King, Catherine. *Renaissance Women Patrons*. Manchester: Manchester University Press, 1998. Studies women who commissioned tombs, chapels, and altarpieces to commemorate fathers, husbands, sons, and even themselves.

Musacchio, Jacqueline M. *Art, Marriage, and Family in the Florentine Renaissance Palace*. New Haven, CT: Yale University Press, 2008. Explores the objects that accompanied the business of marriage in the Renaissance, including furniture, clothing, jewelry, and useful objects along with painting and sculpture.

O'Malley, Michelle. *Painting under Pressure: Fame, Reputation, and Demand in Renaissance Florence*. New Haven, CT: Yale University Press, 2014. Studies the challenges facing artists who worked under commission during the Renaissance, exploring the practices engaged in to ensure a quality product while containing costs and managing time.

Rosenberg, Charles M. *The Este Monuments and Urban Development in Renaissance Ferrara*. Cambridge: Cambridge University Press, 1997. Shows how rulers employed artists to express in monumental forms the legitimacy of their dynastic governance.

Rowland, Ingrid D. *The Culture of the High Renaissance: Ancients and Moderns in Sixteenth-Century Rome*. Cambridge: Cambridge University Press, 1998. Explores how artists, thinkers, and patrons interacted to create a High Renaissance culture.

Starn, Randolph, and Loren Partridge. *Arts of Power: Three Halls of State in Italy, 1300–1600*. Berkeley: University of California Press, 1992. A close study of government halls, showing how power is reflected in space and form.

FIVE

AT HOME AND IN THE PIAZZA
(c. 1350–c. 1530)

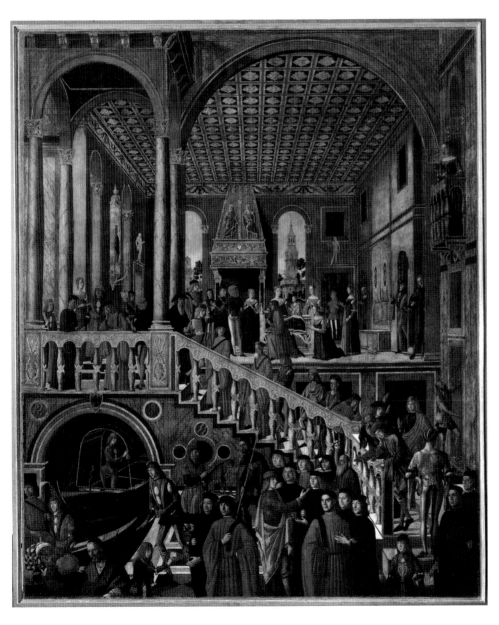

Mansueti, *Miraculous Healing of the Daughter of Ser Benvegnudo of San Polo* (detail), c. 1502–1506, oil on canvas, 11 ft 6 in × 9 ft 7 in (3.56 × 2.96 m). Gallerie dell'Accademia, Venice.

In this depiction of a miraculous healing, the lush panoply of Venetian life overwhelms the sacred event: palace architecture in classic style, marble columns, decorated ceiling, and grand staircase; the arrival of guests at the canal side; the rich costumes worn by dignitaries, fine ladies, and workers.

Artists, humanists, thinkers, authors, and builders constituted only a tiny fraction of those living in Italy during the Renaissance from its origins until about 1530. The historian Peter Burke identified about 600 major figures. Yet at their population peak, the cities of Florence, Venice, Milan, Rome, and Naples each numbered about 100,000. Another 30 to 40 cities numbered 10,000 to 50,000 people. Many other people lived in towns and villages and scattered throughout the countryside. The productivity of a minuscule creative elite rested on the much larger populations that labored and managed the daily tasks of life in their homes and in the piazze, the charming open spaces that punctuate the stonework of Renaissance Italian cities. Their experience is the subject of this chapter.

A look at the diverse careers of Braccio di Giovanni Bernardi and Nencia di Lazerino suggests the range of social experience that a city—here Florence—contained. Braccio, who had spent his whole career as a worker in the wool industry under different masters, in 1399 petitioned to be admitted to the guild himself, so that he might "better himself and achieve a more honorable status." Braccio's hard work and strong record made it possible for him to aspire to the rank of his employers and gave him a real opportunity to gain in wealth.

Whereas Braccio had a genuine possibility of social mobility, Nencia was less fortunate. A servant girl in a respectable Florentine household, in 1475 she was impregnated by a neighbor, thus casting dishonor on her master, who told the tale of these events, and his associates. Through an intermediary, he pressured the guilty man to fund her **dowry**. She was then sent away to deliver her baby, after which she would be married to whoever would take her. Her destiny was not promising, and it lay in the hands of others.

The wool worker who succeeded, the young woman who might not, mark two different points on the spectrum of social roles in the urban society of the Renaissance. This chapter deals with the complex patterns of that society. It turns first to public life, analyzing social structure, the diverse associations to which residents might belong, and the mechanisms of social control (of sexual behavior, criminality, and perceived outsiders) imposed to ensure civic harmony. The chapter then turns to private life, examining household structures, gender roles, and childbirth and childrearing.

Although Renaissance society did not provide the opportunities for freedom and self-definition afforded by modern Western societies—and especially not to women—it was diverse and fluid. These qualities made it an ideal setting for the flowering of ideas and the arts that characterizes the Renaissance.

PUBLIC LIFE

The public realm was the realm of work, ceremony, fellowship, and discipline. Rich and poor, citizens and non-citizens, men and women made up its patterns and experienced its pressures and pleasures.

Social Structure

This exploration of the different social roles that people performed in the public realm will begin with those in the middle: the productive and enterprising artisans. Attention will then turn to the very wealthy, the nobility, and the high clergy and finally to the working poor, the wandering poor, and the special classes of poor women and children.

Merchants and Artisans The activity of merchants and artisans was critical in creating the conditions for Italy's commercial ascendancy and communal autonomy (see Chapter 1). Merchants began to cluster in the remnant of ancient cities in the eleventh and twelfth century, often forming an association, or guild. These newly affluent merchants, the cives of the city, were mostly bankers and long-distance traders of luxury goods. They intermarried with city-based nobles and imitated their customs.

Their descendants in the fourteenth through sixteenth centuries engaged in similar enterprises. They were bankers and jurists, for the children of wealthy merchants could attend university and gain licenses to practice civil or canon law, both highly respected professions. They were also dealers in textiles and metal manufactures (the West's most valuable exports) and luxury goods, especially spices, from Byzantium, the Islamic lands, and East Asia. Their sons were trained in abacus schools where, already literate in the vernacular, they learned to manage numbers and to keep meticulous records of debits and credits in the ledger of the family or firm, entities that were barely distinct. A small portion of them were introduced to the new curriculum of the humanities and became amateur readers and authors of classical and humanist works. In their adolescence, these heirs to merchant enterprises traveled abroad to learn the business of long-distance trade, often residing in one of the Italian merchant colonies planted in major western European cities or in the regions of the East. After the risk and adventure of this experience, they returned home and eventually took up their place as head of the family firm.

The sons of merchants most often became merchants as well. But many, educated at the expense of their affluent families, became physicians; lawyers (including notaries); professors of law, medicine, philosophy, or theology; or members of the clergy (see Chapter 6). In these positions, they formed a respected, but noncommercial, sector of the urban elite, the ancestors of the professionals of modern Western societies. Humanists and professional authors were also likely to come from the middling classes, as was the new class of government secretaries and bureaucrats, both lay and ecclesiastical.

Like that of the merchants, the class of artisans had its origin in the medieval period of emerging urban centers. From the late twelfth century, artisans grouped themselves in guilds in imitation of the older merchant guilds, just as the merchant guilds themselves became differentiated. Not so wealthy or powerful as the upper merchant guilds of textile dealers, bankers, and judges, artisans formed guilds of goldsmiths, carpenters, butchers, and the like. The guilds set standards of craftsmanship and rules for membership, limiting the number of masters who could compete with those already guilded, while providing many social services as well, such as funeral insurance and charitable endeavors. Guild membership in many cities also amounted to citizenship, qualifying the member to participate

PROSTITUTES AND COURTESANS

If women feared death in childbirth, they also feared prostitution, the destiny of so many poor women. Prostitution was the career course available to women who had no fathers, husbands, or brothers to protect them. It was especially a phenomenon of urban society, since peasant communities watched illicit pregnancies carefully and generally compelled the responsible male to marry the woman he had made pregnant. In the city, in contrast, there were many opportunities for men to impregnate and abandon their victims. The young girls who worked as domestic servants were especially vulnerable. In addition,

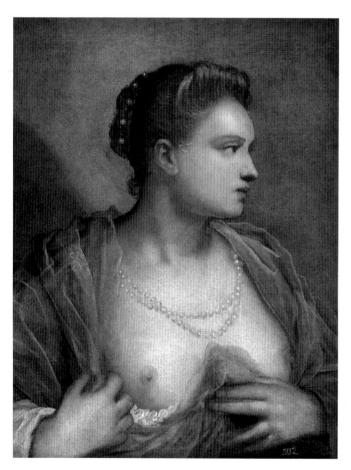

Tintoretto, *Portrait of a Woman with Bared Breast* (thought to be Veronica Franco), c. 1590, oil on canvas, 24 × 21½ in (61 × 55 cm). Museo del Prado, Madrid.

especially among the poor, men might desert their wives who then might turn to prostitution. Widows who had been left no means of subsistence might join the company of prostitutes. Even married women in need of money might engage in prostitution.

Among the salaried and respectable, as well as in elite households, the possibility that a daughter might be raped or seduced was a terrible specter. Such an event would dishonor the household. Ideally, the dishonored daughter would be given a dowry, sometimes funded by the man who was the cause of her downfall. The dowry would permit her to marry a man of inferior rank, whose need for money might permit him to overlook the cause of her dishonor. Women who had had out-of-wedlock sexual experience and were not dowried and married would most likely join the ranks of the prostitutes.

Prostitutes were numerous in the cities of the Italian Renaissance, sought out by the many men—workers, artisans, and adolescents from elite families—who would not or could not marry. Since the circumstances of urban life created a demand for prostitutes, city governments generally tolerated them. They were permitted to work as individuals and in groups resident in brothels. Their existence was a constant source of tension, however, and magistrates attempted to restrain prostitution by regulating it. In some cities, prostitutes had to wear distinctive clothing or practice their trade in special places.

Churchmen, too, tried to stem the tide of prostitution. By the sixteenth century, there were shelters for repentant prostitutes and women who were *malmaritate* (badly married), that is to say, abused or abandoned by their husbands. Such women were taken into residence in a semi-monastic setting, trained in marketable skills, dowried, and then released to marry and work.

Courtesans (in Italian, *cortigiane*, ironically the female form of the word for "courtier") formed the highest stratum of prostitutes. These were women of elevated social skills; they might be witty conversationalists or fine musicians, splendidly dressed and housed. They served such upscale populations as the presumably celibate clerics in Rome and those nobles in Venice who chose not to marry in order to prevent the dispersion of patrimonial wealth. The homes of the most famous courtesans became salons, where wealthy men and intellectuals resorted for witty conversation and to see and be seen.

Among such courtesans were two of the finest women writers of the sixteenth century: the Roman Tullia d'Aragona (c. 1510–1556) and the Venetian Veronica Franco (c. 1546–1591). D'Aragona authored, among other works, the eloquent *Dialogue on the Infinity of Love*, one of the first works in the modern European tradition to discuss sexual love. Franco (see opposite) was the author of a large body of poems about her own experience of love. Courtesan literature was one of the pathways by which women's voices entered into the modern European mainstream.

Yet Franco did not recommend prostitution as a way of life. In the 1570s when a courtesan acquaintance proposed to introduce her own daughter to a life of prostitution, Franco discouraged her. In a famous letter, she rebuked the mother for not having accepted her earlier offer to assist her daughter in gaining entrance to the Casa delle Zitelle (a Venetian refuge for young girls considered at risk for prostitution):

> You know how many times I have begged and warned you to protect her virginity; and since this world is so dangerous and frail and the homes of poor mothers are not immune from the temptations of lusty youth, I showed you how you can shelter her from danger and assist her in settling her life decently and in such a way that you will be able to marry her honestly.

> (M. Rosenthal, *The Honest Courtesan: Veronica Franco*. Chicago: University of Chicago Press, 1992, p. 128)

The life of a prostitute, she argued, was the worst possible one for a woman:

> To become the prey of so many, at the risk of being despoiled, robbed, killed, … exposed to so many other dangers of receiving injuries and dreadful contagious diseases…. What riches, what comforts, what delights can possibly outweigh all this? Believe me, of all the world's misfortunes, this is the worst.

> (Rosenthal, *The Honest Courtesan*, p. 133)

In 1577 Franco petitioned the government to establish a refuge for repentant women who could not join the Zitelle or the Convertite (for rescued prostitutes) or who were unwilling to live under the semi-monastic regime practiced in those institutions. Such a refuge might prevent "the further abomination," she wrote, "of mothers who, being destitute, secretly sell the virginity of their innocent daughters." The Casa del Soccorso (House of Help) was founded according to Franco's wishes, although she had no role in its administration.

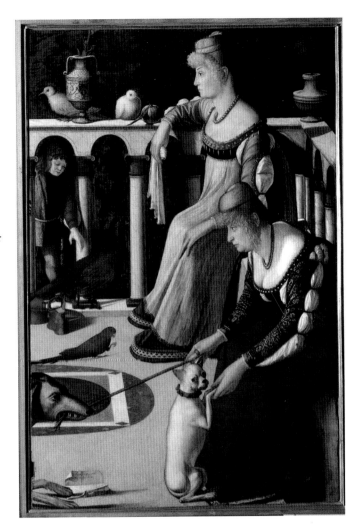

Carpaccio, *Two Venetian Ladies (Courtesans)*, c. 1495, oil on panel, 37 × 25 in (94 × 64 cm). Museo Correr, Venice.

in government councils—although lists of those eligible were "scrutinized" and reduced prior to election by lot. The sons of artisans, like those of merchants, might be educated in the abacus schools, and were often literate as well as numerate. Although less wealthy than the great merchants, artisans were substantial citizens who had a stake in their society.

Nobles and Patricians As early as the eleventh century, the Italian nobility was in contact with urban life (see Chapter 1). The Italian countryside was the home of a large number of minor nobles—sometimes called vavassors, men whose property resulted from the break-up and redistribution of large noble estates. The same process resulted in the commercialization of rural property and encouraged the flow of money. Many nobles from this milieu found cities attractive places to live and to invest in wealth-producing enterprises. They did not abandon their rural properties, but used their commercial wealth to sustain their agricultural enterprises and agricultural produce to sustain their urban households. The household was often a complex structure and interlinked with other households related by blood, sometimes occupying the same neighborhoods and even houses or architectural complexes. As a consequence of these economic circumstances, the Italian nobility developed a character quite distinct from that of the nobles of northern Europe. Often literate, like the merchants with whom they intermarried, their education was not restricted to military skills. Their outlook was urban.

In the Renaissance centuries, the social role of nobles varied from center to center. In republics like Florence, which saw very strong popular (merchant-led) revolutions in the thirteenth century, nobles might actually be disadvantaged. The Florentine Ordinances of Justice famously targeted the nobility and clan solidarity, which were regarded as potentially violent elements in society. In Florence and other republics, nobles were banned—and often rallied in exile to plot against the city that had banned them. In contrast, in the signorie, the despotisms that formed in many cities during the fourteenth and fifteenth centuries, the nobles found a new role as the supporters and defenders of the ruler (see Chapters 2 and 7). In this context, their military training and capacity for violence became an asset.

Meanwhile, the cities produced a new species of nobility. Wealthy merchants surrounded themselves with large households and built lavish residences, or palaces. They invented coats of arms and other devices and traced their genealogies. They patronized artists, musicians, and humanists. In the urban republics, these men also exercised significant political power. This stratum of the merchant elite became, in effect, a nobility, like the magnate nobility that republican governments feared but without the tradition of military violence. This kind of urban elite is considered a "patriciate," a term evoking the upper stratum of the society of ancient republican Rome. In Venice, this merchant elite not only constituted an effective nobility but legally defined itself as such after 1297, when it closed its doors to new members for most of the rest of the Renaissance era after the admission of some 30 families for wartime contributions in 1381. Only from the seventeenth century, well beyond the scope of this chapter, might an aspirant for the nobility purchase the necessary credentials.

Wealthy merchants, patricians, urban nobles—all were products of the commercial revolution led by the Italian cities. Yet from the sixteenth century, they began to turn back from the urban tide. They invested in land large portions of the fortunes they had won in commerce, retiring to the countryside for part or all of the year. They supplied their large households from the fruits of the land and in some cases undertook more intensive cultivation. They withdrew other capital from risky or unprofitable commercial ventures—the Ottoman Turks had choked off much opportunity for trade in the Mediterranean, and Atlantic-based Portugal outpaced the Italian cities in the lucrative spice trade. Instead, they invested that wealth in urban properties or government bonds and lived on rents and interest, forming the characteristically early modern elite of *rentiers*, whose concern was more to live graciously and at ease than to turn a profit.

Workers, Prostitutes, and the Poor Urban nobles, patricians, merchants, and artisans, together with their wives and families, formed an upper social stratum in the cities of the Italian Renaissance—a stratum comprising between one-third and two-thirds of the population. The rest of the population consisted of workers, servants, prostitutes, and the desperately poor. In republics and despotisms alike, these sectors of the population were excluded from political power, although they did not lack all protection from the urban states.

Workers included those we would consider unskilled or semi-skilled today: transporters of goods, construction workers, and shop assistants. Generally, they worked by the day or the week, and were especially subject to the shifts and turns of the marketplace, not owning their own shops or equipment in most cases. In Florence's wool industry and in Venice's Arsenal, where large numbers of these workers were employed, they prefigure in some ways the proletariat of the Industrial Revolution that would begin in the eighteenth century in England.

Another category of workers were servants, a numerous group in all the cities of premodern Europe. Even relatively poor and middling households employed servants, as did both rural and urban households. Wealthy households employed a large servant staff. Servants were haulers of water, cooks, stewards, couriers, stable hands, valets, nursemaids, and companions. In Mediterranean port cities especially, they might be slaves, generally of Dalmatian origin. Alternatively, they might be the poorer kin of the householder— Cinderellas serving their more privileged cousins or half siblings. They were both male and female, and they were often children as young as eight and nine years old who had been sent out from their own families that would or could no longer house them.

Female domestic servants or slaves were often the victims of the sexual advances of their masters or masters' sons. The resulting pregnancy might be viewed as a cause of dishonor to the household. Depending on the status of the woman and the wealth of the master, the offended woman could be provided with a dowry so that she could marry, and thus remove the stain of dishonor. Alternatively, she might be ejected, alone and pregnant, to join the contingents of beggars or prostitutes.

Prostitution was the refuge of women who were not protected by a father, a brother, a husband, or an institution such as a convent, a hospital, or an asylum. During the fourteenth

In 1427 the Florentine state levied a universal tax in the city and surrounding countryside. Tax assessors visited each household and prepared a statement of assets (all property owned) and liabilities (personal exemptions, debts owed). The tax was a percentage (0.5 per cent) of the net. Given here are the principal statistics for representatives of three classes of men: the first wealthy, the second of middling fortune, and the third a struggling worker. Of these, only the first, Compagni, was required to pay a tax. The declarations starkly show the great differences in wealth between members of these different social groups, as well as the differences in their tax liabilities. Amounts are in florins, rounded. At the time, a university professor might earn 100 florins per year.

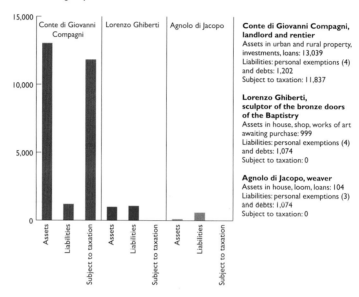

Conte di Giovanni Compagni, landlord and rentier
Assets in urban and rural property, investments, loans: 13,039
Liabilities: personal exemptions (4) and debts: 1,202
Subject to taxation: 11,837

Lorenzo Ghiberti, sculptor of the bronze doors of the Baptistry
Assets in house, shop, works of art awaiting purchase: 999
Liabilities: personal exemptions (4) and debts: 1,074
Subject to taxation: 0

Agnolo di Jacopo, weaver
Assets in house, loom, loans: 104
Liabilities: personal exemptions (3) and debts: 1,074
Subject to taxation: 0

(Based on G. Brucker, ed., The Society of Renaissance Florence: A Documentary Study. *New York: Harper and Row, 1971, pp. 6–8, 10–12)*

and fifteenth centuries, prostitution flourished in urban Europe generally. City governments tolerated the phenomenon, in some cases insisting that prostitutes be confined to certain neighborhoods or certain houses, elsewhere requiring that some outward distinguishing sign be worn so that a prostitute was not mistaken for a respectable woman. Although some prostitutes were talented musicians or poets, and others were protected and wealthy courtesans, most were ordinary sex workers, who could sometimes eke out a reasonable sustenance in this occupation.

Below workers, servants, and even well-employed prostitutes in the social hierarchy was an urban underclass of those who could not or would not gain a minimum sufficiency from their own labor. Catholic Europe considered the poor to be a special charge and attached no stigma to the floating mass of beggars who gathered at known times in front of churches or public buildings to receive a ration of bread. General purpose hospitals (not yet specialized as places to house the sick) also tended to the needs of the chronically poor. Despite the prevailing benevolent attitude toward the poor, however, the wretchedness of those without home or security remained.

The social groups just described were fluid categories. Individuals might pass through several social roles, ascending or descending in the social hierarchy. Over a lifetime, a woman might be a worker, a wife, a prostitute; a man might be first an artisan, later a merchant. The ranks of the nobility could be entered through marriage, especially from the wealthy merchant or professional groups. Impoverished nobles, or branches of noble families, might descend over generations into the peasantry. Enterprising and skilled artisans might gain merchant status. Women's status was not fixed at birth by the status of their fathers; they might acquire a new social identity through their husbands or descend into lower ranks if fathers, brothers, and husbands all failed them. Although the barriers to social mobility remained high, Renaissance society allowed considerable mobility for a premodern society, a mobility unmatched in some parts of the Western world until the nineteenth century.

Associations

Once basic needs are satisfied, people generally long to have a sense of secure belonging to the world they inhabit. Renaissance people could enjoy many opportunities to belong to associations based on relation, friendship, religious activity, residence, and citizenship. Belonging to such groups enriched the identity of individuals and stretched networks of affiliation across the city that in complex ways linked individuals to the community of the whole.

The first group to which an individual belonged—if to any at all—was his or her family. Not only the immediate members of the nuclear family—parents, siblings, children— but all relations, both maternal and paternal, formed part of one's kin, the whole social universe of those to whom one had a relationship by descent or by marriage. Kinsmen and kinswomen would gather for births, marriages, and funerals. Although kin relationships could deteriorate, for the most part you could trust them to assist you in business, defend you in a lawsuit, relieve you in poverty, defend and preserve your children in your absence.

As important as kin were friends, who could be trusted as much as relations. Young men often made lifelong friends in the new humanist schools, where they spent several years residing together, committed to common goals and values. Powerful friendships are known between comrades in arms, for example, between one Venetian procurator (an official commissioned to supervise mercenary armies) and the great condottiere he accompanied to the battlefield. Wealthy merchants might count among their trusted friends their agents or their notaries—witness the famous correspondence between the mogul Francesco Datini (c. 1335–1410) and his friend and advisor Lapo Mazzei. Friendships among women also crossed class boundaries. Some women formed close relationships with humbler neighbors, or with their own servants.

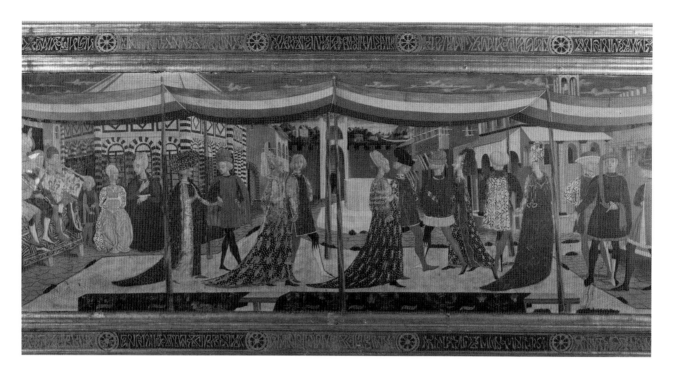

Giovanni di Ser Giovanni (called lo Scheggia), *Wedding Procession,* **c. 1440, panel, 24 × 110 in (63 × 280 cm). Galleria dell'Accademia, Florence.**

Marriage connected two lineages and was thus a central event in Renaissance society. Marriage scenes were often painted on a *cassone* (wedding chest), as here, which a bride then brought to her husband's home.

Beyond the sometimes intense personal relationships of kinship and friendship, Renaissance people associated in other groups that offered comfort and security but were perhaps not so intimate. Everyone belonged to a parish, the community of those who attended a particular church under the supervision of its clergy. There they attended mass, sometimes on a daily basis and on many special occasions. There they visited a confessor and buried their dead. The parish was the primary geographical frame of reference, the small locale that would be named when a person was called upon to state his residence.

There were other religious affiliations beside the parish for the professional religious (see Chapter 6). Some laypersons who wished to dedicate themselves to charitable deeds and pious acts became tertiaries (the "third" category of membership) of religious orders. They did not reside in a monastery or convent, but at home, and did not wear a religious habit, although special costumes were devised to indicate **tertiary** status. Even more common was membership in a confraternity, or brotherhood. Confraternities were groups linked by nothing more than their common dedication to piety and charity. They might include women as well as men and generally enrolled members across class lines. In Venice the confraternities became important, permanent institutions performing essential welfare functions. The six *scuole grandi* (great schools), as confraternities were termed in Venice, became wealthy patrons of the arts and were housed in magnificent and conspicuous buildings. But even in small towns, a confraternity could look after a particular chapel and commission the works of art that adorned it.

Practitioners of trades and professions belonged to guilds, which performed not only economic and political, but also social functions (see p. 29). Guilds provided security to the widows and children of members in a form of life insurance. They often required members to attend their fellows' funerals, assuring that no one would go to his eternal

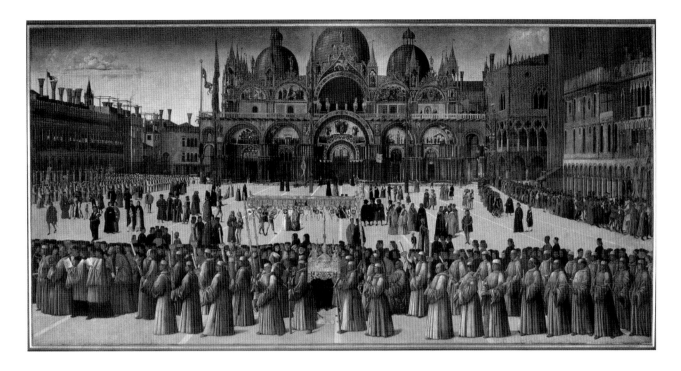

rest unmourned. They offered opportunities for leadership, since guilds had officers and a minimal bureaucracy. They arranged for banquets on special occasions, staged theatrical presentations, or marched as an element of giant civic processions.

A guildsman's training prepared him for the guild, but a more serious education prepared some young men (and eventually a few women) for another kind of association: a conversational circle, the forerunner of what in the later sixteenth century would become the salon or the **academy**. Some early humanist circles in Venice, Milan, Florence, or Rome—glimpsed in the pages of Petrarch, Bruni, or Poggio Bracciolini—performed this role. So did the floating group of "philosophers" who gathered at the Villa Careggi that Cosimo de' Medici bestowed upon the translator of Plato, Marsilio Ficino; informally they called themselves an "academy." The Venetian noblemen and prestigious courtesan friends who gathered to compose and recite poetry were another kind of academy or, perhaps, a more informal salon. After 1500 academies specifically dedicated to the arts, history, poetry, or music, sprang up.

Another social group of importance was that of the neighborhood. Neighbors participated in events of family passage—births, weddings, funerals. Men were organized in militias by neighborhood, or by district, quarter, or *sestiere* (sixth) of the city. When Florence was in danger, at the signal of a bell they would instantly assemble behind the neighborhood leader, or gonfaloniere. Neighborhood allegiances were so strong that even in Renaissance cities, which could be crossed on foot in 15 or 20 minutes, they had their own distinct rituals and even idiosyncrasies of language. A good example of the power of neighborhood identification among the mass of the population were the ritual performances of violence—the "war of the fists"—that were staged in Venice on the boundaries between adjacent neighborhoods.

Gentile Bellini, *Procession in the Piazza San Marco*, 1496, oil on canvas, 12 ft × 24 ft 5¼ in (3.7 × 7.5 m). Galleria dell'Accademia, Venice.

Venetian civic ritual consisted of several annual events developed to enhance social cohesion. Here in the city's greatest public space, Venetian officials progress in hierarchical order, beginning with the doge and magistrates, followed by bureaucrats and leaders of civic associations.

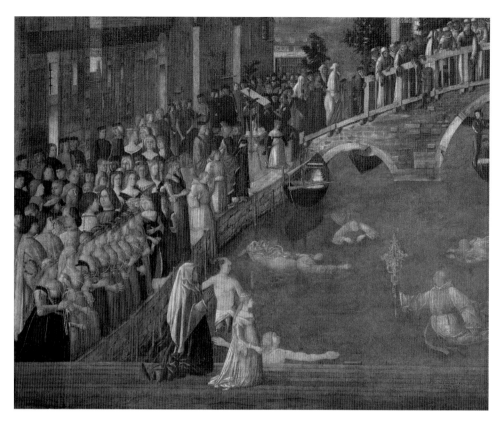

Gentile Bellini, *Miracle of the Cross at the Bridge of San Lorenzo* (detail), 1500, oil on canvas, complete 10 ft 6 in × 14 ft 1 in (3.23 × 4.3 m). Gallerie dell'Accademia, Venice.

As with Mansueti's depiction (see p. 153), Bellini's painting of a sacred event becomes an opportunity to observe a cross-section of Venetian society in action. Crowds gather to observe the rescue of the relic of the cross fallen into the canal.

The largest association, of course, to which the citizen might belong was the city itself. Loyalties to the city were intense in Italy, where for centuries ideals of citizenship and freedom went together. No duke, monarch, region, and certainly no nation ranked above the city in the hierarchy of political forms. Each city's distinct architectural style, speech, and even cuisine is evident even today, more than one century after the unification of Italy.

City loyalty was cemented to a great extent by the participation of the citizens in civic and religious rituals which involved the entire population. These occurred several times a year and were different in each setting. Some ritual celebrations were especially famous. In Florence the feast of St. John the Baptist (the city's patron saint) was the occasion for games and performances. The city of Siena honored the Virgin Mary with a set of horse races, with each city district, fitted out in its own livery, competing against the others. In Venice, which had an especially rich liturgy of civic ritual, urban neighborhoods competed in an enormous boat race each September, and on Ascension Day each spring, the whole city celebrated the marriage of the doge with the sea. Engaging in these civic celebrations, precise in their formulae and repeated year after year, drew residents into identification with the city itself and engaged profound and enduring loyalties—enriching both the city and its citizens.

In sum, the society of the Italian Renaissance offered many opportunities for individuals to engage in local, civic, religious, intellectual, professional, or vocational communities. Here they could freely associate with friends and fellows and develop their abilities and their visions. Renaissance society also limited opportunities, however. Public agencies, both secular and ecclesiastical, vigilantly supervised behavior and were prompt to correct those who spent too lavishly on fashion, explored forbidden areas of sexuality, or engaged in crime or insurrection.

Social Control

Even a free society sets limits on its members. The governors of Renaissance society appear to have been primarily concerned with the issues that any ordered society must be ready to confront: crime, epidemic, and insurrection. Although generally open to contact with foreigners, premodern societies, and the Italian cities as well, did not easily extend the benefits of citizenship to outsiders. In addition, religious traditions fostered hostility to Jews and called for the strenuous regulation of sexual behavior. Christian ideals and a certain social conservatism combined to produce the **sumptuary laws**, which limited the amounts that the affluent members of society could spend on certain luxuries.

Sumptuary and Sexual Control Feudal monarchies and autonomous republics both issued sumptuary legislation, which was commonplace from the thirteenth through eighteenth centuries. In Italian society, the main object was to restrict excesses in dress and jewelry. Sumptuary laws were overwhelmingly directed against women, whose fashion excesses were seen as especially harmful to social order—even though the fashions of elite men were equally extreme. The elaboration of sleeves, the length of trains, the height of shoes, the use of extraordinarily expensive textiles—all were objects of control. Prostitutes, in addition to their other liabilities, were also targeted by sumptuary laws. These prohibited their wearing the kinds of costume and jewelry which were normal for elite women and, in addition, often required their wearing a special sign of their occupation. Men, too, were subject to legislation, notably in Venice, where noblemen were required to wear sober black robes. Clearly the intent of the sumptuary laws was not only economic but also moral. They would protect the economy by preventing wasteful spending but also ensure social order by prohibiting display that was inconsistent with rank.

If sumptuary legislation involved both moral and economic considerations, the regulation of sexuality had a specifically moral rationale. Church rules, household custom, and public law combined to limit the sexual freedom of women. Sexual activity by unmarried women living in their father's household was absolutely not permitted. Their involuntary sexual activity, as the result of rape, would trigger harsh civic penalties and possibly also private revenge on the perpetrator. Similarly, the violation of a married woman invited severe punishment. So would a woman's voluntary adultery. And so would a man's adultery if the honor of a respectable householder was injured by it, although it was held of no account if the woman concerned was of ill repute. Equally, the rape of such a woman by a man of high status would be considered only a light offense.

Beyond the protection of the reputable wives and daughters of householders, the main force of sexual regulation in Renaissance society was directed against two targets: prostitutes and males engaging in homosexual activity. Prostitutes, as has been seen, might

The Renaissance had no concept of "homosexuality." Acts of sodomy, however, defined as sexual acts "contrary to nature," were prosecuted diligently and punished severely. Most accused sodomites were male and were charged with engaging in activity that would today be called homosexual. Contrary to present-day patterns, homosexual relationships were mostly pederastic, involving an older male in the active role, and a younger, generally adolescent male in the passive role; they rarely involved two mature males. The age-curve of sodomites investigated by one magistracy, the Ufficiali di Notte, during the period 1478–1502 was skewed toward the young; more than 80 per cent were under the age of 30.

Ages of Males Accused of Sodomy by the Florentine Officials of the Night

Age	Number	Percentage
> 18	562	44.9
19–30	476	38.0
31–40	138	11.0
41–50	51	4.1
51–60	17	1.4
< 61	8	0.6
Total	**1,252**	**100**

(M. Rocke, *Forbidden Friendships: Homosexuality and Male Culture in Renaissance Florence*. New York: Oxford University Press, 1996, p. 244)

be required to live in certain sections of town or in officially sanctioned brothels, to wear distinctive clothing or insignia, and to obey sumptuary restrictions. Males engaging in same-sex activity—almost a rite of passage among the late adolescents of elite strata—might be subjected to severe penalties. Sodomy was a crime that could and sometimes did warrant the penalty of execution by burning. That penalty was rarely exacted, however. Although there was great anxiety among the moral overseers of Renaissance society about male homosexuality, its practice was common.

Crime, Insurrection, and Disease Those guilty of ordinary crimes were also diligently pursued in the complex judicial systems of the Italian state. Crimes of violence aroused more outrage than crimes against property, although perpetrators of both were subject to investigation and prosecution. Crimes against property were typically punished by the imposition of a fine. Violent criminals were also often fined. Execution, a showy affair that gathered a large public audience, was rarely used. Torture, on the other hand, was routinely used by both secular and ecclesiastical officials. The inquisitorial procedure for the investigation of malfeasance established by Roman law—the common heritage of both secular and church courts—called for confession to establish guilt where there were no credible eyewitnesses to a crime. Torture was generally employed in these cases to extract the necessary confession.

RIOT, PLAGUE, AND PUNISHMENT

The relative harmony of urban life was obtained only by constant surveillance and control. These excerpts show the Renaissance state on the job in an attempt to control crime, prevent riot, and deal with the threat of plague.

The Venetian Council of Ten acts to prevent riot during a scarcity crisis (1569):

On 11 October the Council of Ten and the Zonta [additional advisors], *wishing to alleviate the great dearth of grain which had occurred in Venice, decreed that everyone ... must declare all the grain and flour in the country possessions of noblemen, citizens, prelates, friaries, monasteries and convents ... of the city of Venice. They were to bring all this grain to Venice by the end of the month of October, and they were also obliged to declare all the grain which is here in Venice and sell it here, and likewise to declare all the mouths in each household.... Furthermore, all persons who, after the proclamation of this decree, sold abroad any corn or flour which belonged to anyone other than the bodies listed above were to be banished for ever from Venice and its district.*

(D. Chambers and B. Pullan, eds., *Venice: A Documentary History, 1450–1630*. Toronto: University of Toronto Press, 2001, p. 111. © RSA)

The Venetian Health Office (Provveditori alla Sanità) orders measures against plague (1541):

Ordinances to be observed when plague is discovered in the city, that steps may be taken to ensure that, by God's grace, it does not spread further.

When the [Health] Office has been notified that a death has occurred in the city ... the doctor of the Office must be sent to view the body ... to see if there is an abscess, carbuncle or other symptom.... If plague is found, the whole house must immediately be placed under a ban.... Then the notary and an attendant at the Office must be sent to examine the inhabitants on oath and under threat of punishment.... The notary must take special care to ask if the sick or dead person has been in any house where anyone has died; whether foreigners have lodged with him ... for how many days he has been ill ... whether any relative or friend has been there to visit and how many times ... whether any of the neighbours has come in to help around the house, as often happens; whether any goods have been taken out of the house, and where, and to whom.

(Chambers and Pullan, *Venice*, pp. 115–116)

Florentine judges condemn a woman for infanticide (1407):

We condemn ... Monna Francesca ... of Pistoia ... a most cruel woman and murderess.... During ... the past year, Francesca ... had conversations with a certain Jacopo of Romagna ... who told her that he wanted to take her for his wife. So Francesca, persuaded by his words and his arguments ... became pregnant by Jacopo.... Then Francesca, knowing herself to be pregnant, promised to marry ... Cecco Arrighi ... and after their wedding they had intercourse together, as is proper between husband and wife. Cecco did not realize that Francesca was pregnant by Jacopo.... In the month of March of the present year, Francesca was approaching the time of delivery and with God's help, she gave birth to a healthy male child in the house of her husband Cecco.... But inspired by an evil spirit and so that no one would know that she had given birth to that child, she threw him in the river ... and as a result this son and creature of God was drowned.

[Francesca confessed. She was led through the streets of Pistoia on a donkey, with the corpse of her child tied to her neck, and was then burned to death.]

(G. Brucker, *The Society of Renaissance Florence*. Toronto: University of Toronto Press, 1997, pp. 146–147. © RSA)

THE JEWISH COMMUNITY IN THE ITALIAN RENAISSANCE

Jews constituted a tiny minority of Italians during the Renaissance: about 20,000 in the late sixteenth century, most living in Rome and the Papal States. Some, like many of the Roman community, were descendants of Jewish inhabitants of late ancient Italy. The *Tedeschi* (German, or Ashkenazi Jews) had arrived from the north. Some had recently arrived from Spain and Portugal, major centers of medieval Jewish life from which they had been expelled in 1492 and 1497 respectively. Some had come from the Levant in the eastern Mediterranean, then under Ottoman rule, where Jewish communities thrived.

Different cities of Italy had different policies with regard to the Jews. In general, they were welcome when their supplies of capital made them useful as sources of loans or as pawnbrokers for the populace. When they were no longer needed for these purposes, they might be expelled. At times, anti-Semitism spiraled, as at Trent in 1475, when a blood libel charge fomented a cruel pogrom. All the Jewish males were executed; the women and children were forced to convert.

A rich Jewish cultural life flourished despite the harsh regulations imposed on Jewish residents. The following is an extract from Florentine regulations for the Jewish community issued in 1463:

> Every Jew, male or female above the age of twelve ... shall be required to wear a sign of O in the city of Florence. This yellow O shall be worn on the left breast, over the clothing in a visible place; it shall be at least one foot in circumference and as wide as the thickness of a finger....
>
> To prevent any large concentration of Jews in Florence, or a greater number than is necessary, in future the Jews engaged in moneylending in Florence may not number more than seventy persons in their houses and in their shops, working as factors and apprentices. Included in this number of seventy are Jews of both sexes, masculine and feminine, large and small.
>
> *(Brucker, The Society of Renaissance Florence, p. 242)*

In Venice in 1516, the Jews were required to live in an area of the city called the *ghetto*—the first such place to which European Jews were confined.

> Given the urgent needs of the present times, the ... Jews have been permitted to come and live in Venice.... But no god-fearing subject of our state would have wished them ... to disperse throughout the city, sharing houses with Christians and going wherever they choose by day and night, perpetrating all those misdemeanours and detestable and abominable acts which are generally known and shameful to describe.... Be it determined that, to prevent such grave disorders ... the following measures shall be adopted, i.e. that all the Jews who are at present living in different parishes within our city, and all others who may come here ... shall be obliged to go at once to dwell together in the houses in the court within the Geto at San Hieronimo, where there is plenty of room for them to live.
>
> *(Chambers and Pullan, Venice, p. 338)*

Amid the many restrictions and discouragements to normal existence, the Jews of Italy persevered in their ancient traditions while creating new works of philosophy, art, and literature. They contributed to the Renaissance culture of their neighbors which, in its Christian assumptions, was in many ways antithetical to the Jewish way of life. The Christian humanist Hebraists, for instance, among them Manetti, Pico, and Valla (see Chapter 3), necessarily acquired that language from Jewish teachers.

Meanwhile, Jewish philosophers had an affinity for the Platonic and Neoplatonic ideas that were fused with humanist themes in the work of Pico and Ficino. One of the major works of sixteenth-century Platonism, wholly integrated with Jewish Kabbalism, was the *Dialoghi dell'amore* (*Dialogues on Love*, 1535) by the Sephardic (Spanish) Jew Leone Ebreo (Judah Abravanel, c. 1460–c. 1521). Its influence extended to Giordano Bruno and the seventeenth-century philosopher Baruch Spinoza (1632–1677). The dialogue features the interlocutors Philo (Greek for love) and Sophia (Greek for wisdom), in which Philo explains that his love had its origin in a longing for a universal good:

> Love is of two kinds. Of these, one is engendered by desire or sensual appetite: a man may love a woman

because he desires her. Such love is imperfect, deriving as it does from a source both inconstant and vicious: for it is a child born of desire…. But the other love itself generates desire of the beloved, instead of being generated by that desire or appetite: in fact we first love perfectly, and then the strength of that love makes us desire spiritual and bodily union with the beloved…. For the love I bear you is no child of desire, but my desire is the child of love, which begot it.

(L. Ebreo, *The Philosophy of Love*, trans. F. Friedeberg-Seeley. London: Soncino Press, 1937, p. 56)

Jewish authors also pursued the genres of poetic and epistolary composition that were key for humanists. Sara Copio Sullam (c. 1592–1641), a Jewish woman thinker of the seventeenth century and resident of the Venetian ghetto, was a poet and a *salonière*, in whose home the learned gathered to talk about the latest ideas. Her most famous work was a defense of her belief in the immortality of the soul, against a Christian accuser. The inscription on her tomb in the Jewish cemetery of San Nicolò del Lido, composed by the scholar Leon da Modena, her teacher, reads in part:

A lady of great intelligence
Wise among women
Supporting those in need
The poor found a companion and friend in her …
May her soul enjoy eternal beatitude.

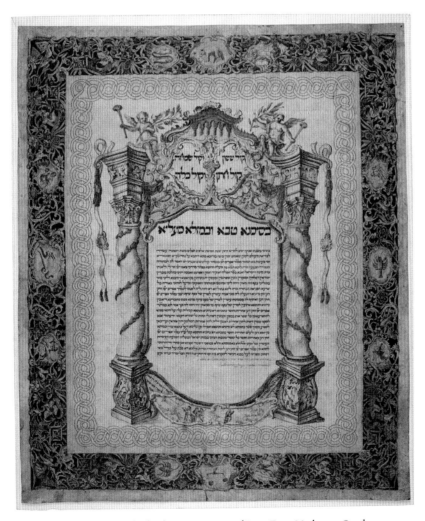

Ketubah (marriage contract) of Ephraim Sanguini and Luna Faro, Modena, 1 October, 1557. British Library, London.

In common with other premodern societies, Renaissance Italy faced danger, not only from individual criminals, but from masses of enraged citizens. Such insurrections might have political and economic causes, such as the famous revolt of the Florentine ciompi in 1378 (see Chapter 2). More commonly, they were riots triggered by scarcity. Famine in the countryside put pressure on prices in the marketplace, provoking angry responses both to the high cost and to the corruption that it engendered, such as the profiteering sale of inferior or adulterated grain. Prudent regimes kept stores of grain on hand in the event of shortages. Even so, they needed to manage those reserves cautiously and often used force to control crowds of hungry and enraged rioters.

Plague, endemic throughout the Renaissance period after its first arrival in 1348 (see Chapter 2), also threatened social disruption. The urban authorities sought to avoid this by isolating plague-stricken households or sections, by the mass burial of bodies, and by trying to control looting and profiteering. Special permanent commissions were formed in some cities to deal with such matters. The Renaissance period saw the creation of specialized institutions for the housing of plague victims: the Lazaretto Vecchio in Venice, for instance, was established on an isolated island in 1423. Hospitals continued to grow and to specialize in this era because of the persistent problem of plague.

Jews and Other Groups Beggars, foreigners, and Jews were also often seen as a social problem requiring supervision and control by government institutions. For centuries, as elsewhere in Europe, cities tolerated and meagerly sustained a fluctuating group of the desperately poor, who were dependent on the generosity of church-related institutions. Foreigners—principally Greeks, Slavs, and other Mediterranean peoples who had come to trade or who sought refuge—tended to gather in communities of the major port cities, Venice and Genoa, where they built their own churches and service institutions. Jews were another story.

Although their European presence had been uninterrupted since antiquity, Jews were sporadically targeted for persecution and repression, especially in crisis times of famine or plague. Italian cities intermittently expelled and welcomed Jewish communities. Jews were welcomed and hated for the same reason: they provided a source of credit for loans to enterprises and individuals and then insisted upon being repaid at stated rates of interest. The Jewish community, too, provided many of the physicians available to diagnose and treat the illnesses of those able to pay for such services.

The fifteenth century, the age of humanism's great advance, was ironically an era of marked anti-Semitism in Italy. There was resentment toward Jewish moneylenders and physicians, and the terrible blood libel (that accused Jews of killing Christian children to obtain blood for their Passover rituals) exploded in the notorious case of Simon of Trent in 1475. By the early 1500s, however, that sort of hysteria appears to have abated. Italy absorbed many of the Sephardic Jews escaping persecution in Spain and Portugal after the expulsions of 1492 and 1497. In Rome and elsewhere, and especially in Venice, they settled in separate neighborhoods. In the latter city, partly to contain them and partly to protect them, Jews were required to live in one section, called the *ghetto*, after the iron foundry that had been that area's principal activity. It was the first ghetto in Europe, where

400 years later this phase of the history of anti-Semitism would culminate in an attempt to exterminate all Jews.

PRIVATE LIFE

Under subsistence conditions in the earlier Middle Ages, most Europeans retired from their labors to sparse one-room huts. In this context, the concept of "private life" has little meaning. Nobles and kings were the first householders to develop a more elaborate domestic existence. Their castles became residences as well as fortresses; they gathered about them family members, servants, close friends, protégés, and dependents; and they developed the arts and rituals that gave meaning to leisure. From the eleventh century, the urban bourgeoisie also began to develop a more complex private life. By the fourteenth century in Italy, a sizable part of the population had done so. Alongside the social interactions that took place in the streets and the piazzas of the city, within the confines of their homes, Renaissance people gathered in domestic communities, distributed property to rising generations, distinguished male and female realms of action, and reared and taught their children.

The Household

The Renaissance household was first a material, second a social entity. The house and its contents were the material foundation on which private life rested. Although poorer workers might rent rooms, successful artisans and those higher in the social hierarchy more likely owned their houses. Furniture could be minimal: a table, stools, some cooking utensils, and a bed. A more substantial household would contain two or more rooms. Often the artisan's workshop was located in the front room facing the street, from which wares could be sold to the public passing by. The wealthy burgher's house would boast more and more elaborate furniture—finely crafted tables and chairs, tapestries and carpets—and separate bedrooms, with related linens and bedding. The residences of the very wealthy flourished during the Renaissance, their lavish furnishings complementing the elegant architecture and finely decorated walls and ceilings of their splendid palaces.

As domestic space grew and became more specialized, it is likely that people's attitudes and feelings became more complex as well. The addition of bedrooms—first that of the householder and his wife, then subsidiary bedrooms—was both the sign of a developing sense of reserve and intimacy and the condition that made those sentiments possible. The enlargement of the hall (or salon, or parlor—the modern living room) enabled a richer leisure life, when family members and invited guests could engage in conversation or music making. As the ritual of dining became more elaborate, so did the tableware; this was another setting for conversation among household members, neighbors, and kin.

DEATH AND CONSOLATION

From the fourteenth to sixteenth centuries, urban people traumatized by repeated experience of plague paid increasing attention to death. In works of art, in literature, and in the rituals that surrounded illness and burial, the preoccupation is apparent. Long before the moment came—for none knew, as preachers reminded their audiences, the hour of their death—people readied themselves for a "good" death, one that was prepared, penitent, and holy. In this project, they were guided by a new genre of how-to books which advised on the *ars moriendi* (the art of dying). Humanism added to the conversation of death, introducing the letter or treatise of consolation. From these works, stylized though they were and determined by religious and rhetorical conventions, something can be learned of how people felt about those they lost.

In the first passage below, the humanist Francesco Barbaro informs his learned daughter about the death of her kinswoman. In the second, a humanist pen-for-hire describes the grief felt by the Venetian nobleman Jacopo Antonio Marcello at the death of his young son.

Francesco to Costanza Barbaro (1447) *I believe, dear Costanza, you have heard that Luchina Miani, in Padua, after a long and serious illness, departed from this fragile and vulnerable life in such a way that her death gave assurance of her salvation…. Even before she had despaired of her life she had … so composed her soul, and so spoke of God with mixed joy and tears that one could perceive that she did not fear death but piously hoped for it. Then, kneeling on the bare floor while imminent death shook her trembling limbs and tears flowed down her face, she received the sacraments of the church…. Without surcease the force of the sickness so tormented her and tortured her limbs and flesh that she was forced to live, it seemed, who was already dead. She could neither lie still nor stand, and she thrashed around the entire bed with her pain…. [Therefore], beloved Costanza, we should … rejoice that she lived and died in such a way that there can be no doubt that she moved to a better life. We may censure ourselves if, in the meantime, we do not conquer by reason the sorrow that time will soften. Let us balance against the brief span of this life eternal memory and so compose ourselves that we learn to live by dying well and to die by living well.*

(M.L. King and A. Rabil, trans. and ed., Her Immaculate Hand: Selected Works by and about Women Humanists of Quattrocento Italy, *2nd rev. ed. Binghampton, NY: SUNY Press, 1991, pp. 106, 109–111*)

Giorgio Bevilacqua, writing for Jacopo Antonio Marcello (1463) *When I saw him, I scarcely thought that it would result in death, that my son would desert me, his father; unthinking me, it never entered my mind. At that time I believed that the beginning of his illness was nothing, a trifle, and I thought that his good health would soon return. But when I saw that the situation slipped into serious illness, oh me! What effort did I expend to save him! How I exhorted the doctors to cure him! How assiduously I urged them! What vows did I offer for his safety not only with tears but with rivers of tears! I believe I canvassed all the judges in heaven in order to make all the saints friendly to me. I called for the help of mortals and immortals; vainly I tried everything…. I approached all the monasteries of our city, and all the most religious men of the religious orders I wearied with my importunity.*

(M.L. King, The Death of the Child Valerio Marcello. *Chicago: University of Chicago Press, 1994, p. 20*)

The private study appeared as the wealthy and educated sought a space to read and think (see Chapter 3).

Only the wealthiest families inhabited residences with multiple specialized rooms and furniture and furnishings dedicated to the functions of eating and sleeping. Most of the population managed these activities with minimal accoutrement. The wealthiest families were also those likely to have the most children. In Europe, generally, the largest families were wealthy families, an effect due in part to the capacity of their households to absorb extra kin and non-related strangers, including servants. This pattern appears also to be generally true for Italy. It is an established fact for the region of Tuscany, dominated by Florence. Because of the extraordinary requirements for the collection of a tax on assets in 1427, modern historians David Herlihy and Christiane Klapisch-Zuber were able to assemble an extensive statistical profile of Tuscan households. The average household size for the region, both urban and rural, was 4.42 persons. But wealthy Florentines—those with assets amounting to over 1,600 florins—had households that numbered five, six, or more persons. And even a more modest group of those with assets of 400 florins or more was five times as likely as the very poor to live in households numbering 11 or more persons. What was true of Florence and Tuscany was not necessarily true of other regions of Italy, but the Florentine evidence confirms a pattern of correlation of larger households with wealth that is also evident elsewhere.

It is likely, then, that Renaissance households on average were not enormously large, relative to modern household sizes, but that large households did exist and were concentrated among the wealthy. Household structure also related to wealth and occupation. Just over 10 per cent of Florentine and just over 20 per cent of Tuscan households were "extended" or "multinuclear." Those terms signify that more than two generations of a family or that more than two married adult males were co-resident. Both of these patterns occurred most often among the propertied upper strata of society and more often in the countryside than in the city. Small percentages of households consisted of a single resident or had no discernible nuclear structure. Most households, however—64 per cent in urban and 77 per cent in rural areas of Tuscany—were organized around married couples, one of whom might be widowed for a period during the household's existence. The proportion is likely to be even higher in other parts of Italy where multinuclear arrangements were less common.

Patriarchy, Property, and Marriage

The dominant form of household was thus the nuclear household, a procreative entity in most cases headed by a married couple. This is the context in which the principal features of family existence described below would most likely be encountered. Here the presence of a patriarchal figure and the decision to preserve property by limiting its descent to the male lineage had important consequences for the lives of all family members.

Fathers and Sons The male head of the nuclear family—the patriarch—was above all concerned with property. His property, or wealth, sustained his family and permitted their survival and welfare. A poor householder was concerned primarily with sustenance, or subsistence. His family, ideally, was small so that there would not be too many mouths to feed. Children were few, as a consequence of high mortality (see pp. 178–179) or an early exit from a household that could not sustain a child beyond the age of 8, 10, or 12. Children also provided labor, however, and so to the extent that they were helpful and could be sustained, they might remain. Wives, too, provided labor. If a poor householder lost his wife, which would occur most frequently through death in childbirth, he generally remarried. In consequence of that decision, a new generation of children was born. Inheritance issues were not pressing, unless the householder owned land that he farmed in the countryside. That land would generally descend to his son or sons.

A wealthy man did not concern himself with mere subsistence. His aim was to protect and maximize his household wealth and to bestow it as an inheritance upon one or more sons so that it might be preserved and increased. As the cost of daily bread was of less concern, a wealthy man's household might contain several children—his own, by one or more marriages, and perhaps those of his less affluent kin. In addition, many servants lived in a wealthy household, providing domestic service, supervision of children, and assistance with the householder's occupation and related needs, such as the care of his horses. Thus the wealthy household tended to be large.

Its members were not, however, equal. Not only were adults more valued than children and the householder's kin than non-kin or servants, but males were valued more than females. Wives could bear legitimate children to the householder (among them a principal heir) and were on that account highly respected. But daughters, however valued for their personal traits, were in this era destined to exit the household to one of two fates: to marriage or to a convent for lifelong residence instead of marriage. Sons, on the other hand, were potential heirs, the future administrators and nurturers of the householder's property. Although in individual cases, strong emotional bonds would link fathers and daughters, family strategic objectives argued for a greater investment in the future of males.

In Renaissance Italy, one or several sons might inherit their father's wealth. The wealthiest families in Venice and Florence, like some of the noble clans, would expect their sons to continue to possess household wealth collectively, perhaps even living together in one palace or complex. Other families might designate one son as the heir to the family enterprise, placing other sons in promising positions during their parent's lifetime, assuring their future careers. Arranging for sons to gain high positions in the church—especially as bishops or cardinals—was a particularly good solution. These clerical sons, officially celibate, not only received an income from outside the family but could confer benefits upon their immediate family and kin. Even an illegitimate or "natural" son might inherit paternal wealth, although not in preference to his legitimate brothers. A fond father might pay for the education of a particularly treasured illegitimate son and even redirect wealth to him if all his other sons were to die.

Daughters and Dowries Unlike her brothers, a daughter did not expect to inherit a major or equal share of paternal wealth. Even if all her brothers died before her, it was likely that the family wealth would be transferred to the male line nearest in relationship. In European society generally, daughters were married to men from families remote in relationship. They brought with them a certain amount of paternal wealth in the form of a dowry. The dowry might consist of cash, jewels, and clothing, as well as linens, textiles, and other fine objects. Normally, it consisted of only a small part of the bride's family's wealth. The bride might also possess some personal wealth beyond the dowry, most likely in the form of gifts from her father or her mother. She was free to dispose of all her wealth—the dowry wealth and her personal wealth—as she willed. Women of the propertied classes often distributed their property very carefully, with bequests characteristically to female servants, acquaintances, and kin. During her lifetime, however, her dowry wealth remained at the disposition of her husband. Theoretically, its management was transferred to him because it helped support the cost of incorporating a wife into his household. In reality, many families managed as well as they did because of the profits made from the dowry of the householder's wife.

Was marriage merely a business arrangement? It seems clear that nearly all marriages among the propertied classes were in fact businesslike. For example, the marriage process began with agreements among male kin on both sides about property arrangements. But there were religious and sentimental aspects of marriage as well. It seems that many husbands and wives were devoted to each other, and certainly that they cooperated for the welfare of their families. Divorce was not a legitimate option, but desertion was possible; yet most marriages remained intact during the lifetimes of the members. Among artisan households, where a woman's labor was essential to the welfare of the family and the prosperity of the family enterprise, husbands and wives might become even more closely tied to one another.

Money intruded again as a factor in marriage at times of transition: when a woman died and when her husband died. Then the marriage relationship was broken, and the dowry again became an important issue. The circumstances were most difficult when the husband died and there were surviving children. In Italy a wife had no permanent place in the household in which she raised her children except through the presence of her husband. In some cases, men included specific instructions in their wills that invited their wives to remain in their households and to be provided with food and clothing, so they might continue as mothers to their children. If a woman stayed in her deceased husband's household under these circumstances, however, she might be subjected to coldness and resentment from her husband's kin.

If she (or her parents) decided that she should leave, she would leave her children behind—presumably at some significant personal cost to her or her children. If she was still young and marriageable, she might remarry. If not, she always had the *tornata* (right of return) to the household of her father, who was obliged to support her. Young or old, the widow would take her dowry with her. In doing so, she would deprive her former household, and her own children, of the profits that had customarily been received from the

THE DUTIES OF A WIFE

Marriage in the Renaissance, as in premodern societies generally, served the interests of the male householder. A man chose a wife to bear legitimate children and maintain the honor of his lineage. Her duties were to be obedient, manage the household, rear children, and nurse the ill.

This is the vision of marriage expressed by the Venetian humanist Francesco Barbaro, who in 1415 wrote the first modern treatise *On Marriage*, from which the excerpt below is taken. His work defines the expectations of the institution held by his generation and rank.

> *Three things, then, are required of a wife to make a marriage praiseworthy and admirable: that she love her husband; that she live virtuously; and that she manage domestic affairs soberly and diligently. I shall explore the first of these, once a little has been said about a wife's capacity for obedience—than which nothing is more pleasing, nothing more desirable—for it is the master and guide of her capacity for love.... A wife who wishes, therefore, to settle differences among her children and servants, first let her settle those with her husband, lest she be criticized for doing that for which she faults others. If she is to perform her duty of maintaining and securing peace and quiet in her marriage, then nothing should more occupy her mind than the need in all matters to assent to her husband.*
>
> (Francesco Barbaro, The Wealth of Wives: *A Fifteenth-Century Marriage Manual, trans. and ed. M.L. King. Toronto: Iter Press, 2015, pp. 96, 99)*

In 1592 another Venetian, Moderata Fonte (pseudonym of Modesta da Pozzo, 1555–1592), the daughter of solid citizens of the professional class and married to the same, completed her dialogue *The Worth of Women*. She died in childbirth the very same day. Her lengthy and multifaceted work (see also Chapter 11, p. 391) touches on many issues concerning women, marriage being only one of them. This statement on marriage by Corinna to Helena concerns the dowry, the sum given to a groom by the bride's family upon marriage. Fonte's critical tone distinguishes this passage sharply from Barbaro's.

> *[Helena]: Dowries are paid to husbands because when a man marries, he is shouldering a great burden; and men who are not rich could not maintain a household without the subsidy of a dowry.*
>
> *[Corinna]: You've got it all wrong.... On the contrary, the woman when she marries has to take on the expense of children and other worries; she's more in need of acquiring money than giving it away. Because if she were alone, without a husband, she could live like a queen on her dowry (more or less so, of course, according to her social position). But when she takes a husband, especially if he's poor, as is often the case, what exactly does she gain from it, except that instead of being her own mistress and the mistress of her own money, she becomes a slave, and loses her liberty and, along with her liberty, her control over her own property, surrendering all that she has to the man who has bought her, and putting everything in his hands—so that he can run through the lot in a week? Look what a good deal marriage is for women! They lose their property, lose themselves, and get nothing in return, except children to trouble them and the rule of a man, who orders them about at his will.*
>
> (Moderata Fonte, The Worth of Women, *trans. and ed. V. Cox. Chicago: University of Chicago Press, 1997, pp. 113–114)*

dowry she had brought with her at marriage. In those cases where her deceased husband's kin would not release her dowry, she was forced to sue for its restitution.

If a wife died before her husband, the consequences were simpler. Her dowry wealth, subject to the arrangements made in her will, would largely remain in the family of her husband and descend directly to her sons by that marriage. Then the object of the dowry system would have been achieved: a portion of one man's wealth would have been transferred through his daughter to the sons of another man. The purpose of the dowry—as opposed to an open share of paternal inheritance—was to ensure that the loss of paternal wealth to the male line was limited and controlled. Dowries could be enormous; but if so, the aim was to secure the most advantageous marriage connection for the parents of the bride, not to transfer more wealth to another family.

In fact, many daughters, sometimes several in a family, were not married with a dowry. Instead, they were sent to a convent to pursue a professional religious career. Although they might have had no original inclination for this, sometimes they developed a liking for the institution and found it a relief to have been spared the difficulties and dangers of marriage. This practice of sending superfluous daughters to convents became very common in some Italian cities, especially after 1500 when dowry values soared. A daughter consigned to a convent also brought a dowry with her; its value, however, was considerably less than a marital dowry.

Women and Children

Marriage in the Renaissance, certainly among the prosperous, was always constrained by considerations of property. The roles women played were similarly limited and not only by property considerations. Medical and biological realities and the shifting patterns and demands of society all affected women and the children they bore.

Childbirth In the Renaissance, as in premodern societies generally, childbirth was a prominent part of a woman's life. Most women gave birth regularly during all the years of their fertility, from early adolescence through their early forties. In the absence of modern contraceptive measures, only a woman's poor health or lack of nutrition prevented pregnancies, so long as she was readily available to her husband or to other men. There were some contraceptive practices which were condemned, such as non-vaginal intercourse and coitus interruptus; others were not reliable, such as various herbal remedies that caused abortions. Breastfeeding, too, made pregnancy less likely, but its contraceptive effect was not dependable.

Women faced the possibility of death with each birth, as maternal mortality rates reached 10 per cent at times. Even though a woman survived one birth, if she gave birth 12 or 15 times in her lifetime the chances of a fatally unsuccessful birth were high. Childbirth was the leading cause of death among younger women. The frequent remarriages of European men, which have left their mark in genealogies, notarial documents, and diaries, witness the sacrifices made by women in the process of giving birth to new life.

A woman who inherited wealth from her father at last exercised her right to dispose of it when she died. Women's testaments, as free statements of their wishes, are important records of how they saw the world. This exceedingly wealthy woman, who with her husband and sons was a patron of projects in the Basilica of the Frari in Venice, made these bequests by her first will of July 2, 1432. It is notable that Franceschina left her *residuum*—the bulk of her fortune, everything left after the laundry list of tiny or modest bequests—to *all* her children, both male and female.

2 ducats for masses at Saint Gregory to be said "for my soul"

3 ducats to Corpus Christi "for my soul"

3 ducats to S. Andrea "for my soul"

3 ducats to S. Alvise "for my soul"

3 ducats to S. Gerolamo "for my soul"

3 ducats to the nuns of A.M. degli Angeli of Murano "for my soul"

3 ducats to the nuns of S. Bernardo "for my soul"

6 ducats "so that a person of good reputation [may] be sent to Assisi to pray to God for my soul"

4 ducats "that masses of the Madonna be said for my soul"

3 ducats "to be given to some good person to go to S. Pietro di Castello to worship for one year to get pardon for my soul"

2 ducats "to be given to some person of good conscience to go one year to get pardon at S. Lorenzo"

6 ducats "that a prayer be offered for my soul"

10 ducats "to be given to the poor who are of the greatest need for my soul"

6 ducats "for the poor of S. Lorenzo"

2 ducats "to S. Brigida that they pray God for my soul"

2 ducats to S. Maria della Carità "for my soul"

3 ducats to S. Giorgio "to require that masses be said for my soul"

40 ducats to my mother

25 ducats to my brother

23 ducats to my sister

100 ducats to my husband

"And I leave all my residual [possessions] to my children, both boys and girls, equally."

(R. Goffen, Piety and Patronage in Renaissance Venice: Bellini, Titian, and the Franciscans. New Haven, CT, London: *Yale University Press, 1986, pp. 35–36)*

Even more fragile than mothers were the babies they bore. Infants died frequently not only in childbirth but also in the first few days and weeks of life and then still in their first two years. Even as children and through adolescence to age 20, they continued to be more susceptible than adults to disease and hardship. Infant mortality rates in Europe generally fluctuated from around 25 per cent to as high as 50 per cent. The causes were multiple, but underlying them all were poor sanitation and poor nutrition, which left these vulnerable beings prone to infection. Endemic plague was a further problem but by no means the only cause of fatal illness. With the exception of the plague, which ceased to be endemic after 1720, these patterns persisted into the nineteenth century.

Midwives Despite the uncertainty of infant life, in secure families a new baby was welcomed into the world by a group of adults more numerous than the infant's own family. Just before and during the birth, men were absent. The new mother was surrounded by women: her own kin, her servants (in affluent households), her neighbors, and the midwife.

Midwives had no formal training, but acquired their expert knowledge from earlier generations, often from their own mothers. They attended uncomplicated deliveries, but they managed all manner of complicated and risky births as well. They could rotate the infant in the womb or encourage or assist in labor. When all assistance failed, they could perform an emergency baptism for a dying infant or surgically dismember a stillborn child in the womb in order to remove the remnants and save the mother's life. They could also perform a caesarean—always on a dead woman—to save a living infant.

Midwives were acquainted not only with the mechanics and psychological aspects of birth but also with the properties of herbs, as indeed were many of the women present, especially in a rural setting. When not managing childbirth, midwives were "wise women" or natural healers, tending the illnesses of women and children and sometimes of adult men as well. They used herbal remedies for problems relating to birth, reproduction, sexuality, and love, among others. Of these, some were efficacious, according to modern pharmacology, and some not; some were downright dangerous.

The company of women that presented itself when a woman gave birth in all but the lowest strata of society performed the functions today carried out by a university-trained and licensed physician. Until the eighteenth century, male physicians were detached from the birthing process and, indeed, from all gynecological concerns. The most important medieval manual of obstetrics and gynecology was named *Trotula*, after the famous and partly legendary female physician of that name (c. 1100) from Salerno, a center of medical learning south of Naples influenced by Arab medical practice. Only in the fifteenth and sixteenth centuries did male physicians, such as the Paduan physician Michele Savonarola (1385–1468) and the German physician Eugenius Rösslin (d. 1526) respectively, begin to write manuals of instruction specifically directed toward midwives. Not only were male physicians not directly involved in the birthing process, it is unlikely that male physicians could have performed better than the experienced midwives. Neither male nor female practitioner had an accurate understanding of the processes of insemination, fetal growth, and birth; neither knew anything about infection or its prevention. Without this knowledge (acquired only in the seventeenth through nineteenth centuries), the outcomes of the birthing process could not have been greatly improved.

Legitimacy and Illegitimacy Another kind of outcome related to social, rather than medical, circumstances. A baby's destiny depended on its mother's status. The child of a married woman was legitimate; the child of an unmarried one was illegitimate. In the modern West, this distinction has lost most of its force. During the Renaissance, however, the distinction was important. An illegitimate child rarely enjoyed the privileges

CHILDBIRTH AND CHILDREARING
IN RENAISSANCE ITALY

Among the propertied classes of Renaissance society, women had one principal function: they were to bear babies who, as the offspring of legitimate marriages, could inherit patrimonial wealth. When a woman of this social rank gave birth, therefore, it was a cause of great celebration. At no other point in her lifetime, except perhaps at her wedding, did she receive so much attention.

Most women did in fact marry and most gave birth. Since there were no modern means of contraception, a woman gave birth repeatedly during the whole period of her fertility, from her mid-teens to early forties. It was common for women to produce eight to a dozen children, not uncommonly 20 or more. Few, however, survived. Overall, infant and child mortality stayed between 25 and 50 per cent for the whole premodern period. It was rare for a woman to see all her children survive her and not unusual for all to predecease her.

Women, too, died in childbirth. The moment of birthing was highly dangerous. Childbirth was the leading cause of death among women during the years of their fertility. Many feared death and prepared their last testaments as the birth approached. Most feared the pains of labor, which even men understood to be severe and terrifying.

Management of the process of birth was the business of an informal community of women consisting of household members, neighbors and kin, the midwife, nurse, and other servants. It was a community of women of different ages, social origins, kinship, and experience—thus quite unlike the communities of men, which were highly stratified by age, class, and profession.

Domenico Ghirlandaio (c. 1448–1494) painted two scenes on the walls of the Tornabuoni Chapel in the Church of Santa Maria Novella in Florence showing such a female birthing community. One, shown here, depicts the birth of John the Baptist; the second depicts the birth of the Virgin Mary. In both cases, the birth of sacred infants is transposed to a contemporary setting. In the scene shown here (see facing page), the eldest of the three women visitors is a portrait of Lucrezia Tornabuoni (1427–1482), whose family commissioned the fresco, herself a poetess and patron and the mother of Lorenzo the Magnificent, then unofficial Florentine ruler.

Dominant among the women attending a birth (she seems not to have been included by Ghirlandaio) was the midwife, who through long practical experience, sometimes learned from her own mother, had acquired the skill of delivering babies. Midwives of this era performed their duties quite apart from the official profession of medicine, whose practitioners required university training. Men were not invited into the birthing chamber. The midwife recognized the pattern of labor pains, guided the parturient woman to a birthing chair or stool, and pressed on her uterus

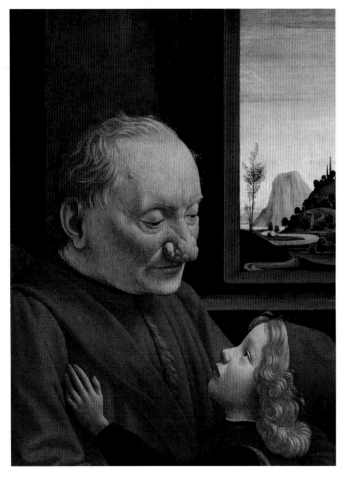

Ghirlandaio, *Old Man with a Young Boy*, c. 1480, oil on panel, 24½ × 18¼ in (62.7 × 46.3 cm). Musée du Louvre, Paris.

or applied unguents thought to be capable of soothing pain or speeding delivery. She introduced her hands into the womb to position the fetus more propitiously. If the child died, the midwife had the job of extracting the stillborn fetus, if only in pieces; if the mother died, the midwife could perform a cesarean section and remove a live infant; if the life of a newborn seemed precarious, she could conduct an emergency baptism. Women trusted mightily in the skill and wisdom of the midwife.

Another figure in attendance at some births was the wet nurse. There are two in the Ghirlandaio representation, one of whom holds and nurses the newborn. A wet nurse is a woman paid to breastfeed someone else's child. She has herself, necessarily, recently given birth and has either lost her own child or handed that infant on to other caretakers. Wetnursing was commonplace in premodern urban societies. In Renaissance Italy the wet nurse contract was commonly arranged by the father of the child. If there were protests from mothers at the removal of their infants (most were sent out to nurse, locally or in the surrounding countryside,

although a few, in the wealthiest families, were nursed by a servant at home), we do not hear of them.

Despite the practice of wetnursing, there is some evidence in Renaissance society of protective and affectionate attitudes toward children (although there is certainly much evidence, too, of neglect or indifference). The second painting shown here, also by Ghirlandaio, is of an unidentified man with a young child, perhaps a grandson. There is clearly a tremendous bond of affection between the two.

A large number of the children of the poor—often, not always, illegitimate—were abandoned as infants or young children. They were left at the doors of churches in front of patrician houses or at the first foundling hospital in Europe, the Ospedale degli Innocenti, opened in Florence in 1419. In addition, poor and desperate women might destroy their own infants if they were unable or unwilling to care for them. Infanticide was principally a crime committed by women—and mothers—and was increasingly prosecuted from the late fifteenth century.

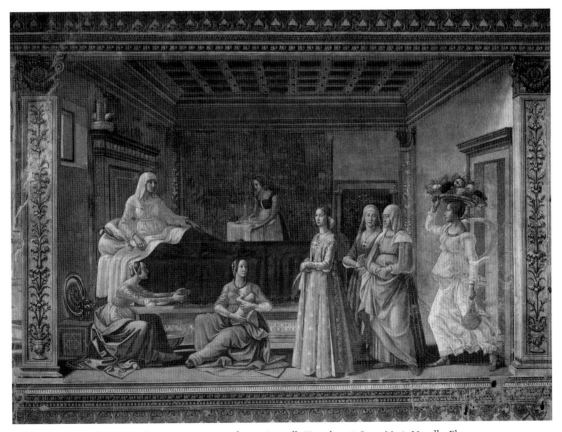

Ghirlandaio, *Birth of Saint John the Baptist*, 1485–1490, fresco. Cappella Tornabuoni, Santa Maria Novella, Florence.

of legitimate siblings, although among the wealthy, a "natural" child might be educated and placed in a worthy vocation. More often, among the far more numerous mothers from the lower social ranks, an illegitimate child was at very high risk of poverty, homelessness, and insecurity; there was a lesser but still significant risk of abandonment and murder. Infanticide, the murder of an infant, was nearly always a woman's crime, and most often a mother's—and the victim was more often than not illegitimate. Infanticide was the one crime (besides witch allegations; see Chapter 11) for which women were often indicted. Abortion was identified both with maternal infanticide and with witchcraft, although the means women had to commit abortion were few in the Renaissance era.

Infants born of legitimate marriages, in contrast, were normally welcomed—perhaps with strained enthusiasm by the very poor, for whom joy might be intermixed with anxiety. Legitimate children could inherit property, although both mothers and fathers could designate specific bequests to illegitimate children in their wills. They could also marry in accord with parental status. The importance that wealthy families attached to a new birth was signaled by the elaborate textiles and trappings assembled in the birthing room, the valuable gifts that the child received, and the lavish celebrations held for the birth or for baptism.

Wet Nurses Nonetheless, among the very same families whose wealth permitted the joyful reception of a new infant, infants were routinely sent away from their homes in the first days of life to live with wet nurses until weaned at the age of 18 to 24 months. For urban families, these wet nurses might be located in the same city but were more commonly residents of the nearby countryside. Rather than sending an infant away, the wealthiest families might employ a wet nurse to live in the household. If so, she was likely the best paid of the household servants. The wet nurses might be married or unmarried, free or slave, well-off peasants adding to the family income or desperately poor. They all shared, necessarily, one feature: all had recently given birth. Since it was not common in this era for women to handle multiple nurslings simultaneously, the wet nurse's own infant must have been handed on to another nurse, or it had recently died.

This wetnursing pattern was well established when the Renaissance dawned in Italy, and it would continue into the eighteenth and even the nineteenth century in some regions of Europe. In those later centuries, the preference for wetnursing would soar among the lower ranks, as it did in Paris, and was associated with very high rates of death. Meanwhile, elite women had turned away from the custom and begun nursing their own babies. In Renaissance Italy, however, families from the upper ranks of society engaged wet nurses. Although infant deaths did occur at high rates during wetnursing (more for girls than for boys), it is not clear that the mortality was significantly greater than infant mortality in the maternal home. In any case, there is no evidence that Renaissance families sent their infants to wet nurses because they sought their offspring's death. On the contrary, as is known in the case of Florence, fathers of households seem to have taken great care when making wetnursing arrangements for their infants.

Many reasons have been offered for the European custom of mercenary wet nursing among elite families. Among them are the woman's desire to be free of breastfeeding duties after the stress and pain of pregnancy and birth; the husband's desire to have his wife sexually available to him (she was not available while breastfeeding, since it was believed that a new conception would spoil the breast milk and injure the infant); or to have more children. Further, recourse to a wet nurse might have been an indicator of high status. Whatever the reasons or incentives for the practice, it contradicted all the medical, clerical, and humanist advice of the time, which said with one voice that a woman, ideally, should nurse her own child.

The Role of Women Although women, at least of the upper social strata, did not nurse their own children, they were responsible for the child's rearing and education after weaning and through to age seven. Women were considered primarily responsible for the child's innate character. That character, experts believed, was informed by the mother's milk, which was regarded as substantially the same as blood. (This assumption lies at the foundation of one of the arguments for women nursing babies themselves.) But even if she did not nurse her infant, she could mold her child's character, especially by offering religious training. When the child reached seven, however, which was considered the "age of reason," the mother would no longer be charged with its intellectual and moral formation. Those tasks were now conferred upon men: fathers, tutors, and schoolteachers.

Women had other responsibilities besides giving birth to children and supervising their early rearing. After their husbands, they were the managers of their households. In both mid- and upper-level households, they arranged for the storage of foodstuffs and other goods. In more modest households, they would also cook and mend; in wealthier ones, they oversaw a staff of servants and were responsible for their comfort, nursing them when they were sick. They would be important consumers of luxury goods. The value of a matron's clothing and jewelry (two categories of expenditure especially targeted by the sumptuary laws; see p. 165) advertised her husband's wealth and established his prestige in the public eye.

The roles prescribed to women were clearly circumscribed—and diminishing. The male experts who expressed the customs of the time, such as Francesco Barbaro and Leon Battista Alberti (see Chapter 3), would have been truly astonished at the notion that women could successfully run enterprises or engage in politics. In the fifteenth century, for the first time, a few pioneers recognized that women could be educated, as did Leonardo Bruni and Lauro Quirini (see Chapter 3). Women, too, began to demand a fuller participation in Renaissance society. They were capable of education, they claimed, and therefore of reasoning—and reason, following Cicero and other ancients, was perceived as the key trait distinguishing the human from the animal kingdom. Indeed, women authors would soon claim that they were intrinsically as worthy as men—perhaps worthier (see Chapter 11). With those claims, the assumptions that supported and justified the assignment of social roles described here began to weaken. Why, then, should a woman marry? Remain subordinate to a husband? Or mother children who were legally his and not hers? The age of feminism dawned before the age of the Renaissance closed.

CONCLUSION

The public life of the Renaissance—the life of the streets and piazzas of the flourishing cities—was diverse, abundant, and pluralistic. People could perform any number of social roles. The opportunities to explore, create, initiate, and communicate were ample. People might associate more or less intimately with their kin, their friends, their neighbors, their guild fellows, their confraternity brothers, their academy or club. Although controls were more rigid than in modern Western societies and rights and liberties were not yet observed as they are today in some sectors, the social world that Renaissance people inhabited was intense and exciting.

The same cannot be said of the private life of the Renaissance, the life that unfolded within households. Here, although both privacy and luxury were more available than in the past, the social roles of women were highly constrained. Those constraints were in part natural, such as the forces that brought death to so many children, and in part artificial, such as the limits imposed on women's behavior by the householder, whose moral position was essentially sustained by the church. Women in their private lives could participate in the Renaissance only in so far as they could become part of the public sphere. As yet, few did.

SUGGESTED READINGS

Primary Sources

Alberti, Leon Battista. *The Family in Renaissance Florence.* Translated by Renée Neu Watkins. Columbia: University of South Carolina Press, 1969. Written ironically by an illegitimate son, an extended dialogue by Alberti on the management and meaning of the household.

Barbaro, Francesco. *The Wealth of Wives: A Fifteenth-Century Marriage Manual.* Translated and edited by Margaret L. King. Toronto: Iter Press, 2015. A guide to choosing a wife, not for her wealth or beauty, but for her capacity to shape the moral and biological character of the offspring on whom the survival of the family depends.

Grubb, James S., and Anna Bellavitis, eds. *Family Memoirs from Venice (15th–17th Centuries).* Rome: Viella, 2009. Five family memoirs, a genre unusual in Venice, and even more unusually, it reflects the lives of members of the "original citizen" rank, a stratum below the nobility but deeply engaged in the political and social life of the city.

Strozzi, Alessandra Macinghi. *Letters to Her Sons, 1447–1470.* Translated and edited by Judith Bryce. Toronto: Iter Press, 2016. Strozzi's 73 letters, one of the most important surviving collections, document a widow's attempt to rear her sons in exile, marry her daughters, and further her family's fortunes.

See also Chapter Two for Gene Brucker, *The Society of Renaissance Florence* and David Chambers and Brian Pullan, eds. *Venice: A Documentary History, 1450–1630.*

Secondary Sources

Ajmar-Wollheim, Marta, and Flora Dennis, eds., *At Home in Renaissance Italy*. London: V. and A., 2006. An essay collection exploring the urban home in different Italian centers, casting light on the outlook and values of those who lived there from the investigation of their furnishings, fireplaces, jewelry, clothing, and even kitchen utensils.

Brown, Patricia Fortini. *Private Lives in Renaissance Venice: Art, Architecture, and the Family*. New Haven, CT: Yale University Press, 2005. Explores the life of patrician families behind the modest exteriors of their palaces, the site for the collection of material objects that enhanced status and shaped cultural trends.

Chonjacka, Monica. *Working Women of Early Modern Venice*. Baltimore, MD: Johns Hopkins University Press, 2000. Shows how women of the "popular" classes could exercise control over their careers, their wealth, and their life choices.

Cohen, Elizabeth S., and Thomas V. Cohen. *Daily Life in Renaissance Italy*. Westport, CT: Greenwood Press, 2001. Examines a cross-section of social groups and contexts to give a rounded picture of ordinary life.

Cohn, Samuel K., Jr. *Women in the Streets: Essays on Sex and Power in Renaissance Italy*. Baltimore, MD: Johns Hopkins University Press, 1996. Examines women in a full range of contexts: city law courts, village communities, property, crime, convents, dowries, death.

Crabb, Ann. *The Merchant of Prato's Wife: Margherita Datini and Her World, 1360–1423*. Ann Arbor, MI: University of Michigan Press, 2015. Examines hundreds of letters from Datini to her husband, a wealthy wool merchant, revealing the world of a Renaissance woman enmeshed in the family business and relationships with friends and kin.

Crawshaw, Jane L. Stevens. *Plague Hospitals: Public Health for the City in Early Modern Venice*. London: Routledge, 2012. Ventures inside the isolation hospitals designed by the city of Venice to contain the sick and protect the healthy, with a rare look at the patients' daily routines and medicines used to treat their diseases.

Frick, Carole Collier. *Dressing Renaissance Florence: Families, Fortunes, and Fine Clothing*. Baltimore, MD: Johns Hopkins University Press, 2002. Looks at the fashion industry as it operated in Florence, a textile manufacturing city, covering the workers and workshops where clothing was made as well as the fabulous wardrobes assembled by wealthy consumers.

Gavitt, Philip. *Gender, Honor, and Charity in Late Renaissance Florence*. New York: Cambridge University Press, 2011. Explores the impact of the pursuit of family wealth on women and children and the charitable institutions developed to care for those disadvantaged by that pursuit.

Goldthwaite, Richard A. *The Economy of Renaissance Florence*. Baltimore, MD: Johns Hopkins University Press, 2009. A comprehensive look at Florentine economic history by a leading expert, including coverage of the textile industry, artisans and guilds, merchants and investors, and the distribution of wealth.

Herlihy, David, and Christiane Klapisch-Zuber. *Tuscans and Their Families: A Study of the Florentine Catasto of 1427*. New Haven, CT: Yale University Press, 1986. Originally published as *Les Toscans et leurs familles: une stude du "catasto" florentin de 1427* (Paris: Fondation nationale des sciences politiques. onale des sciences politiques Press, 1986). This groundbreaking analysis of the records of the Florentine *catasto* (universal tax on assets) reveals much about household structures and family values.

King, Margaret L. *Women of the Renaissance*. Chicago: University of Chicago Press, 1991. A synthesis of women in relation to family, church, and high culture.

King, Margaret L. *The Death of the Child Valerio Marcello*. Chicago: University of Chicago Press, 1994. Studies the interrelations of war, politics, class, household, humanist culture, and grief in mid-fifteenth-century Venice.

Klapisch-Zuber, Christiane. *Women, Family and Ritual in Renaissance Italy*. Translated by Lydia G. Cochrane. Chicago: University of Chicago Press, 1985. A collection of studies probing marriage rituals, dowries, female servanthood, widowhood, and wetnursing.

Musacchio, Jacqueline Marie. *The Art and Ritual of Childbirth in Renaissance Italy*. New Haven, CT: Yale University Press, 1999. Examines childbirth rituals and their social context in art.

Pullan, Brian. *Rich and Poor in Renaissance Venice: The Social Institutions of a Catholic State, to 1620*. Oxford: Basil Blackwell, 1971. Examines the ways in which Venetians provided for the poor through lay confraternities and Jewish moneylending.

Romano, Dennis. *Patricians and Popolani: The Social Foundations of the Venetian Renaissance State*. Baltimore, MD: Johns Hopkins University Press, 1987. Examines how the social foundations of Venice lay in associations of neighborhood, parish, gender, and occupation.

Ruggiero, Guido. *The Boundaries of Eros: Sex Crime and Sexuality in Renaissance Venice*. Oxford: Oxford University Press, 1985. Explores Venetian society through the lens of sex crime, including rape, fornication, sodomy, and convent misbehavior.

Strocchia, Sharon. *Death and Ritual in Renaissance Florence*. Baltimore, MD: Johns Hopkins University Press, 1992. Examines civic funerals from the post-plague era to the advent of the Medici principate, tracing links between funerary display, wealth, and cultural ideals.

SIX

THE CHURCH AND THE PEOPLE
(c. 1350–c. 1530)

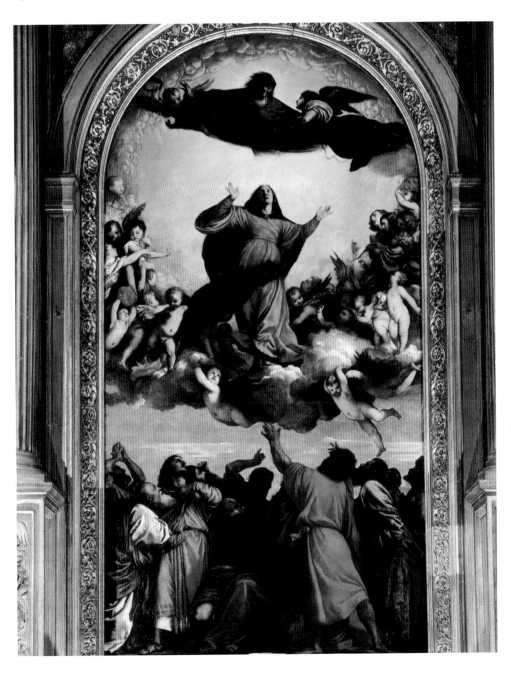

Titian, *Assumption of the Virgin*, 1516–1518, oil on panel, 22 ft 6 in × 11 ft 10 in (6.9 × 3.6 m). **Santa Maria Gloriosa dei Frari, Venice.**

The cult of the Virgin emerged in the twelfth century, and in the Renaissance representations of the Virgin were as common as those of Jesus. In a surging upward rush, an ecstatic Virgin is welcomed by a beneficent God, while apostles on earth are astonished by her assumption, or reception, into heaven.

On June 16, 2002, half a millennium after the Italian Renaissance reached its peak, the pope, leader of the Roman Catholic Church, declared Padre Pio a saint. Some 300,000 people from all parts of Italy and other Western nations crowded into the square in front of St. Peter's Basilica. The *New York Times* reported that it was "one of the largest crowds in memory." Born Francesco Forgione, Padre Pio won the enthusiastic devotion of so many people because of his saintly life and because he showed the signs of divine grace. Since 1918, he had bled from wounds in his hands and side, in imitation of Jesus Christ; he could occupy two places at once; he predicted the future; and he healed the sick. He died aged 81 in 1968.

In this contemporary scene appear some features that characterized the religious life of the people of the Renaissance. These include a powerful pope, who can confer sainthood in the name of a universal church; a saintly figure who has performed documented miracles; and a crowd of believers for whom the canonization of a beloved leader overshadowed other concerns, including the war on terrorism in the wake of the September 11, 2001, attack on the World Trade Center and soccer's World Cup competitions then in progress.

The religious figures and feelings that could motivate hundreds of thousands of people in 2002 motivated millions in Renaissance Italy. At that time, the Roman Church dominated the religious life of western Europeans, while the Eastern Church was dominant in the Byzantine Empire, parts of the Balkans, and eastern Europe, including Russia. Rival Protestant churches did not emerge until after 1520 (see Chapter 9), and Jews formed a scattered and persecuted minority. This chapter explores the development of church institutions and hierarchies during the Renaissance period, including the papacy, the Papal State, and the college of cardinals. It then describes the course of popular religious observance and the emergence of both male and female **charismatic** religious leaders.

PAPACY AND PAPAL STATE

The papacy emerged early in the Christian era, reached a peak with the pontificate of Innocent III (r. 1198–1216), faltered in the fourteenth and early fifteenth centuries, then consolidated its power and potential during the Renaissance. The later part of that story belongs to the Protestant Reformation and Catholic response (see Chapter 9). The earlier stages will be reviewed here.

The Rise of the Papacy

Initially, the bishop of Rome was elected like any other bishop by the members of his flock. By the time of Gregory the Great he had been elevated to pope, assumed the ancient Roman title *pontifex maximus* and the more recent one of Vicar of Christ, and was understood to have inherited the authority that Christ himself gave Peter (see Chapter 1 for the early development of the papacy). With the collapse of Byzantine power following the Lombard advance of the sixth century, the popes called upon and won the support of the Carolingian Frankish kings, whose successors became emperors themselves with papal support, in the ninth and tenth centuries. The Germanic emperors largely controlled the tenth-century papacy, which in turn responded, in the eleventh, with initiatives for moral and political reform. These permitted the popes of the twelfth and thirteenth centuries to achieve a high point of influence on the continent. During these last two centuries, as has been seen, the conflict between popes and emperors on the Italian peninsula became entwined with the parallel process by which urban communes sought their own local autonomy.

Papal authority in Italy dropped sharply when, in 1309, the entire papal court migrated to Avignon, a city in Provence in southern France. Under the influence of the French kings, the papacy remained detached from the concerns of the Italian cities. In the regions technically under papal authority, people rebelled and formed independent states under their own despots, or signori. The attempts of papal diplomats to reassert the pope's authority failed in the long run. This period from 1309 to 1377 is known as the Babylonian Captivity of the Church. Although the papacy undertook fundamental reforms in this era, including the expansion and reorganization of its bureaucracy, its policies were influenced by French royal interests. Notably, all seven of the popes who ruled at Avignon were French.

The interval of Captivity was followed by another period still more damaging to papal prestige. This was the Great Schism of 1378–1417, during which two rival popes (and at one point three) ruled simultaneously. Not surprisingly, during this period the popes failed to recover their authority in the lands they had previously ruled. Europe was scandalized. Reform-minded leaders called for a council of the church, a representative body that would hold greater authority than the pope, and would be capable of deposing him. It convened at Constance (Konstanz, modern Germany) in 1414. By 1417 three holders of the papal title had resigned or been deposed, and the council appointed Martin V as sole pope, who then proceeded to rule at Rome.

Martin V returned to a Rome that had not had an effective ruler for more than a century. It was necessary to reorganize papal governance; establish papal superiority in the symbolic realm, using the tools of humanism and the arts; deal with external threats, such as heresy, the Turkish advance, and **conciliarism** (see p. 194); and reassert authority over the Papal States in central Italy. From 1417 to 1534 (the death of Pope Clement VII), the Renaissance popes successfully managed these tasks—while neglecting pastoral and pious duties, to the distress of reformers and observers throughout Europe.

During its stay in Avignon, the papacy expanded and modernized its bureaucracy, becoming the most sophisticated in Europe. In Renaissance Rome, following the Great Schism, the development of the church bureaucracy resumed. The papal curia, or court, became a highly developed system of committees and councils that handled the tasks of communication, accounting, and policy creation with clerical and secular leaders throughout Europe. The bureaucrats who staffed these offices included laymen as well as clerics. These men were largely distinct from the high prelates, the bishops and cardinals.

The papacy also sent legates throughout Europe on diplomatic missions like those under-taken by secular states. The bureaucracy functioned well, despite its corruption by the Renaissance popes, who sold offices and regularly increased the number of offices so that there would be more available for sale.

The college of cardinals, established in the eleventh century as the body responsible for the election of the pope, had also gained in stature during the Captivity and increas-ingly so during the fifteenth century. It also grew in size. Church councils in the fifteenth century attempted to limit the number of cardinals to 24, and to insist on some minimum standards of competence and a reasonable minimum age, but their number swelled beyond that point. In the sixteenth century, 40 to 50 cardinals might participate in the election of a pope. The cardinalate was an immensely attractive prize, and the sons of important fami-lies throughout Europe contended sharply for the red hat, as it meant the attainment of enormous wealth. Bishoprics and archbishoprics were also valuable plums, sought after by the most ambitious, politically astute, and well-placed clerics. Cardinals often appointed their relatives to these while they used their wealth and influence to arrange advantageous marriages for others. Or they might hold one or two such positions simultaneously with their cardinalate. The resulting income was spent on pensions for relations and friends but above all on their households, which employed thousands of servants, entertainers, stable hands, secretaries, accountants, companions, and the like. Although the papal court was unmatched in its splendor, the retinues and residences of the Renaissance cardinals were impressive.

The wealthy and powerful men who dominated Rome loved magnificence. It was not for that reason alone, however, but also from a desire to establish papal supremacy that they employed artists and thinkers to make Rome a center of cultural innovation in the age of the Renaissance. The patronage of pope and cardinals supported the creation of memo-rable works of painting, sculpture, and architecture, in which the greatest artists of the era participated (see Chapter 4). One of their greatest accomplishments was the construc-tion of a new Vatican complex of basilica, offices, and papal residence. The Renaissance popes also redesigned the city of Rome, cutting broad boulevards through tangled streets to highlight key intersections and marking these by monuments. In doing so, they were the pioneers of early modern urbanism (see pp. 133–134). In the promotion of letters, as in arts, the popes took a leading role. They surrounded themselves with humanists, who found employment in the papal bureaucracy, but who then met informally and in semi-official academies. (Their secular culture was sometimes suspect and, under Pope Paul II, censored.) Some of the popes were themselves learned. The scholarly Pope Nicholas V launched the Vatican Library, which became a principal repository in Europe of manu-script works.

1350–1399

1363 Catherine of Siena becomes a Dominican tertiary.

1377 Pope Gregory returns papacy to Rome, ending the Babylonian Captivity.

1378 Two popes are elected, Urban VI in Rome and Clement VII in Avignon, beginning the Great Schism.

1378 Publication of Catherine of Siena's treatise on religious life, the *Dialogues of the Soul*.

1380 Death of Catherine of Siena.

1384 English religious reformer John Wyclif dies.

1400–1449

1402 Bernardino of Siena joins the Franciscans.

1409 John XXIII is elected a third pope, rivaling those in Rome and Avignon.

1414 Council of the Church assembles at Constance.

1415 Council of Constance declares Bohemian reformer Jan Hus a heretic and burns him.

1417 Council of Constance appoints Martin V pope, ending the Great Schism.

1431 Venetian nobleman Gabriele Condulmer is elected Pope Eugene IV.

1433 Francesca of Rome forms a community of religious-minded women.

1433 Lorenzo Giustiniani is made bishop of Venice.

1438 Bernardino of Siena becomes head of the Franciscan Order in Italy.

1439 Council of Florence declares union of the Greek and Catholic churches, but this is rejected in Constantinople.

1446 Antonino Pierozzi (Antoninus) becomes archbishop of Florence.

1450–1499

1450 Bernardino of Siena is declared a saint, only six years after his death.

1451 Giustiniani becomes the first patriarch of Venice.

1452 Birth of Girolamo Savonarola.

1453 Fall of Constantinople to the Muslim Ottoman Turks.

1459 Pope Pius II convenes a congress at Mantua to launch a crusade to recover Constantinople.

1461 Catherine of Siena is canonized.

1463 Death of Catherine of Bologna.

1464 Pius II sets out on his crusade but dies before leaving Italy; the crusade is abandoned.

1474 Savonarola joins the Dominican Order after a visionary experience.

1489 After preaching at the Church of San Marco, Florence, Savonarola is hailed as a prophet.

1492 Rodrigo Borgia is elected pope as Alexander VI.

1493 Savonarola is appointed vicar-general of the Dominicans in Tuscany.

1494 The Medici rulers are expelled from Florence, which becomes a republic dominated by Savonarola.

1495 Savonarola refuses to go to Rome to answer charges of heresy.

1497 Savonarola is excommunicated by the pope.

1498 Savonarola is publicly hanged and burned in Florence.

1499 Cesare Borgia begins the conquest of Romagna on behalf of his father, Pope Alexander VI.

1500–1535

1500 Aldine Press publishes Catherine of Siena's letters.

1503 Guiliano della Rovere is elected Pope Julius II.

1507 Julius II begins the sale of indulgences to finance building St. Peter's.

1513 Giovanni de' Medici is elected pope as Leo X.

1534 Alessandro Farnese becomes Pope Paul III; he will launch the Counter-Reformation.

1535 Angela Merici founds the Ursulines, a women's religious order for the teaching of girls.

POPES AND CARDINALS

The pope, *papa* (father) of the Roman Church resided, necessarily, in Rome. He was the successor to the bishops of Rome during the late years of the Empire, who guided and protected the citizens when the imperial government could no longer do so. The first popes claimed to be successors of the apostle Peter, who legendarily suffered martyrdom in Rome.

Yet, from 1309 to 1377, the popes lived not in Rome but in Avignon, and from 1378 to 1415, at first two, and then three popes reigned. The Council of Constance deposed all current claimants to the title of pope and appointed Martin V (r. 1417–1431), who returned to Rome unchallenged.

From 1415, when the Schism ended, to 1527, the year of the devastating Sack of Rome (see Chapter 8), the papacy grew in splendor. The popes rebuilt Rome and their own Vatican palace complex. The papal bureaucracy

mushroomed as it employed the secretaries and treasurers necessary to carry on the pope's foreign affairs and manage his fiscal empire. A few highlights of the careers of the most important Renaissance popes are given below. Note that most were Italian-born.

As the papacy gained importance and in wealth, so too did the cardinalate. The cardinals were magistrates of the church whose prime duty was to elect the next pope. Since the interests of many nations hung on the identity of the next pontiff, the function of the cardinals was enormously important. Kings and princes contended to have their candidates appointed cardinals, so that they could influence the election of a pope presumed to be favorable to them. Although there was a theoretical limit of 24 cardinals, of whom no more than one-third might be Italian, the popes steadily increased those numbers. In 1586, when an attempt

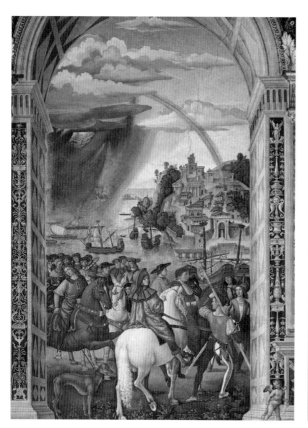

Pinturicchio, *Pope Pius II Leaving for the Council of Basel*, 1503–1508, fresco. Piccolomini Library, Cathedral, Siena.

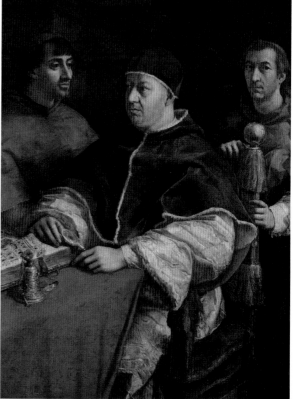

Raphael, *Portrait of Pope Leo X with Cardinals Giulio de' Medici and Luigi de' Rossi*, 1517, on panel, 60½ × 47 in (153.7 × 119.4 cm). Galleria degli Uffizi, Florence.

was made to limit the number to 70, the majority were Italian. Italian princes (from the houses of Gonzaga, Este, Medici, and the like) steadily promoted the presence of their kin among the cardinals: from 1420 to 1520, such figures accounted for five per cent of new cardinals appointed; from 1520 to 1620, six per cent.

Cardinals were granted sky-high incomes drawn from papal revenues. To be named a cardinal was a guarantee of wealth and power. Establishing their households in Rome (as most did), where they regularly attended the papal court, they amassed enormous households of secretaries, stewards, favorites, and servants. A document from 1509, for example, shows that 26 cardinals' households then surveyed had an average of 154 such "familiars." To support these princely households—and what other city in Europe had to sustain the expenses of more than 20 princes?—the church provided a package of benefits that yielded an income in the range of 4,000 to 6,000 ducats per year, which was a massive fortune. With this great wealth, the cardinals followed the popes in the construction of luxurious palaces and gardens, the commissioning of works of art, and entertainments on a grand scale.

The Renaissance in Rome had a different character from the Renaissance in Florence or Venice or other Italian cities. The patrons were churchmen, who in their aggregate constituted a society of male celibates, attended not by their wives, daughters, and heirs but by their familiars and their favorites—and nephews (some of them, in fact, illegitimate sons), who were often promoted precociously to important benefices in preparation for their own successful careers in the ecclesiastical corporation. The many courtesans resident in Rome (see pp. 156–157) were also a consequence of the asymmetrically masculine nature of the city's elite.

Popes of the Renaissance

Pope	Pontificate	Name (City of Origin)	Key Events or Achievements
Eugene IV	1431–1447	Gabriele Condulmer (Venice)	Opposed the Council of Basel, hosted Council of Ferrara/Florence. Learned but puritanical; collector of antiquities.
Nicholas V	1447–1455	Tommaso Parentucelli (Liguria)	Humanistically trained. Renovated Vatican palace. Established the Vatican Library. Supported Peace of Lodi (1454), Italian League (1455; see Chapter 7).
Pius II	1458–1464	Enea Silvio Piccolomini (Siena)	Called for new crusade against Ottoman Turks.
Sixtus IV	1471–1484	Francesco della Rovere (Rome)	Commissioned the building of the Sistine Chapel. Doubled the number of venal offices in the papal secretariat for sale. Uncle of Giuliano della Rovere, later Pope Julius II.
Alexander VI	1492–1503	Rodrigo Borgia (Valencia, Spain)	Nephew of previous Pope Calistus III (r. 1455–1458). Furthered his family's interests through the marriages of daughter Lucrezia Borgia and exploits of son Cesare.
Julius II	1503–1513	Giuliano della Rovere (Rome)	To protect the Papal States, guided an aggressive foreign policy and led papal armies during the invasions of Italy by French and imperial armies. Commissioned Raphael to paint papal apartments and Michelangelo to paint Sistine Chapel ceiling.
Leo X	1513–1521	Giovanni de' Medici (Florence)	As pope, promoted the return of the Medici to rule in Florence. Condemned as heretical 41 propositions of the German monk Martin Luther (see Chapter 9).

Challenges to the Papacy

The Renaissance papacy was not wholly given over to luxury and high amusements. It faced genuine challenges, such as heresy, which had flared up in the thirteenth and fourteenth centuries. In the fifteenth century, the papacy supported the suppression of the English **Lollards** and the Bohemian **Hussites**. These were the followers of John Wyclif (c. 1330–1384) and Jan Hus (c. 1370–1415), respectively; the latter had been condemned and burned at the stake during the Council of Constance.

The popes also had to deal with the threat of conciliarism. The conciliar movement had triumphed at Constance, establishing its authority as superior to that of the papacy. One of the provisions of the Constance settlement was that the pope would meet regularly with a council of the church. When delegates assembled at Basel (modern Switzerland) in 1431, however, Pope Eugene IV (r. 1431–1447) resisted them and was deposed (a deposition that he ignored). He dismissed the Council of Basel in 1437, although a rump council remained and elected an antipope. A new council met at Ferrara, then at Florence, and finally at Rome from 1438 to 1445, which had a more limited mandate: to attempt to come to a resolution with the Eastern church, in view of the impending threat to the Byzantine Empire from the Turkish advance in Asia Minor and the Balkans. One of the leading Greek representatives to the council, John Bessarion, a scholar himself and supporter of humanism and philosophy (see p. 81), decided to convert to the Latin church and was made a cardinal of the church. The Council of Ferrara-Florence also condemned the Council of Basel and reaffirmed the pope as the supreme authority in the church.

On May 3, 1453, a little more than a decade after the Council of Ferrara-Florence dispersed, Ottoman Turkish forces besieged, captured, and sacked Constantinople. This put an end to the Byzantine Empire in the East and posed a new threat to the West. Should there be a counter-offensive or should western Europeans wait to see what Turkish intentions were? Pope Pius II, the first to be elected after the fall of Constantinople, planned a new crusade. In 1459 he convened an international congress at Mantua to rally supporters and in 1464, since the support was lukewarm, attempted to launch the crusade himself. Frescoes by Pinturicchio (1454–1513) in the Piccolomini Library in the Cathedral of Siena celebrate in joyous colors the pope's summons and the departure for the crusade (see p. 192). He died en route to Ancona, the place of embarkation. With his death, the venture ended.

The major political ventures of the Renaissance popes, though, were closer to home, as they struggled to regain sovereignty of the Papal States. That ambition had a long past. The popes had claim to the lands of central Italy from at least the eighth century (and the ninth-century forgery that Lorenzo Valla exploded would have dated that claim from as early as the fourth; see Chapter 3). They reaffirmed their claim during the eleventh-century reform and fought for that territory during the turbulent twelfth and thirteenth centuries when papal Guelf and imperial Ghibelline armies disputed it. Papal sovereignty diminished during the Avignonese period. The French popes sent their legates to manage the bloody and dangerous task of taming the feudal despots who had seized papal territory and reducing them to the rank of papal "vicars." The slight progress made was lost again during the Schism, and the task was resumed once more after 1417. Nicholas V and Pius II made significant progress toward the consolidation of the Papal States. The Spanish-born Alexander VI (r. 1492–1503) managed to establish real authority over parts of the Papal States through the efforts of his illegitimate son, Cesare Borgia (c. 1475–1507), captain of the papal armies, whose ruthless occupation of Romagna brought the region to obedience.

While Borgia's mission was ultimately to make central Italy his own, the Borgia pope's successor, Julius II, waged a relentless war to reestablish full sovereignty over the Papal States and then to extend them. Amid the larger conflicts between the Italian city-states and their foreign allies and taskmasters—imperial, French, and Spanish—Julius drove Venice out of the northeastern regions of the states he considered his, then embraced the cause of Italy against the foreigners. "*Fuori i barbari!*" ("Away with the barbarians!") was his battle cry. By the time of the accession of his successor, Leo X (r. 1513–1521), the expanded Papal States securely incorporated Perugia, Bologna, and Ravenna and reached from the Adriatic to the Tyrrhenian Sea. The states were unified within a troubled, war-torn peninsula. The Renaissance popes had succeeded in making themselves sovereign in their territory, which was perceived as one of Italy's leading states, and behaved according to purely secular principles.

POPULAR RELIGION

Although the papacy was Europe's largest court and a center of civilization, neither it nor the cardinals, nor even the bishops and archbishops, were the source of religious inspiration for most people of the Renaissance. And yet this was an intensely religious age. Another religious universe, one more attuned to the spirituality of ordinary people, occupied the same Italian peninsula as the Church of Rome.

Paganism and Heresy

The dubious behavior of the official church did not disconcert many Renaissance people because many of them remained quite distant from its prescribed doctrine and practice. During the late centuries of the Roman Empire, Christianity spread rapidly and established itself in the cities. The Christianization of the countryside was never effective. The word *paganus* (pagan) used by late Roman and medieval Christians to describe nonbelievers betrays this fact: the Latin word means "country dweller" and is directly related to the word "peasant" in modern Romance languages.

In the premodern centuries after Rome's fall, country-dwellers still formed the vast majority of all Europeans, and even of all Italians, and they were often still effectively "pagan," that is, unassimilated to the dominant Christian culture. Although the entire population was organized into a system of parishes and dioceses used by the church to consolidate the regions under its authority, in fact, regular religious observance was cursory, misunderstood, or neglected altogether. Christian festivals, in contrast, won widespread attention. And so too did magic (the belief in charms and incantations), the use of healers and potions, the worship of relics and icons (as opposed to the allowable reverence for them), and the enthusiasm for unauthorized "holy" personalities, both saintly and heretical. As in other regions of Europe, the religious life of many peasant communities was a stew of folk belief laced with dimly understood official ritual and dogma.

In this setting, heresy flourished. In the twelfth and thirteenth centuries—the period of the communal revolution in northern Italy, followed by revolutions of the popolo— several popular movements swept through the region. One was the movement launched by Peter Waldo (c. 1170) from Lyons in France. He had renounced his considerable wealth, and his followers aroused the condemnation of the official church because of their public lay preaching and anticlerical and anti-sacramental beliefs. Another was the belief centered on the prophesies of Joachim of Flora (1132–1202), a Cistercian abbot from Calabria in southern Italy. Joachim prophesied an imminent Third Age of the Spirit, following the Old Testament age of the Father, and the New Testament age of the Son. In that Third Age the rules of the church and the commands of the Bible would dissolve and all would live at peace in the reign of the Eternal Gospel. Other seekers joined the Guglielmite heresy, or Brethren of the Free Spirit, both of which involved extreme reversals of social and sexual conventions.

The Mendicant Movements

During the same period, two new religious movements emerged that were, after some uncertainty, deemed acceptable by the official church. These, too, had great appeal for ordinary people and were especially directed toward the large Italian population of city-dwellers. These were the mendicant movements of men who took on the vows of monastic discipline but who did not join the traditional Benedictine or Cistercian orders or their offshoots. Instead, they moved into the cities, where they lived by begging (the word "mendicant" comes from the Latin verb for "beg") as a sign of their renunciation of property and commitment to poverty and service. The two mendicant orders had two different founders and two different missions.

The elder of these two religious innovators was Dominic (Domingo de Guzmán, c. 1170–1221), born a nobleman's son in Castile (modern Spain). As a cathedral canon and assistant to a bishop, he witnessed the effects of the Albigensian heresy in the south of France. He committed himself to root out heresy by preaching to those mistakenly lured by its promises. Officially approved by the pope in 1216, his new order became active not only in the drive against heresy but also in the schools and universities of Europe and in the cities from which so many new (and sometimes threatening) ideas came. When Dominic died in Bologna in 1221, strongholds of his **Dominican order** had been established throughout Italy.

Dominic's younger contemporary Francis of Assisi (Francesco di Pietro di Bernardone, c. 1181–1226) was the son of a textile merchant and thus born into the growing commercial economy of central and northern Italy. Whereas Dominic's mission was to preach the true faith, informed by advanced study, to a larger community, it was Francis's to preach poverty to the urban populations of Europe's wealthiest region. He himself experienced a conversion in late adolescence, rejected his father's wealth and connections, and wandered the roads and streets of Italy with his followers. After a struggle to gain papal approval, the **Franciscan order** was officially founded in 1210. Its rule was reconfirmed in 1223, and Franciscan houses were founded throughout Italy during the thirteenth century.

It was common for a city to have one Franciscan and one Dominican foundation at different ends of the city. These became nodes of religious energy. The sons of middling and upper-level families joined these orders to engage in the exciting task of interpreting and communicating the Christian message in a new way to a new population. Both Franciscans and Dominicans developed a new style of preaching, designed especially to reach an audience of urban workers, artisans, merchants, and bankers. They preached in Italian and used anecdotes and examples from daily life. People thronged into the piazzas to hear a popular preacher and might listen for hours. Some members of the audience took notes, or transcribed whole sermons, so that these energizing words could be heard at another time and place. Forty-five sermons preached by the charismatic Franciscan preacher St. Bernardino of Siena (1380–1444) in his native city in August and September, 1428, have reached us in this way. A textile worker attended faithfully each day, recording the sermons on wax tablets which he later transcribed on paper.

The older religious orders had been bulwarks of civilization during the worst centuries of Western history, when Roman institutions crumbled, invaders threatened, the economy lagged, and warring nobles held back the formation of new states. Now the mendicant orders brought messages of hope and consolation to urban peoples venturing on the path of entrepreneurial innovation and profit-seeking, a path which Jesus of Nazareth, the Christian founder, had never commended to his followers. The Dominican and Franciscan friars were an effective guide to laymen and laywomen who wished to overcome their religious fears and to expand their spiritual vision.

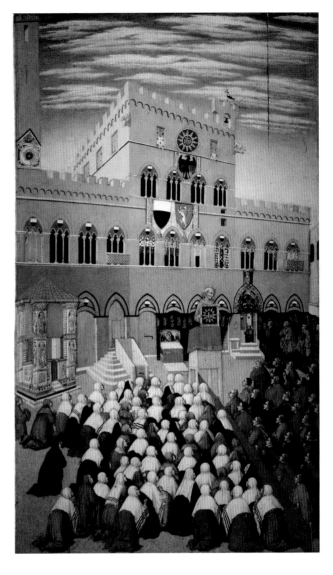

Sano di Pietro, *St. Bernardino Preaching in the Campo*, 1445–1447, tempera on panel, 63¾ × 40 in (162 × 101.5 cm). Cathedral Chapterhouse, Siena.

In the main square of Siena, throngs of people—many of them women—fall to their knees, a posture they would hold for hours on end as they absorbed Bernardino's electrifying sermons.

This bar graph shows the number of confraternities founded in Florence for different periods from 1240 to 1499. For some, the exact date of founding is known; the number of these, within each bar, is indicated by darker shading. For others, the date used is that of the first reference to them in contemporary documents; the number of these, within each bar, is indicated by lighter shading. Note that in the thirteenth century—still "medieval"—only about 15 confraternities were founded. During the half-century after 1450, corresponding to the height of the cultural movement of the Renaissance, over 50 were founded—more than in the 150 years prior to 1350.

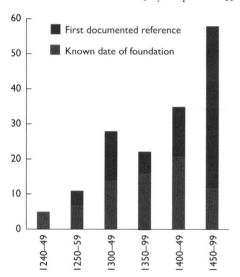

(Based on J. Henderson, *Piety and Charity in Late Medieval Florence*. Oxford: Clarendon Press, 1994, Figure 2.1, p. 39)

Confraternities

Some deeply committed laypersons desired to take on some of the discipline and duties of members of these orders even though they remained active within the secular world. Both the Franciscans and Dominicans, therefore, set up "third orders," to which these laypeople, called "tertiaries," might belong. Although only a few laypersons took on the serious commitment of membership in a third order, many—perhaps as many as one-third of the adults in an Italian town at one point in their careers—joined a confraternity. These organizations flourished especially in Italian and some other Mediterranean regions of Europe.

In some ways, confraternities resembled the other associations to which urban people might belong in Renaissance Italy (see Chapter 5). They especially resembled guilds, which had both religious and charitable functions. Yet they were distinct. The confraternities existed because numerous laypersons across the social spectrum desired to find spiritual assurance. Many were women, many others adolescents. Initially, they appear to have been two types: the *laudesi* (praising) and *battuti* (beating or flagellant) societies. The first engaged in singing hymns, mostly in Italian, some specially composed for the purpose. They were, therefore, important in developing an Italian-language genre of religious poetic expression distinct from official church music and often drawing on popular melodies. The second engaged in self-flagellation, often in processional groups. Flagellant processions were especially frequent in times of crisis such as epidemic or war. The participants believed that by inflicting pain on themselves they atoned for their sins, removing from themselves and their city the punishments inflicted for their collective misdeeds.

Beyond the activities of praise and self-flagellation, members of confraternities met for worship and meditation. Some said the rosary, a practice which became common from the fifteenth century, which involved saying prayers in a sequence aided by counting off the beads on a string or necklace. Confraternity members also said prayers for the dead. Many people left bequests specifically to fund the prescribed manner and times of remembrance to benefit a soul thought to be in purgatory (believed to be a realm of the afterlife where souls atoned for earthly sins in preparation for their ascent to heaven). Some modern observers have seen in this aspect of the confraternal movement a kind of "cult of death," a morbid fascination with dying and the afterlife.

The most visible and characteristic activity of the lay confraternities, however, was their participation in acts of charity. Confraternities founded many hospitals in the early

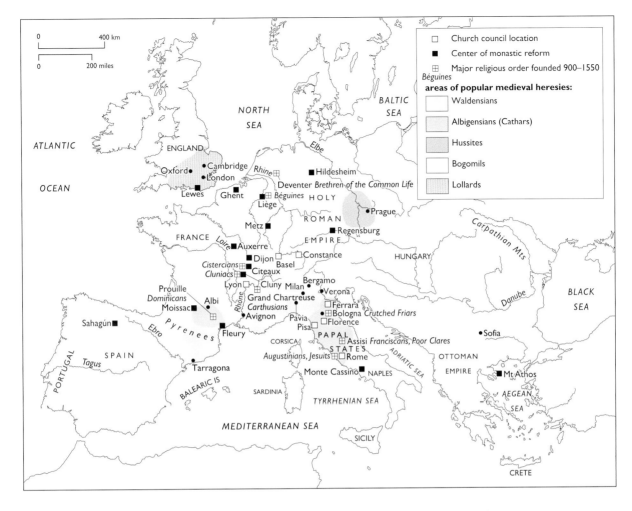

Renaissance period, when hospitals were still general-purpose refuges for the sick, the failing, and the desperate. Their members cared for lepers and plague victims. They organized assistance to women and girls at risk of prostitution (poor women without family protection). They recovered prostitutes and provided dowries and places of asylum. They went into prisons to pray for and with criminals, and attended their executions, comforting them to the end, sometimes holding before their eyes a painted sacred image. Robed in distinctive costume, the teams of "brothers" and "sisters" were conspicuous in the streets of the city as they tended to these tasks and as they marched together in civic processions at times of public celebration.

The Italian confraternal movement was part of an international surge in lay piety, the deep seeking by the general population for the spiritual goods that an earlier age had left to the clergy in their monasteries, cathedrals, and hermitages. In Europe's other major urban zone, centered on the County of Flanders (modern Belgium and the Netherlands), the **Devotio Moderna** (New Devotion) won many adherents in this same period. The Devotio Moderna was a movement of pious laypersons (the New Devout) who practiced inward meditation and scriptural study. There was, therefore, a strong focus on education as a

The Renaissance Church

In a tumultuous time for Christian Europe, new religious orders and new heresies took root. Heresies originating elsewhere found a home in Italy. The Franciscan Order, native to Italy, shared the stage with contemporary movements originating in France and northern Europe: the Dominicans, the Béguines, and the Brethren of the Common Life.

BROTHERS (SISTERS) IN CHRIST

The proliferation of confraternities, which sometimes enrolled old and young, male and female members, and members from different social ranks, is one of the distinctive features of Italian Renaissance society—and certainly brings up short anyone clinging to older views of the Renaissance as "pagan" or "secular." The purposes of confraternal association emerge from the rulebooks that the members created for themselves.

The excerpt here is from the *mariegola*, or rulebook, of the Venetian Scuola di San Chiereghino e del Rosario. (The confraternities of Venice were called *scuole*.) It was established in the Church of San Simeone Profeta on September 12, 1535. Note that the primary purpose of the *scuola* is understood to be a fellowship of Christians seeking salvation. It is also an organization that institutes its own system of governance, which provides for the needs and the spiritual well-being of its members.

[I] Clearly and manifestly do we see how brief, how fleeting and how transitory is the present life amidst the frailty of humankind, for wretched beings in this world are ... oppressed and engulfed in sin, and so each man lives all his days in sin.... Hence ... we ... have thought and conceived of gaining the salvation of our souls through the love of brotherhood and the aid of prayer, and have thought fit to appoint to be our advocate in Heaven the glorious Mother of God, Our Lady Mary, the refuge of us miserable sinners.... And we have now established this blessed Scuola and fraternity ... that, by drawing on the merits of all the saints of God, both male and female, we may attain the glory of eternal life.

[II] First, it is our wish and command that ... an oil lamp shall always be burning by day and by night before the altar of Mary, our holy lady of grace....

[IV] It is likewise our wish and command that every [first?] Sunday of every month throughout the year shall be regarded as our appointed day for transacting the business of the Scuola....

[VI] ... We decree and ordain that from all the brothers one shall be elected to serve as our bailiff (gastaldo) *and two others to be our deans* (degani), *and they shall be men of good life and reputation and experience, and they shall be sure to ... manage the affairs of our Scuola ... with all possible zeal and devotion to duty....*

[VIII] Furthermore, because it is a pious act ... to visit the sick, especially if they are our own brothers, it has been decreed ... that, if any of our brothers falls ill and is in such poverty that he needs aid and support, our bailiff and deans shall be bound to pay him frequent visits and to assist him in his needs by drawing on the funds of the Scuola....

[IX] Furthermore, because the burial of the dead is a work of mercy and charity ... it is our wish and command that ... when one of our brothers passes from this life to the next (and all of us will one day make this journey, one after the other), we should all go to him and wash his body and pityingly accompany it to burial, bearing the cross, the banner, and our great candles and tapers.

(D. Chambers and B. Pullan, eds., Venice: A Documentary History, *1450–1630. Oxford: Blackwell, 1992, pp. 210–213)*

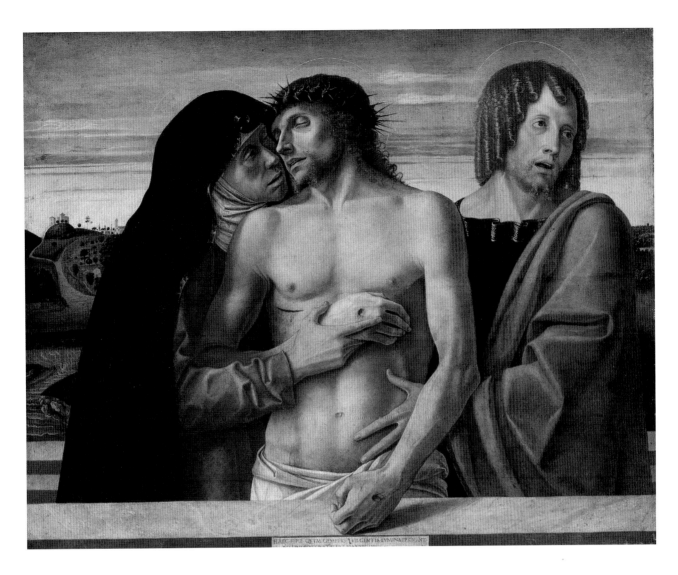

preparation for the Christian life. The northern movements of lay piety tended to avoid ritual and to stress the Bible and the inner life.

In contrast, the Italian confraternal movement valued ritual and objects that aided the religious experience. Along with most Italian Christians, they engaged enthusiastically with the cult of saints and the collection and veneration of relics. Every city, every neighborhood, even streets and alleyways, were dedicated to a particular saint or saints, whose feast days dominated the calendar. Relics of saints were proudly collected and displayed in local and larger churches, and the cities themselves took pride in the number of saints' relics that resided in and protected their cities. The cult of saints was particularly strong in Venice, where the inhabitants believed they were protected by St. Mark, the apostle said to have come to their lagoon during his lifetime. According to legend, some eager merchants had snatched his body from Alexandria and brought it back to Venice in the ninth century.

Giovanni Bellini, *Pietà*, 1460, tempera on panel, 34 × 42 in (86 × 107 cm). Pinacoteca di Brera, Milan.

In this moving example of Italian Renaissance piety, Christ, dead yet upright, stands in or behind a marble sepulcher. He is supported by his mother, with whom he communes face to face as she holds his pierced hand up to view. The beloved disciple John, unable to bear the pain, looks away.

HOLY WOMEN AND UNWILLING NUNS

From Catherine of Siena, born between the generations of Petrarch and Leonardo Bruni (see Chapter 3), to Catherine of Genoa (1447–1510) and Angela Merici (1474–1540), contemporaries of Machiavelli (see Chapter 8), to Maddalena dei Pazzi (1566–1607), contemporary of Galileo (see Chapter 8), Italy teemed with holy women. For all of its classical enthusiasms, the Renaissance was an age of intense spirituality, in which a typically female form of religious experience was highly valued—as is seen here in Annibale Carracci's painting of the mystic marriage of St. Catherine.

At the same time, however, there were women in convents who had no taste for the religious life to which, it seemed to them, they were condemned. Many families sent their daughters to convents, sometimes at a very young age, because they were not able or were not willing to pay the high cost of dowering them. They were required to pay a sum to the convent upon their entry to the religious life but it was cheaper than marriage.

The regular practice in Renaissance Italy of sequestering young girls and women in convents regardless of their aptitude for a religious life had the predictable consequence that many nuns did not behave as convent rules required. Church commissions and city governments constantly strove to reform the convents and compel the nuns to conform to expectations. In 1435, a Florentine court responded in this way:

> There are many nuns, bridges of God and dedicated to Him, who are enclosed in convents in order to serve him with their virginity, but who through carnal desire have failed in their reverence to Him. As a result of this, divine providence is perturbed and has afflicted the world with the evils of wars, disorders, epidemics, and other calamities and troubles. In order to avoid these, the severity of the Florentine people has decreed that no one is permitted to enter any convent, and that a heavy penalty be meted out to delinquents.... Thus, these nuns will not be transformed, by the audacity of evil men, from virtue into dishonor, from chastity into luxury, and from modesty into shame.

> (G. Brucker, *The Society of Renaissance Florence*. New York: Harper and Row, 1971, p. 207)

Nearly a century later, when the shameful laxity and luxury of the Venetian convents was well known, the Venetian state lawyers (*avogadori di comun*), in consultation with the highest councils of state, took action against one of the errant convents: they appropriated part of the building the convent occupied, walled it off, and installed a congregation of strictly observant nuns, who, it later emerged, were not only painfully pious but of inferior social status, which greatly angered the dispossessed nuns of Santa Maria delle Vergini. The incidents of June 20, 1519, are described by the Venetian diarist Marino Sanudo (1466–1536):

> This morning the Avogadori di Comun, by order of the Collegio and the heads of the Ten, in obedience to the wishes of the Patriarch, to whom the Doge had granted all his own authority over the nunnery of the Vergini that it might be reformed, went with constables, officials and masons to that nunnery, which is the second to be enclosed. There they made a forcible entry, breaking down doors, and by walling up doorways and so on they partitioned off a section of it, i.e. the new part of the building which looks towards the Patriarch's palace. This part they intend to give to the observant nuns of Santa Giustina, who will move into it. The nuns of the Vergini protested that they had been the victims of violence and had been cast out from their own hearths and so on, but they have to resign themselves to it.

> (D.S. Chambers and B. Pullan, eds., *Venice: A Documentary History, 1450–1630*. Oxford: Blackwell, 1992, p. 338)

More than a century later, the young women who found themselves trapped in a religious vocation they would not have chosen for themselves discovered a champion in the Venetian Arcangela Tarabotti (1604–1652). Sent to a convent as a child, she was made a nun in 1620 against her will. In her later writings, most notably her *Paternal Tyranny* (published posthumously in 1654 under the title *Simplicity Betrayed*), she lambasted the greed and arrogance of fathers who so mistreated their daughters. Tarabotti presents the case of the coerced nun thus:

> It is well known that the majority of nuns cannot attain perfection because they are forced to the religious life by the force exerted by their fathers and kin.... Most of them are not moved ... by the call

of the Gospel … and surely God has shown himself to hate any act which is not born of a voluntary disposition…. Only those who are willing nuns … even if against the will of their relatives, like Clare of Assisi and Catherine of Siena, who renounce the world even if they must be buried behind holy walls; but men imprison others so as not to bear expense and so as to be able to surround themselves with every sort of luxury, delicacy, and superabundant vanity, even in order to have more means of satiating their vile desires with swollen whores, to dissipate their wealth at the games, drowning themselves in the consummation of every one of their unjust desires.

(M.L. King, *Women of the Renaissance*. Chicago: University of Chicago Press, 1991, p. 89)

What if a woman who had been forced into the religious life wanted to renounce the convent? A letter to such a woman, written in 1399 by the Florentine humanist Coluccio Salutati (1331–1406), is most discouraging. Caterina, daughter of Vieri di Donatino of Arezzo, was placed in a convent at the age of 11. She acquired an education, developed other ambitions, and fled. Addressing Salutati, seemingly expressing her ambition to marry and raise children as well as to pursue her studies, she apparently expected his approval and encouragement. Instead, he mocked her pretenses to learning and rebuked her for leaving the convent: "Do not enter into the depravity and incest that you call marriage, but allow yourself to be brought back to the cloister, not to the service of a man but of Christ, not to carnal delights but to the joy and happiness of the spirit." Caterina ignored Salutati. In 1403 she won papal approval for the dissolution of her childhood vow.

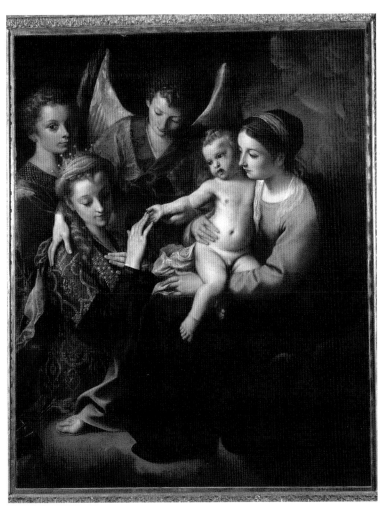

Carracci, *Mystic Marriage of St. Catherine*, c. 1586, oil on canvas, 63¾ × 46½ in (162 × 118 cm). Museo di Capodimonte, Naples.

Renaissance people also revered the holy who were in their midst: miracle-workers and preachers, healers and prophets, both male and female. Long before the church conferred its official verdict of sanctity in the rite of canonization, ordinary people had decided that the female Dominican tertiary Catherine of Siena (1347–1380), or Lorenzo Giustiniani (1381–1456), the ascetic patrician patriarch of Venice (both discussed below), embodied something of the divine; much as the crowds who thronged the Vatican in June 2002 had venerated Padre Pio before Pope John Paul II performed the official act of sanctification.

HOLY WOMEN

Several studies of saints and sanctity in the recent decades have pointed to the prominence of female sanctity as an extraordinary feature of the religious life of the period 1300–1600 in Europe generally but especially in Italy. More women were perceived as holy, living saints (and many were later canonized), and holy women aroused intense interest in the general population. The phenomenon of female sanctity is a significant feature of the Italian Renaissance.

Saints and Martyrs

The first saints were martyrs slaughtered in the arenas of the Roman Empire in witness to their faith. They were buried near the place of their death, and their burial sites became magnets for Christian travelers, called pilgrims. The pilgrims came to marvel at the martyrs' tombs but also to seek from them healing, strength, or contact with God. The very bodies of the fallen martyrs were seen as holy, or *sancti*, and thus they became saints. In time, magnificent churches replaced many of the informal tombs and shrines adorned by the visiting faithful and pilgrimage routes became busy and populous.

Martyrs were both men and women, poor and wealthy, young and old, free and slave. During the first part of the Middle Ages, however, most saints were male. At the same time, those canonized came largely from the elites of church and state: bishops, abbots, kings, and, occasionally, abbesses and queens.

This profile of a largely masculine, largely elite roster of saints changed in the later Middle Ages and during the Renaissance. From 1300 to 1600, although most of those sanctified remained male, the proportion of those who were female doubled. In 1100, considering all of Latin Christendom, women constituted just under 10 per cent of all saints, rising to 15 per cent in 1250, to 24 per cent by 1300, and to 29 per cent in the fifteenth century. Considering only lay saints (because all members of the clergy were male so were the saints drawn from their ranks), between 1350 through 1500, women constituted more than half—55 per cent—of those canonized. If we add to these saints the greater number of those considered holy, the "living saints" who were never canonized, the female component swells again. One scholar identified 152 holy women for Italy alone, including those later canonized, whose date of death fell in the fourteenth through seventeenth centuries. That number may be compared with the total of 87 officially canonized saints (male and female) who flourished anywhere in Latin Christendom in the period 1350 to 1500. Of these, 40 per cent were female.

This storm of statistics (a bit disconcerting because different scholars considered different groups for different subperiods) shows the increasing importance of women among those considered holy in general and among those officially canonized during the period 1300 to 1700, and especially during the period 1350 to 1500, the epoch of the Renaissance. Why this increase? How can we explain the fact that in this era of sophisticated, scholarly, literary, and artistic creation there was a surge of female religious commitment, supported by public enthusiasm for female sanctity?

One clue to this puzzle is the character of women's religious behavior in the period 1300 to 1600. Whereas female sanctity in earlier centuries had been expressed mostly in the convent, female sanctity in the Renaissance centuries was expressed in the home and out in the streets. It was another manifestation, it seems, of urbanization and of public attention to the civic arena of all dimensions of culture.

In this era, women seeking to commit themselves to a religious life did not have to enter a convent but could live at home with their family. Here they could engage in charitable activities or experience mystical encounters. Some joined the mendicant third orders and pursued their religious careers in this partial identification with mainstream religious organizations. Others lived in community with other women, in domestic settings distinct from a convent that would have been affiliated with one of the regular orders. Such communities of religious women also engaged in charitable and educational as well as devotional activities.

In northern Europe, women seeking this kind of unofficial, communitarian existence often were named **Béguines**. In Italy, no specific name was applied, although women engaging in any of the variety of unofficial forms of religious commitments were called *pinzochere*. In the later sixteenth century, as Latin Catholicism strengthened the role of the established orders in response to the challenge of Protestant reform (see Chapter 9), these women were generally forced into convents under stricter rules of segregation than had been imposed earlier. But for more than two centuries, there were many opportunities for women seeking a realm of religious expression apart from the supervision of the male orders and male hierarchy. A closer look at a few of the prime examples of female sanctity in this period will help make that point. The five holy women profiled here span the period from 1347, when the first was born on the eve of the Black Death, to 1540, two years before the establishment of the Roman **Inquisition** and the Catholic Church's riposte to the Protestant Reformation (see Chapter 9).

Catherine of Siena

The most famous of the women saints of the Italian Renaissance was Catherine of Siena (Catherine Benincasa). The daughter of a wool dyer and granddaughter of a poet, Catherine took up a religious vocation in childhood, experiencing mystical visions while refusing to indulge in the few comforts that her household provided. At age seven, she committed herself to virginity; at 16, she became a Dominican tertiary. Affiliated with the order, but not a cloistered nun, Catherine pursued her devotions in a room in her father's house. Her mystical experiences included conversations with Jesus and a mystical marriage in which she saw herself as his bride. Not only a visionary, Catherine pursued an active career of service to the sick, the poor, and the imprisoned. Apparently a person of great charisma, she attracted a circle of followers, among them many men, who saw her as their spiritual mother.

Enraged by the state of the church, Catherine boldly wrote to Pope Gregory XI (r. 1370–1378), then in Avignon, urging his prompt return to Rome. He came, as she commanded, putting an end to the Babylonian Captivity of the church (although the Schism would begin immediately upon his death). She wrote many other letters as well to princes and prelates—some 400, all through the hand of a scribe, as she herself was probably illiterate—and tried to rally support for a new crusade. She also dictated her *Dialogues of the Soul* to her scribes, a book recording her meditations and mystical experiences.

One of Catherine's followers (and her confessor) was Raymond of Capua (1330–1399), later the head of the Dominican Order. He composed her biography, one of the bases of her canonization. In 1461 she was declared a saint of the church, never having been nun or abbess. Thus, she completed one of the briefest known paths from bodily death to canonization. In 1500 the Aldine Press of Venice published a collection of her letters.

Francesca of Rome

Francesca of Rome (Francesca Bussa di Lioni de' Ponziani, 1384–1440), born to a noble family, was, like Catherine, a great mystic who had been committed to a religious vocation from childhood. Yet she married (at the age of 12), and reared three children, of whom two died in childhood. Francesca herself died on the day she had foreseen during a visit to her surviving son. This holy woman faced the particular problem of pursuing a religious career in the midst of a household with its sexual, emotional, and domestic demands. Her task was especially difficult in a Catholic context that associated heightened religious experience, especially for women, with virginity and seclusion. She pursued her devotions privately and publicly dedicated herself to charitable work—care of the sick, the poor, and the desperate. She experienced visions, and she engaged in a life of self-denial, punishing herself for the sexual activity to which her marriage committed her.

In the end, Francesca gained her husband's permission to refrain from sexual activity so that she could more freely pursue her vocation. In 1433 she won approval to form a

In their wills, both men and women gave the bulk of their goods to kin, usually children.
But many also specified large amounts for pious purposes. As men were the greater possessors
of wealth—although women possessed considerable property—they outweighed women
in every one of the following categories of pious bequests made in six Italian cities between
1200 and 1425. Male testators (writers of testaments) outweighed female testators, most
strikingly however, in gifts to priests and parishes and to dowry funds. (The latter gifts
reflected men's concern with the potential cost to male honor of unregulated—unmarried or
nonclaustrated—women.) Although as testators, women were still outnumbered by men, their
average gifts were very high in the categories of nuns and nunneries (where the value of their
average gift exceeded that of male testators) and servants. Since most servants were female
(as were all nuns), it can be concluded that for this sample, at least, women especially favored
bequests to female recipients.

Type of Bequests	Number of Bequests	Average Value (florins)
Priests and Parishes		
Men	2,094	6.24
Women	1,107	3.41
M/F Ratio	1.89	
Monks and Monasteries		
Men	797	7.72
Women	608	2.15
M/F Ratio	1.31	
Nuns and Nunneries		
Men	1,322	2.84
Women	1,175	3.19
M/F Ratio	1.13	
Hospitals		
Men	1,525	19.56
Women	1,117	5.08
M/F Ratio	1.37	
Dowry Funds		
Men	170	115.59
Women	88	46.01
M/F Ratio	1.93	
Servants		
Men	234	10.43
Women	155	8.29
M/F Ratio	1.51	

(S.K. Cohn Jr., *Women in the Streets: Essays on Sex and Power in Renaissance Italy*. Baltimore, MD: Johns Hopkins University
Press, 1996, Table 5.1, pp. 79–81)

religious community with like-minded women, with no vows or strict claustration (seclusion within convent walls), which was loosely affiliated with the Benedictine Order. Upon her husband's death, she took up residence in the community and became its leader. Long before she was canonized in 1608, the local population venerated the body of this holy woman.

Catherine of Bologna

Like both Catherine of Siena and Francesca of Rome, Catherine of Bologna (Caterina Vegri, 1413–1463) won enthusiastic public notice during her lifetime and after her death. From a noble family, she was raised at the court of the dukes of Este at Ferrara where she was educated to a high standard, becoming a lover of books and of manuscript illumination. When her companion, the duke's daughter, married in 1427 and her own father died, Catherine joined a community of 15 religious women in Ferrara, which was later converted to a convent of Poor Clares, the second or female order of Franciscans. She was later transferred to a convent of Poor Clares in her native city of Bologna, of which she became abbess. Deeply contemplative, she wrote *The Seven Spiritual Weapons* (1438; one of the first books printed in Bologna, and printed often thereafter), both a guide to novices and a record of her own spiritual journey. She was also an artist of note—one of the earliest known women artists in the Western tradition—leaving frescoes, altarpieces, and illuminations, which are still studied by art historians. Upon her death, her body was found to perform miraculous cures and to remain incorrupt, and the relic attracted throngs of the faithful. She was canonized in 1712.

Catherine of Genoa

Catherine of Genoa (Caterina Fieschi Adorno), like her predecessors, sought a religious career early in life; but like Francesca of Rome, she was compelled by the interests of her noble family to marry. She did so at age 16. At first she was tormented by her adulterous and abusive husband. Later, she converted him, and together the two pledged themselves to a life of abstinence and service as Franciscan tertiaries. Before she died, Catherine became the manager of the main hospital in Genoa. A mystic and a writer, Catherine was in a state of almost constant religious ecstasy and vision, punctuated by episodes of illness and extreme pain, for more than 25 years. The products of her extraordinary visions were two books, *Dialogues of the Soul and Body* (1551) and *Treatise on Purgatory* (1551), in addition to her *Memoirs* (1551) composed with the aid of her confessor and spiritual guide. She was canonized in 1737.

Angela Merici

The last of the holy women to be examined here, Angela Merici, also sought to lead a religious life from childhood. Orphaned at age 10, she was raised, along with her siblings, by a wealthy uncle in Saló, not far from her birthplace of Desenzano, both small towns attached to the larger city of Brescia. By age 13, she was a Franciscan tertiary determined to own nothing and to eat very little, embracing bodily deprivation in imitation of Jesus. She returned to Desenzano on her uncle's death when she was 20, and she began to teach the catechism (Christian instruction) to the children of the city. Wealthy patrons encouraged her to form a school in Brescia, to which city she moved. There she became the center of a community of devout men and women who were impressed by her knowledge of Latin scripture, of which she had mastered long passages by memory. In 1535 she founded a community of women dedicated to the teaching of girls. Its patron saint was Ursula, and the new teaching order came to be called Ursuline. It was Angela's intention that her organization would require no vows or claustration but that its members would live in the world. A generation after her death, however, the **Ursulines** were required to accept claustration. They remained dedicated to the education of girls. Angela was canonized in 1807.

Every one of these holy women is a saint of the Catholic Church, officially canonized years after their deaths. But they were also living saints, charismatic holy women who won followers and admirers during their lifetimes and veneration immediately upon their death. With the exception of the middle-class Catherine of Siena, all were from the nobility; two married. All lived and worked in the world, engaging in charitable service while associated with mainstream religious orders. Vegri (Catherine of Bologna) alone acquiesced when the community in which she lived was converted to the order of the Clares. Three were authors of works by their own hand or by dictation; one (Merici) was committed to teaching. These women were all citizens of their cities, committed to service, explorers of the spirit and seekers of truth, and largely resistant to the mainstream organizations of the contemporary church. They form a part of the story of lay civic commitment that underlies so much of Renaissance civilization.

The period of greatest opportunities for female religious endeavor corresponded to the period of greatest dynamism for lay piety in general and especially for lay confraternities. Indeed, although some of the holy women who flourished in such abundance during the Renaissance were affiliated with clerical orders, many more were not. The movement was essentially lay and is therefore best seen as a response, not only to the inadequacies of the official church in this period, which invested so much energy in the accumulation of wealth, prestige, and territory, but also to the liberating force of civic life.

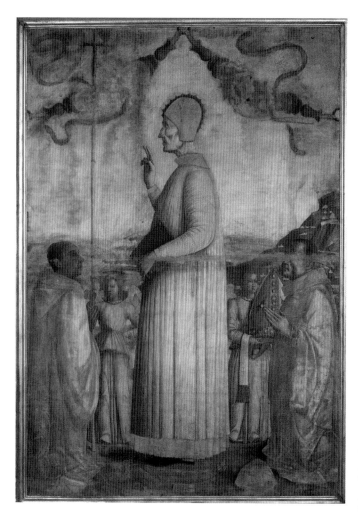

Gentile Bellini, *San Lorenzo Giustiniani*, 1465. Oil on canvas, 7 ft 4 in × 5 ft 3 in (2.2 × 1.6 m). Gallerie dell'Accademia, Venice.

Lorenzo's austere face is shown in strict profile, his hand raised authoritatively to bless his flock, while the figures surrounding him, drawn to smaller scale, sink below the horizon.

PASTORS OF THE FLOCK

The people of the Renaissance certainly found inspiration in these holy women who suffered austerity, underwent torments, tirelessly served the poor, the sick, and the outcast, and whose visions and ecstasies marked them as intimates of the divine. In their daily lives, however, they more often encountered religious leaders who were male, literate, demanding, and in charge. These were the bishops (or archbishops or patriarchs) who directed the religious lives of their city or region and the forceful preachers and visionaries, mostly Franciscan or Dominican, who summoned them to more perfect observance.

Archbishops and Bishops

The important role played by Italy's bishops in the Middle Ages has already been noted (see Chapter 1). The bishops were spiritual and secular leaders at the same time. They ruled cities when kings and lords were absent, inadequate, or abusive. They rallied the populace in times of crisis—plague, famine, war—to city-wide celebrations of penance and prayer. They lost their secular functions as the communal revolution progressed from the eleventh century. But the moral and religious leadership of the bishops remained important in the Renaissance.

A case in point is the Bishop of Venice, Lorenzo Giustiniani, from 1451 the first patriarch of Venice. In tightly run Venice, where the closed caste of adult noble males constituted the state, the bishop had no political power. Nor did he enjoy much prestige, in that the bishop's cathedral and palace were assigned a marginal position (geographically and socially), while the doge's own huge "chapel" of San Marco dominated the city's religious life. Nevertheless, Giustiniani stood out. Born to one of Venice's foremost ruling clans and brother of two major statesmen, his austerity and commitment compelled attention. In his youth, he had joined a number of other young noblemen in search of a more profound religious experience. They lived together in an uncloistered community on the island of Alga in the Venetian lagoon, governed loosely under the Augustinian rule with Giustiniani as their leader. He carried these ideals of deep spirituality and self-denial into his later career. Made Bishop of Venice in 1433, and patriarch in 1451, he proved to be a good administrator, reordering and reforming convents and monasteries. He was better known, and celebrated, for his own practice of voluntary poverty and for the extensive programs of charitable aid that he directed to benefit the poor of the city. He was also an author—like his brother Leonardo, an early humanist and patron—and left two volumes of sermons and ascetical works. Giustiniani was canonized in 1690.

Florence, like Venice, was fortunate in its religious leadership at the middle of the fifteenth century. Holding the position of archbishop for the period 1446 to 1459 was another pious and learned man who was also a skilled administrator: Antonino Pierozzi, known as Antoninus (1389–1459). Antoninus was a follower of the Dominican reformer and visionary Giovanni Dominici (1356–1420), a builder of monasteries and convents, papal legate, cardinal (appointed 1408), and a well-known moralist and opponent of what he saw as humanist secularism. Antoninus, too, was deeply concerned with ethical questions and wrote important works on moral theology. After organizing or leading several monasteries, he founded the Dominican abbey of San Marco in 1436 in Florence, where he hosted some of those who attended the Council of Florence in 1439. As archbishop, he labored to raise moral standards in the community at large and coordinated charitable services to the poor. He was especially loved for his leadership during the crises of plague in 1448 and earthquake in 1453. His compendium of moral theology, the best known of several works, was printed in 15 editions within 50 years of its first printing in 1477. Antoninus was canonized in 1523.

In a period when the papacy was given over to such concerns as papal supremacy and territorial sovereignty, and many bishops and archbishops pursued personal advantage over the needs of their flocks, some local religious leaders were responsive to the needs of the lay population. They guided in times of crisis, they supported charitable activities, and they insisted upon high moral standards. In their performance of this last function, the maintenance of moral discipline, episcopal leaders could rely upon the mechanism of church courts, which operated according to canon law and adjudicated cases involving usury, marriage, and related personal and sexual issues. Through their example of leadership and maintenance of church discipline, they could be forces for solidarity within their cities.

VILLANI'S LIST: RELIGIOUS INSTITUTIONS IN FLORENCE BEFORE THE BLACK DEATH

Churches in Florence and suburbs, including abbeys and churches of friars	110
Among these, parishes with congregations	57
Abbeys with two priors and about 80 monks each	5
Nunneries with some 500 women	24
Orders of friars	10
Hospitals with more than 1,000 beds to receive poor and sick	30

(from Kenneth Bartlett, *The Civilization of the Italian Renaissance: A Sourcebook*. Lexington, MA: D.C. Heath, 1992, p. 41)

Preachers and Visionaries

Other religious leaders were preachers and visionaries who dedicated themselves to arousing their audiences to a more intense religious life. Two in particular, whose lifetimes spanned the fifteenth century, won an enthusiastic response to their message of responsibility, self-denial, and religious commitment. The first was St. Bernardino of Siena (Bernardino Albizeschi); the second was the Florentine Girolamo Savonarola. Bernardino's great success and Savonarola's extraordinary rise and fall testify to the intensity of religious feeling in Italy during the age of the Renaissance.

Bernardino of Siena

An orphaned son of a prominent Sienese statesman, Bernardino sought a life of religious seclusion when still adolescent. At age 20, as a member of a confraternity assisting at Siena's main hospital during an onslaught of plague (which he contracted, but survived), he demonstrated his perseverance and leadership. In 1402 he joined the Observant branch of the Franciscan Order (those more strictly dedicated to the original ideals of the founder) and would eventually serve as their vicar general (chief leader) from 1438 to 1442. He was ordained as a priest in 1404, and during his career was offered three times, but each time rejected, a bishopric. He died in 1444 and was declared a saint of the church only six years later—an extraordinarily rapid canonization.

In 1417 Bernardino took off on the mission that defined his career: the evangelization of Italy. He crisscrossed the country, often on foot, preaching to large crowds of sometimes tens of thousands of listeners in the large public squares of their cities. The churches could not accommodate the magnitude of the audience. His message was the need for penitence: he confronted his listeners with the reality of the many sins they committed and aroused their desire to repent and to change the way they lived their lives. He chastised his listeners for their malicious gossiping, their sexual misdeeds, their addictive gambling, and their attachment to their finery and prized possessions, or "vanities." His audiences (mostly female) would weep in response to his words, surrender their vanities to the flames, or join in a sharing of the *bacio di pace* (kiss of peace). A few diligent listeners faithfully recorded the sermons (see p. 197) and their transcriptions total more than 1,000 pages in a modern edition. In addition, his Latin sermons and ascetical works survive.

If it is puzzling that so stern a message as Bernardino's could arouse such a passionate response, the answer lies in the power of Bernardino's presentation, his lively examples, his folksy speech, and his evident knowledge of the daily lives and secrets of ordinary people. In a sermon delivered in Siena, for example, one of a series of those delivered daily during August and September 1427, Bernardino urges his audience (largely of women, apparently) to bring their daughters with them the next day, so that he can warn them of the "sins" (certain sexual acts then considered sinful) that were often committed in marriage: "wherefore I bid you bring your daughters tomorrow, for I promise you that I believe you have never heard a more profitable sermon.... I believe so few are saved among those who are in the married state, that, of a thousand marriages, nine hundred and ninety-nine ... are marriages of the devil.... You shall come tomorrow and know the truth."

Although Bernardino's warnings about proper sexual behavior may have attracted mostly female listeners, another concern of his also reached men, and important and powerful men. Committed to peace (a Franciscan issue), Bernardino objected to the coats of arms that appeared painted, engraved, or sculpted on public and private buildings. These spoke of pomp and arrogance and threatened to disturb civic concord. Instead, he urged his followers to vaunt the name of Jesus. When he preached, he held before him a wooden tablet with the capital letters IHS (an abbreviation of the Greek form of "Jesus") within a radiant sun. Small painted cards and tablets with this inscription circulated throughout

Italy in response to Bernardino's movement. Prominent intellectuals, including humanists, inscribed the symbol at the top of each letter or work that they wrote.

Girolamo Savonarola

Later in the century, the Dominican Girolamo Savonarola (1452–1498), another popular Christian leader, would also find disciples among the learned and the powerful. Born to a noble Ferrarese family eight years after Bernardino's death, Savonarola was trained for a secular career in philosophy and medicine. A religious experience in 1474 moved him to join the Dominican Order in Bologna, where he followed a strictly ascetic regime and taught philosophy to the novices. During the 1480s he began to preach in various northern Italian cities about the sinfulness of the time and the coming apocalypse. In 1490 he was invited to speak at the Dominican Church of San Marco in Florence and was hailed as a great preacher. He stayed in Florence, where he became prior of San Marco and, from 1493, vicar general of the reformed Tuscan Dominican Order.

Savonarola gathered about him a large number of followers, called *piagnoni* (weepers) because they wept for their sins and the sins of the world. Among the *piagnoni* were some members of the ruling Medici family's clients and circle, including the humanist Pico della Mirandola (see Chapter 3) and the artist Botticelli (see Chapter 4). Like Bernardino, Savonarola preached to the Florentines about their sins: greed, unruliness, impiety, usury, gambling, and lust. Sharing the anti-Semitism of the day, he cautioned them against association with Jews. He called them to repentance and urged them to bring their vanities, those material objects—combs, mirrors, books of classical poetry, dice, and playing cards— that represented the things they loved more than God, to be burned in the bonfires lit in public places. He spoke of the apocalypse; the whole city listened.

Just as there was a political element—the concern for peace, the condemnation of faction—in Bernardino's message of moral regeneration, Savonarola's message contained both moral and political elements. In Savonarola's case, however, the political mission became dominant. He preached not only personal repentance and renewal but civic repentance and regeneration. In a restored republic, Florence would be a New Jerusalem.

Savonarola's rise occurred during the late years of the Medicean republic. In the background were the stirrings of a political cataclysm that would transform Italy as well as Florence. Savonarola was keenly aware of these occurrences and prophesied, among other events, the invasion of Italy by the French King Charles VIII (r. 1493–1498). When that invasion transpired in 1494, Savonarola welcomed it as divinely ordained vengeance. Charles swept through Florence and southward on to Naples before returning to France. On Savonarola's persuasion, Florence did not restore the Medici. Instead, it proclaimed a new republic with God as its sole ruler. A Great Council of the citizens ruled in accord with Christian law. The preacher and prophet Savonarola, who held no official title, was the force behind this theocracy, bolstered by his supporters, the *piagnoni*.

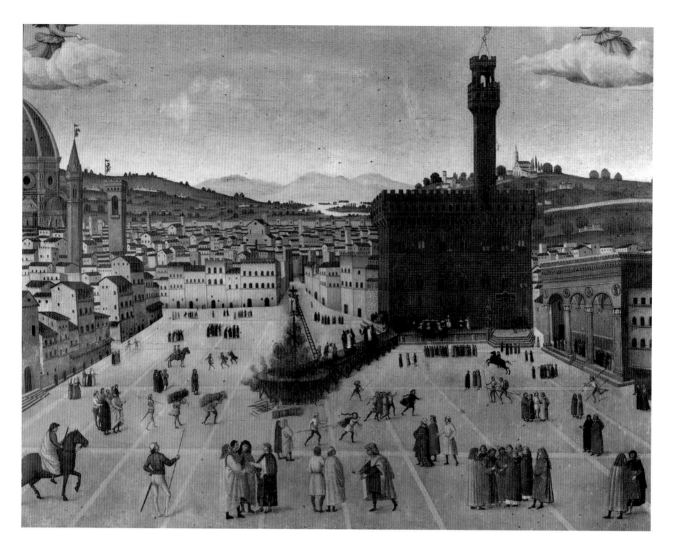

The Execution of Girolamo Savonarola on the Piazza della Signoria, c. 1600, oil on panel, 39⅓ × 45¼ in (100 × 115 cm). San Marco, Florence.

Before the Palazzo Pubblico (symbol of Florentine republicanism), near Brunelleschi's dome (at left) and in the square where he had commanded the Florentine elite to burn their "vanities," Savonarola was hanged and burned in 1498.

Difficulties began to multiply. In 1495 Savonarola was called to answer charges of heresy in Rome and when he did not go, was banned from preaching (a ban he did not obey). In the same year, a pro-Medicean conspiracy erupted. The five perpetrators were captured and executed, for it was a crime to challenge the Christian republic. But Savonarola was losing power. He spoke fiercely against the papacy in Lenten sermons in 1496 and 1497. He was excommunicated in 1497, and responded defiantly to the papal decree in writing and in deed—celebrating Christmas mass while under the ban in 1497.

The next year, Savonarola's bonfire of vanities triggered popular rioting. A rival preacher—a Franciscan—denounced him from the pulpit. Elections were held that returned Medici supporters to power. Savonarola was arrested, tortured, and condemned for falsely prophesying, a crime to which he confessed under torture but later renounced. His own supporters turned on him. On May 25, 1498, along with two companions, he was hanged, then burned at the stake in the piazza in front of the Signoria, the Florentine government palace.

CONCLUSION

What amazes about Savonarola's story, beyond the horror of its closing and the boldness of his political vision, is the power that he could exercise over his followers—at one point a large part of the population of Florence—through his preaching. Bernardino, too, reached many thousands with his preaching, while even the more conventional, and equally saintly Patriarch Lorenzo and Archbishop Antonino won substantial public admiration. [The Italian Renaissance was clearly not, as some commentators once claimed, "pagan" in its outlook. It was fiercely Christian; and that devout piety was shared even by most of those authors and artists who created the civilization of the Renaissance with its classical and secular concerns.]

Yet the Christianity of Renaissance Italy was different from that of the Middle Ages at its height. It was lay and civic, not clerical or official. It took its inspiration from the modernizing, innovating mendicant orders, more than the older established pillars of the church. It valued charitable activities, penitential rituals, and visionary experience more than the conventional rituals and ceremonies of the church. It, too, was revolutionary, as were Renaissance thought and art; no doubt because Renaissance religious sensibility was born of the same kind of urban experience.

SUGGESTED READINGS

Primary Sources

Ferrazzi, Cecilia. *Autobiography of an Aspiring Saint*. Translated and edited by Anne Jacobson Schutte. Chicago: University of Chicago Press, 1996. A laywoman grasps at sanctity in sixteenth-century Venice, and is silenced.

Modena, Leon. *The Autobiography of a Seventeenth-Century Venetian Rabbi: Leon Modena's Life of Judah*. Translated and edited by Mark R. Cohen. Princeton, NJ: Princeton University Press, 1988. A unique autobiography of a Jewish scholar.

Pius II, Pope (Aeneas Sylvius Piccolomini). *Commentaries*. Edited by Margaret Meserve and Marcello Simonetta, 2 vols. Cambridge, MA: Harvard University Press, 2003–2007. A humanist pope comments on the explosive events of his age, now available in a complete and authoritative translation.

Pulci, Antonia. *Saints' Lives and Bible Stories for the Stage: A Bilingual Edition*. Edited by Elissa B. Weaver, translated by James Wyatt Cook. Toronto: Iter Academic Press; Centre for Reformation and Renaissance Studies, 2010. In public theatrical events such as these scripted by Pulci, the lay public came to know and relate to Bible stories and the heroic adventures of the saints.

Riccoboni, Bartolomea, Sister. *Life and Death in a Venetian Convent: The Chronicle and Necrology of Corpus Domini, 1395–1436*. Translated and edited by Daniel Bornstein. Chicago: University of Chicago Press, 2000. Life on the inside of a Renaissance convent, told by one of the resident nuns.

Sulam, Sarra Copia. *Jewish Poet and Intellectual in Seventeenth-Century Venice: The Works of Sarra Copia Sulam in Verse and Prose, along with Writings of Her Contemporaries in Her Praise, Condemnation, or Defense.* Translated and edited by Don Harrán. Toronto: Iter Academic Press, Centre for Reformation and Renaissance Studies, 2009. The writings of a Jewish woman intellectual fully immersed in the mainstream Christian culture of Venice.

Secondary Sources

Bonfil, Robert. *Jewish Life in Renaissance Italy.* Translated by Anthony Oldcorn. Berkeley: University of California Press, 1994. Examines how Jews lived in their own communities and interacted with Christian society.

Bornstein, Daniel, and Roberto Rusconi, eds. *Women and Religion in Medieval and Renaissance Italy.* Chicago: University of Chicago Press, 1996. Originally published as *Mistiche e devote nell'Italia tardomedievale* (Naples: Liguori, 1992). Recent work by Italian scholars, especially on the activity of "living saints."

Cohn, Samuel K., Jr. *The Cult of Remembrance and the Black Death: Six Renaissance Cities in Central Italy.* Baltimore, MD: Johns Hopkins University Press, 1992. Studies more than 3,000 wills to trace the impact of plague on patterns of charitable giving.

Davis, Robert C., and Benjamin Ravid, eds. *The Jews of Early Modern Venice.* Baltimore, MD: Johns Hopkins University Press, 2001. Interdisciplinary studies on the cultural life within the Jewish ghetto of Venice.

D'Elia, Anthony F. *A Sudden Terror: The Plot to Murder the Pope in Renaissance Rome.* Cambridge, MA: Harvard University Press, 2009. Explores the multiple dimensions of a controversy turned violent between humanists and the papacy in 1468 Rome.

Hallman, Barbara McClung. *Italian Cardinals, Reform, and the Church as Property, 1492–1563.* Berkeley: University of California Press, 1985. Demonstrates that clerical abuses were left uncorrected by Counter-Reformation reforms.

Henderson, John. *Piety and Charity in Late Medieval Florence.* Oxford: Clarendon Press, 1994. Studies the devotional activities of Florentine confraternities.

Hollingsworth, Mary. *The Cardinal's Hat: Money, Ambition, and Everyday Life in the Court of a Borgia Prince.* London: Profile, 2004. Based on archival documents and inventories, tracks the rise to the cardinalate of Ippolito d'Este, his vast possessions, household routine, and later career.

Martines, Lauro. *Fire in the City: Savonarola and the Struggle for Renaissance Florence.* Oxford: Oxford University Press, 2006. Dramatic and authoritative narration of Savonarola's rise and fall, by a master historian.

Polecritti, Cynthia L. *Preaching Peace in Renaissance Italy: Bernardino of Siena and His Audience.* Washington, DC: Catholic University Press of America, 2000. An up-to-date study of the greatest preacher of the century of humanism.

Polizzotto, Lorenzo. *Children of the Promise: The Confraternity of the Purification and the Socialization of Youths in Florence, 1427–1785.* Oxford: Oxford University Press, 2004. Traces the history of a youth confraternity in Florence from its fifteenth-century foundation into the era of Enlightenment, showing its importance for the education and disciplining of the young and the maintenance of social solidarity.

Ruderman, David B. *Preachers of the Italian Ghetto*. Berkeley: University of California Press, 1992. Identifies attitudes toward Christian society as well as religious belief.

Sperling, Jutta Gisela. *Convents and the Body Politic in Late Renaissance Venice*. Chicago: University of Chicago Press, 1999. A study of Venetian convents, to which many noble women were consigned to support the interests of family and class.

Strocchia, Sharon T. *Nuns and Nunneries in Renaissance Florence*. Baltimore, MD: Johns Hopkins University Press, 2009. Explores the surge of female conventualization from 1348 to 1530, when a large proportion of the daughters of the city's elite lived in nunneries. This book examines cultural life and economic activity within convent walls.

Terpstra, Nicholas. *Lay Confraternities and Civic Religion in Renaissance Bologna*. Cambridge: Cambridge University Press, 1995. Discusses confraternal organizations in Bologna, in which the aristocracy increasingly gained ascendancy.

Weinstein, Donald. *Savonarola and Florence: Prophecy and Patriotism in the Renaissance*. Princeton, NJ: Princeton University Press, 1970. A classic study that examines Savonarola as religious leader and as the prophet of Florence's future as a New Jerusalem.

SEVEN

STATECRAFT AND WARCRAFT

(c. 1350–c. 1530)

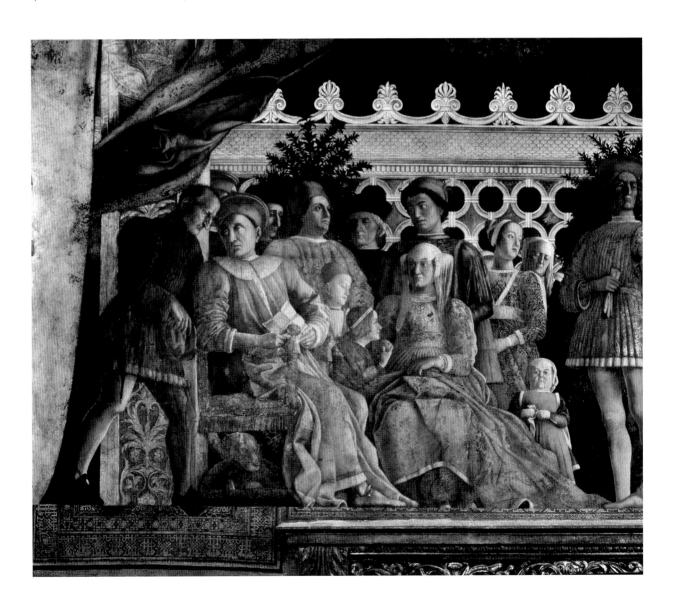

Of unknown parentage, a foundling without heirs, Castruccio Castracane gained mastery of the city of Lucca, defended it against the Florentines, and died from battlefield injuries after a heroic triumph. Lucca passed into the hands of the son of his own benefactor, whose incompetence would mean the loss of all that the great general had won. So he is described by Niccolò Machiavelli in the fictionalized biography that he dashed off in 1520. Despite its brevity and hasty composition, the work is rich in profound Machiavellian themes (see Chapter 8). Castruccio had toiled all day in the sun in a decisive battle, won "with great honor and glory." In the evening, as he stood in a chill wind greeting and thanking his soldiers one by one, he fell ill. As he lay dying, he advised his successor, a man he knew to be less able than himself, how to preserve the independence of Lucca:

> You must not, therefore, trust in anything except your own cleverness and the memory of my ability, and in the reputation brought to you by the present victory.... It is in this world of great importance to know oneself.... He who knows that he is not suited to war ought by means of the arts of peace to endeavor to reign. To them, in my opinion, it is well that you apply yourself, and that you strive in this way to enjoy the results of my labors and dangers ... and to me you will have two obligations: one that I have left you this realm; the other that I have taught you how to keep it.
>
> (N. Machiavelli, *The Life of Castruccio Castracane of Lucca*, trans. A.H. Gilbert, vol. 2. Durham, NC: Duke University Press, 1965, p. 554)

Here Castruccio sums up the two requirements of statecraft in Renaissance Italy. It was necessary first to gain power whether by force, fraud, or genius. Then it was necessary to keep it. The arts of war and peace combined to create this complex web, a dynamic that contributed hugely not only to the arts and thought but also to the political life of the West.

Castracane's Lucca briefly regained its independence, rocking from despotism to freedom and back. Its experience represents one dimension of Italian politics in the Renaissance. States won their autonomy and rulers won mastery, generally through force. Other dimensions included the complex machinery of government and law; the networks of alliance, diplomacy, and maneuvering that were required to keep what was in effect a federation of willful states in balance; the startling achievements of very small states that could not, in the end, withstand the assault of much larger ones. This chapter will explore these themes, examining first the rising tide of despotism in the fourteenth and fifteenth centuries, then the creation of a fragile balance of power in the fifteenth, and finally the tragic disruption of the careful, intricate political structures of Italy by waves of invasion from the late fifteenth to early sixteenth centuries.

THE TIDE OF DESPOTISM

By 1450 despotism—the signorie—had triumphed in Italy (see Chapters 1 and 2). Despotism arose, in fact, from the same conditions that had nurtured the republics—even though the two political forms were apparent opposites. In the signorie, power was concentrated in the hands of one person or dynasty, whereas in a republic, although power was not shared equally by all, it was distributed to the numerous members of a variety of councils and committees.

Yet in other ways the despotisms resembled the republics, with which they shared an essential kinship. Both were revolutionary and illegitimate in origin. They had also both emerged from the unique amalgam of political, social, economic, and historical circumstances that characterized northern Italy from the eleventh century (see Chapters 1 and 2). They were modernizing forms of political organization, distinct from the feudal networks that prevailed in northern Europe. They both pointed the way to the development of the modern European nation-state in the sixteenth century.

The city-states of Italy, both republican and despotic, had an intrinsic flaw; they were the products of struggle and retaliation. Each political form came into being when one faction—nobles, cives, popolo—overcame another. The victory of one faction meant the rout of the other, first through violence, then through exile. The exiled party would regroup, scheme, and make alliances with rival cities. When they were able to do so, they would recover power in their own city and exile their enemies. The ancient pattern of vendettas, still prevalent throughout this period in remote country areas, was replicated on the stage of the city-state.

Some states were able to put an end to the cycle of violence through the machinery of republican government. In so doing, they employed the tools available to modern states: the repression of dissent and the consolidation of power in the hands of a trusted elite. By these methods, Florence avoided turmoil and a recourse to despotism. Its Ordinances of Justice expelled the magnates who were the main source of anti-government violence. Its Guelf party constantly monitored any activity seen as inimical to what it perceived as the public interest. Finally, from the late **trecento** to early quattrocento, it defined and organized an ever-narrowing oligarchy as the political class.

Venice, the only other wholly successful Renaissance republic, used similar organizational methods. It prevented civic disorder through a combination of measures: the creation of repressive institutions (such as the Council of Ten) and the consolidation of the oligarchy as a permanent political class.

Other city-states fell permanently or spasmodically under the yoke of despotisms (or were eventually absorbed by one of the other great city-states). In Venice the signore imposed order by force, whereas the oligarchies had imposed rule by employing the repressive capacity of republican institutions. Both political forms sacrificed civil liberty to the overriding need, as they perceived it, of order.

Republics and despotisms were equally illegitimate, having seized sovereignty that theoretically belonged to a preexisting and legitimate authority. They had no lineage, although the signori themselves might derive from old noble families or from new ones for whom a lineage could be devised. Their political bastardy called for legitimization. Here may be found the point of intersection between Italy's political history and its humanist movement. It could be argued that the city-states sought legitimacy by evoking the more positive, and less barbaric, aspects of their Roman past, just as the humanists diligently modeled their new culture upon the more cultivated examples of their Roman forebears.

Republics and despotisms were also equally revolutionary. They toppled old political orders by force. The eventual triumph of new over old was signified in that moment at Legnano in 1176 (see pp. 30–31) when upstart communes defeated the Holy Roman Emperor in the field of battle.

The Organization of Violence

To be revolutionary, it was necessary to be violent. Republics and despotisms were also alike in their marshaling of force. The signori, all noblemen, were masters of violence from the outset. A nobleman in medieval Europe was a trained warrior. War was the beginning and the end of his training. The nobleman had not yet become a gentleman, a courtier, and a composer of sonnets or compliments. Those refinements had their ancestry in the Provençal courts of southern France in the twelfth century and would develop further in the Italian courts of the quattro- and cinquecento. From there, aristocratic civility was exported to the rest of Europe and to other social strata (see Chapters 8 and 10). In this earlier period, however, a nobleman learned to manage horses, weapons, subordinates, and the chaos of war.

The republican city-states, in contrast, had no native military leader. Instead, a militia made up of the whole body of the citizens would march to the battlefront to defend the city against aggressors. Within the walls, this citizen militia was organized by parishes or neighborhoods, each unit with a gonfaloniere. These civic standards, not the heraldic banners flown by the forces of a nobleman's retinue, were raised and defended in combat. The local unit of the militia was one of the several associations to which a citizen might belong, along with their guild, confraternity, or other kin- or neighborhood-based sodality. The civic militia was a feature of the Italian city-state but rare in Europe north of the Alps, where nobles, knights, and retainers were summoned to war by their feudal superiors.

The citizen militias of the late medieval Italian city-states prefigure the national armies, recruited by conscription, of modern states. However, the development from the early to the later phenomenon was interrupted. By the middle of the fourteenth century, republican governments no longer sent their armed citizens to war. Instead, they hired companies of professional soldiers. Sometimes these were groups of foreign soldiers who were available in the interlude between wars elsewhere. French or Spanish (Catalan) soldiers normally engaged in southern Italy would serve between engagements for northern city-states. The Hundred Years' War, which occupied the English and the French intermittently from

1337 to 1453, gave rise to several freebooting companies. The English knight Sir John Hawkwood, for instance—the Florentines rendered his name Giovanni Acuto, or John the Sharp—commanded the company that defended Florentine interests for years before his death in 1394. In gratitude for his services, the government had the renowned artist Paolo Uccello paint a fresco on the interior wall of the Cathedral showing him in equestrian pose. This avoided the expense of a bronze or marble statue, such as Venice would erect for its most admired generals (see pp. 224–225).

In time, however, the republics sought out Italian companies to hire, whose generals were usually minor noblemen. Sometimes they were themselves signori in smaller towns or papal vicars for towns of the Papal States—necessary because the pope, like the republics, had no standing army. Having such a local base was an asset for a condottiere. Here his company could spend the winter rent free and feed themselves from the fields in the summer.

The agreements reached between city governments and mercenary generals became formalized in the fourteenth and fifteenth centuries. The contract was the *condotta*; the contractor was known as the condottiere. The terminology associated with the contract to hire thus lends its name to the phenomenon of mercenary warfare in the Italian Renaissance.

The condottiere was not merely a general; he was also a prudent entrepreneur whose investments could yield great wealth. From the enormous sums paid him, he withheld enough for his soldiers' food, clothing, equipment, and to subcontract with other condottieri. He paid his soldiers promptly (and not just with the promise of booty, although sometimes that was an additional incentive). An unpaid army was unruly and liable to desert. In the field, the condottiere was cautious, inclined to strategy and maneuver, reluctant to commit his forces to hopeless enterprises. But he took risks where necessary, and many condottieri and their men died in battle. City-state employers were sometimes exasperated by the poor or tardy performance of their condottieri. In 1432 Venice famously executed one of its generals as a traitor, an event which seems to have inspired profound loyalty among subsequent hires. Often, however, employers were grateful to the men whose competence bought their survival.

The condottiere thus became the complex hero of the age, or at least, in retrospect, a heroic figure to later ages. While no public monuments were built to Cosimo il Vecchio ("the Old"; 1389–1464), effectively the first Medici ruler of Florence, or to any Venetian doge, statues of condottieri count among the great sculptures of the age. Among them are the thoughtful, controlled Gattamelata (Erasmo da Narni), a Donatello masterpiece (see p. 224), which dominates the piazza in front of the cathedral in Padua and the passionate, ferocious Colleoni, designed to adorn the great piazza of San Marco in Venice, but reallocated by wary politicians to the still magnificent *campo* of Santi Giovanni e Paolo (see p. 225).

The phenomena of the condottiere and the signore are closely intertwined. Some signori sold their services, and those of their followers, to other states and so became condottieri. Some condottieri were minor noblemen who hoped to acquire a state. Others were loyal servants, who boosted their paymasters to power and gained rich rewards for

WARRIORS FOR HIRE: THE AGE OF THE *CONDOTTIERI*

Mercenary soldiers today are often seen as ruthless and unprincipled fighters who prop up dictators or terrorists. But mercenary armies were a necessity in Renaissance Italy. The city-states lacked a native nobility, at a time when the nobility constituted the only trained warrior class. Citizen militias could not manage the escalating crises of the fourteenth and fifteenth centuries. The captains of the military companies, trained professionals who negotiated for a *condotta* (contract), and were thus called condottieri, were often loyal and long-time servants of the Italian states. A few famous figures are introduced here.

Imported from England: Sir John Hawkwood (1320–1394) Son of an English tanner, Hawkwood acquired the skills and title of a knight during the Hundred Years' War. Demobilized after the Treaty of Brétigny in 1360, he accepted employment by Pisa (where his name was altered to the Italian as "Giovanni Acuto") in 1364. At the head of his White Company, he later fought for the popes and for Milan and became Florentine captain general in 1382. He used the fortune he had accumulated to purchase lands in the Florentine countryside where he resided, always hoping

to return to England. In 1436, a generation after his death, the overseers of the Cathedral commissioned Paolo Uccello to paint Hawkwood's portrait in the style of an equestrian monument in recognition of his service to the state.

Italian warlords: Muzio Attendolo Sforza (1369–1424) and Braccio da Montone (1368–1424) Both offspring of the minor nobility of central Italy, Muzio and Braccio became the leading condottieri of their generation. Muzio fought for Florence and Milan until, in 1412, he took up service with the Kingdom of Naples, where he fought for King Ladislas and Queen Joanna II. Braccio captured his native city of Perugia and made himself its lord, the first condottiere to acquire a state. In 1420 his position was legitimized by Pope Martin V, who gave Braccio the title of "papal vicar." Then he, too, went south to Naples, site of the principal conflict of that generation, in the employ of Alfonso of Aragón. The two combatants died the same year: Muzio by drowning, Braccio from wounds inflicted in battle by Muzio's son Francesco.

Servants of Venice: Gattamelata (1370–1443) and Bartolommeo Colleoni (1400–1475) In the 1430s military

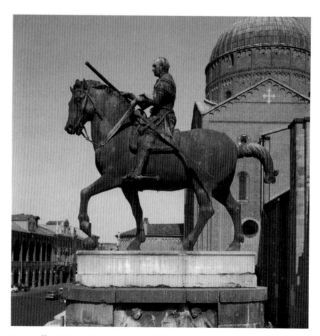

Donatello, *Gattamelata*, c. 1445–1456, bronze, height 12 ft 1 in (3.68 m). Piazza del Santo, Padua.

action shifted northward to the Lombard plain, theater of the ambitions of the Milanese duke Filippo Maria Visconti. When the Venetian captain general Francesco Carmagnola (1380?–1432) seemed only lackadaisically to be pursuing Visconti, the Venetians' mortal enemy, he was arrested, tortured, and executed. Venice had more success with the condottieri they hired subsequently, if only because they operated under the powerful deterrent of Carmagnola's example.

Gattamelata (a nickname meaning "honeyed" or "tabby cat"), born Erasmo da Narni, son of a miller, fought for Florence and the pope before joining the Venetian forces as captain general in the early 1430s (see opposite). In 1439, aged nearly 70, he suffered an apoplectic stroke and retired to Padua with a generous pension from the Venetian government. Venice also gave him a splendid funeral at his death in 1443, attended by the doge and adorned by humanist eulogies. His family commissioned Donatello to erect a bronze equestrian statue in front of the Church of San Antonio in Padua (1447–1450) and built a splendid tomb. Having married within the profession, as did many of the condottieri, Gattamelata left his company of *gatteschi* (followers of "the cat") to his brother-in-law Gentile da Leonessa and his son Giovanni Antonio.

Meanwhile, Bartolommeo Colleoni, the orphaned son of a minor nobleman, yearned for preferment in the Venetian military during the struggles of the 1430s but was disappointed. Later he fought for Milan and for Sforza, returning to Venetian service and winning, in 1454, the coveted title of captain general. The rewards of his Venetian employment were great and permitted him to live like a great lord at his castle in Malpaga. His will bequeathed 300,000 ducats to Venice to pay for a great bronze equestrian statue to be erected in the Piazza San Marco. Upon his death, Venice took the money and commissioned the statue—but erected it instead in front of the Church of Santi Giovanni e Paolo.

The big prize: Francesco Sforza (1401–1466) Sforza (see p. 135), illegitimate son of Muzio, reached the zenith of achievement for the Renaissance condottieri: not just great wealth, but a state of his own—the Duchy of Milan—that he ruled and bequeathed to his descendants. Having gained early experience in the conflicts of central Italy, he came to Lombardy in the 1430s and fought alternately for Venice and Milan. In 1441 he married the illegitimate daughter, and sole direct heir, of Filippo Maria Visconti. Soon thereafter, he was in Venetian employ. In 1447, when Visconti died intestate, Sforza made his claim for the inheritance, as did other powerful contenders, including Alfonso of Naples. But the Milanese revolted and declared themselves a republic, hiring Sforza as their captain general. Soon he, Venice, and the Milanese republic were engaged in a triangular struggle, which ended when, having besieged and starved the city to submission, Sforza took power in 1450.

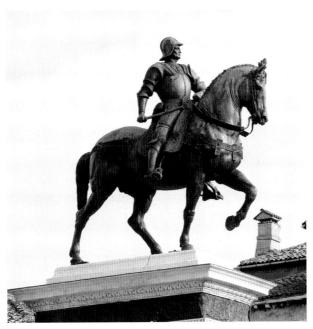

Verrocchio and Leopardi, *Equestrian Monument to Bartolomeo Colleoni*, 1481–1488/1495, gilded bronze on Carrara marble base, height 13 ft (395 cm). Campo Santi Giovanni e Paolo, Venice.

their loyalty, including lands and palaces. Colleoni, for instance, went quietly into retirement in 1456 to live handsomely on the fiefdom of Malpaga granted him by his grateful employer, Venice. There he devoted his sunset years to the patronage of arts and letters. All gained or maintained their own status through the intelligent and effective use of force. A closer look at the careers of some of these amphibious figures—part mercenary general, part sovereign ruler—will help illumine the contours of the political world of the Italian Renaissance.

Padua and Verona

The city of Verona (some 70 miles west of Venice), prosperous and independent from the twelfth century, suffered in the thirteenth under the tyrannical rule of Ezzelino da Romano, immortalized in Dante's *Inferno* for his cruelty. The agent of Emperor Frederick II and his heirs, Ezzelino was the prototype of the signore. Further torn by the factional struggles after Ezzelino's death, the city turned to a local noble family, the della Scala. Mastino della Scala (d. 1277) served as *podestà* (governor) from 1277. Over the next generation, he and his successors transformed the podestariate into full sovereignty. The Scaligeri established themselves as a dynasty of signori, brushing away the republican pretense and becoming the hereditary rulers of the once-free city. Can Grande della Scala (see p. 65), holding the title of imperial vicar, extended his authority over Vicenza and Padua and other nearby cities. He also prefigured later signori in his dedication to cultural pursuits, becoming the patron of Dante (who addressed a Latin treatise on poetic interpretation to him) and the subject of an important early work of Renaissance sculpture. A series of Scaligeri ruled for more than 100 years, until in 1387 they succumbed to Milan. In 1405, the city was taken by Venice.

Nearby, Padua (also in modern Veneto) had eyed the Veronese experience glumly. Padua was a major center well before the Scala takeover, the proud possessor of the miracle-working relics of St. Anthony and home to the gemlike Scrovegni Chapel, adorned by Giotto. Padua was also the site of a university, which was challenged for primacy in Italy only by Bologna, as well as conventual schools for advanced theological study. Ezzelino's brutality, which extended well beyond his center at Verona, aroused resentment and stimulated the thinking of at least one of Italy's early humanists, Albertino Mussato (1261–1329), whose Latin verse *Ecerinis*, modeled on Senecan tragedy, was an indictment of that tyrant.

Fearful of the looming power of the neighboring Scaligeri, Padua called on one of its own noblemen, Jacopo da Carrara, to become "perpetual captain" in 1318, a position subsequently transformed into a signory. The city thus won immunity from Scrovegni designs by subjecting itself to the Carraresi, until, in 1405, Venice snapped up Padua along with Verona in its bid for power on the *terraferma*. Although the dominion of the Carraresi was briefer than that of the Scaligeri in Verona, and it suffered from dynastic rivalries, these rulers, too, devoted themselves to building and to literature. Francesco il Vecchio the Elder

(r. 1355–1387) was a patron of Petrarch, who spent the last years of his life in a small hill-town nearby as a guest of the Paduans.

The Visconti in Milan

The Visconti takeover of Milan, the chief city of the region of Lombardy, followed the pattern of Scala and Carrara advances in Verona and Padua, and then exceeded their model. In 1277, after a period of strife between Guelf and Ghibelline parties, the latter consisting chiefly of the local nobility, backed Archbishop Ottone (1207–1295) of the noble Visconti family in taking control of this wealthy commercial city. His great-nephew Matteo I (1255–1322), as captain general and imperial vicar, established the dynasty as an enduring signory. The Visconti gradually extended their sovereignty across the rich Lombard plain until, in the 1380s, they had extended far enough eastward to take over Verona, threaten Padua, and awaken Venice. Their dominion was confirmed by the emperor, who, in 1395, granted the prestigious title of duke upon Giangaleazzo Visconti upon the payment of a large sum. Giangaleazzo would soon drive southward toward Tuscany and menace its chief city of Florence (see p. 231).

Although the ambitions of the Visconti were stalled by the Florentines and the Venetians in the first half of the fifteenth century, Filippo Maria Visconti (1392–1447) was still the premier ruler in Lombardy. In 1447, however, he died, with no clearly designated heir. This permitted the Ambrosian revolt and the eventual takeover by the greatest of the condottieri, Francesco Sforza (see p. 232). In the signorial pattern, the Visconti were important patrons of the arts and letters. Under their aegis, the gigantic late Gothic Milan Cathedral was begun. They also founded the University of Pavia, established an important library, and supported a first generation of humanists at their court.

Ferrara, Mantua, and Urbino

The Este, Gonzaga, and Montefeltro signori of Ferrara, Mantua, and Urbino have already been encountered as intelligent and generous patrons of arts and letters (see Chapter 4). But it was their control over their cities that permitted them to foster the civilization of the Renaissance, and it was military skill that won them sovereignty. In the cases of the Este and Gonzaga, local nobles seized power during the fourteenth century, establishing dynasties that lasted for over three centuries.

Descended from a long noble lineage with roots in Lombardy and connections to the German emperors, Obizzo d'Este II (d. 1293) became signore of Ferrara (modern Emilia-Romagna) in 1264 and of neighboring Modena and Reggio in 1288 and 1289, respectively. In fact, he controlled much of the eastern Po valley region, which he and his descendants held as papal vicars. The Este patronized building projects as early as the fourteenth century, notably the imposing Este Castle of 1385, and saw to the founding of the University of Ferrara in 1391. The family's patronage activities peaked under the fifteenth-century rulers Niccolò III (1210–1280) and his legitimated bastard sons Leonello (1407–1450) and Borso (1413–1471), the latter capturing for his family the prestigious title of duke in 1471. The Este court remained one of the most brilliant in Italy into the sixteenth century and nurtured the talent of the epic poet Ludovico Ariosto, author of *Orlando Furioso* (see Chapter 8). The last Este duke died without heir in 1597, and Ferrara was reincorporated into the Papal States.

The Gonzaga became signori of the Lombard city of Mantua in 1328, when Ludovico I (1267–1360) served as captain and expelled the then-ruling Bonacolsi clan. Whereas the Este were technically papal vicars for the entire three centuries of their domination, the Gonzaga were imperial vicars, who kept their German contacts alive through diplomatic exchange and marriages. They retained their role as captains of Mantua, too, arranging for their own reelection to that office in each generation. As patrons, the Gonzaga supported many churches, and, even more, the building of luxurious palaces on the edge of the city, which employed leading artists from all over Italy. Although they had no university to support, at the invitation of Gianfrancesco Gonzaga, Vittorino da Feltre established what was perhaps the most famous humanist school in Europe in 1423: the Casa Giocosa, or House of Joy (see Chapter 3). Gonzaga prestige climbed with the acquisition of the titles of marquis in 1433 and duke in 1530. The dynasty endured to 1627, when the last Gonzaga descendant died. The city of Mantua fell three years later to an imperial army. A collateral line was later restored to the title and ruled until 1707.

The Montefeltro clan had dominated Urbino (in the modern region of le Marche) since the twelfth century. Staunch Ghibellines, they had long resisted papal attempts to take over the region around Urbino when, in 1377, Antonio da Montefeltro (d. 1403) returned from exile and became an obedient legate of his former enemy. His son Guidantonio (1378–1443), an able papal condottiere, won the title of duke for the family in 1419. After the death of Guidantonio's legitimate male heir, his legitimated bastard son, the burly condottiere Federico, built up the city and incorporated it seamlessly into the huge palace complex he built into the hillside. Under Federico's son Guidobaldo (1472–1508), the Montefeltro court became one of the most sparkling in Italy. It was the setting for Baldassare Castiglione's *Il cortegiano* ("The Courtier"), a manual for courtly behavior. In 1508, however, Guidobaldo died childless and the Montefeltro family ceased to rule. Now under the control of the della Rovere family, which ruled from nearby Pesaro, Urbino was reincorporated into the Papal States.

The Papal States and the Two Sicilies

Northern Italy was the realm of the commercially successful city-states that had gained their autonomy in the communal revolution. To the south, the Papal States and southern Italy, dominated by the Kingdoms of Sicily and Naples, underwent a different political

A DESPOT'S ADVICE AND A REPUBLICAN'S LAMENT: MALATESTA AND RINUCCINI

As most of the cities of northern Italy succumbed to despotism in the fourteenth and fifteenth centuries, political rhetoric changed to reflect changing circumstances. Here are two examples.

In the first passage, written in 1408, the experienced signore Carlo Malatesta gives advice on rulership to the novice Giovanni Maria Visconti. Although the stated assumptions about the ruler's role are benign, there is little doubt that the ruler, and no one else, will be in charge of the state.

> Love your subjects and they will love you; busy yourself with your government; refrain from excessive gifts and expenses, especially in times of war; do everything you can to avoid wars; beware of using cruelty ... retain only loyal and trusting councilors, letting no others interfere ... see to it that your judges always adjudicate justly ... let corrupt officials be put to death; keep your fortresses in the hands of foreigners and out of the hands of citizens and local men; show no mercy to confirmed rebels, but punish them in accord with justice ... let no one build castles or forts, and tear down those that are built, keeping only the ones necessary to the public good.
>
> (L. Martines, Power and Imagination: City-States in Renaissance Italy. New York: Alfred A. Knopf, 1979, p. 109)

The next passage is drawn from the 1479 dialogue *On Liberty* by Alamanno Rinuccini (1426–1499). Liberty has given way to despotism, one speaker laments, and the people themselves have lost the will to resist.

> We have degenerated so much in our time from the virtues of our ancestors.... They founded, cherished and increased this Republic. They gave it excellent customs, sacred laws, and institutions that further an upright way of life.... As long as our state lived in accordance with its own law, it enjoyed preeminence among the other Tuscan cities in wealth, in dignity, and in power. All that time this city was a model, not of power alone, but of moral principles. Now I see the same laws despised by everyone till nothing stands lower. The desires of a few irresponsible citizens, instead, have gained the force of laws....
>
> Isn't it well known that the basic principle of all liberty is citizen equality? This is a fundamental to keep the rich from oppressing the poor or the poor, for their part, from violently robbing the rich. On this basis everyone keeps what is his and is secure from attack. Judge for yourselves how secure things are in our country. Shall I describe the sale of justice? Most carefully, as long as our state was free, was justice kept clear of corruption. Now it is managed in a way that is sickening even to talk about....
>
> Why compare the freedom of speech that used to prevail in the senate and in all public meetings with the present silence? There once did shine the wisdom, the eloquence, and the fervent patriotism which graced some of our best citizens.... And what about the way public officials are chosen these days? You know as well as I that, in free states, offices are filled by chance selection from certain lists.... But now all the positions that bestow some dignity on a man and yield some profit are filled, not by lot, but by appointment....
>
> Liberty has been uprooted and thrown away.... The people seem to despair of themselves. They submit to an alien will and let the wishes of certain people subvert their lives.
>
> (R.N. Watkins, trans. and ed., Humanism and Liberty: Writings on Freedom from Fifteenth-Century Florence. Columbia: University of South Carolina Press, 1978, pp. 204–207)

experience. There, too, however, powerful men seized control in the fourteenth and fifteenth centuries and established personal rule.

The Papal States were a distinctive but important zone in Italian politics (see Chapter 6). To support the institution of the papacy—an institution with continental, indeed universal responsibilities—the popes needed to control a broad swath of territories extended across the mid-section of the Italian peninsula. This region included parts of the modern provinces of Lazio, Umbria, Emilia-Romagna, and le Marche. This was their concern in the thirteenth century, when the papal monarchy reached its medieval highpoint. It remained their concern in the fourteenth century, during the years 1307 to 1415, when the pope's retreat to Avignon, and then the disruption of the Schism, allowed the local strongmen of Umbria, le Marche, and Romagna to seize what land they could. From 1353 to 1367, the competent Spanish-born Cardinal Albornoz (Egidio de Albornoz, 1310–1367) served as papal agent in Italy, reclaiming lost territories and setting up some reliable nobles as papal legates.

Effective as this solution was in the short term, in the long term it meant, once again, that local dynasties became even stronger. The Malatesta established themselves in Rimini; the Bentivoglio in Bologna; a branch of the Sforza family in Pesaro. Later in the fifteenth century, addressing the same problem, Pope Alexander VI made his son, Cesare Borgia, chief papal legate. By terror and arms, Borgia slashed through Romagna and reestablished his own (rather than the papacy's) supremacy. When Alexander died, and Cesare not long afterwards, the task fell to the next pope, Julius II, who did not shirk conflict. Julius reasserted his authority in the Papal States, at the same time becoming deeply embroiled in the wars of the Italian states in the early sixteenth century (see p. 247).

The papacy was also thoroughly involved with the politics of southern Italy, and had been for centuries. It was the pope, in the eleventh century, who summoned Norman (French) warriors to seize Naples from the Byzantine Empire, which had held it since the sixth century, and the strategic island of Sicily from the Arabs, who had held it since the eighth. When in 1197 the Norman throne of Sicily and Apulia (Naples) passed through marriage into the hands of the German Hohenstaufen Emperor Frederick II, a serious threat to a succession of popes, the pope searched elsewhere for military muscle (see Chapter 1).

In 1266 Pope Clement IV (r. 1265–1268) invited Charles d'Anjou (r. 1262–1285), brother of the French King Louis IX (St. Louis), to reclaim the kingdoms from the German emperors. Thereafter, Angevin kings reigned in Naples, as an autonomous kingdom occupying the peninsula south of the Papal States, until 1442. In Sicily they ruled only until 1282. In that year, the King of Aragón (modern Spain), married to the heiress of the house of Hohenstaufen, crossed a small stretch of the western Mediterranean to seize Sicily from the Angevin rulers. For more than a century, the Aragonese ruled Sicily, and the Angevins ruled Naples, until the last Angevin claimant, René, duke of Anjou and count of Provence (1409–1480), was decisively defeated by the Aragonese armies. In 1442 Alfonso V of Aragón seized Naples (as Alfonso I the Magnificent) and reunited it with Sicily, the combined state being called the Kingdom of the Two Sicilies. Upon Alfonso's death, the two kingdoms divided again under monarchs both in the Aragonese line. The line of Anjou became extinct in France on the death of the unlucky René. Its possessions passed to the crown, which would return in 1494 to press its claim to Italian states (see p. 243).

After Norman adventurers displaced the Byzantine, Lombard, and Arab overlords of the regions of Sicily and southern Italy, foreign kings ruled and scrambled for power, sometimes assisted by and sometimes countered by the popes. Unlike the signori of northern Italy, they were legitimate, not mere strongmen taking over faction-ridden free communes. Yet in both regions, autocracy was the norm.

Freedom versus Tyranny

The signori advanced on every front in the four-teenth and early fifteenth centuries. Only a few republics still stood in 1400: Florence and Venice,

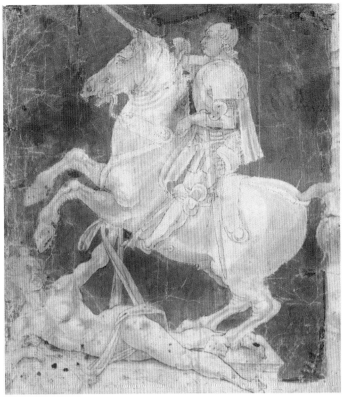

Pollaiuolo, *Study for Equestrian Statue to Francesco Sforza*, c. 1489, pen and bistre wash, 11 × 9½ in (28.4 × 24.5 cm). Metropolitan Museum of Art, New York City, NY.

The condottiere Sforza, truly a self-made man, rose from the minor nobility to become Duke of Milan by luck and talent.

the giants; and Lucca, Genoa, and Pisa. In turn, Venice created its own territorial state on the mainland as a buffer against its rivals (see p. 241). Florence responded, in 1402, by directly confronting the enemy. The citizenry of Milan, which had been under Visconti rule for nearly two centuries when the last Visconti died, fought valiantly to reestablish a republic. These two episodes of resistance will occupy us here, before the narrative returns to the activity of state building which resumed heatedly in the fifteenth century.

Florence The ambitions of the Visconti despots of Milan led to a grand confrontation with Florence, the most dynamic republic of mainland Italy. By 1400 Milan had expanded well beyond the limits of its original city and its *contado*, or neighboring country region: it had incorporated the north-central region of Lombardy, invaded the north-eastern Veneto, and was encroaching southward into Tuscany, which reached across most of Italy north and west of the Papal States. As Duke Giangaleazzo approached Florence, the leaders of that republic were determined to resist. In this determination they were supported by a cohort of humanists, as humanism was just crystallizing as an intellectual movement, following the example of Coluccio Salutati, then Florentine chancellor. In a famous invective directed against the Milanese courtier and humanist Antonio Loschi, Salutati defined the things that made Florence great. Foremost among these was freedom. The Florentines perceived their republican state, which had been forged in the experience of two centuries of civic struggle, as the paradigm of political liberty. They viewed it as the direct descendant of the ancient Roman Republic before that republic—like much of northern Italy—succumbed to tyranny.

These ideas circulated and aroused great passions as Giangaleazzo circled the city and laid siege in 1402. The situation could not be more desperate nor the issues involved—freedom versus despotism—more starkly drawn when, in June 1402, the tyrant himself suddenly caught the plague and died. His death preserved Florence for the century of its greatest achievements. It appeared to be a miraculous vindication of the political principles espoused by Florentine intellectuals.

Milan No miracle saved the people of Milan, however, when nearly half a century later, they banded together to resurrect the republic they had lost. Now the last Visconti had died: the dour and ruthless Filippo Maria, who left no direct descendants but his illegitimate daughter Bianca Maria, who had been given in marriage to the condottiere Francesco Sforza. On his deathbed, Filippo Maria declared as his heir Alfonso I of Naples, to Sforza's astonishment and great displeasure. More legitimate but more remote claimants to Milan, both German and French, announced themselves. As the potential rivals circled about shouting "Liberty! Liberty!" the people of Milan, led by a small cadre of patricians, declared themselves the Republic of St. Ambrose (the city's patron saint). Would it be possible for a republic to reclaim its freedom after two centuries of signorial rule?

For three years, the Ambrosian Republic resisted the pressures exerted by the would-be Visconti heirs—although it had appointed one of them, Francesco Sforza (see p. 225), as their captain general. They continued to negotiate with Venice, however, which did not wish to see a restored duchy and whose own armies were picking off bits of Lombardy as territorial prizes. In 1449, although it had previously contracted with Sforza against the interests of the republic, Venice now leagued with Milan, leaving Sforza apparently deprived of the prize he coveted. The Venetian betrayal infuriated him. Turning against his former employer and determined to seize the Visconti legacy for himself, Sforza besieged Milan in 1449. For a year the citizens struggled and starved, while its leaders conducted a reign of terror against those who defected to Sforza. Then one faction, which had already negotiated with the man it had once despised, betrayed the republic and threw open the city gates. On February 26, 1450, Sforza entered Milan, unarmed and triumphant, and was hailed as duke. Freedom had grappled with tyranny and lost; the republic ceded to the tyrant.

BALANCE OF POWER

Whether republics or signorie, the cities of northern Italy evolved during the first half of the fifteenth century into miniature states that in many ways prefigured the modern nation-states of Europe. They refined their government structures and absorbed neighboring cities and regions. They waged war among themselves for territory and for primacy. In 1200 there were some 40 autonomous cities in the Italian regions north of Rome. After 1400 these succumbed to the emerging territorial powers of the region. In 1454, when the Peace of Lodi resolved a generation of warfare, five principal states dominated the peninsula: in the north, Milan, Venice, and Florence; in central and southern Italy, Rome (the Papal States) and Naples (the Kingdom of the Two Sicilies). A fragile balance of power was maintained for nearly 40 years after Lodi. It was interrupted only by the vicious duel between Venice and Ferrara, which prefigured, in its appeals for the intervention of foreign powers, the debacle that would follow after 1494. This section examines the developing state system of the fifteenth century and the brief moment of political balance that it achieved.

Councils and Commissions

During the centuries of communal and popular rule, the cities of northern Italy developed republican forms of government (see Chapter 2). They shared certain features: a series of standing councils or assemblies supported by another series of ad hoc commissions. The councils ranged from the very large, such as the Maggior Consiglio (Great Council) in Venice with some 2,000 members, to small groups of five, six, nine, or twelve, with names such as the Council of Ten, The Eight of War, the Forty of Justice, and the Adjunct of Sixty. These governing councils discussed and decided matters of policy, war and peace, plans to provision the city or manage crime or riot, the construction of walls or public buildings, and the like. The ad hoc commissions also ranged in size, with groups of six, nine, twelve, or even forty quite common. These commissions might be charged with special projects, such as the conduct of a particular war or the collection of a particular tax. In addition to the regular councils and ad hoc commissions, various other groups were brought in to add wisdom or perspective on a particular knotty issue. The number of public offices was great—in Florence in 1400, about 3,000 were filled annually—and the pool of possible candidates was small, since only adult males of a certain standing were eligible.

The members of these councils and commissions were elected, even in the signorie, where the formal machinery of government was under the control of the despot. Names of eligible citizens would be assembled, with the criteria for eligibility differing from city to city. In Florence, guild membership was a prerequisite for political participation; in Venice, membership in the noble caste. Those names would be kept closely guarded to prevent manipulation by any but the duly appointed officials. The list would be subject to the *scrutinio* (scrutiny). Here is where mischief took place as cabals or oligarchies carefully excluded the names of their enemies from the lists of those eligible for office. In most cities, the final decision was made by lot. From a stockpile of scrutinized names written on slips of paper and placed in a *borsa* (purse or bag), a blindfolded official would draw the winning candidates. In Venice a famous variation on this process took place in the election of the doge. There, a series of committees would vote on the constitution of further committees. There was a total of 9 committees, consisting of 30, 9, 40, 12, 25, 9, 45, 11, and 41 electors in turn; it was the last of these bodies that chose the doge from approved candidates (see pp. 234–235).

THE MACHINERY OF GOVERNMENT IN VENICE

At once a republic and an oligarchy, with access to offices limited to the descendants of a legally defined nobility, Venice had an elaborate system of government that mixed open and exclusive councils and built in safeguards—not always successful—against manipulation and corruption. Although many important deliberations were restricted to such smaller bodies as the Senate or the Council of Ten, the Great Council, to which all adult male nobles belonged, was the heart of Venetian government. It was here that most elections took place, elections that opened the path to major political office in some cases or to high-paying sinecures in others. Here a contemporary describes the electoral process, which is depicted in these images:

When the said [Great] Council is fully assembled and the doors are shut, the … Grand Chancellor … reads out all the magistracies and offices which must be filled on that day in the said Council and he pronounces them in a loud voice so that everyone knows what is to be done. Afterwards, the Councillors take as many ballots of silvered copper as … there are noblemen present, and add to the said silvered ballots 36 gilded ones and place them in two urns.

Nobles are called up to choose ballots from the urns until 36 are selected, who go in groups of nine to four separate rooms, where they nominate candidates for the vacant offices. The names proposed are then sent to the main chamber.

Sequence of Committees in the Doge's Election

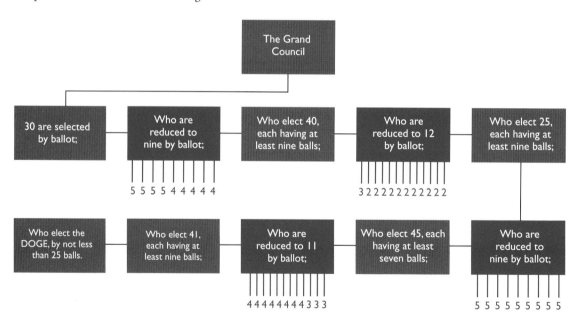

The Grand Council

30 are selected by ballot;

Who are reduced to nine by ballot;
5 5 5 5 4 4 4 4 4

Who elect 40, each having at least nine balls;

Who are reduced to 12 by ballot;
3 2 2 2 2 2 2 2 2 2 2 2

Who elect 25, each having at least nine balls;

Who elect the DOGE, by not less than 25 balls.

Who elect 41, each having at least nine balls;

Who are reduced to 11 by ballot;
4 4 4 4 4 4 4 4 3 3 3

Who elect 45, each having at least seven balls;

Who are reduced to nine by ballot;
5 5 5 5 5 5 5 5 5

The lower figures denote the number of provisional Electors which each Member of a preceding Committee is entitled to name, according to his order in that Committee.

And the slips of paper on which the names are written are carried to the dais where the Doge sits, and the names of the first persons proposed for the first office are read out in a loud voice by the Grand Chancellor. The said four are then balloted one after another by everyone in the Great Council who is eligible to vote; ballots made of fabric are used, and red and green voting-urns. These urns are carried up all the benches of the Great Council by appointed persons. And everyone in the Council casts his vote without moving from his seat, and those who place their ballots in the green urn reject the candidate. Afterwards the bearers of the urns come up to the dais and place the ballots which are in the red urns in front of the Councillor who sits on the right hand of the Doge, and those [ballots] in the red urns in front of the Councillors on the left of the Doge. And the said ballots are very carefully counted, and the number of them, both red and green, is checked by the authorized secretaries…. And he who has the most ballots in the red urn is elected to the first office, provided always that the ballots in the red urn are more than in the green one—that is to say, more than half the nobles in the Great Council approve and elect them.

(D.S. Chambers and B. Pullan, eds., Venice: A Documentary History, 1450–1630. Oxford: Blackwell, 1992, pp. 58–59)

It was in the Great Council, too, that the doge was elected by an exceptionally elaborate process. A panel of 30 was elected, from whom 9 were chosen. These 9 elected a panel of 40, from whom 12 were chosen who in turn elected a panel of 25, from whom 9 were chosen. These 9 elected a panel of 45, from whom 11 were chosen who elected a group of 41. These 41 comprised an electoral college that chose the doge, who had to receive at least 25 votes. The seventeenth-century diagram reproduced above illustrates this process. The many "hands" of the election were meant to ensure that no single clan or faction could control the result.

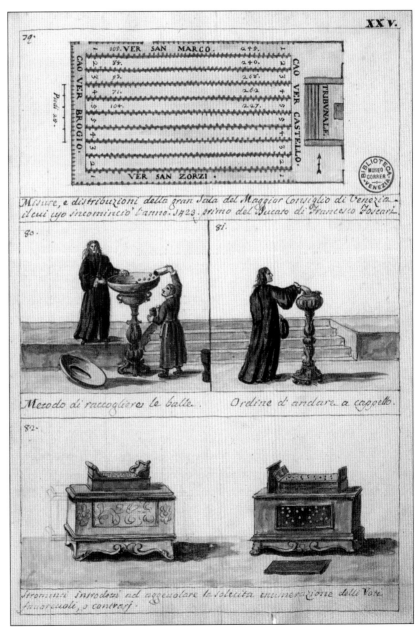

Jan Grevenbroch, *The Voting System in the Great Council*, from *Varie Venete Curiosità Sacre e Profane*, 1755, watercolor. Museo Correr, Venice.

The terms of office to which citizens were elected were exceedingly brief, from the perspective of twenty-first-century democracies. Terms of six months were common, and terms longer than one year were rare. Often there were bars to reelection for a period of *contumacia* (literally contumacy, signifying a leave of absence), generally a period as long as the original term of office. The purpose of these short terms was to prevent any concentration of power in the hands of individuals. The effects were various. On the one hand, a government that consisted of the rotation through an office of numerous persons, none of whom was able to gain control, permitted unofficial cabals or powerful individuals to manipulate government as they preferred. On the other, the regular rotation of the same political elite—of, perhaps, two or three hundred persons—through a series of offices meant that an oligarchy could control the organs of government while presenting an appearance of electoral niceness.

The Trend toward Oligarchy

Oscillating between a perpetual distrust of their own citizens and the entrustment of serious decisions to a narrow elite, city governments managed to run effectively during the fourteenth and fifteenth centuries. Yet there was a steady trend toward greater oligarchy where there was not an actual shift to signorial rule. The political class of Florence, for instance, steadily shrank from the mid-fourteenth century to the late fifteenth century, when, after a period of conservative patrician rule, the Medici family manipulated government through the careful reshuffling of its supporters (and exclusion of its enemies) in government councils. While the members of the noble caste constituted all the political class of Venice, a small group of a few hundred experts was recycled through the main government councils. The signori, as has been noted, carefully preserved the appearance of republican government, while stocking the councils with their kin and cronies. In effect, therefore, the difference between a republic and a signoria faded to invisibility.

Nowhere was this ambiguity more apparent than in Florence. In 1434 Cosimo di Giovanni di Bicci de' Medici, inheritor of the city's greatest banking fortune, returned from exile to take charge of Florence. From 1434 to 1464, Cosimo directed the city's fortunes through his supporters, handsomely rewarding them with his patronage and with the usual spoils of power. Yet he never held a major office for more than a brief term and never claimed lordship of the city. Thus Florence remained superficially a republic, though it was more realistically an oligarchy. And by the time that Cosimo's son Piero (1416–1469) inherited his father's role, ruling from 1464 to 1469, and his son Lorenzo the Magnificent (1449–1492) exercised leadership from 1469 to 1492, it was very nearly a monarchy. Yet the republican forms remained, and when, only two years after Lorenzo's death, his son Piero II (1472–1503) fled Florence in disgrace, the republic was "restored."

Administering Justice

City governments also administered justice through their republican organs, as opposed to elsewhere in Europe where criminal justice was often the responsibility of local feudal lords. Since the eleventh century, Italy had been the principal site of the study and interpretation of Roman law, the principles of which governed the administration of justice. The system was inquisitorial. Once the appropriate body was informed that a crime had been committed (or if it chose to investigate that possibility on its own), the state would seize and prosecute the accused. Conviction depended upon the confession of the alleged wrongdoer, and torture was used to elicit confession when it was not forthcoming voluntarily. Penalties were generally fines, though corporal punishment, including physical mutilation and execution, was also used.

While all of these procedures are foreign to those readers accustomed to an Anglo-Saxon system of law, they were not particularly abusive or cruel in most cases. But they were by no means fair. The definition of crime and the assignment of punishment varied enormously according to social rank, gender, and even profession (the clergy were exempt from secular judicial processes). A woman was more likely to be convicted of adultery than a man; a worker was more likely to be convicted of rape, and punished more harshly, than a member of the elite.

Raising Revenues

To run their government machinery, and even more, to prosecute the wars that were nearly constant in the fourteenth and fifteenth centuries, cities needed to devise ways to extract wealth from their citizens. The most obvious source of revenue for the cities as for the feudal lords of the European countryside was to tax commodities and services. Such indirect taxes could be levied on certain goods; salt was a nearly universal choice, since it needed to be purchased and almost everyone purchased some. Authorities levied tariffs on goods brought into the cities and charged tolls at gates for the use of roads. Special groups and projects were subject to targeted taxes, such as the Jewish community, the alum mines of Tolfa, and the migrations of sheep from hillside to lowland pasture.

These methods of indirect taxation were time-honored, but they were insufficient for the increasingly complex cities of the Italian Renaissance. By the fourteenth century, some cities had developed the "forced loan." This was an unusual mechanism because it targeted, but eventually profited, the wealthy. It required those with assets greater than a stated level to lend money to the government. In exchange, the government promised to pay regular interest on the loan. The forced loan became, in effect, a kind of government bond providing steady and dependable interest income in the range of three to eight per cent. Elite families counted loan paper as an asset that could be distributed to heirs.

The forced loan was, in sum, an imaginative innovation of the Renaissance city, providing a revenue stream while it solidified the support of the wealthiest citizens.

THE MEDICI: BANKING, POLITICS, AND PATRONAGE

No family is more closely associated with the Italian Renaissance than the Medici of Florence. Of modest origin, they became wealthy bankers and powerful politicians. In time, they came to dominate the political as well as the cultural life of their city. Evicted in 1494, they returned as masters in 1512 and again in 1530. Under their rule as grand dukes of Tuscany, Florence would enter the modern era—a city very different from the Florence that had welcomed the unruly freedom of the republican age.

The Medici loomed large in the fourteenth century because of the expanding fortunes of the family bank, an international operation with offices in Lyon, Bruges, and London, as well as several Italian cities. By the end of the century, the Medici had emerged as the leaders of one of two rival factions. The elections of 1433 brought victory to the Albizzi opponents of the Medici, spurring Cosimo

(1389–1464), then head of the family, to seek voluntary exile. He returned to Florence the following year when new elections favored the Medicean party.

After 1434 Cosimo was unofficial master of Florence. The machinery of government was left in place; he exercised power covertly. Medici loyalists scrutinized the lists of names of eligible voters and removed those of opponents. The men who ran Florence were linked to the Medici by innumerable ties of friendship, kinship, and patronage. Even mercenary generals and foreign diplomats received personal favors from the Medici rulers behind the scenes.

Upon Cosimo's death in 1464, his son Piero, called "the Gouty," took over briefly until his own death in 1469, when his son Lorenzo inherited the Medici mantle of leadership. Unlike his self-effacing grandfather, Lorenzo looked and acted like a prince, winning the sobriquet *il Magnifico* (the

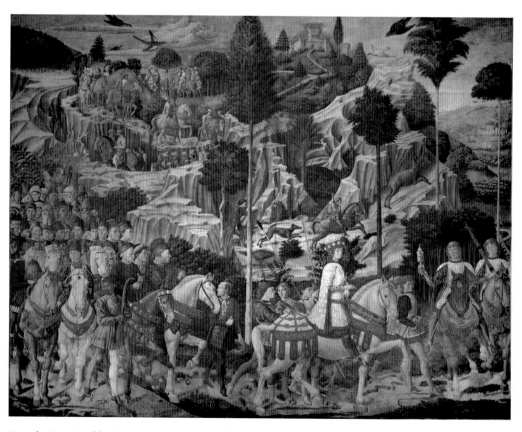

Gozzoli, *Procession of the Magi*, 1459–1462, fresco. Medici Chapel, Palazzo Medici, Florence.

Magnificent). Unofficially or not, he was indisputably ruler of Florence, showing considerable deftness and foresight at least in the area of foreign affairs and introducing some political reforms. Within Florence, there were those who bemoaned the loss of republican "liberty," but most accepted what was in fact dictatorial rule.

Lorenzo was still young when the one major revolt against Medicean domination took place. This was the Pazzi conspiracy of 1478, engineered by the related Pazzi and Salviati families and perhaps known in advance to Pope Sixtus IV, a Medici opponent. The bloody episode began with the murder, during mass in the Cathedral of Florence, of Giuliano (1453–1478), Lorenzo's younger brother, and the attempted murder of Lorenzo himself. It continued with rioting by the Pazzi supporters and ended with the ruthless suppression of the rebels.

The years of Medici rule from Cosimo's rise to Lorenzo's death (1433–1492) corresponded to the most dynamic phase of the Renaissance in Florence. The Medici themselves were key contributors to its vitality. They were the patrons of many artists—Fra Filippo Lippi, Benozzo Gozzoli, Sandro Botticelli, and Michelangelo Buonarroti, among others. They commissioned the architect Michelozzo Michelozzi to build a palace that was then the most splendid in the city. It housed many works of art and was the setting for political intrigue and philosophical conversation. Medici patronage of art was so substantial that when, in 1968, the historian Peter Burke created a taxonomy of the Renaissance "creative elite" (see p. 142), he attributed patronage in all of Italy to only one of two sources: Medicean and non-Medicean. Lorenzo the Magnificent understood the value of patronage on such a scale and considered it well worth the high cost.

Medicean patronage was not confined to the arts. Cosimo purchased and circulated books and created the state library from the legacy of books the humanist bibliophile Niccolò Niccoli had bequeathed to Florence. He supported the intelligent son of his physician, Marsilio Ficino, in the project of translating the complete works of Plato (see Chapter 3). Lorenzo followed Cosimo's lead. Although no profound thinker, he was a poet of some distinction in the vernacular tradition modeled for him by his poet-mother, Lucrezia Tornabuoni.

On Lorenzo's death, his son Piero (1471–1503) succeeded. But Piero fled Florence in 1494 when, having made the wrong political gamble, French forces were poised to invade the city. Inspired by Savonarola (see Chapter 6), Florence exiled the Medici and restored the republic, which preserved its independence during the tumultuous first phase of foreign invasions. Supported by Spanish armies, the Medici returned to Florence in 1512, led by a son and a nephew of Lorenzo

the Magnificent, both cardinal princes of the church. In 1513 the former, Cardinal Giovanni (1475–1521), became Pope Leo X; in 1523, the latter, Cardinal Giulio (1478–1534) became Pope Clement VII.

In 1527, when the tide of battle permitted, the Florentines restored their republic. In 1530, supported by the emperor, the Medici reentered Florence and did not leave again until the dynasty failed in 1737. In the coming years, Medici offspring would marry into the Valois, Bourbon, and Habsburg dynasties, the leading families of Europe. As grand dukes of Tuscany, the Medici would continue to support the cultural ventures of an astonishing city whose creative energies did not lag even after its loss of political autonomy.

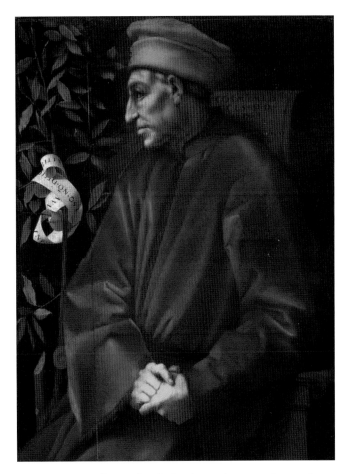

Pontormo, *Portrait of Cosimo il Vecchio* (posthumous), c. 1519, oil on panel, 34 × 25 in (86 × 65 cm). Galleria degli Uffizi, Florence.

Another form of borrowing from the citizens to support the state, while benefiting the contributors, was the dowry fund, such as the Monte delle Doti (dowry mountain) instituted in Florence in 1425. Upon the birth of a daughter, householders paid a sum into the fund, in the expectation that, with interest added to principal, it would fund a dowry at her marriage. In the meantime, the state had use of the funds.

More imaginative was the creation of a comprehensive system of direct taxation, devised first by Venice, then imitated on a grander scale by Florence. The Florentine tax, based on assets, required a complete accounting of the current holdings of every single Florentine household in the city and the *contado*. A special commission scrupulously collected data from 1427 to 1430. Based on this data, the state extracted its levy of 0.5 per cent of assets, less deductions for home and dependents, from each household. This *catasto* (tax survey) was repeated once and then suspended. Nevertheless, these tax efforts represented a milestone in European fiscal history and pointed the way to modern systems of taxation. In addition, the data collected by fifteenth-century bureaucrats—which has wondrously survived and been meticulously analyzed by historians—is a windfall for contemporary scholars.

Diplomacy

The Italian states were also innovative in another area, that of diplomacy. Once again, it was their particular circumstances which spurred imaginative solutions. European monarchs and great lords had long sent their messengers, or heralds, to foreign counterparts or to enemy commanders in the field with the expectation that such agents would be allowed to pass without injury. The Byzantine Empire had maintained the system of sending envoys to foreign courts and of receiving such representatives ceremonially at their own. Following this model, popes from the Middle Ages sent their representatives— legates and *nuncii* (messengers)—to Byzantium and eventually other European courts.

By the fourteenth century, the great Italian cities, led by Venice, sent out professional ambassadors, the first to do so of secular states in Europe. Ambassadors served for brief terms of one or two months or for several years. They were generally drawn from the most elevated social strata of the city and were expected to entertain lavishly (generally at their own expense) and possess high cultural and social skills. They were often granted enormous authority, including the capacity to negotiate treaties. By the fifteenth century, ambassadors from the major Italian cities were resident in other cities—in Rome, at the court of the Holy Roman Empire, as well as in Paris, London, and other capitals. Venetian ambassadors were provided with a full written statement of objectives for each mission and were required to file a full report on their return (originally oral, later written) on events at the courts where they were resident. These *relazioni* (reports) are among the most informative documents that survive about political and social behavior in many European centers.

Diplomacy protected the interests of many states and may in many cases have averted war. The nearly constant wars of the first half of the fifteenth century did lead, in 1454 and 1455, to crucial settlements, negotiated by the ambassadors of the participating states, which bought a few years of peace before the tragedy of Italy began in earnest in 1494.

Venice and Florence Expand

The struggles between the popes and upstart signori in the Papal States, and those between the Angevin and Aragonese contenders for the Kingdom of Naples, had roots in earlier times. But the expansionist wars waged by Florence and Venice in the last years of the trecento and first years of the quattrocento had been triggered by the aggression of Milan. It was the Visconti thrust eastward into the Veneto and southward into Tuscany that pushed Venice and Florence, respectively, to extend their own dominions beyond their limited urban and suburban cores.

Before Giangaleazzo's advance, Venice had controlled only a maritime empire consisting of its lagoons, depots along the eastern coast of the Adriatic, and several strategically important eastern Mediterranean islands and ports. After his death in 1402, however, Venice embarked on a mission to win sufficient *terraferma* (mainland) dominions to act as a buffer from Milanese aggression, and incidentally, to open up new opportunities for trade and agricultural production. Having absorbed nearby Treviso in 1389, Venice conquered Padua and Verona in 1405 from their Carraresi and Scaligeri rulers (see p. 226). By 1420 it had conquered the large territories controlled by the patriarch of Aquileia and, by 1428, the two outpost cities of Brescia and Bergamo, sited not too far from the powerhouse of Milan. The Venetian *stato di terra* (empire on land) was now as great a factor in the city's success as its *stato di mar* (empire at sea). By this date, the Visconti had recovered from the territorial losses resulting from Giangaleazzo's death and defeat. They countered Venetian advances, and the Po valley, stretching from west to east across Lombardy and the Veneto, became a battleground. Florence, too, joined in the fray.

Barely pausing after its miraculous delivery from Giangaleazzo's onslaught, Florence resumed the mission of territorial expansion it had begun some years before. Florence had already absorbed the smaller towns in its orbit before it reached out to seize nearby Volterra in 1361 and Arezzo in 1384. In his advance, Giangaleazzo Visconti had taken Siena and Pisa. After the Visconti menace subsided, Florence seized the port city of Pisa in 1406 and in 1421, purchased the port of Livorno, just to the north, from Genoa. (Florence was centrally located in Italy, with river access to the west shore of Italy, but no seaport of its own.) Florence then joined Venice in its struggle to contain Visconti within his older Lombard domains. Both cities sent their condottieri into this melee. The foremost of these was Francesco Sforza, who had fought at times for all three combatants, but became a loyal servant of the Venetians in the last years of the war.

Military Organization

During the third and fourth decades of the fifteenth century, the greater ambitions of expanding states promoted developments in military organization beyond the fourteenth-century system where a threatened city hired a company or companies of soldiers. The cost of war became the city-state's major expense, and tax systems were adapted to fund combat. In addition, cities devised ways to supervise the performance of condottieri, sending knowledgeable overseers into the field. These changes were accompanied by changes in military hardware and deployment.

The key fighting unit was still the lance, a heavily armed horseman with spare horses and perhaps 12 or 16 servants to tend the weapons and the animals and to carry light arms as needed. The lance was a descendant of the armed knights of the medieval cavalry. In addition, Italian armies of the quattrocento employed sizable infantry components and mounted skirmishers armed with crossbows. From the Swiss, the Italians, as well as imperial and French armies, learned to mobilize pikemen in square formations that served both for offense and defense. The age of gunpowder had arrived, and armies now featured heavy cannon (used primarily to batter down the gates of enemy cities and fortresses) and some hand firearms (arquebuses and muskets by the last years of the century). The existence of cannon inspired the creation of a new type of fortification: one polygonal or pentagonal in shape with low sloping walls, rather than the vertical curtain walls of medieval castles, easily pierced by cannonballs. Each angle extended into spiny bastions from whose outcropping a few men could defend a length of wall. Other features of modern warfare, including espionage and the use of cypher, played an important role in the mercenary armies of northern Italy in the heart of the Renaissance.

War and Peace

It was in this context that the Italian wars of the 1420s to 1450s were waged by a shifting alliance of Venice and Florence against Milan, with Sforza switching allegiance among all three. Once Sforza had defeated the Milanese citizens of the Ambrosian Republic and made himself Duke of Milan, he and Cosimo de' Medici began negotiating a general truce. Those negotiations yielded an important settlement, which signaled not only the end of the northern wars, but a general Italian peace in an agreement that prefigured significant later settlements in European political history. In 1454 the Peace of Lodi was signed by the five principal states that had emerged from the northern wars of the 1420s to 1450s and the struggle for Naples in the 1430s and 1440s. In 1455 all five further joined together in the Italian League, binding each other not to initiate war for a renewable term of 25 years (renewed in 1484) nor to summon foreign assistance in conflicts with the other powers.

A momentous event in the development of modern international relations, the 1455 agreement was observed for not quite 30 years. From 1455 to 1459, Naples attacked Genoa, which sought the aid of the French and in the end regained its fragile independence. From 1482 to 1484, Venice went to war to acquire Ferrara, technically a papal fief which had the support of Pope Sixtus IV. In a dangerous moment, Venice approached the French to exercise their claims to Milan and Naples, establishing the precedent for an Italian state's summoning the army of a foreign power in an internal matter. That precedent would be followed in the period 1494 to 1530 and beyond, when foreign armies entered Italy, destroyed its state system, and stayed to dominate the region that had in the previous four centuries produced more political innovations than any other in Europe.

INVASION AND CONQUEST

A tidal wave of invasion and conquest overcame the Italian peninsula and shattered its hard-won balance of power during the 64 years from 1494 to 1558. Among its multiple causes were the very old pattern of relying on powers outside Italy for political and military support and the very new phenomenon of modernizing, centralizing national states in northern and southwestern Europe.

For centuries, the popes at Rome, without an army of their own, had looked to the north for assistance against their enemies. Eighth-century popes summoned the Carolingian Frankish kings to their aid against the Lombards; eleventh-century popes summoned Norman armies to save southern Italy and Sicily from Byzantine and Arab rule; and thirteenth-century popes invited the Angevins to assist in their struggle against the Hohenstaufen. In the 1430s and 1440s, some cities, along with the papacy, supported Angevin claims to southern Italy, while others welcomed the Aragonese. During the War of Ferrara, Venice explored an alliance with the French to pressure their Italian neighbor. As signorial regimes developed, marriage alliances between Italian and foreign royal families made the intervention of foreign powers in Italian politics more likely. The most fateful of these was the 1387 marriage of Valentina Visconti, daughter of Giangaleazzo and his French royal bride Isabelle, to Louis de Valois, the Duke of Orleans and brother of King Charles VI of France (r. 1380–1422). Through Valentina, the later French kings Louis XII (r. 1498–1515) and Francis I (r. 1515–1547) would claim the Duchy of Milan; through their Angevin ancestors, they would also claim the Kingdom of Naples. All of these precedents and connections had consequences beginning in 1494.

At this juncture, foreign powers had developed to the point where they were ready to expand. Expansion into Italy, a region of huge wealth and high cultural assets, had powerful appeal. France had emerged from the Hundred Years' War satisfactorily, rebuilding its economy, centralizing its bureaucracy, and enhancing the authority of kingship especially during the reign of Louis XI (r. 1461–1483). The Spanish, under the joint monarchy of Ferdinand II of Aragón (r. 1479–1516) and Isabella of Castile (r. 1474–1504), had, in 1492, completed the centuries-long struggle of the *reconquista* (reconquest), with the capture of the last Moorish outpost of Granada. (North African Muslims, called Moors, had invaded

1350–1399

1377 Sir John Hawkwood, English mercenary, is made captain-general of Florence.

1380 Victory over Genoa at the sea battle of Chioggia gives Venice Mediterranean naval supremacy.

1384 Florence takes over the city of Arezzo.

1385 Giangaleazzo Visconti succeeds his father, Galeazzo II, as ruler of Milan.

1387 Verona is conquered by Milan, ending Scaligeri rule.

1395 The pope grants Giangaleazzo Visconti the title of Duke of Milan.

1400–1449

1402 Milanese forces besiege Florence, but the siege ends when Duke Giangaleazzo dies of plague.

1405 Venice seizes control of Padua and Verona, gaining power on the Italian mainland.

1406 Florence takes control of the port city of Pisa.

1421 Florence acquires the port of Livorno by purchase from Genoa.

1428 Venice extends its rule over Brescia and Bergamo.

1434 Cosimo de' Medici returns from exile to rule Florence.

1442 Alfonso, King of Aragón, seizes Naples, rules Naples and Sicily.

1450–1499

1454 The Peace of Lodi largely avoids war in Italy for the next 30 years.

1455 Venice, Florence, Milan, Naples, and the papacy form the Italian League.

1464 Piero de' Medici takes over the rule of Florence from his father Cosimo.

1469 Lorenzo de' Medici (the Magnificent) succeeds as ruler of Florence.

1481 Ludovico Sforza (*il Moro*) usurps the dukedom of Milan from his nephew.

1492 Lorenzo the Magnificent dies; his son Piero II becomes ruler of Florence.

1494 French King Charles VIII invades Italy, occupies Florence; Piero de' Medici flees the city.

1495 Charles VIII occupies Naples but then returns to France, defeated by Italian forces at Fornovo.

1499 French King Louis XII seizes Milan; Ludovico il Moro is imprisoned in France.

1500–1530

1501 The Kingdom of Naples is partitioned between France and Aragón.

1503 Aragonese commander Fernández de Córdoba defeats the French at Garigliano.

1504 By the Treaty of Lyons, France recognizes Aragonese rule over Naples.

1508 Pope Julius II organizes the League of Cambrai to attack Venice.

1509 The Venetian army is destroyed at the Battle of Agnadello.

1511 Pope Julius II forms a Holy League with Venice and Aragón to drive the French from Italy.

1512 The French defeat the Holy League at Ravenna but withdraw from Italy.

1512 The Congress of Mantua restores the rule of the Medici in Florence and Sforza in Milan.

1515 French King Francis I defeats Swiss and Venetian armies at Marignano, reoccupies Milan.

1522 The French are again driven out of Milan.

1525 Francis I is defeated, taken prisoner by Emperor Charles V at the Battle of Pavia.

1526 Pope Clement VII forms the League of Cognac (Venice, Florence, Milan, and France) to oppose the emperor.

1527 The Medici are again expelled from Florence, and a republic is formed.

1527 Rome is occupied and sacked by Charles V's army.

1529 The Treaty of Cambrai makes peace between Francis I and Charles V.

1530 The Gonzaga rulers of Mantua are granted the ducal title.

1530 Florence is restored to the Medici after a siege by imperial forces.

1530 Pope Clement VII crowns Charles V as Holy Roman Emperor.

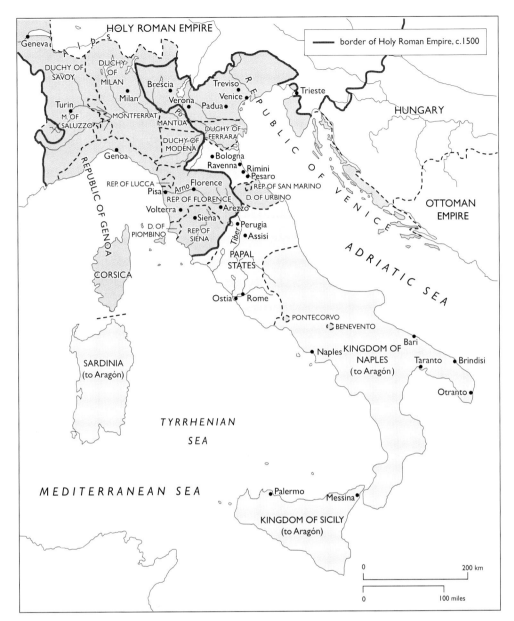

Italy, c. 1500

This map shows the state system of Renaissance Italy on the eve of its disruption by French, Spanish, and imperial armies. The whole of southern Italy, including Sicily and Sardinia, was in Aragonese (Spanish) hands. The papal states had been extended and secured, and to the north, the independent cities of the communal and popular eras had largely been consolidated within a handful of larger states (Milan, Florence, Venice) and smaller ones (Ferrara, Mantua, Modena, Urbino, Genoa).

the Iberian Peninsula in the eighth century and, by 711, reduced the Christian kingdoms of Spain to a tiny sliver of territory south of the Pyrenees.) In 1492, as well, the Genoese admiral in their employ, Christopher Columbus (1451–1506), had opened up a new imperial venture on the far side of the Atlantic Ocean that would, in the short term, greatly enrich and strengthen the Spanish state. Both nations were bulging with energy in September 1494 when the French King Charles VIII set off for Italy. He had been urged by Ludovico il Moro (1452–1508), de facto ruler of Milan, to reclaim the Neapolitan inheritance (which had fallen to Aragón in 1442) for the throne of France.

The French Invasion to the Battle of Fornovo

Il Moro had summoned the French army to punish his enemy, Ferrante II (1495–1496), the Aragonese King of Naples. He had not anticipated that Charles would in a few brief months conquer the whole of Italy nor that the aftermath of his short-lived invasion would be more than 60 years of war. Charles cut through Italy like a knife through butter. Cities threw open their gates to him and offered obedience. Even Florence capitulated peacefully to the French king, guided by the pro-French vision of the theocrat Savonarola (see Chapter 6). The pro-Aragonese Piero de' Medici, the last of the line of Cosimo il Vecchio, fled in disgrace. In February 1495, Charles reached Naples, and Naples, too, capitulated.

The next month, Charles wheeled around, leaving some troops in garrison behind him. Il Moro had thought better of his summons to the French and in the Treaty of Venice allied with other parties alarmed by Charles's advance: Venice, the pope, and the foreign monarchs Emperor Maximilian I (r. 1493–1519) and Ferdinand II of Aragón. Their combined forces met Charles's retreating army at Fornovo (modern province of Parma) in July 1495. The French broke through boldly and returned home, having accomplished nothing, or so it seemed. In fact, Charles VIII's invasion set off a spiraling sequence of events, two features of which were already apparent: the rapidly shifting patterns of alliance and enmity and the increasingly prominent role of foreign rulers and armies.

The Great Captain and the Conquest of Naples

King Ferdinand II of Aragón could not tolerate the continued French presence in Naples, the kingdom now restored to Ferrante II, descendant of Naples' first Aragonese ruler. He sent the brilliant military commander Gonzalo Fernández de Córdoba (1453–1515), known as the "Great Captain," who had recently achieved the 1492 victory at Granada. In league with the Venetians, Fernández scattered the remaining French garrisons and returned to Spain. He was sent to Naples again in 1500, this time to defend the region against a threat from the Ottoman Turks. In league now with French forces under King Louis XII as well as with Venice, Fernández beat back the Ottoman threat. In 1501 he arranged with the French to partition the Kingdom of Naples. The French would hold the northern areas of Campania and Abruzzi (including the city of Naples); the Aragonese the southern areas of Puglia and Calabria. When the French broke the treaty, Fernández expelled them altogether. Thus southern Italy, along with Sicily, came under direct Aragonese (and henceforth Spanish) rule in 1503. It would remain under Spanish rule, with some interruptions, until 1860.

Julius II and the Battle of Agnadello

By 1503, when Julius II (r. 1503–1513) became pope (see Chapter 6), the Aragonese ruled in southern Italy and the French ruled Milan—for, with Venetian support (in exchange for some Lombard properties), Louis XII had crossed the Alps in 1499 and taken Milan from Ludovico il Moro. The papacy had, moreover, largely lost control of the Papal States, thanks to the activities of Cesare Borgia (1475/1476–1507), son and agent of Julius's predecessor Alexander VI. Warrior Pope Julius swept through Romagna and le Marche reasserting papal control. Then, in 1508, he cemented the League of Cambrai (in France) with Florence, the emperor, France, and Spain against the city of Venice, which he identified as the cause of Italian turmoil and foreign dominion on the peninsula. Venetian forces were overwhelmingly defeated at Agnadello in 1509. The land and cities that Venice had incorporated into its *terraferma* dominion in the 1400s surrendered to the allies. Venice faced catastrophe.

The Holy League and the Battle of Marignano

Alliances shifted once again, however, due, in part, to the inspired diplomacy of the desperate Venetians. Now the combined powers of Italy, with Spain and the empire, would turn on France. This new alliance, which called itself the Holy League, restored its mainland possessions to Venice. It also restored the Sforza to power in Milan and the Medici in Florence in 1512. (The Medici had been expelled in 1492, and the city was a republic in the interim; see Chapter 8.) It failed, however, to defeat the French. In 1512 Louis XII's brilliant general Gaston de Foix (1489–1512), who died in the battle, smashed the League forces at Ravenna. The French temporarily withdrew from Italy to deal with dangers at home. They returned under Louis's successor Francis I, who swept south in the year of his accession with a mammoth force of 40,000 men, took Milan once again, and defeated a papal army of Swiss mercenaries at the Battle of Marignano.

Habsburg versus Valois to the Battle of Pavia

Victorious at Marignano, the young Valois King Francis I would need to confront a new pope, Leo X of the Medici family, and a new Spanish Habsburg king, Charles I (r. 1515–1558), who would also acquire the title of Holy Roman Emperor (as Charles V, r. 1519–1558). In 1521 pope and emperor allied with the exiled Sforza Duke of Milan to oust the French from Milan. They did so in 1522, but the French returned in 1524. Then Charles defeated Francis I decisively in 1525 at the Battle of Pavia, which left the king a prisoner on the battlefield at his enemy's mercy. Imprisoned in Madrid, Francis renounced all his Italian claims and ambitions, among other significant concessions, all of which he repudiated when he was released the following year. In 1526 he formed the League of Cognac, in which the French were joined by Florence, Venice, Milan, and the papacy, the latter abandoning the Spanish alliance, for which treachery it would suffer retaliation.

Despite Cognac, the Spanish dominance of Italy was already assured. Spain would remain dominant, despite some free or semi-autonomous pockets of territory, into the eighteenth century. A peace treaty signed at Cambrai in 1529 reaffirmed the status quo. The following year, another Medici pope, Clement VII (r. 1523–1534), crowned Charles Holy Roman Emperor. The French and Spanish would continue to struggle for nearly 30 years, with the French attempting three more invasions to parry the Spanish advance in Italy. With Charles and Francis both dead, a final peace was signed in 1559 at Cateau-Cambrésis (France). It did not alter the reality of Spanish dominance that had been established in 1525.

The Sack of Rome

The turning point of Italy's fortunes, however, was not 1559 but 1527. In joining the League of Cognac in 1526, the pope had turned on Charles V, at a time when the French armies were nowhere in the field. Charles redirected his Spanish and imperial forces toward Rome. It was a body of 12,000, and they were restive and dangerous because they had not been paid. The imperial forces, moreover, consisted mainly of German followers of Martin Luther who had launched a revolution against the Catholic Church in 1520 (see Chapter 9). For Lutherans, Rome was "Babylon"—the city symbolizing all earthly sins, an enemy of the Germans to boot and worthy of annihilation. They gave expression at once to their religious preferences and their desire to be paid when they sacked the city of Rome in May 1527. The pope took refuge in his fortified Castel Sant'Angelo, dignitaries fled, palaces and homes were looted, and the streets were scenes of torture, slaughter, and rape. It was a humbled Pope Clement who, in 1530 in Bologna, crowned Charles V as Holy Roman Emperor, the last emperor to receive his crown from a pope.

The Return of the Medici

Clement was well advised to return to the Spanish allegiance. His Medici kin who had been restored to rule in Florence in 1512 were expelled in 1527 when the humiliation of a Medici pope looked to militants in Florence like an opportunity for the recovery of republican liberty. That renewed Florentine republic survived from 1527 to 1530 when, once again, Spanish power and the backing of the pope enabled the Medici to reclaim sovereignty in Florence. Florence remained under Medici rule for two centuries more, until, in 1737, the dynasty died out, and the city reverted to Habsburg rule.

THE REPUBLICAN SPIRIT IN FLORENCE: SAVONAROLA AND GUICCIARDINI

In 1494, prodded by the inspired preaching of Girolamo Savonarola (1452–1498; see Chapter 6), the Florentines expelled the Medici and reestablished a republic. It endured until the Medici returned, with the backing of Spanish arms, in 1512. In 1527, with Medici fortunes again in reverse following the catastrophic sack of Rome, the Florentines restored their republic. It was to last only three years before being finally extinguished. An imperial army brought the Medici back to power, breaking the determined resistance of the republicans. The two passages here comment upon this series of events.

In the first passage, Savonarola argues that the Florentines were not by nature inclined to be ruled by either prince or tyrant (although Savonarola himself favored a divinely ordained monarchy) but rather to be free.

The Florentine people ... is the most intelligent of all the people of Italy and the most farsighted in its undertakings. It has, as its history has shown again and again, a vigorous and audacious spirit.... This the chronicles show when they relate its wars against various great princes and tyrants, where Florence has absolutely refused to yield and finally, in self-defense, has carried away the victory. This people's character, then, will never tolerate the rule of a prince ... and ... they would either overthrow or kill him.... Alternatively, the prince would have to become a tyrant....

Now the Florentine people, having established a civil form of government long ago, has made such a habit of this form that, besides suiting the nature and requirement of the people better than any other, it has become habitual and fixed in their minds. It would be difficult, if not impossible to separate them from this form of government.... We conclude, therefore, that in the city of Florence the civil form of government is best, although in itself this is not the best form, and we assert this both because divine authority created its present civil

government, and because of the reasons given above. The rule of one, though in itself best, is not good, let alone best, for the Florentine people.

(R.N. Watkins, trans. and ed., Humanism and Liberty: Writings on Freedom from Fifteenth-Century Florence. Columbia: University of South Carolina Press, 1978, pp. 236–238)

In this second passage, historian Francesco Guicciardini (1483–1540), with characteristic cynicism, marvels at the tenacity of the republicans' doomed resistance to the Medici takeover of 1530.

The pious say that faith can do great things, and ... even move mountains. The reason is that faith breeds obstinacy.... A man of faith is stubborn in his beliefs; he goes his way, undaunted and resolute, disdaining hardship and danger, ready to suffer any extremity.... Now, since the affairs of this world are subject to chance ... there are many ways in which the passage of time may bring unexpected help to those who persevere in their obstinacy.

In our own day, the Florentines offer an excellent example of such obstinacy. Contrary to all human reason, they prepared for an attack by the pope and the emperor, even though they had no hope of help from any quarter, were disunited, and burdened with thousands of other difficulties. And they have fought off these armies from their walls for seven months, though no one would have believed they could do it for seven days. Indeed, the Florentines have managed things in such a manner that, were they to win, no one would be surprised; whereas earlier, everyone had considered them lost. And this obstinacy is largely due to the faith that they cannot perish. [The Florentines succumbed at last in the eighth month of the siege.]

(F. Guicciardini, Maxims and Reflections of a Renaissance Statesman (Ricordi). New York: Harper and Row, 1965, pp. 39–40)

CONCLUSION

From the eleventh through the fifteenth centuries, Italy was a zone of important political and military innovation, whose achievements would become part of the common European legacy in the following centuries. To the West, Italy passed along the legacies of the communal revolution, the popular republic, the heroic careers of condottieri and signori, the higher organization of the bureaucracy and the military, and the principle of the balance of power. But the Italian political venture could not remain in the ascendant. After 1494 a more powerful northern nation invaded and illuminated a hard truth that a city-state, or a consortium of city-states, with their armies of a few thousand men, could not withstand the force of a nation-state with an army of tens of thousands.

The problem of insufficient numbers is only one dimension of a more profound problem. Italy would lose its primacy in the sixteenth and seventeenth centuries, as first Spain and Portugal, then France, the Netherlands, and England expanded economically and matured politically. As they did so, they would learn from Italy: from its art, its music, its literature, its philosophy, its humanist model. For the Renaissance did not end in Italy when its political independence ended. It continued, in a later phase, long enough to perform the role of tutor to all of Europe (see Chapter 8). Even the example of Castruccio Castracane would be influential, through the intermediary of Niccolò Machiavelli, upon ultramontane students of the political art.

SUGGESTED READINGS

Primary Sources

D'Este, Isabella. *Selected Letters*. Translated and edited by Deanna Shemek. Toronto: Iter Press., 2016. A selection of 830 of the thousands of letters written to rulers, agents, artists, petitioners, and friends, composed by Isabella d'Este, consort of the ruler of Mantua, daughter of the Duke of Ferrara, and one of the leading patrons of the arts in Italy.

Gouwens, Kenneth, ed. *Remembering the Renaissance: Humanist Narratives of the Sack of Rome*. Leiden: E.J. Brill, 1998. Examines the impact of the 1527 catastrophe on the humanist circle of papal Rome.

Guicciardini, Francesco. *History of Italy*. Translated by Sidney Alexander. Princeton, NJ: Princeton University Press, 1984. A hard-headed, state-centered history that details the Italian crisis from 1492 to 1534.

Sanudo, Marino. *Venice, Città Excelentissima: Selections from the Renaissance Diaries of Marin Sanudo*. Translated and edited by Patricia H. Labalme and Laura Sanguineti White. Baltimore, MD: Johns Hopkins University Press, 2008. Extracts on a range of topics from the matchless diary that fills 58 volumes in its modern edition (1879–1903) and in lively prose, depicts public life in Venice in the early 1500s.

Secondary Sources

Black, Jane. *Absolutism in Renaissance Milan: Plenitude of Power under the Visconti and the Sforza, 1329–1535*. Oxford: Oxford University Press, 2009. Shows how first the Visconti and then their Sforza successors claimed supreme power previously wielded with legitimacy only by popes and emperors.

Bourne, Molly. *Francesco II Gonzaga: The Soldier-Prince as Patron*. Rome: Bulzoni, 2008. An exemplary Renaissance ruler, this Marquis of Mantua (whose consort was Isabella d'Este; see her letters, above) moved easily from the battlefield and halls of power to the commissioning and adornment of residential building projects.

Brachtel, M.E. *Lucca 1430–1494: The Reconstruction of an Italian City-Republic*. Oxford: Oxford University Press, 1995. A portrait of a republic in the High Renaissance.

Chastel, André. *The Sack of Rome, 1527*. Translated by Beth Archer. Princeton, NJ: Princeton University Press, 1983. The events and significance of the 1527 catastrophe expressed in art.

Dean, Trevor. *Land and Power in Late Medieval Ferrara: The Rule of the Este, 1350–1450*. Cambridge: Cambridge University Press, 1988. Demonstrates how the Renaissance rulers of a miniature state gained and held power.

Epstein, Steven A. *Genoa and the Genoese, 958–1528*. Chapel Hill: University of North Carolina Press, 1996. Discusses the evolution of a Renaissance state from its early medieval beginnings.

Finlay, Robert. *Politics in Renaissance Venice*. New Brunswick, NJ: Rutgers University Press, 1980. Competition between families and factions enabled Venice to achieve stable governance.

Fletcher, Catherine. *Diplomacy in Renaissance Rome: The Rise of the Resident Ambassador*. Cambridge: Cambridge University Press, 2015. Situates, in Rome, the development of a permanent, professional diplomatic system, from the time of the return of the papacy from the Captivity and the Schism into the period of sixteenth-century crisis.

Ianziti, Gary. *Humanistic Historiography under the Sforzas: Politics and Propaganda in Fifteenth-Century Milan*. Oxford: Clarendon Press, 1988. Shows how the conqueror of Milan, Francesco Sforza, and his successors employed humanist pens to legitimize their rule.

Kent, Dale. *Cosimo de' Medici and the Florentine Renaissance*. New Haven, CT: Yale University Press, 2000. Explores Cosimo's patronage of art and architecture as an expression of civic commitment.

Lubkin, Gregory. *A Renaissance Court: Milan under Galeazzo Maria Sforza*. Berkeley: University of California Press, 1994. A portrait of Renaissance court society, a model later imitated by the royal courts of the north.

Martines, Lauro. *April Blood: Florence and the Plot against the Medici*. Oxford, New York: Oxford University Press, 2003. A master historian unfolds the many dimensions of the attempted coup against Medici rule in 1468, pursuing the conspirators both domestic and foreign, and showcasing the victor, Lorenzo.

Muir, Edward. *Civic Ritual in Renaissance Venice*. Princeton, NJ: Princeton University Press, 1981. A classic study of the use of ritual by the Venetian state to consolidate civic consciousness.

Murry, Gregory. *The Medicean Succession: Monarchy and Sacral Politics in Duke Cosimo dei Medici's Florence*. Cambridge, MA: Harvard University Press, 2014. No sooner had Florence suffered the downfall of its republic (as told by J.N. Stephens [see below]), it underwent a second transition as Cosimo de' Medici acquired and consolidated monarchical power in the former republic.

Romano, Dennis. *The Likeness of Venice: A Life of Doge Francesco Foscari, 1373–1457.* New Haven, CT: Yale University Press, 2007. Although Venice tended to discount the importance of individual actors, one fifteenth-century doge does stand out as the man who executed Venice's rise as a territorial imperial power.

Rubinstein, Nicolai. *The Government of Florence under the Medici, 1434–1494,* 2nd ed. Oxford: Clarendon Press, 1997. A classic study of how the Medici manipulated the machinery of government to secure control of Florence.

Shaw, Christine, ed. *Italy and the European Powers: The Impact of War, 1500–1530.* Leiden: E.J. Brill, 2006. A collection of essays exploring multiple ways in which the Italian wars reshaped the cultural as well as the political and military fortunes of the region, including studies of effects on courtly culture, music, concepts of citizenship, sovereignty, and Italian identity.

Stephens, J.N. *The Fall of the Florentine Republic, 1512–1530.* Oxford: Oxford University Press, 1983. Discusses how the Medici manipulated crises to seize control of the Florentine state.

Tuohy, Thomas. *Herculean Ferrara: Ercole d'Este, 1471–1505, and the Invention of a Ducal Capital.* Cambridge: Cambridge University Press, 1996. Examines the creation of Ferrara as a ducal capital through Ercole's cultural patronage.

EIGHT

THE CRISIS AND BEYOND (c. 1500–c. 1650)

So, as a prince is forced to know how to act like a beast, he must learn from the fox and the lion; because the lion is defenceless against traps and a fox is defenceless against wolves. Therefore one must be a fox in order to recognize traps, and a lion to frighten off wolves. Those who simply act like lions are stupid. So it follows that a prudent ruler cannot, and must not, honor his word when it places him at a disadvantage and when the reasons for which he made his promise no longer exist.

(N. Machiavelli, *The Prince*, trans. G. Bull. Harmondsworth, UK: Penguin, 1981, pp. 99–100)

In the same year, the nobleman and diplomat Baldassare Castiglione (1478–1529) began his handbook of manners for the courtier, a gentleman residing at or visiting the court of a prince, whose goodwill he sought. Castiglione advised the courtier to cultivate, along with other polite manners and skills, a certain air of sophistication and wit:

To practice in all things a certain *sprezzatura* so as to conceal all art and make whatever is done or said appear to be without effort and almost without any thought about it…. Therefore we may call that art true art which does not seem to be art; nor must one be more careful of anything than of concealing it, because if it is discovered, this robs a man of all credit and causes him to be held in slight esteem.

(B. Castiglione, *Book of the Courtier*, ed. D. Javitch. New York: Norton, 2002, 1:26, p. 32)

Both authors recommended guile, indirection, and the appearance of probity where candor was impossible. The prince and the courtier both inhabited a world of uncertainty, danger, and shifting realities, where the individual who best employed his intellect for self-protection was most likely to succeed. Italy had long been home to political disruptions, and these had not before inspired such caution. What was new was that Italy had entered a new age. Machiavelli and Castiglione wrote during the same period of crisis, when Italy lay prey to the armies of Spain, France, and the Empire and daily suffered devastations to people, to property, and to political autonomy. Machiavelli's response was to call desperately for a native prince to save Italy from the "barbarians" who were plundering its liberty. Castiglione's was to accept the new limitations of power. Princes ruled everywhere. The prudent man learned how to please them.

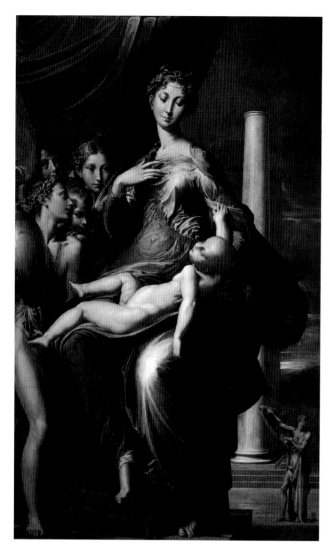

Parmigianino, *Madonna of the Long Neck* (detail), begun 1534, oil on panel, 85 × 52 in (215.9 × 132 cm). Galleria degli Uffizi, Florence.

The elongated body of the Madonna and the lassitude of the equally elongated child almost slipping off her knees, the chilling sheen of surface textures, the column that supports nothing behind the figures at right, characterize the refined but disturbing late-Renaissance style called Mannerism that succeeded the High Renaissance (see Chapter 4).

The age of the late Renaissance was an age both of crisis and anguish and of accommodation and indulgence. In the reorganized states of Italy, the arts and ideas continued to flourish and to inspire developments beyond the Alps. Italy was still a laboratory of culture for Europe, but at first political, and later ecclesiastical restrictions, as well as economic pressures, altered the message that it broadcast. This chapter is concerned with the continued cultural vigor of the late Renaissance in the context of the structural changes triggered by the crisis of invasion and conquest from 1494 to 1530. It considers, first, the contributions of Machiavelli and Castiglione, who envisioned modern politics and courtier society in the changed world of post-invasion Italy. The chapter then describes the configuration of states around 1530 and developments in the visual and performing arts, literature, and thought during the late Italian Renaissance into the first half of the seventeenth century.

THE MACHIAVELLIAN MOMENT

Machiavelli was the principal observer of the dismemberment of Italy by the armies of foreign states. They were all monarchies, whereas Machiavelli was himself a republican, first by party allegiance and then by principle. Born in Florence to a patrician family, the son of an unsuccessful lawyer, Machiavelli was too poor to join the flock of bright young men who studied Greek and Latin with the greatest humanists of the age. Instead, he learned Latin from ordinary masters and taught himself from the cherished collection of books available in his household. His university-trained father was an enthusiastic reader; his mother, who wrote poetry, dedicated to him a book of her works (which has not survived). Both may have contributed to his powerful and sensitive command of language.

Machiavelli's Career

Machiavelli was in his early twenties when the inspired, unofficial ruler of Florence Lorenzo de' Medici died in 1492 and when Charles VIII entered Florence in 1494 and Girolamo Savonarola took charge of a restored republic. Old enough to experience these powerfully important events, he was too young to play a public role. Four years later, when

Savonarola was executed and the republic was reorganized, Machiavelli won a key position in the new government. He served the Florentine republic in many capacities from 1498 to 1512. After 1502 he became the close associate of Piero Soderini (1452–1522), the man declared *gonfaloniere a vita* (standard bearer for life), or permanent president of the state.

He also served on many diplomatic missions. These included an extended one in 1500 to France, where he had first-hand experience of the operations of a major nation state; another to the German court of the emperor in 1508; and further journeys to France in 1510 and 1511 on missions of great importance. His missions to Romagna in the early 1500s exposed him to the character and actions of Cesare Borgia, son of Pope Alexander VI, whose vigor and cruelty won him a large portion of the papal lands in that region. Machiavelli was critical of the laxity and duplicity of the mercenary armies that served the Italian states. In 1505 he was given permission to implement a pet project, to create an army of citizens drawn from the whole province of Tuscany. He saw action in 1509 when his militia recaptured rebellious Pisa, a strategically important city.

Machiavelli's allegiance to the Florentine republic ended when that government fell in 1512 with the return of the Medici backed by the arms of Spain. His loyalty to Florence exceeded his loyalty to the republic; now he sought to serve the Medici. His plea was rejected, however, and Machiavelli was not only banned from government but arrested and tortured in 1513 on suspicion that he was involved in a conspiracy. Released, he returned to his family property outside the city. There in 1513 he wrote his two most important works of political theory and two of the most important works of political theory in the Western tradition: *The Prince* and *The Discourses on the First Ten Books of Titus Livy*. The former is a succinct manual for seizing and retaining power. The latter, referring to historical events described by the Roman historian Livy, is an extended meditation on maintaining republican rule. During this period he also wrote *Mandragola*, a comedy that evinces many of the same attitudes as his other works. In 1521, but based on his earlier experience, he wrote *The Art of War* which defended citizen militias over mercenary forces.

With the assumption of power in Florence by Cardinal Giulio de' Medici (1478–1534), Machiavelli regained notice. He was sent on some legations and from 1520 was named the official historian of Florence. The product of this assignment was his *History of Florence and of the Affairs of Italy*, left unfinished in 1525 when Machiavelli left Florence for Rome. In 1523 Cardinal Giulio was raised to the papacy as Clement VII, and in 1525, he rewarded Machiavelli for the eight books of the history he had completed.

From 1526 to 1527, Machiavelli was engaged in the field with the forces of the League of Cognac, advised by the other great historian and papal emissary, Francesco Guicciardini (1483–1540). They were preparing to counter the advance of imperial forces. Instead, a detachment of imperial troops marched south and unleashed its soldiers in the sack of Rome of 1527. In Florence, a revolution of republican loyalists put an end to Medici rule and restored the republic. The new government rebuffed Machiavelli, tainted as they saw it by his association with the Medici. This was a cruel blow to a man who had always favored republican rule but who could not be sure that in the end republics would prevail over principalities.

1500–1549

1500   Florence sends Niccolò Machiavelli on a diplomatic mission to France.

1505   Machiavelli begins the creation of a militia in Tuscany.

1512   The Medici are restored to control of Florence.

1513   Machiavelli is arrested, tortured by the Medici. He writes *The Prince*.

1516   Ludovico Ariosto produces his epic poem *Orlando furioso*.

1518   Baldassar Castiglione completes *The Courtier*, a manual of court life.

1520   Giulio de' Medici appoints Machiavelli official historian of Florence.

c. 1520   A new Mannerist style is visible in the works of artists such as Jacopo da Pontormo and Francesco Parmigianino.

1521   Machiavelli writes *The Art of War*, claiming the superiority of citizens' armies over mercenaries.

1525   Pietro Bembo writes *Prose della volgar lingua*, establishing the Tuscan dialect as the basis for the Italian vernacular.

1527   Death of Machiavelli.

1528   Genoese commander Andrea Doria enters Genoa, establishes an independent republic aligned with Spain.

1529   Death of Castiglione.

1534   Mannerist architect Baldassare Peruzzi designs the Palazzo Massimo alle Colonne, Rome.

1535   After the death of the last Sforza ruler, Milan comes under Spanish rule.

1536   Pietro Aretino writes *Ragionamenti*, fictional conversations between Roman prostitutes impugning powerful men.

1537   Cosimo I de' Medici becomes Duke of Florence.

1540   Palladio designs his first villa, the Villa Godi-Porto at Lonedo.

1545   Alessandro Farnese, Pope Paul III, creates the Duchies of Parma and Piacenza to be ruled by his own family.

1547   Death of Vittoria Colonna, celebrated Italian woman poet.

1550–1599

1550   Giorgio Vasari publishes his celebrated biographies, *Lives of the Artists*.

1551   Giovanni Palestrina is appointed master of music at St. Peter's Basilica, Rome.

1554   Female artist Sofonisba Anguissola paints a famous self-portrait.

1559   By the Treaty of Cateau-Cambrésis, France recognizes Italy as falling within Spanish/imperial influence.

1561   Castiglione's *The Courtier* is first translated into English.

1569   Cosimo de' Medici is granted the title of Grand Duke of Florence.

1576   Death of Venetian artist Titian.

1593   Sculptor Giambologna creates Mannerist masterpiece *Rape of the Sabine Women*.

1596   Jacopo Peri's *Dafne*, one of the first operas, is performed in Florence.

1597   Ferrara is absorbed into the Papal States after the death of the last Este ruler.

1600–1650

1600   The Inquisition burns Giordano Bruno at the stake for heresy, in Rome.

1600   Posthumous publication of Moderata Fonte's defense of women, *On the Worth of Women and the Defects of Men*.

c. 1602   Tomaso Campanella writes *Città del sole* ("City of the Sun") while imprisoned for heresy.

1607   Claudio Monteverdi's opera *Orfeo* is performed.

1613   Monteverdi becomes choirmaster for life at San Marco, Venice.

1626   Campanella is released after 27 years in prison.

1629   Baroque sculptor/architect Gian Lorenzo Bernini becomes principal artist at the papal court.

1633   The Inquisition forces Galileo Galilei to retract statements affirming the Copernican view of the universe.

c. 1650   Death of female artist Artemisia Gentilleschi, painter of *Judith and Holofernes*.

Machiavelli's Thought

Although the *Discourses* and the *Prince* have different objectives, they exhibit many common features. Machiavelli's capacity for generalization, his sharp contrasts and bifurcations, his estimation of human nature, his valuation of the state as an entity above others—the principle for which other principles must be sacrificed—are all manifest in both works. The following discussion of Machiavelli's views, however, rests primarily on the *Prince*. In that condensed work, the characteristics of taut logic and incisive prose are especially prominent, as is the author's desperation at the condition of Italy and its autonomous state system.

Generalization and Antithesis Chapter 1 of *The Prince*, beautifully condensed, illustrates Machiavelli's tendencies to both generalization and antithesis, or contrast:

> All the states, all the dominions under whose authority men have lived in the past and live now have been and are either republics or principalities. Principalities are hereditary, with their prince's family long established as rulers, or they are new. The new are completely new … or they are like limbs joined to the hereditary state of the prince who acquires them…. Dominions so acquired are accustomed to be under a prince, or used to freedom; a prince wins them either with the arms of others or with his own, either by fortune or by prowess [*virtù*].
>
> (Machiavelli, The Prince, p. 33)

In five statements, each building on the preceding, Machiavelli presents propositions that are breathtaking in scope. The first sentence of this excerpt is a generalization about "all states." This is bold enough, but Machiavelli pushes his theme even further, specifying all states that ever have been or now are. The second sentence theorizes about all principalities, one of the two types of states introduced. The third theorizes about all new principalities. The fourth theorizes about the historical condition of such states; and the fifth theorizes about their manner of acquisition.

Not only do these few sentences create a parade of general statements, increasingly precise and delineated, but they are also a parade of antitheses. The first statement introduces the term "states," and then its bifurcation into republics and principalities. In the Machiavellian universe, these two are equally possible, and no other possibilities are envisioned. The second statement introduces and divides the term "principalities": they are either old or new. Beyond these antinomies the mind does not dare explore. The third introduces and bifurcates the term "new principalities": they are entirely new or new but joined to old ones. The fourth introduces the more complex concept of the state's prior experience, which also is resolved to antinomies: it had previously been free or not free. The fourth introduces the issue of acquisition, which is given two alternate bifurcations: the principality is acquired by a prince acting alone or with others; alternatively, it is acquired by good luck or great ability.

Machiavelli's generalizations in this opening chapter are remarkably broad and abstract and his antitheses razor sharp in their oppositions. Although this chapter is extraordinary in the density of such features, the features themselves are not unique but commonplaces of Machiavelli's style. Throughout the *Prince*, broad claims and bristling antinomies are everywhere. They are found, too, in the *Discourses*: consider, for example, the wording of the title to Chapter 10: "Those who found a republic or a kingdom deserve as much praise as those who found a tyranny deserve blame." Here are antitheses between republic and kingdom, between free republics and kingdoms on the one hand and tyrannies on the other, and between praise and blame, all embedded in a broad generalization about the evaluation of political action.

Human Nature and History Another characteristic of Machiavellian analysis is the author's assumptions about human nature. In a famous passage in Chapter 17 of *The Prince*, Machiavelli gives one of his famous in-a-nutshell estimations of human nature:

> One can make this generalization about men: they are ungrateful, fickle, liars, and deceivers, they shun danger and are greedy for profit; while you treat them well, they are yours. They would shed their blood for you, risk their property, their lives, their children, so long … as the danger is remote; but when you are in danger they turn against you.
>
> (Machiavelli, *The Prince*, p. 96)

Striking here is the inclusiveness and the negativity of Machiavelli's observation. As a generalizer, he does not hesitate to speak about all "men" (human beings, in the context of that age). He does not care to consider that there might be exceptions. What he says of human behavior, moreover, is harsh. Human beings are not only disinclined to the practice of common virtues; they are at heart deceptive and unstable.

For Machiavelli, the essential falsity of human character suggests the need for stern rule. The permanency of human character, however, permits politics to be a science. If human beings always behave in a certain way, then when circumstances are repeated, the same outcomes will follow. Analysis becomes possible. Thus, in Chapter 9 of *The Prince*, Machiavelli argues that, based on the dynamics of human nature, the prince who comes to power with the support of the nobility will face one set of circumstances and the prince who does so with the support of the people, another:

> A man who becomes prince with the help of the nobles finds it more difficult to maintain his position than one who does so with the help of the people. As prince, he finds himself surrounded by many who believe they are his equals, and because of that he cannot command or manage them the way he wants. A man who becomes prince by favor of the people finds himself standing alone, and he has near him either no-one or very few not prepared to take orders. In addition, it is impossible to satisfy the nobles honorably, without doing violence to the interests of others; but this can be done as far as the people are concerned. The people are more honest in their intentions than the nobles are, because the latter want to oppress the people, whereas they want only not to be oppressed.
>
> (Machiavelli, *The Prince*, pp. 67–68)

Human nature causes nobles to behave one way and commoners another, but both predictably. Thus politics can be a rational pursuit and a guide to future action.

The Political Principle Politics, then, is a rational pursuit, and it has one end: the success of the state. This is an end in itself for Machiavelli. Medieval thought was saturated with the notion that kingdoms or cities were divinely protected. Not only did they enjoy the favor of God, but they generally each had a patron saint. Rulers were answerable to God. If the state failed to prosper, its neglect of religious duty might be offered as explanation. Machiavelli, however, viewed the state as a self-sufficient entity, detached from the divine realm. Even the *stato della chiesa* (the state of the church) was a political entity. Although the term *ragione di stato* (reason of state) was coined only after Machiavelli's death, it aptly describes one strand of his thinking. If the needs of the state dictated a certain action, that action should be taken.

The imperative of state-building and state-preservation is so great, in fact, that rulers must devote themselves wholly and unreservedly to these goals. This is the whole message of *The Prince*. Rulers do well only when they preserve the state and badly only when they lose it—whether they themselves have behaved well or not in so doing. Success and failure are the only boundaries of Machiavelli's political universe, which admits no other moral standard. In this sense, in the conventional phrase often used to describe Machiavellian logic, the ends justify the means.

Republics and Principalities Successful states, like unsuccessful ones, can be either republics or principalities; this is the disjunction with which Machiavelli opens *The Prince*, defining the whole universe of political possibility (see p. 262). The republic is ruled by a consortium of the citizens and the principality, necessarily, by a prince. Machiavelli does not at all in this work discuss which form of state is superior. The discussions in his *Discourses* show him to be sympathetic to republics. At the moment he wrote *The Prince*, however, Italy and his own city of Florence were in the hands of princes. Machiavelli accepted the world that was and not the world of his fantasies and focused, instead, on principalities: what kinds were there; how they could be won, preserved, and lost; what qualities a prince must have to be successful. Famously, Machiavelli did not explore the moral issues pertaining to the existence of one-man rule or the forceful acquisition of power. It is not that Machiavelli was an immoral man; the evidence we have about his life testifies that he was not. For him, rather, the political project was more important than matters of morality.

The Prince as Person While he withheld judgment about the relative merits of republics and principalities, Machiavelli did not withhold judgment on the prince himself. He must possess, above all, *virtù*. *Virtù* is an extraordinary quality, which cannot be translated by the modern term "virtue." An Italian word, it is close to the Latin *virtus*, a word related to "manliness." It means something like "great ability" or "excellence," and involves components of strength, boldness, speed, rationality, and ruthlessness. It is a potent emotional quality that is the only force with which people can oppose the "unremitting malice of fortune." These terms—*virtù* and *fortuna*—were presented in opposition in the opening of the *Prince* in the last words of Chapter 1, already examined: "Such dominions ... are acquired ... by fortune [*fortuna*] or by ability [*virtù*]."

In what consists the *virtù* of the prince? While his boldness and rationality are implied in the first 14 books of *The Prince*, which advise the new ruler on how to acquire his new principality, the next nine books further guide his behavior. The first of these, Chapter 15, defines "the things for which men, and especially princes, are praised and blamed." Here Machiavelli names a string of vices and virtues (in the conventional sense), and then comments:

> I know everyone will agree that it would be most laudable if a prince possessed all the qualities deemed to be good among those I have enumerated. But, because of conditions in the world, princes cannot have those qualities, or observe them, completely. So a prince has of necessity to be so prudent that he knows how to escape the evil reputation attached to those vices which could lose him his state, and how to avoid those vices which are not so dangerous, if he possibly can; but, if he cannot, he need not worry so much about the latter. And then, he must not flinch from being blamed for vices which are necessary for safeguarding the state ... because ... some of the things that appear to be virtues will, if he practices them, ruin him, and some of the things that appear to be vices will bring him security and prosperity.
>
> (Machiavelli, *The Prince*, pp. 91–92)

The prince should avoid those vices which, if they were known, would lose him his state, and equally, should avoid those virtues which, if pursued, would do so. He may, however, commit those vicious acts which yield "security and prosperity." In these statements, the moral structures of the Christian universe are not refuted, but simply ignored. The state itself is a greater good than moral action, and can even, for its preservation, warrant the commission of evil deeds. The ends do appear to justify the means.

This principle informs the other eight chapters which advise the prince on his behavior. Chapter 16 discusses generosity, urging the prince to engage in that good practice so long as it benefits the state but not if it leads to the state's impoverishment. Chapter 17 discusses cruelty, urging the prince to avoid that vice unless it is absolutely necessary for the good of the state. Chapter 18, on good faith, urges the prince to keep his word when it is beneficial to do so, but to break it when reasons of state so require. Chapter 19, rich in historical examples, warns the prince to avoid the hatred or contempt of his subjects, a sure pathway to the loss of power. Chapter 20 considers to what extent the prince should put his faith in fortifications, and concludes, to no great extent; far more important a good is to avoid the hatred of the people. Chapter 21 suggests various ways the prince may gain the people's esteem, while Chapters 22 and 23 warn him not to trust too much in secretaries or flatterers, the latter an inevitable, but dangerous, consequence of power. With regard to secretaries, there is a certain rule of thumb: "when you see the servant thinking more of his own interests than of yours, and seeking inwardly his own profit in everything, such a man will never make a good servant, nor will you ever be able to trust him." With regard to flatterers, the key is that the prince, and not his courtiers, should be the provider of good counsel.

In sum, Machiavelli's prince must be always alert, ready to deceive, ready to strike, a man alone, trusting no one. It is not surprising that such qualities should be defined as ingredients of success. It is startling, however, that they should be identified as the components of *virtù* in a Christian world where people longed for heaven and feared hell. Machiavelli ignored these fears and longings, seeming not even to inhabit the Christian universe of his fellow Florentines. He longed only for the freedom of Italy and feared only the force of fortune.

The River of Fortune Machiavelli had witnessed the invasions of French, Spanish, and imperial armies and the destruction of the states of Italy by these massive foreign powers. For him, they represented the force of Fortuna, an ancient Hellenistic goddess whose wheel symbolized the inevitable cycle of success and failure that was the human condition. Machiavelli revered ancient Rome and the great Italian cities, both republics and signorie, that had gained the status of autonomous states through the resolve and courage of their citizens and leaders. Just as Rome had fallen to barbarian forces, an event brought about by hostile fortune, it appeared that the states of Italy, too, would succumb to that force. The new "barbarian" incursions by European states, like a rushing river, could be stopped, Machiavelli thought, only by an equivalent force—the unassailable *virtù* of a redeemer-prince. In a famous passage (which modern feminists understandably deplore for its violent misogyny), Machiavelli imagines the defeat of Fortuna by the prince as a kind of rape of irrational female power by bold masculine strength:

> I conclude, therefore, that as fortune is changeable whereas men are obstinate in their ways, men prosper so long as fortune and policy are in accord, and when there is a clash they fail. I hold strongly to this: that it is better to be impetuous than circumspect; because fortune is a woman and if she is to be submissive it is necessary to beat and coerce her. Experience shows that she is more often subdued by men who do this than by those who act coldly. Always, being a woman, she favors young men, because they are less circumspect and more ardent, and because they command her with greater audacity.
>
> (Machiavelli, The Prince, p. 133)

Machiavelli lived to see the restoration of the Florentine republic, although he was not permitted, given his cooperation with the Medici regime, to join its leadership. He did not live long enough to see the republic dismantled once again, and finally, in 1530, a last Medici restoration. Nor did he know that the foreign invaders he hated would indeed destroy the Italian state system. This system, which had evolved over centuries, prefigured the republican states of the modern world—in their autonomy, at least, and to some extent in their systems of government. The prince he summoned to halt the devastations of fortune did not appear, and did not preserve Italy from the "barbarians."

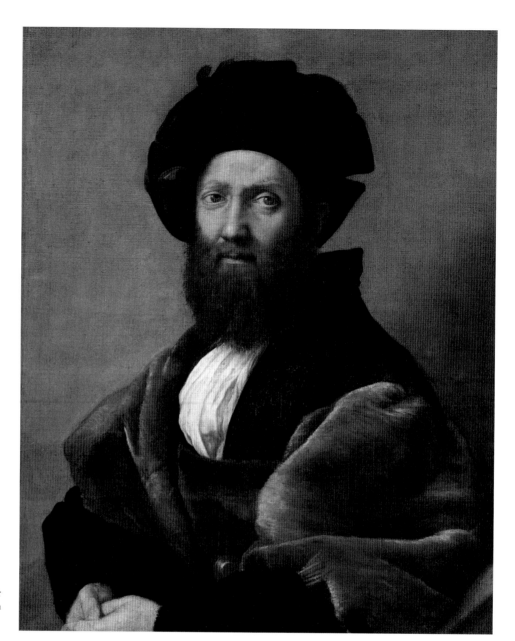

Raphael, *Portrait of Baldassare Castiglione*, c. 1514–1415, oil on canvas, 32 × 26½ in (82 × 67 cm). Musée du Louvre, Paris.

In an era when the Italian court system was primed to serve as the prototype for the great royal courts of Europe beyond the Alps, Castiglione was both the model of the perfect courtier and the author of the bestselling handbook on how to be one.

Machiavelli's Political Vision

Although Machiavelli's prince did not materialize, Machiavelli's political vision prevailed. He conceived of the state as an entity in itself, detached from the person of the king or the intentions of divine providence and thus laid a foundation for all modern Western political thought. As well, his understanding of republics displayed in the *Discourses* would be available to later thinkers who began to see republican governments on the national scale as the best constitutional format for human societies.

Machiavelli's immensely original and powerful thought was shaped by the particular moment in which he lived and wrote—a moment of danger, of uncertainty, of crisis, in which the formal structures of the world in which he was born and reared seemed in peril of crumbling. It was also shaped by his experience as a citizen of Florence, as a reader of classical texts, and as a historian. The author's lucid formulations of the behavior of republics and principalities are rooted in a history he knew well, the evolution of the Italian states since the eleventh century. His desperate faith in the *virtù* of a single individual, the redeemer-prince, derived from his close reading of ancient history, which was full of examples of such behavior. It derived, too, from the conversations of the humanists, whom Machiavelli knew though he was not of their circle, about the active life, civic virtue, and human dignity (see Chapter 3). All these words and concepts were available to Machiavelli the thinker. Machiavelli the man of action saw how they could be employed to build a game plan to rescue Italy from political annihilation.

COURTS AND PRINCES: CASTIGLIONE'S *THE COURTIER*

In the same year that Machiavelli wrote *The Prince* and began *The Discourses*, Baldassare Castiglione began *The Courtier*. He finished it by 1518, but it was not printed until 1528. Like *The Prince*, *The Courtier* draws on the experience of political struggle and humanist thought that Italy had known in the previous centuries. Like *The Prince*, too, *The Courtier* responds to immediate circumstances: the tendency everywhere in Italy, as in Europe, toward monarchy. Whereas Machiavelli called for a native prince to save Italy from an invasion of foreign kings, Castiglione advised the nobles of Italy how to position themselves in a new social situation, where advancement came only by pleasing the prince. It was three times the length of *The Prince*, and discursive where *The Prince* was incisive, but *The Courtier* would become a handbook of correct behavior for the European aristocrats who learned, over the next three centuries, to flourish within the framework of the nation state.

Trained in humanist schools, the nobleman and diplomat Castiglione perfected his own skills as a courtier by serving at the courts of Milan, Mantua, Urbino, Rome (the papal see), and Spain. His *Courtier* records a fictional conversation in the historical setting of the court of Urbino, which the author knew well first-hand. Guidobaldo Montefeltro, the Duke of Urbino, ruled, and the Duchess, Elisabetta Gonzaga (daughter of the ruling family of Mantua), presided over nightly conversations between residents of and visitors to that hospitable palace, intellectuals and diplomats alike. Composed after Castiglione had left Urbino, but set in 1507 when he was still in residence there, *The Courtier* breathes an idealism tinged by nostalgia.

The gathered company includes the Duke himself, a silent figure afflicted by ill-health who retires each night after supper; his wife, the Duchess, who guides the evening sessions of music, dancing, games, and conversation; her companion and aide, the vivacious Lady

Emilia Pia; and, among "countless other very noble gentlemen," the Venetian prelate and author Pietro Bembo, an expert and advocate of the Italian vernacular; the noble Veronese prelate Count Ludovico da Canossa; the brothers Ottaviano and Federico Fregoso, the Duke's nephews, the former destined to become the Doge of Genoa, the latter just appointed archbishop of Salerno; Giuliano de' Medici, the "Magnificent Giuliano," the Medici heir in exile and brother of Pope Leo XIII; and Castiglione's friend, a noble Lombard, Gasparo Pallavicino. The discussions among these participants span four books of *The Courtier*, which take place on four successive evenings.

Book One

On the first evening, the men and women gathered in the Duchess's rooms decide that their subject shall be the nature of the perfect courtier. The discussion that follows not only delivers information about the role of the courtier it is itself a model of how courtiers and court ladies behave. A man who was considered to be a model courtier, Count Ludovico, leads the discussion. He pauses frequently, when another participant asks a question or voices an objection and digressive conversation follows. The main theme is resumed, however, by the count, sometimes at the prompting of Emilia Pia, who serves as the directress of the entertainment. When the discussion concludes, those gathered enjoy a session of music and dance before retiring for the night.

The courtier, according to Count Ludovico, must, in the first instance, be of noble birth. When the objection is raised that some low-born men rise to high position and perform worthily, the count maintains that noble birth is nonetheless essential: "since it is our task to form a Courtier free of any defect whatsoever, and endowed with all that is praiseworthy, I deem it necessary to have him be of noble birth … because of that public opinion which immediately sides with nobility." He should also be attractive in appearance: "endowed by nature not only with talent and with beauty of countenance and person, but with that certain grace which we call an 'air,' which shall make him at first sight pleasing and lovable to all who see him." He must be accomplished in arms, and skillful with all kinds of weapons used on foot and on horseback, as well as in all kinds of related skills—swimming, jumping, running, and throwing stones. But he should not be a sullen warrior unequipped for the life of the court, who might be reproved by a lady thus: "I should think it a good thing, now that you are not away at war or engaged in fighting, for you to have yourself greased all over and stowed away in a closet along with all your battle harness, so that you won't grow any rustier than you already are."

Indeed, the courtier is to wear his physical attainments lightly, as well as all his others, cultivating a kind of nonchalance which seems, in pretending that the task is easy, to make its accomplishment all the more impressive: "to practice in all things a certain *sprezzatura*, so as to conceal all art and make whatever is done or said appear to be without effort and almost without any thought about it." The term *sprezzatura* is as famous as it is untranslatable. Coined by the speaker, it implies an attitude of easy superiority, an elegant disdain

Castiglione's *The Courtier* became a European bestseller. Its curve of popularity and its diffusion to a non-Italian readership can be known from the number of editions published in the original Italian and in translation.

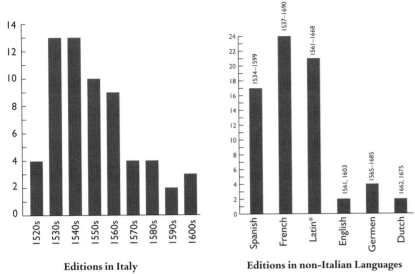

Editions in Italy   **Editions in non-Italian Languages**

* The Latin editions were published in Wittenberg, Strasbourg, Zurich, London, and Cambridge, their publication attesting to the continued importance of Latin as an international language.

(Based on Peter Burke, The Fortunes of the Courtier: The European Reception of Castiglione's *Cortegiano. University Park: Pennsylvania State University Press, 1995, Appendix 1.)*

for the difficulty of the task. If there is one quality that characterizes Castiglione's courtier, it is this one.

However, it is not the only skill the courtier must possess beyond the traditional characteristics of noble birth and skill in arms. He must also command language skills of a high order and an education in the humanities both in Latin and the vernacular. He must be able to sing pleasantly, accompanying himself on an instrument, and even to draw and paint. This man of the Renaissance was thus expected to be a "Renaissance man" in the modern sense of a person broadly trained and able to shine in any context.

Book Two

Gathering for a second evening, the ladies and gentlemen of the court continue their discussion of the requirements of the courtier, this time led by Federico Fregoso. Fregoso is concerned more with appearances than with skills. How must the courtier behave? In all his pursuits, he must show caution and prudence—in dress, for instance, preferring to be "grave and sober" rather than "foppish." In pursuing physical sports, he should choose those that are appropriate to his rank—tennis rather than wrestling with village toughs—and should not seem to try too hard to excel. When dancing, for instance, "he should maintain a certain dignity, though tempered with a fine and airy grace of movement; and even though he may feel himself to be most agile and a master of time and measure, let him not attempt those quick movements of foot … which would perhaps little befit a gentleman."

The same reserve and calculation required of the courtier in these activities are necessary in his interactions with the prince. He will not be presumptuous to the prince, or obstinate, spiteful, idle, or boastful. He will always be pleasant, seeming to ask nothing for himself. His aim is at all costs to please the prince:

> And I would have our courtier bend himself to this, even if by nature he is alien to it, so that his prince cannot see him without feeling that he must have something pleasant to say to him; which will come about if he has the good judgment to perceive what his prince likes, and the wit and prudence to bend himself to this, and the considered resolve to like what by nature he may possibly dislike.
>
> (Castiglione, *The Book of the Courtier*, p. 81)

The courtier, therefore, is expected to shape his whole personality to that of a master. The second book turns in its second half to a discussion of those witticisms and pleasantries which adorn conversation, laced with examples. The great weight given to this discussion befits a social context where the candid expression of personal views is little esteemed—indeed, silenced.

Book Three

On the third evening, the "Magnificent Giuliano" describes the qualities of the lady of the court, though he is often interrupted by the misogynous Gasparo Pallavicino. The presence of the lady is essential to the court, as she is the indispensable counterpart of the courtier: "just as no court, however great, can have adornment or splendor or gaiety in it without ladies, neither can any Courtier be graceful or pleasing or brave … unless he is moved by the society and by the love and charm of ladies." Whereas the courtier is to possess "a certain solid and sturdy manliness," the lady must display "a soft and delicate tenderness, with an air of womanly sweetness in every movement, which, in her going and staying, and in whatever she says, shall always make her appear the woman without any resemblance to a man." The gender division between the courtier and lady could not be more starkly defined. It is this perception of gender difference that will characterize not only the courts of Europe, but European society more generally, for the next three centuries.

Besides being beautiful—"for truly that woman lacks much who lacks beauty"—the court lady must be a pleasant conversationalist who puts people at their ease and skillfully guides, but does not dominate, the discourse. Gossip, however, the use of language to a base end, is roundly discouraged. Neither should the lady engage in the "strenuous manly exercises" that engage the courtier. Dress is important. Whereas men need only choose garments restrained in style, women must make an art of fashion:

> This Lady must have the good judgment to see which are the garments that enhance her grace and are most appropriate to the exercises in which she intends to engage at a given time, and choose these. And when she knows that hers is a bright and cheerful beauty, she must enhance it with movements, words, and dress that tend toward the cheerful; just as another who senses that her own style is the gentle and grave ought to accompany it with like manners, in order to increase what is a gift of nature.
>
> (Castiglione, *The Book of the Courtier*, p. 154)

Besides these guidelines for the court lady's behavior and appearance, Book Three of *The Courtier* is devoted to two lengthy conversations. The first and longer one is a debate on women's worth, beginning with the standard philosophical arguments praising and condemning female nature and ending with many examples from ancient and contemporary times of female courage, skill, and chastity. The briefer one is about the court lady and the courtier in love, which stresses the need for discretion—and dissimulation—in the expression of emotion.

Book Four

The fourth evening, which begins late and does not end until the break of dawn, is devoted to two discussions. The first, led by Ottaviano Fregoso, returns to the courtier and inquires what his main role might be. The second, led by Pietro Bembo, is a discourse on Platonic love.

Whereas Count Ludovico and his brother Federico had inquired into who a courtier must be and how he should behave, Ottaviano seeks to define what the courtier must do—for surely, he must have a purpose: "For indeed if by being of noble birth, graceful, charming, and expert in so many exercises, the Courtier were to bring forth no other fruit than to be what he is, I should not judge it right for a man to devote so much study and labor to acquiring this perfection of Courtiership as anyone must do who wishes to acquire it." It is, in fact, the courtier's vitally important task to advise the prince:

> Therefore, I think that the aim of the perfect Courtier … is so to win for himself … the favor and mind of the prince whom he serves that he may be able to tell him, and always will tell him, the truth about everything he needs to know, without fear or risk of displeasing him; and that when he sees the mind of his prince inclined to a wrong action, he may dare to oppose him and in a gentle manner … dissuade him of every evil intent and bring him to the path of virtue. And thus … the Courtier will in every instance be able adroitly to show the prince how much honor and profit will come to him and to his from justice, liberality, magnanimity, gentleness,

and the other virtues that befit a good prince; and, on the other hand, how much infamy and harm result from the vices opposed to these virtues.

(Castiglione, The Book of the Courtier, p. 209)

In a world where so many princes are predisposed to vice and ignorance, reducing their subjects to ruin, the courtier can be a valuable asset indeed.

Ottaviano's claim for the courtier's significance is interrupted by two digressions. The first of these pursues the question whether virtue can be learned. If good and evil are innate, then, of course, a courtier, however perfect, could not sway the mind of a prince intent on vice. Ottaviano argues persuasively the humanist position that, although much is innate, the mind can direct the human personality: "reason has such power that it always brings the senses to obey it, and extends its rule by marvelous ways and means." The second digression is about the available forms of political rule, referring to Aristotle's description of three good and three bad forms of rule, and whether a princely or republican regime is to be preferred. Although Bembo (a native of the republic of Venice) argues in favor of republican liberty, Ottaviano defends monarchy:

> I should always prefer the rule of a good prince because such rule is more according to nature, and … more like that of God who singly and alone governs the universe…. Note that deer, cranes, and many other birds, when they migrate, always choose a leader whom they follow and obey; and bees, almost as if they had discourse of reason, obey their king with as much reverence as the most obedient people on earth; and hence all this is very certain proof that the rule of a prince is more in keeping with nature than that of republics … thus, men have been put by God under princes, who for this reason must take diligent care in order to render Him an account of them like good stewards to their lord.

(Castiglione, The Book of the Courtier, p. 220, 222–223)

It is not surprising that monarchy is praised in this work, since monarchy and courtier-ship must go together. At the end of this discussion, Ottaviano is asked by the Magnificent Giuliano whether he has not elevated the courtier above the prince in making the former the latter's moral guide. By no means, he responds. Both Plato and Aristotle, the two greatest philosophers of antiquity, Ottaviano points out, had been courtiers: Plato had served Dion of Syracuse (409–353 BCE); Aristotle, Philip of Macedon (382–336 BCE).

Having introduced these ancient sages, Ottaviano has cleared the path for the final discussion of Castiglione's work: Bembo's discourse on Platonic love. Drawing on the Neoplatonic philosophy of Marsilio Ficino (see Chapter 3), Bembo sees Platonic love not only as a cosmic force, but as a kind of emotional state that exists between earthly lovers as a real alternative to a love based in sensuality. For Bembo, love is the desire to enjoy beauty, which is achieved by a union of souls, not of bodies. He summons the courtier to this higher form of love, saying that he "must firmly resolve to avoid all ugliness of vulgar love, and must enter in to the divine path of love, with reason as his guide." The courtier

(FACING PAGE)

Europe, c. 1530

During the late Renaissance, Italy suffered a series of invasions and foreign domination. By 1530 and into the eighteenth century, much of the country, north and south, would lie under direct Spanish rule or indirect Spanish control. The states of Europe beyond the Alps now came to the fore as the sixteenth century saw the consolidation of the Spanish, French, and English nations.

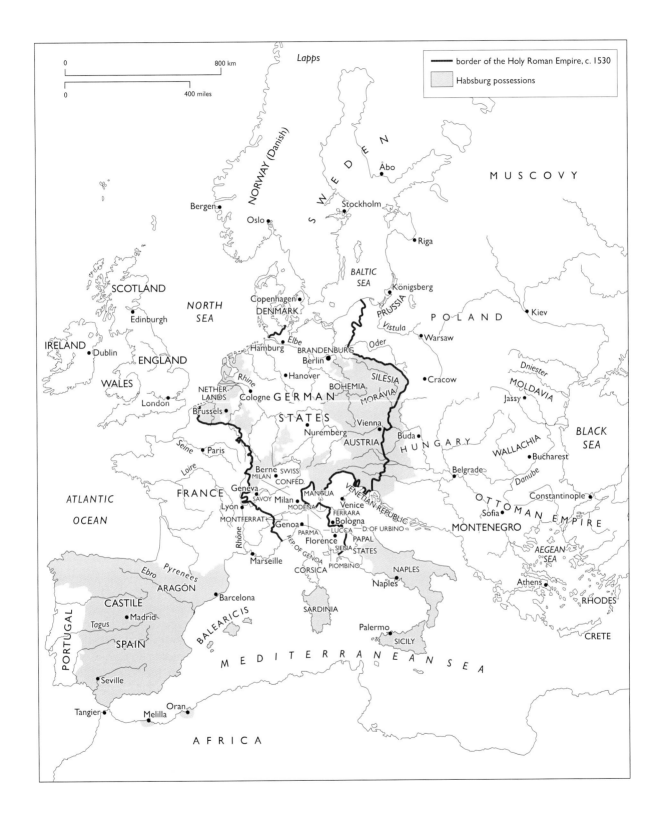

Lapps

border of the Holy Roman Empire, c. 1530

Habsburg possessions

0   800 km

0   400 miles

MUSCOVY

Åbo

NORWAY (Danish)

S W E D E N

Bergen

Oslo

Stockholm

Riga

BALTIC
SEA

Königsberg

POLAND

Kiev

SCOTLAND

Copenhagen

DENMARK

PRUSSIA

Vistula

Warsaw

NORTH
SEA

Edinburgh

Elbe

Hamburg

BRANDENBURG

Oder

Cracow

IRELAND

Dublin

ENGLAND

Rhine

Berlin

Hanover

BOHEMIA

SILESIA

Dniester

MOLDAVIA

WALES

NETHER-
LANDS

Cologne

GERMAN

MORAVIA

Jassy

London

Brussels

STATES

Vienna

BLACK
SEA

Nuremberg

AUSTRIA

Buda

H U N G A R Y

Seine

Paris

Berne

SWISS

Belgrade

WALLACHIA

ATLANTIC

Loire

MILAN

CONFÉD.

VENETIAN·REPUBLIC

Bucharest

Constantinople

OCEAN

FRANCE

Geneva

SAVOY

Milan

MANTUA

Venice

Danube

Lyon

MODENA

FERRARA

MONTENEGRO

O T T O M A N

E M P I R E

Sofia

MONTFERRAT

Genoa

Bologna

D. OF URBINO

Rhône

PARMA

LUCCA

AEGEAN
SEA

Marseille

REP. OF GENOA

Florence

SIENA

PAPAL
STATES

PIOMBINO

CORSICA

NAPLES

Athens

RHODES

SARDINIA

Naples

CRETE

Pyrenees

Ebro

ARAGÓN

Barcelona

CASTILE

BALEARICS

Palermo

SICILY

PORTUGAL

Tagus

Madrid

SPAIN

M E D I T E R R A N E A N   S E A

Seville

Tangier

Oran

Melilla

A F R I C A

must have the resolve to understand that the desire beauty arouses cannot be satisfied by touching, but only by seeing, for the eyes are the gateway to the soul. In this final section of *The Courtier*, the civilizing mission of the court, carried on by its courtiers and court ladies, culminates in a civilized, spiritualized vision of love.

Influence

Thus ends *The Courtier*, one of the most important and most widely read books composed during the Renaissance. It was written just at the time when the nations of Europe were primed to acquire and digest the civilization of the Italian Renaissance and at a time when the Italian princely court could still serve as a model for the monarchical courts of northern Europe. Written in the vernacular, it could be read by women and men, by the learned and the not so learned. It was reissued in approximately 130 editions—about one per year for the century after its 1528 publication and 59 before 1600 in Italy alone (see box, p. 265). It circulated further through translations into Spanish (1534), French (1537), English (1561), Latin (1561), German (1565), and Polish (1566; an adaptation). There were copies in libraries all over Europe, including Scandinavia and eastern Europe as well as Iberia and the western kingdoms. It appears to have been read by virtually every major English writer of the century, including William Shakespeare. Its assumptions about social and gender relations informed European culture and society down through the nineteenth century. In Italy, however, it marked an end as well as a beginning.

While the many conversations that take place in the court of Urbino over the four evenings described in Castiglione's *Courtier* drew on humanist and literary models, the work departs from the republicanism of earlier Italian history. Its hero is a man dependent on a prince, and the prince, not the citizens, rules. The whole work functions as an affirmation of hierarchy: the superiority of the great men assembled at court to all others; the superiority of men to women; the superiority of the prince to the courtier, born and trained to serve the prince.

THE STATES OF ITALY AFTER c. 1530

Castiglione's understanding of the perfect courtier belonged to an age which had surrendered to princes. Although emperors, popes, signori, and kings had long ruled the states of the Italian peninsula, the characteristic political form of the most dynamic part of that region from the eleventh through the fourteenth century was the republic. A few republics, moreover, survived into the era of the Renaissance proper, the late fourteenth to early sixteenth centuries, and were principal centers of cultural innovation. This tradition is obscured in Castiglione's *Courtier*; it is abandoned altogether in Machiavelli's *Prince*.

Between 1494 and 1530, with a final settlement delayed until 1559 (see Chapter 7), foreign armies scourged the Italian peninsula. When the cloud lifted, Spain dominated the peninsula, but it was still a patchwork of unequal states. In the north, the Duchy of Milan maintained its local traditions but under the rule of a Spanish governor after 1535, when the last descendant of Francesco Sforza died. Milan remained in Spanish hands until 1713, when it passed to Austrian rule, which prevailed except for the revolutionary intervals of 1796 to 1814 and 1848. In 1858, Milan was united with the Kingdom of Piedmont-Sardinia, soon afterwards the Kingdom of Italy. In the south, too, Spain ruled through viceroys the Kingdoms of the Two Sicilies—Sicily itself and Naples, including much of Italy south of Rome. These dominions remained under Spanish rule until 1860, when the last Spanish fortress fell to the liberator Giuseppe Garibaldi (1807–1882) and were incorporated in the new Italian kingdom.

Lying between these two poles of Spanish power, the Papal States remained under papal control but the Spanish presence was heavy. A permanent group of Spanish diplomats, bureaucrats, soldiers, and prelates resided in the ecclesiastical capital and influenced, although they did not govern, those states. The popes continued to rule, defended by their Swiss guards and other mercenaries, until 1870, when Rome was claimed by King Victor Emanuel II of Italy, and the pope retreated to the precincts of the Vatican.

Spanish influence also predominated in the Italian states that retained some autonomy, including even the small Republic of Lucca, which remained independent until Napoleon handed it to his sister's husband in 1805. Genoa was also a republic in the Middle Ages but became faction-ridden in the earlier Renaissance and was dominated alternately by France and Milan. Genoa reestablished its autonomy under Spanish influence in 1528. In the eighteenth century, it fell under Austrian and French domination until it was absorbed into the Kingdom of Sardinia in 1814 and thus into the Italian kingdom organized under the kings of Piedmont-Sardinia.

Florence was more successful. In 1530 the Medici regained power as the rulers of Tuscany, the region which the Florentine republic dominated in the earlier Renaissance. In 1559 the region became a duchy, always under Spanish influence, with the Medici ruler accorded the title of grand duke. With the death of the last Medici in 1737, Tuscany fell to Habsburg rule, which continued, despite the interruptions of the French Revolution, Napoleon, and the 1848 revolution, until the region's incorporation into the Kingdom of Italy in 1860.

Smaller duchies followed a similar pattern. The Gonzaga dukes and their descendants in junior lines continued to rule Mantua and Montferrat until 1708, when Mantua passed to the Austrian Habsburgs and Montferrat to Savoy. The Este continued to rule Ferrara, Modena, and Reggio until 1597, when the last duke died, and Ferrara was absorbed into the Papal States. A collateral branch of the Este continued to rule in Modena and Reggio, with interruptions, until the region was incorporated into the nation of Italy in 1860. The Roman Farnese family ruled as the dukes of Parma and Piacenza from 1545 until 1748, when a branch of the Spanish Bourbons took over. In the northwest, the region of Savoy became a duchy under its ancestral house from 1559, with a magnificent capital established at Turin. The dukes of Savoy were one of the most successful dynasties in Europe, acquiring and merging with the Kingdom of Sardinia in 1815 and becoming, as the kings of Piedmont-Sardinia, the rulers of Italy from 1860 to 1946.

Of the major states of Italy surveyed here, Venice remains. Venice alone survived as an autonomous republic, enjoying full independence until 1797. In that year, Napoleon, true to his promise that he would be an Attila to the Venetians (referring to Attila the Hun, who terrorized ancient Rome in 451–453 CE), seized the city and reordered its constitution, its buildings, and its society. With the defeat of Napoleon, Venice remained under Austrian rule (interrupted by the failed revolution of 1848) until it became part of the Italian kingdom in 1866.

Thus over the centuries from 1530 to the French Revolution, the states of Italy lost their independence and the memory of a republican past became increasingly remote. At the same time, Italy lost its economic dominance, retreating in the Mediterranean with the expansion of Ottoman Turkish power to the east and the opening up of oceanic trade and American colonization to the west (see Chapter 11). Soon the dynamic states of northwestern Europe would take the lead. In the meantime, the Italian Renaissance was not over, and its legacy would continue to exert a powerful influence on other regions of Europe and beyond.

IDEAS AND THE ARTS IN LATE RENAISSANCE ITALY

The civilization of the Renaissance, which derived from the vital civic experience of the states of northern Italy in the thirteenth and fourteenth centuries (see Chapter 2), did not cease when the crisis of 1494 to 1530 radically transformed the political landscape. Even as its political and economic importance faded in a Europe whose focus shifted to the northwest, Italy remained a center of the arts and music, literature, religious thought, science, and philosophy. In these endeavors, artists and intellectuals were increasingly constrained by the demands of conformity that came from princes and from the church. Those demands were variously acknowledged, avoided, or resisted, but Italian preeminence in the arts continued for more than a century after the crisis of invasion and conquest. In painting, sculpture, and architecture, Italy remained the font of innovation for at least a century more and the training ground for European artists through the eighteenth century. In music, where Italy had imitated rather than led through the fifteenth century, the peninsula would now take precedence. Henceforth, and up to modern times, Italian would be the language of music theory and performance. In theater, where Italy had been a pioneer, she would continue to experiment, although nations beyond the Alps—especially England, France, and Spain—would soon bound ahead.

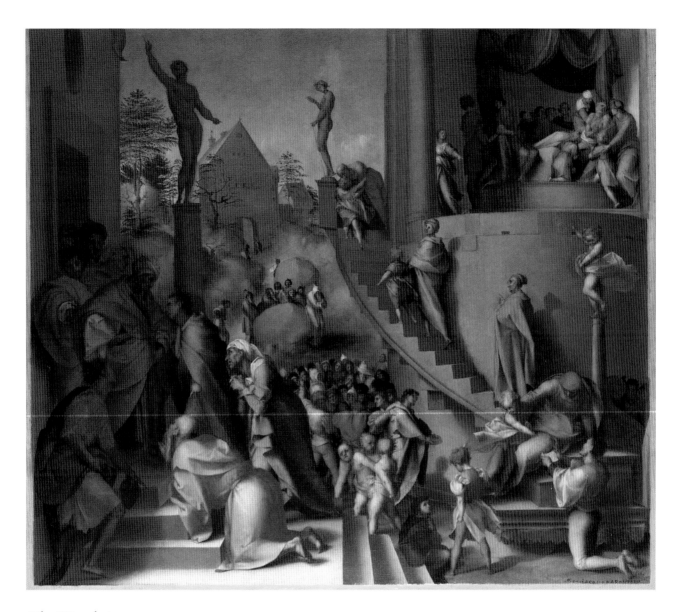

The Visual Arts

The consensus in the visual arts for harmony, balance, and economy, which marks the High Renaissance style (see Chapter 4), broke down from about 1520, amidst the experience of political and military crisis. The new Mannerist style never gained the dominance of the earlier Renaissance or later Baroque, but its practitioners created works so distinctive, and sometimes so shocking, as to disrupt the consensus and trigger new streams of development.

Mannerism displayed itself in painting, sculpture, and even architecture. In painting, Mannerism was characterized by formal distortions, unusual color, extraordinary spatial effects, and a general delight in the bizarre. Two examples must suffice. *Joseph with Jacob*

Pontormo, *Joseph with Jacob in Egypt*, 1518, oil on wood, 38 × 43⅛ in (96.5 × 109.5 cm). National Gallery, London.

In the Mannerist style (see also p. 254), Pontormo assembles figures in different scales, random statuary, a staircase leading nowhere, and a compressed death scene in the upper right.

WOMANLY PERSPECTIVE: THE OTHER WORLD OF THE FEMALE ARTIST

During the Middle Ages, European artists were craftsmen, the practitioners of a skill such as masonry or glass-making, and they were anonymous. It was only from the late thirteenth century in Italy that artists begin to become known to modern audiences. It is not surprising, then, that few women artists are known to us before the full Renaissance. Women were not likely to be trained artisans, and as their social actions were generally more constrained than men's, even if they attained the training necessary to create a major art work, it was unlikely that they would boldly declare themselves as its author.

Certainly women created art in the centuries before the Renaissance. As nuns, they painted, or illuminated, the margins and initial letters of manuscript books in their convent libraries. By the fifteenth century, like the holy woman Caterina Vegri of Bologna (see Chapter 6), they might also be involved in painting altarpieces or other ambitious works.

As the wives, daughters, and resident kin in a noble or comfortable burgher household, women engaged in textile arts. Not being required to produce raw cloth, they were free to utilize the needlework skills that were the essential accomplishments of all women to embroider cloth with fine silk or gold or silver thread to create exquisite items for the church or the home. Like the medieval artisan's work, however, these too are unsigned. Moreover, many have deteriorated and can no longer be admired.

By the sixteenth century in Italy (and in the Low Countries as well), some women had acquired the training necessary to become recognized as artists in the same genres as male counterparts. Most of these were the daughters of artists. Their success is understandable, since they would have access in a family-managed workshop to the skills and materials necessary to develop their talents.

Best known of these women artists trained by their fathers are Marietta Robusti, Lavinia Fontana, and Artemisia Gentileschi. Robusti (c. 1552–1590), daughter of Jacopo Tintoretto, participated in her father's workshop until her marriage. Fontana (1552–1614), daughter of Prospero Fontana, developed considerable fame and autonomy as a painter, pursuing a career fully comparable to that of a man's. Gentileschi (1593–1652), born later and whose style should properly be described as Baroque rather than Renaissance, was the most successful and prolific.

Gentileschi will occupy us below. First, note should be made of Sofonisba Anguissola (c. 1532–1625), who was one of the first women artists to win an international reputation. She was the daughter not of a painter but of a wealthy and indulgent nobleman who provided his six daughters with a humanistic education. As was also often true of later women artists, Anguissola specialized in portraits, very often portraits of women sometimes depicted with children or pets. Perhaps a woman artist was an appealing choice for portraiture, since executing a portrait required admitting a painter to a domestic setting for protracted sessions. Or perhaps it was thought that a woman painter had special empathy that would permit a truthful and intimate

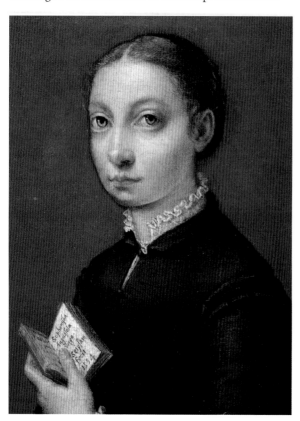

Anguissola, *Self-Portrait*, 1554, oil on poplar wood, 7⅔ × 4⅞ in (19.5 × 12.5 cm). Kunsthistorisches Museum, Vienna.

understanding of the subject. Anguissola's own self-portraits, of which she painted several, as though she were searching for the identity of this person who was both painter and woman, are particularly haunting.

We return to Gentileschi, who by no means confined herself to portraits for wealthy patrons, although she, too, often painted her own portrait and bestowed her own image upon female characters depicted in her art. Gentileschi studied with her father, Orazio, himself a follower of the Baroque innovator Caravaggio (Michelangelo Merisi, 1573–1610). She painted many of the same subjects as her father, using the same techniques. The many soft and lustrous female nudes she produced may have found their way onto the walls of the private studies of their purchasers, where they titillated and pleased audiences.

Gentileschi, however, did more than purvey standard products for an elite audience craving scenes of flesh and drama. Her understanding of women's social role—the limits upon them, the ambitions they still nurtured, their striving for security and dignity—infused her work. In her several depictions of the biblical scene of Susanna observed bathing in the nude by lecherous male onlookers, the figure of Susanna does not titillate but withdraws from the male gaze into a personal inner sanctuary. In her numerous portrayals of the heroic slaying of the enemy General Holofernes by the chaste widow Judith, Judith seems to take vengeance not only for her injured people but for the injury she and all women suffer at the hands of violent men.

Gentileschi's own experience may have taught her the insights displayed in her mature work. In 1612, when she was 19, she was raped by her father's associate, another painter. The case was prosecuted; Gentileschi testified, exposing herself to public shame and to torture imposed as a test of her veracity. She won the case, but the memory of the rape and prolonged trial no doubt remained. It was her presence as an artist in the company of men that especially exposed her to exploitation and abuse, and that reality, it seems, continued to inform her thoughts and her artistic conceptions.

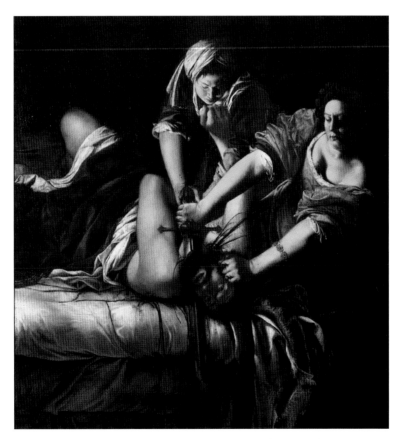

Gentileschi, *Judith Slaying Holofernes*, c. 1620, oil on canvas, 6 ft 6¼ in × 5 ft 4¼ in (1.99 × 1.63 m). Galleria degli Uffizi, Florence.

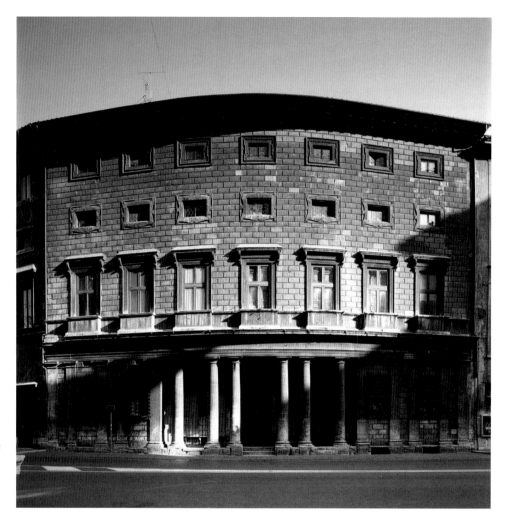

Peruzzi, Palazzo Massimo delle Colonne, Rome, c. 1533–1535.

A Roman palace built on the burned ruins of another after the sack of Rome in 1527, this edifice in the Mannerist style is curved to follow the orientation of the street and features unevenly spaced columns.

in Egypt, painted in 1518 by Jacopo da Pontormo (1494–1557), features as its most prominent motifs a spiraling staircase that goes nowhere, fleshy and flaccid statues on top of scattered columns, and figures depicted in different spatial scales within the same setting. The main narrative theme—the reconciliation of Joseph with his brothers—is tucked into the lower left-hand corner, while a secondary one—the aged, dying Joseph—takes place on a circular balcony from which there is no descent. *Madonna of the Long Neck* (see p. xxx), painted in 1534–1540 by Parmigianino (Francesco Mazzola, 1503–1540), is just as disturbing. Wholly unlike the calm madonnas of Raphael or the holy virgins of the quattrocento, Parmigianino's care-free virgin is perched uneasily on a support that cannot be seen or understood and hedged about with angels who seem less than divine in origin. Dressed in shimmering, billowing garments, adorned with an elaborate headdress, languidly elegant in posture, with a long, slender neck and tilted head, she holds her child at arm's length, his form also elongated and limp. In the background, without reason, are a glistening, freestanding column and a man, holding a scroll, entirely out of scale. The observer can admire the luster and finish of these paintings while still suspecting that their object is to perplex.

In sculpture, the Mannerist impulse caused forms to spiral and twist, whereas Renaissance sculptors positioned their figures to be viewed frontally. The *Rape of the Sabine Women* (1593) by Giambologna (1529–1608) is representative. The Roman aggressor stands astride the Sabine defender, twisting while he holds aloft his captive bride. The three figures are united in one continuous spiral. In architecture, Mannerism expressed itself by disrupting the harmonious alternation of proportional elements and even in the defiance of the principle of the flatness of the wall, as in the Palazzo Massimo delle Colonne (1534) in Rome designed by Baldassare Peruzzi (1481–1536; see left). Its oddly placed columns look like jagged teeth, while the facade swells out in a narrow arc.

By 1600, Mannerism and late Renaissance styles together yielded to the Baroque, the last great artistic style conferred by Italy to the European tradition. The forms of the Baroque also twisted and turned, while the spatial settings could be extravagant, and all in pulsing, surging motion. But the Baroque avoided the distracting colors and surfaces of Mannerism, along with its deliberate distortions and mystifications. Its aim was to be grandiose. It was the style appropriate for great men (and great women) and important times, wholly suited to an era defined, in the political realm, by monarchy. Born in Italy, it flourished in the expanding nations of northern Europe and Iberia through the whole of the seventeenth century.

It was during this later period of the Renaissance and the transition to the Baroque that Italy's most important women artists emerged (see Chapter 4). Of these, the most note-worthy were Sofonisba Anguissola and Artemisia Gentileschi. Anguissola worked mainly as a portraitist, a role that was more easily adopted by a woman than that of a creator of monumental paintings. Her self-portrait of 1554, a frank and sensitive image, is an early example of the genre of self-representation by a woman. Gentileschi also painted self-portraits and often painted herself as the heroic female figure of her assertively feminist narratives. In her well-known painting of the heroic Jewish widow Judith beheading the enemy general Holofernes, one of several she painted on the same theme, it is Gentileschi herself who wields the sword.

The Performing Arts

The sixteenth and seventeenth centuries were also the era of the rapid development of theater. Under humanist influence, the first formal plays performed were either revivals of ancient works or modern works closely imitative of them, produced in court settings for elite audiences. Popular theater developed alongside elite theater, however, and native folk traditions were incorporated into the theatrical lexicon through the **commedia dell'arte**, in which highly skilled actors improvised in groups to produce humorous entertainments. Women performers also excelled in this genre, notably Isabella Andreini (1502–1604), who

THE ORIGINS OF OPERA

Opera was born in Florence around the year 1600. It was the product of the fusion of humanism with the traditions of Western music that had been nurtured by more than a millennium of triumphant Christianity. A Renaissance creation, opera opened the door to the musical and artistic future of the Western world.

For the ancient Greeks, music was part of the cosmic design. The movements of the heavens and the proportions of geometrical figures corresponded to musical relationships. The Greeks also recognized that music could express and evoke emotion. Poetry was recited or chanted to a musical accompaniment, and different instruments were used for different kinds of poetry. The Greek tragedies were chanted or sung by the solo voices of the main characters but also by the group called the chorus.

Only some elements of these Greek notions of music reached medieval Europe, which had taken a different road in the fourth century after Christianity was first legitimated and then instituted as the universal religion of the Roman Empire. Now the main focus of musical creation and performance related to Christian worship, which had adopted the rituals and musical norms of Judaism.

In medieval Europe, the purpose of music was to celebrate God's mercy and judgment. The words were drawn from the psalms and the liturgy, and the singers, a group performing in chorus, were clergy, trained ministers of the word of God. Monks and nuns in their monasteries and convents sang in the choir several times daily. Monasteries housed schools, which had as one of their principal functions to train novices to sing in the choir. Cathedrals in the burgeoning cities of medieval Europe housed a company of choristers. The choir sang or chanted with one voice, the main goal being to deliver sacred words clearly and beautifully. As they did so, they created the vocabulary of sounds and rhythms that would thereafter characterize Western music.

Meanwhile, there were other types of music—unofficial, unauthorized by the awesome prestige of the church, unfixed by writing and tradition. There was the music of the village: songs of love and experience, danced and sung to the accompaniment of simple string, wind, and percussion instruments. The rhythms and melodies of village—or "folk"—music, always in flux and innovative, were a source of renewal for musical performance in other settings, as in the courts of the great nobles and kings and even in the churches.

In time, a specialized class of skilled composers emerged. These experts often borrowed a melodic theme from the secular repertoire to invigorate a sacred work. In further elaboration of inherited chant, they wrote variant themes for several voices to sing at once, different lines of sound that were related in complex rhythmic and melodic patterns. This was polyphony, which reached its artistic zenith in the fourteenth and fifteenth centuries in the type of sacred composition called a motet. The ecclesiastical and worldly princes of Italy vied with each other to hire the composers, concertmasters, and choristers who could perform such polyphonic masterpieces in their splendid Renaissance chapels.

Alongside the elaborate musical productions designed for chapel and cathedral, less formal musical events were organized by the residents of princely courts or by citizen families whose members formed an impromptu chorus. A popular use of leisure time was singing: love songs, ballads, and comic songs. The amateur participants sang in polyphony, using melodies that were more intricate and inventive, more bent to the sense of the words, and rhythms that were more lively and playful than in the formal motets. Composers, too, wrote for these audiences and performers. The new genre to emerge from these settings was the madrigal.

In liturgical chant, words and meaning were paramount. In motet and madrigal, words were lost in the complexities of the several voices that each pursued separate, though intertwined, melodic, and rhythmic courses. It was at this point that opera emerged to privilege the expressive word once more but in a secular setting and with a regrounding in the ancient Greek understanding of the emotional intensity that music added to meaning.

In the late 1500s, a group of composers and intellectuals gathered in the Florentine *camerata*—one of the many groups of intellectuals and practitioners who gathered in the manifold informal settings of academy or salon. They sought to recover the dramatic intensity of Greek theater by developing a new musical form based on the solo voice, which could confer emotional range to words in a melodic aria (air) or convey exact and complex meanings in a half-spoken, half-sung form that would later come to be called *recitativo* (recitative, or recited words). They introduced these innovations in the intermedi of theatrical and civic events. These experiments gave rise to the first operas, the *Euridice*

(1600) of Jacopo Peri (1561–1633) and *Orfeo* (1607) of Claudio Monteverdi. Both were based on the ancient Greek fable of the honey-voiced Orpheus and his beloved Euridice, which demonstrated the overmastering power of the two forces music and love.

From these beginnings, opera became king of the musical forms of the Western world. Its emphasis on the importance of the emotional expression of an individual voice and the communication of meaning led to the development of the solo performance. Sidestepping complex polyphony, opera called on the resources of musical instruments to create sophisticated musical accompaniments and so contributed to the later development of the symphony and concerto. Opera called for the creation of a new performance setting, the opera hall, in preference to the sacred space of the cathedral or the private reserves of court and chapel. In its search for grand narratives emerging from the collision of personalities, opera pioneered a new kind of epic art. Immensely popular since its birth in 1600 until the present day, opera continues to impress by its care for the expressive possibilities of words and its respect for the emotional complexity of the human predicament.

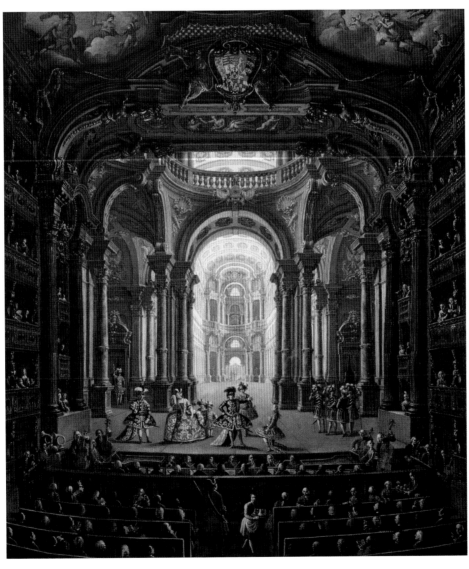

Oliviero, *Teatro Reale Opening Night, December 26, 1740*, 1740, oil on canvas. Museo Civico, Turin.

was not only the foremost actress of the era but a dramatist and poet of note. Religious theater, moreover, deriving from medieval traditions, still flourished in productions managed by guilds or religious communities and performed to enthusiastic audiences. It was in England and Spain, however, late in the sixteenth century, where a theatrical tradition that bridged the gap between elite and popular traditions most flourished.

Although Italy's leadership in art dated from the fourteenth century and in theater from the fifteenth, Italy only took the lead in the development of musical style and performance in the sixteenth century (see Chapter 4). Churches and courts commissioned increasingly elaborate polyphonic compositions whose authors were now mostly native Italians. Conspicuous among them was Giovanni Pierluigi da Palestrina (1525–1594), a master of the new contrapuntal style, who composed more than 105 masses (for church performance) and 250 motets (for secular audiences). Alongside this formal composition, leisured amateurs improvised and performed madrigals in homes and other intimate settings. The variety and capacity of musical instruments of all types increased and began to look like their modern descendants: keyboard, bowed string, woodwind, and brass. The voice was still the main form of musical production, the characteristics of which instruments imitated, although composers now began to write for specific instruments.

An important innovation of the sixteenth century was the incorporation of music with theater. Initially, this marriage took the form of simple *intermedi* ("in-betweens") where, between the acts of performances, musicians would perform to amuse the audience. The *intermedi* became increasingly elaborate, however, involving large numbers of singers and instruments, staging, sets, and costume. Many followed a theme: they were, in effect, theatrical performances in their own right. This tendency culminated in the invention of opera by 1600 (see pp. 278–279). It came into being when the independent developments in music and theater merged with the humanist and literary traditions. The material of the first operas was classical. The theorists behind the creation of opera believed they were recreating ancient theater that had been, initially, entirely sung or chanted. To recapture that tradition, they devised a style of sung speech, the recitative, which was based on the rhythm of the words. The voice varied in pitch, but recitative was not as melodic or as organized as song so as to accentuate the meaning of the text and recapture the dramatic power of antiquity. In 1607, with the performance of *Orfeo* ("Orpheus") by Claudio Monteverdi (1567–1643), opera was securely launched.

The Florentine *camerata*, the informal discussion group from which emerged the idea of opera, was one of a great number of groups that met outside of professional, church, or court circles. These are the academies of the late Renaissance, gatherings of greater or lesser formality where noble amateurs and gifted professionals discussed the arts, literature, and philosophical and scientific ideas. By 1530 we know of 12 such academies in Italy, including the Platonic Academy, centered on the circle of Marsilio Ficino (see Chapter 3), and the Orti Oricellari, a group that met for political discussions in the gardens of a prominent Florentine patrician. By 1600 there were 377; by 1700, an additional 870. The relatively free and spontaneous network of academies was the vital setting for the development of new ideas and the circulation of new literary creations.

Literature and Literary Trends

The modern Italian language began with Dante, whose elevated Tuscan dialect would become the standard for the subsequent written form of the vernacular (see Chapter 2). In the next generation, Dante's successors Boccaccio and Petrarch would, like Dante, compose works in both Latin and Italian and further dignify the vernacular as a written language. For the next century, however, the humanist surge put the development of vernacular literature on hold in Italy, while Latin became the vehicle, not only for prose treatises, but also for lyric and dramatic verse. Toward the end of the quattrocento, however, just before the tide of invasions began, the Italian language was explored again as a vehicle for literary expression.

Influential promoters of Italian were the Ferrarese court poet Ludovico Ariosto (1474–1533), whose *Orlando furioso* ("Roland the Mad") was the most important European epic since Dante's, and Pietro Bembo (1470–1547), the Venetian advocate of the vernacular language, presented above as a participant in the discussions described in *The Courtier*. Ariosto was a diplomat, administrator, soldier, and courtier

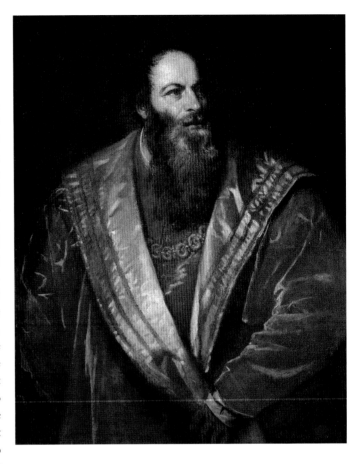

Titian, *Portrait of Aretino*, 1545, oil on canvas, 38 × 30 in (96.7 × 76.6 cm). Palazzo Pitti, Florence.

Like Raphael's *Baldassare Castiglione* (see p. 262), Titian's painting of this "scourge of princes" conveys the prestige and towering self-confidence enjoyed by cultural leaders of the Renaissance.

until he was able to retire to Ferrara to write full-time. Bembo also played many roles: statesman, historian, humanist, cardinal, literary critic, proponent of Platonic love, and author of poems, dialogues, and treatises. Of special importance is his *Prose della volgar lingua* ("Discussions on the Vernacular," 1525), which standardized the literary Italian of the fourteenth century—the age of Dante, Boccaccio, and Petrarch—as a modern vernacular.

Regarding the vernacular as a literary language meant a larger population of authors and an expanded audience of readers—for Latin was always the special preserve of a closed, highly educated group of intellectuals. Likewise, the first generations of printing focused on the Bible and classical texts, but the printing houses were now ready to publish more contemporary works. This shift resulted in an explosion of literary activity in the middle of the sixteenth century, giving rise, not only to more works composed in the familiar genres, but to new genres and new kinds of literary authorship with them. Typical of this period is the appearance of the ***poligrafi*** (polygraphs), those closely connected to the publishing business who wrote on many topics, sometimes provocatively, in tune with the demands of the market place. While many of the *poligrafi* were minor literary figures, some won great renown.

Foremost among these was Pietro Aretino, *l'Unico Aretino* (the unique Aretino), as Castiglione called him. Aretino, like Bembo, participated in the Urbino court conversations

PIETRO ARETINO, "SCOURGE OF PRINCES"

The political catastrophe that befell Italy in the early sixteenth century evoked despair and cynicism among intellectuals. They gave voice to these feelings in a new language, the Italian vernacular, first shaped by Dante but now enriched by classical elements. They published those feelings in print, by the thousands of volumes, as publishers competed to snare those authors who would shock, inspire, and amuse a discerning and demanding public. Among this new generation of pens for hire, Pietro Aretino (1492–1556) was especially bold. His sharp wit that spared not even the powerful won him the sobriquet "scourge of princes." Two dimensions of his work are apparent in the passages here.

The first passage is taken from his dialogues, the *Ragionamenti*, in which Nanna, mother and whore, instructs Pippa, her daughter and whore-to-be, in the nature of their business.

> NANNA: *Now you shall go to the house of the good man ... and I shall come with you. When we arrive, he will hasten out to meet you.... Be sure your entire person is neat and set to rights ... and then ... fix your eyes humbly on his, make a perfumed bow all around, and then greet [his companions] as do brides and women who have just given birth....*
> PIPPA: *And perhaps I should blush as I am doing it.*
> NANNA: *If you do I shall be very happy, for the cosmetic which modesty paints on a young girl's cheeks tears men's souls right out of their bodies.*
> PIPPA: *All right, I understand.*
> NANNA: *When the greetings are over, the first thing that the man with whom you are going to sleep will do is make you sit at his side, and he will caress me too.... And if ... he bends over to kiss your eye or forehead, turn gently toward him*

> *and heave a soft sigh which he can barely hear; and if you can manage another blush at the same time, you will burn him to a crisp from the very start.*
> PIPPA: *Ah, really? ... And the reason?*
> NANNA: *The reason is that simultaneously sighing and blushing are the signs of love and set the passion hammers throbbing. And ... the man who will enjoy you that night will begin to imagine that you are really gone on him.*

> (P. Aretino, Dialogues, trans. R. Rosenthal. New York: Stein and Day, 1972, pp. 168–169)

The second passage is from a letter in which Aretino defends his own work and lambasts the ignorant public which fails to recognize his merit.

> *My happiness would be too great ... if anyone who doubted whether the talent given me by God were true gold or not were to assay it for himself; for then I feel certain that everyone would give me my due as you have done in the letter you kindly sent me. So I bless the fact that you previously disdained reading my writings, because as a result of this I have acquired a true friend.... I laugh at the vulgar mob that has found fault with them, because it is its usual custom to blame what is praiseworthy and praise what is disgraceful; and it is the nature of the mob to try to stir things up if it possibly can. You see, if I have a go at someone important, as I lay into him this or that fawning courtier starts to fume and contrives to grow purple with anger.... Another does the same in order to appear important, and not because there's any sense or decency in him. And in this way the countless tribe of ignoramuses wickedly besmirch the honor of others.*
> (K.R. Bartlett, The Civilization of the Italian Renaissance: A Sourcebook. Boston, MA: Houghton Mifflin, 1992, p. 342)

and wrote journalism, satire (inspiring the poet Ariosto to name him "the scourge of princes"), and pornography. In the latter genre, his *Ragionamenti*, consisting of a series of dialogues between two Roman prostitutes, initiated a new literary genre while cleverly mocking all that the humanists had done in an older one. Although he was notorious in the sophisticated literary world of the cinquecento, he was not scorned. A portrait of him by Titian depicts a vibrant, but wholly respectable, figure of the cultural elite.

In this permissive cultural setting, women authors also flourished. Some, like Aretino, skirted the edge of respectable society, such as the courtesan poets Veronica Franco (c. 1546–1591) and Tullia d'Aragona (c. 1510–1556; see p. 284). Others, like the noblewoman Vittoria Colonna (1492–1547), a composer of both religious and love lyrics, were highly respectable. They were only a few female authors of poems, letters, plays, and treatises whom the printers of the day clamored to publish. The participation of these talented women in literary academies and other informal circles stimulated the discussion already underway among quattrocento humanists about women's nature and capacity for learning. The works by both men and women on this matter joined a longer literary debate that reached beyond Italy. It is referred to as the **querelle des femmes** (debate about women), and it was a major theme in several languages into the eighteenth century (see Chapter 11).

The most famous Italian contributors to this debate were three Venetian women, whose works were all published in the decades after 1600. Moderata Fonte (pseudonym for Modesta da Pozzo, 1555–1592) completed her work *On the Worth of Women and the Defects of Men* on the day she died in 1592; it was published posthumously in 1600. It is an elegant debate with seven participants, all women of different ages and marital status, which strongly advocates the cause of female autonomy. *The Nobility and Excellence of Women and the Defects and Vices of Men* by Lucrezia Marinella (1571–1653) is a more technical, though impassioned, treatise that draws on a host of medical, scientific, and philosophical authorities to prove the case that her title announces. *Paternal Tyranny*, written by Arcangela Tarabotti (1604–1652), who was unwillingly sent to a convent as a child, is a scathing attack on men—particularly fathers—who sacrifice their daughters in order to bolster family connections and fortunes. In these three works, the main feminist claims of later centuries were already germinating.

Science, Medicine, and Philosophy

If one legacy of humanism to cinquecento culture was the literary tradition, which turned in a vernacular direction, another was the philosophical tradition, which blossomed into a broad range of endeavors in the areas of science, medicine, and philosophy. With the availability now of a large number of ancient Greek works, many of them printed, university-based thinkers fully explored the possibilities of that tradition, including Aristotle and Plato but also the later Hellenistic thinkers: mathematicians and scientists, Neoplatonists, mystics. From that late Greek tradition came a renewed basis for the study of the occult, including astrology and alchemy, which the modern world has rejected as pseudo-sciences

WOMEN AND LOVE: TULLIA D'ARAGONA AND MODERATA FONTE

Women were active members in the intellectual life of sixteenth-century Italy. According to one recent reference work, Rinaldina Russell's *Italian Women Writers: A Bio-Bibliographical Sourcebook*, sixteenth-century female authors numbered 14 of 51—more than 25 per cent of the total and more than in any other century except the twentieth. Not only were women authors celebrated, but they spoke more audaciously than at any time before the modern era. Here are two examples.

In the first the courtesan writer Tullia d'Aragona talks frankly about carnal love—people who, having experienced it, love no more, and people who, having done so, yearn even more for union with the lover.

> *What I'm stating is that once the carnal purpose has been attained people are inevitably bound to lack the thrust and the stimulus that tormented and eroded their being up to a moment previously. This follows from the universal and self-evident proposition ... that anything that is moving toward a particular goal, once it reaches it, no longer moves. This is also because the senses of touch and taste, in the pleasure of which these lovers principally delight, are material rather than as spiritual as sight and hearing, and so they are satiated with immediate effect. Indeed, there are times when these senses surfeit the lovers so that they cause their love not just to stagnate but to mutate into hatred....*
>
> *As for the second issue, it is quite obvious that in the very moment when humans attain their desire, they automatically cease from their movement but do not discard their love; in fact, they often cause it to increase, because apart from their never being able to derive complete gratification from it, they retain the desire to enjoy the beloved object on their own, and by [continuing] union (hence this kind of love can never be completely lacking in jealousy). What is more, its acolytes become still more intemperate in their longing for carnal intercourse; they want to enjoy the thrill one more time, and still one more time after that.*
>
> (T. d'Aragona, Dialogue on the Infinity of Love, trans. and ed. R. Russell and B. Merry. Chicago: University of Chicago Press, 1997, p. 103)

Below, Moderata Fonte (1555–1592), pseudonym of Modesta da Pozzo, mother of four and the daughter of Venetian citizens and wife of the same, has one of the interlocutors in her work, *The Worth of Women*, make the case that women must avoid the love of men.

> *I've said before and I'll say again that even if a woman does find a man who is genuinely in love with her ... she should refuse to love him and should stay out of his way so as not to fall into those dangers and errors women fall into so often....*
>
> *A woman in love is in danger, whether she conquers her desire or is conquered by it. If she stands firm ... what greater emotional turmoil can be imagined than the battle taking place within her and the anguish of knowing that she will never be able to fulfill her desire? Death would be a thousand times more welcome to her than continuing to live in such torment. But, then, if she lets herself be vanquished by her desire, won over by the flattery and pleading of her lover, you can very well imagine the dangers she is laying herself open to: her reputation is at stake, her life, and gravest of all, her immortal soul. So ... women should avoid the love of men—though ... many find it hard, because they are so kind and good that they cannot spurn men, however bad men are.*
>
> (M. Fonte, The Worth of Women, trans. and ed. V. Cox. Chicago: University of Chicago Press, 1997, p. 97)

but which in the Renaissance context were fully respected. Medicine, too, made strides. In the theoretical sphere, medicine profited from further appropriation of the works of the medieval Iranian philosopher Avicenna (Ibn Sina, 980–1037) as well as those of the Greek physician Galen. In the practical sphere, the academic study of anatomy progressed dramatically through the dissection of cadavers pioneered by the Flemish-born Paduan university professor Andreas Vesalius (1514–1564). In these endeavors, Italian thinkers of the late Renaissance were part of a wider European reinvention of science and thought that would continue into the Enlightenment (see Chapter 11).

The discussions of the scientists and philosophers reached the ears of the church—a church engaged in its own reconstruction as it responded, from about 1540, to the cataclysm of the Protestant Reformation (see Chapter 9). As the sixteenth century turned, the ecclesiastical institution commissioned to root out heresy and apostasy in Italy, the Inquisition, turned its wrath against three prominent intellectuals whose investigations threatened the cosmological vision of traditional Christianity. The Neapolitan-born former priest, philosopher, astronomer, and mathematician Giordano Bruno (1548–1600), who proposed that the universe was infinite and included multiple world systems, was burned at the stake in 1600, a martyr to the principles of free thought and free speech. Tommaso Campanella (1568–1639), also from the Kingdom of Naples, escaped death for views that the church found dangerous but was imprisoned by the Spanish Inquisition for 27 years (1599–1626) for the ideas that he expressed in, among other works, his utopian *Città del sole* ("City of the Sun"). Finally, Galileo Galilei (1564–1642), a principal figure in the development of modern astronomy and the scientific method (see Chapter 11), also faced charges before the Roman Inquisition for his public defense of the Copernican, or heliocentric, theory that the sun was at the center of the universe. He was not tortured, imprisoned, or executed, but in 1633 he was compelled to denounce the theory that he knew to be true.

The repressive tenor of Italian life in the seventeenth and eighteenth centuries did not put an end to the cultural dynamism of the region. Whereas conditions in northern Italy about 1300 had been welcoming to cultural explorations, conditions on the peninsula in these late Renaissance centuries, increasingly, were not. Italy remained a place of innovation and the guardian of taste, but leadership passed to nations beyond the Alps.

CONCLUSION

Machiavelli and Castiglione, witnesses from their different vantage points of the crisis of Italy during the invasions of the peninsula by foreign powers from 1494 to 1530, distilled many of the main themes of Renaissance thought in their important books *The Prince* and *The Courtier*. As the warfare ceased, even before the final settlement of 1559, the curtain lifted on a transformed Italy. Except for pockets of political autonomy and even republican government, Italy was dependent on Spain, one of the major nation-states of Europe that emerged triumphantly in the sixteenth and seventeenth centuries. In that transformed political setting and as Italian economic power faded as well (see Chapter 11), the civilization of the Renaissance continued to be creative and resilient. In the arts, literature, scholarship, philosophical and scientific thought, and other fields of endeavor, Italy was innovative. Just as important, as her material wealth and power diminished, she became the instructor of Europe, passing on her brilliant cultural legacy to the artists, intellectuals, and elites beyond the Alps.

SUGGESTED READINGS

Primary Sources

Campanella, Tommaso. *The City of the Sun*. Translated and edited by Daniel J. Donno. Berkeley: University of California Press, 1981. A Utopian vision of a communistic state, administered by a great metaphysician.

Castiglione, Baldassare. *Book of the Courtier*. Translated by Charles S. Singleton, edited by Daniel Javitch. New York: W.W. Norton, 2002. A bestselling guide for those who must compete for influence in princely courts.

Cellini, Benvenuto. *Autobiography*, rev. ed. Translated by George Bull. Harmondsworth, UK: Penguin, 1999. The individualist Cellini details his personal and artistic adventures.

Fonte, Moderata. *The Worth of Women, Wherein Is Clearly Revealed Their Nobility and Their Superiority to Men*. Translated and edited by Virginia Cox. Chicago: University of Chicago Press, 1997. A dialogue among seven female interlocutors questioning the social evaluation of women in Venice around 1600.

Machiavelli, Niccolò. *The Prince*. Translated and edited by Peter Bondanella. Oxford: Oxford University Press, 2005. A recent and fluid translation of Machiavelli's often-translated masterpiece; the fundamental Renaissance treatise on the state.

Tarabotti, Arcangela. *Paternal Tyranny*. Translated and edited by Letizia Panizza. Chicago: University of Chicago Press, 2004. The harrowing denunciation of a coerced nun who excoriates the patriarchal strategy of warehousing unwanted daughters in convents.

Secondary Sources

Biagioli, Mario. *Galileo, Courtier: The Practice of Science in the Culture of Absolutism*. Chicago: University of Chicago Press, 1993. Examines the courtly context for Galileo's ideas.

Black, Christopher F. *The Italian Inquisition*. New Haven, CT: Yale University Press, 2009. Development and career of the Inquisition in Italy and its impact on society and culture.

Burke, Peter. *The Fortunes of the Courtier: The European Reception of Castiglione's* Cortegiano. University Park: Pennsylvania State University Press, 1996. Analyzes the diffusion of Castiglione's work in Italian and other languages.

Connor, James A. *The Last Judgment: Michelangelo and the Death of the Renaissance*. New York: Palgrave Macmillan, 2009. Shows how Michelangelo's Sistine Chapel ceiling frescoes reflect the religious and political crises of the time and foretell the end of the Renaissance.

Cox, Virginia. *Women's Writing in Italy, 1400–1650*. Baltimore, MD: Johns Hopkins University Press, 2008. A fundamental work tracing the origins and development of the many strands of women's literary endeavor over the whole era of the Italian Renaissance.

Dandelet, Thomas James. *Spanish Rome, 1500–1700*. New Haven, CT: Yale University Press, 2001. Studies the impact of Spanish rule on Roman society.

Garrard, Mary D. *Artemisia Gentileschi: The Image of the Female Hero in Italian Baroque Art*. Princeton, NJ: Princeton University Press, 1989. Classic and path-breaking study of a female artist and the effects of gender on artistic creation.

Glixon, Beth Lise, and Jonathan Emmanuel Glixon. *Inventing the Business of Opera: The Impresario and His World in Seventeenth-Century Venice*. Oxford: Oxford University Press, 2006. Studies the creation of opera as a theatrical genre and a business in the mid-seventeenth century in Venice.

Grendler, Paul F. *Schooling in Renaissance Italy: Literacy and Learning, 1300–1600*. Baltimore, MD: Johns Hopkins University Press, 1989. Traces the spread of private and public schooling both for elite and popular audiences.

Marino, John A., ed. *Early Modern Italy, 1550–1796*. Oxford: Oxford University Press, 2002. Essay collection exploring the tangled history of the late Renaissance states and of regions, the economy, the family, and intellectual life.

Robin, Diana. *Publishing Women: Salons, the Presses, and the Counter-Reformation in Sixteenth-Century Italy*. Chicago: University of Chicago Press, 2007. Studies the literary lives of women in major Italian centers where the institutions of the salon and the press encouraged and publicized their activity.

Ross, Sarah G. *The Birth of Feminism: Woman as Intellect in Renaissance Italy and England*. Cambridge, MA: Harvard University Press, 2009. Looking at two different national settings over 300 years, connects women's education and literary production to a changing conception of "woman," opening the path to modern feminism.

Saslow, James M. *The Medici Wedding of 1589: Florentine Festival as* Theatrum mundi. New Haven, CT: Yale University Press, 1996. Describes a month-long celebration of a Medici wedding at the intersection of politics, art, and ritual.

Testa, Simone. *Italian Academies and Their Networks, 1525–1700: From Local to Global*. New York: Palgrave Macmillan, 2015. Italy bequeathed to modern Italy not merely the entire legacy of the Renaissance but the model of important cultural institutions, notable among them, the academy, whose evolution and diffusion is studied here.

Viroli, Maurizio. *Machiavelli's God*. Translated by Antony Shugaar. Princeton, NJ: Princeton University Press, 2010. Following up on his classic 2001 biography, further explores the relations of Machiavelli's thought to the civil religion of the northern Italian republics.

NINE

THE RENAISSANCE AND THE TWO REFORMATIONS (c. 1500–c. 1650)

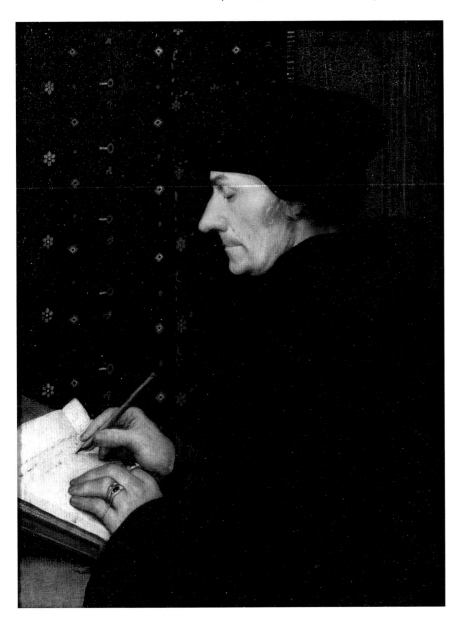

Holbein the Younger, *Erasmus* (detail), c. 1530, oil on panel, 16½ × 12⅔ in (42 × 32 cm). Musée du Louvre, Paris.

Compared with Raphael's *Baldassare Castiglione* and Titian's *Portrait of Aretino* (see pp. 262, 281), the more austere and Christian spirit of the northern Renaissance is conveyed in this painting. Modestly attired and starkly profiled against a somber background, Erasmus is intent on his mission to inscribe on a blank page the words by which the human mind seeks to apprehend truth.

In 1524, while in poor health, Desiderius Erasmus wrote a brief autobiography and sent it to his friend. At the end of its few pages, the author describes himself:

> His character was straightforward, and his dislike of falsehood such that even as a child he hated other boys who told lies, and in old age even the sight of such people affected him physically. Among his friends he spoke freely—too freely sometimes.... Having a touch of pedantry, he never wrote anything with which he was satisfied.... For high office and for wealth he had a permanent contempt, and thought nothing more precious than leisure and liberty.... In promoting the study of the humanities no one did more, and great was the unpopularity he had to suffer in return for this from barbarians and monks. Until his fiftieth year he had attacked no man, nor did any man attack him in print. This was his intention: to keep his pen absolutely innocent of what might wound.

(E. Rummel, ed., The Erasmus Reader. Toronto: University of Toronto Press, 1990, p. 20)

In a few brushstrokes, we have a portrait of the leading humanist of Europe beyond the Alps. Erasmus was a Christian and a moralist who more than any other carried on the intellectual traditions of the Italian Renaissance. In the different setting of Europe beyond the Alps, however, humanism took on different forms. Unlike Italian humanism, the phenomenon of northern humanism had to reckon with the **Reformations**: the radical Protestant break with the Roman church and the forceful efforts of that church to regain its supremacy. Erasmus was centrally involved in that confrontation, his involvement culminating in a lengthy exchange with Martin Luther, the first leader of the Protestant revolt. The concluding words of Erasmus's *Compendium vitae* ("Brief Outline of His Life") refer to that confrontation: "The sad business of Luther had brought him a burden of intolerable ill will; he was torn in pieces by both sides, while aiming zealously at what was best for both."

Erasmus was born in Rotterdam (modern Netherlands), but referred to himself as "Erasmus of Christendom." He is therefore a fitting focus for the present chapter, as he represents not merely the transfer to the whole of Europe of the humanistic mission first announced in Italy, but, more profoundly, its culmination and realization. Beyond this, he represents the plight of the thinker and moralist caught between two churches in the century when the Christian tradition underwent fragmentation and redefinition. This chapter considers, first, the transmission of humanism from Italy to other European regions. It then turns to the print revolution as a mechanism of cultural change and profiles the three Christian humanists Erasmus, More, and Vives. The chapter closes by exploring the relationship between **Protestant** and **Catholic Reformation** and humanism and Renaissance civilization.

VISITORS AND EMISSARIES

During the fifteenth to seventeenth centuries, the innovations of the Italian Renaissance traveled to other parts of Europe, where they took root in foreign soil, supported by a different array of institutions and serving a new spectrum of purposes and community of interests. The diffusion of these ideas, encouraged by the internationalism of European civilization, was effected by travelers, Italians and non-Italians, specialists and non-specialists, who circulated between Italy and key points in the rest of Europe.

European civilization from the fifth through the sixteenth century was both unified and international. The two sources of its unity were the Latin language and the Roman Church: it was the achievement of Rome, republic and empire, to knit the Mediterranean world and a large part of western Europe into a single civilization. That civilization had Latin as its main administrative language. Its literature, too, was Latin, although Latin coexisted with the much greater Greek literary and philosophical corpus. With the collapse of Roman political institutions in the western part of the empire from about 500 CE, this linguistic legacy was transferred to the Roman Church. As the church struggled to bind the European regions together in loyalty to the faith, it spoke, wrote, sang, worshiped, and legislated in Latin.

In the absence of Internet, telephone, or postal connections, communication was always personal. It depended on the existence of a traveler, a person who journeyed from one place to another and delivered a message. Very often, the message was delivered orally in the form of a conversation, a sermon, or a speech. Even when information was conveyed in written form—always manuscript, or "written by hand," prior to the late fifteenth century—the letter or the book was carried by a human being and delivered into the hands of the recipient. Readers from the age of modern communications are often charmed, in reading the correspondence from the premodern past, to see quaint references to the trusted courier who carried and delivered the author's letter. Not only letters, but ideas in a broader sense were communicated by the same medium: a human voyager. Civilization was sustained by the circulation of human bearers of knowledge.

Those agents of civilization often crossed boundaries: rivers, seas, forests, mountain ranges, linguistic barriers, and toll collection depots. These, more than political boundaries, demarcated the regions of Europe. In the eighth century, the English-born Alcuin (c. 732–804) taught at Charlemagne's court. In the twelfth, the father of Francis of Assisi traveled as a merchant to France, from where he brought home a wife, the saint's mother. In the thirteenth century, the Holy Roman Emperor Frederick II, a German-speaking Hohenstaufen born of a Byzantine mother, gathered intellectuals and artists from Arab and Provençal lands to promote the arts and letters. Later in the century, Thomas Aquinas (1224/1225–1274), born near Aquino in southern Italy, journeyed to Paris to study and remained a scholar at that university.

In addition, university students traveled far from home to seek advanced training and lived with their compatriots as distinct groups, called "nations," within the university student body. Merchants, too, journeyed great distances, such as Marco Polo (c. 1254–1324) whose memoirs offer to the Western world a first glimpse of China. The crusaders who in the twelfth and thirteenth centuries explored the eastern Mediterranean and the Italian sailors and merchants who transported and equipped them, returned with new perceptions and ambitions. Multitudes of pilgrims journeyed to the holy sites of Compostela, Canterbury, Rome, and Jerusalem, to name only the most important, and returned with stories to tell. Thus, communication was achieved by the movement of persons who were observers, reporters, consumers, and distributors of ideas, and this was the context in which the Renaissance took place.

Although the Renaissance was Italian in origin, from the first it was touched by information from other regions. Dante and Petrarch (see Chapter 2) spent important formative years in Paris and Avignon, while Boccaccio's mother was probably French. The presence in Italy of the Greek statesman and scholar Manuel Chrysoloras was of pivotal importance, opening the gateway to Greek learning in the West (see Chapter 3). A generation later, Greek scholars in attendance at the Council of Ferrara/Florence stimulated further explorations of the ancient literary and philosophical traditions. Toward the end of the fifteenth century, Greek scholars were essential employees in the print shops then engaged in the publication of ancient texts.

The universities of Bologna and Padua, among others, trained students from the many "nations" of Europe, defined linguistically. Among those who came to study in Italy were Conrad Celtis (1459–1508), the founder of humanistic studies in the German lands; Reginald Pole (1500–1558), an Englishman of royal descent who declared himself a supporter of the Roman Church and pope when King Henry VIII (r. 1509–1547) committed his nation to the Reformation; and the Polish priest Nicholas Copernicus, originator of the modern planetary system (see Chapter 11).

The Englishmen William Grocyn (c. 1446–1519) and John Colet (c. 1467–1519), contemporaries of Erasmus, studied for years in Italy before returning to England, where they played pivotal roles in launching the humanist tradition in that nation. Artists, as well as intellectuals, came to Italy and took back to their homelands the methods and ideas of the Italian Renaissance. Among these were the German Albrecht Dürer (1471–1528) and the Fleming Peter Paul Rubens (1577–1640), both strongly influenced by Italian models. It would later be obligatory for foreign-born artists to study at some point in Italy, as it would become common for young gentlemen from abroad to finish off their aristocratic educations with a "grand tour" that included Italy. This was a custom that the English humanist Roger Ascham (1515–1568) deplored in his 1570 educational manual *The Scholemaster*.

Others came not to study but to work: Erasmus came to work in Aldus's print shop in Venice in 1507–1508. His admirer and follower, the Spanish humanist Juan de Valdés (c. 1490–1541), an exile from the Inquisition, took refuge in Naples, where he became a participant in the intellectual and spiritual movements of Italy's own truncated Reformation.

Just as foreigners hungry for knowledge or experience of Italy's Renaissance descended over the Alps, Italians journeying abroad communicated their new consciousness to residents of foreign capitals. When in England from 1418 to 1423, the humanist Poggio

Bracciolini brought news of the new learning to a region that was, by his standards, quite laggard, and encouraged Duke Humphrey of Gloucester (1391–1447) to endow the library that is still the core of the Oxford University collection. The humanist Enea Silvio Piccolomini, later Pope Pius II, spent the years 1442 to 1447 in Vienna. Other Italian intellectuals abroad included **evangelicals** (see p. 316), heretical or unorthodox thinkers in flight from the Inquisition, who settled in several different northern European centers according to the pattern of their religious beliefs.

Several Italian artists were tempted abroad by foreign patrons. Among them was the multi-talented artist Leonardo da Vinci (see Chapter 4), who accepted the invitation of King Francis I to go to France in 1516, where, holding the title of "first painter, architect, and engineer," he stayed until his death in 1519. The acclaimed sculptor and goldsmith Benvenuto Cellini (1500–1571), similarly, lived and worked in France from 1540 to 1541, also under the patronage of Francis I, who actively recruited Italian talent to refurbish his *châteaux* (country residences) and palaces. Other European monarchs, including those of eastern Europe and the new czars of Russia, also summoned Italian artists and architects to their capitals.

PRINTING, HUMANISM, AND REFORM

The greatest cultural emissary of the era, however, was the printing press. It was in its infancy in the 1400s, but by 1500 the technology of print made a massive contribution to European civilization. Printing speeded up the circulation of ideas. More, it transformed the ideas themselves, as intellectuals thought and expressed themselves differently and as audiences multiplied and readers reinvented the process of reading as a silent, private pursuit. The printed book, multiplied in its translations and editions, contained not only abstract ideas but a whole new ideal of life.

The Manuscript Book

The distinction between the preprint age and the age of print is one of the sharpest lines in Western history. The manuscript book was a unique object; the printed book was a replicable image of a standardized, approved text. It was an epochal "agent of change," as the author of an important print history has named it, that transformed a Western civilization already reshaped by a Renaissance and soon to undergo a Reformation.

The manuscript book, or **codex**, consisted of parchment or, after about 1200, paper sheets stitched together at one side. It stored much more information than the papyrus scroll of the Romans and replaced that earlier form of the book in the late antique period. A manuscript was written by one person (the scribe) for one person (the patron) or one community (monastery, cathedral college, or school). It was a private communication that

1450–1499

c. 1455 Gutenberg's Bible, first printed book in Europe, is published.

1474 William Caxton, working in Bruges (modern Belgium), prints the first book in English.

1478 The Spanish Inquisition is founded to root out and extinguish heresy.

1500–1549

1504 Dutch humanist scholar Desiderius Erasmus publishes *Handbook of the Christian Soldier*.

1511 Erasmus publishes his satirical masterpiece, *The Praise of Folly*.

1514–1517 The Complutensian Polyglot Bible, in parallel Hebrew, Greek, and Latin texts, is published in Spain.

1516 Erasmus's *New Testament* in Greek is printed by Johannes Froben's press in Basel.

1516 English humanist Sir Thomas More publishes *Utopia*.

1517 Martin Luther nails his 95 theses against the sale of church indulgences to a Wittenberg church door.

1520 Luther's *Babylonian Captivity of the Church* attacks the papacy.

1521 Luther defends his views at the Diet of Worms, but is excommunicated.

1523 Spanish humanist Juan Luis Vives publishes *The Education of Christian Women*.

1525 Luther condemns a peasant uprising partly inspired by his religious teachings.

1529 Erasmus publishes *On the Education of Children*.

1529 Lutheran princes set up the Schmalkald League to defend their faith.

1529 Ottoman Turks besiege and nearly capture the city of Vienna.

1534 King Henry VIII is declared supreme head of the English church.

1534 John of Leyden rules a short-lived Anabaptist egalitarian state in Münster, Westphalia.

1535 More is executed for refusing to recognize Henry VIII as head of the church.

1536 Death of Erasmus.

1536 First printed edition of John Calvin's *Institutes of the Christian Religion*.

1539 Ignatius of Loyola's Society of Jesus (the Jesuits) is approved by the pope.

1541 Calvin establishes religious rule in Geneva.

1542 The Roman Inquisition is created to stamp out heresy.

1545–1563 The Council of Trent affirms papal prerogatives, the cult of saints, sacramental orthodoxy.

1550–1599

1553–1558 Mary Tudor briefly reestablishes Catholicism in England.

1555 Peace of Augsburg leaves German princes free to choose between Lutheranism and Catholicism.

1558 Elizabeth I becomes Queen of England, returning the country to Protestantism.

1559 The Vatican produces the first Roman index, the Index of Prohibited Books, condemning Erasmus's works.

1562–1598 Wars of Religion in France between Catholics and Calvinist Huguenots.

1563 First English-language edition of John Foxe's *Book of Martyrs*.

1598 French King Henry IV grants religious toleration to Huguenots by the Edict of Nantes.

1600–1650

1618–1648 The Thirty Years' War between Catholics and Protestants in Europe.

1642–1648 The English Civil War leads to the fall of Catholic-leaning King Charles I.

1649 Puritan domination of Britain under Cromwell's Commonwealth begins.

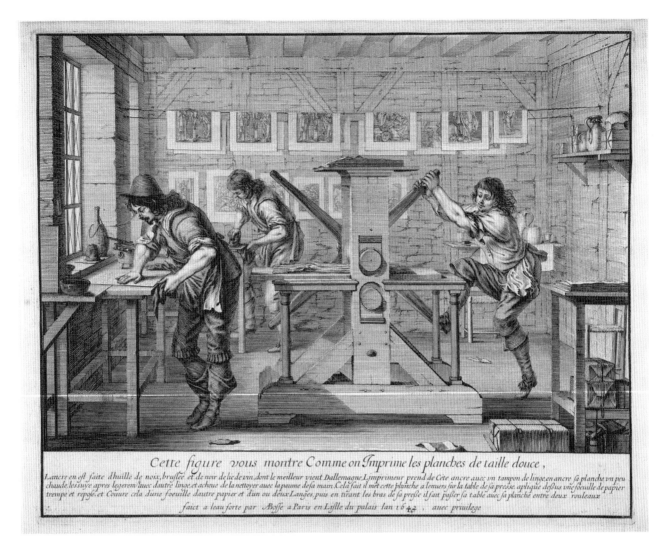

Cette figure vous montre Comme on Imprime les planches de taille douce,

Lancre en est faite dhuille de noix, bruslee, et de noir de lie de vin, dont le meilleur vient Dallemagne, L'imprimeur prend de Cete ancre auec vn tampon de linge, en ancre sa planche vn peu chaude, les suye apres legerem/auec dautre linge, et acheue de la nettoyer auec la paume de sa main, Cela fait il met cette planche a lemure sur la table de sa presse, aplique deßus vne foeuille de papier trempe et reposé, et Couure cela d'une foeuille dautre papier et d'un ou deux Langes, puis en tirant les bras de sa preße il fait paßer sa table auec sa planche entre deux rouleaux

faict a leau forte par Bosse a Paris en L'Isle du palais l'an 1642, auec priuilege

reached a larger audience mainly by being read aloud. In the monastic refectory (dining room), one person read aloud to instruct the community. In the university classroom, the professor read aloud; the reading, or *lectura*, is the origin of our concept of the academic lecture. The manuscript book took a long time to copy, which—beyond the sacredness of the text itself—accounted for its rarity and its value. Moreover, they were often illustrated, or illuminated, by expert miniaturists, whose beautiful work added to the objects' prestige.

The advent of the university after 1200 created an audience of students and professors insatiably hungry for books, and manuscript production became more routine. Professional stationers subcontracted the work of copying and illustrating sections of text and of binding and distributing. This was the system in place when the Italian humanists began to revive the study of classical texts and to circulate new commentaries or translations of them. Even with this standardization, prestige manuscripts for important patrons continued to be produced and became more splendid and numerous than before. Wealthy men   not

Bosse, Interior of an intaglio printer's shop, 1642, etching.

Print technology was nearly 200 years old when this etching of a print shop was made. Note the apprentice working the press, other craftsmen setting type and readying sheets, and inked sheets hanging to dry overhead.

just ecclesiastical institutions or individual scholars—began to gather books in personal libraries (see table p. 75). Whereas once the possession of just a few books was common, now humanists or patrons owned libraries of hundreds of books. Petrarch, who collected his famous personal library at the outset of the Renaissance, owned several hundred.

The Printed Book: Early Years

The demand for university books, which stimulated the acceleration of book production through subcontracting and outsourcing, lay behind the invention of the printing press by several individuals during the 1440s. Early progress toward printing with movable type had been made in China and Korea by the fifteenth century, but it was Europe that progressed beyond that technology to devise a machine that could print text rapidly on two sides of multiple sheets of paper from movable letter forms set in a frame. Johann Gutenberg (c. 1397–1468) is generally given the credit for this invention, which drew on several technologies borrowed from other crafts such as papermaking and the minting of coins. He opened a commercial print shop in Mainz that published such items as papal letters of indulgence and, in 1455, the first printed Bible. Printing remained an affair of German entrepreneurs for a further two decades, and it was they who planted the new technology in Italy, fertile ground for that innovation. In 1465 two German printers established a press at Subiaco, about 50 miles from Rome, which provided an enormous pool of potential book buyers in the vast army of papal secretaries and bureaucrats. In 1469 the German Nicholas Jenson (c. 1420–1480) opened the first print shop in Venice. Italy thus took the lead in printing in precisely the generation when Italian humanism reached the climax of its development. By 1480 there were about 50 print shops in Italy, to about 30 in Germany. In France there were only a few shops in Paris and Lyon. Likewise there was only a scattering of print shops in England, where the entrepreneur William Caxton (c. 1421–1491) printed the first English book in 1477, or in Poland and Hungary, which opened their first presses in the 1470s. Other regions in Europe only entered the print age in the decades after 1500.

Books were published in editions of several hundred at first, then 1,000 or more, and sold commercially. Printers might seek a patron to underwrite the cost of the edition, promote its sale, or protect its author from attack. The audience of the book, however, was understood from the outset to be far greater than a single individual or community. The process of publication was now a mechanical task (although it involved the intellectual labor of proofreaders, copyeditors, and compositors), which established a new form of text. Over the first 50 years of printing—the era of *incunabula*—printing served the academic and religious establishment, as had the stationers who organized the production of manuscript books in the decades before. The books needed were, above all, religious works, and principally the Bible. Secondarily, course books for the study of grammar, philosophy, medicine, theology, and law were in demand. The first books printed and the last books mass produced in manuscript met the same market needs and were the same books.

By the era of Aldo Manuzio (see Chapter 3), who established a Venetian print shop in 1493, the terrain had changed. Generations of humanists had gathered, examined, and corrected numerous texts of Latin, Greek, and Hebrew authors, and humanists were busy codifying the classical tradition for the first time since antiquity. Purged and polished editions of Cicero and Tacitus, Aristotle and Plato slid off the presses, in inexpensive **quarto** and octavo formats that anyone could buy and slip into their pocket, and were snapped up by a European-wide readership. They were accompanied by commentaries and soon by translations into those European vernaculars that had crystallized into modern languages: Italian, Spanish, French, English, German, Dutch, Polish, and more.

The Printed Book: Later Developments

By the early years of the sixteenth century, the religious and secular classics were still staples of printing. Modern, secular works, however, were increasingly published as printers discovered that the public's appetite was building. Volumes of Boccaccio and Petrarch, Ariosto and Erasmus, Machiavelli and Castiglione spun off the presses. The mounting availability of print texts encouraged literacy, and the expanded audience also sought out the lighter fare of popular romances, travel literature, and history. In time, they would read the new literary reviews and news reports printed serially monthly, weekly, or even daily.

Often popular vernacular works were illustrated with woodcut prints, a technology that matured alongside the development of print type. Books laid out so that large illustrations were explained by the accompanying printed text were attractive, especially to new readers. Some of the era's greatest artists created such book illustrations and cartoons: Albrecht Dürer; Lucas Cranach (1472–1553), called "the painter of the Reformation"; and Hans Holbein the Younger (c. 1497–1543), painter of Erasmus, Thomas More, and King Henry VIII. For those readers not ready for books, single sheet **broadsides** carried enough text to deliver a simple message. That message could strike fear in the hearts of the powerful, as in 1534–1535, when printed handouts attacking the Catholic mass circulated. King Francis I responded by closing print shops and sending large numbers of printers and intellectuals into exile. The presses could also set texts in musical notation. Ordinary ballads were popular in a world where music was most often performed by amateurs and at home; members of reformed churches snatched up hymnals, which contained the Psalms translated into the vernacular and set to music for group singing.

Print technology spread rapidly from Italy and Germany. The printer Johannes Froben (1460–1527) had established an important house in Basel (Switzerland) by 1516. By 1500, too, printing was underway in Spain. Cardinal Jiménez de Cisneros's polyglot Bible, printed in 1514–1517, was an early product (see Chapter 10). In France the humanist reformer Lefèvre d'Etaples (c. 1455–1536) published vernacular translations of the New Testament and the Psalms. In 1476 the entrepreneur William Caxton had brought the art to England, encouraged by royal and noble patrons. He completed about 100 editions in his lifetime, many of

THE ENGLISH CENTURY: REFORMATION AND RENAISSANCE FROM HENRY TO ELIZABETH

Renaissance and Reformation coincided in England in a way not experienced elsewhere in Europe. In Italy, the Renaissance took shape nearly two centuries before the Protestant challenge evoked a **Counter-Reformation** response. In the German lands, humanism preceded and encouraged the germination of Reformation ideas. In Spain, there was no Reformation. Instead, an aggressive Inquisition targeted mainly *conversos* (converted Jews) and Moors during the years when Reformation ideology took hold further north. In France, as in the German lands, humanism prepared for the Reformation, but then the reform movement went underground, and tensions between Protestant and Catholic erupted into war. In England, in contrast, Reformation set the stage for Renaissance.

Despairing of a legitimate male heir, the English King Henry VIII took advantage of the mounting Reformation movement to restructure the church in England, removing it from the influence of the papacy. With the king (rather than the pope) as head of the church, two benefits would accrue: first, Henry would strengthen his regime with the added authority residing in religious supremacy; second, more urgently, he would be free to cast off his first wife (whose one child was female) and marry a second whose apparent fertility augured well for a male heir to the throne.

Henry broke with Rome, the English Parliament enacting the rupture by approving his divorce. In 1533 Henry married Anne Boleyn. In 1534 Parliament passed the Act of Supremacy, making Henry head of the church in England.

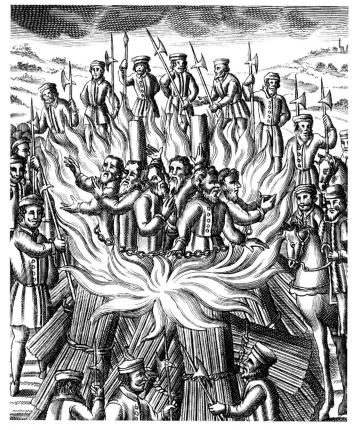

Foxe, from the *Book of Martyrs: Containing an Account of the Sufferings and Death of the Protestants in the Reign of Queen Mary the First*, c. 1555.

The Ten Articles of 1536 and Six Articles of 1539 established the principles of correct belief in this new church established for the sake of the king. Further, Parliament dissolved the monasteries and convents, whose land titles went to the king and whose treasure found its way into the royal coffers. The beautiful windows, vestments, bells, all the sacred objects a loving people had bestowed upon these sacred institutions, were stolen, lost, or ruined. The buildings themselves, sold to eager bidders, became the country houses of the nobility and gentry.

The king and his supporters were fervent Protestants, or at least fervent opponents of Rome. Thomas More was one of the few to resist the royal decision. Many ordinary people, too, remained Catholic in outlook and habit, even as the order of worship changed as directed from the top. When Henry died, the regent and advisors of his young son Edward VI (r. 1547–1553)—not a child of Anne Boleyn, but of Henry's third wife (of six)—sought earnestly to institutionalize the Protestant faith.

Edward died young, to be succeeded (after the nine-day rule of a rival claimant) by Henry's elder daughter. An ardent Catholic, Mary (r. 1553–1558) soon married Philip II, King of Spain, to the distress of both Protestants (who feared Philip's aggressive Catholic agenda) and nationalists (who resented having English policy dictated by Spain). Mary moved swiftly to reverse the tide of Protestantism. Many Protestants recanted and returned to the Catholic fold, while thousands fled to asylum in Protestant parts of the Netherlands or the German lands. Hundreds were martyred. Their heroic resistance and deaths were celebrated in the mammoth *Book of Martyrs* by the Protestant apologist John Foxe, published in Latin in 1559, then in an English translation as *Actes and Monuments of These Latter and Perillous Dayes* in 1563, and in revised editions in 1570, 1576, and 1583. For English readers it was the most important of the many martyrologies that this bloody century produced.

When Mary died, Henry's second daughter and middle child came to the throne. Elizabeth (r. 1558–1603) was the daughter of Anne Boleyn and of questionable legitimacy. Twenty-five years old at her succession, she had spent much of her youth in fear, vulnerable to exile, torture, or execution because of dynastic and religious turmoil. Would she, whose own religious observances tended to the Catholic, reverse Mary's terror and restore Protestantism and her father's Church of England? Was she capable of ruling, or, as the leader of the Scottish reformers charged, was governance by women intrinsically unnatural and doomed to failure? Would she marry and deliver England's destiny to the master of some other nation?

Elizabeth in fact ruled brilliantly, cognizant of the limits on a female monarch but determined to uphold the dignity of the throne and the prerogatives of the monarch. She considered several suitors, both royal and noble, foreign and domestic, but determined not to marry, no doubt so as to preserve both England's autonomy and her own. By two Acts of Supremacy and Uniformity of 1559, she restored England to the Protestant fold—although it was a very moderate Protestantism, and Elizabeth's own beliefs remained private and unknowable.

It was during Elizabeth's reign that the English Renaissance flowered, producing William Shakespeare and Edmund Spenser, Sir Philip Sydney and John Donne, among many poets, playwrights, and humanists. In music and philosophy, as well, the Elizabethan age was a peak of innovation and dynamism. From the terrors of religious crisis and the uncertainties of national identity, a new consciousness emerged that was wholly English and largely Protestant. In a setting very different from that of the city-states of Italy in the age of Petrarch, the Renaissance in England was shaped by the Reformation and the political structures that summoned it into being.

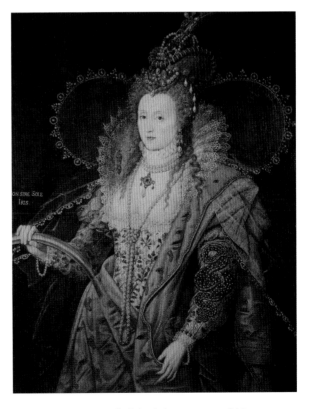

Oliver, *"Rainbow Portrait" of Elizabeth I*, c. 1600. Hatfield House, Hertfordshire. Collection of the Marquess of Salisbury.

What kinds of things did early printers print? Here are two snapshots of printing output in two different settings. The graph on the left shows the main categories for late-fifteenth-century Venice. The graph on the right shows very different categories for Strasbourg, 1515–1548. A major reason for the difference was the impact in the northern city of the Protestant Reformation. Protestant devotional and polemical works dominated the printing enterprise during this first generation of the Reformation. Also notable is the quantity of vernacular and school-text publications. Strasbourg, now a city in modern France, was a free city within the Holy Roman Empire in Renaissance times.

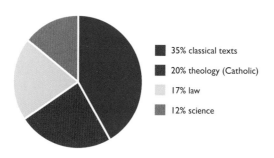

- 35% classical texts
- 20% theology (Catholic)
- 17% law
- 12% science

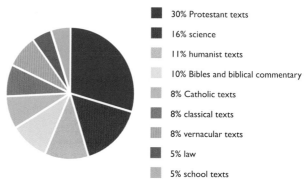

- 30% Protestant texts
- 16% science
- 11% humanist texts
- 10% Bibles and biblical commentary
- 8% Catholic texts
- 8% classical texts
- 8% vernacular texts
- 5% law
- 5% school texts

Editions in Venice, 1469–1480

(B. Richardson, *Print Culture in Renaissance Italy: The Editor and the Vernacular Text, 1470–1600*. Cambridge, MA: Cambridge University Press, 1994, p. 28; taken from Victor Scholderer, *Fifty Essays in Fifteenth- and Sixteenth-Century Bibliography*, ed. D.E. Rhodes. Amsterdam: Menno Hertzberger and Co., 1966, p. 88.)

Editions in Strasbourg, 1515–1548

(M.U. Chrisman, *Lay Culture, Learned Culture: Books and Social Change in Strasbourg, 1480–1599*. New Haven, CT: Yale University Press, 1982, Appendix, p. 298.)

works he translated himself from French, Dutch, and Latin. Print shops were founded in Mexico City in 1539, in Goa (India) in 1556, in Moscow in 1563, and in Nagasaki (Japan) in 1590. The print revolution coincided with the era of European exploration, and printed material accompanied those ventures from the outset (see Chapter 11). Indeed, it was in Anglo-America in 1734, with the libel trial of the German-born printer and journalist John Peter Zenger (1697–1746), that the principle of press freedom made its first appearance.

The development of print after 1500 also coincided with the Protestant Reformation, which some scholars have argued would not have succeeded without the medium of print. The works of Erasmus and other early reformers were snatched up by a public hungry for an alternative to the often incomprehensible announcements of the old church. Luther's three revolutionary tracts of 1520 (see p. 313) were sold in thousands of copies. *Institutes of the Christian Religion* by John Calvin (1509–1564), an encyclopedia of the principles of Calvinist, or Reformed Protestantism, circulated throughout Europe in several editions completed between 1536 and 1559.

Cartoons and broadsides effectively spread the message of religious revolution to a large audience. When the defenders of the different faiths had destroyed large numbers of their enemies by fire, drowning, and sword, the stories of those who proved their loyalty with their lives filled the printed volumes of martyrologies. The most famous of these was almost a second Bible for English-speaking Protestants: the *Book of Martyrs* (see p. 298), published by the clergyman John Foxe (1516–1587) in Latin in 1559, and, an expanded edition in English in 1563. The Catholic Church responded in kind, making ample use of the press to circulate the decrees of the Council of Trent, the records of the spiritual heroism of the saints, and the history of missionary ventures. The papacy employed Paolo Manuzio (Paulus Manutius, 1512–1574), the son of Aldo, as its official printer in 1561, paying him the large salary of 500 ducats per year to keep Rome supplied with devotional and theological texts. On both the Protestant and Catholic sides, the spate of publishing encouraged literacy, and it was the churches that more than any other institution took on the challenge of basic education for the masses.

ERASMUS, MORE, AND VIVES

Among the first authors to write for the printing press were the three great Christian humanists of the northern Renaissance: Erasmus, More, and Vives. Like the Italian humanists, they looked to the classics of Greece and Rome as a standard of thought and imagination. Even more than most Italian humanists, however, their concerns ranged beyond what could be learned directly from ancient texts. They saw in the revival of these texts the basis for the moral regeneration of society.

Erasmus

For Erasmus, the new humanistic learning was the path to a life that was joyous, pious, and pleasant. Old learning was characterized by rote memorization and the angry debates of scholars in the university; these practices pointed the way to ignorance, laziness, and corruption. For Erasmus, truth and goodness coincided just as much as they did for Petrarch (see Chapter 2) or, long before, for the Greek philosopher Plato.

Classical and Christian Texts The young Erasmus pursued the humanist mission with enthusiasm. His collection of *Adagia* ("Proverbs," 1508) from classical texts, requiring a thorough mastery of ancient literature, won him his reputation as a scholar. Later, his *De copia* ("Foundations of the Abundant Style") provided writers in Latin with models of a rich variety of sentences and expressions. Published by Aldus in 1509, the *De copia* was seen through the press in person by the author, who lived in the printer's residence with his staff of editors and proofreaders. Beyond these works that drew on secular texts, Erasmus turned to classics of the Christian tradition. His edition of the New Testament in Greek (accompanied, beginning with the second edition of 1519, by a new Latin trans-lation) derived directly from early manuscripts. It was a controversial text, inspired by Valla's scriptural criticism, that revised many of the readings that had been accepted as authoritative in the Latin Vulgate. Printed at Basel in 1516, it was the foremost product

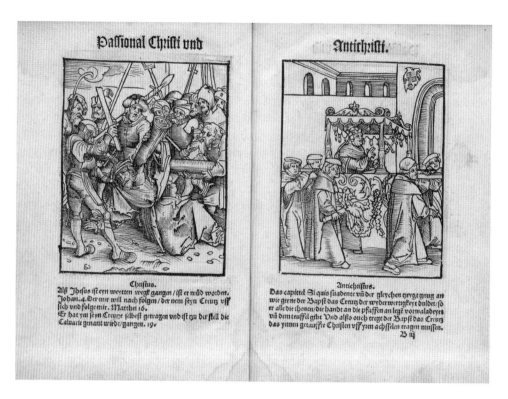

Cranach the Elder, from
Passional Christi et Antichristi,
texts by Melanchthon
and Schwerdtfeger, 1521,
engravings. Wittenberg.

On the left, Christ crowned with
thorns is suffering under the
burden of the cross, while on the
right, the pope is conveyed in
pomp on his litter.

of Froben's press, and the revised 1519 version was used by Martin Luther in his German translation of the Bible of 1522. In 1516, too, Erasmus published his edition of the works of St. Jerome. Jerome was a kindred soul to Erasmus: a scholar and a Christian who reconciled his love of learning and his love of God. Jerome was the author of the Vulgate translation which Erasmus had now superseded and was a critical reader and translator of Scripture in his own right.

The *Philosophia Christi* Erasmus's scholarly commitment to a joint classical and Christian antiquity was the foundation of his moral commitment to a sincere and demystified Christian life. According to Erasmus, Jesus in the New Testament taught simple truths about leading a pious life, doing good deeds, and trusting in God. What the Bible offered, in fact, was the *philosophia Christi* (philosophy of Christ), plainer and purer than all other philosophies. Christians who sought to draw close to God and to win the salvation of their souls, had only to adhere to the simple golden truths of the *philosophia Christi*. All else meant nothing—the elaborate rituals of the church, the panoply of saints, relics, and pilgrimages, the thundering and artful sermons of the friars, the litter of papal bulls, **excommunications**, indulgences, and decrees. Erasmus did not urge that they be abolished, merely that they be understood for what they were: irrelevant to a truly pious life.

This was the message that Erasmus conveyed to a Europe hungry for direct communication about Christian experience. In his *Enchiridion militis christiani* ("Handbook of the Christian Soldier") of 1504, Erasmus laid out the principles of the Christian life: a menu of sincere repentance, good deeds, and deep meditation on the word of God. In *Julius exclusus* ("Julius Excluded from Heaven"), published in 1517 or 1518, anonymous but most likely his, Erasmus offered a biting satire on the corruption of the Renaissance papacy and especially that of Julius II, the warrior pope. His *Colloquia* ("Colloquies"), published after 1518, brief dialogues written for the classroom instruction of Latin, were also witty and pointed critiques of the rituals of the church and the misguided, ignorant beliefs of the faithful.

The *Praise of Folly* The *Moriae encomium* ("Praise of Folly"), published in 1511, is Erasmus's masterpiece. In this extended monologue by the character "Folly"—a mythological female figure in jester's garb—everything in Erasmus's world is subjected to criticism: both things he thinks are wrong, corrupt, or misguided, such as self-indulgent monks, pompous schoolteachers, and ignorant theologians, and those that he considers holy, such as sacrificing oneself to God and trusting in the mystery of the cross. Since in either case—as in any of the statements of this brilliantly shifting, multi-faceted work—the spokesperson is Folly, what is said is not to be believed; or perhaps it is to be believed because the profound wisdom of the fool, paradoxically, is greater than the pretenses of those who think themselves wise. In any case, with Folly as his intermediary, Erasmus intended to escape responsibility for his scathing attack on the contemporary church and society.

Two examples may illustrate Erasmus's versatile use of the character Folly to convey, indirectly, his perception of the world. Folly mocks schoolteachers who:

> Forever hungry and dirty in their classrooms—classrooms, did I say? No, "think-tanks," or rather sweat-shops or torture chambers—tending flocks of boys, they grow old in their labors, grow deaf from the noise, waste away in the stink and stench, and yet … imagine they are the luckiest of mortals—so powerful is their flattering delusion while they terrify the timid band of pupils with threatening words and scowls and beat the poor wretches bloody with rods, switches, and straps.

> (D. Erasmus, *The Praise of Folly*, trans. C.H. Miller. New Haven, CT: Yale University Press, 1975, p. 79)

Here, Folly is a critic, pointing out the problems of ignorance, cruelty, and self-importance among those who teach the young. In this next passage, however, she mocks something which, for Erasmus, is the summit of worthiness:

> No fools seem more senseless than those people who have completely taken up, once and for all, with a burning devotion to Christian piety: they throw away their possessions, ignore injuries, allow themselves to be deceived, make no distinction between friend and foe, shudder at the thought of pleasure, find satisfaction in fasts, vigils, tears, and labors, shrink from life, desire death above all else…. Can such a condition be called anything but insanity?

> (Erasmus, *The Praise of Folly*, p. 132)

This Christian folly, for Erasmus, was wisdom.

Educational and Social Ideals Although the Christian message was paramount in Erasmus's works, he blended it with other moral and social concerns. He was deeply concerned with education, a theme that pervaded his *Colloquies*. In a sense, his textual studies all served educational purposes as well. His most important educational work, however, was his *De pueris instituendis* ("On the Education of Children"), published in 1529. Like the pedagogical works of Pier Paolo Vergerio and Enea Silvio Piccolomini addressed to the young children of rulers (see Chapter 3), this work was dedicated to the 13-year-old son of the Duke of Cleves.

Erasmus's *Institutio principis christiani* ("The Education of the Christian Prince") was published in 1516 and dedicated to the future Emperor Charles V, whom Erasmus served as advisor. Here too the educational theme was explicit. The advice Erasmus gave, however, was suited not just for princes, but for any family undertaking the education of a child. The baby should be nursed and taught by his mother, not a hired nurse. Although necessarily in women's care in infancy, the child should be removed from women's authority as early as possible and put in the hands of a tutor of sound morals and judgment to be protected from immorality, rudeness, and brutality. From an early age, he should be instructed in Latin and Greek, and introduced to the great works of the classical and Christian traditions. Beyond these specific recommendations, Erasmus urged the civilizing task of education in a larger sense:

> Nature, the mother of all things, has equipped brute animals with more means to fulfill the functions of their species; but to man alone she has given the faculty of reason, and so she has thrown the burden of human growth upon education. Therefore it is right to say that the beginning and the end, indeed the total sum of man's happiness, are founded upon a good upbringing and education.
>
> (Rummel, *The Erasmus Reader*, p. 68)

The Education of the Christian Prince also advises a young prince on how to rule. Erasmus calls on the prince to act according to the high standards of morality. He should not, for instance, overtax his subjects—indeed, he should be especially conscious of the condition of the poor: "For it is perhaps politic to summon the rich to austerity, but to reduce poor people to hunger and servitude is both very cruel and very risky." The prince should avoid flatterers: if anyone calls him "your Highness" or "your Majesty," he should recall that these titles "are valid only for someone who governs his realm according to the example of God." Rather than marry a foreign princess, creating a tie and obligation that can result in conflict, the prince should marry a woman "who is distinguished among her fellows by her honesty, modesty, and prudence ... and will bear him children worthy of both parents and of their country." War is the great scourge of nations: "the good prince will never start a war at all unless, after everything else has been tried, it cannot by any means be avoided."

Erasmus returned to the theme of war in his *Querela pacis* ("A Complaint of Peace"), published in 1517, and his *De bello turcico* ("On the War against the Turks"), published in 1530. In *Querela*, the character "Peace," reminiscent of "Folly" but far more somber, delivers a monologue on the evil of war. In just the last 10 years, "where in the world has there not been savage warfare on land and sea? What land has not been soaked in Christian blood, what river or sea not stained with human gore?" Peace calls on princes to find ways to make peace: "You see that hitherto nothing has been achieved by treaties, nothing advanced by alliances, nothing by violence or revenge. Now try instead what conciliation and kindness can do." In the latter work, Erasmus acknowledged the aggression of the Ottoman Turks—in 1526 they had vanquished a European army at Mohács (modern Hungary) and in 1529 besieged and nearly captured Vienna—but still responded with a plea for peace:

> Whenever the ignorant mob hear the name "Turk," they immediately fly into a rage and clamour for blood, calling them dogs and enemies to the name of Christian; it does not occur to them that … the Turks are men…. [Victory over the Turks] will be all the more acceptable to Christ if, instead of slaughtering the Turks, we manage to join them to us in a common faith and observance.
>
> (Rummel, *The Erasmus Reader*, p. 324)

Turning from the darker subject of war, Erasmus also concerned himself with how middle-class boys, armed with humanist educations, should manage themselves in elite settings and polite society. His widely read *De civilitate* ("On Good Manners") was published in Latin in 1530 and quickly translated into English (1532), German (1536), French (1537), and Czech (1537). Dedicated to 11-year-old Henry of Veere, it counseled the young sons of the urban middle classes how to eat politely and comport themselves in society. He recommended, for instance, that "the nostrils should be free from any filthy collection of mucus, as this is disgusting." Aspiring gentlemen should avoid yawning in public, keep their teeth white, and refrain from immediately devouring food served at table: "That is the behaviour of wolves." Yet good manners were not just a matter of rules for Erasmus, who did not like rules, but of moral character: "The essence of good manners consists in freely pardoning the shortcomings of others although nowhere falling short of yourself."

Erasmus and Reform Erasmus's commitment to the study of ancient texts, to the *philosophia Christi*, and to education as a solution for social ills, led him into a conflict he did not seek. His criticisms of the Roman Church delighted the advocates of a growing movement that ended not with reforming the old church, but creating new ones. Erasmus's humanist mission, in fact, coincided with the early stages of the Protestant Reformation. To his distress, the reformers counted him as one of theirs. The Church of Rome did so as well. Erasmus did all he could to avoid identification with the reform movement and feared the vengeance of either Protestant or Catholic crowds, the fear shifting as he changed his place of residence. His works were banned in Catholic Spain from the early days of the Reformation and were promptly listed in several of the versions of the *Index librorum prohibitorum* ("The Index of Prohibited Books") published in the sixteenth century.

Although Erasmus attempted to avoid the issue of reform, he could not ignore one central principle that it embraced: the "bondage of the will" as Luther phrased it. In Luther's theology, the human will was committed either to good or to evil, either God or the devil. It could not act freely, other than to accept, if it was offered, the grace of God.

THE ENCHANTMENTS OF NOWHERE

Among the inventions of the Renaissance was a place called Nowhere, the meaning behind the Greek words *ou* (not) and *topos* (place) that the English statesman and humanist Sir Thomas More used in his compound neologism "Utopia," the title of his epochal book published in 1516. The significations of the word are manifold: Utopia exists, but in a mental realm that has no real place; Utopia is perfect, but does not really exist; since Utopia does not exist, More cannot be blamed for admiring it; etc.

More was not alone in thinking up alternate societies. Many other Renaissance authors and artists were busy inventing imaginary places. The strange landscape of forests and gardens and castles depicted in the Italian epic *Orlando Furioso* (by Ludovico Ariosto), or the equally strange "fairyland" depicted in the English epic *Faerie Queene* (by Edmund Spenser, 1552/1553–1599) were magical worlds. So were the imagined urban and rural landscapes of Italian artists or the woodcut images in the pioneering fantasy by the monk Francesco Colonna: the *Hypnerotomachia Poliphili* ("The Strife of Love in a Dream of Poliphilus"; published by Aldo Manuzio in 1492).

But More's *Utopia* was different. It was not just an amusing fantasy but an imaginary society whose institutions critiqued those of his own. With the writing of his book, his achievement was closer to that of Greek antecedents than to those of his contemporaries. Plato's *Republic* had presented a utopian society where the most talented and best educated—male or female—ruled the state, suggesting that such an arrangement was not already available; and the idealized Sparta that hovered in Greek literature, as, for instance, in the works of Plutarch, implicitly critiqued the deficiencies of physical and moral training in other Greek cities.

More, too, had much to critique. In *Utopia*, no one owns anything, gold has no more value than a cheap trinket, and all face life chances based on their own capacity rather than inherited wealth. No king is elevated without special merit, denying power to the many capable of exercising good judgment in public affairs. And war is seen as an abomination; the Utopians buy off the enemy, send mercenaries against them, or assassinate the guilty ruler—all methods preferable to the actual horror of war.

Relations between men and women were flawed, *Utopia* audaciously suggested, and the whole institution of the family needed reconstitution. In More's imaginary Nowhere, a young man is able to examine his naked bride before the wedding, and only those who must—because it is their turn—or want to, cook dinner and care for crying children. Quarrels over religion and the pretense that there is one truth offend the Utopians. In *Utopia*, even as Europe readied itself for more than a century of religious violence, all were free to worship as they pleased.

Seventeen years after the publication of *Utopia*, the French monk, physician, and writer François Rabelais described a Utopia of his own in a brief episode of his vast history of *Gargantua and Pantagruel*. The giant Gargantua, bestowing gifts upon his company, endowed a monk with the country of Thélème so that he could build an abbey to his liking. The monk in turn asked Gargantua to constitute its rules.

> "First of all, then," said Gargantua, "you mustn't build walls round it. For all other abbeys have lofty walls." … And because in the religious foundations of this world everything is encompassed, limited, and regulated by hours, it was decreed that there should be no clock or dial at all, but that affairs should be conducted according to chance and opportunity. For Gargantua said that the greatest waste of time he knew was the counting of hours—what good does it do?— and the greatest nonsense in the world was to regulate one's life by the sound of a bell, instead of by the promptings of reason and good sense.
>
> (F. Rabelais, *Gargantua*, trans. J.M. Cohen. London: Penguin, 1955, p. 150)

The Abbey of Thélème, with no walls, clocks, or bells, was to be a place where each resident could live as he desired—or as she desired, since it would also be well stocked with beautiful women. Rather than take vows of poverty, chastity, and obedience, as did ordinary monks and nuns, the residents of this abbey could grow wealthy, marry, and leave whenever they wanted. They lived in luxury (since the abbey was well endowed by Gargantua) and in absolute freedom:

> All their life was regulated not by laws, statutes, or rules, but according to their free will and pleasure. They rose from bed when they pleased, and drank, ate, worked, and slept when the fancy seized them…. So it was that Gargantua had established it. In their rules there was only one clause: DO WHAT YOU WILL.
>
> (Rabelais, *Gargantua*, p. 159)

Freedom—from ignorance, repression, and want—also reigned in the *La città del sole* ("City of the Sun") described in 1602 by a third inventor of Renaissance utopias, the Dominican monk Tommaso Campanella, then a prisoner of the Inquisition. The City of the Sun was a place where God's love and human reason reigned under the guidance of the great Metaphysician. There was no private property, and all citizens contributed according to their abilities and were promoted (but not paid) according to their merits. Women had considerable freedom, and sexual restrictions were loosened beyond any possibility in contemporary society. Children were suckled by their mothers but raised from the age of weaning by publicly appointed teachers. Education was valued, and scientific knowledge—all of it inscribed on the seven walls that enclosed the solarian city—was treasured.

These three Renaissance utopias have some points in common: they dispense with property and labor and honor merit over rank; they envision a different kind of relationship between the sexes; and they value intellectual freedom. The ideas they propose will reappear over the next four centuries in the many utopian visions produced by their successors, beginning with the philosopher Francis Bacon, whose *New Atlantis* was published in 1627. It is precisely the intellectual and moral freedom they envisioned that fell a casualty to totalitarian societies in the dystopias of the twentieth century—negative reversals of utopian visions found in Aldous Huxley's *Brave New World* (1932) and George Orwell's *1984* (1949).

Utopiae Insulae Figura ("Plan of the Island of Utopia"), 1516, illustration to an edition of More's *Utopia*.

Erasmus wrote his *De libero arbitrio* ("On Free Will"), published in 1524, to counter this notion. For Erasmus, as for all humanists, the human beings were principally distinguished by reason, which could prompt them to choose good or evil. The proper use of reason would lead to a choice of the good, and an improper use would lead to the choice of evil. Education could train the rational faculty, and the result of not training it was ignorance. But the human will, guided by the rational faculty, must be free. Luther's *On the Bondage of the Will* (1525) sharply attacked Erasmus's position. On this issue, which was central to their different understandings of the Christian faith, they could not be reconciled.

More and Utopia

In 1535 the English scholar Sir Thomas More was executed because, as a Catholic, he would not support King Henry VIII in his separation from the Roman Church and establishment of the Church of England. Famous for his martyrdom, he already enjoyed wide renown as a humanist and author before his terrible persecution began. His household was a gathering place for intellectuals fired by the new learning, which he imparted even to his daughters. Indeed, his daughter Margaret (1505–1544), who could converse in Latin and Greek, was one of the most learned women in Europe, and Erasmus celebrated her as such. She was her father's chief correspondent in his last years and was herself the author of poems and devotional works. These included a partial edition of the church father Cyprian (c. 200–258 CE), a translation of Eusebius (r. 264–340 CE), and a translation of Erasmus's work on the Lord's Prayer, which circulated widely in her English version. It was her husband, William Roper (1496–1578), a regular member of the More circle, who wrote the biography upon which most of our knowledge of this remarkable man rests.

In addition to Roper's biography, More's own works inform us about this thoughtful and courageous intellectual. His *History of Richard III*, which Shakespeare used in composing his play *Richard III*, is a model of historical writing, showing the author's study of the Roman historian Tacitus. He also composed devotional and polemical works on mostly religious issues and a collection of letters. More's most important work, however, so Erasmian in tone, yet so unlike the others, is his *Utopia*. It was published in Latin for a humanist audience, in 1516.

The word "utopia," in Greek means literally "no place": it either does not exist, or, in an Erasmian tease, the author declines to let you know where or if or whether it ever may someday exist. Utopia today, of course, means more than that: it designates an ideal place, either far away, the creation of another kind of being, or in some future world, where the ills of contemporary society are resolved. The term has acquired that meaning because of More's book, although More himself drew on ancient writings which were in the modern sense utopian. It is he, however, who created the concept and the genre of utopia, and all subsequent utopias refer to his, if only implicitly.

Utopia consists of two books, or parts. The first is a "frame" story, a likely sounding narrative that sets up the circumstances under which the second unfolds. It describes an after-dinner conversation among More and his friends while he is abroad on a diplomatic mission to Antwerp. The conversation begins with a discussion of current happenings in England, including the rise in crime resulting, according to More, from the unabated poverty of the people who have been unfairly victimized by lazy and irresponsible aristocrats. This critique of contemporary society sets the stage for the narration in the second book by one of the guests, the fictional character Raphael Hythloday, who has recently returned from a sea journey. Hythloday mentions that things are done quite differently on the island of Utopia. He is invited to describe its distinctive institutions.

Utopia is a society without private property, which thus avoids the evils of injustice and inequality that More so deplores in the first book. It despises gold and silver—metals that are associated with slaves, who are secured by golden fetters, and chamber pots, which are made of the precious substance. Freedom from property unlocks all its other goods. The citizens live in planned city and country communities, with laborers rotating between work assignments. Private families exist, but marriage is detached from the considerations of dowry and status that burden it in European society; for instance, Utopians believe that the groom should be able to view his naked bride before consenting to the match. Childrearing and dining are communal. Government is representative; there is no king. While border defenses are strong, war is avoided by all possible strategies—including the use of assassination to eliminate the ruler of the state threatening aggression. Utopians are thirsty for knowledge, open-minded, and rational. Freedom of religion is absolute—another clear contrast with Europe at that era which was about to indulge in an orgy of bloodshed in the name of religious conformity to which *Utopia*'s author would soon fall victim.

Like Erasmus, More's commitment to humanistic studies was the foundation of his social vision. Without in any way challenging the idea of God and the tenets of the Christian faith, More believed that human beings could use their reason to build a society that was both moral and just. Utopia was no place; it was just a vision. But something of that vision could be made real, he implied, by human beings on this earth.

Vives and the Erasmian Mission

Like More, Juan Luis Vives (1492–1540) shared Erasmus's intellectual values and his hopes for moral and social regeneration. Born in Valencia (southern Spain), a descendant of rabbis, Vives was the son of Jews who had converted to Christianity as a result of a coercive religious policy. In 1524, when Vives was a student at the University of Paris, his father was condemned by the Inquisition and executed for apostasy (reverting to Jewish practices). Four years later, the body of his mother (who had died in 1508) was exhumed and burnt. These events struck the young man with horror and fear, as we know from his letters. In later life, Vives was properly Catholic in his public statements, and, in the Christian humanist vein, published a commentary on the works of St. Augustine in 1522. The work was dedicated to King Henry VIII and won him an invitation to England, from where, after failing to support the king in his divorce from Catherine of Aragón, he was banished in 1528. He spent the rest of his life as a citizen of Bruges (modern Belgium).

A committed and prolific humanist, Vives rejected what he saw as the narrow technicalities of Scholasticism and advocated a thorough reading and understanding of classical texts. Only such reading would build the capacity for stylistic eloquence and provide the foundation for wisdom. This was the basic outlook of Vives's *Adversus pseudodialecticos* ("Against the Pseudo-Dialecticians") of 1520, an attack on the Scholastic method, and in his educational works. Among the latter, his *De disciplinis* ("On the Disciplines of Knowledge") of 1531 is a vast plea for the preservation and communication of the accumulated wisdom of the species. Published several years earlier, in 1523, his *De ratione studii puerilis* ("On the Right Method of Instruction for Children") is a guide written for the education of Mary Tudor, the daughter of King Henry VIII by his first wife, Catherine of Aragón, and later Queen of England, for whom he served as tutor. In the same year, he published a work of special interest to today's feminist scholars and cultural historians: the *Institutio christianae feminae* ("The Education of a Christian Woman"), dedicated to Catherine of Aragón. In it, Vives does not advise women to defy the narrow social limits imposed on them; indeed, by repeating the view that the preeminent virtue for women is chastity, he assents to prevailing notions of women's inferiority (see Chapter 10). Although he does not urge women to pursue university education or to seek professional or public roles, he does recognize their aptitude for learning and prescribes a serious curriculum that includes not only Latin but the study of the most advanced subjects—philosophy and theology.

Another of Vives's works, one of supreme historic importance, belongs to quite a different genre. His treatise *De subventione pauperum* ("On Assistance to the Poor") of 1526 is a discussion of an important social issue, in which it resembles such works as More's *Utopia* and Erasmus's *Complaint of Peace*. The Catholic Church was the main provider of charity during the Middle Ages. Its schools, hospitals, and refuges of all sorts could not solve all the pain and suffering of the poor, sick, and abandoned in a premodern society, but it relieved a great deal. The problem of urban poverty became critical in the Renaissance era, as urban populations expanded from the eleventh through fourteenth century. Here, too, the church stepped in, and took responsibility for the relief of the poor. It was assisted by wealthy burghers and by city governments that distributed cheap or free food in times of crisis, if only to prevent riot.

By the sixteenth century, however, the zeal to serve a general population of the poor was waning. An urban underclass, which included able-bodied men, seemed to become dependent on poor relief and aroused the anger and resentment of thrifty burghers. Beggars must have included imposters in their number, as well as a great number of impoverished women and children who had no other recourse than to beg. Luther hated beggars, and many newly Protestant towns expelled them or limited their access to relief. In this climate, Vives's response was different. He was not repelled by poverty but moved to find a solution: "The extreme poverty of so many compels me to write how I think they might be assisted." The work was addressed to "the councillors and senate of Bruges," as Vives believed the state, not the church, should take responsibility for the welfare of the poor.

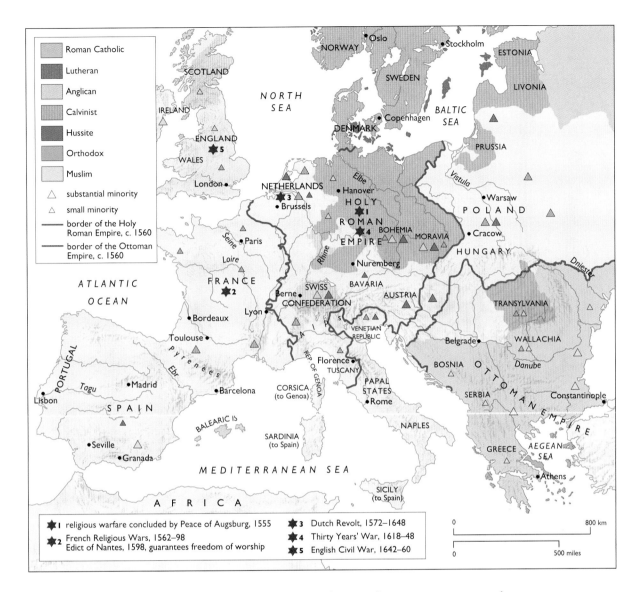

Legend

- Roman Catholic
- Lutheran
- Anglican
- Calvinist
- Hussite
- Orthodox
- Muslim
- △ substantial minority
- △ small minority
- —— border of the Holy Roman Empire, c. 1560
- —— border of the Ottoman Empire, c. 1560

★ **1** religious warfare concluded by Peace of Augsburg, 1555
★ **2** French Religious Wars, 1562–98
Edict of Nantes, 1598, guarantees freedom of worship
★ **3** Dutch Revolt, 1572–1648
★ **4** Thirty Years' War, 1618–48
★ **5** English Civil War, 1642–60

0 — 800 km
0 — 500 miles

Vives recommended the use of funds gathered from voluntary donations to survey and identify the poor. Those who could work should be put to work; those who could not should be sustained with cash subsidies. Abandoned children—girls and boys—should be raised in well-ordered orphanages and taught by the best teachers available since "no greater danger for the sons of the poor exists than a cheap, inferior, and demoralizing education."

For Erasmus, More, and Vives, the reading of ancient texts led to the cultivation of a more rational human being and a more just society. These humanists beyond the Alps saw the goal of classical study to be moral regeneration and not the destruction of the Roman Church or the institution of a Protestant one. They held this position even as Europe was fragmenting into different churches and "confessions," communities of faith sharing a particular creed.

Sixteenth-Century Religious Heterogeneity and Conflict

Northern Europe became largely Protestant. Much of southern Europe remained Catholic. Protestantism also subdivided into several groups (more than are shown here). Calvinists, Lutherans, Orthodox Christians, Hussites, Catholics, and Muslim minorities are shown here.

THE REFORMATIONS AND THE HUMANIST TRADITION

The Protestant Reformation and the Catholic Reformation that it engendered are giant historical processes that effected a radical restructuring of the church in Western Europe. Their many and complex relations to Western thought, politics, and society fall outside the compass of a history of the Renaissance. For the purpose of this narrative, however, it is important to identify those ways in which the Renaissance and Reformation movements intersected and interrelated. To do so, an outline of the two Reformations is provided.

Protestants

The Protestant Reformation had two main causes. First, the people themselves craved a different kind of church. Second, that church was failing the people it was pledged to serve. In a time of rapid change, many people craved a more personal and profound spiritual experience than found in the rituals and messages of the Roman Church. As in Italy (see Chapter 6), lay pious movements abounded in other regions of Europe, and voluntary religious organizations such as confraternities and the communities of the New Devout attracted many followers. Above all, the fear of damnation or the penalties of purgatory gripped the minds of many Christians. To allay this fear, some sought to attain a better outcome in the afterworld by adopting regimes of self-denial, service, and charitable giving, while others made testamentary provisions funding funeral masses or sought other forms of relief from purgatorial punishments. Their needs and anxieties called for a new church order.

So, too, did the abusive practices of some church officials, to turn to the second cause of the Protestant revolt. The papacy seemed to be more interested in restoring the city of Rome and extending its hold over territorial states than in administering the church for the benefit of the people of God. Bishops and archbishops too often delegated their responsibilities to vicars and absented themselves from the diocese to which they were assigned, while skimming its revenues for their own benefit. Many prelates promoted their close kin to positions of eminence and power, disregarding the procedures for choosing the most qualified candidate, or simply purchased such positions for themselves (the practice of simony) or their favorites. Parish priests, meanwhile, were often incompetent or negligent, and the mendicant friars whose preaching tours propelled them into the midst of communities of the faithful were sometimes avaricious or corrupt.

The reformers addressed both issues, as did Martin Luther in 1517 with the publication of his *Ninety-Five Theses*, the opening salvo of the Protestant revolt. Triggering the angry response of this Augustinian monk, ordained priest, and professor at the University of Wittenberg (modern Germany), was a campaign to sell papal indulgences (documents promising release from purgatorial punishment for sins committed and absolved) in the German lands to raise funds for the construction of the new St. Peter's Basilica in Rome. Luther's critique was complex. He faulted the pope for draining the wealth of ordinary people—he had, after all, plenty of his own—to support a lavish building project. But he went further, challenging the theory underlying the sale of indulgences, the notion that an extrinsic act, requiring no self-examination or transformation of will could actually benefit the soul. His first thesis already revealed that direction of his critique: "When he said 'Repent,' Jesus Christ, our lord and master, wished the entire life of the believer to be one of repentance." Even if the clerical establishment were not greedy and unresponsive to the wishes of the people, the people, however much they feared the prospect of damnation, could only gain forgiveness from God himself, who forgives the sinner who repents.

Luther's diatribe against the practice of the sale of indulgences soon broadened into a larger critique of Catholic rituals, sacraments, hierarchy, and creed. He announced his mature doctrine, now constituting a rival theology, in three electrifying treatises in 1520. The first of these, his *Address to the Christian Nobility of the German Nation*, raised national, as well as, religious issues, as Luther summoned the princes of Germany to resist papal tyranny. The second, the *Babylonian Captivity of the Church*, attacked the institution of the papacy and the sacramental system of the Roman Church. The third, *The Freedom of a Christian*, elaborated the central points of Luther's theology. These included the principles that human beings achieve reconciliation with God (justification) *sola fide* (by faith alone); that they learn about God *sola scriptura* (by scripture alone); that individual Christians must therefore be their own interpreters of Scripture, and their own priests—the doctrine of the "priesthood of all believers." In 1520, as well, Luther and his followers burned the papal bull which excommunicated him, along with a copy of the books of canon law, before an enthusiastic Wittenberg audience. When an imperial diet (parliamentary session) condemned his views in 1521, he took refuge in the Wartburg Castle under the protection of a princely patron. When he returned to Wittenberg the following year, he instituted a reformed preaching, liturgy, and congregational hymn singing in the churches. The Reformation was launched.

Luther's ideas spread rapidly through the German lands, carried by associates—humanist scholars, former priests, and trained theologians—deeply committed to the reform program. In the absence of a central government, individual cities governed by councils of magistrates pivoted to the reform agenda by hiring Lutheran pastors who preached the new program and instituted a liturgy shorn of the rituals and ideology of the Roman Church. They closed the monasteries and convents that were the main institutional residue of Catholic practice, and though they did not tear down but rather repurposed the old cathedrals, they sometimes stripped the images of the saints that adorned the walls and altars.

Much of the German-speaking part of central Europe adopted the Lutheran confession, as did the kingdoms of Denmark and Sweden, whose monarchs imposed the new faith by decree. In England, meanwhile, while the Lutheran model was not adopted, King Henry VIII disowned the pope and made himself, as king, the head of a reformed Church of England.

Meanwhile, from the Swiss cities emerged a different strand of the Reformation movement, with strength in, among other cities, Zurich, Berne, Basel, and especially

LUTHER AND CALVIN ON LIBERTY AND FREE WILL

For both Martin Luther and John Calvin (1509–1564), the Roman Church's claim to absolute authority over the lives of Christians and their hopes for salvation intruded upon the authority of God. It was God who decided whether a person was saved from the sin that plagued the human race.

For Luther, writing in 1520, this understanding of divine omnipotence was, ironically, liberating. The human being was freed from the petty demands of the Roman Church: if people were saved by God through faith, they were free; if not, they were lost.

First, let us consider the inner man to see how a righteous, free, and pious Christian, that is, a spiritual, new, and inner man, becomes what he is. It is evident that no external thing has any influence in producing Christian righteousness or freedom, or in producing unrighteousness or servitude.... It does not help the soul if the body is adorned with the sacred robes of priests or dwells in sacred places or is occupied with sacred duties or prays, fasts, abstains from certain kinds of food, or does any work that can be done by the body and in the body. The righteousness and the freedom of the soul require something far different since the things which have been mentioned could be done by any wicked person. Such works produce nothing but hypocrites. On the other hand, it will not harm the soul if the body is clothed in secular dress, dwells in unconsecrated places, eats and drinks as others do, does not pray aloud, and neglects to do all the above-mentioned things which hypocrites can do....

One thing, and only one thing, is necessary for Christian life, righteousness and freedom. That one thing is the most holy Word of God, the gospel of Christ.... The Word of God cannot be received and cherished by any works whatever but only by faith.

(M. Luther, On the Freedom of a Christian, in Martin Luther: Selections from His Writings, ed. J. Dillenberger. Garden City, NY: Doubleday, 1961, pp. 53–55)

In the 1559 edition of his *Institutes of the Christian Religion*, Calvin remained unrelenting in his proclamation of divine omnipotence. Above all, the Christian must recognize and acknowledge the supremacy of God.

Book II, Chap. I: Therefore original sin is seen to be an hereditary depravity and corruption of our nature, diffused into all parts of the soul ... wherefore those who have defined original sin as the lack of the original righteousness with which we should have been endowed ... have not fully expressed the positive energy of this sin. For our nature is not merely bereft of good, but is so productive of every kind of evil that it cannot be inactive. Those who have called it concupiscence have used a word by no means wide of the mark, if it were added (and this is what many do not concede) that whatever is in man, from intellect to will, from the soul to the flesh, is all defiled and crammed with concupiscence; or, to sum it up briefly, that the whole man is in himself nothing but concupiscence....

Book III, Chap. XXI: No one who wishes to be thought religious dares outright to deny predestination, by which God chooses some for the hope of life, and condemns others to eternal death.... By predestination we mean the eternal decree of God, by which He has decided in His own mind what He wishes to happen in the case of each individual. For all men are not created on an equal footing, but for some eternal life is pre-ordained, for others eternal damnation.

(Calvin, The Institutes of the Christian Religion, ed. and trans. Henry Beveridge. Edinburgh: Calvin Translation Society, 1845)

Geneva, perched on the French border. In Geneva, the French native and refugee John Calvin emerged, in 1541, as head of the church council, or consistory, that was distinct from but closely related to the city council. A humanist and theologian of immense erudition and remarkable lucidity, without abandoning the Lutheran principles of *sola fide* and *sola scriptura*, Calvin presented in his *Institutes of the Christian Religion* (final edition, 1559) a systematic presentation of Protestant belief that rivaled the Catholic compendia produced by Scholasticism, guided throughout by the assertion, as first principle, of divine omnipotence. Calvin established an academy in Geneva to train Reformed pastors who fanned out over the continent, establishing pockets of Calvinist observance in the German lands, the Netherlands, Poland, Hungary, Scotland, among the Puritan minority in England, and to him most significantly, in his native France. Here a strong Calvinist movement based in the often heterodox south of France resisted Catholic domination, an opposition that broke forth in open conflict from 1562 to 1598. Calvin

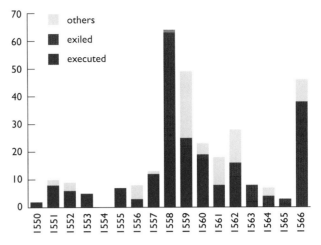

Calvinists, Anabaptists, and Persecuted Others in Antwerp, 1550–1566

A center of commerce in the sixteenth century and a town of very mixed religious allegiances, Antwerp would suffer enormously from Spanish repression, beginning with the murderous sack of Antwerp in 1567, and the institution of the Duke of Alba's Council of Troubles from 1567 to 1573. Even before the Spanish fist descended, Catholic town leaders engaged in the sporadic persecution of Protestants of all sorts—Calvinists (the leading group), Anabaptists, and others. This graph shows how many suffered persecution in each year from 1550 to 1566 and whether they were executed, exiled, or suffered some other fate.

(G. Marnef, *Antwerp in the Age of Reformation: Underground Protestantism in a Commercial Metropolis, 1550–1577*, trans. J.C. Grayson. Baltimore, MD: Johns Hopkins University Press, 1996, Graph 5.1, p. 85)

and his associates guided pastoral leaders and influential laymen in all these regions by their letters and visits, building up an international Calvinist presence that stretched further than the region of Lutheran adherence.

Even as followers of Luther and Calvin established new churches across central and western Europe, popular religious movements emerged that, although they adopted many Reformation principles, broke radically with the historical traditions of Christianity. These movements, or **sects**, aroused nearly universal opposition—from rulers, Catholics, and both Lutheran and Calvinist reformers. Many of these were Anabaptists, as they were labeled by their opponents: those who urged adult or "believer" baptism only, amounting generally to a heretical second baptism, since most adult Europeans had been baptized as infants. Anabaptists often advocated, as well, a deeply personal reading of scripture and active imitation of Christ, rejecting any official creed or church institution. Other Anabaptist beliefs adopted by some but not all adherents included the refusal to bear arms or swear oaths and the common ownership of property. Anabaptist communities spread throughout the Low Countries and German regions, but harsh persecution took its toll. By the seventeenth century, they were in retreat. Other radical sectarians were spiritualists, who believed they were to be guided not by the Bible but by the direct illumination of the Holy Spirit, or anti-Trinitarians, who denied the divinity of Jesus Christ.

The Catholic Response

Meanwhile, the Roman Church responded to the growing Reformation movement. Even before Luther's break with Rome, reformers had pushed an agenda that shared many features with Reformation principles. These made up the "evangelical" movement that stressed an inward-looking piety based on a personal reading of Scripture, which was to be translated into the vernacular languages of the people. Evangelicals called, as well, for reforming the office of bishop, an essential step in establishing a new standard of competence and accountability and eliminating such abuses as absenteeism, nepotism, and simony. Both in Italy and France, evangelicalism flourished, enlisting the support of reformers among the clergy and the learned elites, including prominent noblewomen.

But though evangelicalism seemed to foreshadow a larger Reformation, Luther's challenge to the pope from 1517 resulted in the suppression of this proto-reform. In France, the king cut short the incipient challenge to the church in 1534, causing many reformers to flee to safety elsewhere. In Italy in 1542, the institution of the Roman Inquisition to identify and prosecute heresy stopped the nascent reform movement in its tracks. The evangelicals, as it was said, "fled or bled": they were imprisoned, executed or forced to recant, or, more frequently, they went into exile in friendlier lands, especially Switzerland, Poland, and England. In their new homes, several became the intellectual leaders of radical sectarian movements.

Protestantism would make no inroads in Italy, therefore, nor on the Iberian Peninsula, where a severely repressive climate already prevailed before the Reformation. It was marked by the expulsion of hundreds of thousands of Jews from Spain (1492) and Portugal (1497), followed by the persecution for the next century and more of New Christians (Christian converts from Judaism) and Moors. In a quest to impose orthodoxy, the joint rulers King Ferdinand II of Aragón and Queen Isabella I of Castile launched the Spanish Inquisition in 1478 and, in 1536, pressured by Spain, Portugal would introduce its own Inquisition. In this context, Protestant reform had no chance of success.

The rest of a once-Catholic Europe, however, was penetrated by the Protestant Reformation to some degree. It made inroads not only in the western regions of France, the Low Countries, and the German lands, as has been seen, but further east as well, in Poland, Hungary, and Croatia. Protestant advances in these latter regions were later largely reversed by the vigorous response of the Jesuits, members of the Society of Jesus, a new religious order founded in 1540 by St. Ignatius of Loyola. The main goals of the Jesuits were to support the authority of the pope, especially against the challenge posed by the Reformation; to turn back the Protestant tide in Europe, both through missionary efforts and by the creation of a network of highly regarded secondary schools; and to extend the missionary outreach of the Catholic Church in Asia and the newly opened American

THE CATHOLIC RESPONSE: THE COUNCIL OF TRENT, IGNATIUS OF LOYOLA, AND TERESA OF ÁVILA

In responding to the Protestant challenge, the Roman Church reasserted its authority, reaffirmed the validity of its sacramental system, and offered new exemplars of a renewed spirituality. These passages show how all three aims were achieved.

In the first passage, Ignatius of Loyola (1491/1495–1556), founder of the **Jesuit** order, presents rules (from his *Spiritual Exercises*, 1541) for his followers.

> 1. *Always to be ready to obey with mind and heart, setting aside all judgment of one's own, the true spouse of Jesus Christ, our holy mother, our infallible and orthodox mistress, the Catholic Church....*
>
> 9. *To uphold especially all the precepts of the Church, and not censure them in any manner; but, on the contrary, to defend them promptly ... against those who criticize them....*
>
> 13. *That we may be altogether of the same mind and in conformity with the Church herself, if she shall have defined anything to be black which to our eyes appears to be white, we ought in like manner to pronounce it to be black. For we must undoubtingly believe, that the spirit of our Lord Jesus Christ, and the Spirit of the Orthodox Church His Spouse ... is the same.*
>
> (Ignatius Loyola, "Spiritual Exercises: Rules to Have the True Sentiment in the Church," from The Spiritual Exercises of St. Ignatius Loyola, trans. Elder Mullan. New York: P.J. Kennedy & Sons, 1914.)

This passage "On the Most Holy Sacrament of the Eucharist" from the decrees of the Council of Trent defends from Protestant attack the doctrine of transubstantiation, which held that the bread and wine of the Eucharist were physically transformed during the mass into the body and blood of Christ.

> *Canon I. If any one denieth, that, in the sacrament of the most holy Eucharist, are contained truly, really and substantially, the body and blood together with the soul and divinity of our Lord Jesus Christ, and consequently the whole Christ; but saith that He is only therein as in a sign, or in figure, or virtue; let him be anathema.*
>
> *Canon II. If any one saith, that, in the sacred and holy sacrament of the Eucharist, the substance of the bread and wine remains conjointly with the body and blood of our Lord Jesus Christ, and denieth that wonderful and singular conversion of the whole substance of the wine into the Blood ... which conversion indeed the Catholic Church most aptly calls Transubstantiation; let him be anathema.*
>
> (Ignatius Loyola, "Spiritual Exercises")

In her extraordinary *Autobiography* (1562–1565), St. Teresa (1515–1582) provides an account of her progress toward God, marked by experiences of divine grace. Here she describes the vision of an angel who pierced her body and soul with a golden spear, causing pain and rapture.

> *Beside me ... appeared an angel in bodily form.... He was not tall but short, and very beautiful; and his face was so aflame that he appeared to be ... all on fire.... In his hands I saw a great golden spear, and at the iron tip there appeared to be a point of fire. This he plunged into my heart several times so that it penetrated to my entrails. When he pulled it out, I felt that he took them with it, and left me utterly consumed by the great love of God. The pain was so severe that it made me utter several moans. The sweetness caused by this intense pain is so extreme that one cannot possibly wish it to cease, nor is one's soul then content with anything but God.... Throughout the days that this lasted I went about in a kind of stupor. I had no wish to look or to speak, only to embrace my pain, which was a greater bliss than all created things could give me.*
>
> (Teresa of Ávila, The Life of St. Teresa of Ávila by Herself, trans. J.M. Cohen. Baltimore, MD: Penguin, 1957, p. 210)

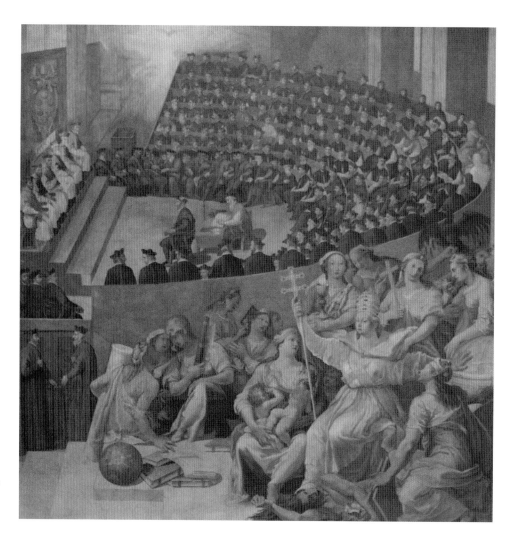

Cati da Lesi, *Council of Trent*, 1588, fresco. Chapel of Cardinal Marco Sittico Altemps, Santa Maria in Trastevere, Rome.

A heavenly company watches on as the dignitaries of the church meet to reaffirm the tenets of the Catholic faith and the privileges of the clergy.

continents. The Jesuit order served as a principal arm of what is often called the Counter-Reformation of the Catholic Church.

Meanwhile, the Catholic Church also responded to the Protestant challenge by a thorough program of self-evaluation and reform—the movement often called the Catholic Reformation—accomplished in the lengthy debates and resulting decrees issued by the Council of Trent (1545–1563, intermittently). The Tridentine decrees made no concessions to Protestantism, as this brief summation makes clear:

- They reaffirmed the authority of the pope and the authority of the church as the interpreter of Scripture;
- They denied the Lutheran principles of *sola fide* (justification by faith alone) and *sola scriptura* (truth derives from Scripture alone);
- They maintained the doctrine of transubstantiation, the view that the bread and wine that were the elements of the Eucharist (Lord's Supper) were physically

transformed into the blood and body of Christ in the priestly celebration of the mass;

- They validated the practices of pilgrimages, indulgences, and veneration of the saints, relics, and the Virgin Mary;
- They called for the reform of the clergy and elimination of the abuses that had aroused mass criticism, as well as the strict enforcement of claustration (enclosure) and other regulations for women in religious orders.

In this way, the Roman Church reasserted its historic mission while instituting reforms that required higher standards of performance and probity among its personnel. Yet how was the Roman Church to respond to the spiritual cravings of the multitude that had welcomed the message of the Reformation? It addressed these as well, reaching into the personal lives of the faithful to nurture and enhance ties to the church. It did so, in part, through the confessional: priests in direct conversations with parishioners encouraged approved kinds of behavior, especially within the family unit. It did so, as well, by encouraging an ideal of lay devotion, or commitment to a program of charitable engagement. The movements launched in seventeenth-century France, especially, by Sts. Francis de Sales and Vincent de Paul, inspired laywomen in particular to devote time and energy to works of mercy, such as aiding the poor and tending the ill. To Luther's summons of the populace to faith, these movements responded with a summons to love.

What was to be done, finally, with the unruly ideas, now empowered by the printing press, that had sprung from the minds of Europe's intellectuals? The Roman Church knew that they had to be brought into conformity. The first papal *Index librorum prohibitorum* ("Index of Prohibited Books"), a guide to those books that were dangerous for the faithful to read, appeared in 1559; among the thousand or so works condemned were all the works of Erasmus. Many subsequent versions followed into the twentieth century; final suppression came in 1966. The inquisitions, too, pursued thinkers with dangerous, unorthodox ideas, including Bruno, Campanella, and Galileo (see Chapter 8). The arts, too, were censored. The proud nudes of Renaissance art were tactfully, if minimally, clothed in the interest of decorum. The war on free expression extended from the sixteenth century through the eighteenth and is the background for the vehement declaration of freedom of speech as a constitutionally guaranteed right in the new republic of the United States of America.

In addition to the war on free thought, a number of real wars broke out between states advocating Catholic, Lutheran, Calvinist, or other confessional positions. The Peace of Augsburg of 1555 terminated a phase of early religious warfare in the German lands. It famously guaranteed to each ruler the right to determine the official religion of his subjects. In France, Protestant (called **Huguenot**) and Catholic leagues of nobles and their followers fought from 1562 until 1598. In that year, the Catholic Henry IV (r. 1589–1610), who had converted from Protestantism in 1594, issued the Edict of Nantes, guaranteeing freedom of worship to his former coreligionists.

The most devastating war of the era, the Thirty Years' War (1618–1648), began as a central European religious conflict of Lutheran and Calvinist states against the emperor and allied Catholic powers. By the time the Pcacc of Westphalia of 1648 put an end to the slaughter, the religious issues had fallen away, as the war had become a wrestling match between the great territorial states of an emerging modern Europe. Religious issues also played a part in the English Civil War (1642–1660), which resulted from a traumatic attempt to create a **constitutional monarchy** in that nation. These were the conflicts that the French thinker Voltaire (François Marie Arouet, 1694–1778) would mock in the age of the Enlightenment. These were also the conflicts that Erasmus feared, as he nimbly avoided identification with any religious party, and these were those of which he fore-warned, without effect, the princes of Europe. At the close of this terrible era of warfare, Catholicism remained the majority religion in Europe; Protestantism was established securely in England and Scotland, the Scandinavian countries, and much of central Europe. Toleration was the norm only in the Netherlands.

Intersections

The Renaissance and Reformation movements intersect in a number of ways. The printing press, as has been seen, served and promoted both movements simultaneously. In the visual arts, Renaissance and post-Renaissance (Baroque) styles gave expression to Protestant outlooks. The musical genres and instruments that developed in Catholic Italy were put to use by Protestant composers, including that most Protestant of musicians Johann Sebastian Bach (1685–1750). Literary genres, too, would cross confessional borders: English Protestants as much as Italian Catholics would write Petrarchan sonnets, and Protestants Edmund Spenser and John Milton (1608–1674) would develop the Renaissance epic inherited from the Catholic Ariosto and others (see Chapter 8).

It was humanism, however, the major intellectual movement of the Italian Renaissance, that was most entwined with the Reformation. The reformers were inspired by humanist works, especially those of Erasmus and Lorenzo Valla (see Chapter 3). Most of them were trained in humanist schools, or at least had a secure command of Latin and classical liter-ature, both secular and Christian. They used humanist methods, insisting on a return to the earliest possible texts, on the critical emendation of those texts and on their analysis in a historical context. They wrote works in the genres developed by the humanists—especially treatises, but also letters, orations, and dialogues. They were not, of course, humanists; they were theologians, pastors, and controversialists, warriors for a faith that they believed correct. But there were four areas in which humanism coincided especially with the Reformation mission.

First, humanism encouraged the examination of sources. The reformers turned to the Bible itself and to the works of the ancient fathers of the church, thereby skipping over the previous 1,000 years of theological writings which, they believed, had introduced false ideas. Thus the reformers continued a project begun by the humanists, especially

Valla and Erasmus. Luther began his translation of the Bible into German while in hiding in Wartburg Castle in 1522, using the edition Erasmus had published a few years earlier. His theology was sturdily based in the reading of Scripture, especially the Gospel of John and the letters of Paul, and of some of the church fathers, especially Augustine. Many reformed scholars followed his lead. The biblical and patristic (that is, related to the church fathers) studies of Protestant and (later) Catholic scholars to a great extent laid the foundations for the development of modern historical research methods in the nineteenth century.

Second, humanism encouraged the questioning of authority. From the outset, humanism had challenged the status quo: the low quality Latin of contemporary writers; the elevation of Aristotle and the method of disputation by the Scholastics; the theories of papacy and empire; the pretensions of monks, priests, and prelates; the methods of education; and the conduct of princes. These two centuries of questioning, recorded in the treatises, dialogues, and letters of persuasive authors, gave weight to the reformed project when it took up its frontal assault on the Roman Church. Erasmus, of course, who had done his share of questioning and criticizing, balked at joining in open conflict. By then, the reformers had learned what they needed from the humanist tradition and proceeded alone.

Third, humanism had placed a renewed emphasis on what it was to be human. The human being, in distinction from the beasts, was a rational creature and in the act of reasoning most resembled God. For the reformers, especially Luther, the capacity to reason independently freed the individual from the decrees and formulas of the Roman Church. Believers could read the Bible and form their own relationship with God—such was the monumental claim to a priesthood of all believers. Salvation came from God alone and by a faith that God imputed to the struggling human being. But seekers reached for that relationship through their own study and meditation on Scripture.

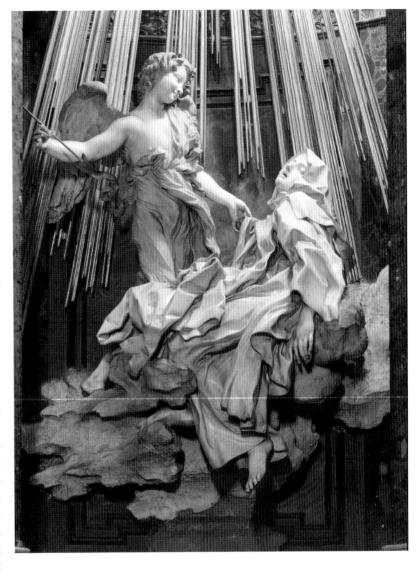

Bernini, *The Ecstasy of St. Teresa*, 1645–1652, marble, height 11 ft 6 in (3.5 m). Cornaro Chapel altar, Santa Maria della Vittoria, Rome.

Catholic Reformation spirituality is imbued with classical expression in this sculpture that portrays the moment—as St. Teresa recounts in her *Autobiography*—when a "very beautiful" angel from God, his face aflame, transfixed her heart with a golden spear.

Finally, humanism had promoted education as uniquely important, the path to the perfection of human beings and human society. For the humanists, only a literate, thoughtful person was fully human. For the reformers, only an educated person was fully equipped for an understanding of God. Both Protestant and Catholic reformers stressed the educational project. The Lutherans attempted to provide, through local institutions, at least an elementary education for all, girls as well as boys. Schooling was also a priority in Calvinist communities. In Catholic Europe, energetic attention was given to providing basic literacy to the laity. Several religious orders, but especially the Jesuits, committed themselves to education. There were 372 Jesuit secondary schools, or "colleges," in Europe by 1615. These provided a carefully graded curriculum, based on humanist ideals, which trained many of the elite of European society. Beginning with the Ursulines, orders of nuns also provided schooling for girls. Thus the humanist educative mission was carried on by both Protestant and Catholic churches, and contributed to the modern achievement of mass education.

CONCLUSION

Europe beyond the Alps learned much from the artists and humanists of Renaissance Italy. In the northern Renaissance, however, each region's local traditions blended with imported ones, developing a distinct variant of the now international Renaissance enterprise. In these regions, too, the emergence of humanism coincided with the outbreak of religious controversies that culminated in the Protestant Reformation and the Catholic response. Both humanist and Reformation debates found a wide audience through the increasingly powerful medium of print. Beyond the Alps, moreover, the Renaissance flowered in a social and political world quite different from the world of the Italian peninsula in the fourteenth and fifteenth centuries. As the following chapter describes, the environment of kings, courts, and cities in Europe outside of Italy would shape Renaissance traditions in novel ways.

SUGGESTED READINGS

Primary Sources

D'Albret, Jeanne. *Letters from the Queen of Navarre, with an Ample Declaration*. Translated and edited by Kathleen M. Llewellyn, Emily Thompson, and Colette H. Winn. Tempe: Arizona Center for Medieval and Renaissance Studies, 2016. The Queen of Navarre, niece of French King Francis I, explains why she must support the Huguenot cause against the monarchy.

Erasmus, Desiderius. *The Erasmus Reader.* Edited by Erika Rummel. Toronto: University of Toronto Press, 1990. A selection from translations in the Toronto edition of collected works.

Erasmus, Desiderius. *Erasmus on Women.* Edited by Erika Rummel. Toronto: University of Toronto Press, 1996. An intelligent selection displaying Erasmus's attitude toward women.

Luther, Martin. *Martin Luther: Selections from His Writings.* Edited by John Dillenberger. New York: Doubleday, 1972. A classic selection.

More, Thomas. *Utopia.* Translated by Paul Turner. Harmondsworth, UK: Penguin, 1976. An accessible translation.

Teresa of Ávila. *The Life of St. Teresa of Ávila by Herself.* Translated by J.M. Cohen. Harmondsworth, UK: Penguin, 1957. One of the first modern autobiographies.

Vives, Juan Luis. *The Education of a Christian Woman: A Sixteenth-Century Manual.* Translated and edited by Charles Fantazzi. Chicago: University of Chicago Press, 2000. A pioneering work on the education of women.

Secondary Sources

Eisenstein, Elizabeth L. *The Printing Press as an Agent of Change: Communications and Cultural Transformations in Early Modern Europe*, 2 vols. Cambridge: Cambridge University Press, 1979. Abridged ed. *The Printing Revolution in Early Modern Europe*. Cambridge: Cambridge University Press, 1984. A groundbreaking work on the impact of print.

Ginzburg, Carlo. *The Cheese and the Worms: The Cosmos of a Sixteenth-Century Miller.* Translated by A. Tedeschi and J. Tedeschi. Harmondsworth, UK: Penguin, 1980. Uses Inquisition documents to tease out the surprising worldview of an ordinary sixteenth-century person.

Gregory, Brad. *Salvation at Stake: Christian Martyrdom in Early Modern Europe.* Cambridge, MA: Harvard University Press, 1999. Argues the centrality of martyrdom to the Reformation experience, studying Anabaptist, Protestant, and Catholic martyrs in parallel.

Guy, J.A. *Thomas More.* Oxford: Oxford University Press, 2000. Carefully reconstructs More's views on monarchy and Parliament on the one hand, church governance and papacy on the other.

Hart, D.G. *Calvinism: A History.* New Haven, CT: Yale University Press, 2013. Considers the full chronological and geographical sweep of Calvinism, seeking the explanation for its global success.

Hendrix, Scott H. *Martin Luther: Visionary Reformer.* New Haven, CT: Yale University Press, 2015. A new biography looking at Luther in full complexity, not as a saint or hero, but as an educated and resourceful man undertaking a mission that could not be allowed to fail.

Hsia, R. Po-Chia. *The World of Catholic Renewal, 1540–1770*, 2nd ed. New York: Cambridge University Press, 2005. Explores the broad, long-term relations between Catholic reform and early modern culture.

Jardine, Lisa. *Erasmus, Man of Letters: The Construction of Charisma in Print.* Princeton, NJ: Princeton University Press, 1993. Focuses on Erasmus's self-representation through the new print medium.

MacCulloch, Diarmaid. *The Reformation.* New York: Viking, 2004. A massive and comprehensive overview, delineating the various stages of the Reformation well into the seventeenth century while carefully avoiding an identification with any of the multifarious confessional participants.

McGrath, Alister E. *Reformation Thought: An Introduction*, 4th ed. Malden, MA: Wiley-Blackwell, 2012. A careful and thoughtful disentanglement of the principal intellectual themes of Reformation and Christianity, especially good on such key issues as the doctrines of justification by faith, the sacraments, and predestination.

Mullett, Michael. *The Catholic Reformation*. London: Routledge, 1999. A comprehensive narrative of the Catholic experience from the late Middle Ages.

O'Malley, John W. *Trent and All That: Renaming Catholicism in the Early Modern Era*. Cambridge, MA: Harvard University Press, 2000. Analyzes various interpretations (and namings) of the Catholic Reformation.

Pettegree, Andrew. *Brand Luther: 1517, Printing, and the Making of the Reformation*. New York: Penguin Press, 2015. Presents Luther as a great communicator, whose ability to change the direction of European culture was closely linked to the availability and exploitation of print technology

Tracy, James D. *Erasmus of the Low Countries*. Berkeley: University of California Press, 1996. Places Erasmus securely within the cultural context of the Netherlands, his native country, by an author expert in the history of that region.

Yoran, Hanan. *Between Utopia and Dystopia: Erasmus, Thomas More, and the Humanist Republic of Letters*. Lanham, MD: Lexington Books, 2010. Provocatively relates Erasmian humanism, centered on the ideal of a disembodied intellectual, and More's construction of Utopia, a celebration of "no place."

TEN

THE RENAISSANCE BEYOND THE ALPS: CITIES, COURTS, AND KINGS (c. 1500–c. 1700)

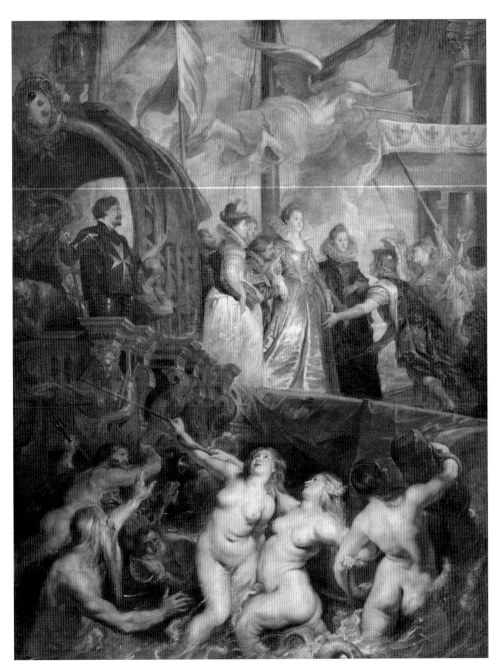

Rubens, *Marie de' Medici, Queen of France, Landing in Marseilles, 3 November 1600* (detail), 1622–1625, oil on canvas, 12 ft 9 in × 9 ft 7 in (3.94 × 2.95 m). Musée du Louvre, Paris.

This Baroque painting, one of a cycle of 24 celebrating the life of Queen Marie de Medici, exemplifies the enlarged conception of monarchy. A vassal sent by the French king bows before the queen, whose ship is escorted by exuberant sea gods and goddesses.

In August 2002, the worst floods in a century afflicted central and eastern Europe. In Dresden (Germany), the magnificent collection of Italian paintings in the Zwinger Gallery was evacuated. In Prague (Czech Republic), an aluminum barrier, called the Wall of Hope, was erected to save the Old Town—its buildings and monuments including synagogues, Baroque palaces, and the medieval complex of university, castle, and churches adorned with altarpieces and statuary. Hundreds of miles from Venice, the Renaissance had taken root in these centers, whose citizens spoke German or Czech.

The cultural transformation of these distant cities was part of a broader process throughout Europe whereby the artistic style and patterns of thought that were developed in the small walled cities of Italy migrated to the kingdoms, the courts, and the capital cities of a continent on the verge of modernization and expansion. This chapter considers the various political and social contexts constituted by kingdoms, courts, and cities characterizing Europe beyond the Alps. It traces the story of how Renaissance civilization sprouted anew in the centers of European life from Spain and Portugal in the southwest to the Slavic lands in the east.

CONTEXTS: KINGDOMS, COURTS, AND CITIES

The civilization of the Renaissance developed in Italy in the cradle of that peninsula's northern cities. The political and social striving of urban elites from the eleventh through the fourteenth century was the foundation of the thought and art of the Renaissance of the fifteenth through seventeenth century. Beyond the Alps, the contexts were different. Here, powerful monarchies and luxurious courts emerged from the ongoing struggle of nobles and kings. At the same time, the expanding network of trade and the coincidental shift from a Mediterranean to a north Atlantic focus for the European commercial system nourished the urban capitals of the European northwest—above all, Amsterdam, London, and Paris. In these settings, Renaissance civilization flourished anew.

Kingdoms

When Boccaccio and Petrarch were writing in Italy, only one kingdom in Europe had established its modern national boundaries, and in only one did the monarch hold clear sovereignty—the kingdom of England. At the same time, royal courts had become more luxurious, but they were not yet the permanent centers of cultural display that they would be by the eighteenth century. Though there were many towns outside of Italy, few had more than 20,000 residents. Only in the Low Countries was there the kind of intense urbanization that had characterized northern Italy since the eleventh century. Over the Renaissance centuries, these conditions changed. Monarchical power expanded in Europe.

Kings who had once shared power with territorial lords now established their sovereignty over larger territories by a variety of means.

Advised by their ministers, kings exploited their prerogatives, winning privileges that had been usurped by nobles. Sometimes they were fortunate or prudent enough to acquire territories through inheritance or strategic marriages. The French kings gained direct control over Provence when René d'Anjou (1409–1480), its territorial lord, died without heirs and the duchy reverted to the crown. Charles I of Spain (1500–1558, Charles V of the Holy Roman Empire) acquired control over Spain, the Low Countries, and the Habsburg lands, not to mention Mediterranean and colonial possessions, through inheritance from a carefully arranged marriage.

Other kings seized lands by military action—as Machiavelli would have urged them to do—at a time when military power was becoming more formidable. The availability of gunpowder encouraged the rapid development of artillery and small arms, which in turn prompted a greater reliance on infantry over cavalry. Soldiers now marched in formations—squares, columns, and lines—which were deliberately designed for maximum offensive or defensive strength or for flexibility or speed. They were required to wear uniforms and to drill the precise maneuvers that made this new kind of warfare possible and deadly. Cannons made the curtain walls of medieval castles obsolete. They were now wheeled into place before low, thick, powerful fortresses with sloping walls ringed by a barren *glacis*. The unlucky soldiers who charged up that inclined, open space to storm the ramparts encountered deadly gunfire from protected positions. Such fortifications were no longer the isolated castles of a feudal lord. They were part of a system of national defense, strung out along the frontiers of a sovereign state.

Large professional armies and sturdy, state-of-the-art fortifications cost vast sums, and kings obtained these resources from their subjects. To levy taxes, however, they generally needed to consult the assemblies or parliaments that had emerged during the Middle Ages. These included representatives of the three "estates" of medieval society, the clergy, the nobility, and the burghers. Parliaments, however, were weighted in favor of the first two of these social groups, those that had greatest power but paid the least in taxes. But even these top-heavy assemblies did not automatically grant kings what they requested. They had their own interests to promote and demanded concessions before they agreed to new taxes. Monarchs were compelled to negotiate, which in itself gave authority to their rivals, or find alternate means of funding their military ventures.

Yet the monarchs pulled ahead of competing groups during the Renaissance era. These powerful kings, tutored by advisors armed with the concepts of political thought from Plato to Machiavelli, developed a grand self-concept. They began to see themselves as "absolute" monarchs, who could make and enforce laws, and whose persons and personalities merged with the state itself—as the greatest king of the era, Louis XIV of France (r. 1643–1715), is said to have assumed in these words: "L'état, c'est moi" (I am the state). Theorists of **absolutism**, drawing on ancient and medieval political philosophy, argued that the king represented on earth the authority of God (the theory of divine right) and for that reason must be obeyed. The king, in turn, must be obedient to God and his laws.

In two regions of Europe, however, coalitions of nobles and burghers defied absolutist kings—in England and the northern states of the Low Countries. Without abolishing the monarchy, they elevated an enforceable body of law above the royal party in a system modern scholars call constitutional monarchy. The monarch ruled, but he ruled in accord with the laws created by a parliament or assembly. The English thinkers Thomas Hobbes (1588–1679) and John Locke (1632–1704), each drawing upon the earlier Western tradition of theories of political right, devised a new basis for the legitimacy of a sovereign's rule. It was a contract, a political agreement by which a human community surrendered its own interests to a sovereign (Hobbes), or surrendered its rights to a law-making body, which might work through a constitutional king (Locke). Thus the resistance to absolutist theory triggered the creation of modern, secular political theory. Unlike Machiavelli, Hobbes and Locke insisted on the legitimacy of the ruler, yet opened the pathway to republican and democratic forms of government.

Most kings and lesser princes, however, clung to their claims of absolute power, which remained unchallenged until the French Revolution (1789–1795). In pursuing their political aims, they often allied with the forces of the church. Whether Catholic or Protestant and whether Lutheran or Calvinist (Reformed), the church was "established" in most of Europe, that is, it was declared to be the sole acceptable confession for the population and one over which the monarchy itself had some kind of authority. The Spanish and French kings saw themselves as defenders of the Catholic faith, while the king of England viewed himself as head of what came to be called the Anglican Church. In the German lands, according to the principle established by the Peace of Augsburg of 1555, each territorial ruler could choose which religion would be officially established in the state that he ruled.

To bolster their power further, European monarchs engaged in extensive programs of self-presentation in painting, sculpture, architecture, and performance. They marked their entrances to the principal cities of their realm with processions for which artists designed elaborate structures that lined the routes. There were rituals of speechmaking, the recitation of formulas of mutual respect and obligation between monarchs and those who welcomed them, and a great deal of pageantry, music-making, and theater. Such entrances were common in an era when not only the monarch, but even the court traveled about the countryside. In the Renaissance era, monarchs also built themselves magnificent residential palaces, as the task of fortification was displaced to the ring of fortresses that defended the borders. The grandiose architectural programs according to which these palaces were constructed, complete with paintings, tapestries, and sculptures, alluded everywhere to the greatness of the monarch. Thus monarchs required, and paid for, the services of artists, authors, and musicians. They became the most important patrons of arts and letters, and thus the promoters of Renaissance civilization in Europe beyond the Alps.

(FACING PAGE)

Europe, c. 1650

After the shocks of the Reformations, Ottoman advances, and the Thirty Years' War, Europe in 1650 differed from 1530 mainly in the north and east. England and Scotland were now united. The Netherlands had split into the independent northern Dutch Republic and the southern Spanish Netherlands. Sweden expanded across the Baltic Sea to absorb the regions previously held by the Teutonic Order. The medieval state of Muscovy had become Russia, ruled by the Romanov dynasty until 1917. Further south, the Ottoman Empire had expanded through the Balkans and into Hungary.

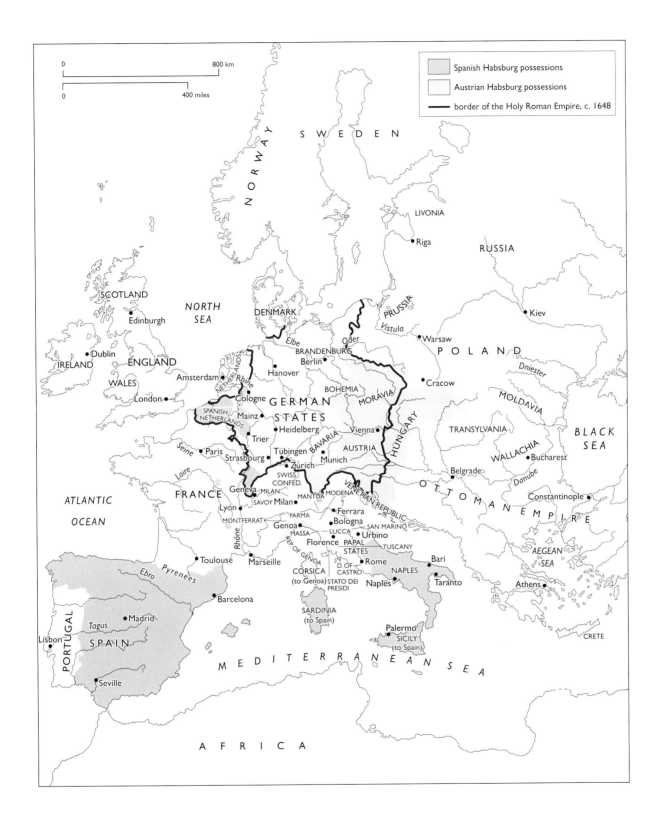

Courts

We have already encountered the princely courts that flourished during the Italian Renaissance and the kind of behavior expected of the courtier, a person who resided at court and sought the favor of the prince (see Chapter 8). Royal and princely courts outside of Italy preexisted the Renaissance but in that era became more lavish and more central to both political and cultural life. In many ways, they followed the Italian model, by which a ruler employed the visual and performing arts, as well as the services of intellectuals, to enhance his image and power. They also became the place where the power of the nobility—never as vast in Italy as in the north—was made to give way to the power of the king.

At its origins in the years following the fall of Rome in the West, the nobility was a warrior class, made up of Germanic warlords and armed provincial landowners. A nobleman's rank was established by his ability to fight. Over time, as nobles were rewarded for military service by grants of land in usufruct, they gained territorial toeholds that collectively eroded the power of kings. By the eleventh and twelfth centuries, noblemen attempted to make their tenure of these lands both permanent and inheritable. The nobility now constituted a formidable social caste, with an independent economic base and valuable military skills. They flexed their muscles in their relationships with kings. The English barons in 1215 required of their monarch, King John, the Magna Carta, or "Great Charter," which bound the king to consult his nobles. The Aragonese nobles gave this defiant oath of loyalty to the King of Spain: "We who are as good as you, swear to you who are no better than we to accept you as our king and sovereign lord, provided you observe all our liberties and laws; but if not, not." The advancing power of the kings, however, soon challenged the social triumph of the nobility.

As kings became more effective rulers of sovereign states from the fifteenth and sixteenth centuries, they sought to control the nobility by summoning them to court. The French King Louis XIV surrounded himself with thousands of nobles at his new suburban palace of Versailles, 12 miles from the capital at Paris. They resided at court, sometimes winning salaries or pensions for doing so. Court was where the king was and was therefore the center of power. Important decisions were made here and important commissions and positions could be won. The days were consumed with an endless series of ritual performances: greeting the king at his rising, going to lunch or to recreation, riding or strolling through the gardens, formal dinners and an evening of theater or ballet, the latter—an innovation—performed by the courtiers themselves.

Schooled at court, the proud nobles of Europe learned the new arts of civility. Civility involved far more than showing reverence to a monarch. It involved a code of manners and attitudes that would become the standard of proper behavior for the next several centuries. Nobles at court needed to know how to behave at table, in the bedroom, in the garden, and in the great halls; in what way and where to bow, speak, or attend to bodily functions; how to adjust behavior to the rank of the person addressed and how to recognize that rank; how to dress for each occasion and what the fashion was in doublets or

1450–1499

1453   The Hundred Years' War between England and France ends in French victory.

1469   The marriage of Ferdinand of Aragón and Isabella of Castile unites most of Spain.

1477   The Low Countries come under the rule of the Habsburg Holy Roman Emperor.

1485   Henry Tudor defeats Richard III at Bosworth Field and takes the throne as Henry VII.

1498   Albrecht Dürer produces his first series of woodcuts, *The Apocalypse*.

1500–1549

1519   Charles I of Spain is elected Holy Roman Emperor, as Emperor Charles V.

1532–1534   François Rabelais writes *Pantagruel* and *Gargantua*.

1536   Hans Holbein is appointed court painter to Henry VIII.

1550–1599

1556   Emperor Charles V abdicates; his son becomes King Philip II of Spain and his brother Emperor Ferdinand I of Austria.

1564   Birth of English poet and dramatist William Shakespeare.

1572   In the St. Bartholomew's Day Massacre, French Catholics kill their Protestant compatriots.

1579   The Union of Utrecht founds the Dutch Republic, with Holland as its main component.

1580   Philip II of Spain takes the throne of Portugal, uniting the Iberian Peninsula.

1580   Michel de Montaigne publishes the first two volumes of his essays.

1589   Bourbon Henri of Navarre (Henry IV) succeeds the Valois as ruler of France.

1590   Edmund Spenser's epic *The Faerie Queene* is published.

1600–1649

1600–1608   Peter Paul Rubens visits Italy and learns from the Renaissance masters.

1600–1605   Shakespeare writes *Hamlet*, *Othello*, *King Lear*, and *Macbeth*.

1603   James VI of Scotland comes to the English throne as James I.

1605   Miguel de Cervantes publishes part one of *Don Quixote*.

1606   Ben Jonson's comedy *Volpone* appears.

1610   French King Henry IV is assassinated by a Catholic fanatic.

1616   Death of Shakespeare.

1619   Architect Inigo Jones designs the Banqueting House, Whitehall, London.

1623   Diego Velazquez becomes court painter to King Philip IV of Spain.

1624   Cardinal Richelieu becomes minister of state to King Louis XIII of France.

1632   Anthony Van Dyck becomes court painter to King Charles I of England.

1635   The Académie Française is founded by Cardinal Richelieu.

1642   Jules Mazarin succeeds Richelieu as chief minister of France.

1643   Louis XIV comes to the throne of France aged five; his mother Anne of Austria is regent.

1649   King Charles I is executed.

1650–1700

1651   English philosopher Thomas Hobbes publishes *Leviathan*, advocating strong government.

1660   The monarchy is restored in Britain, Charles II ascending the throne.

1662   Louis XIV orders a new royal palace to be built at Versailles.

1667   English poet John Milton publishes *Paradise Lost*.

1675   Architect Sir Christopher Wren begins work on the new St. Paul's Cathedral, London.

1685   Louis XIV revokes the Edict of Nantes; the persecution of French Huguenots follows.

1688   Dutch ruler William of Orange invades England; King James II flees.

1689   The English Parliament draws up a Bill of Rights.

1690   English philosopher John Locke publishes his *Two Treatises of Government*.

bodices, footwear or coiffure, this year or this week. Toward the end of the Renaissance era, the rearing of a young aristocrat culminated in the grand tour of European capitals. Its object was to view the great cities and works of art that could be found abroad, to meet and mix with important people from other cities and nations, and to be introduced discreetly to the customs of the world.

Meanwhile, the nobles who were not grand enough or were not willing to attend the king at court remained on their lands, often deprived of the means of advancement. In Spain and France, noblemen were barred from engaging in trade. As a result, with the expansion of both domestic and colonial trade, the increase of manufactures, and steep inflation in the sixteenth century, the revenues that nobles received from their lands diminished. In Spain, an impoverished nobility required financial assistance from the crown, which artificially propped up a nonproductive elite. The situation was different in central and eastern Europe, where a much larger nobility—in Poland as much as 10 to 15 per cent of the population—profited from the intercontinental trade in grain. The English and Dutch nobility, in contrast, did engage in commercial investments. The English nobility was limited to a tiny "peerage," and although it controlled a disproportionate share of the country's wealth, it did not overwhelm the other social strata by its numbers.

In this new context, the nobleman was still a warrior—nobles filled the officer ranks of most European armies into the nineteenth and twentieth centuries—but he was not primarily a warrior. Instead, the nobility found new ways to define itself. Noblemen were noble because of their descent from great ancestors over many generations, it was argued; thus they were noble by blood. The wealthiest among them demonstrated their status in the same way that kings did, by building magnificent palaces and townhouses, which they filled with works of art and where they hosted musical performers and the sparkling conversation of the wise and well-placed. In addition, noblemen had mastered the arts of civility, which were learned from their upbringing in a noble household, attended by nursemaids and tutors, and then perfected by residence at a royal or princely court. Few commoners, even from wealthy burgher families, were able to obtain quite the same polish as a product of this aristocratic rearing. Finally, after the humanist movement had distilled its first principles into a curriculum that was taught in the finest schools of Europe (see Chapter 11), the nobleman possessed the grace of a classical education, which enabled him to write eloquent letters, compose sonnets, and even compile useful reports.

Some offspring of wealthy burgher families who obtained the skills conferred by humanist training were able to gain employment as clerks, accountants, or advisors in newly complex national bureaucracies. With the further payment of a cash sum into the royal treasury, a few were raised into the nobility. In France, these were the "nobility of the robe," referring to the sober garments worn by a professional, merchant, or bureaucrat. They formed a stratum just below that of the "nobility of the sword," the traditional nobility, with its claims of privilege by blood and warrior training. Except in England, nobility could be purchased nearly everywhere. The sale of title was a prime source of revenue for the cash-starved monarchs of Europe. Commoners who were able to buy such titles were generally the product of an urban civilization and of commercial enterprise.

Cities

The cities of Europe beyond the Alps flourished in the Renaissance era, although in a pattern different from that of urban northern Italy. Italian urbanization began as early as the eleventh century, awakened by commerce, which brought accumulating wealth and the increased circulation of money (see Chapter 1). In the twelfth and thirteenth centuries, the cities of northern Italy were at their most autonomous. The largest of them reached 100,000 and more in population by the 1340s (when the Black Death struck); many had 20,000 to 50,000 inhabitants. These cities were powerhouses of trade and manufacture. Many of the luxury products purchased by the elites of Europe were shipped from eastern Mediterranean ports by Italian carriers. The large-scale manufacture of high quality wool and silk textiles—the most important manufactured products in Europe before the Industrial Revolution—was centered in northern Italian cities. These activities yielded huge profits, which funded large building projects, both public and private, and the development of urban design. There was no equivalent level of urbanization anywhere else in Europe.

Yet cities and towns had long existed north of the Alps, which were productive in their own way. From the earliest Middle Ages, towns concentrated in the area of the Low Countries, a conurbation that endures to the present day. Others dotted the routes traced by the Rhône and Rhine Rivers and were scattered along the coast of the North and Baltic Seas. In England, outside of the archiepiscopal sees, the main urban center was and would remain London. Northern European towns and cities rarely exceeded 20,000 or 30,000 in population. The majority had fewer than 10,000 inhabitants and many towns of 2,000 or 3,000 had an important role in commerce and were counted as urban centers.

From the twelfth century, these northern towns gained charters from kings and local secular and ecclesiastical lords that enabled them to create urban governments. As in Italy, they established magistracies and elected councils that debated policy and made key decisions. In the major towns, an urban patriciate developed from which most of the civic leaders were chosen. Guilds organized merchant and artisan activities and played an important public and cultural role. Guildhalls and town halls, the major public buildings of northern cities, dominated the urban landscape in many cities, sharing architectural dominance with the cathedral and major churches. Northern European cities, however, never attained the level of autonomy enjoyed by the great Italian cities.

Northern European towns were centers of local and regional commerce. Some, especially in the Low Countries, also engaged in long-distance trade and supported manufacturing enterprises. The regional trading systems often followed rivers, as they did for the Rhône–Seine sequence (France) and the Rhine (Germany). In the Low Countries, the commerce of a cluster of towns was centered on Bruges through the fifteenth century, but upstaged by Antwerp in the sixteenth and by Amsterdam in the sixteenth and seventeenth. In England, smaller regional centers looked to London as the dominant commercial center. For its part, London hooked into the French and Netherlandish trade networks and, most importantly, the Hanseatic League.

EARLY MODERN CITIES: PARIS, AMSTERDAM, LONDON

The northern Renaissance coincided with a shift in the pattern of European urbanization. In the thirteenth and fourteenth centuries, northern Italy was the most urbanized part of Europe, and it was in that setting that the Italian Renaissance emerged. After 1500, however, the center of gravity of urban development shifted to the northern and western parts of the continent, which absorbed the cultural trends radiating from Italy and became home to the later phase of the Renaissance.

This shift corresponded to the seismic change in trade patterns that occurred following the events of 1453 and 1492: the conquest of Constantinople by the Ottoman Turks, making the Mediterranean Sea increasingly hostile to Italian and Spanish trade; and the opening of the Atlantic to trade as a result of the Columbian discovery and conquest. Other changes encouraged the big cities of northern and western Europe to get bigger still, while Italian urban populations stagnated. Incorporated into developing nation-states, cities lost their autonomy (and often their walls). As part of the process of proto-industrialization, they constructed extensive relationships with the surrounding region, which enhanced the wealth of both urban center and rural periphery. Some cities became capitals of nations, acquiring new buildings and spaces associated with political and military needs. Foremost among those capitals were Paris, Amsterdam, and London, the leading cities of early modern Europe.

The site of royal government and the oldest university in Europe, Paris was already a large town during the Middle Ages. It played a pivotal role in the religious wars of the sixteenth century. A center of early Reform activity in the 1520s and 1530s, as the century waxed, it became a city torn between Catholics and Protestants. On the eve of St. Bartholomew's Day in 1572 the infamous massacre of thousands of Protestants occurred in Paris. It was Paris that the new King Henry IV (r. 1589–1614) had to enter and rule in order to establish sovereign authority in France after decades of religious strife. He did so, becoming Catholic in order to win the citizens' support. Once established, he supervised the most important building projects in the city since the Middle Ages, notably the Pont Neuf (New Bridge) across the Seine and the Place Royale, a residential square. The population of Paris, which had been about 80,000 in 1300, near its medieval peak, approached 200,000 by 1600, 600,000 by 1700, and nearly 1,000,000 by 1800.

Whereas Paris had Roman origins, Amsterdam was probably founded no earlier than the thirteenth century, an

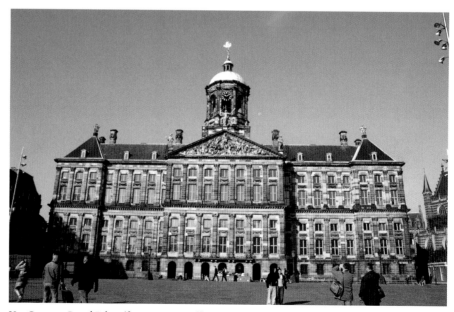

Van Campen, Royal Palace (former Town Hall), Dam Square, Amsterdam, 1647–1655.

unprepossessing depot in a marshy wilderness. The project of reclaiming land from the water began immediately with the construction of dikes and canals. By 1500 Amsterdam was a thriving but modest center of about 10,000 people; its population had doubled by mid-century. From the first, its main business was trade, the concern of both the residents and the town governors, for the town had won effective autonomy from the local nobility.

In 1578, as part of the first stage of a struggle for the independence of the northern Low Countries from Spanish rule, in what was decorously called the "Alteration," Amsterdam adopted the Reformed faith. In the later decades of the sixteenth century, it absorbed large numbers of Jewish and *converso* refugees from the Portuguese Inquisition. By 1618, as the city profited from the fall of Antwerp in 1585, its population had swollen to about 100,000. In 1602 the Dutch East India Company, which would soon administer commercial operations around the globe, was founded with its main office in Amsterdam. The Bank of Amsterdam and the Stock Exchange, founded in 1609 and 1611, were world financial centers.

The seventeenth century saw the Dutch mastery of the seas reach its apogee. Yet after a series of wars with England from 1652 to 1674, its importance began to diminish. By the opening of the eighteenth century, Amsterdam had fallen behind both Paris and London, yet was still an important center, with a population of some 200,000 at the time of the French Revolution.

A small town on a remote and thinly populated island during the Middle Ages, London was the northwestern most outpost of the Hanseatic League ports. With a thriving population of about 80,000 in 1300—up from between 10,000 and 15,000 in 1085, not long after the Norman Conquest—it engaged in the trade of wool (from sheep raised on the lush grass of rural monasteries) and other raw commodities that were the staples of the medieval commercial system. During the sixteenth century, when the establishment of the Tudor dynasty put an end to two centuries of disruptive warfare, London began to export finished cloth as well as raw wool, reaping the profits that had previously gone to Flemish or Italian merchants. By the age of Elizabeth I (see p. 299), London had become a major political and cultural as well as commercial center, with a population that approached 200,000. It was, moreover, the only important city in England; the large proportion of the English population who were urban lived in or circulated through London. In the seventeenth century, as the home of Parliament as well as royal government, London experienced at close quarters the shock of the English Revolution, Cromwellian Interregnum, and Restoration. Under Oliver Cromwell, who engaged the Dutch in the maritime wars of 1652–1674, London benefited from its now unchallenged supremacy at sea. The city reached a population of about 500,000 by 1700 and about 1,100,000 in 1800, in the midst of the Industrial Revolution.

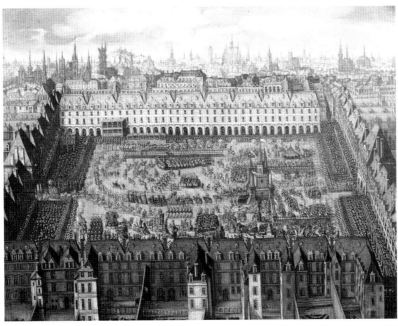

Anonymous, The Great Carrousel Held in the Place Royale (now Place des Vosges), 5–7 April 1612, to celebrate the marriage of Louis XIII to Anne of Austria, 17th century, oil on canvas. Musée Carnavalet, Paris.

The Hanseatic League was an association of mostly northern German merchants and merchant companies ("Hanse" was German for "guild" or "association"), protected by a common law code and their own defense organization. It connected about 100 cities and ports on the North and Baltic Seas ranging in size from Trondheim (Norway) and Kolberg (Poland), to Bruges, Bergen (Norway), and Novgorod (Russia). Across this swath of northern Europe, the merchants of the member cities exchanged the commodities of the northern or eastern European interior—metal, timber, fish, grain, honey, furs—with the textiles of England and the Netherlands. From the seacoast, commerce extended inland to such important centers as German Cologne and Lübeck, Prague, and Cracow (Poland). This trading system, although it handled cheaper goods, prevailed in northern Europe from the thirteenth through the fifteenth century, and was exceeded only by the Venetian maritime empire in extent and in sophistication.

Like the Venetian empire, and like other smaller trading systems, the Hanseatic League was a collection of cities and towns. Its borders did not correspond to those of any single nation-state; indeed, in the northern and eastern fringes of Europe, national boundaries were inchoate in this era. As in Italy, cities preceded nations, the main exception being the precocious English nation. Before the modern kingdoms of Europe clearly defined themselves and before modern vernacular languages crystallized, systems of towns and cities functioned together, had legal and management systems, and brought prosperity to the continent.

As in Italy also, by the fifteenth century, these urban–regional systems began, not merely to exchange commodities, but to manufacture them. Over the next centuries, these manufacturing enterprises would knit together laborers and skills in both country and city, constituting what historians call "proto-industrialization." They were a necessary basis for the spurt of accelerated manufacturing capacity in the eighteenth and nineteenth centuries known as the Industrial Revolution.

In the sixteenth and seventeenth centuries, the autonomous cities of the Middle Ages, like the nobility, yielded somewhat to the power of kings. The growing power of the kingdoms of Lithuania, Sweden, the Netherlands (under Habsburg rule), and England sent the Hanseatic League into decline, as each nation nurtured its own mercantile enterprises. In France and Spain, the elevation of a capital city associated with the monarch—Paris (Versailles) and Madrid—recentered the national map. The need to establish and defend a nation, moreover, meant that fortifications were required on the frontier, where there were few or no cities. Strong walls were no longer needed as defensive rings around the cities themselves. Indeed, such walls might persuade an urban populace that it could defy a monarch's authority. The walls came down, at least those of the major cities. New straight avenues sliced through the city centers and boulevards ringed them in the pattern of the once-encircling walls.

By the seventeenth and eighteenth centuries, three European cities had grown to exceed all others in wealth, rank, and population: Amsterdam, London, and Paris. The great Italian cities of the Renaissance remained, but they did not grow and were forced to give way to these newcomers of northwestern Europe.

The successor to Bruges and Antwerp as megalopolis of the Low Countries, Amsterdam had only 30,000 inhabitants at the time of the Reformation in the early sixteenth century but more than 200,000 when it reached the apex of its importance as an international merchant shipper in the mid-seventeenth century. The Dutch lost their primacy to the English in the late seventeenth century, as London came to the fore, surpassing the 500,000 mark in population by 1700. London was capital not only of England, but, like Amsterdam, of a far-flung colonial empire, yet it was rivaled by Paris in political, commercial, and cultural importance by the mid-eighteenth century. Although the French, too, had colonies, Paris's proximity to the court of an absolutist king meant more than empire. Paris took the lead as the intellectual and artistic capital of Europe, the seat of the movement known as the Enlightenment.

These huge European capital cities—Paris and London more than Amsterdam— were adorned with fine architecture, huge government buildings, schools, theaters and museums, shops and promenades, elaborately designed gardens and parks, and luxurious residential areas for the elite who now felt it was necessary to live at least part of the year in town rather than at their country residences, where the principal pleasure that remained was hunting. It was this urban context that nurtured modern theater and a profusion of salons and academies—all based on Italian Renaissance models—and above all, the conversation of the learned and the powerful.

CENTERS OF THE RENAISSANCE BEYOND THE ALPS

There was no single "European Renaissance" outside of Italy but several different local and national expressions of the Renaissance phenomenon. The remaining pages of this chapter will review the main settings and features of the Renaissance beyond the Alps, beginning with the Iberian Peninsula and ending with the northern and eastern borderlands of the continent.

Spain and Portugal

On the Iberian Peninsula, the Renaissance era saw the building of strong national monarchies and the influence of the Inquisition.

Spain When the Italian Renaissance began, the kingdom of Portugal was an independent state on the Iberian Peninsula, but there was no kingdom of Spain. Instead, there was a collection of small kingdoms, each with its own *cortes* (assembly). The 1469 marriage of Ferdinand II of Aragón (1452–1516, considered Ferdinand V of Spain) and Isabella of Castile (1451–1504) united the two major kingdoms of the peninsula outside of Portugal. Their long and successful joint monarchy saw the completion of the *reconquista* of the remaining Islamic states by the warrior nobility, reversing the Islamic conquest of the Iberian peninsula accomplished in 711. It also saw the establishment in 1478 of the Inquisition, which was formed to police recent and possibly insincere Jewish and Moorish converts to Christianity. (Jews and Moors who did not convert were expelled from Spain in 1492 and from Portugal in 1497.) Finally, it saw the opening up of the Americas by the Genoese navigator Christopher Columbus, the first step toward the construction of the European maritime empires (see Chapter 11).

During the sixteenth century, the joint monarchy determined the modern nation of Spain. Charles I, the grandson of Ferdinand and Isabella by their daughter Joanna the Mad, commanded the allegiance of all the Iberian states, excluding Portugal, though they were still partly autonomous. As King of Castile, Charles ruled the Spanish maritime colonies. As King of Aragón, he fought the French Valois King Francis I to a standstill in Italy (see Chapter 7).

Charles had other burdens as well. He inherited title to the Habsburg lands from his grandfather, the Holy Roman Emperor Maximilian I. These included not only Austria and other territories in German-speaking central Europe but also the Low Countries, which he had earlier inherited from his father, Philip the Handsome, and some other possessions. He gained title to these and to the imperial throne as Charles V in 1519. During his long reign, Charles's responsibilities included those he incurred as emperor as well as those he incurred as King of Spain. Among these were the need to confront the expanding Ottoman Empire and to deal with Martin Luther's revolt against the Catholic Church in imperial territory.

Under Charles's son Philip II (r. 1556–1598), Spain reached the height of its prestige and territorial expanse. It then ruled over Naples and Milan in Italy, the Balearic Islands, the Philippines, and a vast American empire. For the 60-year period 1580–1640, it included Portugal as well. In the style of other absolutist monarchs, Philip II gave expression to his sovereign status in building—notably the Escorial, a huge residence and monastery complex not far from Madrid, where future Spanish monarchs would be entombed. He intervened, albeit unsuccessfully, in the political affairs of the French and the English. In France, he supported the Catholic party against the Huguenot opposition. In England, as spouse of Queen Mary (r. 1553–1558), he pressed for the defeat of Protestantism. Mary Tudor was the eldest child of King Henry VIII but a devout supporter of the Catholic Church of her mother, Catherine of Aragón, the daughter of Ferdinand and Isabella. Under the persecution carried out during her rule with Philip's approval, many Protestants fled to safety on the continent, and many were executed. Philip survived Mary, while England returned to an official Protestantism under her successor Elizabeth I (r. 1558–1603). To turn England Catholic again, in 1588, Philip sent the great Spanish fleet, or Armada, against the much weaker naval forces of the island nation. The latter prevailed, however, aided by the weather.

The great Spanish empire of the sixteenth century faded in the seventeenth despite the considerable skill of royal advisors. Philip III (r. 1598–1621) and Philip IV (r. 1621–1665) were ineffective rulers; and Philip IV's son Charles II (r. 1665–1700) was entirely incompetent. With the latter's death, the throne passed to a junior branch of the Bourbon family which had once bitterly opposed the Spanish king.

SPANISH SKETCHES: A NOBLEMAN ON THE SKIDS AND A DISHONORED WIFE

The Spanish *Siglo de Oro* (Golden Age) of the sixteenth and seventeenth centuries saw a great outburst of splendid literature (poetry, drama, narrative prose) characterized by patriotism, piety, and fearless realism. The plight of the poor, the degeneration of the nobility, and the suppression of women were frequent themes.

In this excerpt from the anonymous picaresque novel *Lazarillo de Tormes* (1554), the boy Lazarillo has found employment with a member of the fading nobility, only to learn that the grandly attired aristocrat is as wretched as he is, as starved and gaunt as the miserable bed on which he slept:

I stood at one end and he at the other, and we made up the filthy bed.... The bedclothing was about as dirty as the mattress, which had a whole lot less wool in it than it needed.... The wretched pad did not have a bit of stuffing in it. With everything on top of the framework the reeds showed through, so that it looked exactly like the backbone of a very skinny pig. Over that hungry pig went a cover of about the same leanness.... It was night when the bed was made. He said to me, "Lazaro, it is late, and the market place is quite some distance from here. Besides, there are many footpads in this city who will steal the clothes off a person's back at night. Let us get by as best we can, and tomorrow, when it gets light, God will provide.... The past few days I have been eating out, but now we shall have to manage some other way."

"Sir," I said, "do not worry about me. I certainly know how to spend one night, and even more if necessary, without eating."

"You will live a longer and healthier life," was his answer, "for ... there is no better recipe in the world for a long life than to eat sparingly."

(J.G. Markley, trans., The Life of Lazarillo de Tormes. New York: Liberal Arts Press, 1954, pp. 37–38)

In the next excerpt, from a story by Maria de Zayas y Sotomayor (1590–1661/1669), a jealous husband describes the awful punishments he has heaped upon his innocent wife, whom he has starved, humiliated, and enslaved:

Blinded with furious rage, the first thing I did ... was to burn alive Helen's treacherous cousin. I took special pains to preserve his head so that it could be put to the use which you yourselves have seen. It was his skull that Helen was carrying in her hands. Let it serve as a cup from which she may partake of bitter drinks, just as formerly she imbibed sweet ambrosia from her paramour's lips!... I have to take away Helen's life also, as I intend to do before she dies a natural death.... I did not kill her on the spot, because a quick death is too small a punishment for a woman who has committed such a heinous crime.... In conclusion, I have held her penned up, in the condition that you have seen, for two years. She eats and drinks no more than that ration which was allotted to her today. A heap of straw is her only bed.... Her sole companion is the skull of her treacherous, beloved cousin. She is to remain in this condition until the moment of her death.

(K.M. Wilson and F.J. Warnke, eds., Women Writers of the Seventeenth Century. *Athens: University of Georgia Press, 1989, pp. 219–220)*

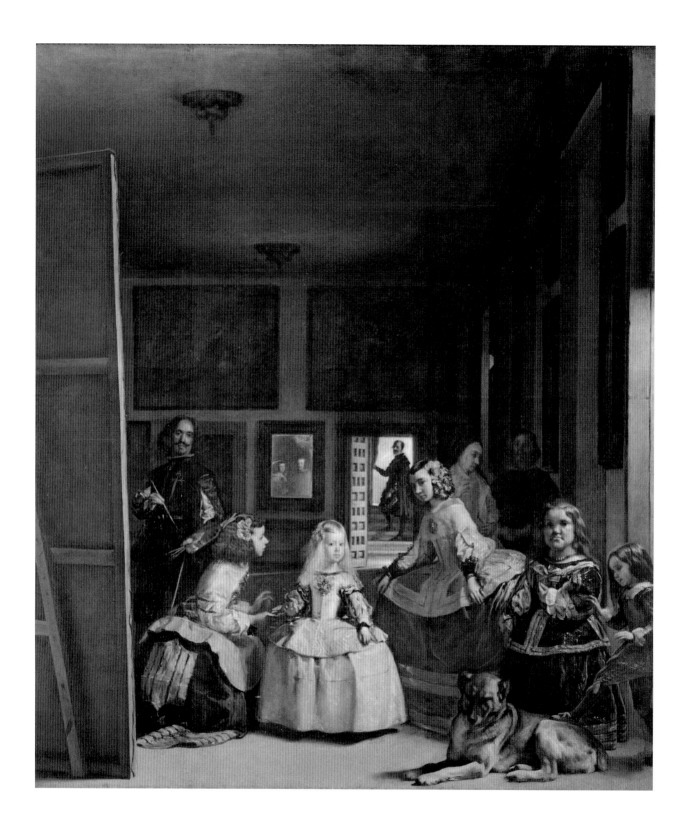

Portugal Portugal, meanwhile, also traced a pattern of decline after a period of growth and achievement. Independent from the twelfth century, the kings of the fourteenth and fifteenth centuries were effective rulers who saw Portuguese rule extend in the Mediterranean region. Under the guidance of the king's brother, Prince Henry the Navigator (1394–1460), Portugal became the foremost European innovator in methods of shipbuilding, cartography, and navigation, which laid the basis for the explorations that opened up Asia and the Americas and won for Portugal a great maritime empire (see Chapter 11).

The Portuguese monarchy became increasingly autocratic as it defended its authority against feudal lords, on the one hand, and the kings of Castile on the other. Following the Spanish lead, Portugal expelled its Jews in 1497, five years after the expulsion of the Jews from Spain and forced any who wished to remain to convert to Christianity. In 1536, again on the Spanish model, Portugal instituted the Inquisition and began the process of purging Jewish and Moorish converts. In 1580, with the death of the last of the Aviz dynasty, who was a cardinal and a celibate, Philip II of Spain, a distant kinsman, claimed the Portuguese throne. Portugal remained merged with Spain until 1640, when a successful revolution brought the Braganza family to power. The Braganza monarchs continued to struggle to maintain their new position through the rest of the century, aided greatly by an alliance with England. This alliance was cemented by marriage between the two royal houses: the daughter of King John IV, the first Braganza monarch (r. 1640–1656), and Charles II (r. 1660–1685), the restored King of England.

Iberian Humanism and the Arts Thus Renaissance civilization developed on the Iberian Peninsula in the context of centralizing monarchy and a crusading church. Spanish intellectuals were in close contact with Italian currents of thought and the arts through the Kingdoms of Sicily and Naples, both under Aragonese rule. The works of Dante, Petrarch, and Boccaccio had reached the Iberian Peninsula by the fifteenth century, where they stimulated an interest in classical antiquity. Early humanists translated some Italian works into Castilian, the leading Spanish dialect and the basis of modern Spanish. They wrote new works in Castilian as well, leading some to refer to this stage of intellectual culture as "vernacular humanism."

At the same time, Spanish humanism was strongly tinged by religious interests. A notable achievement, spearheaded by the humanist Cardinal Jiménez de Cisneros (1436–1517) at the new University of Alcalá, was the Complutensian Polyglot Bible, printed in 1514–1517, which provided the biblical text in Hebrew, Greek, and Latin. ("Complutensian" derives from the Latin name of the city of Alcalá, "Polyglot" from the Greek for "many languages.")

Erasmianism was a prominent feature of early Spanish humanism. Erasmus enjoyed an early popularity in the circle of intellectuals who were the administrators and advisors to King Charles I. Charles had been reared in the same Netherlandish environment as Erasmus, and Erasmus had dedicated to him his *Institutio christiani principis* ("Education of the Christian Prince"). The ardent Erasmianism of the Spanish humanists came to a quick halt, however, when the Dutch humanist's ideas became the target of the Inquisition. It

(FACING PAGE)

Velázquez, *Las Meninas (The Maids of Honor),* 1656, oil on canvas, 10 ft 5 in × 9 ft½ in (3.2 × 2.74 m). Museo del Prado, Madrid.

The Infanta Margarita, sole heir to the throne of Spain, is surrounded by her maids of honor, while the artist in the background paints himself painting a portrait of her parents, the monarchs Philip IV and Mariana of Austria. The work not only portrays a court scene but also affirms the principle of dynastic continuity.

became dangerous to possess his books, which were officially banned in the 1559 *Index of Prohibited Books* (and later editions). Meanwhile, Juan Luis Vives, the most Erasmian of the Spanish humanists, had already gone north—to France, England, and Flanders (see Chapter 9).

Whereas Spain faced the Mediterranean, where Italy lay a short voyage away, Portugal faced the Atlantic. Its intellectual culture remained primarily traditional and Scholastic, although humanistic influences were felt in the fifteenth century and peaked in the early sixteenth. Prince Henry, the promoter of navigation and cartography, was also a patron of humanists and a collector of books, and Italian humanists were active at the court of Henry's nephew, King Afonso V. Several Portuguese-born scholars studied and wrote in Italy, including the Jewish exile Leão Hebreo (Leone Ebreo, 1465?–1521?), author of the *Dialoghi d'amore* ("Dialogues of Love"), which were heavily influenced by Neoplatonic philosophy. But there was little room for inquiry or innovation in Portugal once the Counter-Reformation established itself. There was still less in the New World lands occupied by the Portuguese, where both printing and advanced university study came much later than to the Spanish colonies (see Chapter 11).

Spanish and Portuguese literature, however, flourished in the sixteenth and seventeenth centuries, stimulated by the influx of humanist works, by Erasmian texts and debates, and by the translations now provided by the printing press (see Chapter 9). Both vernacular languages became crystallized in the literary texts of this period, with the Castilian dialect winning out as the basis of modern Spanish. Contacts with foreign cultures encouraged the study of linguistics and the composition of vernacular dictionaries.

In both languages, poets wrote in lyric and epic genres, while prose masters produced travel tracts and scholarly works. Devotional and mystical works were numerous, including those of St. Teresa of Ávila (1515–1582), author also of an important autobiography. The summit of Spanish literature in this period was reached in the seventeenth century with *Don Quixote* (1605, 1615), the prose epic, or novel, of Miguel de Cervantes (1547–1616), and the comedies of Lope de Vega (1562–1635). Both in their way reflect the grand issues of contemporary Spanish society, including the role of the nobility and the condition of women. Portugal's experience of empire deeply colored that nation's literature. Asian, African, and American themes fill a body of works ranging from travel narratives to the great epic poem *Os Lusíadas* ("The Lusiads," 1572) by Luis de Camões (1524/1525–1580), narrated by the explorer and admiral Vasco da Gama (c. 1469–1525) who had opened the Indian Ocean to Portuguese commerce.

In the arts, the powerful visual style of the Moorish civilization that flourished from the eighth through fifteenth century had already impressed the Iberian imagination prior to the arrival of Italian models. In addition, artists were influenced by French Gothic in the fourteenth century and the painting of the Low Countries in the fifteenth. By the mid-sixteenth century, however, when Italian style had become international and dominant, its forms were visible not only in painting, but in the design and facades of churches, monasteries, palaces, and the monumental retablo altarpieces favored in the region.

Among the native artists in the region, most influenced by Renaissance patterns were the father-and-son painters Pedro (c. 1450–c. 1504) and Alonso Berruguete (1488–1561), both of whom had worked in Italy. A visitor from abroad, Doménikos Theotokópoulos (1541–1614), born on the Venetian-ruled island of Crete and thus known in Spain as "El Greco" (the Greek), won the favor of rich patrons in Toledo for his dramatic large-scale oil paintings, whose style was conditioned by his years of study in Italy. In the next century, with Baroque style succeeding to late Renaissance, the paintings of Diego Velázquez (1599–1660) depicted both the court in Madrid and scenes of daily life in Seville.

The Renaissance that took form in the Iberian kingdoms of Spain and Portugal was ultramontane (beyond the Alps) and distinct from the Italian. Deeply Catholic and suspicious of innovation, it was also distinct from the different varieties of Renaissance that developed in the regions shortly to be visited. It is these that are normally intended by the term "Northern Renaissance": the Renaissance of the Low Countries, France, England, the German lands, and to some extent, their neighbors to the north and east.

The Low Countries

This region—constituted in modern times by the Netherlands, Belgium, and Luxembourg—has never been a single nation, neither in the Middle Ages, the Renaissance, nor since. It was an assemblage of ecclesiastical and secular principalities, studded by semi-autonomous towns. The northern part of the region, consisting primarily of the provinces of Holland and Zeeland, looked to the North Sea and the Baltic and the largely German merchant community that dominated the Hanseatic League. The southern part, consisting primarily of the provinces of Flanders and Brabant, looked to France and the Duchy of Burgundy. It was a dynamic region, where urbanization set in early, although on a smaller scale than in Italy. With an unusually large proportion of the population of the Low Countries engaged in commerce or manufacture, conditions were ripe for substantial cultural innovation.

From 1384 to 1477, the different components of the Low Countries fell under the rule of the dukes of Burgundy. Upon the death of Duke Charles the Bold (r. 1467–1477) in 1477, the Low Countries passed to his daughter Mary, who married the Habsburg king and Holy Roman Emperor Maximilian I in that year. From 1477 to 1579, they were a Habsburg possession and drawn into the politics of the empire. Emperor Charles V was challenged in the German lands by Lutheran reformers (see Chapter 9) and attempted to impose religious uniformity on the Low Countries. His son, Philip II, pushed that agenda still further as, coincidentally, the Inquisition was at work in Spain, and Philip's wife, Queen Mary of England, was attempting to turn back the Protestant tide there.

Philip's anti-heresy campaign aroused stiff resistance. In 1648, after a long and violent struggle, the northern provinces united in a largely Protestant and Dutch-speaking federation called the Dutch Republic. The largely Catholic and southern provinces (where both Flemish, a Dutch dialect, and a French dialect were spoken) became the Spanish

THE LOW COUNTRIES: INTERIORS AND EXTERIORS

The scenes painted by Italian artists of the Renaissance were located in abstract spaces (around a throne or a tomb framed against an open sky) or in stony stage-sets (at one end of a city street or in front of a hill). Netherlandish art of the fifteenth to seventeenth centuries, by contrast, perhaps because of a powerful heritage of manuscript illumination, tended to be meticulous in its description of setting. Artists rendered details as precisely as possible—in which project the new use of oil paints assisted greatly—creating scenes that were lifelike in their depiction of context as well as in their portrayal of the human figure. Interiors were distinct from exteriors. The former were busy places, with floors, walls, windows, and occasional objects with special attention being given to texture and finish. By contrast, the latter, painted with the same meticulous detail and attention to objects and textures, were open and restful. These characteristics make the art of the northern Low Countries, which was in many ways as splendid as the art of Italy, altogether distinct.

Netherlandish artists paid special attention to interior spaces as early as the first decades of the fifteenth century, as seen in this painting of the *Arnolfini Marriage* (1434), or *Arnolfini Betrothal*, by Jan van Eyck. Realistic details abound in this scene showing the betrothed pair, an Italian merchant and another merchant's daughter. Note the rich colors and textures of the clothing worn, down to the hems and fringes and the elegant gatherings of the bride's sleeves; the delicacy

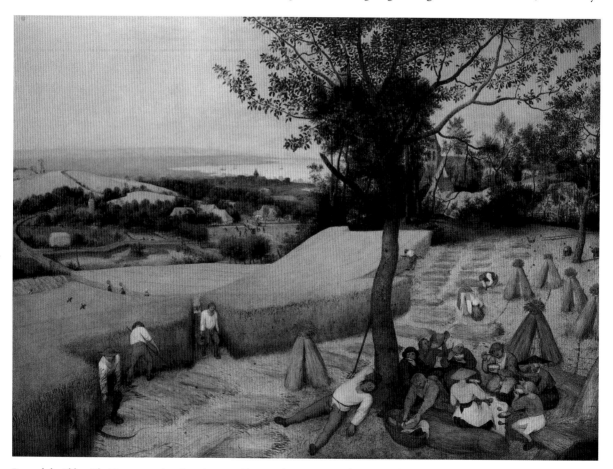

Bruegel the Elder, *The Harvesters*, 1565, oil on canvas, 46½ × 64 in (118.1 × 162.5 cm). Metropolitan Museum, New York.

and intricacy of her headdress; the careful delineation of all the parts of the chandelier; the polished broad planks of the floor and the wooden frame of the window; the lustrous convex mirror, containing within its circle the images of the bride and groom as well as the two witnesses to the moment (one of them thought to be van Eyck himself). The fine realism of the detail does not detract from the symbolic value of many of the objects: the red draperies of the bedstead hanging in womb-like folds, suggestive of fertility; the single lit candle bespeaking the presence of God; the rosary hanging on the wall, a reminder of prayer; and the little dog, an emblem of fidelity. Through the precise depiction of objects, the painting serves its dual purpose of description and metacommunication.

The masterful van Eyck and others of his generation were succeeded by painters who continued the tradition of attentive detail to interior space. The interiors painted by the seventeenth-century artists Pieter de Hooch (c. 1629–c. 1677) and Jan Vermeer, more secular in tone, still show the same attention to patterned floor tiles, wooden door frames, and tapestries and draperies. Some painters specialized in the genre of still life, where the focus on the interior narrowed to a still-narrower focus on the opulent forms of a bowl of fruit or a display of flowers.

The exterior world in the Netherlandish art of the fifteenth century is often glimpsed through a window, as in the Arnolfini portrait, where a shaft of sun enters through the open window to warm the colors and the faces. Sometimes whole worlds, removed in a perspective achieved through shadings of light and color, are evident beyond the framework of windows or archways. In the sixteenth and seventeenth centuries, complete focus on the exterior world was seen in the new genre of landscape painting. Seen here is *The Harvesters* (1565) of Pieter Bruegel the Elder, a painting in which one senses that the heavy scaffolding of doors and windows of the Netherlandish house have been exuberantly surpassed. It speaks of spaciousness: the gold zone of the wheat field and harvested stacks of produce, the green zone of grass, hedges, and trees in the middle distance, and, far away, a light-flooded, gentle gray of water and sky. Amid this lush display, people and their props are small, almost comic in their insignificance: workers pass through an alleyway cut through wheat stalks that, uncut, are nearly as tall as they; others sleep, glean, or enjoy their lunch in the shadow; in the distance, some other figures, barely discernible, seem to play on a green field, and a few boats are just gray blurs on a gray backdrop.

The foregrounding of background is a theme that will occupy Dutch painters into the seventeenth century as well, in paintings where the undulations of the fields or the mottled patches of the sky are the subject that engages the artist's attention. The subtle interplay of water and sky became a specialty for Aelbert Cuyp (1620–1691), whose nautical scenes recorded the harmonious ports and waterfronts of a region that was, as he painted, the commercial center of the world. Appealing to the eyes and hands of Jakob van Ruisdael (c. 1628–1682) were country scenes that figured windmills and cottages that were as compelling as the faces and bodies that had been the central concerns of the Renaissance artist, absorbed in the merely human.

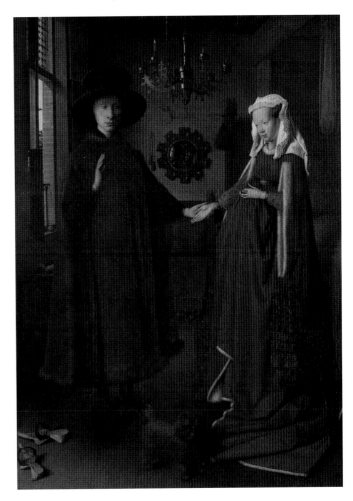

Jan van Eyck, *Arnolfini Marriage*, 1434, oil on panel, 32½ × 23½ in (82.5 × 59.7 cm). National Gallery, London.

Netherlands and accepted submission to Spain. In the north, the experience of cruel repression encouraged an attitude of toleration in matters of religion and freedom of thought and expression.

Art In this vibrant region, an artistic and intellectual Renaissance occurred that was at first independent of Italian models. Italians and others purchased works of art and borrowed elements of style from Netherlandish artists and thinkers. (This was especially the case in music; see Chapters 4 and 9.) Albrecht Dürer, the leading German Renaissance artist who journeyed to Italy to learn from its experts, also journeyed to the court of Margaret of Austria (1480–1530) in Flanders to learn from Netherlandish masters. As in Italy, the luxury goods sold in world markets by the merchants of the Low Countries were themselves works of artistry, while the entrepreneurs who became wealthy in that commerce were patrons of prestige objects—tapestries, gold and silver work, sculpted wooden altarpieces, and paintings. While an elite of burghers and nobles supported artistic works for their own consumption, the ecclesiastical and secular courts encouraged and supported the musical personnel—choirs, composers, and conductors—who transformed medieval musical traditions into new Renaissance patterns.

The painting of the Netherlandish Renaissance contrasts in several ways with the contemporary painting of the Italian Renaissance. It is characterized by an intense interest in detail, especially of natural and domestic objects, and by the use of oil paints. Netherlandish artists delighted in representing the texture and weight of the luxury textiles produced in their region, the reflection in mirrors or metallic items of objects in a room, the petals of flowers or intricately patterned leaves in a garden, glimpses of the outside world through the sunlit windows of interior spaces, and the contrasts of household surfaces: tile, wood, iron.

Their use of oil paint facilitated the execution of this detail, all on the flat surfaces of wood or canvas. Oil permitted exceptionally rich colors, which could be built up in successive layers of glazes to give the appearance of great depth. Oil required the artist to work slowly and with care (in contrast to Italian fresco painters who covered large surfaces of damp plaster with rapid-drying pigments), at the same time enabling the artist to render each object with a maximum of precision. Among the masters of these techniques were Jan van Eyck (c. 1395–1441), Rogier van der Weyden (c. 1399–1464), and Hans Memling (1430/1435–1494). The emphases on nature, homely domestic objects, interior space, and landscape persisted in the Netherlandish tradition in the later work of Pieter Bruegel the Elder (1525/1530–1569), Jan Vermeer (1632–1675), and many others.

Peter Paul Rubens (1577–1640) acquired a classicizing style after traveling to Italy. He painted grandiloquent religious and mythological scenes and tributes to the powerful and prosperous, mostly in his native Antwerp, but also in Spain and France. Rubens's student Anthony van Dyck (1599–1641) painted elegant portraits of wealthy patrons at home and in England, where he worked during the last years of his life. In Amsterdam, meanwhile, Rembrandt van Rijn (1606–1669) depicted in somber, demystifying tones scenes from bourgeois life and from biblical narrative.

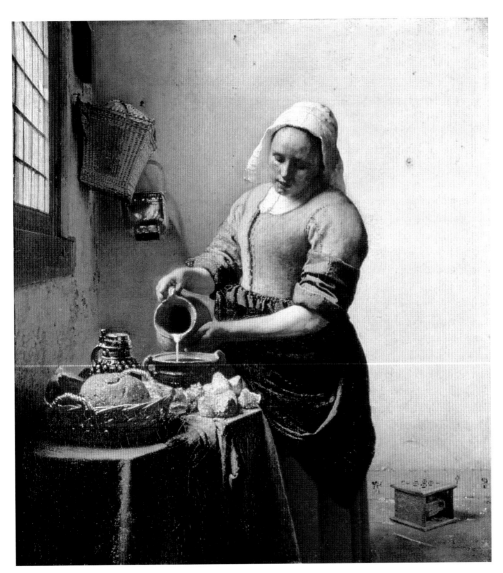

Vermeer, *The Milkmaid*, 1658–1660, oil on canvas, 18 × 16 in (45.5 × 41 cm). Rijksmuseum, Amsterdam.

Characteristic of Dutch painting is a concern for meticulous detail. Note the delicate stream of milk poured from the jug and the sunlight entering the window to brighten the milkmaid's headdress and the wall behind her.

Ideas The Low Countries were a vibrant center for the exchange of ideas, as well as for the arts. Humanism took an original and characteristic form and produced the genius of Erasmus (see Chapter 9). Influencing the humanism of the Low Countries was an earlier movement called the Devotio Moderna, which flourished from the fourteenth century and eventually merged with the Reformation movements in the sixteenth. The Devotio Moderna valued the spirituality of the inner life over the formalistic rituals and abstract theorizing common at that time. Lay adherents of the Devotio Moderna (the New Devout) called themselves the Brethren of the Common Life. Although the Brethren did not, as once was thought, form an intellectual movement, many of the later religious and intellectual leaders of the region—including Erasmus and other humanists—received their training in schools founded by the Brethren.

Netherlandish culture became deeply imbued with the spirit of the Devotio Moderna. Against this background the Dutch thinker Rudolphus Agricola (Roelof Huysmann, 1443–1485), who had spent several years in Italy, introduced humanistic studies. The young Erasmus was strongly influenced by Agricola and became, in the next generation, the major figure of Dutch, and indeed European, humanism. It was to be a humanism strongly religious in character—often called "Christian humanism"—and deeply committed to the educative function of language and study. Erasmus's legacy was a humanist tradition that valued the dignity of the individual, an interior and questioning spirituality, and an earnest commitment to classical studies.

Erasmus helped to found the Trilingual College at the University of Louvain (modern Belgium), which fostered classical studies. Here the Spanish-born humanist and refugee Juan Luis Vives spent many productive years (see Chapter 9). Although the university itself tended toward Catholicism in the Reformation struggles, later prominent Protestant (specifically Calvinist) intellectuals in the Erasmian tradition emerged in the Netherlands. One such was Jacobus Arminius (Jacob Harmansen, 1560–1609), who argued within the Calvinist community for an enlarged concept of human freedom. Another was Hugo Grotius (1583–1645), whose *De jure belli et pacis* ("On the Law of War and Peace") was the first great work in any language defining principles of international law based on natural law and the essential dignity of the human individual.

Although a local literary tradition emerged in both the northern and southern zones of the Netherlands, Latin remained the primary language for the communication of ideas. Nonetheless, considerable energy was devoted to the study and standardization of the Dutch language, and in 1637 a *Statenbijbel*, an officially approved Dutch translation of the Bible, was published for the largely Calvinist Christians of the Netherlands. Poets, play-wrights, and political writers also produced important works in Dutch in the seventeenth century, which was the Netherlands' Golden Age.

Academies and informal groups flourished in Antwerp in the sixteenth century and in Amsterdam in the seventeenth, providing a home for the discussion of ideas. Having suffered so much from religious warfare and confessional strife, Amsterdam became the freest city in Europe, and many foreign authors who could not safely publish in their own countries did so here. Toward the end of the seventeenth century, both Pierre Bayle's (1647–1706) *Dictionary* and John Locke's *Two Treatises of Civil Government*, important works of early Enlightenment thought, were published in the Netherlands.

France

The French Renaissance, like the Spanish, developed in the context of a centralized state and a powerful monarchy, one of the earliest to develop in Europe. It reached its height in the Middle Ages under the late Capetian kings Philip II, called Augustus (r. 1180–1223); his pious grandson Louis IX, later sainted (r. 1226–1270); and Louis's grandson, the aggressive Philip IV, called the Fair (r. 1285–1314). The monarchy suffered setbacks in the fourteenth and fifteenth centuries, as the new line of Valois monarchs struggled with England and her allies in the Hundred Years' War (1337–1453). In the last years of that struggle and the first years of the peace, Kings Charles VII (r. 1422–1461) and Louis XI (r. 1461–1483) moved rapidly to reduce the power of the feudal lords and reestablish the sovereignty of the king.

Under Francis I, France was largely unified and pacified. Even Francis's misadventures in Italy did not weaken his regime. Upon his death in 1547, however, four monarchs followed in quick succession whose reigns were marked by tragedy and turmoil: Francis's son Henry II (r. 1547–1559), and Henry's sons Francis II (r. 1559–1560), Charles IX (r. 1560–1574), and Henry III (r. 1574–1589). Henry II died in a tournament in 1559. His widow, Catherine de' Medici (1519–1589), a daughter of the Medici Duke of Urbino, held power as regent for her son Charles IX and remained active during the reign of Henry III.

During these years, France was convulsed by religious warfare between a Catholic majority, headed by one group of nobles, and a Calvinist or Huguenot minority (see Chapter 9), headed by another. A third party, that of the *politiques* (politicals), wished to elevate political considerations—and the welfare of the French state—above religious matters. The struggle culminated in 1572 in a massacre of Protestants, beginning with those gathered in Paris for a royal wedding, by the forces of the Catholic party. Named for the day on which it began, the St. Bartholomew's Day Massacre (August 23–24) was one of the bloodiest moments in the awful history of sixteenth-century religious strife.

When the last son of Catherine de' Medici was assassinated in 1589, the Valois line died out. Next in line to the throne was the leader of the Protestant party, Henri de Bourbon, King of Navarre—a circumstance that led to renewed turmoil. To win control of Catholic Paris and pacify and unify the country, in 1593 Henry agreed to convert to Catholicism. His reign (as Henry IV, r. 1589–1610), from his unexpected accession to his assassination by a Catholic fanatic, was marked by his dual commitment to the restoration of monarchical power and to the principle of religious toleration. The nation's finances recovered under his trusted prime minister, the Duc de Sully (Maximilien de Béthune, 1560–1641). In 1598 Henry issued the Edict of Nantes, which granted the Huguenots, his former coreligionists, political rights and freedom of worship. This freedom would be denied them by Henry's grandson Louis XIV, who revoked the Edict in 1685.

The reigns of Louis XIII (r. 1610–1643), Louis XIV, and Louis XV (r. 1715–1774) saw the greatest development of the royal claim to power. Louis XIII enjoyed the services of one of Europe's most effective prime ministers, Cardinal Richelieu (Armand Jean du Plessis, 1585–1642), who worked to support royal authority against the nobility and the Huguenots in domestic matters. In international affairs, he sought to build French prestige and military readiness and saw the Thirty Years' War through to a conclusion (finalized after the Peace of Westphalia of 1648) that was favorable to France.

In the meantime, Louis XIV had ascended to the throne. The influence of his mother, the regent Anne of Austria (1601–1666), and the guidance of Richelieu's successor as chief minister, Jules Mazarin (1602–1661), colored his early years as king. Louis established his

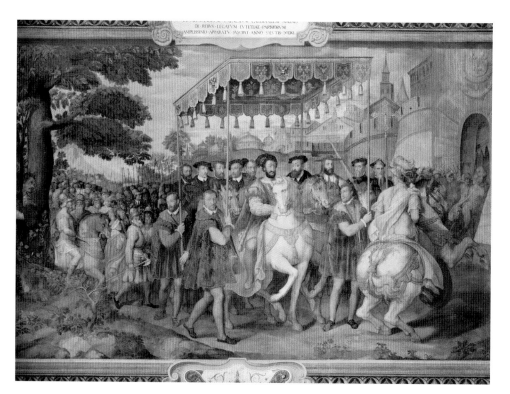

Taddeo and Federico Zuccari,
Francis I Receiving Charles V
and Cardinal Alessandro Farnese
in Paris, **1554, fresco. Palazzo**
Farnese, Rome.

A display of pageantry—the
trappings of the horses, the
courtiers in full dress, the official
baldachin held over the mounted
dignitary—was an essential
element of diplomacy in the
sixteenth century.

royal court in the Parisian suburb of Versailles. Here his magnificent palace and gardens
became the prototype of the absolutist residence. From Versailles, Louis ruled France
and threatened Europe, surrounded by the domesticated nobility of the nation who were
summoned to the royal court and who obeyed that summons if they were to have hope of
advancement. Louis XIV lived so long—his reign lasted 72 years—that he was succeeded
not by his son or grandson, but his great-grandson, who as Louis XV ruled autocratically
and lived extravagantly, though aware of the restiveness of his nobles and the mounting
problems that faced the regime.

Art It was in the arts that the hand of monarchy was most evident in the unfolding
of the French Renaissance. Francis I brought back many fine examples of Renaissance
workmanship and imagination from his many years on campaign in Italy—artists as well,
such as Leonardo da Vinci, Benvenuto Cellini, and Andrea del Sarto. At home in France,
he had many residences built and decorated in Renaissance style, executed by native and
foreign artists, most famously his palace of Fontainebleau. Henry IV brought new dynamism to the Parisian cityscape, rebuilding parts of the royal palace of the Louvre, and
constructing on a grand scale the Pont Neuf over the Seine and the Place Royale (now
Place des Vosges) as a private residential square. Louis XIV's grand venture of Versailles
has been mentioned above.

Ideas In 1529 Francis I founded the Collège de France for the promotion of humanistic
studies, and Richelieu, under Louis XIII, organized the Académie Française to promote
the French language and literature. Royal patronage, however, was less important for
humanism and literature than it was for the arts. French intellectuals came into contact

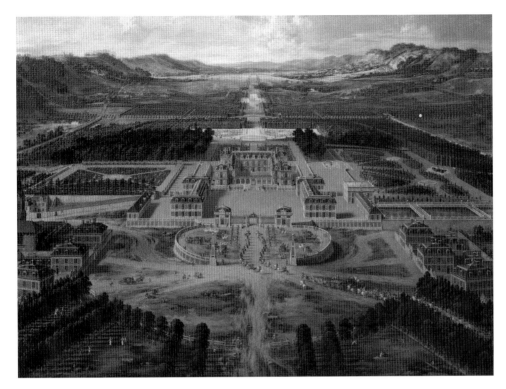

Patel the Elder, *View of Versailles*, 1668, oil on canvas, 3 ft 10 in × 5 ft 3 in (1.15 × 1.61 m). Châteaux de Versailles et de Trianon, Paris.

The enormous Palace of Versailles opened up to an equally grandiose park adorned with gardens, grottoes, fountains, and statuary, in which the royal family and thousands of courtiers took their leisure.

with the early currents of Italian humanism at the papal court in Avignon during the fourteenth century. When the popes returned to Rome in 1378, French humanism shifted north to Paris. In the fifteenth century, Guillaume Fichet (1433–c. 1490) and Robert Gauguin (c. 1433–1501) introduced humanism to the University of Paris and pursued the humanistic disciplines of rhetoric and history.

Their contributions were overshadowed by the humanist circle of the early 1500s, which included the humanist reformer Jacques Lefèvre d'Etaples and the lawyer and humanist Guillaume Budé (1467–1540), both major authors and scholars. A priest who had studied in Italy for some years, Lefèvre produced editions and commentaries on Aristotle, the Psalms, the Gospels, and the letters of St. Paul, blending the Christian tradition with humanist values. Like Erasmus, an exponent of Christian humanism, he became involved in early reform circles in France. Budé devoted his critical skills to the books of Roman civil law, on which he wrote a massive commentary. Following his lead, French humanism was characterized by legal scholarship. In addition, Budé produced a Greek grammar, a history of Roman coinage, and works on philology and literary studies. Both Lefèvre and Budé were important correspondents of Erasmus.

Close to these figures was Marguerite of Angoulême (1492–1549), later Queen of Navarre, sister of Francis I and grandmother of the first Bourbon king Henry IV. Deeply interested in religious reform, Marguerite was herself an author of poems, devotional works, and the story collection *Heptaméron* ("The Seven Days"), an important contribution to French Renaissance literature with strong feminist elements. Marguerite's contemporaries included other women authors: the poet Louise Labé (c. 1520–1566), the novelist Hélisenne de Crenne (d. after 1552), and the mother-and-daughter humanist poets Madeleine (1520–1587) and Catherine (1550–1587) des Roches.

Later in the sixteenth century, a number of scholars engaged in textual criticism, which led to the publication of editions of classical texts and the exposures of forgeries. They included the two Scaligers, the Italian-born father Julius Caesar (1484–1558) and his son Joseph Justus (1540–1609), who joined the Reformation and died in the Netherlands. Julius Caesar edited ancient texts and wrote treatises on Aristotle; Joseph Justus wrote massive and authoritative works on historical chronology.

Meanwhile, humanism had a great impact on literature in France, influencing the poet Clément Marot (1496?–1544), who turned Protestant and wrote the immensely popular French psalter, and the novelist François Rabelais (c. 1494–1553). The relationship of Michel de Montaigne (1533–1592) to humanism is complex. Renowned creator of the essay form and author of the *Essais* ("Essays"), discursive explorations of the self, society, and the past, he certainly drew on the humanist tradition, as he possessed a formidable but selective knowledge of classical texts. However, he also resisted it, rejecting humanism's formal Latin for flowing French prose. During the seventeenth century, French literature was perhaps most noted for its brilliant playwrights. The comedies of Molière (Jean Baptiste Poquelin, 1622–1673) mocked contemporary social types—the bourgeois ambitious to be viewed as noble, pretentiously learned women, greedy misers, and pious hypocrites. Pierre Corneille (1606–1684) and Jean Racine (1639–1699), in contrast, wrote austere, classicizing tragedies which explored enduring human themes, often in classical or historical settings.

The British Isles

In the British Isles, too, the Renaissance centuries witnessed the centralization of government, the growing power of the monarchy, and the stresses of the Reformation. England claimed Ireland from the twelfth century and had absorbed Wales by the thirteenth century. Scotland, a separate nation from the Middle Ages, was unified with England in the person of James VI of Scotland (r. 1567–1625), who ascended the English throne as James I in 1603. England and her rulers were preponderant in the region throughout the Renaissance centuries.

Although the French emerged from the Hundred Years' War ready to centralize and modernize, England then entered a period of civil war that lasted through much of the fifteenth century. In this conflict, known as the Wars of the Roses, Yorkist and Lancastrian factions, representing two branches of the royal family, struggled for supremacy. In 1485 the young half-Welsh nobleman Henry Tudor (the future Henry VII, r. 1485–1509), a descendant of the royal line through his Lancastrian mother, defeated the last Yorkist monarch, Richard III (r. 1483–1485), who fell in the decisive battle of Bosworth Field. This victory established the Tudor dynasty, which would last through three generations and five monarchs in a little more than a century.

IN SEARCH OF AUTHENTICITY: TWO FRENCH VIEWS

Historians no longer call the Renaissance the "age of the discovery of the individual." Individuals and individualism exist in all ages and were not lacking in the Middle Ages which preceded the Renaissance. Yet the Renaissance did see a different kind of inquiry into the self. The humanist attention to the issue of the "dignity of man" and the related insistence by women authors on the "worth of women" (see Chapters 3 and 11) formed part of this exploration. So too were the efforts at self-fashioning, the construction of a public image, apparent in the elaborate self-presentation of monarchs or of nobles contending for recognition, the subject of Castiglione's *Courtier* (see Chapter 8). The playwright William Shakespeare confronted crucial issues about the self and the human condition, as when Hamlet pondered his choices in one of the most famous passages of English literature: "To be, or not to be: that is the question."

In the following passages, two French authors raise the issue of the authentic self: are we who we are or who we seem to be? Michel de Montaigne (1533–1592) asks us to judge the real person and not the outward face that is put on public display in this excerpt from his essay "Of the Inequality That Is between Us":

> But apropos of judging men, it is a wonder that, ourselves excepted, nothing is evaluated except by its own qualities. We praise a horse because it is vigorous and skillful ... not for his harness; a greyhound for his speed, not for his collar; a bird for his wing, not for his jesses and bells. Why do we not likewise judge a man by what is his own? He has a great retinue, a beautiful palace, so much influence, so much income: all that is around him, not in him.... Why in judging a man do you judge him all wrapped up in a package? He displays to us only parts that are not at all his own, and hides from us those by which alone one can truly judge of his value.... Measure him with his stilts; let him put aside his riches and honors, let him present himself in his shirt.
>
> (M. de Montaigne, Complete Essays, trans. D. Frame. Stanford, CA: Stanford University Press, 1958, pp. 189–190)

In this second passage, from the comedy *Tartuffe* by the playwright Molière (1622–1673), the character Cleanthes, speaking to his brother Orgon, distinguishes between a genuinely pious person and a pretentious hypocrite:

> No, brother, I am none of your reverend sages, nor is the whole learning of the universe vested in me; but I must tell you, I have wit enough to distinguish truth from falsehood. And as I see [nothing] ... more noble, or more beautiful, than the fervor of a sincere piety; so I think nothing more abominable than the outside daubing of a pretended zeal.... Those slaves of interest, who make a trade of godliness, and who would purchase honors and reputation with a hypocritical turning up of the eyes, and affected transports ... who show an uncommon zeal for the next world in order to make their fortunes in this, who ... daily recommend solitude, while they live in courts. Men who ... are ... full of artifice; and to effect a man's destruction, they insolently urge their private resentment as the cause of Heaven.... But the sincerely devout are easily known.... They have no cabals, no intrigues to carry on; their chief aim is to live themselves as they should do.... Nor do they ever exert a keener zeal for the interest of Heaven, than Heaven itself does.
>
> (Molière, Molière's Comedies, ed. F.C. Green. London: J.M. Dent, 1929, pp. 87–88)

Henry VII was concerned with reestablishing order and royal authority after a near-century of conflict, as well as providing a sound basis to the nation's finances. His son Henry VIII was driven by his need for an heir to protect the succession (see pp. 298–299). He took advantage of the Reformation arguments for a break from the Roman pope and established the Church of England with himself as head. Upon his death, England was not yet securely Protestant. His young son Edward—the youngest of his children, born to the third of his six wives—succeeded as Edward VI (r. 1547–1553) under the regency of noble protectors and advisors fiercely dedicated to the Protestant cause. By the time of his death, when only 16 years old, Protestantism had taken firmer root. It was confronted and shaken, however, during the reign of Edward's eldest sibling, Mary, the daughter of Henry's first wife. Mary was a devout Catholic who married Philip II of Spain, a zealot for the Catholic cause. She persecuted many Protestants, of whom some fled to the continent and some suffered martyrdom.

Mary, too, died after only a brief reign. The middle of Henry VIII's three legitimate offspring, Elizabeth, daughter of the monarch's second wife, now took the throne. Raised a Protestant, but possibly preserving Catholic rituals in her own private worship, Elizabeth moved swiftly to settle the disruptive religious question, approving the Thirty-Nine Articles that established guidelines for a national Protestant observance that steered midway between the Catholic and the Calvinist positions. Elizabeth's reign was also notable for its resistance to Spain, its participation in colonial exploration, and its consolidation of the monarchy along the line of absolutism. Dying without heirs, Elizabeth had previously arranged for the succession of her cousin's son, James VI of Scotland, to the English throne as James I. The Tudor dynasty ended with Elizabeth, and the new Stuart dynasty began with James.

Henry and Elizabeth had succeeded in protecting the power of the English throne and in managing religious matters. James asserted his power as an absolute monarch, which angered a Parliament then seeking to extend its prerogatives, while he alienated both Puritan (Calvinist) Protestants and Catholics, and irritated many by cultivating a circle of favorites. His son and successor, Charles I (r. 1625–1649), pursued similar policies. More irritatingly, he tended toward Catholicism in worship, at a time when many members of Parliament and other powerful figures were not only Protestant, but often Puritan. The king and Parliament clashed repeatedly. In 1642, angered by Charles's refusal to pursue the reforms it had demanded, Parliament raised an army. War ensued, in which parliamentary forces faced the legitimate monarch—a sight most disturbing to the other monarchs of Europe. In 1649, after a brief trial, King Charles I was executed.

England remained without a monarch until 1660, largely under the control of Oliver Cromwell (1599–1658), an officer in the parliamentary army and himself a Puritan. Cromwell turned against monarchy altogether, and served as Lord Protector of the English government from 1653. Upon Cromwell's death, and that of his son, the people and leaders of England were ready to recall their king; the monarchy was restored in 1660. The new king, Charles II, preserved the monarchy despite the growing demands of Parliament and sought a policy of religious toleration at a time of heightened anti-Catholic feeling.

Although his reign served to unify the nation, Charles himself died a Catholic. His brother and successor James II (r. 1685–1688) was also Catholic. Parliament could tolerate neither his arbitrary manner nor his Catholic faith and deposed him in 1688. In England's second, "Bloodless (or Glorious) Revolution," the joint monarchs William of Orange (r. 1689–1702) and Mary (r. 1689–1694), James's Protestant daughter, were placed on the throne. They swore to uphold the principles of the Bill of Rights (1689).

Art and Ideas The history of England is deeply intertwined with the history of the churches in this era. So is it with humanism. Both those who defended the break with Rome and those who opposed it were humanists. So were those who encouraged the strengthening of the monarchy, who discussed the education of young noblemen, and who participated in the translation of the Bible under James I. The English Renaissance began with the humanist movement, although it had largely outgrown that tradition by the mid-seventeenth century.

Humanism was introduced into England in the fifteenth century, primarily by Italians stationed abroad. Furthered by noble patrons, it flourished in the sixteenth century, influencing the intellectual debates between Protestants and Catholics. William Grocyn (c. 1446–1519) and John Colet (1467–1519), who had both studied in Italy, were the forerunners of the native English humanist tradition. Grocyn brought the study of Greek to Oxford University; Colet taught at Oxford and was dean of St. Paul's Cathedral (in the part of London called the "city," its commercial center). He founded and administered St. Paul's School, which trained youngsters in the classics, including poor students whose fees were waived. Their younger contemporary Thomas More, lawyer and statesman who attained the exalted title of Lord Chancellor of England, was the center of an important circle of humanist scholars, including Erasmus (see Chapter 9). The medical humanist Thomas Linacre (c. 1460–1524), who translated the Greek physician Galen and thus founded the early modern study of medicine in England, was also in More's circle. So was the statesman Sir Thomas Elyot (c. 1490–1546), whose *Boke Named the Governour* ("Book Named the Governor") depicted an ideal ruler and described the classical education required of those who ruled. Also important in More's circle was his daughter and intellectual heir, Margaret More Roper, whom he himself trained in Greek and Latin.

In More's lifetime, the nascent humanist movement in England collided with that of the Reformation. Humanism promoted the critical study of classical texts, with due attention to historical context; it therefore prepared the ground for the intellectual world of the Reformation. At the same time, humanist supporters of the Catholic Church, often in exile on the continent, employed their learning against the Reformation in England. Humanistic culture spread among elite groups, as is evidenced in *The Scholemaster* by Roger Ascham (1515–1568), a treatise on education directed to the sons of the upper classes. Ascham himself was most famous as the tutor of the young Elizabeth Tudor, daughter of Henry VIII, the future Queen of England.

The classical ideals of humanism influenced several important authors of the English literary Renaissance such as Edmund Spenser (1552–1599), Ben Jonson (1572–1637), and John Milton (1608–1674)—notably not, however, William Shakespeare. Spenser and

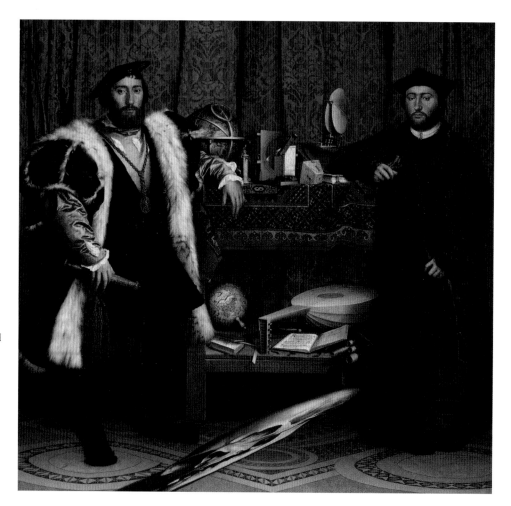

Holbein the Younger, *The Ambassadors*, 1533, oil on wood, 81½ × 82½ in (207 × 209.5 cm). National Gallery, London.

Decked out in sumptuous finery, the ambassadors surround objects associated with human knowledge, heroic endeavor, and mortality—terrestrial and celestial globes, a sundial, a spyglass, books, a lute—and a haunting, distorted skull in the foreground. These objects variously refer to the conditions of harmony and discord in political and natural realms and ultimately to our certain end.

Milton were both lyric poets and creators of two of the major epics of the Renaissance: respectively, the *Faerie Queene*, an allegory centered on Queen Elizabeth I, and *Paradise Lost*, an exploration of the meaning of the Christian vision of the Fall of Man. Jonson was a poet and dramatist, author of many works, such as the astute comedy *Volpone* about avarice and family ties. Shakespeare, of course, was not only a poet of towering importance, but the greatest playwright of an age that produced many greats and who more than any other helped create the modern tradition of public secular theater. In the comedies (*Midsummer Night's Dream*, *Much Ado about Nothing*), tragedies (*Hamlet*, *Romeo and Juliet*), and the history plays that examined the grand political themes of monarchy and nationhood (*Henry IV Parts I and II*, *Richard III*), Shakespeare drew together and brought to life the many problems and paradoxes that Renaissance civilization pondered. Many of his plays were set in Italian cities and courts and attest to his attentive consideration of the legacy of the Italian Renaissance.

The English were not so prolific in the visual arts as in poetry and drama, although they contributed much to both secular and sacred music in the sixteenth and seventeenth century. In the sixteenth century, the German painter Hans Holbein the Younger was invited to the English court, where he completed many official portraits and other works. In the next century, the Dutch painter Anthony van Dyck played much the same role. In architecture and the decorative arts, however, artists explored native traditions fruitfully. In the seventeenth century, architects Inigo Jones (1573–1652) and Christopher Wren (1632–1723) introduced the classical style in a series of prominent buildings in London and Greenwich. Wren built 53 churches, among them the massive St. Paul's Cathedral.

The German Lands

The German-speaking regions of Europe in the Middle Ages were largely incorporated in the Holy Roman Empire, which also included at different times Slavic Bohemia, Moravia, and Croatia; the Low Countries; and parts of northern Italy. The region consisted of hundreds of principalities, ruled by secular or ecclesiastical lords, and some free cities. These were bound together only by their common recognition of the emperor. From the fourteenth century, the Swiss cantons resisted imperial overlordship fiercely and had won effective independence by 1499.

In 1356 the Golden Bull issued by Emperor Charles IV (r. 1355–1378) decreed that the emperor was to be chosen by a prescribed set of electors: the King of Bohemia, the Count Palatine of the Rhine, the Duke of Saxony, the Margrave of Brandenburg, and the archbishops of Mainz, Trier, and Cologne. (After 1623, the Duke of Bavaria, and after 1698, the Elector of Hanover were added to this list.) These states gained prestige accordingly, dignified by their ability to assist in the imperial selection process. After the extinction of the great imperial Hohenstaufen family in 1254, Hungarian, Croatian, and Bohemian princes held the title of emperor. In 1438 the Habsburg family captured the imperial title. It remained in the Habsburg family (with one exception) until the empire's dissolution in 1806.

The Habsburg realm reached its maximum extent early in its history, under Charles V (see p. 269), when it included the Burgundian inheritance of the Low Countries and all the possessions of Castile and Aragón. After Charles's abdication in 1556, the Spanish possessions in Iberia and the Low Countries passed to his son Philip II, while his brother Ferdinand (r. 1558–1564) took up rule of the traditional Habsburg lands in central Europe and assumed the imperial title. In the previous year, the Peace of Augsburg had conferred upon the princes and other rulers of the empire the right to determine the confessional identity of their states, which now divided into Calvinist, Lutheran, and Catholic camps. These religious divisions came into play in the Thirty Years' War (1618–1648), which proved devastating for the region and for the future of imperial power. Later seventeenth-century warfare further eroded the power of the emperor. Meanwhile, the leading German princes profited from the imperial weakness and created miniature absolutist states where they could rule relatively freely.

Art and Ideas In the German-speaking lands of the Holy Roman Empire, humanistic studies were once again influenced by the Italian model. Three key figures in the development of German humanism had made the *italianische Reise* (the journey to Italy) that stimulated the pursuit of classical studies and Renaissance thought. These three figures were Rudolphus Agricola (see p. 348), who spent his last years in Heidelberg; the lawyer Johann Reuchlin (1455–1522), a pioneering Hebraist; and Conradus Celtis (Conrad Pickel, 1459–1508), called the German "Archhumanist."

Whereas Agricola introduced the humanistic study of classical languages and literature, rhetoric, and pedagogy, Reuchlin's interest was in Hebrew texts. The Italian humanists Giannozzo Manetti, Giovanni Pico della Mirandola, and Lorenzo Valla had all become masters of Hebrew through reading and commenting upon scriptural and kabbalistic texts (see Chapter 3). Reuchlin composed the first Christian dictionary of the Hebrew language and defended the reading of classical Hebrew texts so long as they did not attack Christianity. He also advocated the establishment of university positions of Hebrew. Although Reuchlin's views provoked enormous controversy, laced with anti-Semitism, they won the support of a group of pro-humanist, early reformers, who satirized the anti-Reuchlin party with a blistering work, *Epistulae obscurorum virorum* ("Letters of Obscure Men"). Reuchlin himself was not Jewish and died a Catholic.

Celtis's brief but illustrious career took him from the German cities of Cologne, Heidelberg, and Nuremberg to Italy, Poland, and, in his last years, Vienna, where he taught at the university and founded a circle of humanistic studies. Not only did he bring humanistic studies into vogue in the German lands, but he was the author of elegant Latin verse and a pioneering historian of the German states. Celtis discovered the manuscript works of the tenth-century woman mystic poet and playwright Hrosvitha (c. 935–1000) and thereafter promoted her achievements.

In the next generation, German humanism, influenced at first by Erasmus, became wholly involved in the controversies of the Reformation, and is best studied as part of that movement. As the religious traditions crystallized, the humanist mission continued primarily in the area of education. Universal education was one of the aims of Lutheran theology, and the humanists set about the reorganization and founding of schools that would provide both a sound classical education and a sturdy religious training. Active in this field was Philip Melanchthon (Philipp Schwartzerd, 1497–1560), chief deputy to the reformer Martin Luther (see Chapter 9). Melanchthon promoted the humanist curriculum in the schools and revised the Scholastic understanding of Aristotle in the universities in the light of the new generation of Hellenist textual studies. In Strasbourg, later in the century, Johann Sturm (1507–1589) established a famous humanist school that provided a model for secondary education throughout northern Europe. The humanistic transformation of the curriculum also reshaped the universities. In Germany, the Lutheran University of Tübingen, and in Switzerland, the Calvinist academies and seminaries of Geneva, served as sites of advanced training for the Protestant religious leaders of Europe.

At the same time that travelers to Italy brought a zeal for humanism home to the German realms, so did they bring back a taste for Italian style in the arts. The key figure in the transformation of the German artistic tradition was Albrecht Dürer, whose voyage south brought him into contact with the work of Andrea Mantegna and the Bellinis. The Renaissance sense of proportion, the use of perspective, the focus on the human body, the incorporation of classical and mythological elements—all figure in Dürer's work. The son of a goldsmith, Dürer was also an outstanding engraver and graphic artist, who used the medium of the woodcut to new expressive purposes. The two Lucas Cranachs, father and son (1515–1586), also developed a German Renaissance style in painting and woodcut. The elder Cranach, especially, used the woodcut format to popularize the Lutheran message (see p. 302). Hans Holbein the Younger was a member of the Erasmian circle; he created the pen-and-ink illustrations for the great humanist's *Praise of Folly* and won renown for his portraits (see p. 297) and altarpieces. He was called to England, where he painted both Thomas More and More's nemesis Henry VIII.

Northern and Eastern Europe

The great expanses of land on the northern and eastern fringes of Europe were mostly ruled by kings, during the Renaissance centuries often kept in check by a large and forceful nobility. These regions were little urbanized except for national capitals, but Renaissance culture made inroads here, too, depending largely on royal patronage.

Scandinavia was especially receptive to the humanist impulse, which arrived along with the Reformation, and Dutch and German humanists often found patrons in the kings of Sweden (which included Finland) and Denmark (which included Norway). Native humanists were especially active in education, religious reform (the region as a whole adopted Lutheranism by the 1530s), and in the compilation of national histories.

Bohemia (the modern Czech Republic and the most western of the eastern regions) was particularly open to Renaissance culture. A place of shifting dynasties and great religious turmoil, it was the homeland of the early reformer Jan Hus, who was burned at the stake at the Council of Constance in 1415 (see Chapter 6). It was equally receptive to Lutheran reform. Renaissance influence showed as early as the fourteenth century, when the Bohemian King Charles IV was made Holy Roman Emperor. He made Prague, the chief city of Bohemia, an imperial capital, gracing it with a new university, the first in central Europe, and rebuilding the city with the aid of artists brought from abroad, especially Italy. After a lapse, Bohemian kings from the late fifteenth century continued the tradition, and the buildings of Prague Castle and St. Vitus Cathedral were adorned in ambitious Renaissance style. Imitating these efforts, the nobility built Italianate palaces and villas, and the wealthier burghers erected Renaissance chapels in Prague's medieval churches. Under the Habsburg rulers, Prague was a leading European cultural capital, a center not only for the arts, but also for philosophy, science, and literature. In no other region in Europe did Italian models so permeate the arts and letters for so long a period.

Poland was a republic of nobles with an electoral monarchy. Home to large minorities of Germans, Jews, Armenians, and Tatars, its diverse cultures provided fertile ground for both humanism and reform movements. Latin was widely used, although poetry was often written in a vernacular steeped in the classical tradition. Polish intellectuals, many of whom studied in Italy, produced treatises on a range of humanistic issues, especially political ones. In a climate of religious freedom into the seventeenth century, both Lutherans and Catholic Jesuits established humanist schools. Later, the progress of recatholicization limited the freedom of worship and thought. In all, Poland was the greatest center of Renaissance culture in eastern Europe. Its neighbor, Russia, was largely untouched by Renaissance influences, although Italian artists helped to design some key buildings in Moscow, including the Kremlin.

In Hungary, the patron and bibliophile Johannes Vitéz (1408–1472), the Catholic primate, was instrumental in the elevation of Matthias Corvinus (r. 1458–1490) as king. His court at Buda became a sparkling Renaissance center, a magnet for humanists and artists from Italy and the German lands. Vitéz's nephew, the humanist poet Janus Pannonius (Ivan Cesmicki, 1434–1472), who was Croatian by birth, studied at the school of Guarino Veronese in Ferrara (see Chapter 3) before returning to Hungary and becoming a key figure in that region's native humanistic culture. The breakup of the country following the battle with the Turks at Mohács in 1526 led to a diminution of humanist activity and an absorption in battle literature and history.

Dalmatia, which was under Venetian rule from 1409 to 1797, participated in the Italian humanism centered at Venice, where many Dalmatians studied and subsequently printed their works. Among these were translations into Croatian, Croatian–Latin dictionaries, and histories of the Slavic peoples.

CONCLUSION

Renaissance civilization developed in different ways in the very different political and social contexts of Europe beyond the Alps. Although the impetus came almost everywhere from Italy (the urbanized Low Countries being, at first, exceptional), Italian patterns of thought and concepts of style were received differently according to native traditions and were teased and channeled in new directions. By the sixteenth and seventeenth centuries, the Renaissance belonged to Europe as much as to Italy. Distant Prague, Cracow, and London were, like Modena or Urbino, centers of Renaissance civilization and participants in the tide of cultural change that would create a new world by 1700.

SUGGESTED READINGS

Primary Sources

Elyot, Thomas, Sir. *A Critical Edition of Sir Thomas Elyot's "The Boke Named the Governour."* Edited by Donald W. Rude. New York: Garland Publishing, 1992. A political figure advises how to rear and educate a ruler.

Medici, Catherine de'. *Portraits of the Queen Mother: Polemics, Panegyrics, Letters.* Translated and edited by Leah L. Chang and Katherine Kong. Toronto: Iter Academic Press, Centre for Reformation and Renaissance Studies, 2014. Letters of Catherine de' Medici, arguably Europe's most important regent, who dominated French history in the mid-sixteenth century, accompanied by contemporary ambassadorial reports, eulogies, and other documents.

Montaigne, Michel de. *The Complete Essays of Montaigne.* Translated and edited by Donald M. Frame. Stanford, CA: Stanford University Press, 1958. A writer steeped in the classics takes himself as the object of his meditations. The classic translation.

Rabelais, François. *Gargantua and Pantagruel.* Translated by J.M. Cohen. Harmondsworth, UK: Penguin, 1976. Portrays the adventures of two comic heroes.

Secondary Sources

Asch, Ronald, and Adolf M. Birke, eds. *Princes, Patronage, and the Nobility: The Court at the Beginning of the Early Modern Age.* Oxford: Oxford University Press, 1991. Discusses the role of courts as early modern centers of power and patronage.

Bonney, Richard. *The European Dynastic States, 1494–1660.* Oxford: Oxford University Press, 1991. Surveys the European state system in the early modern era.

Bouwsma, William J. *The Waning of the Renaissance, 1550–1640.* New Haven, CT: Yale University Press, 2000. An intellectual historian traces the unraveling of the Renaissance synthesis.

Burke, Peter. *The Fabrication of Louis XIV.* New Haven, CT: Yale University Press, 1992. The quintessential absolute monarch devises his self-image.

Dewald, Jonathan. *The European Nobility, 1400–1800.* Cambridge: Cambridge University Press, 1996. Stresses the resourcefulness and flexibility of this elite class.

Duindam, Jeroen F.J. *Vienna and Versailles: The Courts of Europe's Dynastic Rivals, 1550–1780.* Cambridge: Cambridge University Press, 2003. Parallel study of two major European courts over a long time span, tracking personnel, servants, and rituals, while showing the centrality of the household to the organization of the court.

Elias, Norbert. *The Court Society.* Translated by Edmund Jephcott. Oxford: Basil Blackwell, 1983. Originally published as *Die höfische Gesellschaft: Untersuchungen zur Soziologie des Königtums und der höfischen Aristokratie* (Neuwied: Luchterhand, 1969). A classic work on the "civilizing process" as it emanated from the court to wider social circles.

Fichtner, Paula S. *Emperor Maximilian II*. New Haven, CT: Yale University Press, 2001. A portrait of a Renaissance monarch attempting to deal with the Turkish threat, religious conflict, and an inflexible bureaucracy.

Grafton, Anthony. *Defenders of the Text: The Traditions of Scholarship in an Age of Science, 1450–1800*. Cambridge, MA: Harvard University Press, 1991. The broad stream of humanism is examined as it interacts with science and other cultural trends.

Hohenberg, Paul M., and Lynn Hollen Lees. *The Making of Urban Europe, 1000–1994*, 2nd ed. Cambridge, MA: Harvard University Press, 1995. A comprehensive analysis of the development of European cities across 10 centuries.

Newman, Karen. *Cultural Capitals: Early Modern London and Paris*. Princeton, NJ: Princeton University Press, 2007. Shows how rapid urbanization set in much earlier than the nineteenth century to create busy capital cities that were transformed by commerce and, in turn, transformed culture.

O'Brien, Patrick K., ed. *Urban Achievement in Early Modern Europe: Golden Ages in Antwerp, Amsterdam, and London*. Cambridge: Cambridge University Press, 2001. Collected look at three powerhouse cities that were centers of commerce and of cultural production.

Orr, Clarissa Campbell, ed. *Queenship in Europe, 1660–1815: The Role of the Consort*. Cambridge: Cambridge University Press, 2004. Essays examining the case of 14 queen consorts from the Baroque era through the Enlightenment.

Parker, Geoffrey. *The Military Revolution: Military Innovation and the Rise of the West, 1500–1800*, 2nd ed. Cambridge: Cambridge University Press, 1996. Describes the "military revolution" that enabled Europeans to expand and dominate around the globe.

Williams, Patrick. *The Great Favourite: The Duke of Lerma and the Court and Government of Philip III of Spain, 1598–1621*. Manchester: Manchester University Press, 2006. A master statesman and patron too often overlooked, Lerma is here seen as the principal actor at the Spanish court.

Wilson, Derek. *In the Lion's Court: Power, Ambition, and Sudden Death in the Reign of Henry VIII*. New York: St. Martin's Press, 2002. Traces in parallel the lives of six Thomases, including the well-known Thomas Cromwell and Thomas More, whose experience encapsulates the intrigues and terrors of the Tudor court.

ELEVEN

THE RENAISSANCE AND NEW WORLDS

(c. 1500–c. 1700)

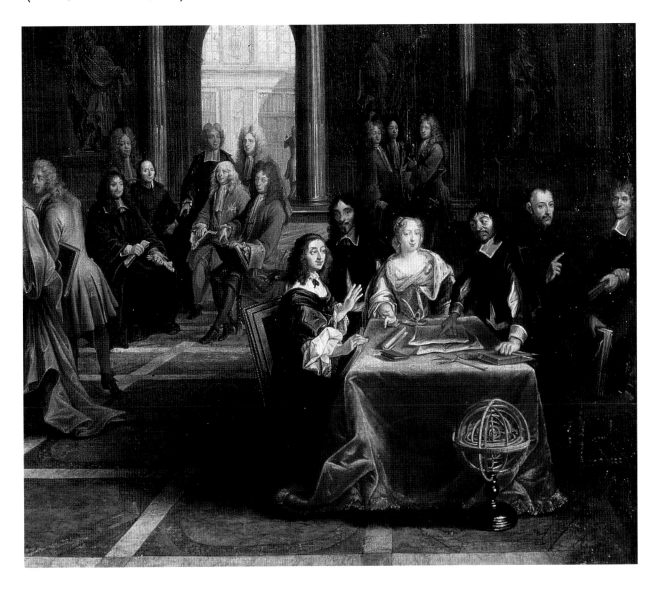

Dumesnil, *Queen Christina of Sweden with Her Court* (detail), 18th century, oil on canvas, 38 × 49⅝ in (97 × 126 cm). Châteaux de Versailles et de Trianon, Paris.

Queen Christina of Sweden (r. 1644–1654), daughter and heir of King Gustavus II Adolphus, made the Stockholm court a center for the arts and ideas. She is here seen in 1649 examining geometrical diagrams with the philosopher René Descartes. By converting to Catholicism in 1654, she surrendered the throne of her Lutheran country.

The Italian banker, navigator, and geographer Amerigo Vespucci (1454–1512), son of a major Florentine family close to the ruling Medici dynasts, spent his last years in the Spanish city of Seville as chief navigator of the Casa di Contratación de las Indias, the organization overseeing the commercial development of Spanish America. In earlier years, he had known another and more famous Italian navigator, Christopher Columbus, also in Spain's employ, who arrived in American waters in 1492, and then made three subsequent voyages to that region. Vespucci, however, also participated in two important expeditions. On the first, for Spain in 1499–1500, he explored the northern coast of South America past the river mouths of the Orinoco and Amazon. On the second, for Portugal in 1501–1502, he explored the Brazil coast, traveling south perhaps as far as Patagonia (Argentina).

These voyages persuaded Vespucci and those who listened to him that the lands Columbus had "discovered" were not in fact part of Asia but a *novus mundus*—a new world. Fictionalized versions of Vespucci's reports on these ventures circulated from 1504. They were available in several languages and 60 editions by 1520. In 1507 the German humanist Martin Waldseemüller (1470?–1521?) produced a completely new map of the world in his *Cosmographiae introductio* ("Introduction to Cosmography"). It represented the old world of Asia, Africa, and Europe, adorned by a portrait of the ancient Greek cosmographer Ptolemy (c. 100–c. 170 CE); and a new world, adorned by a portrait of Vespucci, and named, after him, "America."

Columbus was the first European to encounter the lands and peoples of the Americas (passing by the earlier, transient Viking settlement of Vineland). Vespucci, however, was the first to recognize that what Columbus found on the other side of the Ocean Sea was a land mass separate from Asia, an unexplored new world. A son of the Florentine Renaissance, a civilization whose examination of ancient texts encouraged new values and interests, he pointed to the civilization of the modern age, which looked forward and outward to the future, eager to conquer new challenges with new tools of knowledge and resources of spirit.

This chapter will consider three new worlds, or rather, arenas of radically new thought and experience that opened during the last centuries of the Renaissance: first, global explorations and encounters, especially of the western hemisphere; second, the explosion of scientific investigations known as the Scientific Revolution; and third, the expanding audience for ideas, especially the audience of women, in anticipation of the cultural phenomenon of the Enlightenment. These three series of developments are distinct from the Renaissance yet the Renaissance precedes them and influences them. The relationship between the Renaissance and the modern, a relationship of tension and yet of continuity, will be of special concern for it was the thought and consciousness of the Renaissance that stimulated the explorations, the investigations, and the innovations of the new world of the emergent modern era.

THE NEW WORLD IN THE OCEAN SEA

In 1492 the Italian navigator and entrepreneur Christopher Columbus stumbled unknowingly upon a new world. Over the next centuries, Europeans would conquer and transform the lands Columbus first opened up. At the same time, the New World would in manifold ways transform the politics, economy, and consciousness of European civilization.

The Mediterranean

Western civilization began its career of outreach and expansion in the Mediterranean Sea—that body of water "in the middle of the land" (the meaning of the Latin words composing the name) that had been since the origins of Old World civilization a principal channel of commodities and information. Toward the end of antiquity, the Mediterranean became a Roman sea: *mare nostrum* (our sea). During the early Middle Ages, as Roman power retreated, it became an Arabian sea, at the same time as Arab ships were venturing across the Persian Gulf and Indian Ocean from Africa to India. After about 1000 (see Chapter 1), the Mediterranean was Italian.

The Mediterranean was the source of the wealth that sustained the Italian cities and made them the suitable home of the first stage of Renaissance civilization. From west to east, Italian ships brought European commodities and manufactured goods to Syrian and Black Sea ports: timber, salt, furs, honey, metals and metal products, and woolen textiles. From east to west, they carried the luxury goods of the African interior, the Middle East, and South and East Asia to western ports: gold, gems, spices, cotton, sugar, silks. After 1300 the westward route of Italian shipping reached as far north as Flanders, where the Italian trade system intersected with the Hanseatic League controlling the North and Baltic Seas. Beyond the Syrian ports on the Mediterranean lay another system of land routes to the remote east: the Silk Road to China across the Asian steppes. Here the Venetian merchant Marco Polo had journeyed and returned to describe his adventures. His account remained the principal source of Western knowledge about China through the eighteenth century. Other Italians ventured into Asia as well and knew well what wealth it promised.

The Mediterranean, Europe's gateway to the east, became increasingly closed to Europeans after 1453. In that year, the Ottoman Turks, a Muslim people who had been expanding in Asia Minor since 1281, completed their quest of almost two centuries by capturing Constantinople, the last outpost of ancient Rome and the capital of the medieval Byzantine Empire. Over the next century, the Ottomans incorporated much of the eastern Mediterranean, including strategic islands and port cities of North Africa. These conquests denied the eastern Mediterranean to European merchants, which affected not only the Italians but also the French, Spanish (Castilian and Aragonese), and Portuguese.

THE RENAISSANCE AND GLOBALIZATION

From the last decades of the fifteenth century, Europeans began to expand beyond the frontiers of the world they already knew: the continent of Europe and its northern seas and the Mediterranean and the Byzantine, Arab, or Ottoman lands on its shores. As experiments in navigation gave way to exploration, exploration gave way to economic expansion and exploitation, and to occupation, conquest, and settlement. The reasons for this outward thrust are complex. They include the search for new commercial routes after the closing of the Mediterranean by the Ottoman conquerors of Byzantium; religious zeal fired by Christian reconquest of the Iberian Peninsula from remnant Moorish powers; and the quest for adventure.

An important link in the chain of causation, though, was forged in the realm of theory and was the product of the changes in intellectual culture that distinguish the Renaissance. The recovery of the ability to read Greek and to study ancient scientific texts stimulated new discussions about the cosmos and the earth. These suggested not only that the East—China, Japan, and the Spice Islands (Moluccas)—could be reached by sailing westward, but also that the distances could be calculated and managed.

This was, as schoolchildren are still taught today, the message that Christopher Columbus (1451–1506) brought to Ferdinand and Isabella. He had learned of it from the letter, with enclosed map, that the Florentine physician and astronomer Paolo Toscanelli (1397–1482) wrote to a friend of his in response to an inquiry on behalf of the King of Portugal and the school of Portuguese navigators he supported who were just then testing their updated vessels for ventures on the Ocean Sea. Before Columbus sailed across the Atlantic in 1492, before the Portuguese navigator Bartolomeu Dias journeyed in 1488 down the western shore of Africa past what would become known as the Cape of Good Hope, Toscanelli outlined, in purely theoretical

terms, the goal that might be accomplished. Thus began the pathway to globalization, the process of unification of the regions and resources of planet earth that is ongoing today. Here is Toscanelli's letter of June 25, 1474, which scholar Samuel Y. Edgerton, Jr., considers "one of the decisive letters of history":

> ... I have spoken with you elsewhere concerning a shorter way of going by sea to the lands of spices, than that which you are making by Guinea [west Africa]. The most serene King [Afonso V of Portugal, r. 1438–1481] now wishes that I should give some explanation thereof, or rather that I should so set it before the eyes of all, that even those who are but moderately learned might perceive that way and understand it.
>
> But though I know that this could be shown by the spherical form, which is that of the world, nevertheless I have determined to show [that route] in the way in which charts of navigation show it, and this both that it may be more readily understood, and that the work may be easier.
>
> Wherefore I send to His Majesty a chart, made by my hands, wherein your shores are shown, and the islands from which you may begin to make a voyage continually westwards, and the places [to which] you ought to come, and how much you ought to decline from the pole or from the equinoctial line, and through how much space, i.e., through how many miles you ought to arrive at the places most fertile in all spices and gems. And do not wonder if I call those places where the spaces are "western," whereas they are commonly called "eastern," because to those that sail by subterranean [i.e., in the southern hemisphere] navigation those places are ever found in the west.

For if we go by land and by the upper ways [i.e., the northern hemisphere] they will always be found in the east.

The straight lines, therefore, marked lengthwise in the chart, show the distances from east to west, but those which are transverse show the space from south to north.... [a detailed explanation of the navigational chart follows]

From the city of Lisbon in a direct line to the westward, [as far as] the most noble and very great city of Quinsay [modern Hangzhou, China], there are 26 spaces marked in the chart, each one of them containing 250 miles.... Thus by [these as yet] unknown ways there are not great spaces of the sea to be passed. Many things [perhaps] ought to be explained more openly. But for these things he that [considers] diligently will be able to see the rest for himself.

[Dearest friend], farewell
Florence, June 25, 1474

(H. *Vignaud*. Toscanelli and Columbus: The Letter and Chart of Toscanelli: A Critical Study. *London: Sands and Co., 1902, pp. 277–280, 287–288, 291–292)*

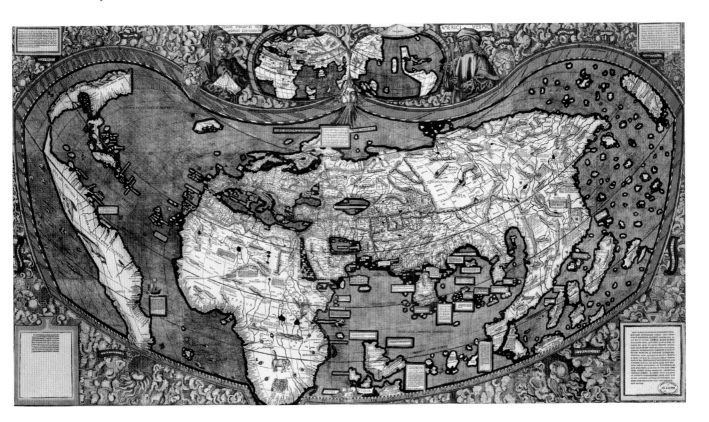

Waldseemüller, Map of the World, 1507. Library of Congress, Washington, DC.
Waldseemüller's renowned map not only shows the land mass of the New World but names it "America" after Amerigo Vespucci.

Portuguese Ventures

The Portuguese were the first to attempt to find another way to access the wealth of Asia. It faced the Atlantic, a sea into which navigators did not venture, and a place of unknowns, beset by unfavorable winds. Yet as the Mediterranean closed down, the Atlantic beckoned.

The activity of Prince Henry the Navigator, younger brother of the Portuguese king, was an essential preliminary to these Atlantic ventures. In 1415 he had fought for the conquest of Ceuta, a port city in Morocco on Africa's Mediterranean shore, not far from the Straits of Gibraltar. This victory facilitated the journey of Portuguese ships through the Straits and into the Mediterranean. In later years, he became the founder and chief patron of a center for the development of navigational and maritime skills near the port of Lagos in Portugal's extreme southwest. Here expert seamen studied maps and charts, ship construction, and the pattern of the winds. And they ventured out into the Atlantic.

Henry's navigators first reached the Madeira Islands in the Atlantic, which they claimed for Portugal, then pecked slowly down the west African coast, past Cape Bojador, Cape Blanco, and Cape Verde (adding the offshore islands to Portuguese territory). By Henry's death in 1460, they had reached almost to the Gold Coast (modern Ghana). By establishing trade depots on the coast, they had already begun the direct commercial penetration of Africa that would characterize the European role in Africa until the late nineteenth century. They also engaged in the capture and sale of slaves—although Henry himself intervened—participating in a commercial practice that predated the Portuguese arrival.

The Portuguese exploration of Africa continued for the rest of the century, culminating in two famous voyages. Bartolomeu Dias (d. 1500) sailed past the Cape of Good Hope at Africa's southern tip to enter the Indian Ocean in 1488. Vasco da Gama (1460–1524) went further and sailed across the open sea to India in 1498. These two journeys opened up Asia to Portugal and were the foundation of the Portuguese Empire. For a century, Portugal would have a leading advantage among European nations in the immensely profitable trade with Asia. The Portuguese had greater access to Asian spices, especially pepper, than even the Venetians, who until that point had held the lead. The 20 per cent tax on every ship-load that came home to Lisbon enriched the Portuguese monarchy. Portugal had set the stage for an era of imperial expansion. Other nations now looked for their own opportunities to open markets and gain extraordinary profits.

Spanish Exploration and Conquest

By the time da Gama reached Calicut, Spain had already ventured in a different direction and found immeasurable wealth at the other shore of the Ocean Sea.

The Spanish would perhaps not have won the race for global expansion if Renaissance scholars had not recovered the text of Ptolemy's *Geography* in the early fifteenth century. Brought to Italy from Byzantium, it was translated into Latin in 1410, in which version it was widely read by scholars. Ptolemy's works included lists of cities and important places by longitude and latitude, and some maps of the known world which even then were obsolete. He underestimated the circumference of the earth (by 30 per cent), for instance, and believed that China, the target of European explorations, extended much further east than it did. However erroneous, Ptolemy's *Geography* reaffirmed the fact that the earth was a sphere—a fact already known to scholars—and advanced the theory that the east could be reached by going west.

Among the readers of Ptolemy was Christopher Columbus. Born in Genoa, Columbus left Italy in his youth and spent much of his adult life in Portugal, where he was a sea-going entrepreneur and chart-maker. By 1484 he had vainly sought the support of the Portuguese king for a voyage across the Atlantic in search of the riches of China, which, according to Ptolemy and his erroneous calculations, lay not too far to the west of the Azores. By 1486 he was in Spain, petitioning the joint monarchs Ferdinand of Aragón and Isabella of Castile for the same venture. In 1492 they commissioned him to go forth in a document that anticipated both territorial conquests and merchant ventures, granting him the status of a noble (and his sons after him) and the title Admiral of the Ocean Sea.

Columbus set out on his voyage in September and in October reached an island in the Caribbean (today called Guanahani) that he claimed for Spain and named San Salvador. He subsequently landed at Cuba and then in Haiti, which he called Hispaniola after his adopted land. Here he set up a fortified depot and leaving a garrison (later destroyed), he returned with some captured treasure and kidnapped natives to Spain. In subsequent voyages in 1493–1496, 1498–1500, and 1502–1504, Columbus explored the whole Caribbean basin, established more trading depots, and launched the twin efforts to convert the natives to Christianity and to exploit the new land's resources for his profit and the benefit of his Spanish patrons.

When Columbus died in 1506, he still believed that he had reached Cipango (Japan) and Cathay (China)—not to mention the precincts of the Earthly Paradise—and that he had found a route to the east superior to the Indian Ocean route of da Gama. Vespucci had already realized that these lands were not the East, but a *novus mundus*, a new world, a continent previously unknown to any of the peoples of the Old World. The Spanish rulers prompted the Spanish pope, Rodrigo Borgia, then reigning as Alexander VI, to suggest a division of this unexplored domain as early as 1493: the Spanish would have dominion to the west of a longitude about 300 miles west of the Cape Verde Islands; the Portuguese would have dominion to the east. By the 1494 Treaty of Tordesillas, the Spanish and Portuguese agreed to a line of demarcation fairer to Portugal, about 1200 miles west of the Cape Verdes (longitude of 46°30'W). Well before the lands themselves were explored, Spain and Portugal had agreed on a division of the New World booty.

The Spanish proceeded to conquer the lands, then exploit them. The process of *reconquista* (reconquest) of the Iberian Peninsula from Moorish occupation had left Spain with a caste of trained warriors and an assumption of justified aggression. These were assets in the Spanish victory over the two advanced Indigenous civilizations that flourished in Mexico and Peru: the Aztec and the Inca. With only a minimal force of well-armed soldiers, but with great audacity and ruthlessness, Hernán Cortés (1485–1547) vanquished

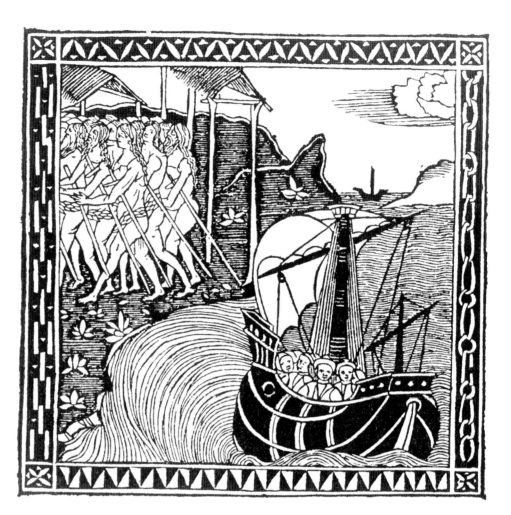

Dati, *Columbus Arriving in the Americas*, 1497, woodcut.

On October 12, 1492, Columbus prepares to set foot on the Bahamian Island of Guanahani. The nakedness of the inhabitants and the construction of their habitations were two among the features of New World life that Columbus noted in his journals.

the Aztec Empire in 1521; Francisco Pizarro (c. 1476–1541) the Incan in 1532. Within the next two generations, Spanish nobles and entrepreneurs established themselves in the American interior, enlisting natives as laborers on ranches and in mines equipped with the latest German technology. Disciplined and earnest Franciscan and Jesuit professionals arrived to convert the inhabitants to Christianity and to establish schools and missions. The settlers founded cities according to European patterns of urbanization, set up universities, and launched printing presses.

Indigenous Peoples, Africans, and the Slave Trade

The Indigenous peoples escaped enslavement, largely through the heroic crusade of the Dominican missionary Bartolomé de las Casas (1474–1566). His attack on the conquerors' cruelty and his belief in the natives' innocence persuaded King Charles I (Emperor Charles V, 1500–1558) to sign the "New Laws" of 1542, which prevented the worst abuses. They did not escape **peonage**, however, which was roughly equivalent to European serfdom. They were forced to work and their mobility was restricted, as they were pressed into the service of the Spanish or creole elites—those fortunate enough to survive, that is. An isolated population without immunity to Old World diseases, they died by the millions from the diseases that arrived with the European conquerors. Smallpox, measles, diphtheria, mumps, and influenza destroyed all but 10 million of the pre-conquest 75 million inhabitants of the Americas.

Not only diseases, but also beneficial flora and fauna arrived with the Europeans: horses, pigs, and draft animals, as well as apples, oranges, and wheat from their homeland and rice, bananas, and especially sugar that they had acquired from Asia. The Europeans in turn brought previously unknown products back from the Americas to the Old World, including the potato, the tomato, coffee, and ears of corn (maize).

Sugar cultivation would remake the society of the Americas. The Portuguese had learned to cultivate sugar from the Arabs and had done so profitably on plantations on the Cape Verde Islands employing African slaves. They introduced sugar cultivation in northern Brazil (settled by the Portuguese after about 1530), from where it spread to the Caribbean. Indigenous laborers were not available as it was forbidden to compel them to plantation labor. They were, in any case, scarce, having been decimated by the onslaught of European pathogens and prone to disease.

The failure of Indigenous labor was an incentive to import slaves, and thus the horrible story of Atlantic slavery began. The Portuguese were the first major importers of African slaves, followed by the Dutch in the seventeenth century and the British in the eighteenth (when the commerce in slaves reached its high point). From the early 1500s until slavery's final obliteration in the western hemisphere in 1870, more than 10 million Africans were brought to lives of harsh servitude in Brazil, the Caribbean, and North America. Millions more died in transit.

Not only did American slavery constitute a forced migration on a monumental scale causing disruption and rootlessness to generations of African-born people and their descendants, it left scars on American societies that are by no means erased today. It is a slight mitigation of this record that the societies that brought the slave trade to the Americas also spearheaded the abolitionist movement that would, after long delay, result in its eradication. In the meantime, to the "encounter" in the Americas of Europeans and Indigenous peoples was added a third group, Africans. Peoples from three continents met in these centuries of exploration and exploitation, creating from their interactions an entirely new society.

North America and the Triangle Trade

Those interactions differed, moreover, from the southern to the northern zone of American colonization. In Spanish South America and Mesoamerica, with a large Indigenous population and relatively small numbers of Africans, there was extensive miscegenation (marriage across ethnic lines) and a strong Indigenous influence. In coastal Brazil (the interior

THE COLUMBIAN EXCHANGE: THE CONTRIBUTION OF NEW WORLD CROPS

To procure the food they need so that they can survive and propagate, our human ancestors engaged in hunting and gathering, and eventually, beginning about 10,000 years ago, developed the skills of pasturage and agriculture. The farmers of the Old World of Afro-Eurasia produced four main crops: rice, wheat, barley, and oats. These yield, at current hypothetical rates, an average of 5.6 million calories per hectare cultivated. The introduction to the Old World of new crops farmed in the Americas brought not only greater variety, but a higher overall benefit to the species. The New World contributed four main staple crops that yielded an average of 7.95 million calories per hectare cultivated: maize, potatoes, sweet potatoes, and manioc.

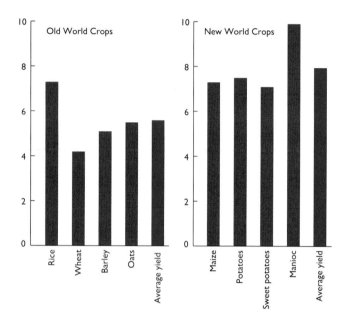

(Alfred W. Crosby, *The Columbian Exchange: Biological and Cultural Consequences of 1492.* Westport, CT: Greenwood Press, 1972, Table 2, p. 175)

remained at first largely unexplored) and the Caribbean, a large slave population determined social relations, and the mixture of "white" and "black" was largely forbidden.

North America was settled somewhat later and developed differently. The southwestern region of North America was settled by the Spanish, as well, and followed the Mexican pattern. European settlement of North America, however, was distinctive. Until the eighteenth century, this was confined largely to the Atlantic coast and along the expansive St. Lawrence and Mississippi waterways. Here a sparse European population (mainly English and French, but also Dutch, Swedish, Irish, and others) encountered indigenous groups with seemingly less sophisticated societies than the Aztecs or Incas of South America. By treaty, manipulation, and force, the settlers gradually pushed these Indigenous populations westward, until, in the late nineteenth century, they had confined the survivors to government-managed reservations. There was little intermarriage of European and Indigenous peoples, and the colonial societies that formed along the eastern seacoast remained outposts of European civilization. African slavery was introduced in North America in the seventeenth century but affected mainly the southern colonies of Anglo-America, especially Maryland, the Virginias, the Carolinas, and Georgia. As in the slaveholding regions to the south, racial mixture occurred through forbidden unions, often of male slaveholders and dependent female slaves.

The commercial ventures of North American settlers were more energetic than those to the south, where the primary concerns were the extraction and export of precious metals. North American products such as ships, timber, and molasses were transported to the Caribbean and to Europe in exchange for slaves (transshipped from Africa), sugar, and rum from the former, and manufactured products from the latter. This commercial exchange formed part of the larger northern Atlantic triangular trade system—a pattern where goods left Britain in ships bound for the African coast, where they were exchanged for slaves, who were then brought to the Caribbean or southern colonies of North America, where agricultural goods were obtained for return shipment to Britain.

Atlantic commerce enriched European merchants, although it did not necessarily enrich nations or their inhabitants. The large amount of treasure in silver and gold shipped back to Spain and Portugal did not nurture new entrepreneurial projects. It caused high inflation, in fact, with a sharp increase in grain prices that impoverished many workers. The Spanish and Portuguese monarchies were both in crisis in the seventeenth century (see Chapter 10), and the bullion that passed through their ports proceeded to the coffers of bankers in Amsterdam, London, or Paris. Those three capital cities, as has been seen, flourished in the seventeenth century, enriched in large part by the colonial ventures of their merchants. By 1700 the dynamic core of European wealth and power had completed its journey from the Mediterranean to northwest Europe. For the next two centuries, England and France were the centers of European civilization; the Dutch, who had figured significantly in the seventeenth century, lagged behind thereafter. New World ventures thus helped form a new Europe.

The Impact on European Consciousness

Neither Renaissance civilization nor the humanist movement triggered the impulse of European exploration and expansion. But the journeys and encounters of Europeans in the Americas, Africa, and Asia had an enormous impact on European civilization from the Renaissance era into modern times. They enlarged Europeans' imagination about the world and themselves in many different ways.

It has already been noted how the shape of the known world changed quickly after 1492 (see p. 365). In 1538 the Flemish cartographer Gerardus Mercator (Gerhard Kremer, 1512–1594) published a map of the world depicting two hemispheres: a western hemisphere containing the two Americas and an eastern one, containing the Old World continents of Asia, Africa, and Europe. In 1569 he published a world map featuring a grid of straight parallels of latitude and vertical meridians. He named this mapping system the Mercator projection after himself, and it is still commonly used today.

Along with new maps came new descriptions of the world. Visitors to faraway places previously unknown to European audiences wrote books about their journeys, while travel accounts became one of the most popular genres of literature. We have already noted Vespucci's report of a *novus mundus*. First-person reports included *Histoire d'un voyage fait en la terre du Brésil* ("The Story of a Journey to the Land of Brazil," 1578) by the Huguenot Jean de Léry (1534–1611). In 1596 the English privateer Sir Walter Raleigh (1554–1618) described his South American venture in *The discoverie of the large, rich, and bewtiful Empyre of Guiana*.

Compilers and narrators followed. The Venetian Giovanni Battista Ramusio (1485–1557) collected and published an anthology of travel narratives related to Asia, Africa, and the Americas. His three-volume *Delle navigationi e viaggi* ("On Explorations and Voyages"), published in 1550–1559, included famous earlier texts such as Marco Polo's journey and the *Description of Africa* by the converted Moorish author Leo Africanus (c. 1485–c. 1554). The English geographer Richard Hakluyt (1552–1616) took as his more narrow focus the English explorations of the Americas, which he related exhaustively in his *Principall Navigations, Voiages and Discoveries of the English Nation* (1589).

To these descriptive accounts must be added the journeys of the mind—fictional accounts of imagined places inspired by travels abroad to new worlds. Thomas More's *Utopia* (1516) described an idealized society inhabiting a distant and previously unknown island (see Chapter 9). After his own circumnavigation of the globe, the Portuguese poet Luis de Camões (1524/1525–1580) wrote his epic poem *Os Lusíadas* ("The Lusiads," 1572), describing the experience of navigator Vasco da Gama. The meaning for the Old World and its way of life posed by the consciousness of a new world was the central theme of playwright William Shakespeare's *The Tempest* (c. 1611).

New World experiences also stimulated Europe's moral philosophers. From the first moment of the great encounter between Europeans and Indigenous peoples—when Columbus commented on their utter nakedness—newly observed people and places called for a new way of thinking. The French essayist Michel de Montaigne was led by reports of other places and customs to consider the relativism of cultural values, most famously in his "On Cannibals." Witnessing the cruelty of his countrymen to the Indigenous people moved Bartolomé de las Casas to argue against their enslavement and thus to lay the foundations for the argument against all forms of slavery. The great seventeenth-century works on international law *De jure belli et pacis* ("On the Law of War and Peace," 1625) by Hugo Grotius (1583–1645) and *De jure naturae et gentium* ("On the Law of Nature and of Nations," 1672) by Samuel Pufendorf (1632–1694) could only emerge in a context where the vision of Europeans, as a result of their global ventures, had become global as well. The visions that the far-sighted nourish today of a world marked by universal human equality, peace, and justice, have their roots in the age of discovery, exploration, and encounter.

NEW HEAVENS, NEW EARTH

At the same time that navigators and voyagers discovered a new world beyond the borders of Europe, philosophers and scientists created a new world of knowledge and a method for knowing it. In less than two centuries, they transformed the fundamental assumptions about the universe: how objects moved, how senses perceived, the components of the human body, and the design of the cosmos.

Led by the humanists, they began their investigations with ancient texts. The geometry and cosmography of the Greeks pointed them in new directions. But they quickly left those texts behind and began to observe systematically, to make calculations, to propose models, and to experiment. Even when they engaged in pure thought (to the extent that such thought is possible), they thought along new lines. They discarded Aristotle, the favorite of the medieval thinkers, and even Plato, the favorite of the Renaissance, as guides to method. The new world of the Scientific Revolution emerged from the civilization of the Renaissance but placed that civilization firmly in the past.

1450–1499

1488 Portuguese navigator Bartholomeu Dias sails around southern Africa into the Indian Ocean.

1492 Seeking a westerly route to China, Christopher Columbus sails across the Atlantic.

1494 Pope Alexander VI divides the New World between Spain and Portugal.

1498 Vasco da Gama sails from Portugal to India.

1499 Amerigo Vespucci embarks on the first of two voyages to the Americas.

1550–1549

1502 The first African slaves are brought to the New World by the Portuguese.

1506 Death of Columbus.

1507 Martin Waldseemüller publishes a map showing the New World as "America."

1509 English scholar John Colet founds St. Paul's School, London.

1515 Spanish missionary Bartolomé de las Casas campaigns to end ill-treatment of Indigenous peoples.

1521 Hernán Cortes leads Spanish conquistadors to conquer the Aztec Empire, Mexico.

1528 Paracelsus writes the first modern manual of surgery.

1532 Francisco Pizarro conquers the empire of the Incas, Peru.

1538 Flemish cartographer Gerardus Mercator publishes a world map showing two hemispheres.

1542 Spain's New Laws give some protection to Indigenous Americans under Spanish rule.

1543 Nicholas Copernicus presents his view of a universe centered on the sun, rather than the earth.

1543 Andreas Vesalius founds the modern study of anatomy with *De humani corporis fabrica*.

1550–1599

1552 Las Casas publishes *Brief Relation of the Destruction of the Indies*.

1569 Mercator publishes a world map using the projection that bears his name.

1570 English humanist Roger Ascham publishes a treatise on education, *The Scholemaster*.

1578 Publication of Jean de Léry's *Histoire d'un voyage fait en la terre du Brésil* ("The Story of a Journey to the Land of Brazil").

1589 Richard Hakluyt publishes an account of English exploration of the Americas, *Voyages*.

1596 Sir Walter Raleigh's account of his South American adventures appears.

1598 Danish astronomer Tycho Brahe publishes the results of his observations of the stars.

1600–1649

1600 Venetian Moderata Fonte publishes *The Worth of Women*.

1609 Johan Kepler produces his first and second laws of planetary motion.

1610 Galileo Galilei publishes *Sidereus nuncius* ("The Starry Messenger") detailing astronomical observations.

1611 Shakespeare's *The Tempest* relates to the discovery of the New World.

1619 Kepler proposes his third law of planetary motion.

1620 Francis Bacon's *Novum organum* argues that knowledge is derived from observation and experience.

1622 Marie de Gournay publishes *The Equality of Men and Women*.

1628 William Harvey expounds a theory that blood circulates through the body.

1632 Galileo's *Dialogue Concerning the Two World Systems* favors the Copernican view of the universe.

1637 In his *Discours de la méthode* ("Discourse on Method"), René Descartes declares: "I think therefore I am."

1650–1700

1654 Moravian scholar John Comenius produces the first educational picture book for children.

1661 In *The Sceptical Chemist*, Robert Boyle lays the foundations of modern chemistry.

1674 François Poulain de la Barre writes *On the Equality of the Two Sexes*.

1678 Madame de La Fayette writes the novel *La Princesse de Clèves*.

1687 Sir Isaac Newton's *Principia mathematica* is published.

1694 Mary Astell's *A Serious Proposal to the Ladies* suggests women develop their talents away from male society.

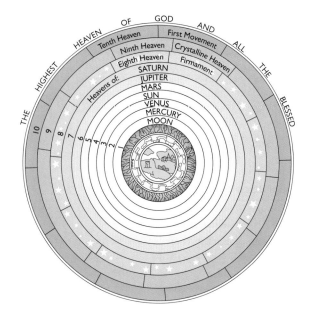

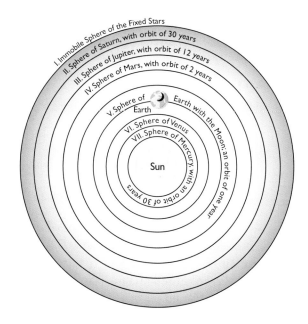

Celestial Maps: Medieval and Copernican

The diagram on the left shows the ten heavens, or spheres, of the medieval cosmological system which, it was believed, rotated around the earth. The diagram on the right shows the Copernican system with the sun at the center, around which the planets rotate.

Cosmographical Revisions

Ptolemy was not only a geographer, but also the most important ancient cosmographer known to the Middle Ages and the Renaissance. The model of the universe he presented prevailed for 1,300 years—until the time of Copernicus.

Copernicus The Polish priest Nicholas Copernicus studied at the universities of Bologna and Padua in Italy and read ancient Greek scientific texts. He wrestled with the Ptolemaic model of the universe, which had become the Christian model during the Middle Ages. According to this model, the earth was at the center of the universe, the planets and stars orbited around the earth, and beyond its limit of a fixed sphere, God and his angels held sway. To make this model square with naked-eye observations of the movement of the planets required a complex apparatus of "eccentrics" and "epicycles." A simpler model could be obtained, Copernicus argued, with a different hypothesis: that the sun, rather than the earth, was at the center of the universe. Copernicus proposed this theory in his groundbreaking work *De revolutionibus orbium coelestium* ("On the Revolutions of the Heavenly Bodies," 1543), withheld for fear of public reaction and published only in the year of his death.

The Copernican theory profoundly challenged the assumptions of European thought. It not only required a rethinking of how celestial bodies moved, it also required a critical rereading of authoritative texts and a direct confrontation with the church. A geocentric (earth-centered) cosmos accorded perfectly with theological views of the relationship between God and humanity. It accorded also with the equally naive cosmography of the Bible, which assumed a moving sun, and a static, central earth.

Brahe and Kepler In the two generations after Copernicus's death, the Danish astronomer Tycho Brahe (1546–1601) and his student, the German mathematician and astronomer Johann Kepler (1571–1630), provided the observations and calculations that lent weight to the Polish priest's hypothesis. Brahe and his assistants were provided with a plush laboratory by the Danish king. Without benefit of the telescope, they plotted minute observations of the motions of the stars and planets, compiling an enormous data bank for later analysis. Although Brahe's observations did not fully support the Copernican heliocentric (sun-centered) universe, they did point to a pattern of planetary revolutions (excluding the earth) around the sun.

On his death, Brahe left his astronomical data to Kepler. Kepler, in turn, used them to test and prove the Copernican hypothesis. He sought to find regular patterns in the planetary motions that could be described by mathematics. His investigations resulted in three laws of planetary motion. The first stated that the planets moved around the sun in elliptical, not circular patterns. The second showed that the speed of the planets in their elliptical orbits varied in a regular pattern: the areas of the ellipses defined by their paths and of the radii of those ellipses drawn to the sun were equal in any period of time. The third showed that the square of the period of each planet's revolution was proportional to the cube of its mean distance from the sun.

Kepler's rules were laws, but for him they were also revelations of the order of the universe transcribed in numbers. Kepler was mystically inclined—his original intent had been to be a pastor—and he found traces of the Christian Trinity in the structures of the cosmos and identified the light and energy of the sun with the power of God. The discovery of regularities of planetary motion, which could be expressed in mathematical formulae, seemed to validate the concept of a divine providence that regulated the heavens—even if the framework was heliocentric and not geocentric. The new scientific cosmos, as much as the old, pointed to the presence of a divine hand.

The solid data and mathematical formulae provided by Brahe and Kepler may have supported the Copernican model of the universe, but that model was opposed by Protestant and Catholic churches alike. In 1600 the Italian visionary philosopher Giordano Bruno was condemned by the Roman Inquisition and burned at the stake. Among the crimes of which he was accused were his proposals that the universe was infinite and that there could exist in that infinity a multitude of worlds—anticipating some modern views of the structure of the universe. His thinking was not so much Copernican as post-Copernican. Once Copernicus had challenged the prevailing Ptolemaic system, backed up by Aristotelian mechanics and logic, the opportunity for exploration and hypothesis opened wide.

Galileo The philosopher, astronomer, and mathematician Galileo Galilei demonstrated the truth of the Copernican hypothesis, while declining to follow Bruno in the path of martyrdom. Galileo was a younger contemporary of Kepler's and a product of the vigorous Renaissance civilization of sixteenth-century Tuscany. He constructed a new device—the telescope—to investigate the heavens (as Brahe had done unaided) and establish the Copernican theory through his observations. He noted that there were spots on the sun and imperfections on the surface of the moon that challenged the traditional notion of the unvarying perfection of the heavens. His recognition that the Milky Way consisted of countless stars suggested—not unlike Bruno—that the universe was far vaster and stranger than had previously been thought. His discovery that Jupiter had moons, and Venus rings,

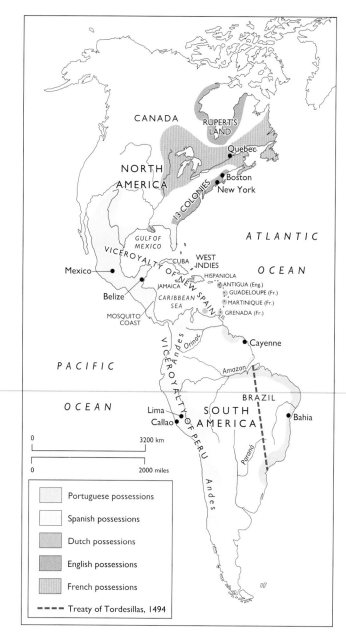

CANADA
RUPERT'S LAND
Quebec
NORTH AMERICA
Boston
New York
13 COLONIES
ATLANTIC OCEAN
GULF OF MEXICO
VICEROYALTY OF NEW SPAIN
WEST INDIES
Mexico
CUBA
HISPANIOLA
JAMAICA
ANTIGUA (Eng.)
GUADELOUPE (Fr.)
Belize
CARIBBEAN SEA
MARTINIQUE (Fr.)
MOSQUITO COAST
GRENADA (Fr.)
Orinoco
Cayenne
PACIFIC OCEAN
Amazon
Andes
BRAZIL
SOUTH AMERICA
Lima
VICEROYALTY OF PERU
Bahia
Callao
Paraná
Andes

0 — 3200 km
0 — 2000 miles

	Portuguese possessions
	Spanish possessions
	Dutch possessions
	English possessions
	French possessions
- - -	Treaty of Tordesillas, 1494

European Colonization of the Americas, 1700.

The European imprint is strong, as in the territories of the Aztec and Inca, now under Spanish dominion.

demonstrated that the solar system was not as Ptolemy had described it. Galileo announced these observations in his *Sidereus nuncius* ("The Starry Messenger," 1610), which won him fame and the suspicious glances of the Catholic Church.

More provocative still was Galileo's *Dialogue Concerning the Two Chief World Systems* of 1632, in which a defender of the old Ptolemaic system debated with, and emphatically lost to, a defender of the Copernican system. Published in Italian rather than Latin, it reached a broad audience of literate, interested readers. It was read, too, by the inquisitors, who arrested him in 1633 and commanded him to reject the Copernican position. Galileo retracted, saving himself from Bruno's fate. His failure to make a public stand for the truth of science against the Inquisition aroused the hostility of some later critics (not themselves at risk of persecution), who labeled it "the crime of Galileo." Galileo's retraction did not, however, prevent the circulation of his ideas, which were made available in the tens of thousands of copies of his books. Only in 1992, 360 years later, did the Catholic Church reverse its condemnation of Galileo.

Galileo made contributions to physics as well as to astronomy. In these, too, he used empirical observation to challenge Aristotelian theories of mechanics and motion. Most importantly, Galileo developed the method of experimentation, in which a set of circumstances is contrived so that regular and repeatable observations of natural phenomena can be made. Using inclined planes and other devices of his own design, he studied the effects of gravity and friction, weight and mass, and pendular motion. Contrary to Aristotle, for whom the natural condition of objects was rest, Galileo demonstrated that their natural condition was motion.

Newton It remained for the English mathematician, scientist, and mystic Isaac Newton (1642–1737) to combine the work of Kepler and Galileo with his own calculations to produce, in 1687, the *Philosophiae naturalis principia mathematica* ("Mathematical Principles of Natural Philosophy"). Written in the Latin of the learned professionals of Europe, this was arguably the most important work of the century and of this whole first era of scientific discovery.

Like Kepler, Newton believed that God ordered the universe and governed it according to three regular, knowable laws—laws of motion tantamount to moral law. The first stated

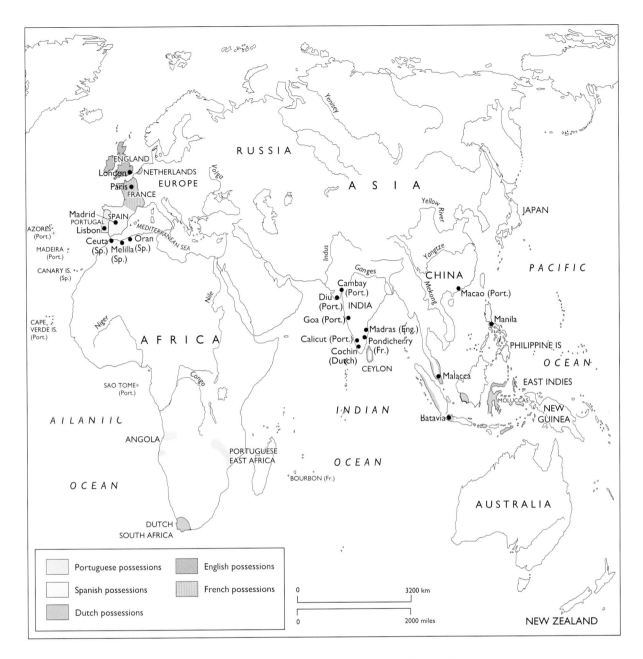

European Colonization of Africa and Asia, 1700.

European outposts exist around Africa, India, the Malay Peninsula, the East Indies, and the Philippines.

that a body at rest remained at rest unless acted upon by an external force. The second stated that a body's change in motion (change in velocity × mass) was proportional to the force that caused it to accelerate (or decelerate). The third stated that every action will cause an equal and opposite reaction. Newton showed that the operation of these laws pointed to the existence of one single principle, the universal force of gravitation that bound and powered the universe. Gravity explained equally the movement of bodies in the heavens and that of bodies on earth. The omnipresence and constancy of the unitary

SCIENTIFIC OBSERVERS: GALILEO AND NEWTON

The Scientific Revolution was marked especially by innovations in astronomy and physics, spanning the period from the publication of Nicholas Copernicus's *On the Revolutions of the Heavenly Bodies* (1543) to that of Sir Isaac Newton's *Mathematical Principles of Natural Philosophy* (1687). These scientists, along with Tycho Brahe, Johann Kepler, and Galileo Galilei, reshaped the cosmos. They replaced the geocentric Ptolemaic model of the planetary system with the heliocentric Copernican model, assailing traditional religious conceptions based on scripture and Scholastic philosophy. They described the movement of heavenly and earthly bodies in the abstract language of mathematics, and they discerned universal laws of motion that prevailed throughout the universe.

In the first of the two passages below, in a letter to Christina, the Grand Duchess of Tuscany, Galileo (1564–1642) distinguishes between scientific and theological inquiry—an essential distinction if scientists were to pursue their investigations even if their conclusions contradicted religious paradigms.

> *I am inclined to think that Holy Scripture is intended to convince men of those truths which are necessary for their salvation, and which being far above man's understanding cannot be made credible by any learning, or by any other means than revelation. But that the same God who has endowed us with senses, reason, and understanding, does not permit us to use them, and desires to acquaint us in another way with such knowledge as we are in a position to acquire for ourselves by means of those faculties—that, it seems to me I am not bound to believe, especially concerning those sciences about which the Holy Scriptures contain only small fragments and varying explanations; and this is precisely the case with astronomy, of which there is so little that the planets are not [even] all enumerated.... I think that in discussing natural phenomena we ought not to begin with texts from Scripture but with experiment and demonstration, for from the Divine Word Scripture and Nature do alike proceed.*
>
> (J.J. Fahie, Galileo: His Life and Work. London: John Murray, 1903, pp. 150–151)

In this second passage, Newton (1642–1727) defines the purpose of his great book, *Mathematical Principles of Natural Philosophy*, and, indeed, of all philosophy: to explain the workings of the universal system.

> *I offer this work as the mathematical principles of philosophy, for the whole burden of philosophy seems to consist in this: from the phenomena of motions to investigate the forces of nature, and then from these forces to demonstrate the other phenomena; and to this end the general propositions in the first and second Books are directed. In the third Book I give an example of this in the explication of the System of the World; for by the propositions mathematically demonstrated in the former Books, in the third I derive from the celestial phenomena the forces of gravity with which bodies tend to the sun and the several planets. Then from these forces, by other propositions which are also mathematical, I deduce the motions of the planets, the comets, the moon, and the sea. I wish we could derive the rest of the phenomena of Nature by the same kind of reasoning from mechanical principles, for I am induced by many reasons to suspect that they may all depend upon certain forces by which the particles of bodies, by some causes hitherto unknown, are either mutually impelled towards one another, and cohere in regular figures, or are repelled and recede from one another. These forces being unknown, philosophers have hitherto attempted the search of Nature in vain; but I hope the principles here laid down will afford some light either to this or some truer method of philosophy.*
>
> (I. Newton, Principia, I: The Motions of Bodies. Berkeley: University of California Press, 1974, pp. xvii–xviii)

VISITORS TO THE NATURAL HISTORY MUSEUM OF ULISSE ALDOVRANDI, 1522–1605

Visitors	Number	Visitors	Number
Popes	1	Professors	21
Cardinals	10	Philosophers	6
Archbishops	11	University graduates	21
Bishops	21	Scholars	907
Theologians	15	Doctors	87
Inquisitors	3	Anatomists and surgeons	2
All other clergy	201	Apothecaries and distillers	7
Princes	6	Mathematicians	2
Nobles	118	Cosmographers	1
Courtiers	4	Antiquarians	1
Diplomats and princely servants	7	Printers	2
Famous men	26	Booksellers	2
Appointed and elected officials	26	Painters	6
Lawyers	43	Poets	1
Secretaries	8	Jewelers	1
Notaries	1	Women	1
Military leaders	6	Unknown	4

(Paula Findlen, Possessing Nature: Museums, Collecting, and Scientific Culture in Early Modern Italy. *Berkeley: University of California Press, 1994, pp. 140–141)*

force of gravity matched the simplicity and coherence of the pre-Copernican universe and definitively replaced it.

Newton's unveiling of the mechanical principles of the universe remains his most momentous achievement. It is only in comparison to this that his other endeavors seem secondary. For example, his mathematical work culminated in the development of calculus by 1669. His studies in optics (a field to which Kepler and Galileo had also contributed) resulted in his demonstration, through the use of a prism, that white light comprised the sequential colors of the spectrum.

Other Scientific Advances

The most dramatic expressions of the new age of science, which some historians call the Scientific Revolution, lay in the field of astronomy, related to which are both physics and optics. However, chemistry and medicine made notable progress in this period as well.

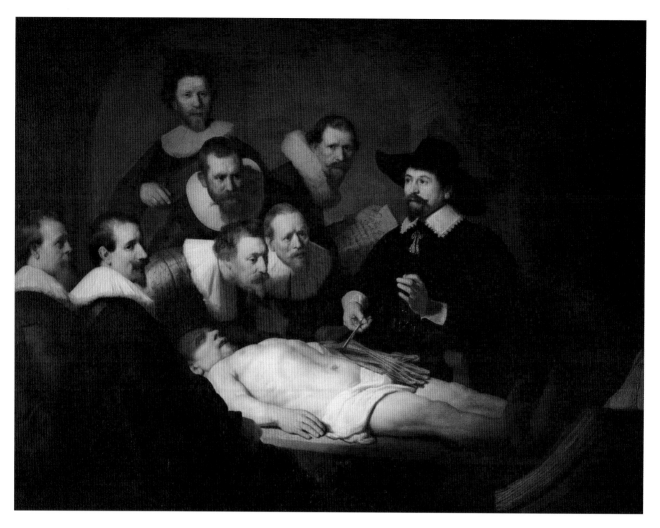

Rembrandt, *The Anatomy Lesson of Dr. Nicolaes Tulp,* **1642, oil on canvas, 5 × 7 ft (1.5 × 2.1 m). Mauritshuis, The Hague.**

The learned scholar and surgeon Dr. Tulp, who had also served as Amsterdam's city treasurer and mayor, commissioned this group portrait of wealthy citizens invited to observe an anatomy lesson on a cadaver rendered with splendid *chiaroscuro*.

Modern chemistry began to detach itself from alchemy, an ancient and universal pursuit by philosophers seeking to find the secret of immortality or, more modestly, a means of changing base metals into gold. An important early chemist was Robert Boyle (1627–1691). He developed the vacuum pump, defined such basic terms as "element," "reaction," and "analysis," and conducted significant experiments to ascertain the nature of gases. The first law of gases—"Boyle's law"—states that the pressure and volume of gas are inversely proportional.

Renaissance philosophers recovered and studied the Greek medical corpus that had been known to Arab physicians, especially the work of Galen. But early investigations challenged Galen's assumptions and greatly extended knowledge of the human beyond what the Greeks had accomplished. The Flemish-born scientist Andreas Vesalius (1514–1564), working in Padua, began the university teaching of anatomy based on the dissection of human bodies. His findings, described in his *De humani corporis fabrica* ("On the Composition of the Human Body," 1543), showed Galen to be wrong and vindicated the method of direct observation in anatomical dissection. Likewise, the Swiss physician Paracelsus

DISCERNING TRUTH: BACON AND DESCARTES

Both Francis Bacon (1561–1626) and René Descartes (1596–1650) grappled with a question that has always occupied inquiring human minds: how do we know what is true? Working at approximately the same time and in the same environment of burgeoning scientific investigation, they proposed two very different ways of reasoning—both of which are fundamental to scientific thought and to all disciplined thinking, even today.

For Bacon, true statements could not be derived from the books of the philosophers and the theologians, which were the authorities that governed the thinking of his day and which had to be discarded. They must derive from concrete things—"particulars"—which are perceived by the senses and about which more general principles can be derived. He defined this as "the true way" in the following passage:

> There are and can be only two ways of searching into and discovering truth. The one flies from the senses and particulars to the most general axioms, and from these principles, the truth of which it takes for settled and immoveable, proceeds to judgment and to the discovery of middle axioms. And this way is now in fashion. The other derives axioms from the senses and particulars, rising by a gradual and unbroken assent, so that it arrives at the most general axioms last of all. This is the true way, but as yet untried.
>
> (H.G. Dick, ed., Selected Writings of Francis Bacon. New York: Random House, 1955, p. 465)

For Descartes, the very "particulars" that Bacon turned to were an inadequate source of truth since knowing them relied on the senses, and the evidence of the senses was itself unreliable. Descartes searched for a sounder basis for certain knowledge. He found it in rigorous and disciplined abstract thought, which, in a chain of reasoning from one unassailable truth to the next, could yield true philosophical statements. The entire chain of reasoning was grounded in one irrefutable truth: the existence of a reasoning mind.

> Inasmuch as I desired to devote myself wholly to the search for truth, I thought that I should … reject as absolutely false anything of which I could have the least doubt, in order to see whether anything would be left after this procedure which could be called wholly certain. Thus, as our senses deceive us at times, I was ready to suppose that nothing was at all the way our senses represented them to be. As there are men who make mistakes in reasoning even on the simplest topics in geometry, I judged that I was as liable to error as any other, and rejected as false all the reasoning which I had previously accepted as valid demonstration. Finally, as the same percepts [i.e. perceptions] we have when awake may come to us when asleep without their being true, I decided to suppose that nothing that had ever entered my mind was more real than the illusions of my dreams. But I soon noticed that while I thus wished to think everything false, it was necessarily true that I who thought so was something. Since this truth, I think, therefore I am, was so firm and assured that all the most extravagant suppositions of the sceptics were unable to shake it, I judged that I could safely accept it as the first principle of the philosophy I was seeking.
>
> (R. Descartes, Philosophical Essays I. Indianapolis, IN: Bobbs-Merrill Co., 1964, p. 24)

(Theophrastus Bombastus von Hohenheim, 1493?–1541) preferred empirical observation of wounds and diseases to the medical theories of the learned. These explorations were preliminary to the critical work of the Englishman William Harvey (1578–1657), whose discoveries of the circulation of the blood by the pumping action of the heart and the structure and functions of animal reproductive systems, corrected the speculations of Aristotle and Galen and opened the era of modern medicine.

Although major advances in the study of biology could not take place until scientists could use microscopes to study cells, tissues, and pathogens, philosophers and amateurs expressed their interest in the biological world by collecting objects such as bones, fossils, and leaves, as well as models of unusual species. They cataloged these collections, much as they also cataloged their collections of important books, making available sets of data about the traces of biological life for eventual study.

New Ways to Reason

At the same time that Kepler and Vesalius, Harvey and Galileo studied the movement of the planets or the composition of the human body, other thinkers were devising new ways to reason. The Renaissance had explored the world—the accumulated knowledge and reasoning of the great thinkers of the past—through the book. The new ways of knowing were not rooted in the study of literary texts but in the asking of a new set of questions. Two seventeenth-century figures directly addressed this issue of method, formulating two distinct (but not opposed) approaches to logic. They were the French philosopher and mathematician René Descartes, and the English thinker Francis Bacon, the modern founders of the deductive and inductive approaches to philosophical and scientific investigation respectively.

Descartes's *Discours de la méthode* ("Discourse on Method," 1637) explained how the author arrived at his concept of the reasoning process. Having traveled broadly, he explained, he found that many things thought to be universally true were in fact relative: true for one culture, but not for another. That uncertainty fueled other uncertainties: how could philosophers know for sure that what they understood to be a fact was indeed true? They must strip all of these preconceptions and supposed facts from their minds, Descartes argued, and begin from very first principles to construct an unassailable sequence of true propositions. The first principle, Descartes famously declared, would then be that he himself—the questioner—did in fact exist: "I think, therefore I am." All further truths were deduced from such basic principles. Hence Descartes's prescribed method of logic is called *deductive*.

Bacon was equally skeptical of received but untested truths. For Bacon, these included the many unfounded assumptions and prejudices with which ordinary human beings operated. They also included the body of purported "knowledge" derived from books: the books of the ancients and especially the books of Aristotle that had for so long been the staple of philosophical and scientific thought in European schools and universities. In his

The acquisition of basic literacy by all citizens is a goal that all developed nations now set themselves (but do not always achieve). It is a very recent aspiration. In ancient societies, literacy was confined to a few specialist scribes, often priests or members of a priestly caste. Subsequently, many merchants also learned to read and write. In the European Middle Ages, literacy was still largely limited to the clergy and upper merchant strata. From the fifteenth to the eighteenth centuries, artisans, women, and workers were learning to read and write. Here are a few landmarks along the way:

1466	England	40 per cent of 20 men who witnessed the will of Sir John Fastolf could sign their names
1587	Venice (Italy)	33 per cent of boys and 12.2–13.2 per cent of girls (23 per cent of total children) were literate, based on school enrollment and estimates for home tutoring
1586–1595	Milan (Italy)	50 per cent of 104 workers and skilled craftsmen on the payroll of the Fabbrica del Duomo (cathedral construction team) could sign their names
1612–1614	England	47 per cent of 204 men sentenced to death for a first offense in the county of Middlesex were literate
1655	Netherlands	80 per cent of 20 bakers working in the Zaan region were literate
1686–1690	France	25 per cent of all people contracting marriage could sign their names
1740	Turin (Italy)	76 per cent of 79 bakers could sign their names

(From Carlo M. Cipolla, *Literacy and Development in the West*. Baltimore, MD: Penguin, 1969, pp. 56–61. For Venice, 1587: Paul F. Grendler, *Schooling in Renaissance Italy: Literacy and Learning, 1300–1600*. Baltimore, MD: Johns Hopkins University Press, Table 2.2, p. 46)

works *The Advancement of Knowledge* (1605) and *Novum organum* ("New Method," 1620) he called for these all to be cast aside—the fairy tales of daily life along with the heavy tomes of Greek thought—so that modern thinkers could begin anew. On what, then, were they to base secure statements of truth? On the evidence of their senses, as they experienced directly the facts and objects about which they wished to theorize. Particular things could be known derived from experience, from which generalizations could be induced. Hence this prescribed method of logic is called *inductive*.

Both Bacon and Descartes were urging rigorous standards of proof and argument in the construction of philosophical and scientific statements. The more empirically based inductive method championed by Bacon was especially useful to scientific investigators, who, from the time of Galileo, constructed experiments to simulate real situations but in carefully controlled conditions so that accurate observations could be made of the behavior of natural objects. Experiment can be both conditioned by and result in a hypothesis

EDUCATING THE FEW—AND THE MANY

In the Middle Ages schools were for future monks and priests, teaching the Latin necessary to read the Bible and learned works. A diverse curriculum, a humane and responsive environment in which to learn, and a gradual approach to learning were not educational goals. Outside of the church schools, young people received the training they needed for their vocations on the job or through apprenticeships. By the thirteenth and fourteenth centuries, many artisans and merchants were acquiring vernacular literacy and basic numeracy—but not Latin—in the new schools that proliferated in cities where these skills were useful.

From the late fourteenth century, the humanists proposed a new educational model. Grounded in the liberal arts, the humanist program involved the study of Latin (and sometimes Greek) literature, history, and moral philosophy, not for vocational purposes, but as a general training of the mind and character. Only fortunate young people were able to acquire a humanist education either because of their social rank and gender (male) or their access to one of the few but multiplying public schools that provided training either free or for a modest fee.

What the humanists proposed was, in effect, a program of secondary education, a training beyond mere literacy and numeracy, that provided advanced linguistic and reasoning skills. It left undisturbed, and did not especially value, the university curricula that trained professionals in law, medicine, and theology. It aimed to prepare future leaders, some of whom might acquire university degrees, become statesmen or diplomats, the ministers and assistants of rulers, or become rulers themselves.

Concerned with shaping the entire person, humanist pedagogy discouraged corporal punishment which, for centuries, schoolmasters had assumed was the only way to teach Latin, the gateway to learning. Erasmus, for instance, who in his *Praise of Folly* had characterized the schoolroom as a "torture chamber," described in his *On Education for Children* the damage done to children by the habit of beating them: "When corporal punishment is applied too harshly the more spirited children are driven to rebellion while the more apathetic ones are numbed into despair."

In the sixteenth century, Protestant and Catholic reformers sought to educate a broader population than the humanists had targeted. Reformed theology insisted that each individual must be able to read and interpret Scripture

himself—or herself. The education of all children at least in basic literacy became a priority. Regions that were primarily Lutheran or Calvinist developed an extensive network of elementary schools. In Catholic areas, this motivated bishops and religious orders to expand the schools of Christian doctrine that provided free instruction in basic literacy and devotional studies.

From the 1630s and 1640s, one refugee from the horrors of religious warfare in central Europe dedicated himself to constructing new systems of learning so that all human beings might cultivate to the fullest the potential for reason that each possessed at birth. John Amos Comenius (Ján Komensk, 1592–1670) was a spiritual leader of the Bohemian Brethren, a Moravian (Czech) Protestant group descended from the heretical medieval Hussites, who anticipated many features of Lutheran thought. Having lost his family, his career, and his books in the turbulence of the Thirty Years' War, Comenius traveled throughout Europe promoting his educational theories and winning wide renown in England, France, and the Netherlands, as well as Sweden, Poland, and Hungary.

In 1631 Comenius published his *Janua linguarum reserata* ("The Gateway to the Knowledge of Languages Unlocked"), a textbook for the early acquisition of Latin. The same concern for young learners is seen in his picture-book guide to the world of knowledge, the *Orbis pictus* ("The World in Pictures") of 1658. Addressed to Czech mothers, Comenius's *School of Infancy* appeared first in German in 1633, soon after in Polish, and in 1653 in Latin. His most important work was the *Didactica magna* ("The Great Didactic"), completed between 1628 and 1638 in both Czech and Latin.

In the *Didactica magna*, Comenius investigated how people learn from infancy through adulthood and how they should be taught. While his recommendations promoted a uniformity that modern pedagogy no longer values, he did so precisely because of his expansive understanding of the educational mission, its service to all of humanity—*rex humanitas* (King Humanity), as he called it, the only king he revered. Comenius wished to educate everyone, regardless of class or privilege. In imitation of the sun, which "lights and warms the whole earth at once" and "gives light to all things with the same rays … [and] causes the same wind to blow on all things," Comenius recommended a disciplined, unified, and progressive system of learning for all—the poor and the rich, both male and female:

In imitation [of the sun]:

(i) There should only be one teacher in each school, or at any rate in each class.

(ii) Only one author should be used for each subject studied.

(iii) The same exercise should be given to the whole class.

(iv) All subjects and languages should be taught by the same method.

(v) Everything should be taught thoroughly, briefly, and pithily, that the understanding may be, as it were, unlocked by one key....

(vi) All things that are naturally connected ought to be taught in combination.

(vii) Every subject should be taught in definitely graded steps, that the work of one day may thus expand that of the previous day, and lead up to that of the morrow....

If these reforms could be introduced into schools, there is no doubt that the whole circle of the sciences might be completed with an ease that surpasses our expectation, just as the sun completes its circling course through the heavens every year.

(Comenius, *John Amos Comenius on Education*. New York: Columbia University Press, 1967, p. 71)

Child of the Reformation, Czech progressivism, and European humanism, Comenius was the first thinker to envision the education of all for the betterment of all and to advocate that project as the moral responsibility of humankind.

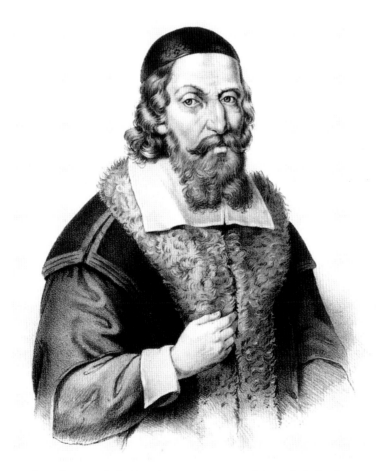

Hanfstaengl, *Portrait of John Amos Comenius*, 19th century, lithograph. Archiv für Kunst und Geschichte, Berlin.

(a preliminary explanation of the data). This hypothesis can then be refined and tested by further experiment, until an unassailable conclusion—a scientific theory or law—is reached. This process, which involves both deductive and inductive reasoning, is called the "scientific method." Its adoption has been central to the project of modern science.

The scientific method was not a feature of Renaissance investigation. On the contrary, many Renaissance thinkers preferred to speculate on the basis of the much more accurate and sophisticated ancient texts that the editorial labors of the humanists had provided—texts to which Descartes was often indifferent and which Bacon firmly spurned. Yet, the Renaissance openness to new areas of inquiry and the rigor of its own methods of investigation and argument were fundamental to the scientific pursuits of the next generations. The Renaissance itself did not produce modern science, but the investigations of modern science depended upon the intellectual contributions of Renaissance thinkers.

TOWARD ENLIGHTENMENT

Navigators and explorers, not Renaissance humanists or artists, opened up the New World of the Americas and Old World Asian markets to Europeans. Similarly, philosophers, astronomers, and physicians opened up a new world of scientific thought that had not been imagined by Renaissance thinkers. There also opened a third "new world" during the period from 1500 to 1700, which culminated in the Enlightenment of the late seventeenth to eighteenth centuries. This was the broadening circle of the literate. Europe became a place where many people—in urban areas often 50 per cent of the population—could read well enough to be made aware of the political, social, and religious issues of the day.

Readers and Learners

The participation of a large proportion of the population in cultural life was a unique feature of Western civilization at this historical moment. Although it was not a goal that Renaissance thinkers had set, it was an outcome of the Renaissance recovery, edition, translation, and circulation of texts, boosted by the advent of print and the development of national languages into a definite form (see Chapter 9).

Books, Academies, and Salons The printing press made available a large number of relatively cheap editions of books, including illustrated books, in addition to song sheets and broadsides that supported a broader reading public. The use of vernaculars made it easier for ordinary people to acquire literacy in a matter of a few years; by contrast, the mastery of Latin or Greek took much longer. The use of the vernacular, too, encouraged authors to communicate clearly to an audience of nonprofessionals. In the pre-print age, in contrast, when the audience of learned works was almost entirely restricted to those trained in universities or humanist schools, authors used the technical jargon of their fields of expertise, unconstrained by any need to engage the public.

Among the moneyed classes, academies and salons now provided a setting where professionals and amateurs could communicate in a common language (see Chapter 8). Academies first flourished from the sixteenth century in Italy, where several women were admitted as members. They then were imitated in regions beyond the Alps, where their constitution was generally more formal and often associated with royal patronage. Salons, which assembled in private apartments generally hosted by a woman, took their inspiration from Castiglione's *Courtier* but first flourished in seventeenth-century France. The latest discoveries in geography and navigation, astronomy and anatomy, were discussed in these relaxed settings, as were poetry, music, and the arts. Through these informal discussions, members became acquainted with scientific matters that they might not otherwise encounter in their reading, and in a readily accessible format. Women, especially, were beneficiaries of the discussions of ideas that took place in academies and salons. Previously, even if they had the opportunity to read, they had no access to settings where they could participate in intellectual conversation.

Education In addition to the broadening circle of the literate, encouraged by the availability of reading material and the opportunity for discussion provided by academies and salons, more people had access to formal education during the sixteenth and seventeenth centuries. In the earlier Middle Ages, schooling was available only within monasteries and cathedrals; its main aim was to train future monks and priests in Latin and other necessary skills. The first universities were extensions of the most important of these cathedral and monastic schools. With the emergence of cities, private lay schools developed as required to teach the skills necessary for artisans and merchants—basic literacy and arithmetic. In addition, municipalities might organize a "public" school, as happened in some Italian cities, headed by a master who taught the skills needed for secretaries and bureaucrats. Humanist schooling took place in a number of settings, including private day and boarding schools, such as Vittorino da Feltre's Casa Giocosa in fifteenth-century Mantua (see Chapter 3) or John Colet's school at St. Paul's in sixteenth-century London (see Chapter 10), which reserved places and menial jobs for poor boys on scholarships.

The Protestant Reformation brought the need for a network of elementary schools to teach basic literacy to both girls and boys, who must, through their own reading of Scripture, achieve a relationship with God. These were supervised by the parish and ecclesiastical superiors. While the *praeceptor Germaniae* (Germany's preceptor) Philip Melanchthon saw to the revision of the university curriculum in the light of Lutheran values, other educators, including Johann Sturm (1507–1589), developed secondary schools that combined humanistic and Protestant ideals (see Chapter 10). In Protestant England, meanwhile, Roger Ascham (1515?–1568) introduced the ideals of humanist education to an elite public in *The Scholemaster* (1570), while Richard Mulcaster (1530–1611), whose London school served a middle-class community seeking mobility for its children, described his aims in his *Positions Concerning the Training Up of Children*.

The Catholic Reformation responded by instituting a variety of Sunday and weekday schools that taught literacy, but also catechism and basic prayers, to the children of the poor. For the middling and elite classes, the Jesuit order created hundreds of private and boarding schools whose carefully structured humanistic curriculum, combined with training in religious doctrine and social skills, moved systematically from elementary through secondary grades (see Chapter 9). Angela Merici of Brescia (1470/1474–1540), later sainted, pioneered a system of schooling for girls. This was originally designed to operate in cities, but ultimately was confined to the premises of the cloistered Ursuline order. The Englishwoman Mary Ward (1585–1645) also created a system of schooling for girls based on the Jesuit model, but she received resistance in Protestant England and from the pope.

By the later sixteenth century, it was clear that the circle of those who were schooled was broadening. Theorists responded, presenting ways of pursuing knowledge appropriate to an expanded audience. The Moravian (Czech) polymath John Amos Comenius (Ján Amos Komensk, 1592–1670) proposed a new pedagogy, many of whose principles have been adopted by modern experts (see pp. 386–387). It had considerable impact on circles in Paris and London where he worked following tragedy in his homeland. He urged that concepts learned should be related to real-world objects, a principle he used in an illustrated picture book for the instruction of children. He insisted that the curriculum must be carefully structured for the step-by-step acquisition of knowledge. Teaching should take place in the vernacular, not Latin, and be taught through conversational methods; scientific, humanistic, and religious subjects should be taught. Moreover, Comenius argued that girls should be taught as well as boys.

Women and the World of Learning

Comenius believed that women were as capable of intellectual activity as men. This assumption was by no means universal in the seventeenth century. The first women humanists of the fifteenth century argued, both in their words and in their behavior, that women were as able as men to master the humanist curriculum and to enter the mainstream of intellectual life (see Chapter 3). Those claims were made again, loudly and in great numbers, in the sixteenth and seventeenth centuries. The claims that women, equally with men, belonged to the human species; that they were of equal worth to men (and perhaps superior, as some participants in this debate proposed); and that they were capable of the same advanced level of education as men featured in a great literary debate that was carried on by various lettered men and women from Boccaccio to Mary Wollstonecraft (1759–1797). French participants referred to this as the *querelle des femmes* (debate about women).

During the Middle Ages, and in antiquity with a few exceptions, women were largely isolated from cultural pursuits. They lived apart, sometimes literally in separate quarters, as in ancient Greece. In medieval Europe, although they lived in households with their families, they gathered together for needlework and storytelling and to engage in the processes and rituals of birth and death. They were the repositories of knowledge about healing and the mysteries of childbirth. They were solely responsible for children's welfare and education through the age of seven. The information they needed to perform these roles they learned from other women—their mothers and the other experienced women of their community. They transmitted this knowledge to their daughters. It is no surprise that one of the widely circulated books of the Middle Ages was the ferociously misogynist *De secretis mulierum* ("On the Secrets of Women"). The world of women was despised and distrusted.

While women had their own "secrets," they did not engage in the dominant masculine culture of writing and reading. In the medieval tradition, the main exceptions to this pattern were the saints and mystics who won great popular support. Some of them were literate (or semi-literate, dictating their ideas) and authored important works recording their visions and precepts. By the twelfth century, some elite women were reading the troubadour verse of Provence (southern France), while some were themselves poets. By the thirteenth century, literate women were reading stories and novellas, and in the fourteenth, women were the audience for Boccaccio's *Decameron*, a collection of stories presumably told over 10 days.

The *Querelle des Femmes* In his *De mulieribus claris* ("On Famous Women"), Boccaccio published brief biographies of 106 women, mostly from pre-Christian antiquity. The figures he profiled were models of womanly greatness, yet even in celebrating these figures, he revealed a misogyny characteristic of the age: his heroines were punished if they exceled too much or they are condemned for lustful excesses.

In the fifteenth century, Boccaccio's work inspired a response in two main traditions. Writing in the French vernacular, Christine de Pizan presented in her *Livre de la cité des dames* (*The Book of the City of Ladies*) her own series of short biographies. She emphasized female virtue and resourcefulness where her Italian predecessor had suggested female hubris and transgression. Writing in Latin, in an independent tradition, Italian women humanists often included in their works brief defenses of women which included a list of female worthies, likely extracted from Boccaccio. Thus in two different linguistic and national settings, defenders of women adopted and modified Boccaccio's method of collective biography to validate women's moral capacity by demonstrating their great achievements in the past.

In the sixteenth and seventeenth centuries, the genre developed in several other languages and many print editions, notably in *On the Nobility and Preeminence of the Female Sex* by Henry Cornelius Agrippa von Nettesheim, a manifesto imitated, and even plagiarized, by several other male authors. The posthumous *Il merito delle donne* ("The Worth of Women") by the Venetian Moderata Fonte (pseudonym of Modesta da Pozzo, 1555–1592), published in 1600, brilliantly revealed the limitations placed on women's freedom by contemporary society. A fellow Venetian, Lucrezia Marinella (1571–1653), published *The Nobility and Excellence of Women and the Defects and Vices of Men*, an extended critique of the misogynous assumptions of the dominant learned traditions.

The French author Marie de Gournay (1565–1645) argued in her concise work *The Equality of Men and Women* (1622) that men and women were equally human, distinguished only by sex, an argument self-evident, perhaps, in the twenty-first century but by no

THE WORTH OF WOMEN: RENAISSANCE VINDICATIONS

When Giovanni Boccaccio (1313–1375) wrote his *De mulieribus claris* ("On Famous Women") in 1364, he inaugurated a debate that would span the Renaissance centuries: the question of the worth of women. Boccaccio's catalog of famous women from ancient times, both real and mythological, featured women creators, inventors, mothers, wives, and rulers.

The Italian-born French author Christine de Pizan (1364–1430) responded to Boccaccio with an alternate listing in her *Book of the City of Ladies* of 1405. Although Boccaccio viewed the figures he profiled as models both of virtue and evil, Christine found heroic virtues even among those he had condemned, as well as among others he had omitted. Boccaccio, Christine implied, understated women's achievements and misunderstood the condition of their lives.

Although they did not explicitly address Boccaccio, the major female humanists of the fifteenth century—Isotta Nogarola, Cassandra Fedele, and Laura Cereta (see Chapter 3)—used the women whose fame he had enhanced as a litany of "women worthies," great women who had brought honor to the female sex. In their works, too, they argued the case for women's dignity and capacity for reason, while in their lives they exemplified female achievement.

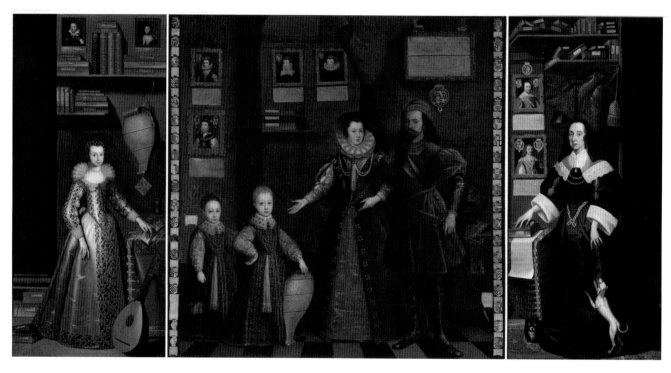

Van Belcamp (attrib.), *The Clifford "Great Picture"* showing the Englishwoman Lady Clifford (left panel) with her books, c. 1646. Abbot Hall Art Gallery, Kendall, Cumbria, England.

In the sixteenth century, as the number of women authors exploded (see p. 394) so too did the discussion of women's worth. Discussion was focused by *The Nobility and Preeminence of the Female Sex* (1509), written by Henry Cornelius Agrippa (1486–1535). Agrippa's extravagant claims, not merely for female equality, but superiority, incline some modern scholars (unnecessarily, most likely) to read his work as a jest. Whatever Agrippa's intent, the learned arguments he presented (from theological, classical, medical, and legal traditions) provided food for thought for the next century and a half.

Agrippa's work was reissued, translated, and plagiarized freely. It also drew refutations by male authors as well as male defenders of female dignity. Women authors, too, joined in the fray. At this stage, the literary discussion of women's worth became a genre of its own, constituting the *querelle des femmes*, which engaged many contenders on both sides of the issue well into the seventeenth century. Two related issues dominated: The ongoing discussion of women's worth—were they equal, inferior, or superior to men? And, with greater focus, the problem of women's education—could women learn what men learned, and as well?

Exploring these issues led two of the later participants in the *querelle*, the Englishwomen Margaret Cavendish (1623–1673) and Mary Astell (1668–1731), to ask a further question: if women were in fact equal in merit and capable of education, just how did men manage to retain their social superiority? Cavendish complained of male cruelty in one of her *Female-Orations* (1662):

Ladies, Gentlewomen, and other Inferior Women, but not less Worthy: I have been industrious to Assemble you together, and wish I were so Fortunate, as to perswade you to make frequent Assemblies, Associations, and Combinations amongst our Sex, that we may unite in Prudent Counsels, to make our selves as Free, Happy and Famous, as Men: whereas now we Live and Dye, as if we were produced from Beasts, rather than from Men: for, Men are happy, and we Women are miserable; they possess all the Ease, Rest, Pleasure, Wealth, Power, and Fame; whereas

Women are Restless with Labour, Easeless with Pain, Melancholy for want of Pleasures, Helpless for want of Power, and dye in Oblivion, for want of Fame. Nevertheless, Men are so Unconscionable and Cruel against us, that they endeavour to barr us of all sorts of Liberty, and will not suffer us freely to Associate amongst our own Sex; but would fain bury us in their Houses or Beds, as in a Grave. The truth is, we live like Batts, or Owls, labour like Beasts, and dye like Worms.

(K.M. Wilson and F.J. Warnke, eds., *Women Writers of the Seventeenth Century*. Athens: University of Georgia Press, 1989, p. 324)

Mary Astell explained how men manage to stay ahead of women in her *Reflections on Marriage* (1700):

There are strong and prevalent reasons which demonstrate the superiority and preeminence of the men. For in the first place, boys have much time and pains, care and cost bestowed on their education, girls have little or none. The former are early initiated in the sciences, are made acquainted with ancient and modern discoveries, they study books and men, have all imaginable encouragement…. The latter are restrained, frowned upon, and beaten … laughter and ridicule, that never-failing scarecrow, is set up to drive them from the tree of knowledge. But if in spite of all difficulties nature prevails, and they can't be kept so ignorant as their masters would have them, they are stared upon as monsters, censured, envied, and every way discouraged.

(B. Hill, ed., *Mary Astell: The First English Feminist— Reflections on Marriage and Other Writings*. New York: St. Martin's Press, 1986, p. 85)

By the time Cavendish, Astell, and the other defenders of women discussed in this chapter had completed their work, the equality of women as a theoretical principle had been largely established in intellectual circles. The vindication of the worth of women must be numbered as one of the most significant achievements of the Renaissance.

means so in the seventeenth. The Dutch mystic Anna van Schurman (1607–1678) made the case for the education of women in her treatise *Whether a Christian Woman Should Be Educated* (1638). In 1700, the English gentlewoman Mary Astell echoed Moderata Fonte in *Some Reflections upon Marriage*, a critique of marriage as an institution that limited women's options. More hauntingly still, in *A Serious Proposal to the Ladies* (Part I, 1694, Part II, 1697), she echoed Christine de Pizan, a voice from three centuries earlier, in her suggestion that women seek the community of other women in a "Protestant nunnery," in which they could pursue their own interests and talents without male intervention. Meanwhile, the Frenchman François Poulain de la Barre (1647–1723), an author of pedagogical works and a forerunner of the Enlightenment, famously declared in his *On the Equality of the Two Sexes* (1674) that men and women were in essence perfectly equal, as both were rational creatures: "the mind has no sex," he wrote.

Poems and Stories While these and other authors continued the discussion begun by Boccaccio about women's worth, women authors of poems and stories in the modern vernaculars proliferated. These included poets of women's experience in love, such as the Italian Veronica Franco (c. 1546–1591) and the French Louise Labé (c. 1522–1566), or more broadly, poets who wrote about women's social and intellectual roles, such as the French mother-and-daughter duo Madeleine (1520–1587) and Catherine des Roches (1542–1587). In French, Marguerite de Navarre (Chapter 10) and in Spanish, Maria de Zayas y Sotomayor (1590–1661/1669) wrote stories that highlighted the social and sexual dilemmas that women faced in the premodern era. Hélisenne de Crenne (c. 1510–after 1552) addressed the same themes in her longer semi-autobiographical *Angoysses douloureuses qui procedent d'amours* ("The Torments of Love," 1538).

In the seventeenth century, employing new literary forms, women novelists, such as Madame de La Fayette (1634–1693) in France, author of *La Princesse de Clèves* ("Princess of Cleves," 1678), and dramatists, such Aphra Behn (1640–1689) in England, also explored the identity and condition of women for a very broad public. Women also participated in the investigations of science and philosophy, such as the Englishwomen Margaret Cavendish, Duchess of Newcastle, who was also a poet of great interest, and Anne Conway (1631–1679), participant in the contemporary circle known as the Cambridge Platonists.

Witch Hunts Ironically, but perhaps not coincidentally, it was exactly during these centuries when women entered forcefully into the mainstream of intellectual discourse that many women were accused as witches and suffered persecution, torture, and death. A set of witch beliefs crystallized in the late fifteenth century, shared by illiterate villagers and learned jurists and theologians alike. These beliefs triggered attempts, more or less vigorous in different regions and eras, to identify and eliminate those charged with committing *malefecia* (evil deeds). The evil deeds included causing harm to people, especially children, and to beasts and crops; bringing about epidemics or other natural disasters; and causing abortions, stillbirths, or impotence. Accused witches were thought to fly on broomsticks, copulate with the devil, and engage with other witches and demons in "black sabbaths" that parodied and blasphemed Christian rituals. The great majority of those charged and executed as witches were women—very often those who were considered abusive in speech or associated with healing in village societies. Male intellectuals were among those who described and transmitted the witch beliefs that injured so many innocents. They were also important in disproving witch theory. By the late seventeenth century, the witch hunt lost momentum. It could no longer survive in an age that saw the triumph of reason in so many fields of endeavor.

CONCLUSION

The Roman author Cicero, a favorite of the Renaissance humanists, had defined reason as the trait which distinguished human beings from animals. In his *De officiis* ("On Duties") he wrote:

> But the most marked difference between man and beast is this: the beast, just as far as it is moved by the senses and with very little perception of past or future, adapts itself to that alone which is present at the moment; while man—because he is endowed with reason, by which he comprehends the chain of consequences, perceives the causes of things, understands the relation of cause to effect and effect to cause, draws analogies, and connects and associates the present and the future—easily surveys the whole course of his life and makes the necessary preparations for its conduct.

> (Cicero, *De Officiis*, trans. W. Miller, London: W. Heinemann, 1913, I.iv)

From 1500 to 1700, the capacity to reason that Cicero and the Renaissance had so elevated as a distinctive human faculty was employed in the exploration of new worlds. It played a part in the seeking of a new world beyond the bounds of the Atlantic, which had previously limited European westward movement. It played a part in the new world of scientific understanding that constituted the beginning of modern thought. It played a part in expanding the audience of the literate and the schooled that for the first time in history included women as creators and not merely consumers of thought. In these ways, just as antiquity fueled the achievements of the Renaissance, Renaissance civilization preceded, preconditioned, and foreshadowed the great explorations of the globe and of the mind in the early modern era.

SUGGESTED READINGS

Primary Sources

Descartes, René. *Discourse on Method and Related Writings*. Translated by Desmond M. Clarke. Harmondsworth, UK: Penguin, 2000. A fundamental rethinking of the relation of self and cosmos.

Galilei, Galileo. *Discoveries and Opinions of Galileo*. Edited by Stillman Drake, rev. ed. New York: Doubleday, 1989. Selections from the seventeenth-century scientist's major works.

Gournay, Marie le Jars de. *Apology for the Woman Writing and Other Works*. Translated and edited by Richard Hillman and Colette Quesnel. Chicago: University of Chicago Press, 2002. Gournay's concise and critical claim to the essential equality of women and men and women's aptitude for intellectual production.

Las Casas, Bartolomé de. *The Devastation of the Indies*. Translated by Herma Briffault. Baltimore, MD: Johns Hopkins University Press, 1992. A Spanish priest speaks out forcefully against the enslavement of Indigenous people in the New World.

Leibniz, Gottfried Wilhelm, Sophia, Electress of Hanover, and Queen Sophie Charlotte of Prussia. *Leibniz and the Two Sophies: The Philosophical Correspondence*. Translated and edited by Lloyd Strickland. Toronto: Iter Academic Press, Centre for Reformation and Renaissance Studies, 2011. Correspondence between the mother-daughter pair of noblewomen with the great philosopher Leibniz on such issues as the nature of substance and universal salvation.

María Rosa, Madre. *Journey of Five Capuchin Nuns*. Translated and edited by Sarah E. Owens. Toronto: Iter Press, 2009. Chronicle of the three-year journey of five nuns from Madrid, Spain to Lima, Peru, in the early 1700s, recording their encounters with war and disease and other perils on the sea and in the high Andes.

Van Schurman, Anna Maria. *Whether a Christian Woman Should Be Educated and Other Writings from Her Intellectual Circle*. Translated and edited by Joyce L. Irwin. Chicago: University of Chicago Press, 1998. Key statement of the case for women's education from a Dutch pietist.

Secondary Sources

Abulafia, David. *The Discovery of Mankind: Atlantic Encounters in the Age of Columbus*. New Haven, CT: Yale University Press, 2008. When Europeans ventured across the Atlantic, they discovered not only new lands, but new forms of humanity, knowledge of which corrected and expanded the consciousness of what it was to be human.

Briggs, Robin. *Witches and Neighbours: The Social and Cultural Context of European Witchcraft*. New York: HarperCollins/Viking Penguin, 1996. How fear-ridden ordinary people, more than magistrates, became the persecutors of accused witches.

Chartier, Roger. *The Order of Books: Readers, Authors and Libraries in Europe between the 14th and 18th Centuries*. Translated by Lydia G. Cochrane. Stanford, CA: Stanford University Press, 1994.

Relates how developments in the tracking, indexing, and ordering of books created a new world of knowledge.

Clossey, Luke. *Salvation and Globalization in the Early Jesuit Missions*. New York: Cambridge University Press, 2008. Shows how the Jesuit missions that reached four continents beyond Europe constituted a decentralized global enterprise, with carefully organized systems of communication and finance.

Crosby, Alfred W. *The Columbian Exchange: Biological and Cultural Consequences of 1492*. Westport, CT: Greenwood Press, 1972. A classic of ecological history.

Dobbs, Betty Jo Teeter. *The Janus Faces of Genius: The Role of Alchemy in Newton's Thought*. Cambridge: Cambridge University Press, 1991. Far from being a rationalist who rejected religion, Newton is here seen as committed to the unification of natural, philosophical, and religious truth.

Findlen, Paula. *Possessing Nature: Museums, Collecting and Scientific Culture in Early Modern Italy*. Berkeley: University of California Press, 1994. Describes the upper-class rage to collect and display items of natural history in a cultural movement akin to the book collecting of the earlier Renaissance.

Grafton, Anthony. *Cardano's Cosmos: The Worlds and Works of a Renaissance Astrologer*. Cambridge, MA: Harvard University Press, 1999. A physician, mathematician, and scientist, Cardano was also courted throughout Europe as an astrologer.

Harth, Erika. *Cartesian Women: Versions and Subversions of Rational Discourse in the Old Regime*. Ithaca, NY: Cornell University Press, 1992. Examines how women authors inserted themselves in literary discourse, creating a female alternative to the universalist Cartesian discourse of male intellectuals.

Houston, R.A. *Literacy in Early Modern Europe: Its Growth, Uses, and Impact, 1500–1800*, 2nd ed. Harlow, UK: Pearson Education, 2002. Investigates the nature, significance, and consequences of literacy across Europe.

Huff, Toby E. *Intellectual Curiosity and the Scientific Revolution: A Global Perspective*. Cambridge, MA: Cambridge University Press, 2011. Looks at the European inventions of the early modern period that, although they were spread abroad to China, India, and the Ottoman Empire, were developed and exploited mainly in Europe, promoting its ascendancy in science and commerce.

Lewalski, Barbara K. *Writing Women in Jacobean England*. Cambridge, MA: Harvard University Press, 1993. Explores the relations of educated women to print culture.

Pagden, Anthony. *European Encounters with the New World: From Renaissance to Romanticism*. New Haven, CT: Yale University Press, 1992. Discusses how Europeans perceived the New World and themselves in the wake of Columbus's achievement.

GLOSSARY

absolutism: In the sixteenth and seventeenth centuries, the political theory that a monarch held power over parliament or assemblies as well as individual subjects.

academy: An association of writers, artists, or scholars, often guided by commonly agreed statutes and sometimes possessing a special meeting place, late fifteenth century to the present; initially mostly private, later often state-funded.

Annunciation: The moment when the Angel Gabriel announced to the Virgin Mary that she would bear a child who would be the son of God.

Babylonian Captivity: The period 1309–1378 when the papacy was displaced from Rome and located in Avignon (modern France); the term is an allusion to the Israelites' exile in Babylon following the Assyrian invasion (586–538 BCE).

baptistry: A medieval Italian building specifically dedicated to baptism, usually adjacent to its church.

Baroque: An artistic style from the seventeenth and eighteenth centuries characterized by grandiosity of scale, rounded forms (in architecture), a vigorous expression of emotion, and the representation of luxurious objects and sensuous surfaces and ornaments.

basilica: In ancient Rome, a public building consisting of a large, long central area used for large assemblies, and often as law courts; adapted by early Christians as the model for their churches.

Béguines: Devout laywomen who formed communities from the thirteenth through fifteenth centuries to lead a pious life and perform charitable service, especially in the Low Countries and northern German lands.

Black Death: The epidemic of plague—most likely bubonic plague, caused by the bacterium *yersinia pestis*—that reached Europe from Asia late in 1347, raged for years, and recurred episodically until 1720.

broadsides: Large sheets containing announcements, cartoons, satire, propaganda, popular ballads, etc., printed on one side, publicly posted, distributed, or sold at low cost from the sixteenth through eighteenth centuries.

Byzantine: Relating to the Byzantine Empire and the Eastern Orthodox Christian Church; called "Byzantine" because it was centered at Constantinople, a city founded on the site of the ancient Greek city of Byzantium.

campanile: Italian for "bell tower," often the tower that stood next to but detached from a church or public building.

campo: From the Italian word for "field," an open space amid the densely packed buildings of a medieval city, distinct from the larger and more formal *piazza (see below)*.

Catholic: Denoting the largest communion of the Christian church, centered in Rome from the early centuries CE under the authority of the pope and a hierarchy of bishops and archbishops; also called the Latin Church because it employed Latin liturgy and the Latin Bible until the twentieth century; increasingly called the Roman Catholic Church from the seventeenth century to distinguish it from other Western churches.

Catholic Reformation (*see* **Reformations**.)

charismatic: A religious observant perceived as having extraordinary spiritual powers or one engaging in practices marked by extreme displays of enthusiasm.

château (pl. châteaux): From the French word for "castle," a large manor house; those from the sixteenth through eighteenth centuries were often examples of splendid Renaissance and baroque architecture and ornamentation.

chiaroscuro: Italian (lit. "light-dark") for a technique in painting or drawing by which, using graded shadings of pencil or paint, an impression of a three-dimensional object is obtained through the representation of the fall of light.

ciompi: (unguilded) wool workers who worked as *sottoposti* (subordinates) to the wool merchants of the Lana guild.

city-states: Independent political entities made up of cities and their surrounding countryside.

cives: The citizens of an Italian town, a status determined by length of residence and other considerations according to local statute.

codex: From late antiquity through the Renaissance, a book initially of parchment bound with wood panels, later of paper bound with wood or leather, which replaced the papyrus scroll of the Hellenistic and Roman eras.

commedia dell'arte: The form of professional theater developed in Italy from the sixteenth through eighteenth centuries, often consisting of improvised comic performances by masked, stock characters for popular consumption, but increasingly based on crafted plays (and opera scripts); performed at courts or other important venues, anticipating modern dramatic productions.

commune: The sworn association of citizens who seized control of many of the cities of northern Italy from the eleventh century, often ousting the ruling bishop or lord.

conciliarism: A movement in Roman Christianity of the fourteenth and fifteenth centuries to limit papal authority by making the pope subject to a general council of prelates and experts.

condottiere (pl. *condottieri*): Literally, a person who has received a contract; in thirteenth- through fifteenth-century Italy, a hired military commander.

confraternity: An association, often formalized by written statutes; in medieval society, often an association of persons dedicated to a particular religious mission and thus distinct from a **guild** (*see below*).

consorterie: The clan-based armed associations of noblemen and their kin, often expressed in residential patterns in medieval Italian cities.

constitutional monarchy: From the sixteenth century, the political theory that the powers of a just monarch were limited by the laws established by a parliament or assembly.

Counter-Reformation (*see* **Reformations**.)

courtier: A person qualified by noble birth or a conferred favor to attend upon a great lord or monarch at his court, exchanging deference, flattery, and advice for housing, sustenance, and sometimes monetary gifts.

Devotio Moderna (New Devotion): From the fourteenth through sixteenth centuries, a lay religious movement centered in the Low Countries that stressed a personal and mystical relationship to God. Adherents were called the New Devout.

dialectic: The art of systematic argumentation based on principles of logic, the aim being to determine truth and falsehood; more recently, in philosophy, the understanding of reality as formed by the tension between and reconciliation of two opposing principles. The characteristic method of Scholasticism.

diocese: From the Greek and Latin words for "administration" and "jurisdiction," the term used by the early Christian churches to designate an administrative unit (comprising several churches) under the authority of a bishop; still used today.

doges: Venetian language form of the Latin *dux* ("duke," or leader), the doge was an elected monarch, chosen from among the leading citizens and subject to the laws of the city.

Dominican order: The mendicant (*see below*) order founded by Dominic in 1216, specifically dedicated to teaching orthodox doctrine and opposing heresy.

dowry: Customary in many ancient societies as well as premodern Europe, the sum in cash, goods, or land paid by a bride's family to her new husband.

ducats: Venetian gold coin first minted in 1284, second to appear in West after the florin of 1252. Widely used as a standard currency throughout Europe and Mediterranean region.

Enlightenment: The intellectual movement of the late seventeenth through eighteenth centuries that championed the capacity of reason to liberate humankind from tyranny and superstition and to enable the construction of a more just society.

evangelicals: Italian proto-reformers who, before Luther, stressed an inward-looking piety based on a personal reading of the gospels and who either recanted once the Lutheran challenge and papal response materialized or fled to refuge in Protestant regions.

excommunications: The exclusion of peoples from participation in worship or the benefit of the sacraments, especially in the Catholic Church.

florin: Florentine gold coin, first to appear in the West since antiquity, minted in 1252 by the victorious *Primo Popolo*. Widely used as a standard currency throughout Europe and Mediterranean region.

Franciscan order: The mendicant (*see below*) order founded by Francis of Assisi in 1209, specifically dedicated to the principle of apostolic poverty.

fresco: A painting technique characteristic of medieval and Renaissance Italy in which water-based pigments were applied to damp plaster, which partially absorbed them.

Ghibelline: One of the two sets of allegiances (*see also* **Guelf**) to which contenders for power often adhered in medieval northern Italy. The Ghibellines tended to be associated with the nobility and with support for an imperial role in Italy.

glacis: From the fifteenth century, the barren area surrounding a fortification with low-sloping walls designed to withstand cannon fire.

Gothic: The medieval European artistic style from the twelfth through sixteenth centuries following the Romanesque. In architecture, characterized by the use of an ogival (peaked) arch and ribbed vaulting, enormous height achieved through the use of external buttresses, or supports, and extensive windows for the admission of light. In sculpture, characterized by a concern for harmony and emotional realism. (*See also* **Goths**.)

Goths: A Germanic people who had migrated into the Roman region by the third century CE, and were soon converted to Christianity; later split into the two groups of Ostrogoths and Visigoths.

Great Schism: Split in the Catholic Church 1378–1417, when allegiance was divided between at first two, then three popes. Also Western Schism, Papal Schism.

Guelf: One of the two sets of allegiances (*see* **Ghibelline**) to which contenders for power often adhered in medieval northern Italy. The Guelfs tended to be associated with the mercantile leaders and with supporters of the papal role in Italy.

guilds: Associations of merchants or artisans at various levels of wealth and importance that, not only organized economic activity, but also served as a gateway to political participation and as the provider of many social and cultural services.

Hanseatic League: From 1241 to 1669, a commercial alliance of free cities with access to English Channel, North Sea, and Baltic ports that flourished especially in the fourteenth century.

heretic: In Christianity, a member of the church who chooses to pursue beliefs at odds with orthodox or official doctrine.

Holy Roman Empire: A medieval empire (962–1806) conceived as a successor to the Roman Empire, with special responsibility to protect and advance the Roman Church; often in conflict with the papacy on that account.

Huguenot: In the sixteenth and seventeenth centuries a French Protestant, usually an adherent of Calvinist Reformed theology.

humanism: A movement dedicated to the study of the classical tradition and the liberal arts; later meanings include Christian humanism, which combined humanist scholarship with reformist religious views, and in modern times, philosophical humanism committed to purely human needs and interests, whose outlook is essentially secular.

Hussites: From the late fourteenth through sixteenth centuries, followers of Czech reformer Jan Hus (c. 1369–1415), whose campaign of anticlericalism and critique of the doctrine of transubstantiation led to his denunciation as a heretic and burning at the stake by order of the Council of Constance.

incunabula (s. *incunabulum*): Latin for "cradle" books, the first books (to 1500) of the print era.

Inquisition: An ecclesiastical commission set up to inquire into and defend against heresy, first established in Italy in 1233, replaced by the Roman Inquisition in 1542; distinct from the state-run Spanish Inquisition, established in 1478.

Islamic: Relating to the institutions and civilization constructed by adherents of Islam.

Jesuit: Member of the Order of the Society of Jesus founded in 1534 by St. Ignatius of Loyola; committed to serving the pope, to education, and to missionary activity.

jurists: People learned in the law, who might serve as a judge or expert; from the eleventh century onward, the universities of Italy became centers of jurisprudence, and jurists trained there were often important contributors to urban constitutions and policies.

kabbalah (kabalah, cabala): Medieval Jewish mystical readings of scripture, using symbolic and numerological interpretations; by extension, any body of esoteric knowledge.

Levant: Geographical term referring to the lands and islands of the eastern Mediterranean north of the Arabian Peninsula and south of Turkey.

Lollards: From the late fourteenth through sixteenth centuries, English supporters of the reform program of theologian John Wycliffe (c. 1328–1384) who had decried numerous church abuses and encouraged the reading of the Bible in the vernacular.

Lombards (Langobards, Longobards): The Germanic people who invaded northern Italy in the sixth century and who established the Italic kingdom as well as some smaller principalities.

magnates: The *grandi*, or "great men" of medieval Italian cities, whose wealth, record of political office, lineage, marital kin, claim to nobility, or other attributes permitted them to claim extraordinary privileges and dominate social subordinates.

Mannerism: An artistic style that developed in Italy in the early sixteenth century; characterized by the distortion of relations between bodies and objects, the juxtaposition of unusual or impossible visual elements, and the use of odd or extreme colors.

mendicants: People who beg for alms for a living; in the history of the Catholic Church, a member of those itinerant orders (*see* **Dominican order** and **Franciscan order** *above*) that renounced the monastic life at an established abbey and whose members lived by begging.

monastery: A community of persons who have taken vows of poverty, chastity, and obedience, living together in seclusion and engaged in worship, study, service, and necessary labor.

Muslims: Adherents of Islam; meaning those who submit to the will of Allah.

nepotism: Term derived from the Latin word for grandson or nephew; denotes the improper transfer of offices or privileges to relatives.

octavo: From the fifteenth century, a whole printer's sheet folded into eight leaves (folios); also the book made up of sheets of octavo size.

papacy: The system of government of the Catholic Church, headed by the pope; the historical lineage of the popes of that church.

peonage: The labor system common from the sixteenth century in South America, in which a peasant farmer becomes bound in servitude to a landholder by indebtedness.

perspective: A way of seeing things; in the Renaissance, linear perspective was a new system of using converging lines on a two-dimensional surface to create the illusion of deep space.

piazza (pl. *piazze*): A large open space in an Italian (or Spanish) town, often with conscious reference to formally designed building façades.

poligrafi (s. *poligrafo*): In sixteenth-century Italy, professional writers connected to publishing houses, who wrote for the marketplace on a variety of topics, sometimes provocatively.

polyphony: From the Greek words for "many" and "sound," a style of musical composition developed from the fourteenth and fifteenth centuries in the Low Countries and later generalized in Europe, in which several independent musical lines or "voices" blend harmoniously and are heard simultaneously.

popolo: Literally, the "people," in medieval northern Italy, the republican movement led by middling merchants and professionals, often organized in guilds and desiring to wrest power from the magnates.

Protestant Reformation (see **Reformations**.)

quarto: From the fifteenth century, a whole printer's sheet folded into four leaves (folios); also the book made up of sheets of quarto size.

quattrocento (*see* **trecento**.)

querelle des femmes: The "debate about women," a series of conversations and print discussions by both men and women attacking and defending women's nature and capacity for learning, carried on in several languages from the fifteenth through eighteenth centuries.

reconquista: From the eleventh century through 1492 when the last stronghold fell, the long process of reconquest by which the Christian kingdoms of the Iberian Peninsula pushed back the Moors who had invaded and occupied almost the whole of the peninsula by 711 CE.

Reformations: Sixteenth-century movements to reform some beliefs and practices of the Roman Church, resulting both in the creation of a variety of Protestant churches and a Catholic or Counter-Reformation involving a clarification of doctrine, reform measures, and increased missionary efforts.

rhetoric: The art of using language to argue or persuade, often based on classical examples; more recently and secondarily, the use of excessively elaborate language.

Romanesque: The medieval European artistic style especially of architecture and sculpture developed in the eleventh and twelfth centuries based on the Roman forms of the arch and column, but elaborated according to Christian theoretical requirements.

sacraments: According to the Christian churches, visible signs (a ritual performance or ceremony) of divine grace, instituted by Christ.

salons: Formal rooms in a private or public building used to receive guests, often including those of distinction, and accordingly the setting for conversation on intellectual, political, or aesthetic matters, especially from the late fifteenth through nineteenth centuries.

Saracen: Term used in Middle Ages to refer to Arab Muslims.

scholastic: Pertaining to a *schola*, the medieval "school," characterizing the kind of logical investigation and argumentation epitomized by the university faculty of the thirteenth through fifteenth centuries, whose work overall is referred to as Scholasticism.

scuola (pl. *scuole*): Italian for "school," which in medieval Italy might denote any number of associations including those with academic purpose; in Venice, particularly, the *scuola* was an association of citizens committed to charitable service and was roughly equivalent to a confraternity.

sects: Especially in the sixteenth and seventeenth centuries, small religious groups distinct from larger ones (generally Protestant), united by a particular set of beliefs and practices (e.g., Anabaptists, Quakers, and Mennonites).

serrata: Beginning in 1297, membership in the Venetian assembly began to be restricted to a prescribed group of families who constituted a nobility, in a process known as the *serrata* (closing) of the Great Council.

signoria (pl. *signorie*): In English, signory, from the Italian *signore* (lord or prince; plural *signori*), denotes the despotisms that emerged in the northern Italian cities of the thirteenth through fifteenth centuries.

simony: Term derived from the name of the New Testament trafficker in miracles Simon Magus (Acts 8:9–24); denotes the sale of church offices or privileges.

sonnets: Fourteen-line poems composed according to a formal rhyme scheme; developed by Petrarch and widely imitated and changed by later European poets in several vernaculars.

studiolo: Italian for "small study," the private room or space that scholars or wealthy amateurs began to demand in their residences for quiet, solitary study.

sumptuary laws: Common in medieval and Renaissance cities, laws regulating expenditures and thus also moral behavior or appearance, differentially imposed on different social groups and on women.

terraferma: The mainland of northeastern Italy, a region with varying boundaries, constituting part of the Venetian dominion from the fifteenth through eighteenth centuries.

tertiary: A member of one of the "Third Orders" affiliated with the Franciscan, Dominican, or other religious orders; often a role assumed by members of confraternities or others seeking sanctification through charitable service.

trecento: "the thirteen hundreds," as Italians refer to the fourteenth century; likewise quattrocento (the fourteen hundreds), and cinquecento (the fifteen hundreds).

Ursulines: Originally followers of St. Angela Merici (1474–1540) who established a lay religious organization of uncloistered women for the education of girls, later organized as a cloistered religious order of the Catholic Church.

vanishing point: In the technique of linear **perspective** (*see above*), the point at which the lines establishing a three-dimensional scene converge.

vavassors: The "vassals of vassals," petty noblemen with small feudal holdings, linked by patronage agreements to other nobles to whom military or other service is owed.

CREDITS

REVIEWERS

In addition to the participation of those individuals credited in the acknowledgments, the author is grateful for the comments and suggestions of the following reviewers: Kenneth Bartlett, Victoria College, University of Toronto; Philip Bebb, Ohio University; Christopher Blackburn, University of Louisiana at Monroe; Robert Blackey, California State University, San Bernardino; Daniel Bornstein, Texas A & M University; Gayle Brunelle, California State University, Fullerton; Robert Butler, Elmhurst College; Cyndia Clegg, Seaver College, Pepperdine University; Tim Crain, Marquette University; Neal Galpern, University of Pittsburgh; Elizabeth Hertzler, Maricopa Community Colleges; Ronald S. Love, The State University of West Georgia; Duane Osheim, University of Virginia; Roger Schlesinger, Washington State University; and Ronald G. Witt, Duke University.

PHOTOGRAPHS AND ILLUSTRATIONS

Sources for illustrations, additional information, and copyright credits are given below. Boldface numbers are page numbers unless otherwise indicated.

Reproduced courtesy of Abbot Hall Art Gallery, Lakeland Arts Trust, Kendall, Cumbria, England **420**; akg-images **398, 415**; Album/Art Resource **27, 247**; Alfredo Dagli Orti/ The Art Archive at Art Resource **39, 87, 153, 215, 282, 378**; Alinari/Art Resource **68, 73 (bottom right), 93, 105, 145**; bpk, Berlin/Bayerische Staatsbibliothek, Munich, Germany/ Art Resource **59 (left)**; bpk, Berlin/Bayerische Staatsbibliothek, Munich, Germany/Lutz Braun/Art Resource **59 (right)**; bpk, Berlin/Hamburger Kunsthalle/Christoph Irrgang/ Art Resource **330**; bpk, Berlin/Kupferstichkabinett/Joerg P. Anders/Art Resource **69**; bpk, Berlin/Kupferstichkabinett/Volker-H. Schneider/Art Resource **49–50**; © The British Library Board. OR6706, f1r. **197**; Cameraphoto Arte, Venice/Art Resource **79 (top right), 104, 181, 185, 191–192, 263**; Erich Lessing/Art **Resource 46, 65, 133, 135, 151 (left), 156, 220 (right), 242, 266, 290, 302, 209, 353, 368, 375, 410**; © Flickr user Richard Leonard **362**; © Flickr user Rodney **346**; Gianni Dagli Orti/The Art Archive at Art Resource **37, 322, 363, 391**; © Heritage/The Image Works, Inc. **326**; HIP/Art Resource **141, 173**; JT Vintage/Art Resource **327**; L. Tom Perry Special Collections, Harold B. Lee Library, Brigham Young University, Provo, Utah **136**; Image copyright © The Metropolitan Museum of Art. Image source: Art Resource **259, 322, 372**; Scala/Ministero per Ibeni e le Attività culturali/Art Resource **209, 231**; James Morris/Art Resource **304**; Copyright of the image Museo Nacional del Prado/Art Resource **184**; © National Gallery, London/Art Resource **166 (left), 301, 373, 384**; Photo courtesy of The Newberry Library, Chicago. Call # Case YD 05 02 **137**; Nicolo Orsi Battaglini/Art Resource **163, 190**; © RMN-Grand

Palais/Art Resource **175, 208, 379**; Scala/Art Resource **24, 44, 55, 86, 97, 101, 116, 123, 146, 161, 166 (right), 168, 220 (left), 225, 229, 238, 252, 253, 267, 303, 307, 349**; Stephanie Colasanti/The Art Archive at Art Resource **29**; © Stock Sales WGBH/Scala/Art Resource **395**; © TopFoto/The Image Works, Inc. **335**; Vanni Archive/Art Resource **19**.

LITERARY EXTRACTS

Every effort has been made to trace or contact all copyright holders. The publishers would be pleased to rectify any omissions brought to their notice at the earliest opportunity.

Columbia University Press from *Medieval Trade in the Mediterranean World*, by R.S. Lopez and I.W. Raymond. Copyright © 1955 Columbia University Press. Reprinted with permission of the publisher. **Editions Droz** from *Isabella d'Este and Lorenzo da Pavia: Documents for the History of Art and Culture in Renaissance Mantua*, edited by C.M. Brown, translated by M.L. King. Geneva: Librarie Droz, 1982. **Indiana University Press** from *Letters from Petrarch*, translated and edited by M. Bishop. Bloomington, IN: Indiana University Press, 1966. **Penguin Random House, LLC.** Excerpts from *The Book of the Courtier* by Baldasare Castiglione, copyright © 1959 by Charles S. Singleton and Edgar de N. Mayhew. Copyright renewed © 1987 by William B. Dulany (Estate of Charles S. Singleton) & Edgar Mayhew. Used by permission of Doubleday, and imprint of the Knopf Doubleday Publishing Group, a division of Penguin Random House LLC. All rights reserved. **Renaissance Society of America** from *Venice: A Documentary History, 1450–1630*, edited by D.S. Chambers and B. Pullan. Toronto: University of Toronto Press, 2001 © RSA. And from *The Society of Renaissance Florence*, by G. Brucker. Toronto: University of Toronto Press, 1997 © RSA. **Renee Neu Watkins** from *Humanism and Liberty: Writings on Freedom from Fifteenth-Century Florence*, translated and edited by Renee Neu Watkins. Columbia, SC: University of South Carolina Press, 1978. **University of California Press** from *Possessing Nature: Museums, Collecting, and Scientific Culture in Early Modern Italy*, by Paula Findlen. Berkeley, CA: University of California Press, 1994. **University of Chicago Press** from *The Worth of Women* by Moderata Fonte, edited and translated by V. Cox. Chicago: University of Chicago Press, 1998. **University of Georgia Press** from *Women Writers of the Seventeenth Century*, edited by K.M Wilson & F.J. Warnke. Athens, GA: University of Georgia Press, 1989. **University of Toronto Press** from *Aretino's Dialogues*, edited by Margaret Rosenthal and Raymond Rosenthal. Toronto: University of Toronto Press, 2005. Reprinted with permission of the publisher. And from *The Erasmus Reader*, edited by E. Rummell. Toronto: University of Toronto Press, 1990. Reprinted with permission of the publisher. **Yale University Press** from L.B. Alberti, *On Painting*, translated and edited by J.R. Spencer. New Haven: Yale University Press, 1956.

INDEX

Maps, illustrations, figures, graphs, timelines, and tables are indicated by page numbers in italics.

Cellini, Benvenuto, 293, 350
Celtis, Conrad, 292, 358
Cereta, Laura, 98–28, 106, 392
Cesmicki, Ivan, *see* Janus Pannonius
charity, 198–99, 200, 310–11
Charles d'Anjou (king in Sicily and Naples), 33, 230
Charles I (Spanish king), *see* Charles V (Holy Roman Emperor)
Charles II (English king), 341
Charles II (Spanish king), 338
Charles IV (Holy Roman Emperor), 357, 359
Charles IX (French king), 349
Charles V (Holy Roman Emperor), 247, 248, 304, 327, 338, 341, 343, *350*, 354–55, 357, 370
Charles VI (French king), 243
Charles VII (French king), 349
Charles VIII (French king), 90, 213, 245–46, 254–55
chemistry, 381–82
Chigi, Agostino, 133
children
    childbirth, 177, 179, 180–81
    daughters, 174, 175, 177, 202
    family roles, 174
    infanticide, 167, 181, 182
    infant mortality, 174, 178–79
    legitimacy, 179, 182
    sons, 174
    upbringing, 181, 183
    wet nursing, 181, 182–83
Christian humanism, 87, 168, 348. *See also* humanism
Christianity
    bishops, 11–12, 12–13
    definitions of terms, 12
    failure to fully assimilate, 195–96
    humanist challenges to, 92–93
    immortality of soul, 87, 103
    in Italy, 11, 13
    maps of divides, *199, 311*
    relationship to state, 328
    in Renaissance, 215
    saints, 12, 201, 204
    timeline of Reformations, *294*
    See also monasticism; papacy; popular religion; Protestant Reformation; Roman Catholic Church; women, holy
Christine de Pizan, 100
Chrysoloras, Manuel, 79, 81, 292
church architecture, 128–29

Cicero, Marcus Tullius, 5, 54, 57, 74, 78, 87, 109, 395
ciompi revolt, 43, 46
cities, 39
    buildings, 51–52
    city planning, 40–41, 133–34
    civic humanism on, 93, 95–96
    in Italy, 333
    in northern Europe, 326, 333, 334–35, 336–37
    walls, 50–51
civic humanism, 90, 92–93, 95–96. *See also* humanism
civility, 330, 332
Clare of Assisi, 203
classical antiquity
    Greek works, 79, 81, 101–2, 292
    revival, 62, 64, 78
    Roman works, 78–79
    See also Aristotle; Plato
Clement VII (pope), 189, 239, 248, 255. *See also* Medici, Giulio de' (cardinal)
The Clifford "Great Picture" (Van Belcamp), *392*
Coducci, Mauro, 129, 133
Cognac, League of, 247–48
Colet, John, 292, 355
Colleoni, Bartolommeo, 137, 223, 224, 225–26
colonialism, 370–71, 371–72, *378, 379*
Colonna, Francesco, 109, 306
Columbus, Christopher, 245, 338, 364, 365, 366, 369, *370*
Columbus Arriving in the Americas (Dati), *370*
Comenius, John Amos, 386–87, 390
commerce
    bookkeeping, 22
    commenda contract, 22
    Hanseatic League, 48, 333, 335, 336, 343, 365
    impact of Ottomans, 334, 365
    impact on Italy, 24–25
    Italian withdrawal, 159
    maritime trade, 23–24
    in Mediterranean, 365
    merchants, 29, 155, 158–59, 291–92
    with North America, 372–73
    Roman decline, 20–21
    in Venice, 40, 44, 48
communes, 25–26
    factions and conflict within, 28
    government system in, 26–27
    Holy Roman Empire against, 27–28, 30–31
    Lombard League, 30–31